Residential
Planning
and
Design

Residential Planning and Design

Jeannie Ireland
Missouri State University

Fairchild Publications, Inc.
New York

Executive Editor: Olga T. Kontzias
Senior Development Editor: Jennifer Crane
Development Editor: Sylvia L. Weber
Production Manager: Ginger Hillman
Associate Production Editor: Beth Cohen
Art Director: Adam B. Bohannon
Assistant Acquisitions Editor: Jaclyn Bergeron
Assistant Development Editor: Justine Brennan
Editorial Intern: Yelana Bromberg
Copyeditor: Annie McDonnell
Illustrator: Jason Dillbeck
Text Design and Layout: Andrew Katz
Cover Design: Adam B. Bohannon
Cover Art: Jeannie Ireland

Library of Congress Catalog Card Number: 2006921195
ISBN-13: 978-1-56367-384-9
ISBN-10: 1-56367-384-3
GST R 133004424

Printed in China
CH06, TP1

To Willa,
who believed

Contents

Extended Contents

Preface

During the thirty years I've been teaching residential design, I've used several texts ranging from drafting books to tomes of specialized material for housing systems. None actually provided the information needed in intermediate design classes, so I continually supplemented reading materials with lecture information. It is vital, however, for students to have important information at hand to allow for concentrated study. It was for this reason that I began this text.

Of great joy to me through the years has been the opportunity to travel to more than 50 countries to examine building systems and cultural mores associated with residences. In the process, my understanding of other cultures has deepened. While this text concentrates on American planning and design, examples from other cultures are used both in the text and in photographs to provide some understanding of the diversity of residential design throughout the world. In an increasingly global community, it is important that professional designers have a basic knowledge of this diversity, not only to work with a variety of clients but to offer design solutions that may incorporate ideas from other cultures.

Rather than simply providing information, I have made an effort to offer a rationale for some of the decisions that must be made during the planning and design processes, in the hope that knowledge could then be transferred to provide information for other decisions. In addition, I have tried to provide information to answer the questions most frequently asked by my students. Many of the tables in this text are a direct result of these questions.

It is imperative that any book describing residential planning and design have numerous illustrations to support the text. Photographs have been used where possible to provide information about finishing features. Drawings are used to illustrate details and broad concepts.

While the text provides information on traditional systems—structural, mechanical, and electrical—it also emphasizes the importance of green design and provides suggestions for employing principles of green design in residences. In a world in which resources are being rapidly depleted and energy is becoming more and more expensive, working with the environment rather than against it in site design and structure orientation makes sense. Further, the structure itself can be designed to use fewer natural resources, conserving them for future generations. Designers can play a significant role in these decisions at any stage of planning and construction.

This text provides, in a single volume, the information needed for residential planning from the beginning to the final stages. It begins with an overview of influences on design. Part One discusses individuals and families, the environment, technology, and materials, each of which affects the final product. With an understanding of the overall influences, Part Two then leads the designer through the construction process, not so they can actually do the work but rather to understand the processes, be able to communicate with contractors and subcontractors, and provide appropriate design solutions. Part Three discusses residential systems for the same reason. Sufficient information on electrical, plumbing, and air-quality control systems is provided so that design decisions can be intelligently made while ensuring that the systems work properly. A discussion of green design as it relates to the energy-efficiency of the structure is the final chapter in Part Three. In Part Four, information is provided to enable the designer to apply the information from the first three parts of the text to specific living spaces: overall space planning including circulation, living areas, service areas, and private areas. The information in this text can be used in a single course, although it lends itself readily to two separate courses.

The text has been written to provide sufficient information for making design decisions in most residential scenarios. Design implications that provide specific suggestions for using information in the design process are highlighted in blue. Ways to improve the relationship of the structure to the environment, including energy-efficiency, are also highlighted in green design features set in green. A large number of photographs and drawings are used to illustrate concepts and details, and a full set of house plans is provided in the appendix. An extensive glossary has also been provided.

An associated instructor's guide provides comments about the topics covered in the text. These are designed to supply additional information that teachers may want to use in the classroom, to offer examples of concepts, and to further explain some material. The instructor's guide also includes an outline, a list of new terms, objectives, suggested test questions, and resources for each chapter.

It is my hope that this text provides not only the information needed for successfully planning and designing residences but also acts as an impetus to more creative and environmentally friendly design.

Acknowledgments

It is the author who receives the credit for writing a book, but there are many individuals without whom the process could not have been completed. Some of these people stand in the wings, encourage, share ideas, and applaud every success without need for acknowledgment. Dr. Michele Granger has been a friend, mentor, and encourager throughout this process. Janet Leighton has not only listened and encouraged but has shared ideas from her very sharp mind. None of this, however, would be possible without the experiences I have shared with hundreds of students through the years. They have encouraged me, laughed with me, and explored possibilities with me. I have learned much from them. Because of them, teaching provides great joy in my life.

Strangers passing like ships in the night have provided encouragement, shared their time, and left a lasting impression. I shall always remember Dorothy Harding, her son Benny, and her son-in-law David Radasky, who shared my life for only a week but who provided significant impetus and encouragement. Deb Berkey, who entered my life for a few hours, showed a stranger great kindness and provided access to information and photographs that I would have been unable to get otherwise.

Willa Gilliam stood by from the beginning, making suggestions and reading every word. It was she who let me know when something didn't make sense, who stopped me from straying beyond the scope of this text, and who made many suggestions for improvements to make the document more readable. Barbara Huffman not only encouraged me but graciously allowed me to use several of her photographs. Jason Dillbeck of Nuclear

Imagery in Springfield, Missouri, an AutoCAD genius, has provided the drawings throughout the text and a complete set of house plans found in the appendix. Southern Materials in Springfield, Missouri, allowed me to photograph their plumbing displays, which greatly facilitated illustrating the plumbing chapter. The contributions of these individuals and businesses is greatly appreciated.

Others have made a significant contribution because they have been willing to share their expertise. Johnny Kurten read the plumbing documents and provided insights garnered from years of experience. Jay Jones shared his knowledge of acoustics. Rod Finkle commented on electrical information, sharing his extensive knowledge of that field. Tom Huffman examined the structural chapters, generously sharing his expertise. I want to express my heartfelt gratitude to these individuals who gave of their time and knowledge to help with this endeavor. Any errors, however, are mine.

The following reviewers examined the plans and manuscript for this text closely and made numerous suggestions that have made the book better than it otherwise would have been: Linda Johnson, Arizona State University; Susan Kirkman, Harrington College of Design; Attila Lawrence, University of Nevada-Las Vegas; Robert Paul Meden, Marymount University; Rosemary Pegram, Texas Tech University; Marilynne Rose, Drexel University; Suzanne Scott, University of Wisconsin; and Patricia Viard, Western Michigan University. I am grateful for the time and effort they expended and hope the results meet the standards and expectations they have set.

I cannot thank the people at Fairchild enough. They have made me feel like family, have brightened many days with their comments, and have accepted me with all my faults. Olga Kontzias opened numerous doors that made this tome a reality and has always shown great excitement about the possibilities. Joe Miranda and Carolyn Purcell worked diligently behind the scenes to bring this project to fruition. Sylvia Weber has to be the most understanding, encouraging, and delightful development editor that ever was. She has made this project fun and has kept me from going too far astray. Beth Cohen encouraged me and kept me working on all the pieces, finally making it all come together. Jaclyn Bergeron worked tirelessly to provide direction and helped greatly in the organization of this text. Thank you to Adam Bohannon and interior designer Andrew Katz for their work with the art and design.

In the end, however, it is my family who deserves much of the credit for who I am and what I do. I am so grateful for a family who understands my flights of fancy, uplifts me when my imagination takes wing, and brings me gently to earth when I have flown too far. I could not ask for more love, understanding, and encouragement than is given to me by those who know me best.

Part One

Influences on Residential Design

Personal
and
Social
Influences
on
Residential
Design

Chapter 1

First and foremost, it is important to design residences for people—not to design sterile spaces that are simply aesthetically pleasing and functional. In a global economy, it is also important to recognize that there are differences in the way cultures interpret housing needs and uses. Regardless of culture, individuals' residences are not just places to eat and sleep but a headquarters—a home. The term *home* combines the ideas of dwelling, refuge, and a place of affection. While there are similar terms in a number of Northern European and Germanic languages derived from the Old Norse *heima*,[1] there is no equivalent term in Latin or Slavic languages. Mark Twain noted that his house "had a heart, and a soul, and eyes to see us with; and approvals, and solicitudes, and deep sympathies; it was of us, and we were in its confidence, and lived in its grace and in the peace of its benediction. . . . We could not enter it unmoved."[2]

The Role of the Designer

Interior designers usually focus on either contract (or commercial) design or residential design, but either specialist may complete projects in both fields. In both types of design, the interior designer works with other professionals, but their roles may be different. In contract design, most of the work is guided by building codes and local regulations. While building codes apply to residential design, the criteria are generally less stringent. For example, hallways in residences need be only 36 inches wide, while in commercial structures, hallway width depends on the number of occupants expected and the amount of time allowed for evacuating the structure in the event of fire. Commercial hallway widths must be sufficiently large to enable two or more individuals to pass; residential hallways need not be as wide. All designers are expected to work within code limitations to ensure that the resulting structure is safe and healthy.

In commercial design, the interior designer will most likely be given a plan that has already been approved by local code officials. The job of the designer then is to ensure the quality of the interior space. Residential designers may have more input from the beginning stages and may indeed even design homes from the ground up. Most of the time, however, designers influence final plans by making small but important changes—directing the swing of a door, suggesting the location of a window or a heating vent, or improving the usability of the structure by recommending added switches to control lights.

Residential designers may work closely with individual contractors—the builder, the electrician, or the plumber, for example. Professional designers must have the knowledge and terminology necessary to communicate with these contractors. The designer, for instance, must understand the implications when a wall is described as load-bearing, must be ready to explain the need to reroute plumbing pipes to ensure sufficient headroom over stairs, or must communicate the need for additional support within the walls for future **moldings** or heavy objects.

It is the designer who must understand the uses to which the residence will be put. If there is to be a home office, for example, the designer can stipulate additional telephone lines for faxes, Internet access, and a business phone so that wires can be concealed during construction. The designer may also be the only one who understands that heavy window draperies may be hung along with additional top treatments such as cornice boards, and that those future items will require support within the structure. Very frequently, much of the design of a home is left up to contractors, who do not consider the best use but rather the ease of installation. The designer must stipulate where grab bars are to be located rather than just that there need to be grab bars. Leaving the location up to a contractor relinquishes design control to individuals who are not appropriately trained. In many instances, that is not a problem, but a professional designer does not leave those decisions to chance.

Most of the work done by residential interior designers is for clients who can afford decent housing. The work may consist of selecting finishes, specifying a new window treatment, or designing the space plan. While it is those who have adequate housing who can afford the services of designers, it may be those who cannot afford designer input who need it the most to improve the quality of their living spaces.

This text is written for the interior designer. It is not a how-to text but rather a description of the processes involved from the planning stage through construction to the end use of the space. Part One discusses issues that must be considered during preliminary design stages: personal and social needs of individuals and families, environmental impacts, technological possibilities, and materials available for use. Part Two begins with the structure and follows through to the completion of structural components. Part Three provides the necessary material for understanding how residential systems work—electrical, plumbing, and heating and air-conditioning systems. The final chap-

Figure 1.1 Even when the structure itself is not a good reflection of its occupants, the landscaping, maintenance habits, lifestyles, interior decoration, and objects displayed in the structure do reflect the occupants' personalities, because people have a significant amount of control over these factors.

ter of Part Three addresses energy issues of concern in residential design. Part Four discusses the types of homes available, as well as designing specific spaces for use by individuals and families.

Designing Residences to Meet Individual Needs

The home reflects the personalities and values of its occupants. *Time* magazine is succinct: "Our homes are where our personalities and imaginations are nakedly on display. . . ."[3] and Kahlil Gibran notes: "Your house is your larger body".[4] As the second-century Greek mystic Artemidorus Daldianus conceptualized, the house is an "image of self." Mihaly Csikszentmihalyi and Eugene Rochberg-Halton state, ". . . Home is much more than a shelter; it is a world in which a per-

son can create a material environment that embodies what he or she considers significant. In this sense, the home becomes the most powerful sign of the self of the inhabitant who dwells within."[5] See Figure 1.1.

In the United States, the average person lives about six years in one dwelling, which means it must be constructed with resale value in mind. This results in houses that are built for the average family. People must select from available alternatives at the time they are seeking housing. Even given this constraint, most individuals and families are able to find housing that meets their needs, that reflects their values and personalities, and that they can make a home.

Functions of Homes

The functions of housing have not changed significantly over the centuries. Changes in the physical structure may improve the way a house functions for a family, but what is demanded of housing is similar regardless of climate, technology, and cultural background. Among the most important functions of the home are protection and security, a visible indication of status, sensitivity to aesthetics, and economy of resources.

The home space provides not only physical protection but also psychological support, becoming a center of abiding affection. People's shelters may provide a home space where there is privacy and freedom from intrusion, a place where individuals make their own rules, a refuge where people can revive their spirits, and a place for intimacy and companionship. The need for such a refuge of peace and security is intensified by societal demands.

Figure 1.2 Among Native Americans in the Southwest, an open-sided structure called a ramada provides shade while allowing individuals to remain outdoors.

Protection and Security

Housing moderates or provides protection from the harmful effects of the environment. The first shelters and those built during the exploration of new territories were, in all likelihood, those that shielded inhabitants from the effects of weather. The sod houses of the American frontier were generally temporary shelters used because they protected against the frigid winter temperatures more effectively than the wagons in which the settlers arrived. As they remained in an area, however, families built more substantial homes.

Once people begin to collect goods, housing also serves as a place to store them. In fact, the two Latin words[6] forming the term *domicile* mean "house" and "to conceal," incorporating in the word itself an aspect of the security expected from housing. While the most obvious security function provided by structures is the physical security of inhabitants, safety is defined broadly and includes psychological security.

Climate. Shelter can provide protection from rain, snow, high water, and wind. A **windbreak** is a simple shelter form that blocks wind from one or more sides. Nambicuara Indians in Brazil use only windbreaks dur-

ing the dry season, although they build thatched huts during the rainy season. Figure 1.2 shows a simple structure used to provide shelter from the sun. During high winds, tornadoes, or hurricanes, people living in the American Midwest retreat to basements or shelters, and those living in coastal areas cover their windows to prevent breakage.

People may elevate their houses on stilts or **piers** to prevent damage from high water. Pile dwellings are frequently found in coastal or swampy areas, such as those in Guiana. There, traditional methods continue to be used even when inhabitants move to hilly terrain. Houston, Texas, experiences hurricanes relatively frequently, and the residents of several exclusive subdivisions have paid for the construction of dikes to prevent future flood damage in their low-lying areas. (See Figure 1.3 for an example of a house constructed to guard against high water.)

Earthquakes present another danger to structures. In northern China, traditional homes use **mortise and tenon** joints for the columns and beams. When an earthquake shifts the building, these joints move slightly, lessening the strain on the structure, which often prevents the collapse of the walls. In San Francisco, California, building codes incorporate clauses

designed to decrease the losses of life and property as a result of earthquakes.

Criminal Activity. Once people begin to store food and accumulate goods, shelter must also provide protection against acts of aggression and criminal activity. Building on high ground provides a measure of security because the elevation offers a command of the surrounding territory, almost precludes surprise attacks, and is easier to defend than land in low-lying areas. See Figure 1.4.

Another technique used to protect a home is to conceal it or to provide a means of escape. The Tanzanian Sonjo build their huts as similar in appearance to the rocky landscape as possible, in the hopes that marauding warriors may overlook them. Originally, residents of the isolated Tunisian village of Matmata constructed underground homes to provide protection from roving bands of outlaws. Since the underground village was not visible on the horizon, the residents hoped that bandits would not notice it. Today, people still live in this underground village, but for

Figure 1.3 (TOP) This beach house is protected from high water by raising it off the ground several feet. Raising the structure does not protect it from the high winds often associated with high water, however.

Figure 1.4 (BOTTOM) Until modern times, security dictated that cities be located on high ground whenever possible for defense.

other reasons primarily associated with health. In ancient Persia, even members of the lower classes had secret doors in their homes to allow them to escape arrest or attack. The Persians also found dogs so useful in guarding their possessions that they made the dog a sacred animal.

Folklore Associated with Security. Not all dangers are real. In most cultures, some people make use of features imbued with cultural symbolism that they believe help to stave off evil or evoke power. In northern Sumatra, the Karo Batak fashion buffalo heads out of palm fibers, add real buffalo horns, and attach them to both ends of the house's roof ridge to provide protection; thus, the house is seen to take on the characteristics of the powerful buffalo. In Guiana, the doorposts of houses belonging to tribal elders are ornately carved and are considered so powerful in protecting inhabitants that unauthorized entry will result in death to intruders.[7]

Today, members of technologically sophisticated cultures rely on locks, alarms, and security systems for protection but also apply other techniques, especially for the safety of children. Fenced yards help improve the security of children at play in American cities, and municipal governments establish lower speed limits in residential sections to help prevent collisions between vehicles and people.

Status

Once security is attained, humans are free to be concerned about their place in society. The ways in which status is made evident vary according to culture, but visibility is a common characteristic. Almost universally, housing is an important way to express status, making status apparent by the dwelling's size, location, and the materials used. Generally, the larger the house, the more it costs, therefore, the more status it bestows on its inhabitants. Typically, higher-status houses not only have an increased amount of space but also more amenities, better protection, luxurious appointments, and a preferable location. Of

course, the housing manifestations through which status is attained vary according to culture.

Social prominence may also be manifested by housing location. Although not universally true, there is evidence that as the ground rises, the status of the inhabitants also rises. Historically, cliff dwellers were the elite; common people lived in flatter, less safe areas. Medieval castles were built on high ground for security, while serfs and common people lived at the base of the castle or in nearby villages on a lower level. In Boston, Massachusetts, many of the elite live in brownstone houses located on steep hills. At night, brightly lit crystal chandeliers proclaim the status of those within. However, altitude is not the only indication of status. The African Hottentots erect the chief's house at the location of the rising sun when the camp is established. From that site, other houses are constructed in hierarchic order in the direction of the movement of the sun.

Individuals concerned with social status desire to live in "correct" neighborhoods. Luxurious areas near community services or recreational facilities are prestigious. Not only are lots on lakes or near country clubs expensive but regulations in such areas may require that houses be of a minimum size or of a specific material. For example, one lakeside area in Texas requires homes constructed on the lots to have brick facades and a minimum of 1600 square feet. Such regulations preclude the construction of homes affordable to average individuals and so retain the monetary value of homes in the subdivision and, by extension, the status of the owners.

In most cultures, new or rare materials may be reserved for the most important people. In the Neolithic Canary Islands culture, which survived until modern times, woodworking tools were not available and cutting trees into boards was difficult and time-consuming. Although all houses were made of stone, the king's house was paneled with wood—an indication of his status. Even in nomadic societies, status becomes obvious through housing form. Since wood is a rare commodity in the desert, high status among

Figure 1.5 Custom entry doors serve as status symbols on contemporary housing for those in upper-income brackets in America. Once these have become common, other symbols will replace them.

Bedouins is indicated by the number of long poles in a person's tent. Further indexes of elevated status are a highly ornamented tent covering and the division of interior space into separate entities.

Status may also be indicated by the space allotted to an individual. In the Buryat Mongol yurt,[8] a circular tent made of felt, the husband and wife are allotted the space to the right of the entrance, and the guest of honor is given the area across from them. Other guests are assigned places to the left of the entrance according to their importance. In some societies, a place near the entry, the least-protected area, is reserved for the person considered most dispensable. Often, the person assigned to that spot is a mother-in-law.

Although status symbols are partially determined by cultural influences, much is left to individual taste. One person may feel that a large house in a secluded neighborhood reflects the most prestige, while another aspires to a luxury apartment in the midst of a crowded metropolis. Inside the home, status may be

achieved by having a collection of the latest appliances, entertainment equipment, and technologically advanced gadgetry—or by having few possessions but impeccably tasteful decor. Status is not always related to expensive material objects. Book-filled rooms —whether they consist of solid oak bookcases holding leather-bound volumes or simple shelves overflowing with paperbacks—can convey that the owner is a person of education and culture. Of course, many people prefer to place their own comfort or individuality above signs of prestige.

In socially mobile cultures, status symbols are continually replaced by new ones. As more individuals obtain status symbols, people with higher status find still other symbols to maintain their elite status. Swimming pools, tennis courts, large landscaped yards, three-car garages, and double front doors have become American status symbols, but these will be replaced by other symbols as they become more affordable to individuals with lower incomes. See Figure 1.5.

Housing reflects not only social status but social mobility. In cultures where people are born into specific social classes, their status and housing form are predetermined. The caste system in India is an example. Other societies, however, may permit mobility from one social class to another. In the United States, upwardly mobile individuals tend to move into larger and better housing in more prestigious neighborhoods with better community services. Because housing reflects social mobility, it is often used to create the illusion of rising status. Some homes in prestigious neighborhoods have lavishly furnished rooms for entertaining guests, but rooms used for family or private functions may be furnished in "early attic."

Aesthetics

Every individual has an aesthetic sense, although some are more concerned than others that furnishings coordinate and interiors look beautiful. Simplicity, harmony, and order may take precedence over other values—even comfort. Ideas about what is pleasing to the senses are extremely personal.

Messy rooms may displease parents but seem unobjectionable to children. Some individuals prefer high-rise apartment buildings, while others see them as impersonal. When given a choice, people live in surroundings they consider aesthetically pleasing. A room that has simple lines, filled with contemporary furnishings and artwork, would not appeal to a person who has more Victorian tastes for extensive carving and detail, plenty of decorative objects, and fringed draperies. John Ruskin, a Victorian art critic and social commentator, proclaimed that ornament is the most important part of architecture; the modernist Adolph Loos said, "Ornament is crime." Modern architects continue to design buildings with straight lines; little, if any, color; and minimal ornamentation. At the other end of the spectrum are the glittering ceiling mosaics of the Byzantine period; carved plaster decorations on the exteriors of buildings ranging from medieval England to modern Hausa quarters in Northern Nigeria; Babylonian glazed brick

Figure 1.6 The extended roofline of this structure appeals to an individual's sense of aesthetics and cannot be explained in functional terms.

with lion and bull reliefs; cone mosaics on Sumerian walls; and the folk paintings of the Ndebele of South Africa on their structures. See Figure 1.6.

Economy

Individuals' housing choices may be based mostly on economic factors, although the ways in which they treat and decorate the space exhibits their personal aesthetic sense. Even individuals in low-income housing may hang pictures from a magazine on their walls or display treasured objects that are indicative of their personalities. Economy is the value placed on anything in short supply, including time, effort, material things, the natural environment, and money. Economy involves setting priorities, such as putting low cost before comfort or time before money.

Effects of Economy on Homes. In the loess plateau of northwestern China,[9] approximately 40 million people live in caves;[10] some are dug into slopes and cliffs, and some are dug around sunken courtyards up to 33 feet deep. These structures use few materials for construction, often requiring only a small number of sun-dried bricks on the facade. But most important, these dwellings are economical in terms of land use. Digging dwellings into hillsides conserves the surrounding arable land for agricultural purposes. Because only 15 percent of land in the People's Republic of China is arable, such conservation is necessary.

Structures designed for spatial economy often make maximum use of available space. Spaces beneath stairs and between roof levels are often used for storage—or even living—in China.[11] In Japan, walls are movable, making all rooms multifunctional. Americans with strong economic values select housing with multipurpose rooms that serve several functions, making them more economical because they are used more frequently.

People who value time and effort may prefer to exchange financial resources for convenience in their homes. Such homes may have laundry chutes, storage for items near their point of use, easy maintenance features, and equipment that saves time and effort, such as self-cleaning ovens, dishwashers, and riding lawn mowers. In valuing time and effort over money, individuals may also select homes that require little maintenance: exterior finishes such as brick or stone that need no periodic painting, ground cover instead of grass to lessen the need for lawn care, or living in an apartment or condominium where residents are not responsible for such tasks.

Economic Factors Affecting Housing Quality. Economic factors dictate to a great extent the location, type, and quality of housing available to families. What consumers cannot pay for, they cannot have. Although most people in the United States have some type of shelter, not all have decent housing. The Census Bureau defines three grades of housing: substandard, minimal, and adequate. Most Americans, however, have housing that is not simply adequate but luxurious by world standards.

Substandard housing lacks one or more of the basic amenities: an interior hot and cold water supply,

a private flush toilet, a private bathtub or shower, a heating system, or cooking facilities. It may have structural defects such as exposed wiring, water leakage, cracks or holes in the walls, peeling paint, or holes in the floors. In addition, substandard housing is often overcrowded. The Census Bureau defines overcrowded conditions as housing with a ratio of 1.01 or more persons per room. Substandard housing offers little of the psychological or physical security associated with home.

Minimal housing at least meets health and safety standards. Plumbing, heating, and other amenities are present, and the home is not defective or overcrowded. Minimal housing provides just that—minimal facilities. Because it is not overcrowded, minimal housing does provide some space for individual and family privacy. Such housing, however, provides few amenities to facilitate the strengthening of family relationships, nor does it provide for long-range security.

Adequate housing provides the necessities plus some comfort and certain conveniences. There may be a yard or family room, space to entertain guests, or even space for hobbies or personal interests. This is not to say that adequate housing is luxurious. However, it does meet the basic needs of the families who live there.

Historically, growing affluence and the development of a strong middle-income group have been reflected in housing. As a family's income rises, its residence typically has more space, more satisfactory amenities, a greater variety of available services, and a more desirable location. Thus, economic differences are apparent through housing.

LOW-INCOME HOUSING. Families with incomes equal to 80 percent or less of the median income for a given area (such as a county) are defined as low-income families. (If the income of every family in the area were listed from lowest to highest, the median income would be the one having as many entries in the list above it as below it.) A family with a very low income has an income of 50 percent or less of the median income for the area. The groups with the greatest percentage of low-income families are the elderly, people with less than a high school education, families with a female head of household, and unrelated individuals forming households.

Inflation and unemployment make it difficult for the poor to obtain anything higher than subsistence levels in housing. Many low-income families live on a fixed income from a pension, Social Security, or welfare payments. During inflationary periods, when prices rise and income remains stable, their financial problems are compounded. Solutions are needed to provide inexpensive yet adequate housing for low-income families, preferably in areas where employment is also available.

One-third of the American people cannot afford adequate housing. Having few affordable alternatives from which to select, they generally live where one or more major problems exist. Low-income housing is often substandard. It may be located in areas that are noisy, polluted, unsafe, or inaccessible to amenities such as libraries and shopping.

Figure 1.7 Large homes in exclusive neighborhoods, on large plots of land, or in gated communities with security controls provide comfort and amenities for those who can afford them.

Often, the central area of a **city** has a large concentration of low-income housing. This is because as cities grow, housing in central areas gets older, begins to deteriorate, and is abandoned by upwardly mobile families. The housing is then gradually modified to meet the needs of those with lower incomes. Large homes are often divided into smaller units that can be sold or rented for less money. Many housing units are allowed to deteriorate to reduce maintenance and operating costs.

MIDDLE-INCOME HOUSING. For many years, middle-income families have been able to spend a large percentage of their income on housing. However, because of the inflation of the past few decades, home ownership is no longer within the financial means of many middle-income families. Land, construction, and materials costs have risen at faster rates than personal income. Those who can afford to buy usually must make compromises. The housing middle-income families can afford is generally smaller than what they want or lacks some of the desired amenities. In fact, many families must choose units in multifamily dwellings even when these are not most suitable for their needs. A person who makes minimum wage cannot afford the average-priced home in America.

Single-family homes may be affordable only if extras are eliminated. Houses may be built in close proximity to one another, sacrificing yard space and privacy. To further allay rising costs, housing is built from similar or identical plans designed for efficiency of construction. As a result, houses in some subdivisions may be identical or very similar.

UPPER-INCOME HOUSING. People in upper-income brackets have sufficient money to purchase the housing they desire. If they cannot locate suitable housing, they can afford to have it built. Housing for upper-income groups is characterized by a desirable location, a large number of rooms, more total space, and luxury features absent in other housing. See Figure 1.7.

Upper-income residences are usually accessible to desirable amenities, including mass transportation systems, cultural activities, and recreational facilities.

Table 1.1 Percent U.S. Population by Age

Age	1980	1990	1995	2000	2003	2005*	2015	2025	2050
Under 5 years	7.2	7.5	7.4	6.8	6.8	6.9	6.9	6.7	6.7
5 to 13 years	13.8	12.8	13.1	13.2	12.6	12.2	11.9	11.9	11.7
14 to 17 years	7.2	5.4	5.6	5.7	5.7	5.8	5.0	5.2	5.1
18 to 24 years	13.3	10.8	9.6	9.6	9.9	9.9	9.3	8.9	8.8
65 years and over	11.3	12.5	12.7	12.4	12.4	12.4	14.5	18.2	20.7

Source: U.S. Census Bureau, Table 11 "Resident Population by Age and Sex: 1980 to 2004" and Table 12 "Resident Population Projections by Sex and Age: 2005 to 2050," *Statistical Abstract of the United States: 2006* (Washington, D.C.: Department of Commerce, 2005), 13–14.

* 2005 figures and beyond are projections. The percentage of population in most age groups has remained fairly consistent over a period of years. Projections, however, show a significant increase in the percentage of the population over 65 years of age beginning by 2015.

They are generally built either at the hub of activity—as in the case of luxury high-rise apartments in downtown areas—or on large lots in other desirable locations. Large lots provide visual and acoustic privacy, space for outdoor activities, and sufficient area for landscape design.

Special Needs in Housing

Typical housing is designed for individuals with the strength, agility, and size of a 30-year-old male. The majority of the population, although of varying ages and physical conditions, can easily use most of the facilities in homes. There is, however, a growing number of people for whom housing adaptations increase independence. Children appreciate some adaptations that can make living in an adult world less challenging. Simple modifications can improve the quality of life for people with limited mobility and those for whom certain senses have somewhat deteriorated. Some of these adaptations are detailed in the chapters that follow.

In 1900, the average life span of Americans was 47 years. Only 4 percent of the population at that time was 65 years of age or older. Medical technology has increased life expectancy to more than 70 years and has also improved the quality of life for the elderly. By 2003, the percentage of the population over age 65 had increased to more than 11 percent and is ex-

pected to continue to rise due to the age of baby boomers and decreased birth rates. See Table 1.1.

The effect of longer life spans is not entirely positive. Most individuals are able to function independently in their homes well into their eighties but as people age, their bodies change. Elderly people are more vulnerable to physical injury, and their bodies heal more slowly. Many have limited small-muscle movement due to arthritis or rheumatism. Heart and circulatory problems can decrease mobility, make extremities cold, and cause sensitivity to drafts. In addition, deterioration of the senses of sight, hearing, smell, and touch can reduce self-sufficiency and enjoyment of life. Stroke, heart disease, arthritis, rheumatism, and other medical problems associated with age may decrease physical mobility to the point where round-the-clock care is necessary. In addition, senility may prevent otherwise active individuals from caring for themselves. Physical impairment also increases the need for security. See Table 1.2.

Handicaps range from the loss of acuity in the sense of touch to the loss of use of all the extremities. Many affected individuals are capable of functioning independently, while others need almost constant attention and care. Modifying the design and equipment of the home or adding special devices can improve the quality of life for many by helping individuals to function more independently than they otherwise could.

Table 1.2 Percent Disability Status by Age

Disability	5 to 15 years	16 to 64 years	65 and over
Total Percent With Some Type of Disability*	5.8	18.6	41.9
Sensory	0.98	2.31	14.2
Physical	1.01	6.24	28.6
Mental	4.61	3.79	10.8
Self-care disability	0.93	1.72	9.5
Go-outside-home disability	—	6.39	20.4

Source: U.S. Census Bureau. http://factfinder.census.gov/servlet/QT-Table?_bm=y&-geo_id=01000US&-qr_name=DEC_2000_SF3_U_QTP21&-ds_name=DEC_2000_SF3_U&-_lang=en&-_sse=on

* On the whole, the greatest percentage of handicapped people is among the elderly. However, physical handicaps are not exclusive to that age group.

Sensory Impairment

Partial or total loss of the senses of sight or hearing, like other handicaps, can to some extent be compensated for by adjustments in housing. Although not as commonly thought of as handicaps, impairment of the senses of smell and touch (the ability to feel objects touching the skin) also require that adjustments be made in the home.

Vision. Visual acuity decreases with age and is, therefore, a common problem among the elderly. However, individuals in any age group may experience visual impairment. The federal government separates visual impairment into two categories: legal blindness and severe visual impairment. People who are legally blind either have a viewing angle of less than 20 percent or have vision corrected to no better than 20/200 in the better eye. (Vision of 20/200 indicates that what people with normal 20/20 vision see at 200 feet, people who are legally blind cannot see until it is only 20 feet away.) Severe visual impairment is defined by the federal government as the inability to read newsprint when wearing corrective lenses, no useful vision in either eye, or blindness in both eyes. For individuals in either of these groups who have some vision, simple modifications in housing can improve living conditions and increase independence.

Increasing lighting to approximately double normal levels often improves safety and visual comfort for those with poor vision although steps should be taken to minimize glare. Night-lights increase nighttime safety. Raised thresholds are often painted a contrasting color to call attention to the change in level. Textural cues also become important as visual acuity declines. A change from carpeting to a smoother, nonslippery surface helps to indicate the beginning of stairs. For those with severe visual impairment, appliances and switch-es can be marked with Braille symbols or other raised markings.

Hearing. Individuals with partial hearing loss must often turn up the volume on televisions, stereos, and radios to enjoy them. The resulting sound may, however, disturb others. Those who wear hearing aids may find that background noises create a confusing cacophony of sound. Hearing aids may improve hearing but volume may still need to be fuller. Sound-conditioning in the home helps to alleviate these problems.

To make alarms, telephone bells, and doorbells more audible to the hearing impaired, it is necessary to lower the pitch and turn up the volume. In cases of extreme impairment, this change may be supplemented by lights or electric fans that are activated by the equipment.

Smell. When the sense of smell becomes less acute, providing protection from gas leakage and fire is important. Automatic gas shutoffs are provided on many newer gas appliances and can be installed on older equipment. Smoke alarms are particularly needed to provide early warning in case of fire.

Touch. The sense of touch can become impaired due to circulatory problems. The primary danger is burns.

A change in the color or texture of walls or floors can be used to indicate stairs ahead, a change in direction, or a dead-end corridor.

Compounding the injury is the fact that people with circulatory problems usually heal slowly. Although children usually have a normal sense of touch, they may not know enough to protect themselves from some of the hazards common in homes. Hot water is the most common culprit in injuries to children and individuals with circulatory problems. Hot water temperatures should be set no higher than 110 degrees Fahrenheit to prevent the possibility of scalding.

In addition, circulatory problems cause individuals to be sensitive to drafts and cold temperatures, therefore, indoor winter temperatures should be kept at approximately 80 degrees Fahrenheit. Heat should be uniform throughout the house, with drafts and cold spots eliminated. In summer, some people are susceptible to heat prostration and dehydration, so indoor summer temperatures should be between 75 and 82 degrees Fahrenheit, and ventilation should be provided.

Mobility Limitations

The American environment presents obstacles for people with limited mobility that few others even notice. Curbs, stairs, and irregular surfaces hamper getting from one place to another, and everyday tasks such as bathing present difficulties. Housing for those with mobility limitations should minimize obstacles.

Limited mobility causes some people to remain in their homes much of the time. In fact, Table 1.3 shows that 12.1 percent of the total population and 26.3 percent of those 65 or older have sufficiently limited mobility to preclude leaving the house. A large window overlooking a pleasant view will provide enjoyment, a sense of spaciousness, and awareness of the environment. Low windowsills enable seated persons to enjoy the view. For the bedridden, a window should be located in view of the bed.

Stairs should be eliminated as much as possible for those who have difficulty walking. The home should be on a single level, preferably on the ground floor. Raised entrances should have ramps with **handrails** on both sides for support. Even raised **thresholds**

should be eliminated if possible. If not, attention can be drawn to them by painting them a bright color.

Easy-to-clean flooring throughout the home makes housekeeping easier, but it should be nonslippery. Falls and injuries can be very debilitating, especially to the elderly. Carpeting helps to cushion falls and is comparatively easy to maintain. Smooth-surfaced kitchen carpeting is both easy to walk on and easy to clean.

Impaired mobility is a consideration not only in getting from one place to another but also in sitting and standing. Furniture should be heavy and stable enough to prevent tipping. Grab bars should be installed near the tub, shower, toilet, and lavatory. Warm air dryers can be installed to make drying off after bathing easier.

A decrease in small-muscle control or other loss of full use of the hands can cause serious problems in everyday living. Levers are easier to handle than round doorknobs or separate faucet handles.

Adaptations for Wheelchair Users

A home for a wheelchair user should be on one floor. Circulation routes should be as direct as possible and wide enough to allow a wheelchair to turn 180 degrees. Usually 5 feet is necessary for this purpose. Doorways should be at least 32 inches wide, but this will not be sufficient for any but electrically driven

Table 1.3 Limitation of Activity Caused by Chronic Conditions 2002

Age	Percent
Total Population	12.1
Under 18 years	6.9
18 to 44 years	6.0
45 to 54 years	13.0
55 to 64 years	21.1
65 to 74 years	26.3
75 years and over	44.0

Source: U.S. Census Bureau, Table 182 "Persons with Limitation of Activity Caused by Chronic Conditions: 2000 to 2003," *Statistical Abstract of the United States: 2006* (Washington, D.C.: Department of Commerce, 2005), 122.

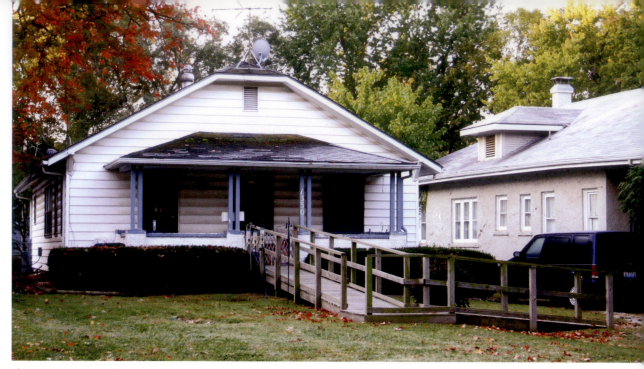

Figure 1.8 For an individual in a wheelchair, the built environment is difficult to maneuver. Ramps at curbs and into buildings, elevators, and large openings all help lessen the difficulty.

chairs. A better solution is for doors to be a minimum of 3 feet in width. Smooth floor surfaces present the least resistance to wheelchair operation, and the use of throw rugs or carpeting decreases mobility. Other accessibility recommendations are given where specific components are discussed. See Figure 1.8.

Designing Residences with Families in Mind

The changes that a family goes through as new members are born, raised, and reach adulthood are part of the family life cycle that greatly influences housing. The family life cycle varies according to cultures. The most common cycle in Western civilization includes four major stages: the beginning family, the expanding family, the launching family, and the contracting family. The family life cycle can differ significantly when adults remain single, when couples do not have children, or when the family is disrupted at any stage

by death, separation, or divorce. Each household has unique characteristics and, therefore, unique housing needs.

The Traditional Stages

Traditionally, the beginning stage of the family life cycle originates when a couple marries. Most newly married couples have little money to spend on "extras." They therefore need inexpensive, private quarters where they can develop responsible independence from parents and establish living patterns.

The expanding stage of the family life cycle begins when the couple has a child. Additional space is needed for the child and all the paraphernalia accompanying babyhood, from diapers and teddy bears to equipment and furniture. The couple who used to do their laundry once a week at a laundromat may decide they need a washer and dryer. The family budget may be strained because there is an extra person to feed, clothe, and house but no additional income. When that is the case, families must make some trade-offs. For example, they can relocate to gain more space but may not be able to afford larger quarters of the same quality.

As children reach school age, parents may move into school districts they believe will provide the desired quality of education. In addition, even more space demands are placed on housing. School-age children expand their outside friendships, begin to develop personal activities such as hobbies, and desire more privacy. These needs continue to increase through adolescence, creating strain on both the family budget and the housing unit. Relocating, remodeling, or adding on to a house may be desirable to provide space for family needs. These alternatives may not be possible, however, because it is also during the expanding family stage that other needs—food, clothing, transportation, and entertainment—require an increased proportion of the family budget.

When children remain at home during college years, or as they begin their careers, the demand for space may continue to be constant. On the other hand, the strain may be periodic if children return only on weekends or during holidays from school or jobs. During this time, the launching stage of the family begins. Eventually, children establish their own households. With the exception of occasional visits, the need for space in the family home decreases.

It is at this point that the contracting stage of the family begins. The couple may spend many years living full and productive lives after their children have moved away from home. Later, one or the other will probably encounter several years of solitude. During the contracting stage, income may be high at first because the expenses associated with raising a family are eliminated. The home may be entirely paid for by this time, leaving more disposable income for nonessentials. Although space is now plentiful, new or expanding interests and the desire to do more entertaining may make different demands on existing space.

After retirement, income decreases. When families remain in a larger home, the extra expenditures for upkeep of unused spaces, plus the labor involved in

maintaining the home, may make it necessary or desirable to move to less commodious quarters. Many people, however, prefer to remain in their familiar homes and neighborhoods with friends and relatives nearby. Renting a portion of the house to someone else can in many cases help alleviate financial problems and make better use of space. Eventually, declining health may require a move to an assisted-living facility.

One of the major motivations for mobility in America is changing family status—adding a family member or having a family member leave the household. A house that can be adapted to changing needs would make it possible for families to remain in a neighborhood with which they are familiar and keep children in the same school if they so desire. Some such houses are constructed with the largest amount of space that will be needed during the life cycle, although not all this space may be utilized at first. Building the house according to the maximum size that will be needed in the future is less expensive than adding on later. Expandable housing offers a solution to the problem of extra space being needed at the same time that the family budget is strained, as happens when children arrive.

A house designed to fill needs throughout the family life cycle might originally have an unfinished upper level. As the family grows, the upper level could be finished into bedrooms and a bath; later, when the children have left home, it could be converted into a rental unit. This type of solution requires advance planning if it is to be feasible. For example, converting part of the house into an apartment involves providing utility hookups, soundproofing, and other adaptations that can mean costly alterations unless provisions were made at the time of original construction.

Variations of the Family Life Cycle

The traditional family stages are based on marriage and children. Indeed, until recently, the definition of a family in American society has also been based on marriage and children. However, Western social values are changing and new patterns have emerged that do not fit traditional molds. These changes are resulting in new ways of defining the family. Single adults, childless couples, and single-parent families do not follow the traditional family life cycle but they do have identifiable characteristics of their own. See Table 1.4.

Single Adults

A significant number of people in the United States postpone marriage until they are established in their careers, while others choose to remain single indefinitely. Single people may have more money to spend for housing than traditional families, since they have no others to support. Although there is no "typical" single lifestyle, single people may be able to devote more time and income to entertaining, travel, or hobbies.

The space needs of single adults do not conform to housing designed for traditional families. Rather than desiring extra bedrooms, singles may find more use for a formal dining room, a large living room, or more outdoor space. It is unusual to find homes with these characteristics that have fewer than three bedrooms. Often, the kitchen does not need to be large, since singles may prepare smaller meals and eat out more often than families with children.

While many singles rent housing, more and more of them are purchasing their own homes. Many share housing with other single adults, although whether this is more often by choice or necessity has not been determined.

Single-Parent Families

Single adults go through a more traditional family life cycle when they adopt or bear children, practices that are becoming more common. High divorce rates are another factor resulting in a greater number of single-parent families. Housing needs for these families are similar to those of traditional families: extra bedrooms, places for family activities, and areas for children to entertain friends. These needs may, how-

Table 1.4 Household Makeup by Percent

Type of Household*	1980	1990	2000	2003
Average household size	2.76	2.63	2.62	2.57
Married couples	49.6	45.0	42.1	40.7
Single-parent families	10.5	11.8	12.7	13.0
Non-family households	21.4	23.4	24.9	25.4
Single-person households	18.5	19.7	20.3	20.9

Source: U.S. Census Bureau, Table 56 "Households, Families, Subfamilies, and Married Couples: 1980 to 2003," *Statistical Abstract of the United States: 2004–2005* (Washington, D.C.: Department of Commerce, 2005), 50.

* The percentage of households headed by single adults is greater than the percentage of married couples. This fact has a significant effect on the housing market.

ever, be combined with the needs for socialization by the adult—requiring more privacy and more room for entertaining guests than many traditional families.

Childless Couples

Married couples who choose not to raise children also have unique housing needs. These couples often have two incomes and can afford to spend more for housing. However, more expensive housing has traditionally meant "bigger" before "better." These couples may not want larger quarters but might appreciate the luxuries usually associated with more expensive housing—formal entertaining space, a swimming pool, a security system, and a prestigious location, for example. Condominiums are one solution to the need for high-quality housing on a smaller scale.

The housing needs of these groups vary widely, depending more on individual values than the housing needs of traditional families. As of yet, the market is not prepared to offer many suitable alternatives.

The Role of the Community

When few others are involved, people maintain more control over the design of their residences, with control decreasing as the number of people involved increases. As people form communities, a complicated network of interdependence develops. A product of this network is that decisions affecting individual residence choices decrease individual control even further. Elected officials determine rules by which individuals must live; bankers influence where people may live, the cars they drive, and the possessions they own; and decisions made by municipal governments affect where people work, the sizes of yards, and sometimes even the materials of which their houses are constructed. See Figure 1.9.

Figure 1.9 Choosing to live in an urban area brings with it many advantages but limits housing choices.

Although the formation of communities means a decrease in personal freedom, it has many advantages. Communities provide the security of the group and opportunities for socialization. They also offer a variety of goods and services that would not be available if individuals had to supply all of their own needs.

Community size is diverse but, generally, the larger the city, the greater the number of goods and services provided. Today, people live not only in cities of various sizes but in **suburbs**, large and small **towns**, and **rural** areas. Each type of community has distinctive characteristics, although every individual community is unique.

It is not a simple matter to categorize and define community types. Most people would agree that life in a sprawling metropolis differs from that in a town of 25,000 inhabitants or a small rural village. But when it comes to actual definitions, people's ideas of community type depend on personal experience. What one person calls a city may seem to another to be only a fairly well populated town.

Even definitions by the Census Bureau change, but in general and for the purpose of this discussion, communities can be divided into the following four types:

- Cities—communities of 50,000 people or more
- Suburbs—towns within the closely settled region surrounding a city
- Towns other than suburbs with populations ranging from 2500 to 50,000 people
- Rural areas, including small towns with fewer than 2500 people

Cities

The structure of modern cities is in part the result of the automobile. It is no longer necessary to live within a short distance of work. City size is, therefore, virtually unlimited, with many cities spread over large areas.

When two or more major metropolitan areas are relatively close to one another, their expansion often results in a **megalopolis**—a built-up area spanning hundreds of miles (also termed a **Standard Metropolitan Statistical Area—SMSA**—by the Census Bureau). One such megalopolis is formed by the population center surrounding the cities of Washington, D.C., Baltimore, Philadelphia, New York, and Boston. This area is 600 miles long, encompassing more than 55,000 square miles.

The demand for land raises its price considerably and makes it available only to those who can afford it. Thus, industrial and commercial areas take precedence over residences in central city areas. Because of the need to house greater numbers of people in small areas, multifamily dwellings are the dominant form of housing. Some central city districts, such as New York's Park Avenue, are made up of luxury apartments; others are some of the worst slums in the country. Faced with high prices and little available housing, middle-income people tend to move into outlying areas, leaving the wealthy and the poor in the central city.

Because land is expensive and desirable in cities, it is necessary to use all of it efficiently. High-rise structures for offices and residences can be built over freeway overpasses, in highway cloverleafs, and in other wasted space. Residences are often constructed above commercial buildings, and many buildings and services are located underground. Germany, Japan, and other countries have large underground shopping areas with residences directly overhead.

Many businesses and industries have located in cities because labor, raw materials, and transportation are available there. Another reason is that the companies believe they can attract better employees by providing the social benefits of urbanization.

Most cities have a particular industrial or commercial activity for which they are known. Pittsburgh, Pennsylvania, for example, is a center for the steel industry. It is attractive to steel manufacturers because it is close to fuel supplies and raw materials needed for production. Other cities have more of an administrative function, and some are known for their cultural activities. Business and industry help support urban areas through taxes, which may help keep residential taxes down.

The concentration of people in large urban areas provides amenities not available in smaller communities. Most businesses have a **threshold size**—the minimum number of people required to support that activity or function. The more frequent and necessary the activity, the lower the threshold size. Smaller communities are limited to low-threshold functions such as churches, restaurants, and grocery stores. Large cities, on the other hand, have enough people to support even those services that only a small percentage of residents will use.

Cities also offer a wide variety of services for the general public. Subways, bus lines, taxi services, and other public transportation systems are available. Hospitals and other health care facilities are close at hand and serviced by ambulances and rescue squads. Urban fire and police departments are relatively large and have facilities not available in less populated areas. Educational systems are generally larger and may offer a greater variety of subjects to students. Other services range from the provision of sewer, water, electric, and gas lines to very high-threshold amenities such as symphony orchestras, operatic and ballet companies, and large theaters.

Cities are not without problems, however. Although a large population makes a wide variety of services possible, it can also interfere with the efficiency of those services. Traffic congestion may cause ambulances to be slow to respond. The large number of paid service workers allows the possibility of a major disruption if a work stoppage occurs. There may be great differences in the quality of several schools in the same city. More alarming than these problems are the reduced health and safety of city life. Urban areas have more air pollution, more traffic accidents, and significantly more crime than rural areas. Psychologists have found that crime is often a direct result of overcrowding, unemployment, and the higher stress levels associated with urban life. Noise and visual pollution are also problems.

Suburbs

American cities have grown considerably, offering the advantages of centralization. However, since World War II, mass moves to suburbs testify to the fact that urban areas may not present a satisfactory quality of life for many families. Suburban living offers many of the advantages of city life and minimizes some of the disadvantages.

Suburban areas are usually less crowded than more urbanized areas. Because the demand for and therefore cost of land is lower, homes can be spread out with more space between them, allowing greater privacy and lower population density. Traffic and parking problems are minimized. Since they are located near large population centers, the suburbs also offer the advantage of accessibility to the variety of goods and services offered by cities. See Figure 1.10.

Because people who work in urban areas but live in the suburbs must be able to afford the cost of commuting, they are often those who earn incomes in the middle and upper ranges. Suburban schools, shopping centers, and other public facilities are usually geared to these groups.

Towns

The category of towns between 2500 and 50,000 in population covers a wide range. Communities in this category can be very different from one another, but all have some characteristics in common. In general, this size range represents communities that offer a distinctly different lifestyle from large cities yet more services than rural areas.

Towns of this size are not as densely populated as large cities. Land is usually less expensive and homes are spread over more space. Lower population density is associated with low crime rates, less pollution, fewer traffic and parking problems, and a less hurried atmosphere. The smaller size of these communities gives them a reputation for being friendlier than cities. Townspeople often are personally acquainted

Figure 1.10 Living in a suburb usually requires commuting to work. Most suburbs do not have a sufficient number of available jobs to support their population and must rely on nearby urban areas. However, many suburbs have grown along transportation arteries radiating from cities, making commuting relatively simple.

with or are familiar with a relatively large percentage of the population.

Towns often have a population large enough for a variety of low- and medium-threshold services. Movie theaters, shopping centers, restaurants, and recreational facilities are offered by most towns. Health care facilities are also available locally, although some smaller towns may not have a sufficiently large population to support specialists such as orthodontists and heart surgeons. Public utilities are almost always available and often public transportation is as well.

Unless towns are located near larger cities, they generally do not offer all of the cultural advantages associated with city living. However, they often have civic music groups, theater groups, museums, monuments, and a variety of civic organizations. They may also be located near natural recreation areas.

Towns of this size usually have enough employment opportunities to support their population, although some may become "bedroom communities" where the majority of residents commute to a nearby city for

Figure 1.11 Large open spaces may surround dwellings in rural areas. While this single farm looks almost like a small village, only one family lives here. Part of the expense of living in rural areas may be the cost of extra structures and their maintenance.

jobs. Commuting is expensive, but the advantages of living away from the city can make it worthwhile.

Rural Areas

Towns with populations under 2500 are considered rural by the Census Bureau. In 2000, approximately 21 percent of Americans lived in rural areas, but there were significant differences by state. In California, only 5.6 percent lived in rural areas, while in Vermont, 61.8 percent lived in rural areas. For the most part, people living in rural areas must commute to urban areas for goods and services. Although circumstances vary, rural communities generally offer only a few of the services of population centers. Few rural communities have doctors or dentists. Very small towns may not even have a grocery store. Most people living in rural areas must commute to their jobs, decreasing effective income unless their work is farm-related. Rural areas may not have public water supplies and sewage systems. Some areas do have rural water districts, although many of these provide only a water supply. See Figure 1.11.

In the past, rural schools have been considered inferior to urban schools, but the consolidation of districts in rural areas has closed the gap. Many rural schools now offer a large variety of subjects and low student-teacher ratios.

Many of the inconveniences of rural living are offset by the advantages. Because there is less demand for land, taxes are lower than in urban areas. For most residents, however, the major advantages of rural life are psychological. Crime rates are lower, the hustle and bustle of the city is absent, and large amounts of space surround homes. People know one another personally and are willing to help when the need arises. Living in rural areas helps to reduce stress and increases the quality of life for many families.

Alternative Community Forms

In recent years, other alternatives to urban life have been tried with varying success. Most are a type of planned community—those for which services are planned and areas defined for specified purposes prior to beginning construction. This allows space to be used efficiently and services planned to serve the greatest number of people effectively. Planning also allows transportation systems, utilities, and other public services to be provided at minimum cost.

Most planned communities use some type of **cluster housing**. Residences are built in clusters and may even share walls (**town houses**). Little space is left between dwellings but compensating green space separates clusters of units, each of which has direct access to greenbelts. Green areas, including playgrounds, parks, and picnic spaces, create the illusion of space. Green space may also facilitate the development of a sense of community. **Planned unit developments** and **new towns** are current alternatives.

Planned Unit Developments

Planned unit developments (PUDs) are planned communities with housing built in clusters and that may be adjacent to existing urban areas. They provide economical living units in higher densities than are usually found in suburbs. They combine the advantages of the suburbs—green space, availability of single-family homes, and recreational facilities—with the advantages offered by urban living. Other advantages include accessibility to a variety of goods and services and freedom from maintaining large yards. Commuting time and costs to urban areas are also lower than typical for the suburbs. Because they use less space, units are often less expensive as well.

Requiring a master plan, PUDs typically provide a mixture of housing types and may even include shopping centers and institutions such as hospitals that provide employment within the development. PUDs are not financed with government funds but through private sources. Large corporations may provide housing for their employees through PUDs and include recreational facilities exclusively for their use. Because of the funding sources, no low-income housing is included, although various price ranges are represented. Some of the dwellings are sold, others rented. A characteristic of PUDs is development by stages over a period of time. Subsequent stages may be replanned prior to development to incorporate innovative technologies or materials or to meet changes in community needs.

New Towns

The concept of new towns came from England, where Letchworth and Welwyn—garden cities established in the early twentieth century—are still thriving communities. During the 1930s, early new towns in the United States were sponsored by the federal government and included Greendale, Wisconsin; Greenhills, Ohio; and Greenbelt, Maryland. Each survives as a successful residential community. Privately financed new towns have also been successful—Columbia, Maryland; Reston, Virginia; and Irvine, California, among others.

New towns are completely planned prior to construction, then built from the ground up on undeveloped land—generally near population centers. Thus, growth and development are orderly rather than haphazard. New towns differ from PUDs in that each is a separate community with a municipal government that can levy taxes.

Modern new towns are not simply residential communities, as many early ones were, although residences in a variety of price ranges and types are common. New towns offer both single- and multiple-family units. To increase their functionality, new towns are designed with all the amenities needed by communities, including recreation and shopping facilities, light industry, public services (schools, libraries, police, and fire protection), cultural activities, and some employment. Lake Havasa City, Arizona, has become a freestanding new town that provides sufficient employment for its residents.

Like PUDs, new towns are designed for high density using the cluster concept. New towns may have access to lakes or other bodies of water, increasing recreational possibilities.

Designed for high densities, new towns generally have defined pedestrian areas where motor vehicles are not permitted. Pedestrian paths designed with under- and overpasses eliminate the need for crossing major traffic arteries, increasing the safety of the community.

Green
Design:
Environmental
Influences
on
Residential
Design

Chapter 2

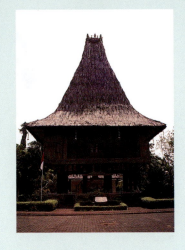

The interrelationships between the environment and people are complex. Over time, people have learned to control their environment and use natural resources to improve their quality of life. Climate, the characteristics of land, energy supplies, and the subsequent consequences of the use of these resources affect people, how and where they live, and, in particular, their housing.

Historically, civilizations have failed because they depleted necessary resources, stripped the land, and polluted the environment. In fact, the survival of the human race may well depend on the recognition of people's interdependence with the environment, including the responsibility for preserving its quality, and the ways in which people solve the complex environmental problems facing them.

Green Design

In less industrialized cultures, housing materials and forms reflect an understanding of and willingness to cooperate with climatic factors. Shelters respond to climatic conditions peculiar to their locations, utilizing nonmechanical means to modify interior environments—often without the use of supplementary heating or cooling systems. See Figure 2.1. While technological developments over the centuries have made living in extreme climates more feasible, they have also made it possible to modify interior environments without regard for climatic conditions, lessening the relationship between climate and housing form. Mid-twentieth-century residential design was characterized by a technological emphasis depending on mechanical control of interior spaces that often ignored the potential energy value of local climatic conditions. Artificial lighting; mechanical heating, cooling, and ventilation systems; and waterproof materials and techniques have eliminated the necessity of cooperating with climate. Each of these, however, achieves comfort at the expense of energy. Some modern

Figure 2.1 Using materials at hand—cow dung, ash, and clay—the Masai in Kenya build houses that blend with the landscape.

buildings are returning to the spirit of environmental cooperation exhibited in most primitive dwellings.

Prior to 1973, energy was inexpensive. The low price created little incentive for efficient use and, in fact, actually encouraged consumption. It was not until the winter of 1977 that energy consumption habits began to hit home to American consumers. During that winter, fuel shortages caused more than a million children to be out of school and a proportionate number of workers to be out of work. These factors, combined with other hardships of the winter, led to a national consciousness of the energy problem.

During the 1980s, interest shifted to more complex global environmental issues, including global warming. Among the decisions that affected subsequent building design were the following.

- In 1989, the American Institute of Architects established a Committee on the Environment.
- The United Nations Conference on Sustainable Development in 1992 focused on the environmental impact of humans living on the planet.
- In 1993, members of the American Institute of Architects met with their counterparts in the International Union of Architects. That meeting resulted in a Declaration of Interdependence for a Sustainable Future that focused not only on the use of energy but also on the interdependence of buildings with the natural environment and with quality of life. This declaration supports reducing the adverse human effects on the environment while improving quality of life for all.
- The U.S. Green Building Council was established in 1993 by government and industry professionals. A resulting task force developed standards for evaluating both the efficiency of structures and their environmental impact by 1998. Other countries, including Canada and Spain, are considering the same type of approach.

The type of construction advocated as a result of this emphasis on cooperation with the natural environment is called **green design**, **sustainable construction**, or **high-performance building** design. The goal of green design is to build, use, and deconstruct healthy buildings that have minimal environmental and energy impact without diminishing the quality of life of future generations. Green design results from an ecologically sensitive team approach to building design, construction, and use. Economically, the life-cycle cost is more important than the initial cost. Green-design structures must consider:

- The site
- The materials used
- The amount of energy required for construction, as well as life-cycle energy requirements for building systems
- The impact of the structure on the environment, including pollutants and generated waste during construction and use, as well as deconstruction
- The effects of the structure on human occupants, including acoustics, indoor air quality, and natural lighting

Energy-conservation techniques employed include:

- The design of the building envelope to reduce heat transfer (See Chapter 10.)
- Implementation of energy-efficient design techniques, including solar and earth contact designs (See Chapter 10.)
- Maximum use of natural and climatological site characteristics to decrease energy use, including landscaping (See Chapter 10.)
- The use of renewable materials and materials that require as little energy as possible for extraction, manufacturing, and transportation (See Chapter 3 and Chapter 5.)
- Maximizing natural lighting and making use of the most energy-efficient artificial lighting (See Chapter 7.)
- Minimizing water use and disposal (See Chapter 8.)

The Effects of Climate on Building Design

Temperature, moisture, and air movement combine to create a variety of climates around the globe. As a result, climate has been an important factor in the development of settlements and the forms of housing throughout history.

Temperature

Civilizations first developed where temperatures were warm. As people learned to use clothing, fuel, and shelter to maintain thermal homeostasis, they were able to spread to colder areas. However, in very cold places, the capacity of the land to produce food in the short growing season is limited, fuel supplies in usable form may be scarce, and climates are made suitable for habitation only by the use of shelters. Even then, such climates are generally sparsely populated and may indeed force a nomadic lifestyle on the inhabitants.

At the other extreme, hot climates may also be sparsely populated. While more favorable temperatures create longer growing seasons, there may still be problems associated with food production. In dry areas, lack of water makes agricultural production difficult, if not impossible. In wet areas, vegetation grows so rapidly and abundantly that the soil is soon depleted of its minerals. Neither type of land will support large population concentrations without intensive reclamation efforts, making nomadic or seminomadic lifestyles common.

A large percentage of the world's population is concentrated in the temperate zones where temperatures are relatively mild. Even in these areas, the temperature may vary over the course of the year by 120 degrees Fahrenheit or more. However, agriculture is more feasible, allowing the support of population concentrations. Buildings protect most people from the effects of temperature extremes.

Moisture

The climate of an area is also affected by humidity and the amount and consistency of rainfall. Rain governs the agricultural stability of land and, thus, the ability of land to support life. Where rainfall is plentiful, food and fibers are easily produced for large numbers of people. Where rainfall is infrequent, few people can be supported by the land unless irrigation systems are used. If water is available in limited quantities, it may be necessary to ration it during certain periods of the year.

Air Movement

Air movement is an important factor in climate. Wind carries heat from warm latitudes to temperate and arctic zones, and cold air from the polar regions into temperate zones. Wind also transports moisture from water to landmasses. This air movement can be beneficial, carrying needed rain and cooling breezes, or it can be harmful, bringing damaging gales, tornadoes, or hurricanes.

Where winds are strong or constant, structures are generally built to withstand the force of the wind. How this is accomplished depends on the culture and on the degree of protection needed. In areas of the United States where tornadoes are frequent, many homes are constructed with basements for protection. On the Melanesian island of Tikopia, houses are designed with a low profile to minimize the effects of gales. Building streamlined structures such as this is one of the most common ways to adapt housing to wind. A streamlined structure allows the wind to continue its forward movement without a drastic change of direction. When wind hits a surface that forces it to change direction abruptly, turbulence results. Turbulent air flow carries heat away more rapidly, increases **air infiltration**, and causes greater stresses on structural surfaces.

Slanted or rounded surfaces are more streamlined than vertical or squared-off areas and allow air to rise smoothly above structures. Some roofs in Normandy and other areas are gabled on the leeward end, but the end that faces the direction of the prevailing wind is rounded, deflecting wind over the structure. The Eskimo snow igloo, a temporary structure used on hunting expeditions and during winter travel, is also a streamlined structure. Its entrance is low, curved, and located away from prevailing winds.

The wind patterns at a home site should be identified prior to construction so that the structure, orientation, and landscaping can be designed for maximum efficiency. In the United States, prevailing winds typically come from southerly directions during the summer and from northerly directions during the winter. However, localized patterns may exist at the site because of nearby topographical features.

Types of Climates

The three distinctive characteristics of the climate of a region are the amounts of heat, humidity, and rainfall it receives. Appropriate building technology depends to a great extent on the particular combination of these factors.

Hot, Humid Climates

People living in hot, humid climates are anxious to take advantage of breezes that carry away moisture and produce cooler temperatures. Buildings constructed without interior and exterior walls invite cross-ventilation. Furthermore, because breezes are impeded by low-growing vegetation and air moves more quickly several feet above the surface, floors are raised off the ground. Thus, breezes can be caught for ventilation and heat radiated through the floor can be carried away. Using building materials that do not retain heat and that "breathe," such as bamboo, leaves, and grass, prevents condensation problems inside the structure. A steep roof acts as an umbrella during seasonal torrential rains. These roofs generally have large **overhangs**, permitting the open structures to remain dry inside while maintaining air circulation. When the

Figure 2.2 This thatched roof structure makes use of indigenous materials that do not store heat. The steep roofline not only sheds water readily but improves the velocity of the warm air leaving the surroundings. Raising the structure off the ground increases the amount of breeze that can be channeled through the living quarters.

sun is shining, the overhang shades the interior of the house. See Figure 2.2.

The Choco houses on the Isthmus of Panama are an excellent example of housing suited to a hot, humid climate. The thatched roof is supported by poles, the floor is raised off the ground, and walls are absent. Using readily available materials and primitive technology, these people build houses ideally suited to their environment.

French-influenced buildings in colonial Louisiana employed many of the same characteristics, adapted to a more technologically advanced culture. They were two stories high: Servants were housed in the lower story while the owners enjoyed the coolness of the upper story. These homes were one room deep, with walls consisting almost entirely of doors or shuttered openings permitting cross-ventilation. A second-story surrounding walkway or **gallery** that was covered by an overhanging roof made it possible to open

the house even on rainy days. See Figure 2.3. The style was reminiscent of that found by the French in the West Indies. There, homes are still constructed on poles with long, one-room-wide floor plans, walls that open, and large roof overhangs.

Hot, Dry Climates

In contrast to the constant heat of hot, humid climates, areas with hot, dry climates experience heat during the day but cool rapidly at night. This temperature fluctuation makes it desirable to have structures that are cool during the day and warm at night. Materials ideally suited to this type of construction are readily available in such regions.

Early in history, people found that thick walls made of materials such as adobe, clay, mud, and stone create a **heat sink**—a substance or object that can absorb and store heat, releasing it when the surrounding area has a lower temperature. Thick masonry walls absorb heat from the sun during the day, keeping the inside of the home comparatively cool. By the time the outside air has cooled at night, heat has

Figure 2.3 The gallery surrounding this house is protected by a large roof overhang, allowing the windows to be opened for air circulation and cooling even when it is raining.

penetrated to the inside of the walls. During the cool nighttime hours, the stored heat is radiated to the interior of the house. Mud houses in the Punjab region of India and Pakistan remain cool during the sweltering heat of the day, as do the adobe apartments of the Pueblo Indians.

In order to prevent the materials from collecting and storing too much heat, a minimum of exterior surface area is exposed to the sun, making compact building shape an advantage. Shading of the structures may also be desirable. Since such climates have little vegetation, shade must be accomplished in other ways. Buildings that are crowded together for reasons of defense, land preservation, or cultural practices have the additional benefit of shielding one another from the sun. Middle Eastern towns and Pueblo Indian villages are good examples of heat control through building proximity.

Others who live in hot, dry climates have sought refuge beneath the earth's surface. For centuries, the entire village of Matmata in northern Africa has existed below the surface of the desert. When the Tunisian government provided the inhabitants with surface housing, the villagers occupied the houses for only a few months. The people soon discovered that they were losing their sense of community and that their lips and skin were becoming dry and cracked. Their solution was to move back into their homes beneath the surface.

Cold Climates

Although dwellings in hot climates are designed to invite outdoor living, houses in cold climates attract people to the inside by providing a central heat source. In fact, the primary concern is the need to keep heat in and cold air out. The same principles used to shelter a structure from wind are effective for this purpose.

Attention to the proper utilization of the principles of heat transfer is also important in cold climates. Doors and windows are small and the house form is compact, minimizing the surface area through which precious heat can be lost. Rural Europeans may house their animals beneath the family dwelling space. The heat generated by the animals' bodies rises and helps to warm the living area. More direct use of animal heat is practiced in other areas. Members of some African tribes bring their goats inside on chilly nights, to the thermal benefit of both goats and people.

In contrast to structures in warm climates, dwellings in cold climates are generally constructed of materials selected for their insulative qualities. The driftwood or whalebone roof framework of the traditional Eskimo house, for example, is covered with an insulative layer of moss sandwiched between two layers of sealskin.

People living in cold climates often take advantage of the same temperature-moderating effects of the earth as people in hot climates. Several variations of earth-contact dwellings are found in cold climates. In the extremely cold climate of northern China, millions of people live underground because the temperature remains warmer than on the surface. Several homes open onto a common courtyard that is situated to catch available sunlight.

Effects of Climate on People

Not only does climate help determine the exterior character of buildings but it also may affect the socialization of entire cultures. In colder areas where houses are compact and small, a central heat source invites residents inside. Because it is more comfortable indoors, most activities take place there, including the preparation of meals. People in cold climates, then, may have fewer opportunities for external socialization. In addition, because climate affects growing seasons and the availability of fuel, people in cold regions tend to be frugal, knowing they must conserve to survive.

People in warmer climates, on the other hand, live in houses that are open. Outdoor activities increase opportunities for socialization, cooking outdoors pre-

Figure 2.4 Courtyards in warm climates often have gardens and pools of water in contrast to the surrounding countryside.

vents heat buildup in the house, and flat roofs invite people to the heights to cool off or to sleep. Many houses are built with rooms opening onto an interior courtyard that often includes a fountain. The greenery, splashing water, and shade of the courtyard make it especially cooling, both physically and psychologically. See Figure 2.4.

Land

Broadly interpreted, land is three-dimensional space. Land includes all of the earth's surface, whether covered with soil, water, or ice; underground mineral and water deposits; and the aboveground phenomena of sunlight, wind, and rain.

The total amount of available land is finite. Although the surface can be altered, more land cannot be produced. Distribution of finite land is controlled by people whose number is not finite but ever increasing; thus, the competition for land and its resources grows constantly.

Land use is affected by green-design principles. Minimizing urban sprawl would result in less pollution

and fossil fuel consumption, due to a lessening of transportation requirements. Reducing the amount of land covered by pavement for pedestrian and vehicular traffic would conserve land for other uses; construction of swales to contain water runoff would minimize the amount of water channeled through storm-water systems in municipalities; and recycling land would bring it back to productive use. Land use recycling includes converting **brownfields**—former industrial zones—and **grayfields**—blighted urban areas—to productive uses.

All land is not the same. Some can support human habitation and supply resources readily, while some cannot. Some land is more suitable for the production of certain foodstuffs, some for the production of fibers, some for producing renewable fuels and building materials, and some produces very little. As population increases, it becomes more difficult to provide food and other resources from a limited amount of land. Although the amount of land available per person in the United States is about the same as for people in the rest of the world, America has a greater percentage of arable land and vast stores of resources. See Table 2.1.

Physical Characteristics of Land

The physical features of land include topography, soil, and subsurface composition, each of which affects housing. Much of the earth's surface is covered with rocky terrain, mountains, deserts, and ice, none of which is suited to agriculture. Water supplies may be abundant in some areas and virtually nonexistent in others.

Topography

Topography, or the "lay of the land," includes manmade features such as buildings and landscaping, as well as natural features such as hills, valleys, and bodies of water. Topography influences housing in three ways: by affecting the location and concentration of

Table 2.1 Percent of Land Use by Country: 2001

Country	Arable land	Permanent crops	Other
Afghanistan	12.13	0.22	87.65
Andorra	2.22	0.0	97.78
Argentina	12.31	0.48	87.21
Bangladesh	62.11	3.07	34.82
Austria	16.91	0.86	82.23
Brazil	6.96	0.9	92.15
Canada	4.96	0.02	95.02
China	15.4	1.25	83.35
Denmark	54.02	0.19	45.79
Egypt	2.87	0.48	96.65
Germany	33.85	0.59	65.56
Japan	12.19	0.96	86.85
Kenya	8.08	0.98	90.94
Kuwait	0.73	0.11	99.16
Nicaragua	15.94	1.94	82.12
Philippines	18.95	16.44	64.28
South Africa	12.08	0.79	87.13
Taiwan	24.00	1.00	75.00
United States	19.13	0.22	80.65
World	10.73*	1.00	88.27

Source: www.odci.gov/cia/publications/factbook/fields/2097.html

* The percent of arable land for growing food crops is relatively low in most parts of the world. When buildings are constructed on arable land, the usable percentage decreases further. In most countries, land conservation is necessary to ensure land for food production for present and future generations.

housing, by forming natural boundaries, and by affecting climate.

Topography and Housing. The location and density of housing depend a great deal on topography. Rough terrain may be suitable for low housing concentrations but may discourage the use of land for urban purposes. Few cities are located in extremely rough areas where other sites are available. The location of cities such as Rome, Italy; San Francisco, California; and Pittsburgh, Pennsylvania, on rough terrain is influenced by overriding factors—convergence of major transportation arteries, a good harbor, or availability of raw materials.

Topography also affects the desirability of individual sites for building construction. High, well-drained sites in any area command high prices. Low-lying sites may be flooded frequently and are therefore less desirable for construction purposes. Additionally, because cold air sinks, low-lying areas may be excessively cold during winter months. Fog may create further problems. However, if well-drained sites are not available and demand is high, the cost of filling or draining low-lying areas may be worthwhile.

Topographical Boundaries. Geographical features that are difficult to traverse—mountain ranges and large bodies of water—minimize the effect of other cultures on isolated people. Unique housing styles may therefore exist within natural boundaries. Although the advent of rapid and easy transportation has lessened the influence of topography on housing style, cultural pockets remain. See Figure 2.5.

Topography and Climate. Topographical features can influence climate over a large area and can also form microclimates in small areas. Rain typically falls more readily on the windward side of mountain ranges, for example, leaving little moisture for the leeward side. In mountainous areas, temperatures fall as altitude increases.

Figure 2.5 Unique regional housing styles were common before the era of mass communication. This residence is typical of some areas of Bavaria and has scenes from fairytales painted on its sides.

Topographical features also influence the direction and speed of air flow. Wind is forced around or over topographical obstructions such as hills and mountains. Since wide valleys have a large surface area over which winds pass, wind speeds are relatively low. Narrow canyons and valleys, however, force wind through small areas, increasing wind speed significantly—an example of the **Venturi principle**. Homes constructed partway up hills or mountains receive the benefits of cooling breezes but not the pounding winds common at the top nor the strong turbulent winds at the bottom. Air flow in turn affects temperature. Valleys parallel to dominant wind patterns tend to be cool because winds carry away warm air. Those at other angles receive less wind and are generally warmer.

Although small bodies of water do not significantly affect climate, large bodies of water moderate the surrounding temperature because the temperature of water changes less readily than that of land. Thus, coastal areas often have more moderate temperatures than do interior regions of landmasses. The climate in much of the British Isles is moderated by the relatively warm Gulf Stream current off the coast.

Air movement, too, is affected by bodies of water. Because warm air flows to cooler areas, breezes generally blow from water to land during the day and from land to water at night. In addition, water provides less resistance to air flow than do landmasses. Thus, major storms may build up over the ocean only to dissipate a few miles inland.

Buildings, highways, and other structures can be considered part of an area's topography in that they affect climate. Wind velocity increases in the narrow spaces between buildings, creating wind turbulence. Concrete buildings and streets serve as heat sinks, absorbing and radiating heat and resulting in an increase in temperatures. During the winter, the heat sinks keep cities warmer than outlying areas and help to melt snow and ice.

Altering Topography. Topography can be altered by leveling, filling, digging, or draining land and by con-

Figure 2.6 In the low countries of northern Europe, windmills have been used to pump water to produce more land.

structing dams and dikes. People in lowland countries of Europe have used dikes for centuries to hold back the sea, creating more land for food production and housing. See Figure 2.6.

Dams may be constructed to provide electricity and to control flooding, but in the process, large areas of land are deliberately flooded. Truman Dam in the Missouri Ozarks and the dams built by the Tennessee Valley Authority during the Depression era are examples. Flooding land precludes its use for agricultural or residential purposes but often results in greater stability of surrounding land because water levels can be controlled.

Not all topographical changes result in land use for the public good. Soil erosion caused by changes in land use can drastically alter topography over a period of time. Ancient Greeks, in using the wood from their vast forests for fuel, denuded the hills surrounding their urban areas. Torrential rains characteristic of the Mediterranean climate then washed away the unprotected soil, leaving rocky terrain that produces little food. In the early twentieth century, American agriculturists plowed natural prairies, which became a contributing factor in the Dust Bowl, affecting food supplies for a decade.

Soil

Soil quality influences whether a region can supply sufficient food for permanent settlements. Cities tend to grow in and near agricultural areas capable of supporting large populations. Land without this capacity is usually sparsely populated.

Where arable land is scarce, people must find ways to conserve the land and make it produce sufficiently. In Jordan, villagers crowd homes in small spaces to conserve precious arable land for crops. The desert regions of Israel and Southern California have been made to bloom by introducing irrigation. These areas now support greater populations. Fertilization improves

Figure 2.7 The entire city of Venice, Italy, continues to sink because the subsurface cannot support its weight. The shifting of the buildings produces cracks in floors and foundations.

crop production, and the use of soil-conservation techniques helps to maintain soil quality and quantity.

Subsurface Composition

Subsurface composition is important to housing. The primary concern is whether the land on which the structure is built can support its weight without undue shifting. Ideally, the weight of the structure should be transferred downward to bedrock or other stable layers. Support is especially important when building on sloping sites. The lack of proper support can lead to building damage and even destruction. In California, massive mudslides have destroyed homes that were not linked to deep subsurface support. Although buildings should be constructed on solid ground, the presence of rock hinders excavation. Building costs are greatly increased when rock must be blasted prior to construction.

Land with water close to the surface is also unstable. See Figure 2.7. In many areas of the United States, basements are precluded because water tables are too near the surface.

Support is the primary concern associated with subsurface composition in certain areas, while expansion and contraction of soil are of major concern in other areas. Clay, for example, expands when wet, increasing pressure on the soil side of basements and foundations, which results in cracks and leaks.

Distribution of Resources

The desirability of land, competition for it, and purchase price depend on location and resource potential. Location with regard to markets, employment, transportation facilities, and other resources affects land cost. Commuting long distances to jobs or community facilities decreases the desirability of land and, thus, its cost. In addition, transporting products to markets increases the cost of goods, lowers profit margins, and increases energy consumption and pollution.

High resource potential, or the capacity of land to provide products or services, offsets some of the adverse factors associated with remote locations. These resources include not only products of the land but services provided. Recreational areas typically produce few goods but land costs are high because of services provided. Usually commercial and industrial enterprises promise higher returns than other functions; therefore, they may pay more for available land. Land for residential use is generally second in the cost hierarchy.

Since population density greatly affects the cost of land, higher prices are commanded in urban areas. In some instances, land is so scarce and so high in price that multistory buildings are erected to "create" more land. Not only is much of the population concentrated in urban areas but most productive activities occur there. Thus, land in urban areas receives intensive use. See Figure 2.8.

Food, trees, water, minerals, arable land, and fossil fuels are all land-related resources used to satisfy people's needs for food, clothing, shelter, and energy. None of these resources is evenly distributed. In the world economy, it would be most beneficial to use all land for the purpose to which it is best suited. However, the distribution of resources is increasingly a political as well as an economic function. While thousands starve in one area, excess food is stored indefinitely in another.

Further complicating the distribution of resources is the fact that people are not necessarily most concentrated in areas capable of supplying their needs most readily. Where population density is low, competition for land use creates few problems. Nomadic Aborigines in Australia establish camps a short distance from water supplies so that others may use the same supply. No one is really interested in controlling specific portions of land or resources. However, when population increases to the point where people must compete for the use of land, control of land and resources becomes increasingly important. People often migrate to areas with richer land and resources. The United States, for example, was established partially as a result of the redistribution of individuals for the

Figure 2.8 In urban areas where land is expensive, it is often more economical to build up rather than out. High-rise apartments make it possible for many more people to live within a given area than would otherwise be possible.

purpose of controlling, using, and enjoying land. The importance of control of land and resources cannot be underestimated. Wars are fought and new nations forged for this reason.

Energy

Land either holds or affects the energy sources available for the production of power. Modern society has become dependent on the comfort and material resources produced through the use of power and energy. The per capita energy use in the United States remains higher than in most other nations. (See Table 2.2.) Much of the energy consumed is used to support the lifestyle of the American people, including a large percentage for residences—for construction, operation of mechanical systems and labor-saving devices, lighting, and myriad other uses. It must also be remembered that the United States produces a significant proportion of the world's goods and food

Table 2.2 Per Capita Energy Use by Country

Area	Per Capita Btus in Millions
World Average*	**66.7**
North America	279.7
Canada	427.9
Mexico	65.6
United States	339.9
Central and South America	49.7
Brazil	49.5
El Salvador	18.3
Netherlands Antilles	702.8
Venezuela	113.4
Western Europe	151.1
Austria	179.2
France	186.9
Germany	172.7
Luxembourg	396.6
Norway	393.0
Portugal	111.0
United Kingdom	166.0
Eastern Europe and Former U.S.S.R.	140.0
Bulgaria	112.5
Georgia	27.2
Russia	202.9
Middle East	107.8
Cyprus	141.3
Israel	138.6
Jordan	43.6
Kuwait	372.3
Qatar	812.9
United Arab Emirates	725.0
Africa	15.7
Algeria	41.9
Burundi	1.1
Ethiopia	1.1
South Africa	108.8
Asia and Oceania	33.8
Cambodia	0.6
Fiji	32.6
Hong Kong	123.8
Japan	175.6
New Zealand	225.5
Pakistan	12.4
Singapore	413.4

Source: www.eia.doe.gov/pub/international/iealf/tablee1c.xls

* Industrialized countries use a much greater percentage of the world's energy per capita than do less privileged nations. It must be remembered, however, that per capita energy use includes the energy used for the production of goods, many of which are exported.

supplies using that energy. The United States, however, consumes more energy than it produces, leaving the country vulnerable to political and economic conditions in other areas of the world.

Energy Use

In the past, energy sources were changed not because people ran out of fuel but because something better was developed. The current situation is different in that supplies are being exhausted before alternative energy sources are fully developed. Conservation provides time to develop technology in areas that have potential as energy resources. Increasing concentrations of carbon dioxide and other gases in the atmosphere caused by the burning of fuels have resulted in global warming.

Energy Sources

Because homes are not totally energy-efficient, much of the energy consumed to maintain comfortable interior spaces is wasted. Energy for homes is obtained from various sources, several of which are being seriously depleted. The most important at present are fossil fuels (petroleum, natural gas, and coal), hydro energy, nuclear energy, and solar energy. Sources of energy that may become more important in the future include **bioconversion**, geothermal energy, nuclear **fusion**, ocean thermal energy, tidal power, and wind energy. Most of these energy sources can be used to generate electricity that can be transported long distances from the source and that is usable everywhere. From past experience, scientists and politicians realize that any energy source used in the future will have to be not only technically feasible but also practical, economical, and environmentally and socially acceptable.

Petroleum

Petroleum, or oil, supplies a greater percentage of energy used in the United States than any other single source. The basic unit of measurement for oil is the barrel (42 gallons). Petroleum is a depletable resource that is unevenly distributed. The United States has large supplies but a major portion of the oil used in the country must be imported.

After refinement, oil can be converted directly to heat by combustion. Many homes, especially in the Northeast and in rural areas, still use oil heaters. A drawback is the need to rely on delivery of home heating oil by truck. Oil can also be burned to produce steam to run electric turbines.

An increasing use of petroleum is the production of petrochemicals. These chemicals are used in fertilizers, insecticides, herbicides, drugs, fibers, plastics, antifreeze, and in the production of building materials such as plywood, insulation, and electrical wiring.

Environmentally, the use of oil has its disadvantages. Massive oil spills create news headlines but are infrequent. More pollution is caused by the combustion of oil than by spills. Oil is not a clean-burning fuel, producing black soot that escapes into the air, causing air pollution. In homes, this soot makes housekeeping difficult.

Natural Gas

Natural gas is a depletable resource that is also unevenly distributed. The United States has large supplies and imports a relatively small percentage of its natural gas needs. Natural gas consists mostly of methane with a small percentage of other gases mixed in. It is found in pockets deep beneath the earth and must be cooled to -260 degrees Fahrenheit before it becomes liquid.

Natural gas is burned to produce heat directly or to produce steam for generating electricity. Little environmental pollution is created through the use of natural gas, although some air pollution is inevitable. Because it is clean-burning, the most frequent use of natural gas is in homes as the fuel for furnaces, water heaters, and ranges.

Natural gas is generally distributed through underground lines. Since it is an odorless fuel, utility companies add an odor to the gas for safety. Natural gas is sold by the cubic foot or by the **therm**, sometimes called a **heating unit**. One hundred cubic feet of natural gas equals one therm.

Liquid Petroleum Gas

Liquid petroleum gas (LP) is a byproduct of the petroleum industry and consists mostly of propane and butane with small amounts of other gases. LP gas is liquid at atmospheric temperatures if it is slightly pressurized. While natural gas is carried through pipelines for long distances, LP is transported in tanker trucks. In areas where there are no natural gas pipelines (especially in rural areas), LP is often used as a fuel for space heating and cooking. It is stored in tanks at the site. LP is cleaner burning than natural gas and produces fewer pollutants.

Coal

Another combustible fossil fuel is coal, which was the primary fuel source during the early part of the twentieth century. As environmental standards were increased and other fossil fuels became cheaper, the use of coal decreased. However, when the prices of natural gas and oil rose, coal again became more important as a fuel source. More than half of the electricity produced in the United States is generated by using coal as a fuel. See Table 2.3.

Coal is the only fuel resource exported by the United States. Although it is a depletable resource, reserve estimates indicate that at present consumption rates, coal supplies should last about 200 years. However, much of the accessible coal has been removed and new sources are farther underground, which increases mining costs.

Coal is not an environmentally desirable fuel. The coal mining process scars the land, permits erosion, and results in the loss of available agricultural land. To combat these problems, mining companies are required by law to plan for the reclamation of land that has been altered by the mining process. Strip mining also causes water pollution when water combines with sulfur impurities in the coal.

Table 2.3 Percent Electricity Generation

Fuel Used	1990	1995	2000	2002
Total billion kWh*	3038.0	3353.5	3802.1	3838.6
Coal	52.5	50.1	51.7	50.2
Petroleum	4.2	2.2	2.9	2.3
Natural gas	12.3	14.8	15.9	17.9
Nuclear	19.0	20.1	19.8	20.3
Hydroelectric	9.6	9.3	7.2	6.9
Geothermal	0.5	0.4	0.4	1.6
Wood	1.1	1.1	1.0	1.0
Waste	0.4	0.6	0.6	0.6
Wind	0.1	0.1	0.1	0.3
Solar	Consistently about 0.5 billion kWh (less than .01 percent per year)			

Source: U.S. Census Bureau, "Electric Power Industry—Sales, Prices, Net Generation, Net Summer Capacity, and Consumption of Fuels: 1990 to 2002," *Statistical Abstract of the United States: 2004–2005*, Table 901 (Washington, D.C.: Department of Commerce, 2005), 582.

* The total number of kilowatt-hours of electricity production in the United States increased more than 26 percent between 1990 and 2002.

Once coal is mined, there are other problems confronting users. Because it is generally not a clean-burning fuel, coal adds greatly to air pollution. Although coal-burning power plants are required by law to have pollution-control equipment, standards are sometimes relaxed when circumstances seem to warrant it. Recent attention to these problems has resulted in a significantly cleaner-burning fuel.

Hydro Energy

Hydro energy results when the gravitational force of falling water is transformed to another energy form. See Figure 2.9. Current usage of hydro energy is almost entirely restricted to that of producing electricity. Unlike early systems, today's hydroelectric production does not depend on the constancy of flowing water in streams and rivers. Water can be stored in **reservoirs** behind dams to allow energy production on demand. The water may even be pumped back up to reservoirs for use again during peak periods.

The number of appropriate sites for hydroelectric production is limited. Hydroelectric plants are often built near mountains or hills where water flows swiftly and can be dammed easily. Most of the promising sites have already been exploited, leaving little room for expansion.

Although hydroelectric production is environmentally clean, it is not necessarily environmentally desirable. Dams and reservoirs require flooding a portion of land. Hydroelectric production may also increase water temperature downstream, resulting in thermal pollution that may harm plants and wildlife.

Tidal, Wave, and Current Power

A second form of energy derived from water movement is the extraction of energy from ocean tides, waves, and currents to power electric generators. The energy from each of these three sources must be extracted differently.

Energy extraction from tides is the most feasible. Tidal power is extracted in much the same way that hydroelectricity is produced by falling water. Tidal basins are dammed and the flow is regulated through gates. The Rance River tidal plant in France is the world's largest, and China has many small plants. The dam at Rance River is about half a mile in length. At

Figure 2.9 The use of waterwheels is a centuries-old method of extracting mechanical energy from water. Waterwheels have been used to grind grain and supply power to textile mills.

high tide, water is trapped behind the dam. At low tide, the water flows back into the sea through turbines that generate electricity. There are few places in the world that have sufficiently high tidal variations to generate energy—over 49 feet. Some of these locations (as in Northern Australia) are located where there is little demand for power. Dammed tidal basins may adversely affect marine life, although there is presently little evidence.

Since waves are much smaller in scale than tides, harnessing their energy is difficult. To date, the extraction of energy from waves has been accomplished only on a small scale. Japan uses more than 300 individual 70-watt wave-powered units for buoys and lighthouses. Great Britain and Portugal are developing wave-power units for more conventional uses.

Energy density in ocean currents is low. Power generation from currents is possible but not yet economically feasible. Extracting energy from ocean movement is not environmentally damaging.

Nuclear Energy

Nuclear energy results from the fusion (joining together) or the **fission** (tearing apart) of atoms. Energy exists in the bond between particles in atoms and is released when that bond is altered.

Nuclear Fission. Fission is used in nuclear power plants that use uranium or plutonium. Although both are depletable resources with limited reserves, nuclear reactors need only small quantities of fuel. The thermal energy released through nuclear fission is used to produce steam, which in turn is used to generate electricity.

The disposal of fission waste products creates environmental problems. One of these waste products is heat. Water warmed by waste heat is dumped into streams and rivers, creating thermal pollution that can alter food chains. The most publicized problem, however, is that of radioactive waste. If such wastes are to be disposed of, problems arise having to do with the stability of the potential waste site. Suggested solutions include disposal in salt mines or in outer space. Radioactive waste can be reprocessed, but doing so increases costs and still leaves the problem of temporary storage.

Because one of the first uses of nuclear energy was the atomic bomb, people immediately recognized the potential danger of nuclear energy as a fuel source. Under normal operating conditions, nuclear reactors do not emit radioactive particles to air or water. However, accidents such as those at Chernobyl and Three Mile Island may cause radioactivity to be released. In that event, water supplies or air become harmful. Some people have become concerned about having nuclear power plants near their homes, and a few plants have even been temporarily or permanently closed.

Several countries, including Switzerland, West Germany, and Sweden, obtain a higher percentage of their electrical needs from nuclear energy than does the United States. See Table 2.4. With the exception of hydroelectric energy, nuclear power production is less expensive than other large-scale forms. The future use of nuclear power depends on public acceptance and on government and industry action to resolve current and potential problems.

Nuclear Fusion. Nuclear fusion is the most common source of energy in the sense that it is the process that powers the sun. Currently, the direct use of the fusion process for production of electricity is not practical. The Department of Energy has estimated that commercial fusion power plants would be developed early in this century. Such plants would be relatively clean, producing smaller quantities of radioactive waste than fission plants. The heavy hydrogen required for the fusion reaction is found in almost limitless amounts in ocean water, while other fuel would actually be generated during the fusion process.

Solar Energy

The amount of sunlight striking the earth each year is equal to 35,000 times as much energy as that

Table 2.4 Percent Electricity Generation by Country: 2001

Country	Total billion Kilowatt-hours	Thermal[a] Percent	Hydro Percent	Nuclear Percent
World total[b]	14,813.3	64.1	17.3	17.0
Australia	204.7	91.3	7.9	—
Belgium	74.4	38.2	0.6	59.2
Bulgaria	41.3	50.6	5.2	44.2
Canada	570.1	28.1	57.8	12.8
China	1,409.3	80.3	18.3	1.2
Germany	547.9	62.5	3.7	29.7
Japan	978.3	58.9	8.5	31.0
Mexico	198.6	78.7	14.2	4.2
New Zealand	38.6	33.9	55.0	—
Paraguay	44.9	Z[c]	99.9	—
South Africa	199.6	93.6	1.0	5.4
Switzerland	68.7	1.2	59.6	37.1
United Kingdom	361.6	73.6	1.1	23.7
United States	3,736.6	71.6	5.6	20.6

Source: U.S. Census Bureau, "Net Electricity Generation by Type and Country: 2001," *Statistical Abstract of the United States: 2004–2005,* Table 1368 (Washington, D.C.: Department of Commerce, 2005), 868.

  [a] Includes electricity generated from coal, gas, and oil

  [b] The fuel or power used to produce electricity differs according to the natural resources of the country. Paraguay, for example, gets almost all of its power from hydroelectric sources, which is not possible in most countries. Total figures show that the United States generates a quarter of the world's power.

  [c] Z = Less than 0.05 percent

consumed by the entire world's population. The development of technology to capture and use some of this energy has made solar power a feasible energy source.

Solar energy can be used to generate electricity through **photovoltaic cells**. Light reacts with silicon or other materials in the cell to produce electricity, but high temperatures are needed. The wide dispersion of the sun's heat over the earth's surface causes only about 429.2 **Btus** of heat to strike each square foot of sunlit earth per hour. (A Btu is a measure of heat—the **British thermal unit**. One Btu is the amount of heat required to raise the temperature of 1 pound of water 1 degree Fahrenheit.) To obtain the high temperatures needed for conversion of sunlight into electricity, the sun's rays are concentrated on the cell by the use of mirrors or lenses. Because sunlight is not constant and varies according to season, geographic location, time

of day, and cloud cover, storage facilities for collected energy are necessary.

Current usage is generally limited to watches, calculators, photographic light meters, and satellites, although some recent buildings have photovoltaic arrays on their rooftops to generate power. This technology holds great promise for future energy generation.

Solar energy has many of the characteristics of the ideal fuel source. Its supply is inexhaustible. It creates no dependence on foreign sources or even local delivery systems. Its use requires no other energy source, results in no environmental damage, and is at least intermittently available everywhere.

Bioconversion

Through photosynthesis, plants convert sunlight into stored energy. In turn, this stored energy can be converted from organic materials to a suitable form through the process of bioconversion. Burning wood to provide heat is the most common example of bioconversion but other materials and methods can be used. Sources of organic materials for bioconversion include:

- Crops grown especially for energy conversion, including trees, sugar beets, sugarcane, sorghum, corn, and water hyacinths
- Wastes from field crops grown for other purposes
- Waste products from other sources, including cities and industries
- Algae and seaweed

Burning is a bioconversion process that can be used for waste products as well as for wood. Burning waste products makes efficient use of substances that would otherwise be unusable. Wastes can be combined with other fuels or burned directly to generate power. In 2003, there were 89 municipal solid-waste plants producing electricity, including one in Baltimore, Maryland. About 0.3 percent of the electricity generated in the United States comes from solid waste.[1] Burning solid wastes reduces the volume up to 90 percent, which saves a significant amount of land that would potentially be used for landfill. The caveats, however, include air pollutants from burning of the wastes and disposal of the ash created.

A second method of bioconversion is the decay of organic materials. For example, sewage and feedlot residue can be organically decomposed to produce methane, a low-grade natural gas. This method, too, is a way to dispose of waste products while at the same time producing useful energy. Waste products suitable for bioconversion are an almost unlimited resource.

The third method of bioconversion is the distillation of grain, sugarcane, sugar beets, or cellulose wastes to produce alcohol that can then be used as a fuel. A disadvantage of this method is the need for a fuel for the distillation process. Although the products to be distilled can be used for other purposes, their use as a fuel may be the most important one in coming decades.

The environmental impact of bioconversion depends on what method is used. When substances are burned, bioconversion produces air pollution. However, that pollution may be less than the pollution caused by other methods of disposal. The use of a bioconversion product such as methane or alcohol produces varying degrees of pollution, depending on how the secondary fuel is used.

Wood is an important supplementary fuel source in the United States. It is used in fireplaces, fireplace inserts, woodstoves, and furnaces. Wood is a renewable resource replenishing itself faster than it is consumed when its production is well managed. Energy plantations harvest quick-growing trees in three- to five-year cycles for use as fuel.

In general, wood is impractical for large-scale energy production. However, in some cases, trees or wastes from logging and milling operations can supply sufficient fuel to power plants. In Tennessee, Maryville College uses the wood byproducts of local sawmills to heat campus buildings. Such large-scale use is limited to areas where wood is abundant.

Geothermal Energy

The natural thermal energy found in the interior of the earth is geothermal energy. The temperature of the earth increases by approximately 100 degrees Fahrenheit each mile toward the core. In certain areas, this heat is transferred to water near the surface, creating steam: Geysers and hot springs are forms of geothermal energy. The steam and hot water produced naturally or through wells can be used to generate electricity. In northern California, the Geysers Field power plant produces enough electricity to power a city of half a million people. Geothermal energy was first put to use in Italy in the early twentieth century. Iceland, Japan, Mexico, New Zealand, Russia, Turkey, and the United States presently harness and use geothermal energy.

Geothermal energy is widely dispersed. To be economically feasible, it must be used where it is. In the United States, a major problem with the development of geothermal energy is that most of the prospective sites are on federal lands that are not available for leasing. Through provisions of a geothermal act in 1970, some of these areas may eventually be developed.

When geothermal energy in the form of water is utilized, some environmental problems occur. The hot water carries minerals and gases that are then discharged into streams and rivers. The chemical composition of the natural waterways is changed, affecting plant and animal life. Extraction of geothermal energy may also cause the surface to sink, contributing to soil erosion.

Ocean Thermal Energy

Ocean thermal energy conversion is the extraction of heat from seawater and the conversion of that heat to electricity. The principles involved were suggested during the 1820s by French scientists. Not until relatively recently, however, was ocean thermal energy seen as economically feasible. A number of ocean thermal power plants are being planned for the future.

The economical conversion of heat energy to electricity requires a temperature differential of 35 to 50 degrees Fahrenheit between warm water near the surface and the colder water beneath. This differential makes it necessary to locate ocean thermal power plants in tropic zones or in the Gulf Stream. The plants would be built on floating platforms similar to those used for offshore oil wells. Warm water from near the surface would be pumped into the plant and used to heat liquid ammonia, changing it to a pressurized gas that drives turbines that generate electricity. Deeper, colder ocean water would cool the ammonia so that the cycle could be repeated. The efficiency of energy production is low but increases as the temperature differential of the warm and cold water increases.

Ocean thermal power is an inexhaustible energy supply, although its extraction would be limited to a few places—all of which are subject to tropical storms. Other potential problems include saltwater corrosion, the clogging of system components with marine life, and the long underwater lines necessary to transmit the electricity to shore. These problems may preclude the large-scale development of ocean thermal power plants.

The environmental effects of ocean thermal energy extraction are not yet certain. Moving warm and cold water to different areas may alter global weather patterns and affect marine life.

Wind Energy

Wind energy has been used for centuries to pump water and sail ships. By 1910, Denmark was also harnessing wind power to generate 20 percent of the electricity used by its citizens. Traverse City, Michigan, Fort Collins, Colorado, and a few other communities have some wind-powered generators to provide a portion of their electrical needs. In the United States, wind machines produce about 10 billion kWh of electricity per year—enough to serve the city of Chicago. Many of the wind farms today are owned by independent power producers who sell the electricity produced to local power companies. Power companies are required to purchase any available wind-generated electricity—even excess power produced by individual units. For the sale of electricity to be feasible, however, wind farms must be located reasonably close to power transmission lines. See Figure 2.10.

The small percentage of wind in the 100 feet of atmosphere closest to the earth provides the force to drive the propellers. Low-speed winds cannot be used economically to produce electricity: Usable wind speeds must range between 10 and 25 miles per hour. Since sufficient wind is not always present, the energy generated by it must be stored to create constant supplies. The components of wind-powered generators are relatively inefficient at producing usable

Figure 2.10 Wind machines designed to generate electricity are often grouped together in wind farms or parks, some of which are offshore.

energy—about 30 to 35 percent efficient—because winds are not constant. Wind-generated electricity is environmentally clean, producing no pollution. The supply is nondepletable, although inconsistent.

Pollution

From the beginning of time, people have caused environmental pollution. When population densities were low, the effect was imperceptible. But as demands for housing, clothing, recreation, food, and energy increased, excessive pollution followed. Because of the populations concentrated there, urban areas have always had more problems with pollution than less populated areas. Ancient Romans recognized the hazards of air pollution; their philosophers extolled the healthfulness of the environment in the country as compared with that in the city. In processing lead, the Romans employed tall chimneys so that gases released would be carried off by wind currents. Babylon and ancient Greece had the same problem with air pollution. Charcoal was burned for heat, metals were forged, and pottery fired—all creating excess heat, smoke, and dust. Air pollution was especially noticeable on calm days, when the air filled with smoke.

The ancient Greeks were also concerned with water pollution. Athenian laws required sewage to be removed to a specified distance beyond city walls, where it was then distributed over large areas as fertilizer.

Pollution has continued to cause problems as technology has expanded. In 1306, English law forbade the burning of coal while Parliament was in session. The Industrial Revolution and the spread of urbanization increased the demand for higher standards of living. These demands necessitated industrial development and the production of goods and services, which in turn increased waste formation. Today, workers in certain industries wear masks to filter pollutants from the air they breathe. Even schoolchildren in Japan wear masks to protect them from pollutants.

There are various types of pollution. Some affect housing spaces directly, others indirectly, and some are a result of housing itself. Others result from the associated demands of individuals.

Air Pollution

The Environmental Protection Agency has identified major air pollutants at which current control efforts are aimed. Most of these pollutants originate as automobile exhausts, energy losses from power plants and industrial processes, and waste products needing disposal. Much potential air pollution is eliminated at the source due to the requirements of the Clean Air Act of 1990. The act also provides for minimum standards of air quality set by the government and gives enforcement powers to the Environmental Protection Agency.

Areas around cities are especially affected by air pollution. However, because wind carries pollutants away from their source, pollution originating in any area becomes a global problem. Australia, England, and the United States all report more deaths due to air pollutants than to automobile accidents each year. In fact, some estimates report that every year up to three million people worldwide die prematurely as a result of air pollution.[2]

When wind does not carry away pollutants in urban areas, smog results. The term *smog*, a combination of the words *smoke* and *fog*, was coined in England when both conditions were prevalent. Smog is unpleasant to look at and to smell, blocks sunlight, and may cause respiratory diseases and even death.

Air quality affects housing as well as the environment. Because oxygen is consumed by housing occupants and by heating and cooling systems, fresh air supplies from outdoors are brought into homes. If this air contains contaminants, including pollen, smoke, dust, and odors, the healthfulness of the living space is affected. Control of air pollution in homes is essential in high-smog urban areas. Foreign particles eventually settle out of the air, creating dust and increasing household chores. Filters or electronic air cleaners effectively clean the air, decreasing pollutants, removing substances that may cause allergic reactions, and keeping interior surfaces cleaner and, therefore, longer-lasting. The initial cost of air cleaners is negligible when compared with the advantages.

Housing, in turn, affects the air quality of the environment. The more power needed for the operation of a household, the more power must be produced, increasing air pollution at generating stations. In addition, most residential climate-control systems add to waste heat and other forms of air pollution.

Water Pollution

People's dependence on water is so great that their distribution over the earth is governed by the availability of water. Modern cultures use water not only for drinking but for cleaning, disposal of wastes, and recreation. These uses interrupt natural water cycles and introduce contaminants in the form of heat and solid wastes. Contamination makes water unfit to drink, threatens forms of aquatic life important in the food chain, and decreases recreational uses of water.

The generation of power with fossil fuels often requires the use of large volumes of water to dissipate heat. In the process, water in lakes and streams is warmed. This warmer water is the beginning of a chain reaction that not only decreases the oxygen content of the water but increases the food and oxygen needs of the fish. The lack of sufficient oxygen in the water causes the death of aquatic organisms.

✿ Individuals who sort solid wastes at home require additional space for storage of recyclable materials prior to collection or delivery. Municipal trash collection costs are often increased when consumers separate recyclable materials because these materials must be kept separate during collection and transportation.

Fish and shellfish are also affected by other wastes dumped in water. Poisons such as mercury and pesticides are eventually concentrated in their bodies, affecting every organism at higher levels of the food chain. Water quality is further affected by air pollution. Rain droplets form around particles in the air, including pollutants, resulting in acid rain. When the contaminated rain falls to earth, it washes additional pollutants from streets, buildings, and the land into waterways. Acid rain is also destructive to building surfaces, including masonry.

The control of water pollution is expensive, and costs are eventually passed on to consumers. Water-treatment methods are not always entirely effective. In towns across the United States, there are times when residents are asked to boil water prior to consumption.

Solid Wastes

Many of the products of the technological age are virtually indestructible by natural processes. Some means must be found to dispose of them, whether by burning, burial, or recycling. Americans generate an average of 3.7 pounds of waste per day, of which 3 pounds is disposed of in landfills.[3]

Before pollution controls were established, individuals incinerated solid wastes at home, but currently, most municipal areas have regulations against the burning of rubbish. The necessity for trash cans and city collection systems adds to individual housing costs and to visual pollution. Waste is produced during all stages of housing life cycles: construction, use, and deconstruction. The Environmental Protection Agency estimates that 2.41 to 11.30 pounds of construction waste are generated per square foot of space (with an average of 6.14 pounds per square foot). For a 2000-square-foot home, the amount of construction waste, then, is approximately 12,280 pounds—more than 6 tons.[4]

Although solid wastes can be used to provide energy through bioconversion, only combustible wastes can be disposed of in this manner. The costs of sorting waste material at the municipal level are prohibitive. It is more feasible for sorting to take place at the consumer level. A similar problem affects the recycling of materials such as paper and aluminum. (See Table 2.5.)

Solid wastes may also be buried for landfill. Through landfill, a more aesthetically pleasing environment can eventually be created. The shielding of current dumping areas is advisable to decrease visual pollution.

Visual Pollution

Typical visual pollutants include large groupings of signs along roadways, destroyed areas of natural beauty, overhead power lines, litter, or almost anything considered unpleasant. Unkempt homes with poorly maintained yards may not be out of place in some neighborhoods but when located beside well-kept homes with manicured lawns, such homes would be visually polluting and may even affect the property values of homes around them. Generally, however, visual pollution is only psychologically irritating and is not hazardous to health.

Olfactory Pollution

Whether odors are considered pleasing or offensive depends on the culture and the individual. Paper pulp plants, oil refineries, and feedlots for hogs and cattle are all responsible for strong odors. To some, the odor is offensive and sometimes physically damaging, but to others, it is the smell of prosperity. Local zoning ordinances often require industries that produce strong odors to be located downwind of urban areas to minimize their olfactory impact and the number of complaints registered against them. However, wind directions sometimes shift, carrying odors from even well-located plants to highly populated areas. These odors can be minimized inside homes by the use of air filtration but outdoor space remains affected.

Table 2.5 Generation and Recovery of Solid Waste Materials: 2001

Waste material	Generated amount in millions of tons*	Recovered amount in millions of tons	Percent recovered
Paper products	81.9	36.7	44.9
Ferrous metals	13.5	4.6	33.8
Aluminum	3.2	0.8	24.5
Other nonferrous metals	1.4	0.9	64.8
Glass	12.6	2.4	19.1
Plastics	25.4	1.4	5.5
Yard waste	28.0	15.8	56.5
Other wastes	63.3	5.4	8.5

Source: U.S. Census Bureau, "Generation and Recovery of Selected Materials in Municipal Solid Waste: 1980 to 2001," *Statistical Abstract of the United States: 2004–2005,* Table 364 (Washington, D.C.: Department of Commerce, 2005), 223.
  * 81.9 million tons = 81,900,000 tons

Odors are also produced within the home, including those associated with kitchens, bathrooms, pets, and smoking. The sale of room deodorizers attests to the perceived offensiveness of such odors. Household odors can also be reduced by venting them outdoors or filtering them through air cleaners.

Electromagnetic Pollution

Electrical energy is carried from power plants through large cables. These cables and towers require wide rights-of-way, taking up many acres of land. See Figure 2.11. The high-voltage cables are surrounded by electromagnetic fields. High-voltage lines interfere with television and radio reception in homes near them. Other radio and television interference is caused by the use of citizens-band and ham radios on various frequencies. Stray signals have been known to operate remote-control garage doors, compromising security. Various devices for reducing electromagnetic interference are available and are successful to varying degrees but add to housing costs.

Buried electrical cables cause groundwater to carry electromagnetic energy resulting in corrosion of underground pipes. Pipes made of materials subject to

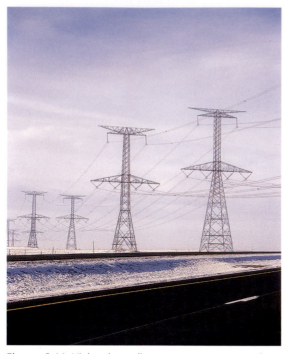

Figure 2.11 High-voltage lines carry power sometimes hundreds of miles from electrical plants to communities.

corrosion must then be replaced at relatively frequent intervals.

Noise Pollution

Noise is unwanted sound.[5] Noise adversely affects quality of life, disrupts communication and other activities, poses a threat to physical and psychological well-being, and affects property values. Because it is generated by humans and detrimental to health or welfare, noise is considered a form of environmental pollution.

Overall noise levels have increased significantly since World War II, and all predictions point to further increases. Noise is often associated with the use of land—traffic arteries, air space around airports, transit systems, factories, construction equipment, refuse collection, sports, and play activities all add to the cacophony of urban areas.

Individuals show a high tolerance for noises they create. Noise generated by others is more likely to be annoying. Much like the proverbial rose being a weed in a vegetable garden, what is pleasing sound to one individual may be noise to another. Much of the noise pollution people experience results from individuals and businesses who believe that it is their right or freedom to make noise. The most common right claimed is a property right. Individuals claim that they should be free to use their property as they see fit without interference from others.[6]

In his keynote address to the 1969 conference on Noise as a Public Health Hazard, U.S. Surgeon General William H. Stewart (1965–1969) said: "Calling noise a nuisance is like calling smog an inconvenience".[7] The urban and suburban population of America and other countries is subjected to noise on a consistent basis, affecting quality of life and often health.[8]

Measuring Sound

Sound intensity or loudness is measured in **decibels (dB)**. One decibel is equal to the smallest change in sound intensity that can be discerned by a person with average hearing. Zero decibels represents the softest audible sound. Decibel scales are logarithmic in nature. For every 10 dB increase, sound intensity is multiplied by a factor of 10. A sound of 20 dB is 10 times as loud as one at 10 dB, and a sound of 30 dB is 100 times as loud as one at 10 dB. Table 2.6 shows the decibel levels of various interior and exterior noises. One of the unique characteristics of sound is that it is not cumulative. If music is playing at 70 dB and a fan is operating at 55 dB, the combined decibel level is not 125 but 70.13.

The perception of loudness by people is also logarithmic, but in this case, a 10-dB increase doubles loudness. Thus, a 30-dB sound is perceived as 4 times as loud as a sound at 10 dB.

Sound spreads out over distance, diminishing the decibel level that reaches the ear. Power, too, affects the distance that sound travels. When power is doubled, loudness increases 3 dB. When distance is doubled, loudness decreases 6 dB.

Table 2.6 Decibel Levels of Selected Interior and Exterior Noises

Source	Decibels*
Human breathing	10
Whisper	20
Quiet conversation	30
Quiet street	50
Normal conversation	60
Average office	60
Average street noise	70
Average factory	80
Subway (rubber wheels)	80
Blender	90
Subway (steel wheels)	100
Loud street noise	100
Power lawn mower	100
Accelerating motorcycle	110
Hard rock band	110
Sonic boom	120
Siren at 100 feet	120
Jet plane taking off	140

Source: http://www.bia.org/BIA/technotes/t5a.htm

  * Many of the everyday sounds in the American environment are sufficiently loud to cause damage to hearing.

Sound is also measured by the frequency or the number of wave peaks or cycles passing a point in one second. This measurement is given in **Hertz (Hz)**—one Hertz is equivalent to one cycle or peak per second. Low-pitched sounds have long wavelengths, resulting in fewer waves per second passing a point, thus lower frequencies; higher-pitched sounds have shorter wavelengths and more waves per second, resulting in higher frequencies. Low-pitched sounds carry farther than those with higher pitches. Young people hear sounds ranging from about 20 Hz to 20,000 Hz, although the human ear is most sensitive to frequencies between 1000 Hz and 5000 Hz.

Effects of Noise

Because noise is not visible and few dramatic incidents have brought attention to the problem, the effects of noise have been recognized slowly. Constant exposure to even low-level noise may have negative effects: Individuals may not be able to sleep when noise levels are as low as 45 dB. Noise has been associated with anger, stress, aggression, hypertension, communication difficulties, productivity losses, and interference with cognition, learning, and language acquisition.

Noise is the number one cause of hearing loss affecting the nerve (hair) cells in the cochlea of the inner ear. Hearing loss occurs beginning at about 80 dB, first in the higher frequencies. Continued exposure to damaging noise results in hearing losses in lower frequencies, eventually affecting the understanding of speech. Noise-induced hearing loss is permanent and cumulative. The louder the sound, the less exposure time is necessary to result in damage. Noises above 85 dB (the approximate dB level of a street in a large urban area) are known to cause damage over time, but noise at 140 dB or above can cause damage after just one exposure. Sounds of 180 dB and over—such as that produced by rockets—can structurally damage buildings and can even be fatal to humans. Because of higher noise levels, individuals in urban cultures have a higher incidence of hearing loss than rural ones.

Individuals in some occupations are more subject to hearing loss than people in the general population because of the noise to which they are subjected at work. Ironically, musicians often exhibit measurable hearing losses.[9] The Occupational Safety and Health Administration (OSHA) requires hearing protection for individuals in some jobs where exposure to noise may be high. OSHA halves allowable unprotected exposure time for every 5 dB increase over 90 dB. For example, a worker who is exposed to 90 dB is allowed to work 8 hours in that environment, while an individual exposed to 95 dB may be exposed for only 4 hours per day; exposure to 115 dB is limited to 15 minutes a day. The National Institute for Occupational Safety and Health halves exposure time for every 3 dB increase in noise. This office also recommends that individuals should not be subjected to noises of 90 dB or more for more than a single hour a day.

While regulations exist to protect individuals from damaging noise in the workplace, there are only a few local regulations concerning the noise produced by recreational activities—speedboats, snowmobiles, all-terrain vehicles, and shooting are examples. At major sporting events, noise levels often reach 120 dB during some moments. The noise generated by construction activities—even those occurring at night—is rarely regulated, nor is the volume of music played by individuals. Some apartment dwellings have rules concerning noise, college dormitories often specify "quiet hours," and some municipal areas have been designated as "quiet zones." More than 150 American communities have banned the use of leaf blowers due to the noise associated with their use.

Noise in the Residential Environment

Sound-conditioning decreases the impact of existing noise levels in the home. Noise control is important not only because of the stress associated with loud or constant noises but also because of the need for privacy in many areas of the home. Sounds from entertainment equipment or the clatter of dishes in the kitchen should not disturb people who are sleeping, nor should conversations be audible through walls between rooms.

Sound-Conditioning

Noise can be reduced at the source, absorbed by barriers, or masked by other sounds. A combination of these techniques can be used to improve the acoustic quality of homes, public spaces, and business environments.

Reducing Sound. Reducing the noise generated by a source is the most effective technique but often the most difficult and expensive to accomplish. The purchase of quietly operating equipment, mounting equipment on pads, and sometimes decreasing the power of a mechanical unit all help to reduce the decibel level of sounds transmitted from one area to another. In some building systems, providing alternative routes to dissipate sounds is necessary.

Absorbing Sound. The most common sound-reduction technique, however, is absorbing sound. This is usually accomplished by installing porous materials—soft, textured materials for interior design and furnishings, acoustic ceilings and panels, and special absorbing materials in structural components and mechanical equipment—disrupting pathways through which sound can travel.

Often, materials and structural components absorb sound waves at some frequencies better than others. For this reason, a noise reduction coefficient (NRC) is assigned—suitable for use in noncritical applications.

The third type of sound-absorptive material is the vibrating panel, which converts sound energy into vibrational energy. These panels are mounted with either an air space or porous material behind them.

Sound Masking. Sound masking is the use of one sound to reduce the effective levels of less pleasing sounds or noises. Masking sounds is a technique used frequently in public spaces—waterfalls, music, and other pleasant sounds often cover the sounds of clattering dishes, motion, and conversation in restaurants and shopping malls. Even household noises themselves help to mask noises from outside. In addition, sounds from radios, television, and stereo equipment help mask noises produced by inhabitants, equipment, and exterior sources. Consumers can even purchase CDs and tapes of jungle sounds, rainfall, flowing water, ocean waves, and other pleasing sounds to use as sound masking.

Sound Transmission Class

As sound moves through a barrier, its intensity is reduced by a predictable amount. The ability of a structural component to block airborne sound depends on the materials used, the type of construction, and the specific design. The measure of this resistance is the

Sound Transmission Class (STC). The higher the number, the greater the effectiveness of resisting the transmission of sounds. If a structural component has an STC of 30 dB, the loudness of the sound at one side of the barrier is reduced by 30 dB by the time the sound reaches the other side. A sound at 50 dB, then, would be heard on the other side of the barrier at 20 dB. A 4-inch framed wood wall with half-inch drywall on both sides has an STC of approximately 30 to 36, which is not adequate to provide privacy across the barrier. The **International Building Code** stipulates the sound transmission class of walls between units in multifamily dwellings as well as walls between elevators or refuse chutes and living units. In the United States, the required STC is 50.

Light Pollution

Artificial lighting illuminates both the indoor and outdoor environments, providing safety, easing tasks, and enhancing decorative appeal. There are, however, downsides to the use of artificial lighting. Lighting can produce glare, it uses energy, and outdoors it can result in night-sky pollution. Some terms are used to describe nondesirable effects of light on the environment—most concerned with exterior lighting. **Light trespass** occurs when lighting spills over into a space where it is not desired—a neighbor's yard or even onto streets and highways. Glare from lights often causes "blindness" to drivers and may result in accidents. **Light clutter** is the confusion of light in urban areas where lighted signs, street and parking lot lights, and sports lighting result in urban sky glow. Both of these conditions can have a negative effect on wildlife and interrupt people's circadian rhythms. **Light pollution** encompasses both these ideas and results in lighting the night sky sufficiently to make fewer stars visible. The number of stars visible de-

Planning lighting to reduce light pollution involves the use of lights that illuminate only what is necessary and do not spread light upward; lights that switch off when not needed; amber-colored rather than clear or white lamps; and surfaces with low reflectance.

pends on the clarity of the sky, the phase of the moon, and light pollution. Under ideal conditions, about 7000 stars can be seen by the naked eye at night in each hemisphere. In the sky over a major city, fewer than 50 stars may be visible and the Milky Way is never visible. In fact, more than half of the American people have never seen this phenomenon. (See Figure 2.12.)

Reducing light pollution is one of the goals of green design. In 1981, Australia established limits for light pollution, but few American cities have been concerned. Tucson, Arizona, is one exception. Because much of the economy of the area is based on astronomy, which requires a clear view of the stars, Tucson has installed street lighting that projects light downward rather than in all directions.

Figure 2.12 The beauty of a city at night is offset by the problems caused by the multitude of lights—light trespass, light clutter, and light pollution.

Technological
Influences
on
Residential
Design

Chapter 3

People in modern society tend to forget or to ignore the technological innovations of the distant past. However, credit must be given to prehistoric and ancient peoples who, over a period of thousands of years, developed the technologies necessary for designing, building, and furnishing structures.

Technology is the application of knowledge or science to achieve a practical purpose. People in a particular culture may be familiar with a form, material, or process, but they cannot be said to have achieved that technology unless they put the knowledge to practical use. The Mayans, for example, built toys with wheels but never applied the wheel to other tasks. Although they lacked that particular technology, they were able to build extraordinarily large monuments that required the transport of stones weighing many tons.

Development of Technology

Technologies change—often as a result of contact with other cultures. The rapidity with which new technologies are accepted depends on whether they help solve a pressing problem, whether their use requires associated changes, and whether society is ready for the new technology. There are times, as well, when technology is lost.

Contact with Other Cultures

Prior to the development of mass communication through radio, television, and periodicals, people in many areas were essentially isolated from the rest of the world, resulting in unique regional housing styles based on locally available materials. In some instances, such as in Japan, China, and ancient Egypt, building styles remained almost unchanged for centuries. Most civilizations, however, have borrowed

Figure 3.1 Modern cities have a similar appearance, not always to the benefit of their inhabitants. This city could be New York, Los Angeles, Berlin, London, or almost any other metropolis, when in fact, it is Kuala Lumpur, Malaysia.

structural ideas from other cultures with whom they have had contact, whether through trade or war. Sun-dried brick was a Mesopotamian innovation carried to Egypt along trade routes. The arch, too, was borrowed by the Romans from Mesopotamia. The Romans must be given credit for expanding the use of the arch and then spreading it throughout their empire.

Now, rather than following local customs, people sometimes build houses similar to those they have seen from other areas. Adobe homes in the United States were originally limited to the dry climate of the Southwest, but homes of concrete designed to appear as adobe are built in every climate zone in America today. Similar-looking structures can now be found all around the globe. See Figure 3.1.

Solution for Critical Need

Sometimes, even though techniques and forms are known to members of a civilization, they choose not to use them because their present methods are satisfactory and no pressing problem exists. Generally, a change must be proven beneficial before people will accept it. Even then, it will rarely be adopted if it is more difficult to implement than existing technologies. Before the 1970s, for example, most people were comfortable with the use of gas and oil for heating homes and few gave any thought to energy-efficiency. Oil shortages prompted the search for alternative energy sources. Much money was invested in the development of alternative-energy systems, but to catch up with need, the technology had to be developed quickly. The time for gradually refining and perfecting these systems was insufficient, and many people paid high prices for systems that did not work well. Nevertheless, once the energy crisis was over, the research and development of energy systems slowed down—waiting for another pressing problem.

The process of research and development is expensive, making the first models of a technological innovation high in price. As the technology is further developed, products become more reliable, their price decreases, and new uses are often found. Photovoltaic cells were at first so expensive that they were used only for the space program. Now watches, cameras, and calculators with photovoltaic cells cost relatively little.

Associated Changes

To further complicate the matter, a new technology often affects not just one aspect of building but several. Parts may not fit together in the same way, and a new method or sequence of construction may be needed. Thus, changes in building technology have almost always been gradual. See Figure 3.2. The nineteenth-century development of central heating systems resulted in the same time lag as did chimneys in the fifteenth century. Central heating requires the installation of supply and return ducts or pipes, which would require tearing out structural components or exposing the heating system components in living spaces. For this reason, central heating was more often incorporated in new structures than in existing ones.

Potential of Technologies

Some technological advances are so ahead of their time that people may not recognize potential applications, and some technologies are simply lost. King Porus[1] of India selected the more valuable gift of tempered steel rather than gold or silver for Alexander the Great, but until modern times, steel was used mostly for blades—the well-known Damascus steel. It was not until the nineteenth century that steel was used in building construction. When modern computers were first developed, they were used for data collection and analysis. Other potential applications were not considered for a number of years. In fact, when the first personal computers were put on the market in 1976, only 150 were sold. But computer technol-

Figure 3.2 A major advance in heating came when the chimney was invented. Although chimneys were gradually incorporated in new buildings, adding them to existing ones was difficult.

ogy has made precision work easier, made possible many time- and labor-saving devices, and made the quality of products more consistent—advances that have made housing more efficient. In 2003, the Census Bureau reported that 61.8 percent of American households had at least one computer and 54.6 percent had Internet access.[2]

Lost Technologies

Technologies may be lost—sometimes permanently. The Romans used hydraulic cement—cement that hardens underwater, a technology that was not rediscovered until the eighteenth century. Ancient Roman glassmaking techniques, too, were lost to Western Europe until the eleventh century. An example of a technology that seems to be permanently lost exists in

India. The fourth-century Delphi pillar in Delhi, India, is made of iron that until recently remained free of rust. While scientists have some theories as to why this is possible, the technology remains a mystery.[3] Modern cast iron readily rusts.

How the ancient Egyptians built the pyramids and how Stonehenge was raised on the Salisbury plain remain enigmas. Modern engineering has solved such problems as lifting large stones but with technology unavailable to those who originally accomplished the task. There were probably a number of other technologies used by prehistoric and ancient people that modern society knows nothing about.

Effects of Technology

Typically, technology progresses slowly but logically. In 1743, French King Louis XV had an elevator known as the flying chair. The elevator was operated by a system of weights and pulleys powered by men. Steam and hydraulic elevators were introduced by 1850, but

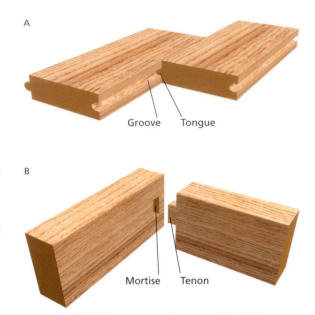

Figure 3.4a–b The tongue and groove joint (a) is an extended version of the mortise and tenon joint (b).

Figure 3.3 At times, inherited conventions are used with new technologies. Stonehenge uses mortise and tenon and tongue and groove joints normally found in wood construction—indicating that wood henges probably preceded those of stone. (A henge is a circle of stone or wood.) Stone construction does not require such joints.

it was the safety brake invented by Elisha Graves Otis in 1852 that made the elevator practical. The elevator continued to be improved and, by 1903, the gearless traction electric elevator made skyscrapers possible. It is this elevator that is still in use today. Escalators and moving walkways are further innovations built using elevator technology.

While its construction remains a mystery, Stonehenge (Figure 3.3) provides evidence of the evolution of construction using mortise and tenon and **tongue and groove** joints. See Figure 3.4a–b.

Technologies can result in significant unrelated changes. While mass communication introduces innovations from other areas, it is transportation technology that makes many of them possible. With efficient transportation methods comes the ability to move building materials and supplies long distances. Thus, wooden homes can be constructed even where wood is scarce. Transportation technology also makes it possible to work farther from home, increasing income and alternatives. The sprawling suburbs are a direct result of this technology.

The Development of Housing Technology

Housing technology has developed over many centuries and more slowly than other technologies probably because present methods were satisfactory and no pressing problem existed. The basic functions of shelter have not changed significantly in thousands of years—a secure place protected from the weather in which to sleep, prepare and eat meals, gather in groups, and sometimes provide privacy. Once a satisfactory shelter design is developed, the shelter's aesthetics, materials, and method of construction may be of less concern than other needs such as security or providing food. People's houses actually vary more according to climate or cultural mores than in structural form. Structural design changes much more rapidly in technologically sophisticated cultures than in less developed or less affluent ones, largely because other needs are satisfied.

As tools are developed and improved and innovative construction methods devised, some changes in housing are inevitable. Technological developments over the centuries have increased comfort levels, decreased the workload of residents, and provided more choices.

Tools

The development of tools increases productivity—facilitating labor or increasing options. For instance, until societies have axes or saws, making paneling is difficult. In the early-twentieth-century Neolithic culture of the Canary Islands, only the chief's house had paneling. Others could not afford a luxury that required so much time and effort. The gingerbread decoration of Victorian-style homes of the nineteenth century was only made possible by the invention of the jigsaw.

Tools affect structural form. The builders of Stonehenge had tools to roughly shape stones, curving lin-

Figure 3.5 Cyclopean walls consist of uncut stones stacked or piled up without the use of mortar. The walls are very thick at the bottom, providing stability through sheer weight and bulk.

tels to fit the intended circle, but both the Egyptian and Incan civilizations developed more precise stone-cutting tools and processes that resulted in finely fitted joints. In cultures where stones unsuitable for cutting are the only ones available, or where stone-cutting tools and processes have not been developed, stone structures are built with **cyclopean** walls. See Figure 3.5.

Methods of Support

A house, no matter how primitive, has to be designed so that it not only stands without collapsing but has a significant portion of the interior space freed for use. The first construction technologies, then, were those of spanning space and transferring weight to the ground. The manner in which this is accomplished affects the shape and form of the structure.

In early structures, walls and roofs were probably formed as a unit. Trees used as vertical posts were arranged in rows or circles and bent inward to meet at the top, where they were tied together. Before walls and roofs could be separated, it was necessary to devise other construction methods. Several problems had to be solved during this process: supporting the load, achieving height, turning corners necessary for wall construction, and spanning space.

Wall Construction

Most early types of wall construction required that materials be stacked. While even small children engage in stacking objects, wall construction is not quite that simple. Stacking individual masonry units requires one of two things—thick bases or mortar between joints. For wood construction, methods had to be developed by which units could be attached to one another, which often required more tools or the development of some attachment device such as pegs or nails. Although buildings have a wide variety of structural designs, all rely on one of three types of support systems: **bearing wall construction**, **framed construction**, or **suspended construction**.

Buildings constructed entirely of masonry typically have bearing wall construction. Walls using this type of construction are built of masonry—rammed earth, sun-dried or fired brick, stone, or concrete—piled up, with each part supporting the weight above it. Walls must be thick and continuous to provide support for the roof and floors. If part of the wall is removed, the upper part of the wall loses its support and may collapse. This characteristic requires that openings be few in number and small in size. The openings may be tall but they must be narrow, and even then they require separate support mechanisms. Bearing wall construction strictly limits design freedom because

---

▦ When remodeling, it is essential to determine whether a wall is load-bearing or non-load-bearing before making changes. If a load-bearing wall is to be altered in any way, support must be provided for the structural components above.

interior walls are often necessary to support the roof structure.

When uncut stones, stone or brick without mortar, or sun-dried brick are used, stability depends on walls having thick bases and tapering toward the top. Before walls could be the same thickness throughout their height, it was necessary to develop mortar to permanently bind blocks together and, when stone was used, tools and techniques to cut the stone. Ancient Mesopotamians used bitumen for mortar but that material was unavailable to most civilizations.

It was in America that light wood framing was developed in the 1830s. Although wood continues to dominate the construction of residences in America, recent innovations have resulted in an increased interest in light steel framing. Regardless of the material used in framed construction (also called **skeleton construction**), the process remains almost the same. In frame construction, the weight of the roof is transmitted to the ground through vertical and horizontal framing members, requiring the use of strong materials. These framing members are like a skeleton over which the inside and outside surfaces are applied like a skin. Even if no surface coverings are applied, the framing members will stand alone indefinitely. The covering, then, supports no weight but its own and can be of any material as long as it resists weather. Sometimes the frame itself may be exposed—as in medieval **half-timbering** and the American Victorian Stick style—but for the most part, the framework is hidden. The strength inherent in skeleton construction makes it possible to plan openings in floors, walls, and roofs without the loss of structural integrity. See Figure 3.6.

Frame construction permits greater design freedom than does bearing wall construction. Most of the interior walls can be located for aesthetic or functional purposes rather than for support. However, some interior walls, called **load-bearing partitions**, may be necessary to support large spans. Such a situation differs from bearing wall construction in that the strength of the partition derives from its frame. The

Figure 3.6 In skeleton construction, the framework stands alone. Although wall and roof coverings may add some dimensional stability, they are not necessary for structural integrity.

number and size of wall openings are relatively limitless as long as support is provided where structural members are cut. Materials that are capable of supporting little weight can be used in walls in large quantities. Such materials include glass, paper, cloth or skins, vegetative matter, or wattle and daub. Most of these covering materials are lighter than structural members, minimizing the weight on the foundation. A wide variety of structural forms can be built using frame construction, and styles range from the Indian tepee to contemporary homes.

Suspended Construction

Structural support in both bearing wall and frame construction is provided from beneath. In suspended construction, the weight of the structure is supported from above by cables or rods. These cables or rods are in turn supported by posts, towers, or arches that then transfer weight to the ground. The use of suspended construction is limited by the strength of the cables or rods that transfer the weight. Primitive rope bridges to modern suspension bridges carrying many lanes of traffic often employ this support mechanism, as do tents.

Corners

In addition to developing methods for achieving height, it was necessary for early builders to develop techniques to turn corners so that space could actually be enclosed. Primitive buildings are often round because they are easier to build and to roof. See Figure 3.7. Round structures are also more stable under some stresses. During the medieval period, builders often constructed round towers on defensive walls and castles because they were more difficult to collapse by tunneling under them. Early in history, however, Mesopotamian builders learned to overlap sun-dried brick at corners to strengthen the structure and provide square corners. The same method was used for cut stone. See Figure 3.8 for an example of

It may be necessary to consult original plans or an engineer before planning for changes to determine whether a wall is load-bearing. It is a much simpler process to modify or eliminate non-load-bearing components than those that bear weight. The load borne by load-bearing walls must be supported at every stage—even during demolition.

corners formed by notched logs. In industrial societies, round walls periodically become fashionable not for their defensive qualities but for aesthetic reasons. Towers on Victorian Queen Anne buildings were often round, and today's structures may have one or more curved walls.

Spanning Space

Methods of spanning space are used to free openings in walls for entry and egress for both people and smoke, and the same methods are used for roof structures to free space on the interior for use. The devices used to accomplish these functions affect the shape of the structure as well as the size of the opening or free space. Four methods are used for spanning space —all of which were well developed by the time of the ancient Greeks: the **post and lintel**, the **arch**, the **truss**, and the **cantilever**. Each method is in use today—sometimes having been changed or improved over thousands of years—but with no new basic techniques.

Figure 3.7 Today, round forms may still be used because of the materials or processes used for construction. Rubble stone construction with a thatched roof is used for this Kenyan home.

Figure 3.8 Notching logs to form corners has been widely used since the prehistoric Swiss lake dwellers. It was a common technique in colonial America and is still used in many parts of the world where logs are used for construction.

Figure 3.9 The interior of Egyptian stone temples often looked like forests because so many posts were needed to support the stone lintels.

Post and Lintel

The post and lintel[4] was the first architectural device used to span space, and it is the basis of most residential construction today. Vertical supports—posts, columns, or walls—are bridged by horizontal lintels. The weight of the structure above openings and the weight of the roof must be carried by the lintels to the vertical supports, which then transmit weight to the ground.

Lintels must be of sufficient strength to support the loads above them. Loads may cause the lintel to bend, creating tension on the lower edge. The post and lintel method is especially suited to steel or wood, although it is also used with masonry construction. While stone can carry immense compression loads, it breaks readily under tension. Thus, the distance spanned is limited by the load-bearing capacity of the

lintel as well as by its length. See Figure 3.9. The post and lintel is often of limited use in areas where large stones or timbers are not available. Structures with post and lintel design have continuous parallel walls and are square or rectangular in shape.

While post and lintel construction may also be called **trabeated**, the more common use of that term refers to posts and lintels that are stacked —often in decreasing lengths. Generally, wood is the material of choice. Brackets (Chinese *tou-kung*) make the transition from one size to the next. Arms of lower brackets carry other brackets, expanding diagonally upward. These brackets are often intricate and highly decorated. This type of trabeated construction is infrequently used in the West. See Figure 3.10.

Figure 3.10 Trabeated construction is common in the Far East, where it is used in traditional Chinese, Japanese, and Korean buildings. This Chinese example of trabeated construction shows brackets supporting shorter and shorter cross members to create a gable roof. Note that the underside of diagonal finishing members are painted as well as the beams themselves.

Arches

The arch was most highly developed in areas where large stones and heavy timbers were unavailable, making post and lintel structures impractical. Arches have been used in building construction for at least 4000 years.

The arch employs a series of small blocks, usually of stone, sometimes brick, to span space. The true arch makes use of radiating wedge-shaped members called **voussoirs**, which push against one another to form a strong support. Such arches are usually built using a temporary framework called **centering** that is removed once the final wedge at the top is inserted. This **keystone** completes the form, making the arch self-supporting. Arches are most often used when building with brick or small stones but are also feasible in wood, steel, or concrete construction.

Since arches always exert outward thrust that must be counteracted, they tend to spread horizontally, but arches are stable and strong when a counterthrust is present. This pressure can be provided with

Figure 3.11 The thrust of one arch can be used to counteract the thrust of an adjacent arch. In an arcade, each arch pushes against the next. Walls or buttresses are used to counteract the thrust of the arches at the ends of the arcade.

buttresses—heavy walls or piers that transmit the weight to the ground, where it is ultimately supported. Because of the outward thrust, at first arches were used only underground or for windows and door openings, with the necessary counterbalance supplied by soil or surrounding walls. Later, buttresses were formed by masses projecting from a wall, making the wall stout enough at those points to serve as counterthrust. Figure 3.11 illustrates an **arcade**, another way of counteracting the thrust of arches. Horizontal tie rods may also be used as support; many examples can be found in Renaissance architecture. Modern engineers have added tie rods to help preserve many ancient buildings that did not originally incorporate them.

The use of the arch allows greater design freedom than does post and lintel construction. Some parts may be higher than others, supports can be widely spaced, and plans can be complex. Interiors may have large open areas that can be wider and higher than possible using post and lintel construction. Roofs can be formed by continuous arches in a single plane, forming vaults called **barrel** or **tunnel vaults**. **Domes** are formed when arches radiate around a center point.

Arch profiles vary considerably but a given civilization or historic period tends to use a single basic arch style, which then becomes a recognizable characteristic of that architectural style.

Trusses

The truss is a triangular form that depends on the geometric principle that the length of any side of a triangle cannot change without changing the angles at the corners. It is, then, the most stable form for spanning space because as long as one corner is solidly attached, its shape will not change. The bottom of the truss—the **tie beam**—ties the sloping sides together, counteracting the outward thrust of the diagonal members, but carries no weight itself. Trusses are used when single members of sufficient length or strength are not obtainable to span the required distance.

Trusses can be used to span wider spaces than can post and lintel construction, thereby freeing more of

Figure 3.12 This house has a cantilevered second-story area. Cantilevering allows for a larger living area without requiring additional ground space.

the interior for use. Interior space can be subdivided in any manner because intermediate supports are unnecessary. Buildings employing truss construction are generally lighter and more open in appearance than those using either post and lintel or arched construction. Walls can be thin with many large openings. Like post and lintel construction, the use of trusses places limitations on form, usually requiring that structures or portions of them be rectangular or square in shape. The triangle forming the end of the building is the **pediment**, a form that has frequently been used by artists and sculptors as a decorative surface. This triangle may be continuous or interrupted (broken).

Trusses exert only vertical pressure on walls, concentrating weight at the points of support, so the wall or support member must be of sufficient strength to carry the load. The large triangular form required for spanning long distances is often subdivided into smaller triangular forms, making it possible to span even longer distances. Indeed, a triangulated framework may even be placed within horizontal top and bottom members, forming floor and ceiling trusses that will span long spaces. Usually, these trusses are incorporated in commercial structures to span great distances. Many gymnasiums have exposed ceiling trusses.

Often, intermediate supports are unnecessary when trusses are used, resulting in the freedom to divide interior spaces as desired.

The Greeks are credited with the invention of the truss, and their early temples use this device. The truss form is most commonly employed today for **gable roofs** in residential structures, although the truss may be used for floors and ceilings in both residential and commercial buildings.

Cantilevers

A cantilever is a horizontal projection that permits a portion of a building to extend beyond its vertical supports. For example, the beams that support the second floor of a house can extend beyond the width of the first floor, forming an overhanging second story known as a **jetty**. Cantilevers are like levers, with the weight of the building exerting downward force behind the fulcrum. Typically, the weighted portion is at least twice the length of the unsupported portion. The House on the Rock in Wisconsin and Fallingwater in Pennsylvania make extensive use of the cantilever.[5] The length of the cantilever depends on the direction of the floor joists and the expected load. See Figure 3.12 for a typical residential example.

The earliest form of the cantilever was the **corbel,** which has been most frequently used to form arches and domes without the use of wedge-shaped members. In corbeled construction, small blocks of stone are laid in successive rows, or **courses**, each of which projects beyond the course below it. The structure gradually curves inward until meeting at the top, enclosing the structure. Ancient people were able to bridge larger spaces with the corbeled arch than with the post and lintel. Today, the beehive houses of southern Italy still survive using this ancient technique for roofing.

Most modern structures make use of a combination of structural technologies. A typical house might utilize frame construction, incorporating the wall and lintel to support the roof, the post and lintel to form openings, the principle of the truss in its triangular roof shape, a large open archway between two rooms, and a cantilevered deck on the second story. All of this is accomplished using a variety of construction methods.

The Building Industry

Housing plays a major role in the American economy. In 2001, almost 6.5 million people worked in the construction industry. In addition, typically, more than a million new homes are constructed each year in the United States. By 1998, the rate had risen to more than 1.5 million homes, and it continues to rise. The exact number depends on demand, which in turn depends largely on the ability of lending institutions to finance homes at affordable interest rates. See Table 3.1.

Each new home built does not add to the total number of homes. Homes become old, deteriorated, and uninhabitable. Fire and natural disasters claim others. Local governments exercise the right of eminent domain (using property for the common good—transportation, community buildings, and other services) to condemn additional homes. Habitable homes are also abandoned, especially in rural areas. The property itself may continue to be used but the home left uninhabited and uncared for.

Construction Methods

For centuries, building construction was an individual responsibility. When people needed a home, they designed a structure to suit the climate and used locally available materials for construction. These factors limited design. Individual home owners generally did the construction work themselves—often pooling their labor to erect buildings quickly. However, few people

Table 3.1 New Housing Starts

Year*	Number of starts	Year	Number of starts
1946	1,015,000	1975	1,160,000
1947	1,268,000	1976	1,538,000
1948	1,362,000	1977	1,987,000
1949	1,466,000	1978	2,020,000
1950	1,952,000	1979	1,745,000
1951	1,491,000	1980	1,292,000
1952	1,504,000	1981	1,084,000
1953	1,438,000	1982	1,062,000
1954	1,551,000	1983	1,703,000
1955	1,646,000	1984	1,750,000
1956	1,349,000	1985	1,742,000
1957	1,224,000	1986	1,805,000
1958	1,382,000	1987	1,620,000
1959	1,554,000	1988	1,488,000
1960	1,296,000	1989	1,376,000
1961	1,365,000	1990	1,193,000
1962	1,492,000	1991	1,014,000
1963	1,635,000	1992	1,200,000
1964	1,561,000	1993	1,288,000
1965	1,510,000	1994	1,457,000
1966	1,196,000	1995	1,354,000
1967	1,322,000	1996	1,477,000
1968	1,545,000	1997	1,474,000
1969	1,500,000	1998	1,617,000
1970	1,469,000	1999	1,641,000
1971	2,052,000	2000	1,569,000
1972	2,357,000	2001	1,603,000
1973	2,045,000	2002	1,705,000
1974	1,338,000	2003	1,848,000

Sources: Figures for 1946 to 1973 from U.S. Census Bureau, *Statistical Abstract of the United States: Bicentennial Edition*, Series N 156-169 "New Housing Units Started, by Ownership, Type of Structure, Location, and Construction Cost: 1889 to 1970," 1975, p. 639. Figures for 1974 to 1998 from U.S. Census Bureau, *Statistical Abstract of the United States*, Table 1195 "New Privately-Owned Housing Units Started—Selected Characteristics: 1970 to 1999," Washington, D.C., Department of Commerce, 2005, p. 713. Figures for 1999 through 2003 from U.S. Census Bureau, *Statistical Abstract of the United States: 2004–2005*, Table 928 "New Privately-Owned Housing Units Started—Selected Characteristics: 1970 to 2003," Washington, D.C., Department of Commerce, p. 599.

* Since World War II, there have been more than a million housing starts per year—even during the period of high interest rates in the 1980s. Figures for 1946 to 1959 exclude farm housing.

constructed a sufficient number of buildings to become skilled at it.

Innovations in materials and processes have both increased and reduced housing choices. On the one hand, most modern homes are designed to be easily constructed anywhere. Materials are easily transported long distances, bulldozers alter the terrain to suit the design, and climate-control systems make it unnecessary to build appropriately for specific climates.

On the other hand, home owners have less personal control over housing than previously. Building construction, having become ever more complex, is largely in the hands of members of the builders' trades. While design is not as influenced by environmental constraints, there are marketplace constraints. Partly because mobility is a characteristic of contemporary society, homes are designed for an "average" family to ensure good resale value. Rarely are homes built for the specific needs of their owners.

The location where construction actually takes place and the processes involved affect costs, time, and design. Alternatives include **conventional construction**, **mass site construction**, and manufactured homes.

Conventional Construction

The most common method of housing construction is conventional construction (also called **on-site** or **stick-built construction**). In conventional construction, almost all of the labor is done on the building site, materials are stored on the site, and materials are cut and assembled as they are used. This type of construction is relatively expensive and inefficient and requires six weeks to six months or more to complete a single home. The average length of time required was 6.2 months in 2003.[6]

The costs of theft, insurance, and transportation increase the price of conventional construction. Materials stored on the site are subject to damage or theft. In making bids, many builders add an extra 10 percent to the cost of materials to compensate for such losses. In addition, property owners must carry insurance to protect themselves in the event that someone is injured on the property during construction. Property owners are liable for any injury, whether to workers, visitors, or trespassers. Costs are further increased when isolated homes are built and materials must be transported long distances.

Conventional construction also suffers from delays. Inclement weather can slow down a project or cause a long postponement. Another problem is getting **subcontractors**—specialized workers, such as plumbers and electricians—to the site at the proper time. If subcontractors are held up elsewhere, construction may have to wait until they arrive. Because many jobs require that other work be finished prior to starting, late subcontractors can set off a chain reaction.

The quality of work in on-site construction depends on the crews employed. Building inspectors make several visits during construction and should detect any potentially dangerous flaws. Nevertheless, errors sometimes go uncorrected.

In spite of the difficulties, conventional construction is popular because of its one major advantage—its versatility. The design of a home is not limited to what can be constructed in a factory or mass-produced, or even to what has been done before. Most builders, however, do construct homes from standard plans.

Custom building using innovative ideas and plans is even more expensive. When submitting bids for custom construction, contractors must add an allowance for error. By building many similar homes, workers become accustomed to processes and methods. When innovative plans are used, contractors must allow extra time and materials for the learning process. Custom building may also require that an engineer or architect be on the site—supervision that is expensive. See Table 3.2 for the percentages of homes built using various construction methods.

Mass Site Construction

Mass site construction is the building of many homes in a single area with skilled workers progressing from

Table 3.2 Construction Method of Single-Family Homes 2003

Region	Stick-Built		Modular		Panelized/Precut	
	Units	Percent of homes	Units	Percent of homes	Units	Percent of homes
Northeast	98,000	85.9	12,000	10.5	4,000	3.5
Midwest	253,000	92.7	11,000	4.0	9,000	3.3
South	604,000	95.0	14,000	2.2	18,000	2.8
West	359,000	98.9	2,000	0.6	2,000	0.6
Total		94.7*		2.8	33,000	2.4

Source: Buildings Energy Databook, 2.1 Residential Sector Characteristics, 2.1.9 "2003 Construction Method of Single-Family Homes, by Region." Their source DOC, Manufacturing, Mining and Construction Statistics, New Residential Construction: Type of Construction Method of New One-Family Houses Completed, March 2005.

   * The popularity of stick-built construction is evident in this data. Only about 6 percent of homes were constructed in 2002 using other methods of construction. It is also obvious that more homes are being constructed in the South than in any other region of the United States.

one house to another as they complete a particular portion. This type of construction is more efficient than conventional construction, using both land and labor more efficiently, which results in lower costs than typical of on-site construction. Streets and utilities can be put in for an entire subdivision before construction even begins. Excavation crews, plumbers, electricians, and carpenters work continuously on different homes in the subdivision.

When builders began mass-producing homes in the mid-twentieth century, entire subdivisions were built using a single design, resulting in rows of what were termed "cookie-cutter" houses. See Figure 3.13. Individuality was achieved through exterior decoration, mostly in color and landscaping. Current mass-site production continues to take advantage of efficiency but with more individualization. Most subdivisions now offer various styles of homes.

Manufactured Homes

The concept of applying assembly-line efficiency to housing construction is taken one step further with manufactured housing. Manufactured homes have

Figure 3.13 Some subdivisions use only a few basic plans, while in others every plan is different and individually suited to family needs. Different exterior styles can be achieved simply by reversing the basic plan or changing the exterior detailing.

evolved through various forms. Two basic types can currently be identified: **precut** homes and **prefabricated** structures—**panelized**, **sectionalized**, **modular**, and **mobile homes**. In actual construction, however, there is much overlapping of types.

Precut Homes

Of the types of manufactured housing, precut homes require the most on-site work. Constructing a precut home is much like putting together a large jigsaw puzzle. The components are cut to size and labeled in a factory, then shipped to the site. Owners are provided with a set of instructions for assembly. Because the components are designed and cut to reduce waste, precut homes reduce material requirements and the amount of labor necessary to size materials on the site. They were especially popular prior to World War II and were even sold by mail. The same basic principle was used by the Egyptians thousands of years ago to build the pyramids. They quarried and cut stone to fit predetermined locations, transported the stone, and put it in place with a minimum of on-site fitting.

Prefabrication

Entirely prefabricated houses have been used throughout history. When Hannibal crossed the Alps with his elephants and armies, he took along prefabricated huts for his troops. During World War II, ready-made homes for defense workers could be set up in an hour and a half. The current boom in the use of prefabricated housing began in the postwar period, when the housing shortage became acute.

Prefabricated houses are constructed from factory-made structural components that are transported to the site and erected. Prefabrication saves time and labor because assembly-line techniques and equipment are used. A system of standardized sizes further increases the efficiency of home construction. Materials are produced in the appropriate sizes, reducing waste and facilitating economical quantity shipments. Rather than sacrificing individuality for efficiency, it is possible to combine various standard-sized components, modifying designs to suit individual needs and tastes. Another advantage of prefabrication is the relative ease of quality control.

Part or all of a house can be prefabricated. Prefabricated roof trusses, prehung doors and windows, and prefinished cabinets became common in the 1940s and are currently used even in many conventionally built homes. An innovation beginning with R. Buckminster Fuller's Dymaxion House was the **core**. Housing cores include some or all of the electrical, plumbing, and climate-control components. Many contain entire kitchens and bathrooms. The core is manufactured in the factory, transported to the construction site, and lifted into the home with a crane. Electrical and plumbing work are simplified, having been already accomplished in the factory.

Generally, prefabricated homes are built according to the modular system. Components in the modular system are designed so that all dimensions are divisible by four. For example, an outside wall might be designed to be 24 feet long rather than 22 or 25 feet. The basis of the system is the standard module: a 4-inch cube. Standard modules are combined to form larger units, such as the major module. Sixteen-inch and 24-inch cubes are minor modules used especially for window and door openings.

Depending on the type of components manufactured, an entirely prefabricated house can be made of panelized, sectionalized, or modular units. Mobile homes are a unique fourth type of prefabricated housing.

Panelized units. When panelized units are used, roof, wall, and floor panels are constructed and prefinished at a factory. The flat panels are then shipped to the building site where the foundation has been prepared. Panelized units require less time for construction on the site than conventional construction. How much less depends on the percentage of work done at the factory. Some panelized units are merely shells, with interior finishes, wiring, plumbing, and heating systems left to do on the site. When only the shell is used, little time is actually saved. Other panelized units have all finish work completed and mechanical systems installed, requiring little on-site work.

Sectionalized units. Sectionalized homes consist of two sections that are placed side by side on a foundation and joined together. Sections are not interchangeable since each is built for a particular home. Sectionalized units are prefinished, including all interior and exterior finishes and all mechanical systems. The length, width, and height of such units are regulated by state law because the units must be moved on highways. Most commonly, sectionalized units are 12 feet wide and as long as the finished home will be. For wider homes, a center section can be added on the site. Because of transportation height regulations, most sectionalized homes have low-sloped or flat roofs and 7½-foot ceilings. Some, however, are designed to allow the roof to be raised to a steeper angle once the home is on the site.

Modular units. Modular units are the most industrialized prefabricated units and are the most finished prior to on-site delivery. Modular units are entire rooms or sections of home that, when attached to similar units, are ready for occupancy. The draperies may already be hung, appliances installed, and even some furnishings put in place. Modular units are not designed for specific homes, as are sectionalized units. Rather, they are designed to be used with identical or similar units, which can be combined vertically or horizontally into many final forms. Additional rooms can be purchased at any time and added to the original units.

Modular units are subject to the same size restrictions as other units that must be transported on highways. Several units can be used together to construct a large home but the rooms will be small. As with sectionalized homes, the roof on some units can be raised on the site.

The site is prepared prior to shipment of the units. Because plumbing and electrical hookups must be connected to the units beneath the floor, modular units cannot be placed on slabs. They require a basement, crawl space, or lower level. Cranes are used to place the modules on the foundation. Joints are then sealed, and within a few hours the house is closed in. With so little time required for enclosing them, modular homes can be erected year-round. Only severely inclement weather will stop or slow construction.

Modular units are becoming increasingly popular for the construction of multifamily dwellings. Habitat, a modular housing complex in Montreal, is an example. In multifamily projects, individual modular units are combined in all three directions. The type of vertical construction determines costs and flexibility. When units are stacked directly on top of one another (the **dependent stack system**), lower modules support the weight of others. Since lower modules must therefore be stronger, all units cannot be constructed identically. The **independent stack system** uses identical units, which can be more easily and less expensively mass-produced. This system is more flexible because each unit is structurally supported separately. Obsolete or damaged modules can be removed and replaced without disturbing others.

Mobile homes. A mobile home is built in one or more sections on a supporting chassis. The steel framework of the chassis includes wheels that allow the unit to be transported relatively easily. All electrical, plumbing, and climate-control systems are factory-installed and ready for hookup to utility supplies. Furniture is often included as a part of the package. Once on the site, the home may continue to be supported by the chassis or may be placed on a permanent foundation. See Figure 3.14.

The mobile home industry developed in response to the housing shortage immediately after World War II. The homes constructed by the infant industry were small and often shoddily constructed. There was a social stigma attached to living in mobile homes, which

Figure 3.14 This double-wide mobile home bears little similarity to the "trailers" of the 1960s. Were it not for its setting—a mobile home park—it could easily be mistaken for a conventionally constructed home.

were considered stopgap housing. As the industry developed, however, minimum standards were adopted for construction and mechanical systems. The stricter government building codes associated with the 1974 Federal Mobile Home Construction and Safety Standards Act decreased shoddy construction even further. Newer mobile homes are often designed in familiar architectural styles and, in some cases, are difficult to distinguish from conventional homes. For these reasons, the stigma attached to living in mobile homes has all but disappeared.

Since the mobile home industry was originally a child of the automobile industry, similar construction methods and materials are used in both. Most mobile homes are manufactured with aluminum siding and metal roofing. The manufacturing method makes mobile homes quick to assemble, with entire walls cut by a machine at once. Like other forms of manufactured housing, mobile homes are less expensive and more consistent in quality than site-built homes.

By definition, mobile homes today must exceed 8 feet in width and 40 feet in length. Structures that are similar to mobile homes but are too small to fit that definition are classified as travel trailers or recreational vehicles. The maximum dimensions for mobile homes are established by transportation regula-

tions, just as in the case of sectionalized and modular homes. Since the size restrictions make it necessary to use space efficiently, mobile and sectionalized homes are often better planned in this respect than other dwellings. The number of new mobile homes has decreased since 1998. In 2003, 137,700 new units were added to the housing market.[7]

Mobile homes may be single-wide or double-wide. Single-wide mobile homes tend to have small rooms because a large percentage of the floor area is required for circulation. Double-wide mobile homes are constructed in two sections, each with its own chassis. The sections are transported separately and attached at the site. Double-wide mobile homes are similar in appearance to conventionally built homes but have lower rooflines. Triple-wide homes are available as well. A single-wide home is 16 feet wide or less, and double-wide homes are 24 feet or more in width.

One or more expandable sections may be incorporated in either single-wide or double-wide mobile homes. These sections fold, collapse, or telescope into the mobile home during transportation and are expanded at the site. Separate sections may be added to any mobile home for a more traditional appearance and increased floor space.

In contrast to early models, today's mobile homes

are rarely truly mobile. According to the Mobile Homes Manufacturers Association, less than 5 percent of the mobile homes in America are moved from their original sites. The cost of moving a mobile home is prohibitive, perhaps even exceeding the value of the home in the case of a long-distance move.

Mobile homes may be set up in communities or parks designed especially for them. Although most of the homes in these parks are owner-occupied, the lots on which they sit are rented. Mobile homes not in parks are set up on the residents' own land.

For years, the economic advantages of mobile homes were offset by the fact that they did not appreciate, or increase, in value as did more permanent dwellings. In fact, they depreciated, or declined in value, relatively quickly. However, many mobile homes now appreciate in value, especially when they are in desirable locations.

While they have many advantages, mobile homes have some unique disadvantages. They are more vulnerable to wind and storm damage than conventional homes, and fire spreads more rapidly in them. Heat loss and cold floors may be a problem in the winter because the home sits up off the ground.

Remodeling Existing Buildings

Remodeling is big business. In 2003, more than $176 billion was spent on remodeling residences—$157 billion of that was for privately owned residences. See Table 3.3. Most remodeling monies are spent on owner-occupied dwellings, and home ownership rates have risen from 55 percent in 1950 to 69 percent in 2003. Three categories of remodeling include maintenance, improvements, and additions. There are several reasons why the remodeling industry is so large:

- The median age of an American home in 2003 was 32 years. Remodeling efforts may be neces-

sary to maintain the physical quality of the home. Roofs, for example, have a life expectancy of 15 to 50 years, depending on the finish material.

- Remodeling an existing home can make the home more competitive with new homes in terms of amenities and comfort at less cost.
- When families move into different housing, they are likely to expend funds for remodeling within the first two years to acquire the amenities they desire or to increase the comfort of the home.
- Prior to selling a home, individuals may opt to alter or improve features of the home to ensure the home is competitive in the marketplace.
- Repair may be necessary in the aftermath of a natural disaster or fire.
- Remodeling can improve the quality of life for mature individuals and may make it possible to stay in their own homes longer. Even small changes such as installing a higher toilet or adding grab bars in a bathroom can make a significant difference.

Table 3.3 Expenditures for Improvements in Residential Property

Year	Amount
1993	$121,899,000,000
1994	$130,625,000,000
1995	$124,971,000,000
1996	$131,362,000,000
1997	$133,577,000,000
1998	$133,693,000,000
1999	$142,900,000,000
2000	$152,975,000,000
2001	$157,765,000,000
2002	$173,324,000,000
2003	$176,899,000,000*

Source: U.S. Census Bureau, *Statistical Abstract of the United States: 2004–2005*, Table 967 "Expenditures by Residential Property Owners for Improvements and Maintenance and Repairs by Type of Property and Activity: 1990 to 2003," Washington, D.C., Department of Commerce, p. 622.

* Residential remodeling expenditures continue to increase as disposable income rises and as the baby boom generation reaches its peak earning years.

Table 3.4 Home Remodeling

Remodeling project	Households		Work done by (in percent)*		Amount spent (in percent)		
	Number	Percent	Household Member	Outside Contractor	Under $1000	$1000–$2999	$3000+
Conversion of attic, garage, or basement to living space	3,785,000	1.8	61	22	21	25	35
Remodel bathroom	13,893,000	6.6	65	22	45	23	14
Remodel kitchen	9,387,000	4.5	54	30	31	15	32
Remodel bedroom	8,656,000	4.1	76	13	60	15	8.7
Remodel/convert room to home office	2,115,000	1.0	81	6	54	13	8
Remodel other rooms	8,143,000	3.9	70	16	55	18	17
Add bathroom	1,606,000	0.8	52	28	27	20	33
Add/extend garage	1,095,000	0.5	51	39	14	16	49
Add other rooms	1,814,000	0.9	41	41	10	11	66
Add deck, porch, patio	5,568,000	2.7	66	30	6	36	22
Roofing	10,408,000	5.0	28	57	24	22	36
Vinyl/metal siding	3,533,000	1.7	31	46	19	19	38
Aluminum windows	1,384,000	0.7	27	53	22	28	19
Clad wood/wood windows	1,007,000	0.5	37	34	21	15	32
Vinyl windows	4,202,000	2.0	36	49	23	32	27
Ceramic tile floors	7,115,000	3.4	52	35	52	16	12
Hardwood floors	4,539,000	2.2	45	36	29	27	21
Laminate flooring	3,697,000	1.8	55	35	48	30	7
Vinyl flooring	4,665,000	2.2	51	37	65	15	2
Carpeting	9,999,000	4.8	26	61	41	32	12
Kitchen cabinets	4,911,000	2.3	43	33	27	18	25
Kitchen countertops	5,130,000	2.5	36	39	34	19	20
Skylights	788,000	0.4	29	53	53	15	15
Exterior doors	6,083,000	2.9	50	37	58	15	15
Interior doors	3,694,000	1.8	55	26	57	11	6
Garage doors	4,412,000	2.1	23	60	53	22	5
Concrete or masonry work	4,959,000	2.4	43	44	43	19	21
In-ground swimming pool	463,000	0.2	8	76	12	10	67
Wall paneling	1,340,000	0.6	61	14	72	11	1
Ceramic wall tile	2,354,000	1.1	55	31	60	16	4

Source: U.S. Census Bureau, *Statistical Abstract of the United States: 2004–2005*, Table 968 "Home Remodeling—Work Done and Amount Spent: 2003," Washington, D.C., Department of Commerce, 2005, p. 622. Their source: Mediamark Research Inc., New York, NY, *Top-Line Reports*, www.mediamark.com.

* Work done by and the amount spent figures represent known quantities and may not add to 100 percent.

The cost recovery for most remodeling projects is relatively high. (The cost recovery is reflected in the increased value of the property due to remodeling efforts.) HomeTech Information Systems reported that in 2003, a deck addition added 104.2 percent of its cost to the value of a home. Most remodeling projects, however, have a cost recovery percentage from about 75 percent to almost full cost. In general, kitchen and bathroom remodeling and additions to the home provide a greater return on investment than other types of projects. See Table 3.4 for the types of remodeling projects done in the United States during 2003.

Regulating Building Construction

Local governments are responsible for housing standards in their areas—including zoning ordinances, building codes, and subdivision regulations.

Zoning Ordinances

Although opposition to early zoning ordinances argued that such ordinances violated individual property rights, today zoning ordinances are a municipal tool used to regulate land use, delineating what are considered compatible uses. Early zoning ordinances affected only isolated areas in large population centers. Modern ordinances generally affect entire communities of any size.

The major purpose of zoning ordinances is to protect residential areas from commercial and industrial development. Each of these categories may be further divided for purposes of regulation. Performance standards may be used to determine the category to which a specific business or industry belongs. Light industry, for example, produces no noise or odor. Smoke, glare, heat, parking problems, and other criteria are often used. Usually, cities allow businesses or light industry at intersections of major streets or roads, and areas near railroads or shipping arteries may have heavy industry. Zoning ordinances also provide buffers between commercial districts and residential areas, preventing commercial establishments from spreading beyond specified limits and softening the impact of commercial districts on residential ones. See Figure 3.15. All land values are affected by activities in close proximity. Gas stations, restaurants, and shopping centers—and the associated traffic, noise, pollution, and danger—decrease the value of residential land.

Because zoning ordinances affect land values through use regulations and because a secondary function of zoning ordinances is improving or maintaining the aesthetic appearance of communities, an overall zoning plan is imperative. This becomes even more true in light of the fact that zoning ordinances are not retroactive. Once a business has been established, for instance, new zoning ordinances making the area residential cannot force the business to move. Zoning boards have an additional right to make individual exceptions and permit occasional deviations from established policies. A common example is the permission to put a beauty shop in a residential area.

Figure 3.15 Zoning ordinances in this area stipulate that lot sizes be a minimum of 3 acres so these homes are not crowded near one another.

Proper zoning maximizes the value of all the land within city limits, making certain that the sum total of property values is the maximum possible. This stabilizes land values and encourages the construction of residences, industrial complexes, and commercial establishments. It also ensures a stable tax base.

Zoning ordinances even regulate the placement of utility lines. Many municipalities now require the underground placement of electrical lines in new areas through zoning ordinances.

Zoning ordinances not only affect land use but stipulate densities. The control of population density is generally accomplished through minimum lot size; by setback requirements—the distance from a structure to the edge of adjoining property; the percentage of lot that can be taken up by the structure; and the number of parking spaces that must be provided. Zoning ordinances also stipulate the maximum number of families per acre. See Figure 3.16.

Zoning ordinances may also control building height. In fact, the first zoning ordinances were a result of a New York City investigation of the relationship between skyscrapers and community health and safety in 1916. The first ordinances restricted building height to ensure that light and air could reach the streets below. An additional function of those regulations was to prevent the spread of industry into commercial districts. Today, building height is especially regulated near airports.

Exclusionary zoning denies access to certain amenities generally associated with living in an area. Exclusionary zoning may include minimum lot sizes that eliminate the possibility of multiple-family dwellings and, at the same time, force economic segregation by precluding the possibility of people with low incomes purchasing the lots. When multiple-family dwellings are permitted, exclusionary zoning practices may stipulate the number of people who may occupy each bedroom. This practice helps to regulate the burden on the community educational system. Other exclusionary zoning forces people who build "different" housing to congregate in specific areas. Earth-shel-

Figure 3.16 Because of space limitations outside the dwelling, there may be no covered parking facilities or children's play areas by multifamily dwellings.

tered housing is often permitted only in certain subdivisions, for example.

The American judicial system may insist that **inclusionary zoning** be practiced—ensuring a variety of housing choices in each area and requiring a percentage of the area to be designed for low- or moderate-income families. When developers comply by constructing a specified percentage of homes in price

---

Zoning ordinances even regulate land on which there are no buildings, setting aside specific areas for agriculture, recreation, or preservation of natural environments. Environmental zones are generally designated to protect fragile ecosystems. Zoning ordinances establish greenbelts in cities, decreasing apparent high density and providing for social interaction. Chicago has vast greenbelts that have not been developed. Many of them retain their natural environments, including woods, flora, and fauna. Others have been established as parks and are maintained—grass is mowed; benches, tables, and trash receptacles are provided; and bicycle paths and pedestrian walkways are established.

ranges that make them affordable to families with low incomes, they are often given bonuses. These bonuses may stipulate that builders may construct housing with higher densities than normally permitted; that municipal governments may accept responsibility for the provision of specified services such as sewer systems, sidewalks, or roads; or that builders may be exempt from paying certain fees.

Building Codes

Building codes are designed to ensure that housing construction meets certain health and safety guidelines. Building codes affect not only new construction but also remodeling, replacement of plumbing and electrical systems, and structural additions. Permits are required for all of these, enabling local officials to enforce building codes. To obtain permits, individuals or builders must submit plans for the project, file an application, and pay a fee. If plumbing or electrical work is a part of the project, separate permits for these must be secured. At specified points during construction, local building inspectors examine the work, making certain it is done according to codes. Once plumbing and electrical work are covered up, it is difficult to determine whether it meets code requirements. For this reason, people who fail to have the interim inspections are often forced to tear out sufficient work to permit inspection. In many localities, tax officials closely monitor **building permits**, assuming that improvements to property will increase its value and consequently, its taxes.

The International Building Code has replaced regional model building codes in some areas, but building codes continue to differ from one locality to another. This code is also divided into separate sections,

---

Even where there are no building codes, model codes should be followed because they ensure the safety and healthfulness of the built environment.

with the **International Residential Code (IRC)** of most interest to residential designers. In order for a model building code to be enforceable, it must be adopted. Some states have adopted codes; others leave building codes up to local governments. In fact, there are still areas of the country with few code regulations. Building codes consist of minimal standards for health and structural safety, including plumbing and electrical systems. **Performance codes** stipulate only that health and safety criteria be met. **Specification codes** dictate which materials are acceptable to meet these criteria. For example, earth-contact housing is difficult to build in certain areas because codes are written in terms of specifications and earth is not on the list of acceptable roofing materials. Plastic plumbing pipe presents another current dilemma. Plastic pipe is acceptable in many areas, while in others it may be used only for drains, and in some places, not at all. Specification codes make it difficult to use new materials or technologies. Variances are often permitted, however, when local officials are knowledgeable about current developments and when individuals requesting variances can present logical arguments at a hearing.

Specification building codes may not only inhibit the use of innovative materials and technology but force costs to remain high. Codes based on performance may lower costs. Plastic pipe, for example, is less expensive than galvanized pipe as well as easier and less time-consuming to install. Performance building codes could conceivably reduce costs or improve housing quality. The difficulty with performance codes, however, is that innovative materials and technology may not have been subjected to sufficient testing to ensure long-term safety.

Subdivision Regulations

While zoning ordinances affect property that is either already built up or protects property from being built up, subdivision regulations deal with undeveloped land. Like zoning ordinances, these regulations may dictate density and minimum lot sizes, but additional features may be added that are not generally a part of zoning ordinances. The design of buildings, materials, number of bedrooms, color, or any aesthetic feature may be regulated. Subdivision regulations are designed to promote orderly as opposed to haphazard growth and to protect property values and the aesthetic appeal of the subdivision. Subdivision regulations ensure that new developments will be structurally and aesthetically consistent with the community as a whole.

Subdivision regulations reduce the responsibility of local governments for the provision of services in new developments while ensuring not only that such services will be provided but that specific regulations concerning only the development will be followed. Municipal governments may make certain stipulations guaranteeing that subdivisions will not impose expenses on the city. Most require that builders furnish water supplies, sewer lines, streets and sidewalks, and street lighting before selling residences in the subdivision. They may also require that certain areas be reserved for the future or present development of schools, recreational facilities, or other public amenities. Municipal governments may prohibit development if they deem the area to have unstable soil conditions or to be in floodplains where citizens' lives or health would be jeopardized. Because city approval is needed before deeds can be recorded for lots in a subdivision, developers have no choice but to follow municipal guidelines.

Housing Codes

Housing codes address the health and safety conditions of housing units in a community. Established as a result of unsafe and unhealthy conditions in urban residences, housing codes are concerned with the provision of heat, the presence and condition of electrical and plumbing systems, ventilation, light, and the control of vermin. For the most part, housing codes are local, but some states have adopted housing codes. In such instances, local codes must minimally comply with state codes but may have more stringent requirements.

Although theoretically, housing codes affect all housing in a community, in practice, rental property is most affected because home owners are not likely to complain about their own housing. Because funds are unavailable in most communities, local officials rarely inspect housing about which no complaints have been received. Even then, it may be difficult to force proprietors to comply with housing codes. Typically, stringent enforcement of housing codes results not necessarily in better housing but in less housing for low-income families. Rather than expend funds to improve deteriorating property, property owners may have the property condemned, abandon it, or sell it.

Types of Dwellings

The largest percentage of Americans live in single-family dwellings, although most are located in urban fringes, smaller cities and towns, suburban areas, and rural areas. Purchasing a single-family dwelling in a large urban area is prohibitively expensive. Modern apartment dwellers enjoy the benefits of living in urban areas at an affordable cost. In ancient and medieval cities, land prices within city walls, where there was greater protection, were higher than land outside the walls. Historically, the benefits of living in an urban area have been not only protection but greater cultural opportunities, job availability, and access to products. As early as ancient Rome, many families lived in smaller units within a larger one. When walls surrounded a city, it was necessary to use land efficiently to provide access for the greatest number of people. Demand was sufficient that higher prices could be charged. Dwelling units were frequently constructed with shared walls and stacked to create more space. The various types of multifamily housing have unique benefits and drawbacks when compared with single-family homes.

Single-Family Dwellings

Single-family detached dwellings are structures designed to house one family and are not attached to other dwellings. Both visual and acoustic privacy are easier to attain in single-family detached dwellings than in other housing types. Each home sits on its own property, providing outdoor living and recreation areas for family use. However, the trade-offs may be high.

Because they are constructed without shared facilities, single-family detached dwellings have higher initial costs, energy costs, and maintenance costs than multifamily dwellings. More land is required to house people in single-family homes than in multifamily housing. Hidden costs result from the additional miles of streets, roads, and utility connections, and the public transportation and other services that communities must provide. Environmental trade-offs include increased land use, added pollution, and energy consumption due to traffic and the need for greater power to deliver utilities and services to consumers.

Despite the continued popularity of single-family detached housing, economic constraints and increased urbanization have resulted in greater numbers of multifamily housing complexes. Multifamily dwellings are those in which two or more families occupy the same structure. There are various types of multifamily dwellings, ranging in density from **duplexes** to apartment complexes.

✳ Due to shared walls, multifamily dwellings are relatively easy to heat and cool. As the number of attached units rises, the cost of climate control generally decreases.

Multifamily Dwellings

Multifamily dwellings are less expensive to construct than single-family homes because they share walls, foundations, roofs, utilities, and land. A number of amenities are available in some types of multifamily dwellings that are lacking in single-family dwellings. These may include building security, shared recreation facilities, and accessibility to schools, churches, shopping areas, and employment.

Multifamily dwellings also have some disadvantages. Most units in multifamily dwellings are smaller than the average single-family detached dwelling and offer less visual and acoustic privacy. Children or pets may be banned. Even when the unit is owned rather than rented, decisions about landscaping, remodeling, or other changes may be affected by a homeowners' association.

Safety and security in multifamily dwellings may be compromised or enhanced depending on the unit. Most multifamily structures have many units under a single roof, with several exits and entrances. If no special security is provided this arrangement facilitates the work of intruders. Tenants may not know one another, and many tenants are away during the day. Multiple exits make it easy for an intruder to disappear quickly. On the other hand, multifamily complexes that have special security measures such as security guards, well-lit public areas, and television monitors are considerably safer than most single-family dwellings.

Duplexes and Quadriplexes

A duplex typically has the appearance of a single-family detached dwelling but houses two separate families. The structure may be divided into left and right halves, with the two dwelling units separated by a **party wall**, or each unit may occupy a separate story. A **quadriplex** is similar to a party-wall duplex but houses four families. **Triplexes**, having three attached dwelling units, are also similar but not as common. See Table 3.5.

Table 3.5 Percent of Housing Units by Number of Units in Structure: 2000

Type of dwelling	Percent
Single-family detached	60.3
Single-family attached	5.6
2 units	4.3
3 or 4 units	4.7
5 to 9 units	4.7
10 to 19 units	4.0
20+ units	8.6
Mobile homes	7.6

Source: U.S. Census Bureau, *Statistical Abstract of the United States: 2004–2005*, Table 948 "Housing Units by Units in Structure by State: 2000," Washington, D.C., Department of Commerce, 2005, p. 610.

Duplexes and quadriplexes provide many of the amenities of single-family detached homes. If the units are divided by a party wall, each has its own yard space and one or more ground-level entrances. A garage or carport is often provided for each unit as well. Many duplex owners live in one unit and rent the other, with the rental income helping them to pay for the duplex.

Row Houses

Row houses consist of three or more individual units in a continuous row with adjoining side walls. When the units are two or more stories tall, they are often called town houses. Row houses or town houses are usually built in relatively small clusters. Some have similar exterior designs and floor plans from one unit to the next. Others have units so different from one another that rooflines may not even match. See Figure 3.17.

Town houses have been constructed at least since the medieval period. During that time, row houses grouped around a courtyard or garden served a protective function similar to city walls. When urban land was scarce and expensive, this solution proved useful. In American cities—Philadelphia, Boston, New York City's Greenwich Village, and others—town houses

In town houses, exposed surfaces can be reduced by as much as 70 percent, making maintenance easier and energy bills lower.

have been constructed in almost every architectural style.

Town houses are popular because they require little land and are therefore suitable for families of modest means who want to live in urban areas. Shared walls make construction more efficient and costs lower. They are easy to heat and cool. Town houses have their own yards or outdoor living areas. The lack of visual and acoustic privacy associated with most multiple-family dwellings can be a major problem. Town houses are usually built in relatively small clusters, however.

Apartments

Modern apartment dwellers enjoy the benefits of living in urban areas at an affordable cost. Apartments

Figure 3.17 Row houses or town houses share side walls but they may have different appearances and even styles on the exterior.

Energy costs in apartments are considerably less than in single-family detached dwellings of the same size. Exterior exposure may be reduced by 90 percent.

are separated both vertically and horizontally from other units, sharing walls and floors with others.

Apartments can be built more efficiently than other housing types, resulting in greater density while requiring less land. When land is at a premium, apartments may be the only way to create affordable housing. Because apartments share walls and floors, and because stacking them requires less foundation and roof area structure, fewer materials are used. Additionally, the concentration of plumbing, electrical, and air-quality-control systems requires fewer materials.

Amenities that would not otherwise be affordable, such as security systems and elevators, are made possible because facilities are shared. Larger apartment complexes may have recreational facilities, restaurants, and shops right on the premises. Apartments may also provide convenient access to major business and shopping areas, since they are often located in urban areas where land is too expensive for single-family detached homes. Maintenance costs are extremely low when apartments are rented.

Despite these advantages, apartments are more likely to suffer from the drawbacks of multifamily dwellings—lack of visual and acoustic privacy, restricted outdoor space, and rulings against pets and children—than are duplexes, quadriplexes, and row houses. With few exceptions, apartments are typically smaller than other dwelling units. Limited yard space, lack of covered parking, and insufficient storage are common problems. Although the reduced exterior surface area increases energy-efficiency, it also provides for less natural light and ventilation. Many apartments do not have direct access at ground level.

Several types of apartments are available.

- Two-story self-contained units are called **maisonettes**.
- **Penthouse** apartments are located on the top floor of a building, generally have luxury features, and may have more than one story.
- **Garden apartments** are located in suburbs or urban fringes and are surrounded by large landscaped areas. They provide a semblance of country living while remaining close to urban conveniences. Because land is generally less expensive, parking may be an added amenity.
- A **studio apartment** or **efficiency apartment** combines a living area, a kitchenette, and sleeping quarters in one room. There is a separate bath and a limited amount of storage space. A one-and-a-half-room apartment adds a small sleeping alcove. A two-and-a-half-room apartment has a separate bedroom, a living area with a kitchenette, and a dining alcove.

Number of Levels

Homes of almost any type, particularly single-family homes, may have one or more levels. See Table 3.6. The number of levels in a home affects living patterns, design efficiency, energy usage, and efficiency of land use.

Single Story

Single-story homes are spread over a larger land area than multilevel homes with the same amount of living space. The need for larger lots may preclude the building of single-story homes in urban areas where land is expensive. Construction costs are high due to the number of linear feet of foundation and the large roof expanse. Single-story homes are also more expensive to heat and cool because of their sprawl. However, the lack of stairs simplifies circulation and makes cleaning easier. Exterior maintenance is also easier because almost everything can be reached with a short ladder.

Table 3.6 Number of Stories in New
One-Family Homes by Percent

Year	One story	Two or more stories	Split-level
1975			
U.S.	**65**	**23**	**12**
Northeast	48	42	10
Midwest	57	22	21
South	78	16	6
West	62	24	14
1980			
U.S.	**60**	**31**	**8**
Northeast	33	58	9
Midwest	53	30	17
South	69	27	4
West	60	29	11
1985			
U.S.	**52**	**42**	**6**
Northeast	25	70	6
Midwest	47	39	13
South	60	37	3
West	55	37	7
1990			
U.S.	**46**	**49**	**4**
Northeast	19	76	4
Midwest	44	45	11
South	57	41	2
West	44	52	4
1995			
U.S.	**49**	**48**	**3**
Northeast	19	78	3
Midwest	44	50	6
South	57	41	2
West	51	45	4
2000			
U.S.	**47**	**52**	**1**
Northeast	19	81	Z*
Midwest	45	50	5
South	53	47	Z
West	48	50	2
2004			
U.S.	**47**	**52**	**1**
Northeast	21	79	Z
Midwest	48	49	3
South	51	48	Z
West	46	54	Z

Source: www.census.gov/const/C25Ann/sftotalstories.pdf, (9/19/05).

* Z = Fewer than 500 units or 0.5 percent.

Multiple-story homes require less energy to heat and cool due to the decreased roof area. ❀

Split-Level

A **split-level home** has approximately one and a half times the living area of a single-story home that takes up the same amount of land. Construction costs are somewhat lower than for single-story homes (per square foot), although framing is more complicated. Energy costs are slightly lower than for single-level homes due to the stacking of some rooms. Split-level homes make good use of sloping lots (which may be less expensive) but do not make as efficient use of level lots. See Figure 3.18.

Good interior circulation patterns can be achieved because areas are functionally separated. Public areas are typically located on the entrance level, bedrooms on the upper level, and family living areas and utilities on the lower level. Although the stairs separating levels present some inconvenience, there is less than a

Figure 3.18 A split-level house is better suited to a sloping lot than to a relatively flat one. Note the entry at one living level. Sometimes the garage is located beneath the second-story section but that is not always the case.

full-story difference in height between consecutive levels.

Two-Story Houses

Two-story homes have a smaller ratio of wall, roof, and foundation area to floor space. Therefore, they are less expensive per square foot to construct than ranch or split-level homes. They also require less land and can be built on smaller lots. Due to the smaller ratio of floor space to surfaces that lose heat, stacking the floors creates some air-quality-control problems. Even temperatures may be difficult to achieve, with second-floor rooms often warmer than those on the first floor. Separate heating and cooling zones for each level help to solve this problem. Stacking the floors also makes two-story homes difficult to expand at a later date, although single-story additions have been common throughout history.

Because bedrooms are typically located on a different level than living areas, visual privacy in both zones is easily attained. Acoustic privacy is more difficult to obtain because noise travels through floors and ceilings easily. Upstairs, there is no direct access to the outside, complicating egress when an emergency exit is necessary.

Hillside Ranch

A hillside ranch is a two-story home built on a sloping lot that utilizes space below **grade level** for living. From the front, a hillside ranch looks like a one-story ranch home. The entry is at grade level and leads directly to the upper-story living areas. The full basement actually opens on at least one side to the lower-grade level in the rear so there is direct access to the outside from both levels. Family rooms or bedrooms may be located on the lower level. From the rear, a hillside ranch looks like a two-story house.

Basement walls are not extended significantly above the ground, if at all, so it may be difficult to provide light and ventilation to portions of the lower level away from exposed exterior walls. The earth

sheltering lowers heating and cooling costs in the lower level, although dampness may be a problem.

Initial construction costs may be lower than for other two-story homes because basements may be left unfinished until they are needed for living space. When finished, it is not necessary to use the entire basement for living space. Portions may be used for storage or for a garage. When a garage is located in the rear, however, a significant portion of the lot may be required for access.

Split Entry

Split-entry homes are also a variation of two-story dwellings. There are two separate living levels but part of the floor space is taken up by the entry. There is no living space on the same level as the entry requiring that all users go up or down stairs.

The basement of split-entry homes is raised several feet above grade level. High windows can be located on basement walls to admit light and ventilation, making basement space functional as a living area. However, because the basement extends above the ground, placement of porches or decks may be awkward and require the use of stairs. The extended basement wall, since it is made of concrete, is not aesthetically pleasing. Shrubbery can be planted to hide the concrete walls but takes several years to do so.

Split-entry homes facilitate privacy and make it possible to divert traffic from certain areas. Because living areas are stacked, split-entry homes cost less initially than ranch homes. Energy costs are lower for the same reason, and additional savings may be realized due to the earth sheltering of portions of the walls.

One- and Two-and-a-Half-Story Homes

When the roof pitch is steep enough, attics can be used for storage or added living area. When used as a living area, the attic needs windows, usually in dormers, to provide light and ventilation. Because the roof slants, much of the space beneath is not high enough to use efficiently. The IRC does not allow areas with angled ceiling lines less than 5 feet in height to be counted as floor area in a habitable room. **Knee walls**—vertical walls that are not high enough to stand under—may be constructed to provide usable wall space. Knee walls decrease apparent space, although they do not affect living area substantially. They do provide extra storage under the eaves. Homes with attic living space are classified as one-and-a-half- or two-and-a-half-story homes, indicating that approximately half a story of usable space is available in a finished attic.

Materials
Used
for
Residential
Design

Chapter 4

Materials used for building must

support the loads placed on them and maintain strength and stability when subjected to the stresses of climate. Materials determine the effectiveness of architectural devices and, to some extent, the building form. The most commonly used building materials are natural substances widely found throughout the world. Almost every imaginable material, including grass, has been used by some culture for the construction of housing. In some cases, it is necessary to combine materials or devise methods of using apparently unsuitable substances to produce structures.

While the materials themselves may not exhibit appropriate qualities, human ingenuity can often make do. Such diverse materials as snow, hides, felted hair, animal bones, reeds, bamboo, grass, and bits of driftwood are used to build structures.

Materials should be evaluated on the basis of life-cycle impacts, including energy consumption during all phases of manufacturing: extraction, transportation, and production. Energy use during the material's life span within a structure, any energy required for installation of the material, and the environmental impacts of the life cycle of the material, including emissions during manufacture and impacts of disposal when the usable life is over, should also be considered.

The materials used for housing may not necessarily be those of choice but rather availability. Locally available materials are generally less expensive and are almost always the choice of individuals without high social status. In fact, certain materials may be reserved for the more prestigious members of a social structure due to cost or social norms.

Where it has been available, the most common building material throughout history has been wood. Masonry construction also dates to prehistoric times. Modern technology has increased the use of metals, plastics, and other materials.

Figure 4.1 The tepee is a ubiquitous structure in many parts of the world and is covered with a variety of materials. This bark-covered tepee form is used by certain ethnic groups in the People's Republic of China.

Wood

In locations where wood is abundant, it was probably the first building material used. The characteristics of wood make it ideal for building construction. It is durable, decorative, relatively easy to work with using a few simple tools, and can be made into almost any form. It has a good strength-to-weight ratio and natural insulative qualities. Wood can be dried or pressure-treated to make it more suitable for its purposes and painted or stained to further improve its aesthetic qualities and to preserve it.

Wood is used as a framing system for the support of walls and roofs made of mud, bamboo, grass, leaves, or other materials. Branches and poles were used in very early windbreaks and sunscreens that are still used today in places like Tierra del Fuego and the tropics. See Figure 4.1 for an example of a wood tepee. Houses made of wood include the log cabin developed in Scandinavia and associated with the American frontier. The log cabin technique of notching logs, however, can be traced to ancient Swiss lake dwellers who used a notched-log framework to support walls of **wattle and daub**.

Classes of Woods

Woods are divided into two major classes—**hardwoods** and **softwoods**—depending on botanical differences, although there is little basis for the terminology. Each species has its own characteristic hardness.

In fact, some softwoods are harder than some hardwoods.

Softwoods come from coniferous trees[1] such as fir, pine, and cedar. Softwoods are used to construct the frame of a house, as well as for siding, roofing, and some trim and finish materials. Softwoods are generally easy to work with and accept most finishes well.

Hardwoods come from broad-leaf, deciduous trees[2] and include oak, walnut, and cherry. Components made of hardwoods can be crafted with sharp details and almost invisible joints, making them ideal for furniture construction.

Lumber

When a log is sawn or planed to size, the resulting material is called lumber. Various sizes and types of lumber are used for different purposes. See Box 4.1 for a guide to the method used for selling lumber.

- **Boards** are less than 2 inches thick and are 2 inches wide or more; they are used for siding, paneling, and furniture.
- **Dimension lumber** is 2 to 5 inches thick and 2 inches wide or more. It is used in home construction as framing members such as studs, joists, and rafters.
- **Timbers** have dimensions of 5 inches or more in each direction and are used for horizontal or vertical support where heavy loads must be carried.

In addition to these broad categories, lumber can be classified according to its use, strength, and appearance.

- **Finish lumber** is characterized by its lack of defects. It is used where appearance is important, such as in cabinets, furniture, and paneling.
- **Pattern lumber** is special-purpose lumber made from finish boards. The lumber is made into special shapes that allow adjoining pieces to fit

Softwoods scratch and dent relatively easily and do not stand up well under hard usage. For this reason, hardwoods are typically used for flooring, furniture, and cabinets.

together snugly or that serve a decorative purpose. Flooring, siding, and molding are examples of pattern lumber.

- **Structural lumber** is used for large supporting members such as joists and beams. Its distinguishing characteristic is its strength, as determined by accepted lumber standards.

Engineered Lumber

Engineered lumber is made with wood fibers, chips, or particles glued together under heat and pressure to form boards, panels, and structural components. Engineered lumber has no directional grain, knots, splits, or checks. Unlike lumber from trees,

---

Box 4.1 Calculating Board Feet

With the exception of molding, which is sold by the linear foot, most lumber is measured and priced by the board foot. A board foot is nominally 1 inch thick, 1 foot wide, and 1 foot long. To calculate the number of board feet in a piece of lumber, use the formula below. The example uses a 2 inch × 10 inch × 6 foot board.

Thickness (in inches) × width (in inches) × length (in feet) / 12
$$2 \times 10 \times 6 = 120$$
$$120 / 12 = 10 \text{ board feet}$$

To find the number of board feet in a quantity of same-sized pieces, calculate for one piece and then multiply by the number of pieces. If there are 5 boards the same size as used above, the total number of board feet is 50.

$$10 \text{ board feet} \times 5 = 50 \text{ board feet}$$

---

engineered lumber is consistent in its hardness and density, resists warping, and is more dimensionally stable. At the same time, engineered lumber is advertised to be stronger than traditional lumber. Some is made of recycled products. Because it resists warping and crowning, engineered lumber can be made in long units that remain straight over time. This quality makes engineered lumber suitable for boards with sufficient length to construct two or more stories with one set of walls.

Pressure-Treated Lumber

Since the 1940s, arsenic, copper, and chromium have been mixed to produce a chemical compound known as chromated copper arsenate (CCA), which is injected into wood under high pressure to protect it from mold, termites, fungi, and dry rot. The pressure-treated lumber is used for utility poles, marine construction, and in building construction. Typically, CCA is used where lumber comes in contact with masonry materials or the earth. It is used where wood framing joins a masonry foundation; for decks, fences, and gazebos; and for children's play equipment. Because of the dangers associated with arsenic, the Environmental Protection Agency ruled that after December 31, 2003, manufacturers could no longer use CCA to treat lumber to be used for deck surfaces, children's play equipment, and other surfaces with which people would be likely to come into contact.

The most popular alternatives to CCA are alkaline copper quat (ACQ) and copper azole. These alternatives are more expensive than CCA due to the increased amounts of copper used for treatment. In fact, the prices of alternatively treated lumber may be up to three times higher than for CCA.

Lumber Quality

Strength is the most important quality of the wood used for housing. The strength required is related to the specific use to which a piece is put, the way the load is distributed, and how long the load must be supported. Lumber strength depends on the species of wood, grain direction, and size.

Defects affect both the strength and appearance of lumber. **Knots** are round or irregularly shaped portions of wood in a piece of lumber, resulting from a branch growing from the tree. Separations of the grain, known as **splits** or **checks**, are likely to develop around or in knots. A split extends through the thickness of the lumber but a check does not. **Warping** is a twist or curve in the plane of the lumber. **Crowning** is a curve in the middle of a board.

Moisture Content

Wood is affected by moisture. A freshly cut tree has a large amount of water in its cells. Once it is cut, the wood absorbs or gives off moisture until its moisture content is in equilibrium with the relative humidity of the air. Wood expands as it absorbs moisture and shrinks as it loses moisture. In winter, when the humidity in homes is low, cracks become more apparent in floorboards, paneling, and furniture as wood members shrink.

Lumber is classified as either dry or green, depending on its moisture content. **Green lumber** has a moisture content greater than 19 percent. Contraction of green lumber as it dries pops nails; causes warping, splits, and checks; and causes cracks in finishes such as plaster. Wood is dried, or **seasoned**, prior to use to prevent these problems. Two methods are commonly used: air drying and kiln drying. Although more expensive, kiln drying is faster and results in a lower moisture content and fewer defects than does air drying.

Because the copper content of ACQ- and copper-azole-treated lumber makes wood more corrosive, designers who specify this material should also specify fasteners and other metals in contact with the lumber made of stainless steel, copper, or heavily galvanized metals. If special fasteners are not specified, less expensive ones may be used.

Lumber Sizes

Lumber is specified by its **nominal size**. Originally, this was the size of the lumber before drying and before it went through final processes such as planing. A plane is used to trim (**dress**) the sides of the boards to smooth them. For example, a common size for dimension lumber is the 2 × 4. This means that the lumber measured 2 inches thick and 4 inches wide when unfinished. (It can be cut to any length.) The actual size of a 2 × 4 ready for use (its **dressed size**) is somewhat smaller than 2 inches thick and 4 inches wide. **Dressed** sizes of softwoods are standardized to dimensions specified by the American Softwood Lumber Standard. The actual dimensions of a softwood 2 × 4 are 1½ × 3½ inches. Hardwoods are usually sold as rough-sawn lumber so that the nominal and actual dimensions are relatively close.

Wood Uses in the Home

The most obvious use of wood in homes is for the structure that supports floors, walls, ceilings, and roofs. But wood is also used for finishing materials, including flooring. Although wood is a nonresilient flooring material, the walking comfort of wood floors is greater than that of other nonresilient flooring types. Softwoods may be used for flooring but do not wear well. More durable hardwoods, such as oak and maple, are the most common materials for wood floors. Wood varieties have a characteristic grain or pattern.

The most common pattern for laying wood flooring is in parallel strips—called **strip flooring** and **plank flooring**, depending on the strip width. Strip flooring uses boards 2¼ inches or less in width, with tongue and groove joints. See Figure 4.2. In addition, wood is an ideal material for creating intricate **parquet** or **marquetry** patterns. Parquet designs are geometric and employ straight edges. Marquetry employs different materials inlaid in a background material. Inlaid shapes may be extremely complex. The

Figure 4.2 Plank flooring makes use of boards 3 to 8 inches in width and results in a rustic effect. (Source: Heather Ireland-Weter)

designs can be formed with a single type of wood, different woods, or wood in combination with other materials.

Sealing and finishing wood make it impervious to many stains. The floor can be finished with varnish, shellac, lacquer, or a polyurethane-based finish, all of which let the wood grain show through. Prefinished wood flooring is also available—some finished with acrylic, others with any of a number of varnishes. When the finish eventually wears off in high-traffic areas, refinishing renews the gloss. Other finishing alternatives include painting the floor a solid color or decorating it with painted or stenciled designs.

Fiberboard, Hardboard, Particleboard, Waferboard, and Oriented-Strand Board

A number of products made from wood fibers—**fiberboard**, **hardboard**, **particleboard**, **waferboard**, and **oriented-strand board** (OSB)—are commonly

---

When pegging plank flooring, a contrasting wood may be used for the pegs for a more decorative floor.

used in home construction. Because they are made from scraps from lumber production, they are relatively inexpensive. These products are usually sold as panels in 4 × 8 feet or 4 × 10 feet sheets.

Fiberboard

Wood is broken down into individual fibers, then re-formed with rollers to make fiberboard. The bond between the fibers is weak since little or no glue, heat, or pressure is used. Fiberboard is lightweight and has some insulative value. It is used for ceiling tiles, as a backing for interior finish materials, and other places where strength is not necessary. Exterior-grade fiberboard has asphalt in its composition to improve moisture-resistance.

Fiberboard ceiling tile is used in new construction as well as to cover existing wallboard or plaster. Mineral-fiber tiles have the same appearance and are used in the same manner. These interlocking tiles are easy to install and cover damaged older surfaces quickly and inexpensively. The tiles can be attached directly to the existing surface with staples or adhesive. If the existing surface is uneven or cracked, or if there is no existing surface, the tiles are stapled to wooden **furring strips** or attached to a metal track with clips.

Square or rectangular tiles in several sizes are available, although 2 feet square and 2 feet × 4 feet rectangular tiles are the most common. Some of these tiles present the appearance of stamped metal tiles. Acoustic tiles have tiny holes in the surface to trap sound. Although most fiberboard tiles are white, board-shaped tiles are available in wood-grain finishes to create the illusion of a wooden plank surface.

Hardboard

Hardboard is made of wood fibers that are expanded and separated in the presence of pressurized steam. Pressure is then applied to formulate the exploded fibers into permanently bonded sheets ⅛ to ⅜ inches thick. No glue is used in the production of hardboard. Denser than wood, hardboard offers strength and durability, although moisture will damage the product.

Hardboard can easily be painted or can be purchased in prefinished form. It has no grain of its own but can be formed with a simulated wood grain. The surface may be smooth, perforated[3], or textured. Hardboard is used primarily for interior surfaces because it shrinks and swells with changes in humidity. It is often used for furniture backs, drawer bottoms, and pegboard.

The addition of heat and certain chemicals in the manufacturing process results in **tempered hardboard**, which is more moisture-resistant. Tempered hardboard can be used as exterior siding and in bathtub enclosures.

Hardboard paneling is an inexpensive material used to finish walls or ceilings in homes. The paneling has a printed design applied to the surface. When panels with printed designs are used, the edges are usually fit into exposed channels between panels. These channels are utilitarian and are not generally aesthetically pleasing. Textured patterns available include grooved wood grain; simulated brick, stone, and marble; and other designs. Grooves are spaced so that they appear on both side edges, hiding the seams. For bathrooms and kitchens, tempered hardboard with a laminated plastic finish provides a waterproof surface.

Particleboard

Particleboard is made of wood fibers that are coated with glue and pressed into sheets using heat and pressure. Particleboard is usually thicker than hardboard—up to 1½ inches thick. Particleboard has excellent dimensional stability. It is not particularly attractive by itself but it can be stained, painted, or used as a backing for surface finishes. Because of its smooth surface, it is often used as an underlayment on floors. Particleboard should not be used where moisture may damage it—including under ceramic and porcelain tile on bathroom floors and walls.

Waferboard and Oriented-Strand Board

Waferboard and oriented-strand board (OSB) are similar materials. Like fiberboard, hardboard, and particleboard, they are reconstituted wood-panel products. Both waferboard and OSB are made of wood flakes. In waferboard, the wood flakes are randomly oriented; in OSB, they are aligned. Strands are mixed with wax and adhesive or resin, then formed into panels. Waferboard panels have random, homogeneous composition; OSB is made in **plies** or layers stacked so that alternating layers have strands that run perpendicular. OSB is stronger and stiffer than waferboard. When exposed to moisture, both expand. For this reason, they are not suitable as an underlayment beneath tile, and care should be taken when these panels are used as roof sheathing.

Laminated Materials

When two or more thin sheets of material are glued together to form a single unit, the result is a laminated product that combines features of the laminates. Laminating thin layers gives the finished product added strength as well as versatility of shape. Laminated construction materials include **plywood** and laminated beams and arches. The most common laminated finish material in homes is a thin plastic layer bonded or glued to particleboard to form countertops.

Plywood

Plywood is made of a number of plies that are glued together. The layers are usually made of **veneer** —very thin sheets of wood that are sliced or peeled from logs—although some of the layers may be made of other materials. The plies are glued together with

the grain running at right angles in adjacent layers. This helps provide the dimensional stability of plywood, makes it equally strong in both directions, and helps to keep it from splitting. Plywood always has an odd number of layers so that the grain of both outside faces runs in the same direction.

The middle layer is called the **core**. Certain core materials give plywood characteristics that make it suitable for specific functions. A core of thicker lumber rather than veneer is usually used in plywood designed for furniture, doors, flooring, and paneling. A mineral or gypsum core is used for fire-resistant plywood that is typically made into paneling.

Although plywood is most frequently left with the natural wood grain, it can be made with a grooved, embossed, or otherwise textured surface. Because the plies are thin, plywood can be molded into various shapes as it is made. Curved furniture pieces such as chairs may be constructed of plywood that is formed as it is glued. Plywood comes in thicknesses ranging from $\frac{1}{4}$ to $1\frac{1}{8}$ inch and is made into 4×8 feet or 4×10 feet panels.

Both softwoods and hardwoods are used to make plywood, but Douglas fir is the most common species used. Softwood plywood is graded in terms of appearance. The grades are N, A, B, C, and D, in descending order. N-grade plywood has few, if any, defects and must be specially ordered. D-grade plywood has knotholes and splits. Because much plywood use requires that only one side be attractive, each side is graded separately. A–C plywood, for example, has one face of high quality for appearance and one of a lower grade for economy.

Softwood plywood is produced in both exterior and interior grades. Exterior plywood is made with adhesives that are insoluble in water and is used for sheathing, siding, and fences. Interior plywood is manufactured with water-soluble adhesives, so it cannot be used where exposed to excessive humidity or moisture. In homes, it serves as subflooring, roof and wall sheathing, and paneling.

Hardwood plywood is desirable for its aesthetic appeal, with more than 250 different species used. Hardwood plywood grades, in descending order, are specialty grade, premium grade, good grade, sound grade, utility grade, and backing grade. In the higher grades, the face veneer is designed so that joints can be matched. In lower grades, grain and color are not matched.

Plywood is often used for finished paneling. Face veneers from a variety of species are available. The panels are usually grooved at intervals ranging from 3 to 10 inches to give the impression of individual boards. Plywood paneling can be installed over studs, plaster, wallboard, backer board, or furring strips. Furring strips are used to apply the paneling over masonry walls or walls that are very uneven.

Laminated Finished Components

Unusually shaped arches and beams can be constructed of thin layers of wood. Although some are made and finished on the construction site, complicated shapes are usually fabricated in factories. Laminated beams and arches are most often used in schools, churches, and other commercial buildings where large spans are desirable, but they are also used for exposed ceiling beams in homes. Railings for curved stairways may also be formed using thin boards laminated together on the building site.

Other Vegetative Materials

Although grass and leaves appear to be unlikely building materials, they are excellent for shelters in hot, humid climates because they do not retain heat. Grass, reeds, or straw are commonly used in less industrialized areas of the world for building or finishing structures. Cork is a less used material derived from the bark of certain trees. Wattle-and-daub structures use a mixture of vegetative materials and mud.

Grass, Reeds, and Straw

To build in the marshlands of Iraq, people bind bunches of reeds together, forming strong ribs to support the tunnel-like structures. The structural use of most vegetative materials other than wood, however, requires a stable framework. To cover the frame, two basic methods are employed: **thatching** and weaving.

Thatching is accomplished by bundling long grass, straw, or reeds and overlapping the bundles when attaching them to the frame. Thatch may be used for only the roof or for the entire house. The Wichita, Caddo, and Shoshone Indians, for example, used thatch to build large cone-shaped structures up to 40 feet in diameter. In areas where shelters have no walls, thatch is the material of choice for the roof. Thatch roofs have also been combined with various wall structures. They can still be found in rural areas of the British Isles and in Africa, South America, and the South Sea Islands. While natural thatch will deteriorate over time, modern thatch made of a plastic-based material will last indefinitely.

The second method of utilizing vegetable material for building is by **plaiting** (various types of braiding) or weaving. Palm fronds are frequently woven or plaited for the walls of houses on tropical islands. In southwest Africa, the Swazis build their huts of woven grass. When one of these dome-shaped houses needs to be cleaned, the people simply lift the house and set it down at a new site. Spring housecleaning takes only minutes. Some buildings in native Fijian villages incorporate mats of woven vegetative materials as walls. See Figure 4.3.

A contemporary use of straw includes straw bale construction where walls are built by stacking bales of straw. The interior and exterior surfaces are finished with **stucco**. The thick walls are highly energy-efficient because the straw provides insulation.

Bamboo—a grass—has been used for centuries in tropical areas for flooring but is relatively new on the

American market. This grass, sliced into strips, is very durable but lacks the grain associated with wood.

Cork

Cork is used for tiles that are very resilient and, therefore, comfortable to walk on and quiet. Indentations made in the tile, however, are permanent. Cork is not recommended for floors in heavy-use areas because it chips easily. Colors are limited to browns. Vinyl cork is less expensive and easier to clean than natural cork but is not as resilient. Cork has many dead air spaces and absorbs sound, so cork tiles can be used on walls to help provide acoustic privacy.

Wattle and Daub

Mud and vegetation are combined as building materials in wattle-and-daub houses. A framework of timbers supports the structure, and much of the framing is exposed on the final building. Branches are interlaced between supporting timbers to form a basket-like lattice called wattle. This lattice is then daubed with mud or clay to complete the wall. A binder—animal hair, straw, or moss—mixed into the daub helps prevent cracking as it dries. The early Scandinavians interlaced branches with supporting posts to form walls. They plastered over these walls with mud or clay. Structurally, these houses are much like an upside-down basket with mud daubed on the outside. Grass or thatch roofs are commonly used on wattle-and-daub structures.

Animal Products

Animal hides and felted hair are commonly used building materials for structures designed to be moved. The tepee of the Plains Indians used a framework of poles covered with animal hides. Felted hair is

Figure 4.3 The walls of this structure are made of woven palm fronds that allow breezes to cool the interior. Raising the structure off the ground allows cool air to circulate beneath the structure as well. Homes such as this are common in tropical areas.

still used for Mongolian yurts, which are supported on a wooden framework with latticelike walls.

Leather is used as a finish material and can be applied to structural surfaces or to furnishings. Leather has been used for centuries on walls to help prevent drafts but today, leather is used for its aesthetic appeal. Wool is used in high-end carpets and rugs designed for use on the floor. Silk carpets are usually designed to be hung on walls.

Masonry

Because most masonry construction is durable, it is the material of choice for structures expected to last indefinitely. Egyptian stone pyramids and Roman aqueducts are only today being harmed by pollution in the air. **Cement** and concrete are used alone and in combination with other materials. **Adobe**, brick, and

While brick and stone can be used to face a wood-framed wall, these materials can be used to construct structural components as well. Concrete block can also be used for this purpose. Each of these materials can be used for heat collection and storage. Planning floor and wall masonry masses inside the home where they are in direct sunlight can significantly improve the amount of heat gain during the winter.

stone are the building materials of choice in many arid lands because of the lack of wood. In addition, these materials absorb and store heat, making the resulting structures especially suited to hot climates. Clay products are used for decorative and utilitarian functions in many homes. Besides their many uses in residential construction, masonry materials are idea for commercial and industrial construction, roads, and certain utilities necessary for the efficient management of modern homes.

Most early masonry construction employed small individual units that were stacked in some manner to form walls. Mud formed into blocks, fired brick, and cut and uncut stone were masonry materials commonly used during the prehistoric and ancient eras. While individual units are still used in construction, they are often used as veneer rather than as support. Most masonry supporting components today are made of concrete.

Brick

Brick is the oldest manufactured building material, with a history of more than 6000 years. There are two basic types of brick—sun-dried brick (adobe) and fired brick. Sun-dried brick was probably developed before 4000 B.C. in ancient Mesopotamia, and it has also been used in arid climates including Egypt, much of the Middle East, the Far East, Africa, and by Indians in the Western hemisphere. The use of sun-dried brick eliminated the need for wood in structures except as support for roofs. While sun-dried brick is not com-

monly used today in highly industrialized areas, it is still used extensively in other parts of the world.

Adobe

When mud bricks dry, they crack and break, but early builders discovered that when a binder such as straw was used, the dried brick was more likely to keep its form. Adobe is a mixture of clay and water with a binder such as straw, animal hair, or moss. It may be used with or without forming it into blocks or bricks.

To insure structural stability, sun-dried brick walls must be thick. Such structures often have flat roofs since there is little need for a roof pitch in areas where rainfall is sparse. Rooftops are high enough off the ground to catch the breezes, and during times when temperatures do not get too cold at night, the flat rooftops make ideal places to sleep in comfort.

Pueblo Indians used sun-dried bricks to build their multistoried apartment complexes. The walls were then plastered with mud on both the interior and exterior to create a smooth surface. See Figure 4.4.

Figure 4.4 This 400-year-old adobe brick is well preserved. Usually, a finish coat of adobe is plastered over the brick, but in this case, the wall was not originally an exterior one. The end walls have been protected with stucco, but this wall has been left in its original condition. The binder used in the adobe mix can be seen in some places.

Since the timbers used to support the roof were difficult to obtain, and to cut with stone tools, they were not cut to length. If the timbers were too long, the ends simply stuck out beyond the walls. These timbers could be used again and again if necessary. When materials for supporting a roof framework are not available, a different form of structure results. In Jordan and Turkey, the clay homes are conical. Modern houses with the appearance of adobe are actually constructed of concrete or stucco applied over a framed structure.

Fired Brick

Because adobe quickly reduces to mud when wet, it is best used in arid climates. In other climates, it is necessary to repair or replace sun-dried brick frequently. Fired brick is much more durable. Firing clay brick at extremely high temperatures for up to 200 hours partially melts the clay particles, then fuses them so that they become strong and hard. Ancient civilizations discovered this metamorphosis around 4000 B.C.

Fired brick is made from pulverized clay and shale mixed with water. The resulting material is then formed into molds, cut, dried, and fired. Fired brick has the strength of stone but comes in standardized dimensions in sizes small enough to handle easily. It is available in a variety of colors and textures and has the added advantage of uniform quality. Brick can be used to construct walls using bearing wall construction or it can be used as a facade over any type of structure. In residential construction, brick is usually a facade on a frame or masonry wall.

The properties of finished brick depend on the type of clay used, the temperature to which it is fired, and the amount of time it is fired. Finished brick color is related to the clay used but is also affected by the length and temperature of firing and the amount of oxygen used during firing. Natural brick colors include reds, buffs, and creams. Blacks and grays are also possible but rarer. For lighter colors, manufacturers underburn brick; for darker ones, they overburn. Chem-

icals may also be added during the firing of brick to change its color. The texture is affected by the mold and the method of cutting, and can be altered by scratching, rolling, or brushing the surface as the brick leaves the mold.

Finished brick is graded according to the effects of freezing and thawing in the presence of water. The ability to absorb water is a function of the amount of time the brick is fired. The hotter the temperature and the longer the time bricks are burned, the less moisture the finished brick will absorb. Decreasing moisture absorption minimizes cracking as a result of freezing and thawing. **Vitrified** brick is extremely hard, absorbs no moisture, and has a high resistance to abrasion. Medium-burned brick absorbs some water, while soft-burned brick absorbs a great deal.

Bricks may also be classified according to their intended use.

- **Building brick**, also called **common brick**, is used for construction where beauty is not an important factor.
- **Face brick** is specially made for a combination of aesthetic and functional purposes. It is graded on the basis of color, size, and texture. Generally, face brick is almost as durable as building brick.
- **Firebrick**—made of heat-refracting clays—is capable of withstanding extremely high temperatures without cracking. Usually, firebrick is larger than other types of brick. It is commonly used to line fireplaces, chimneys, and barbeque pits.
- **Acid-resistant brick** is specially formulated for use in contact with chemicals.

Bricks are laid in rows called courses and are usually held together with mortar. A variety of patterns,

Brick can be painted, but once it is, it must be kept painted. It is extremely difficult to strip paint from brick and rarely is all the paint removed; sandblasting removes the fired surface of the brick, resulting in deterioration.

called **bonds**, can be used in laying brick. Most bonds use alternating joints to improve the strength of the bond. Brick can also be molded so there is a raised design on its surface that extends across many units. Molded brick is being used in commercial establishments but rarely in residences. See Figure 4.5 for various bonds and Figure 4.6 for molded brick.

Glazed Brick. Glazed brick is used in places where ease of cleaning is important, such as in dairies and laboratories. Glaze is a glasslike finish that may be added prior to the first firing or afterward. All glazes must be fired to melt the particles and form a continuous impermeable surface. Since many glazes cannot take the high temperatures required for firing brick, they are applied to previously fired brick that is then refired at lower temperatures. Generally, only one surface is glazed.

Interior Finishing Applications of Brick. Brick can be installed as a walking surface with or without using mortar. In a mortarless installation, the brick is set in a bed of sand. This type of installation is typically used outdoors for patios and sidewalks around the home. Inside the home, brick flooring usually has mortared joints, which facilitate cleaning.

Any of the brick bonds can be used in a floor, although bonds that allow alternating joints are most successful. Brick **pavers** are thin bricks and can be installed using an adhesive. Some brick pavers are saturated with acrylic, making them impervious to moisture and stains. Brick can also be glazed or sealed for this purpose. However, the texture of unglazed brick hides some of the dirt and stains that would show on more highly polished surfaces. Brick may chip or crack but usually can be replaced easily.

The rustic effect of a brick or stone wall can be simulated by applying one of several products to wallboard or plaster. One such wall covering consists of thin masonry units sliced a half inch thick from full-sized brick or molded separately. These thin bricks can be applied individually with adhesive, or panels of bricks premounted on a fiberboard backing can be nailed to the wall. The spaces between the bricks are then filled with mortar for an authentic appearance. A realistic masonry effect can also be achieved with artificial bricks and stones made of plaster or rigid plastic

Figure 4.5 Bricklayers have developed a variety of brick bonds over the centuries. The bonds here are the most common: stack bond (a), common bond (b), and running bond (c).

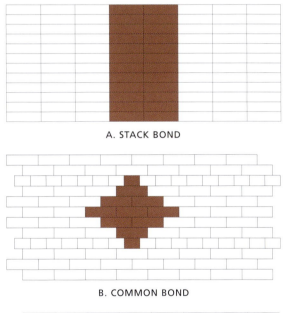

A. STACK BOND

B. COMMON BOND

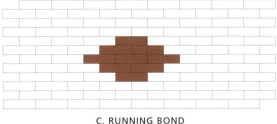

C. RUNNING BOND

❁ The use of individual bricks or stones for paving conserves water because it allows water to drain between the units back into the ground. Not only does this increase the amount of water returned to the water table but it reduces the amount of water that runs into storm drains and municipal sewage-treatment plants.

Figure 4.6 Molded brick is generally used in buildings in the commercial sector rather than in residences. The brick is molded as it is formed and requires precision when installing it to ensure that the final product appears as it should.

foam. These units are inexpensive, lightweight, and easy to install with adhesive. Both real and artificial masonry wall coverings are especially popular in kitchens and family rooms.

Stone

In building construction, stone is used for both construction and veneer. Stone facades can be applied over concrete, wood frame, or even brick construction. On the interior, stone can be used for finishing structural components, such as walls and floors, and for fireplaces and countertops.

Types of Stone Construction

Stone can be used alone or with mortar to create walls. When built without mortar, walls are termed **dry stone**; when mortar is used, walls are called **wet stone**. Many of the dry stone walls around fields in New England are still standing after almost 300 years.

Stone is more expensive to lay than brick because it is irregularly shaped and requires great skill for the building of structurally sound walls. Like brick, stone is

Because of the heavy weight of stone flooring, it is essential to ensure that the floor structure has sufficient strength to support the materials.

often laid in bonds, although uncut stone—called **rubble**—is used for a rustic appearance. Rubble may be partially squared and placed roughly in rows—**coursed rubble**—or left in irregular shapes—**random rubble**. Figure 4.7 illustrates random rubble.

Ashlar stonework uses carefully squared-off stones in specific sizes for a close-fitting formal pattern. The two exposed faces of ashlar stone may be textured, left in a natural state, or treated in some other manner.

Varieties of Stone

Although stone is hard, not all stone has the strength or durability necessary to build structurally sound buildings. Absorbed water freezes and

Figure 4.7 Uncut rubble stone construction is typical of areas where medium-sized rocks abound and there is material for mortar. Because rubble stone construction does not require cutting of the stone, this type of wall has often been used by peasants. Today, rubble stone construction is very expensive because of the difficulty of fitting the stones together.

expands, causing chips of stone to break off, so stone ideal for buildings has few tiny pores and absorbs little water. Strength, durability, and appearance depend on the type of stone used. Even in thin layers, stone is cold to the touch.

Limestone. Limestone is relatively soft so it can be worked and cut easily, making it an excellent building material. The Egyptian pyramids were made of limestone, which ranges in color from white to black. Because it is easily scratched, limestone is not used where a high polish is desired.

Travertine is a porous limestone formed by mineral springs where escaping gases form small holes in the resulting stone. For this reason, it should be sealed with epoxy resin before using. Clear resin gives travertine a three-dimensional appearance, while an opaque resin provides a satin finish. Travertine is used for flooring in formal areas.

Granite. Granite is an igneous rock with visible crystals. Colors include white, gray, pink, red, blue, green, and black, with a variety of shades in each color range. Granite is very strong and capable of withstanding great pressure, making it valuable for support in bridges and buildings. Its hardness makes granite difficult to cut but makes it possible to highly polish the surface. Because it resists abrasion, granite is used for facing the interior and exterior surfaces of buildings that receive high use. The limestone of the pyramids was originally faced with granite, which withstands weathering better than limestone. Granite is used not only for structural support but as a finish veneer on the exterior of buildings, as flooring, and as a countertop material in kitchens and bathrooms.

Sandstone. Sandstone is easy to work with but is less suitable than granite for building construction because it is easily worn by wind and weather.

Slate is slippery when wet so it should not be used for outdoor walking surfaces.

Marble. Marble is hard limestone and can be polished and carved with minute detail and sharp features. Although the finest marble is white, the presence of minerals in the stone results in pinks, reds, yellows, blacks, grays, blue-grays, and greens as well. The colors are streaked in veins.

Marble was a favorite building material in ancient Greece and Rome because of its aesthetic qualities. Today, marble is used for buildings, fireplaces, tables, flooring, and countertops. Marble has been a favored flooring throughout history, although it is more expensive than other flooring materials. Marble veneer applied to a wall results in a formal appearance.

Terrazzo. Terrazzo is a manufactured material made of marble chips and either resin or cement. It may be precast or poured in place. Precast tiles are usually 12-inch squares. Sections of poured-in-place terrazzo may be separated by metal or plastic strips that serve as expansion joints and as dividers between colors in a specific pattern. The colors of terrazzo are usually limited to the natural colors of marble.

Slate. Slate has an almost perfect natural cleavage, splitting into thin sheets with little difficulty, making it suitable for roofs and flooring. Colors usually range from grays to black, although some greens, browns, and reds occur. Slate is less formal than marble but more formal in appearance than other stones, thus lending itself to high-traffic areas in formal spaces. Its dark color makes it ideal for areas where it can be used to collect passive solar energy. See Figure 4.8 for an example of slate roofing.

Flagstone. Flagstone consists of irregularly shaped flat stones, usually in beige, reddish brown, and gray colors. A number of stones, including slate, sandstone, bluestone, and quartzite, may be classified as flagstone. The stones may be cut into blocks for a more formal appearance, but flagstone is usually laid with its natural uneven surface in a random pattern achieved without cutting the edges of the stones.

Flagstone may be used as a veneer on exterior walls or as flooring in informal spaces.

Cement and Concrete

Cement is a mixture of lime, silica, iron oxide, alumina, and other ingredients designed to make cement harden slowly, more quickly, underwater, or with other special features. Cements differ by the source of lime. Common sources include limestone, oyster shells, and clay, although the Romans use burned marble and volcanic ash for lime. Silica comes from sand. The raw materials are finely ground, then heated to a temperature high enough (up to 3000 degrees Fahrenheit) to change their physical and chemical properties. Gypsum is added to the resulting material and the mixture is pulverized. Most of the cement used in construction is portland cement, which has calcium added.

Flagstone has an uneven surface resulting from natural cleavage of the rock, causing furniture placed on a flagstone floor to tilt or rock.

When cement is combined with water, a chemical reaction—hydration—occurs. Hydration causes the cement to harden permanently to a stonelike consistency. Portland cement was developed by the English mason Joseph Aspdin in 1824 and named because when finished, it resembled the quarried stone from the Isle of Portland.

Cement backer board is made in panels from ¼ to ½ inch thick. Backer board may be laid on a subfloor or attached to studs for walls. Because it is impervious to water, it is excellent for use under tile in bathrooms and kitchens.

Cement is rarely used alone for construction purposes. The large amounts necessary for buildings

Figure 4.8 Slate roofs are often found in rural areas, where their rustic appearance blends with the surroundings. Slate roofing ranges in color from tans to darker browns and from light to dark grays, including blue gray.

would be prohibitively expensive, and cement shrinks excessively as it hardens. Therefore, it is usually mixed with **aggregates** such as sand, gravel, or crushed stone to form concrete. In a concrete mixture, the cement-water paste surrounds each particle of the aggregate to bind the whole mass together. Aggregates provide inexpensive bulk while maintaining strength and preventing excessive shrinkage.

Concrete is strong and durable, ideally suited for foundations, walls, floors, sidewalks, and driveways. Other materials can be added to give it special properties, making it lighter in weight or adding insulative value. A major advantage of concrete is its plasticity—the ability to be formed into almost any shape while wet. It can be poured into molds to make plain or ornamental blocks, or into forms made of earth, wood, metal, foam, or fiber to make walls, floors, panels, sidewalks, and paving.

A structural member cast other than in its final position is considered **precast**. Heavy equipment is needed on the site to place precast panels used for floors, walls, or roofs. Precast concrete members are economical because they can be mass-produced, but transportation costs—especially over long distances—may offset any savings. On large construction projects, on-site precasting is common.

Concrete can support heavy loads because it has excellent **compression strength**—the ability to support a weight that bears directly on the material. However, its **tensile strength**—its resistance to being torn apart by longitudinal stresses—is low. Steel has relatively low compression strength but high tensile strength. Reinforced concrete combines concrete with steel bars, mesh, or cables, merging the desirable strength characteristics of both materials. Reinforced concrete minimizes cracking due to changes in temperature and moisture conditions. It can be poured on the site or purchased in precast sections.

Prestressed concrete is poured over steel cables

to which tension is applied. When the concrete hardens, tension on the steel cables is released, permitting them to spring back to their shorter, thicker original shape. The increased diameter serves as a wedge inside the concrete to hold the cables tightly against it under stress. Prestressed concrete prevents cracks, has elastic properties not found in ordinary concrete, and is capable of resisting considerable stress. Prestressed concrete can be hauled without damage over greater distances than other precast concrete products.

Thin-shell concrete is sprayed over an inflated air form made of plastics. The air form is much like a balloon and can be made in any shape. On the job site, the air form is inflated, reinforcement bars installed, and concrete or plastic is sprayed over the form to create the structure of the building. The air form is generally left on the structure after the concrete has hardened.

Uses of Concrete in Residential Interiors

Concrete is often used as a base for other flooring but can also serve as finish flooring. As such, it is relatively inexpensive. Color can be added when the concrete is mixed, or the floor can be painted or stained after it is cured. Concrete often cracks due to temperature changes and settling. Once cracked, it is difficult to repair. If a pattern of grooves is made in the concrete while it is still plastic, the floor will have a more formal appearance and any cracking is likely to occur in the grooves, making cracks less apparent. Because concrete is plastic until it is dry, it can be poured into complexly shaped panels for use as countertops in kitchens and bathrooms.

Concrete Block

The use of concrete block is relatively inexpensive because it does not require forms, as does poured concrete construction. Mortar, a mixture of portland cement, lime, water, and sand, is used between the blocks to bind them together. The mortar also compensates for slight variations in the size of the blocks.

Concrete blocks are durable and termite-proof,

⊞ Waxing a concrete floor gives it a luster suitable even for formal rooms.

Figure 4.9 Concrete block can be quite decorative and is often used in climates like Miami, Florida, because it is not affected by moisture.

meet fire and safety requirements, and offer acoustic privacy. They are commonly used for retaining walls, structural walls, common walls in multi-unit buildings, and fireplaces.[4] They can be covered with a veneer of brick, stucco, or wood. Decorative block is popular for patios and fences. See Figure 4.9.

Clay

Clay can be fired to produce hollow drainage tiles, roofing tiles, ceramic tile, and porcelain. See Figure 4.10 for an unusual use of a clay product in a building. Hollow cylindrical tiles are glazed to make them impervious to water. Such tiles are ideal for use in plumbing systems because they can be buried without damage, will last indefinitely, and will not leak. Glazed and unglazed clay tiles are also used for roofing material. Roof tiles may be rounded, flat, squared off, U-shaped, or a combination of these forms.

Other ceramic tiles are used where their imperviousness to water and resistance to scratches make them desirable. Bathroom walls, kitchen walls, and entry floors are commonly covered with ceramic tiles. Porcelain tiles are made of clay mixed with specific minerals and fired to extremely high temperatures—often exceeding 2400 degrees Fahrenheit. Because of the high firing temperatures, porcelain tile resists moisture better than ceramic tile.

Ceramic tiles are available in a variety of shapes, surface patterns, and textures. Glazed tiles are impervious to stains, although the mortar or grout used between tiles needs to be sealed to prevent it from staining. The glazed surface is easy to clean but does show dirt and dust and may scratch easily. Tile sizes range from 16-inch squares to 1-inch squares designed for use in mosaic patterns.

Ceramic tile is made of fired clay that is glazed with either a gloss or satin finish. The color, therefore, is only on the surface. **Quarry tile** is the same color throughout its thickness and is usually unglazed. **Mexican quarry tile** is less consistent than other types because it is generally made by hand without measuring the ingredients used in the clay. This method of manufacture also results in inconsistent thickness of the tile. Some tiles have imperfections resulting from their outdoor location during drying. Others may have animal footprints, foliage prints, or even marks left by children before the tiles were fired.

Porcelain tiles are usually unglazed and the color runs through the thickness of the material. Because it is fired at higher temperatures than other clay tiles,

Figure 4.10 The glazed clay product used near a roof in Bangkok, Thailand, coordinates with the tiles used on the facade of the structure.

porcelain is extremely durable and can be used for floors in high-traffic areas. Porcelain glaze is impervious to almost any material, so it prevents staining. Glazed porcelain resists the action of acids and corrosion and is easy to clean, but over a period of years, the finishes may dull. Plumbing fixtures made of molded porcelain (also called vitreous china) are heavy and will break when dropped or roughly handled. Porcelain cannot be used for bathtubs because they are too large to be successfully cast.

Glass

Glass materials are translucent or transparent and provide good light transmission. The Romans were the first to use glass for windows. However, it was not until the twelfth century that glass was used in housing to any great extent and even later before it became common.

Types of Flat Glass

Modern glass used in homes includes **window glass**, **plate glass**, and **float glass**. These terms refer to the way the glass is manufactured.

- Window glass is manufactured by drawing a molten silica-based material into sheets that are then flattened by rollers. Most window glass is $1/16$ to $1/8$ inch thick and has some flaws. The thicker the glass, the stronger it is.
- Plate glass is formed by a more complicated and time-consuming process than window glass. Molten glass is poured over a casting table, smoothed with rollers, and further refined by polishing the surfaces. The resulting glass is without the flaws of window glass, virtually eliminating distortion. Plate glass is also thicker and therefore stronger than window glass. For these reasons, plate glass is used for large areas, such as picture windows.
- Float glass is superior to plate glass in strength and freedom from distortion. Manufactured by floating molten glass on molten tin, it is extremely expensive and rarely used in homes except in high-quality mirrors.

Ordinary glass breaks easily, but **tempered glass** is more shock-resistant. Tempered glass is strengthened by reheating followed by rapid cooling. When it does break, it disintegrates into practically harmless blunt-edged pieces. For this reason, tempered glass is commonly used in sliding glass doors. It is also an acceptable material for low windows. The International Residential Code (IRC) requires that glass in windows lower than 18 inches be safer than window glass. **Safety glass** is also acceptable.

Safety glass is made of two sheets of glass between which is sandwiched a thin sheet of transparent plastic. It is essential in automobiles but not widely used in homes. Real or artificial leaves, butterflies, and other foreign objects can be embedded in the plastic layer to create decorative effects.

Obscure glass, also called **patterned glass**, has a textured surface. The glass allows light to pass through but creates visual distortion. In homes, obscure glass is most commonly used for bathroom windows and shower doors.

Glass Block

Other glass materials are used because they, too, are translucent or transparent and provide good light transmission. Glass block is 3 to 4 inches thick and can be purchased in 6-, 8-, or 12-inch squares. End blocks, corner blocks, and curved blocks are available for finishing. Although they are translucent, glass blocks distort images enough to provide some privacy. Glass block is often used for showers, bathroom windows, and even for walls, especially in commercial settings. Because of their small unit size, even an undulating wall can be constructed. Glass block does not have load-bearing capacities, so any openings in which they are installed must be supported independently. A limited number of square feet of glass block can be used in a continuous installation. Glass block can be used on floors as pavers and to cover recessed light fixtures. See Figure 4.11.

Similar blocks are available in acrylic. Acrylic blocks are lighter in weight but scratch easily—often when using cleaning products.

Glass tiles are impervious to acids, alkalis, and grease. Glass colors run throughout the material and are not subject to fading or wear. Glass tiles come in ½-inch squares and are being used for mosaics. They are also being used for covering sculptures and accessories such as lamp bases.

Gypsum Products

Gypsum[5], in one form or another, has been the interior finish material of choice for several hundred years. Gypsum is a common mineral that when processed becomes a powder known as plaster. When this powder is mixed with water, it remains in a pliable condition for a short time, then hardens to its original rocklike consistency. Plaster is used to provide interior finished wall and ceiling surfaces. It is also used on exterior surfaces as stucco. Stucco is usually a combination of plaster or portland cement with sand added.

An important advantage of gypsum is its fire-resistance. When exposed to heat of 212 degrees Fahrenheit, gypsum releases some of its moisture as steam. During this process, the gypsum absorbs heat and delays temperature increases. By releasing moisture, the surface becomes calcined (reduced to a powder). The powder then protects the underlying gypsum surfaces from excessive heat.

Glass block is constructed in two halves that are fused together, leaving a hollow space in the center. This dead air space gives glass block excellent insulating and sound-deadening qualities, making it highly suitable for windows or partition walls.

Plaster can be cast into intricate moldings and trim to be used on stationary surfaces; it has no visible joints, allowing it to cover complex surfaces; and it is relatively inexpensive. Plaster does crack, chip, and soil easily, though.

Plaster and Lath

Because it is pliable, plaster must be applied over a stationary base. It can be applied directly to masonry walls, but frame walls and ceilings require **lath** under the plaster. Lath is a backing installed over structural members to hold the plaster firmly in place. Materials used for lath include wood, metal, and gypsum board.

Wood lath consists of narrow horizontal boards

Figure 4.11 Glass block may have bubbles, ribs, waves, bumps, facets, or other patterns within the block itself. The outside surface of the block remains smooth. Glass blocks are available in a number of colors.

nailed to the studs or joists with about ½ inch of space between boards. The plaster works through the openings in the lath and spreads out on the other side. This allows the plaster to adhere to, or become "keyed" to, the lath. However, plaster applied over wood lath tends to crack easily. This tendency arises because the individual strips of wood react separately to settling of the structure or changes in temperature.

Metal lath comes in large sheets. One type is made of sheet metal that has been slit and expanded to form a pattern of many holes. Another type is made of woven wire. The plaster works through the mesh of the lath and becomes keyed in the same way as plaster over wood lath. Metal lath is most commonly used in nonresidential construction. However, it is often used in homes for bath and kitchen walls, for making repairs in existing plaster, for reinforcement around window and door openings, and in corners. Because of its ability to be shaped to various forms, metal lath is also used for curved surfaces. Plaster applied to metal lath does not crack readily and presents a durable, smooth surface.

Gypsum lath is a type of gypsum board with a specially treated paper facing. The plaster bonds chemically to the facing. Some gypsum lath is perforated to improve the bond.

Wallboard

Plaster has generally been replaced in residential construction by **gypsum wallboard**, also known as **plasterboard**, **drywall**, or **Sheetrock**. Gypsum wallboard is made of hardened gypsum plaster covered on both sides with treated paper or foil. Gypsum wallboard is essentially the same as gypsum lath except for the type of paper facing. It comes in sheets 4 feet wide and 8 feet long or more. Installation goes quickly because the large sheets can be nailed directly to the framing members. The joints between wallboard sheets are sealed and smoothed with layers of joint tape and plaster. Cracking is minimized.

Wallboard is not applied directly to masonry walls but is instead attached to furring strips. Furring strips are wood or metal strips applied vertically or horizontally to the masonry. The furring strips create an air space between the masonry and the finish material and make it possible to attach wall finish materials with nails or screws.

Various types of gypsum board are used for interior wall surfaces, exterior sheathing, and other purposes. **Type X gypsum board** has noncombustible fibers added to the gypsum, making it somewhat fire-resistant. Type X gypsum board is required in garage ceilings when there is living space above. **Green board** has a light coating of asphalt on the back of its paper faces, making it moisture-resistant, although over time, moisture will damage the product. Green board requires the closer spacing of fasteners to prevent slippage of the gypsum crystals.

In general, the paper facing of gypsum wallboard is designed for easy application of paint or wallpaper. Green board or tile backer board is a specially treated moisture-resistant wallboard suitable as a base for tile for walls in bathrooms and kitchens. Gypsum wallboard is also available with a foil backing to serve as a vapor barrier. Both plaster and wallboard typically have additional decorative finishes. Walls and ceilings can be left smooth or can be textured. See Figure 4.12.

Prefinished gypsum board eliminates the need for applying additional coverings. A vinyl surface with a preprinted design is laminated to the gypsum core. Prefinished gypsum board is available in solid colors and a wide variety of patterns, such as simulated wood grain, marble, and designs resembling wallpaper.

Metals

Iron and bronze were used so commonly by prehistoric people that two separate eras were named the Iron Age and the Bronze Age. However, metals were

Figure 4.12 On plaster surfaces, texturing can be done by using a brush, trowel, or other tool to create patterns in the wet plaster; by mixing sand or other material with the plaster; or by applying textured paint. (Source: Heather Ireland-Weter)

generally used for tools and utensils, not construction. By the Middle Ages, metal was used decoratively in gates, grilles, door handles and knockers, and lighting fixtures. In today's homes, metals may be used for structural components, housing systems, mechanical equipment, hardware and fasteners, and decoration.

Uses of Metals in Residences

Metal can be used for structural components, and light steel framing is used in some residences. For the most part, however, metal construction is more popular for larger buildings. Metals are used in homes for heating and air-conditioning ducts, electrical wiring,

fasteners, hardware, and decoration. The decorative uses of metal include lighting fixtures; hardware on doors, windows, cabinets, and furniture; plumbing fittings; and some uses on structural components, including ceilings and walls.

Stamped metal ceiling tiles were popular during the Victorian era and are enjoying a contemporary revival. These tiles can be used on walls and ceilings, covering the entire structural component or only a portion of it. They are especially popular as wainscoting for walls. Manufactured tiles come in 2 × 2 feet or 2 × 4 feet pieces in a variety of finishes. Tiles come in tin, steel, copper, chrome, brass, and molded plastic. Steel tiles must be painted or sealed on all sides prior to installation to prevent rust. Tiles are installed in one of two ways: They may be laid into a standard suspended ceiling grid or nailed to existing ceilings, plywood, or furring strips. The edges of the ceiling tile need to be covered, and a variety of matching trim is available for flat or angled surfaces.

Types of Metals Used in Residential Buildings

In residences, the most commonly used metals are iron, steel, aluminum, and copper. Brass is less frequently used.

Iron

Iron is an element found in abundance in the earth. By itself, iron is not sufficiently strong for structural uses, but when combined with other substances, it becomes quite valuable. Iron rusts when exposed to moisture, although rusting can be prevented by the addition of a coating of tin, zinc, brass, or other nonoxidizing material.

Cast iron is iron that has been combined with a small amount of carbon and heated to the melting point. It has impurities and is brittle, coarse, and nonmalleable. Though it breaks easily when hammered, it can be cast into molds of complex shapes. Cast iron is used for woodstoves, fireplace accessories, bathtubs, radiators, and pipes. See Figure 4.13 for an illustration of a famous cast-iron structure.

Cast iron coated with porcelain enamel is used for lavatories, sinks, and bathtubs. If the enamel chips, the metal is exposed and may rust and corrode. Regular enamel is less expensive than acid-resisting enamel, which is usually available only in white. Cast-iron bathtubs hold heat exceptionally well, keeping bathwater hotter longer. Cast iron is heavy and a bathtub may weigh as much as 400 pounds.

Cast or wrought iron is durable and highly desirable where strength is necessary. This strength makes iron pipe especially suitable for underground installations, even where loads are imposed (such as under driveways) and where soil is unstable. Cast iron pipes resist invasion by tree roots. Its strength often makes cast iron the material of choice for plumbing stacks.

Because cast-iron pipes are rough textured, they cannot be threaded. Joints must be packed with a substance such as lead. This joining method results in relatively smooth interior pathways, permitting the flow of materials without hindrance. However, such joints make pipes unsuitable for water under pressure; therefore, the use of cast-iron pipes is limited to drainage systems.

Ductile iron pipes are even stronger and tougher than cast iron. The addition of magnesium and other materials to molten iron increases the tensile strength to twice that of cast iron and multiplies the impact strength to many times that of cast iron.

Wrought iron has fewer impurities and more carbon than cast iron. It is not as brittle and therefore can be bent into a variety of shapes. Since it is rust-resistant, it is ideal for exterior grilles and railings. Inside the home, wrought iron is used for light fixtures, hardware, and fireplace accessories.

Steel

Steel is composed of iron with between 1 and 2 percent carbon and small amounts of other materials. It is the carbon content that determines the strength of the steel. Rust-resistant steel has chromium added;

Figure 4.13 The Eiffel Tower was constructed of cast iron. Because it has been repainted on a seven-year schedule, the iron retains its structural integrity.

when 10 percent or more of the mass is chromium, the result is **stainless steel**.

Steel is lighter in weight than cast or wrought iron and has greater elasticity. The grain in steel is fine, allowing it to accept a high polish. Steel is used for reinforcing concrete and for beams and columns in structures. It is also used in nails and other fasteners, appliances, housing systems, plumbing fixtures, gutters, and hardware.

Steel pipe is inexpensive, strong, and especially resistant to damage from sudden impacts. Uncoated steel would quickly corrode in the presence of air and moisture, so pipes must be treated to make them suitable for use in water and gas systems. For water pipe, steel is **galvanized**—coated with molten zinc to help minimize rust. It can be used for hot and cold water supply, drains, and vents. **Black pipe** is steel pipe that has been protected with varnish for use in gas lines.

Enamel-coated steel is also used for appliances, bathtubs, and showers; it is less expensive and lighter in weight than cast iron. Steel bathtubs, however, are subject to cracking because they are less rigid than cast-iron tubs, and their use is generally limited to low- and moderately priced homes.

Stainless steel is used for kitchen sinks and occasionally for bathroom lavatories, although it is expensive. Its major advantage is ease of cleaning, and for this reason it is used extensively for institutional purposes. Stainless steel with a shiny finish shows water spots, but on satin finishes spots are not as obvious.

Aluminum

After processing, the surface of aluminum is a soft silvery color. Because this natural finish is subject to corrosion, a protective anodized finish is often applied during manufacture. This coating may be clear or an opaque color. Anodizing is permanent and provides the extra protection necessary in saltwater areas to prevent deterioration.

Because it is lightweight and requires little or no maintenance, aluminum is ideal for window frames, gutters, siding, and doors. It can be successfully used on both interior and exterior surfaces and for decorative details. In warm climate areas where heat reflection is important, aluminum may be used as roofing material. See Figure 4.14. Aluminum foil is used for vapor barriers.

Copper

Copper is easy to work with, malleable, and strong. Since it does not rust and can be made into flexible sheets or tubing, copper is ideal for water and gas pipes. Copper is impervious to corrosive materials, with the exception of acids; therefore, copper is unsuitable for water pipes in areas where water is very soft or acidic. Copper reacts with minerals in water to form a protective coating on the inside of pipes. Although initially expensive, copper pipe is easy to work

with. It comes as flexible or rigid tubing. Flexible tubing can be bent as necessary, making possible long segments of pipe without elbows or other fittings. Because joints are soldered instead of threaded, leaks are less likely in copper than in other types of pipe. Copper is a long-lasting material used for both hot and cold water supply pipes.

Copper wire is also used for electrical systems because the metal conducts electricity efficiently. In addition, it is sometimes used for roofing, although because it is expensive, it is typically used on small areas, such as over bay windows or on cupolas. Copper may be coated with a clear finish to help it retain its reddish brown appearance or allowed to weather to a soft greenish patina.

Brass

Brass is an alloy of copper and zinc. It takes a high polish and, although it tarnishes easily, does not rust. Screws, doorknobs, faucets, andirons, and decorative pieces for the home can be made of brass. The longest-lasting faucets are made with brass internal parts.

Figure 4.14 The metal roof on this house in the southern part of the United States reflects some light and heat away from the structure while providing excellent drainage. Lighter-colored metal roofs reflect even more light and heat.

Plastics

The first plastic, discovered in 1868, was used for billiard balls, dental plates, and shirt collars. Today, plastics have become important materials in homes. Plastics may be rigid or flexible, and some soften when heated. Because plastics are almost indestructible, they are durable and long-lasting. Some plastics have a petrochemical base and therefore require the use of oil for production.

Plastics are used for plumbing pipes, toilet seats, wiring insulation, and in appliance coverings and parts. Plastic foam is used for insulation that is either foamed into place or formed into lightweight boards. Mar-resistant plastic laminates are used to cover furniture and countertops. Plastic tiles are used for sink backsplashes and tub enclosures. Entire houses have even been constructed of plastics. Plastics scratch easily and are difficult to repair.

Vinyl

Vinyl is a type of plastic used for channels in prehung windows and as siding, trim, shutters, gutters, and fences. See Figure 4.15. Vinyl may also be used as a decorative sheet laminated to a backing of another material, such as wood, to form inexpensive paneling used to finish walls and ceilings.

Vinyl is also used for certain flooring materials. Sheet vinyl and vinyl tiles are often used in contemporary homes. Vinyl may be solid with the color running through the thickness of the material, it may have a very thin layer of real wood veneer sealed between transparent vinyl and a backing, or a thin layer of patterned vinyl may be bonded to a backing. Any type of vinyl flooring may have a backing of vinyl foam, making it quiet and resilient. The additional layer of foam

---

✤ **Although aluminum is also popular for some of these purposes, vinyl transfers heat more slowly, resulting in greater energy-efficiency.**

also makes it possible to texture the surface. Texturing helps to hide dirt and stains but also creates indentations that hold the dirt. Vinyl products often have an inherent gloss, requiring little if any waxing or polishing. Vinyl is resistant to stains.

Sheet flooring comes in rolls 6 feet wide or more. Resilient tile is available in various sizes, most commonly 9- or 12-inch squares. Most of these materials are easy to care for, requiring mopping and occasional waxing. Decorative choices are almost limitless. Patterns and colors are printed on or impregnated through the flooring materials.

Acrylic

Acrylic is a plastic that has the appearance of glass. It is lightweight and resistant to weathering, corrosion, and discoloration but scratches easily. Acrylic is seventeen times more break-resistant than glass. When it does break, its light weight causes the relatively large, dull-edged pieces to disperse harmlessly. It can be transparent, translucent, or opaque and comes in colors ranging from clear to solar control tints. Acrylic is also available with textured surfaces and can be safely used in shower and tub enclosures, storm doors, and sliding patio doors.

Rigid Plastics

Rigid plastic is available both as tiles or as panels. Plastics make excellent finishes for kitchens and bathrooms because they can be easily cleaned. Formed plastic is commonly used to enclose showers and bathtubs because it is moisture-proof. When plastic panels are used on an extensive surface area, the channels required to join the panels are exposed and may detract from the wall finish. Panels may be plain in a variety of colors or may have a textured pattern to enhance their appeal.

Although fiberglass is not itself a plastic, translucent fiberglass panels are usually made of plastic reinforced with fiberglass and corrugated for strength.

Figure 4.15 Vinyl siding is durable, never needs painting, and can be easily installed.

The corrugations in plastic panels can be rounded, squared off, ribbed, or V-shaped, providing a variety of decorative effects. Flat panels, designed to be used vertically, are also available. Fiberglass panels are break-resistant and lightweight, making them suitable for use in skylights, as room dividers, and to cover patios and carports. Because fiberglass panels are impervious to rot and vermin, they can be installed directly in contact with the earth to make fences. Fiberglass is often used to form moldings and decorative trim pieces as well.

Fiberglass and acrylic are cast into lightweight shower stalls and tub/shower units. Some models include the tub, shower walls, a seat, soap dish, and shampoo ledge molded into a single unit. Because it is in one piece, the unit is leak-proof and easy to clean. Abrasive cleaners can mar the surface of fiberglass. Acrylic units are more resistant to surface abrasion, but are also heavier and more expensive.

Rigid plastic panels may be used in suspended ceilings or installed on a ceiling surface. Translucent plastic panels may be designed to fit under light fixtures to diffuse the light or may be highly decorative. Some of these panels are designed for use on walls or ceilings and provide interesting textures. When lights are used over translucent and transparent materials in the ceiling, a luminous ceiling results.

PVC (polyvinyl chloride) and **CPVC (chlorinated polyvinyl chloride)** are plastic materials used to make lightweight water pipe that will not corrode or rust, is inexpensive, does not conduct electricity, is easy to work with, maintains water purity, and is durable. Some sizes can be purchased in flexible form to go around obstructions or be pulled through older pipes of a larger diameter to revitalize older systems.

Because it is rated only for cold water, PVC is usually used for drains. CPVC is rated for both hot and cold water, and most plastic water supply pipes make use of this material. The IRC allows the use of any pipe material that meets standards and does not specify individual acceptable materials. Local building codes, however, may permit the use of PVC and CPVC in outdoor sprinkler systems or for drains but not for water supply pipes. Other local codes do not permit the use of plastic pipe for plumbing systems.

The major limitations of plastic pipe are its low strength and lack of heat-resistance. It is suitable for general supply pipe and much of the home's drainage system but its use in underground installations is limited.

Rubber

Neoprene is a synthetic rubber developed in 1931. It is weather-resistant and is not damaged by aging. Since neoprene does not conduct electricity, it is widely used around electrical wiring for safety. It is also used for seals in faucets, toilets, and other plumbing.

Rubber floor tile is more resilient and therefore quieter and more comfortable to walk on than most other flooring materials. Rubber tile resists many stains but may be damaged by grease and oil. It is easily marred by heel marks.

Asphalt

Asphalt is found in large deposits in nature and is also a by-product of gasoline and oil production. Asphalt is a sticky substance with waterproofing characteristics. It was used by ancient Babylonians to waterproof baths.

Today, builders waterproof homes by applying asphalt to the outside of foundation walls. Asphalt is also used for roads, driveways, roofs, and linoleum. Asphalt-saturated paper (**building paper** or **building felt**) has many uses in building construction. **Linoleum** is a flooring material with an asphalt-saturated paper base.

A good-quality carpet pad increases the life of the carpet and makes it more luxurious-feeling when walking on it. Even an inexpensive carpet benefits from a good pad.

Linoleum was the first sheet flooring type, developed more than 100 years ago. Also available as tiles, it is made of a mixture of materials bound to burlap or asphalt-saturated felt. Linoleum is inexpensive and easy to clean. However, it has several disadvantages when compared with newer flooring materials. Because linoleum is not as resilient as other sheet flooring, indentations made by heavy objects remain permanently. In addition, linoleum is not very durable. It has only fair stain-resistance and is damaged by alkalis such as those found in common household products. Colors applied to the surface wear away in high-traffic areas and are faded by the sun. Inlaid linoleum, however, has patterns and colors impregnated through the sheet so that the colors do not wear away as rapidly. Linoleum mildews when subjected to moisture over a period of time, making it unsuitable for floors located below grade level.

Carpet

Carpeting is the quietest flooring material. Resiliency and durability depend on the fiber type, the thickness of the pile, and the padding beneath the carpet. Carpet hides much of the dirt tracked on it, although that, too, depends on color and pile height. Although ordinary soil can easily be cleaned from carpet, some stains may prove impossible to remove.

Wall-to-wall carpeting is cut to fit the room and attached to the floor at all edges. It can be installed over wood, concrete, and other floors. Rugs can be used over wall-to-wall carpeting and other flooring materials. Carpet may have an attached cushion or may be laid over a separate pad.

Carpet comes in rolls or as individual tiles. Installation of rolled carpeting requires stretching and attaching the carpet to tacking strips and is best done by a professional. Carpet tiles are more easily installed and, if not glued, can be reused in another location.

Part Two

The
Structure
of
Homes

Structural
Components
of
the
Home

Chapter 5

In modern Europe, the dominant building form makes use of masonry—brick, stone, or concrete—as has been the case for centuries. When wood is used, heavy timbers predominate. It was in America in the 1830s that light wood framing was developed—first balloon framing and, later, platform framing. Wood is readily available and is easily worked, making it ideal for building construction. Although wood continues to dominate the construction of residences in America, recent innovations have resulted in an increased interest in light steel framing. Regardless of the material used in frame construction, the process remains almost the same.

Structural Loads

Ultimately, the weight of all structural components and the forces applied during the occupation of a building must be transferred to the ground. While the weight of structural components can be calculated with relative accuracy, the forces applied due to natural phenomena are more difficult to predict.

Types of Loads

The structure of every building must be sufficiently strong to support several types of loads, including **dead loads**, **live loads**, and **dynamic loads**. Dead loads consist of the weight of building materials and fixed equipment. This includes structural materials, plumbing fixtures, mechanical system components, and cabinetry. Live loads consist of the weight or force caused by other factors, including furniture, people, and climatic phenomena. Dynamic loads are sudden short-term live loads—usually caused by wind gusts or earthquakes. All of this force must be distributed to the earth, which furnishes the ultimate support for the building. Local building codes consider snow, wind velocity, and earthquake probabilities and provide tables for calculating these loads according to expected events within given areas.

Snow Loads

Snow loads vary from expected loads in a given area, depending on a specific site, microclimate, and building configuration, especially roof geometry. Roof framing members are sized to support expected loads. In areas where there is little snow, it is possible to use smaller framing members than in areas where snowfall is heavier. In years when weather is extreme and these structures are subjected to the weight of excess snow, residents may actually shovel snow from their roofs to preclude their collapse. Steeply pitched roofs shed snow more readily than shallow-pitched roofs; therefore, snow loads on flat and low-pitched roofs are greater, requiring heavier structural members.

Wind Loads

When wind strikes a vertical surface, turbulence is created, and the resulting load can be significant. Most residences in the United States are constructed to withstand wind speeds up to 110 miles per hour. In known hurricane or tornado areas, local building codes may require that walls withstand winds as high as 160 miles per hour for short periods. To resist the lateral pressure of wind loads, the IRC recommends the following:

- Vertical framing members are placed with their greatest thickness perpendicular to the wall surface.
- A minimum of 4 feet of wall is required for every 25 linear feet of surface.
- The placement of anchoring devices is adjusted to counteract the uplifting characteristics of wind.

Seismic Loads

The intersections of floors, walls, and roofs and where openings break up walls are weak points in any structure. In areas of seismic activity, it is critical to tie these components together so the building moves as a unit. Steel straps or ties may be installed at junctions to improve the structural integrity of the building, and anchoring devices may be more closely spaced. Traditional structures around the Pacific Rim, where earthquakes are common, are often built of lightweight materials. In some Asian areas, rice paper is encased in light wood frames to form the walls. While the use of these materials does not help maintain structural integrity during an earthquake, it does help to reduce losses of life and property.

Load-Bearing and Non-Load-Bearing Components

There are two types of walls in frame construction: load-bearing and non-load-bearing. (This is not the same as bearing wall construction.) Any component that bears a load other than its own is considered load-bearing. Weight is transmitted both vertically and horizontally: Walls carry weight downward, while floors and ceilings transmit weight horizontally to vertical structures. Load-bearing walls transfer weight to other bearing walls or to a **beam** or post and ultimately to the ground. Exterior walls are almost always load-bearing because they support the roof. Interior partitions on which floors or ceilings rest are also load-bearing. Non-load-bearing walls—called **curtain walls**—support only their own weight. These walls serve strictly as partitions, providing privacy and dividing large spaces.

Structural Components

Buildings are literally constructed from the ground up. In fact, construction begins below the ground with a support system that transfers the weight of the structure to a stable base. The structure continues upward using either bearing wall construction or frame

Figure 5.1 Houses built of lightweight materials do not require foundations and footings because the soil will support their weight.

Because curtain walls support no weight other than their own, the IRC permits their construction on 24-inch centers with 3-inch lumber rather than 4-inch lumber. In a typical house, about 5 percent of the interior space is consumed by walls. Three-inch walls would free a quarter of that 5 percent for living area.

construction. Residential design generally incorporates frame or skeleton construction. See Box 5.1 for International Residential Code requirements.

Footings

Buildings employ **footings** and **foundations** to distribute dead and live loads fairly evenly to the earth. (See Figure 5.1 for an exception.) A footing is an enlarged base, usually of poured concrete, which supports structural components and minimizes the movement of the structure by distributing the weight of the building over a larger area than would be possible without them.[1] Footings are located beneath exterior walls, interior load-bearing walls, vertical support members such as posts or columns, and heavy structural components such as masonry fireplaces and chimneys. Footings may not be necessary if a structure is built on solid rock.

Footings must be located on undisturbed soil and even then, some soils will not support the weight of a structure. For large buildings and in some geographic areas, soil tests are a prerequisite for obtaining a building permit to determine if there is adequate support. Footings should not be placed on earth that has been previously excavated and filled because filled earth will settle when weight is added.[2] This settling can cause cracks in structures or even more severe structural damage. While most structures normally experience some settling, the proper construction of footings can minimize the problem.

Because the expansion and contraction of the soil as it freezes and thaws will cause walls to move, settle, or crack, footings in colder climates are located

Box 5.1 International Residential Code Requirements for Structural Components

FOOTINGS FOR LIGHT-FRAME CONSTRUCTION

- Recommendations depend on the load-bearing capacity of the soil, and those listed here are for 1500 pounds per square foot. For better soils, the footing width may be less. Standard practice dictates 16-inch footing widths for an 8-inch foundation wall, which exceeds the minimums listed.

FOOTING WIDTHS

Number of Stories	Conventional light-frame construction	4-inch brick veneer over conventional construction or 8-inch hollow concrete block
1-story	12"	12"
2-story	15"	21"
3-story	23"	32"

- Exterior footings must be a minimum of 12 inches below the undisturbed soil surface.
- Footings must extend below the frost line, be erected on solid rock, or meet other specific standards. The IRC specifies that local code boards will stipulate this depth.

FOUNDATION WALLS

- The recommended thickness of foundation walls depends on the height of the wall, the height of the backfill above the floor (unbalanced backfill height) on the interior, the total wall height supported, including gables, and on soil conditions. Again, the following assume the minimum soil conditions and a maximum wall height of 20 feet.

  With minimum soil conditions and an 8-foot foundation height with 7 feet of unbalanced backfill height, the foundation wall must be a minimum of 8 inches thick. When the unbalanced fill height is increased to 8 feet, the foundation thickness increases to 10 inches. For a 9-foot foundation wall height with up to 7 feet of unbalanced fill, an 8-inch wall can be used. When the height of the unbalanced fill is increased beyond 7 feet, the minimum foundation wall thickness is 10 inches. Standard practice uses a minimum 8-inch-thick foundation wall.
- Foundation walls must extend above grade level a minimum of 6 inches unless a masonry veneer is planned. In that case, the foundation wall must extend above grade level by 4 inches.
- A perimeter drain made of gravel or crushed rock must extend at least 12 inches horizontally beyond the outside of the footing. The drain extends vertically from the bottom of the footing to a point not less than 6 inches above the top of the footing. The drainage area should be covered with a membrane that filters soil.
- When a perforated pipe or tile drain is used, the bottom of the pipe or tile must rest on a minimum of 2 inches of gravel and be covered with a minimum of 6 inches of gravel.

FOUNDATION ANCHORAGE

- The wall sole (in slab-on-grade construction) or sill at the top of a foundation wall must be attached to the foundation or slab by anchor bolts located a maximum of 6 feet o.c. In structures over two stories in height, anchor bolts are required every 4 feet.

Box 5.1 (continued)

MOISTURE-PROOFING

- Where usable space is located below grade, suitable damp-proofing is required. Damp-proofing can be accomplished using a coat of portland cement, a double layer of building felt, or plastic sheeting, each with a coating of asphalt. Moisture-proofing must be accomplished from the top of the footing to finished grade level.

FLOOR FRAMING

- Openings in floors require header and trimmer joists. If either dimension exceeds 4 feet, the header and trimmer joists must be doubled.
- The minimum thickness of subfloor material when laid perpendicular to joists is $^{11}/_{16}$ inches when joists are on 24-inch centers; $^5/_8$ inches when joists are on 16-inch centers.
- Slab-on-grade floors must be a minimum of 3½ inches thick.
- Concrete slab floors require vapor-retardant materials beneath them.
- Bridging is required every 8 feet of span when the depth-to-thickness ratio of the joist exceeds 6:1.
- Joists around openings in floors, ceilings, and roofs must be doubled when the dimension exceeds 4 feet.

WALL FRAMING

- Maximum stud spacing is affected by expected wind speed and snow loads. Expected seismic activity also affects stud spacing. When designing structures in active seismic zones, check local building codes. The following chart uses 100 miles per hour or less for a wind factor and a snow load of 25 pounds per square foot or less. See the International Residential Code for 8-inch and 12-inch spacing requirements.

MAXIMUM ALLOWABLE STUD LENGTH

Height	Supporting roof only		Supporting one floor and a roof		Supporting two floors and a roof	
	16" o.c.	24" o.c.	16" o.c.	24" o.c.	16" o.c.	24" o.c.
10'	2 × 4	2 × 4	2 × 4	2 × 6	2 × 6	2 × 6
12'	2 × 4	2 × 6	2 × 6	2 × 6	2 × 6	2 × 6
14'	2 × 6	2 × 6	2 × 6	2 × 6	2 × 6	2 × 6
16'	2 × 6	2 × 6	2 × 6	NA	NA	NA
18'	2 × 6	NA	2 × 6	NA	NA	NA

Walls over 18 feet high cannot be constructed with 2 × 4 or 2 × 6 lumber unless on center spacing is decreased.

- Fire-stopping is required for every 10 feet of height.
- Interior non-load-bearing walls require only a single top plate.
- Either wood structural panels or bracing is required at wall corners.
- Maximum header width varies with the size of the header, the span, the building width, the expected snow load, and whether there are stories above that must be supported. In general, openings less than 5 feet in width require single trimmers; openings 5 feet or greater in width require double trimmers on single-story homes. When there are additional stories, the number of trimmers required increases.

(continued)

- Single-family residential structures must not exceed three stories above grade.
- Studs in exterior and load-bearing walls must be placed so their width is perpendicular to the wall.
- Studs in non-load-bearing walls may be spaced a maximum of 28 inches o.c. and have a single top plate.
- A minimum of three studs is required at corners of exterior walls.
- Doubled top plates are required on all load-bearing walls and exterior walls.

ATTIC AND ROOF ACCESS

- When the ceiling or roof is constructed of flammable materials, there must be access to the attic through an opening with a minimum size of 22 × 30 inches in an accessible location. Above the access, there must be some space with a minimum 30-inch head height. This access is required only for attic areas that have a height of 30 inches or greater and exceed 30 square feet in area.

ROOFS

- The maximum span of roof trusses or rafters is 40 feet between points of support.

Source: International Code Council, *International Residential Code for One- and Two-Family Dwellings: 2003* (Country Club Hills, IL: International Code Council, 2003).

beneath the **frost line**—the depth to which soil freezes in winter. The IRC requires that footings be located at least 12 inches below the frost line to ensure stability during extreme winters, and local codes dictate the specific depth.

Footing size is based on calculated loads, the load-bearing capacity of the soil, whether the concrete is reinforced, the thickness of foundation walls, and the specific characteristics of the building. In small buildings such as residences, the standard practice is to use 8-inch-thick foundation walls with an 8-inch-deep and 16-inch-wide footing. See Box 5.1 for specific IRC requirements, and see Figure 5.2 for an illustration of a footing.

When a poured concrete footing is used, the footing is allowed to dry before pouring the foundation. For this reason, the joint between the footing and the foundation it supports is a weak point in the structure, and soil pressure or seismic activity may push the foundation away from the footing. To insure the stability of the structure, reinforcement bars or **keyways** are used. A keyway is illustrated in Figure 5.3. When steel reinforcement rods—called **rebar**—are used in-

stead, they are placed before the concrete is poured[3] and project above the footing at specified intervals. When the foundation is subsequently poured, the concrete encases the rebar, strengthening the joint between the footing and the foundation.

The joint between the footing and the foundation is also subject to potential water leakage. To divert

Figure 5.2 Diagram of a footing.

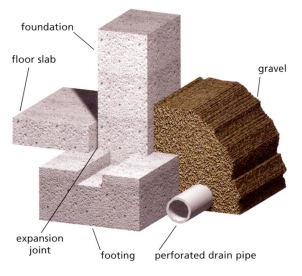

foundation

floor slab

gravel

expansion joint

footing

perforated drain pipe

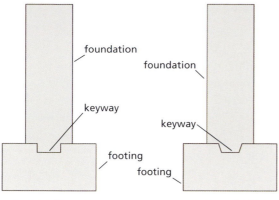

foundation

foundation

keyway

keyway

footing

footing

STRAIGHT KEYWAY   ANGLED KEYWAY

Figure 5.3 A keyway is formed by pressing a dimensioned lumber form along the center line of the wet concrete footing. This form is removed when the footing is dry, leaving a depression. When the sides of the form are beveled, an angled keyway results.

groundwater, a bed of gravel is established beside the exterior of the footing. A perforated pipe[4] or clay tile drain may be laid in the gravel bed with at least 2 inches of gravel beneath and 6 inches over the pipe or tile. The drain slopes to a low point that terminates in a ditch, pit, or storm sewer. Because the drain circumscribes the structure, water is drained from all sides of the building. Besides minimizing leakage at the foundation joint, this practice also helps to maintain stability of the soil around the footing. To further protect the joint from water leakage, the joint should be sealed with a durable caulk, or a coating of asphalt or hot asphalt sprayed onto the foundation exterior from grade level—the level at which the ground intersects the finished building—to the top of the footing.

The footings are constructed on top of the excavated soil, leaving about 8 inches between the soil and the top of the footings. An aggregate such as gravel is used to bring the surface level with the top of the footings. To prevent moisture from getting into the subsequent concrete slab, a waterproof membrane is laid over the aggregate. A layer of rigid board insulation may be used beneath the slab as well to reduce heat loss. The concrete slab is poured over the prepared floor and is reinforced with wire mesh or rebar.

Foundations

The foundation is usually a perimeter wall, largely belowground, that forms the base for the structure. It provides support for both dead and live loads, transferring weight to the footings on which it rests, and it resists the lateral forces of ground movement due to expansion and contraction of the soil. Rebar placed in foundation walls increases the tensile strength of concrete, minimizing cracking.[5] The foundation should also resist moisture and gases such as radon that are found in the soil.

Foundation walls extend to several inches above grade level. Six inches is the minimum distance between grade level and the top of the foundation, although unless there is at least 8 inches of clearance between the top of the foundation and grade level, lumber that has been treated to resist rotting due to moisture must be used in contact with the concrete. When a masonry facade is incorporated, this distance can be reduced to 4 inches (IRC). The gap between grade level and wood framing members helps to protect the structure from termites and ground moisture.

The thickness of the foundation walls depends on the amount of weight to be carried and the length of the wall. In general, long spans require thicker walls and/or more rebar for support. See Box 5.1 for specific size relationships. Foundation walls are centered over footings, which then extend beyond both sides of the foundation. If a masonry facade is to be incorporated, the foundation wall must be sufficiently wide to support both the framed wall and the masonry veneer—generally 12 inches. The additional thickness necessary to support a masonry facade terminates at a lower point than the rest of the foundation wall, forming a **brick ledge**.

Because of the weight of a masonry facade, it is difficult to add to existing structures.

Foundation Materials

Although a variety of materials can be used for foundation walls, those most typically utilized include poured concrete, concrete block, brick, and stone. Brick and stone are found in older homes but are rarely used in contemporary construction because of their expense. Brick, stone, and concrete block foundations are subject to leakage, due to the joints necessary for multiple-unit construction.

Concrete block construction does not require the use of forms or heavy equipment, the blocks can be handled easily by one person, and the work can be spread over several days because interruptions do not affect the quality of the finished foundation. For these reasons, it is especially popular with people who build their own homes. To maximize water-resistance, the IRC requires block walls to be sealed with two coats of mortar on the exterior—a process known as **parging**—with a waterproofing membrane such as asphalt applied over the mortar. Both vertical and horizontal steel reinforcement strengthen concrete block walls, and local codes may require that hollow spaces in the blocks be filled with concrete.

Poured concrete is generally considered the most suitable material for foundation walls. It tends to crack less easily than multiple-unit construction—especially when reinforced with steel—resulting in a more waterproof structure. Frames for any openings, including utility connections, must be placed in the forms prior to pouring the concrete. Typically, all the walls are poured at the same time, maximizing water-resistance. When additional foundations must be poured for extra living space, garages, or porches, both foundations must be tied together. Holes are drilled in existing concrete and short steel dowels are

In multiple-unit construction, cracks usually form over time, often resulting in leaks. Reestablishing and maintaining the moisture-resistant characteristics of the foundation may require pointing—adding mortar to cracks—or stuccoing over the inside of the walls.

placed in the holes so they project into the area of the new foundation. When the concrete is poured, it encases the dowels and provides a connection between the existing and new foundation walls.

Traditional poured concrete foundations are relatively expensive because they require the use of forms into which the concrete is poured. The forms must be set and later removed, resulting in additional labor costs. Expanded polystyrene forms—known as insulating concrete forms (ICFs)—are light in weight and provide significant insulative value. The use of these forms results in significant labor savings because they are less time-consuming to erect than traditional forms and they are left permanently in place. See Figure 5.4.

Foundation Structures

Three structural support systems are used in conjunction with foundations: basement, **crawl space**, and **slab-on-grade**. The major difference is the height or presence of a space beneath the floor.

Basement. Basement construction is the most expensive of the alternatives and is more common in cold-climate areas than in warmer ones. See Table 5.1. Because footings rest on soil 12 inches below the frost line, in cold climates where frost lines are deep, the extra excavation and concrete costs required to make the foundation walls taller can provide relatively inexpensive living space. When the frost line is shallow, the extra costs make basement construction significantly more expensive.

Foundation walls form the basement walls, creating a space 6 feet high or more. A basement provides extra space for storage, utilities, and living areas. Basement temperatures remain more constant—cooler in summer and warmer in winter—than above-grade spaces. During high winds and tornadoes, basements provide a haven of safety if there is no danger of flooding.

Figure 5.4 (OPPOSITE) The hollow foam blocks are erected in patterns similar to concrete block or brick, forming walls into which rebar can be placed and concrete poured.

Table 5.1 Foundation Type Distribution

Foundation Type	National Percent*	Northeast	Midwest	South	West
Full or partial basement	43.2	84.7	76.5	19.2	18.6
Crawl space	26.5	6.1	14.2	36.3	35.5
Concrete slab	29.4	8.9	8.8	43.7	45.3
Other	0.9	0.4	0.5	0.7	0.6

Source: U.S. Census Bureau, "Housing Units—Characteristics by Tenure and Region: 2003," *Statistical Abstract of the United States: 2004–2005*, Table 947 (Washington, D.C.: Department of Commerce), 609. Total number of units nationally is 82,068,000. Data is limited to single-family units of which 74,813,000 are detached, 7,255,000 are attached. Figures may not add up due to rounding.

   * Of the single-family units in the United States, the largest percentage have basements. Numbers for the various types of foundations, however, differ depending on the region in which a structure is located. In colder areas of the Northeast and Midwest, there are more basements, in the South and West, more slabs.

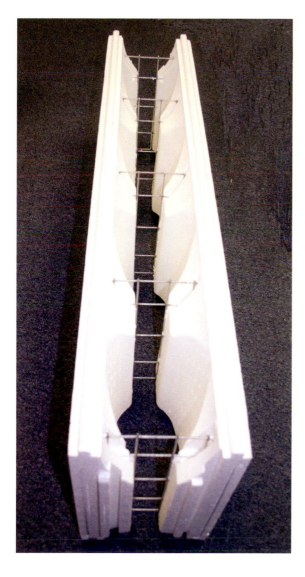

Basements of the past were often damp and smelled of mildew. Contemporary construction methods have minimized these problems and made basements livable. The IRC requires the following to prevent moisture in basements:

• Use of a vapor barrier beneath the basement floor
• Placement of a waterproofing layer such as building felt and asphalt over the outside of the foundation walls from footings to grade level
• A fall in grade level of at least 6 inches within the first 10 feet from the structure
• Gutters and downspouts that carry water from the roof away from the house
• Proper ventilation of the basement area
• Venting of moisture-producing equipment such as clothes dryers

Usually, 8-foot high forms are used for the foundation walls but when the floor slab is subsequently poured, the actual clearance is reduced by 4 inches. Heating ducts and plumbing pipes may extend below the floor above, further shortening the space in the basement. Higher foundation walls will help alleviate the problem and allow additional clearance for living space. Higher foundation walls, however, may make it necessary to increase the thickness of the wall. See Box 5.1 for specifics.

Crawl Space. The major difference between basements and crawl spaces is height. Crawl spaces are a minimum of 12 inches deep and rise to as much as 4 feet above grade but do not have sufficient headroom for living areas. Support for interior load-bearing walls is provided by piers or posts that support beams or by an additional foundation wall. Crawl spaces usually lack a floor and must be properly ventilated to prevent deterioration of wood structural members due to the presence of moisture.

The major advantage of crawl spaces over basements is economy. The reduced amount of materials and labor required for the shorter foundation walls lessens costs. In areas where flooding or high water tables pose a potential risk, crawl spaces provide some protection for the house itself by raising it off the ground. Crawl spaces also provide accessible space for locating pipes, ducts, and some equipment, although when equipment requiring servicing is located in the crawl space, the IRC requires a minimum height of 2 feet in the immediate area. Access is usually provided from the living areas above. In cold climates, crawl spaces must be insulated to prevent frozen pipes, the loss of heat through ducts, and cold floors.

Slab-on-Grade. Slab-on-grade construction requires no extensive excavation—often depending on trenches for footings and foundations, which minimizes both material and labor costs. The slab is constructed in the same manner as a basement floor slab—on a layer of gravel on top of which is a waterproof membrane. The finish flooring of the house is usually laid directly on top of the concrete slab and no floor framing is required.

The exact method of construction depends on the climate. In warm climates, a **thickened-edge slab** (also called a **floating slab**) can be used. The thickened edge serves as both foundation and footing. See Figure 5.5. In areas of the country where the soil freezes, an independent slab and foundation wall must be used with footings constructed in the normal way below the frost line.

The major disadvantage of slab-on-grade construction is the lack of a below-grade area in which to install utilities such as furnaces and water heaters, making it necessary to sacrifice living area for those components. Pipes and ducts may be placed in the gravel beneath the slab, making access difficult if repairs are needed. Often, wiring, pipes, and ducts are installed overhead instead to provide access, although

Figure 5.5 These drawings illustrate two of several alternatives for slab-on-grade construction.

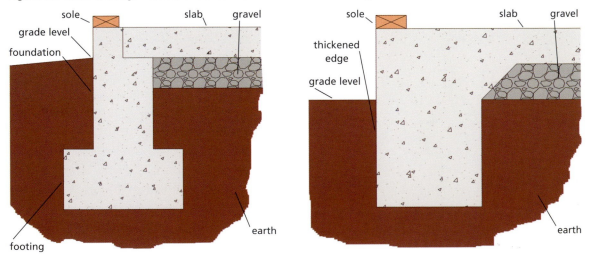

this placement is more expensive due to the longer runs. A standard floor using joist construction can be placed directly on top of the slab or can be attached to the walls and suspended above the slab. Either method provides space for wires, pipes, and ducts beneath the floor without the necessity of locating them beneath the slab. Unless the floor is suspended at least 12 inches above the slab, however, and an opening for access is provided, there is little advantage. The added cost of the floor and exterior finishing materials make this an expensive alternative.

The Termite Shield

To protect wood members from damage by termites, the soil near the foundation can be chemically treated, wood treated for or naturally resistant to termites can be used near the ground, and a **termite shield** can be employed. A termite shield consists of a strip of galvanized iron, copper, or aluminum that is placed around the top of the foundation. The IRC requires some type of termite protection only in areas where there is an established termite hazard.

The Frame

After the footings and foundation are completed, wood or lightweight metal members are used to construct the framework of the floors, walls, ceilings, and roof. It is necessary to securely attach the frame to the foundation to prevent uplift during high winds, resist soil pressure on the foundation wall, and to insure that the frame does not become displaced as a result of ground movement.

Attaching the Frame to the Foundation

The first wood framing member attached to the foundation is the **sill** or **mudsill**. The sill is a board—usually a 2 × 6 or 2 × 8—laid on its side around the perimeter of the building on top of the foundation and interior load-bearing walls.

Some builders eliminate termite shields and place

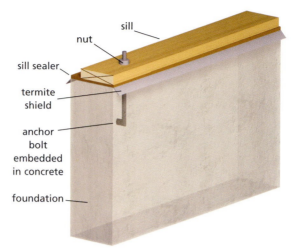

Figure 5.6 Anchor bolt with termite shield.

the sill on the foundation before the concrete dries. Because lumber in direct contact with concrete is subject to moisture in the concrete, the sill is constructed of treated lumber or lumber that is naturally resistant to decay, or it is separated from the concrete by a barrier such as plastic. The resulting joint is relatively weak. An alternative method is to use masonry nails to attach the sill to the foundation after the concrete has set—allowing the use of a termite shield.

Anchor bolts provide the extra strength necessary for stability during high winds and seismic activity and the IRC specifies them for attaching the sill to the foundation. See Figure 5.6. The IRC requires anchor bolts every 4 to 6 feet, at corners, and on each side of door openings.

Sill Sealer

The process of curing results in uneven concrete surfaces that subsequently allow air, moisture, and insects to enter living spaces. Whether or not the termite shield is used, when the sill is placed after the concrete is dried, a **sill sealer** or **sill gasket**—a thin strip of foam or fiberglass—can be applied below the sill.

The sill sealer compresses between building components, sealing openings and reducing heat loss.

Framing Methods

Although there are other framing methods, the two most commonly used for residences are **balloon framing** and **platform framing**. For this reason, they are often collectively referred to as conventional construction. Both make use of the sill but construction of the remainder of the floor differs, as does the construction of walls. The IRC limits frame construction to three stories because of the danger of fire.

Balloon Framing. The use of balloon or **eastern framing** makes it possible to close in a structure quickly—ideal for barn and house raisings common in the nineteenth century and still prevalent within certain cultural groups. Walls that extend from the sill to the roof are raised, the roof constructed, and the external covering applied. Floors are completed later.

Wood expands and contracts little along its length, making continuous vertical framing members dimensionally stable. For this reason balloon framing:

* Is often used for two-story structures with masonry facades.
* Is best for interior load-bearing partitions in homes with exterior solid masonry walls.
* Is preferred for gable end walls and walls supporting cathedral ceilings, allowing them to be constructed as a single unit rather than as two separate ones and providing better wind-resistance than separate platform-framed walls.

The use of continuous vertical framing members, however, poses a significant problem. Each pair of framing members and the interior and exterior coverings form hollow, chimneylike cavities that make it easy for fire to engulf the entire structure. In fact, it was this problem that led to the development of platform framing. The IRC requires **fire-stops**—dimensioned lumber filling the space across the openings—for every 10 feet of vertical wall. See Figure 5.7.

Platform Framing. As the name implies, in platform or **western framing** the floor for each level of the house is a separate boxlike unit. The first-floor platform is constructed on top of the sill before wall construction begins. A **sole** plate is laid on top of the platform to serve as the base for the wall framing. Walls for each story are separately constructed. Floor platforms for upper stories are constructed with the floor resting on the wall framing beneath. This provides a safe, level base from which to work and simplifies wall framing. The framework for wall sections can be assembled on the platform and tilted into place or prefabricated in a factory. It is this feature that makes platform framing the most common method for contemporary construction. A disadvantage of platform framing is dimensional instability.

Figure 5.7 Fire-stops in balloon framing.

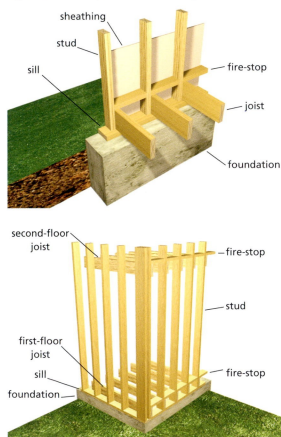

Lumber expands and contracts most readily across the grain (widthwise) causing floor height to change, which can then cause cracks in masonry facades of multiple-story dwellings. See Figure 5.8.

Floor Construction

Floors provide a smooth, level surface on which to walk and place furniture, offer protection from the dampness and cold temperatures of the soil, and prevent the intrusion of animals and insects into living areas. In slab-on-grade construction, the concrete slab itself usually serves as the floor or subfloor. When frame construction is used for floors, they are more complicated structures.

Beams

Floor **joists** are horizontal framing members that transfer the weight of walls above, as well as the floor and loads placed on it, to beams or bearing walls and foundations. Even when lumber of the best species and grade are used and units are closely spaced, wood floor framing members will only span about 24 feet—an insufficient length to span an entire structure. When framing members will not span the desired distance, it is necessary to provide support somewhere within the span—frequently in the middle. The ends of individual framing members may rest on load-bearing walls or, if it is not desirable to have the space divided by a wall, on a beam.[6]

The beams themselves are supported by the foundation walls at one or both ends. Because beams, too, span limited distances, they must be supported by wood posts, steel columns, masonry piers, or bearing walls, each of which rests on a footing. Isolated supports are placed at intermediate points along the span, the distance between them dictated by the size and material of the beam.

Beams may be made of steel, heavy timbers, dimensioned lumber nailed together, a framework of plywood and 2 × 4s to form hollow beams, or laminated wood. Steel beams generally span longer dis-

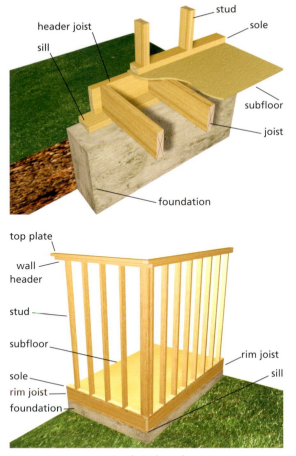

Figure 5.8 An example of platform framing.

tances than wood beams of the same dimensions and are also more dimensionally stable than wood because steel does not absorb moisture. However, steel weakens at relatively low temperatures—about 500 degrees Fahrenheit—and buckles at 1000 degrees Fahrenheit so a fire beneath them can cause loss of support within a short time period. Covering steel beams with 1 inch of cement helps to protect them from heat for a longer period of time. Solid wood beams require a longer time to weaken in the event of fire.

Laminated beams consist of boards glued together. Gluing forms a stronger bond than does nailing, making laminated beams stronger and capable of spanning longer distances than beams made of lumber nailed together. Laminated beams are dimensionally stable and do not twist or crack. They may also be formed to be aesthetically pleasing and then used in exposed places on the interior of structures.

The top of the beams is usually level with the bottom of the floor. This type of construction results in lowering the ceiling in the space below—often a foot or more—so the placement of beams is critical when planning for any living spaces beneath them. Alternatively, joists may be attached to beams using joist

Figure 5.9 (TOP) On center spacing is measured from the center of one framing member to the center of the next one and is designated as o.c.

Figure 5.10 (BOTTOM) A sample floor structure.

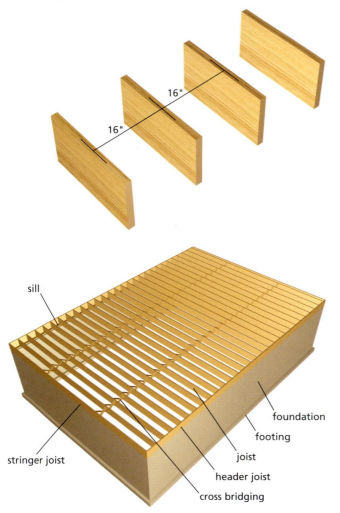

16"

16"

sill

stringer joist

foundation

footing

joist

header joist

cross bridging

hangers or, in the case of steel I-beams, the joists may rest on beam flanges. When this method is used, beams do not project downward.

Floor Construction Using Joists

In balloon framing, joists are attached to the sill and to **studs**—vertical wall framing members. In platform framing, the joists are attached to the sill. Joists are regularly spaced, usually 16 or 24 inches **on center (o.c.)**. On center spacing is used for all framing members. See Figure 5.9.

Joists are installed to run the shortest distance possible to provide the greatest support. Double joists or beams are required beneath load-bearing partitions that run parallel to the joists. Floors that give way or bounce when walked on may have joists that are spaced too far apart or that are of insufficient width.

Joists are placed on edge and may be of a variety of materials. Dimensioned lumber is the most common material used for joists, but steel joists can span longer distances and support greater loads. Wood I-beams[7] are engineered framing members that can be used as joists. They are constructed of a framework of small dimensioned lumber—called **chords**—with a solid **web** of OSB (oriented-strand board), waferboard, or plywood between them. Holes can easily be cut in the I-joist webs for wiring, plumbing pipes, and HVAC ducts, although some have precut knockouts.

In platform framing, floor joists are aligned with the outer edge of the foundation wall.[8] The joists that fall at the two outside edges—called **stringer joists**—are doubled to support the outside walls. The ends of all the joists are fastened to perpendicular **joist headers**. Together, the joist headers and stringer joists are called **rim joists**. Where joists lap over interior walls or beams, it is necessary to install solid blocking between them to maintain their plumb position. See Figure 5.10.

The IRC requires that floor joists be braced by the installation of **bridging** every 8 feet of clear span and nailed in rows across the entire length or width of the structure when the width-to-thickness ratio of the joist material exceeds 6:1. Bridging stiffens the floor, preventing the deflection of joists, and helps to distribute the weight so loads are shared by several joists. Local codes may permit joists to span longer distances when bridging is incorporated. Although required by the IRC, the necessity of bridging is controversial.

Cross bridging, solid bridging, or strap bridging may be used. Cross bridging is formed using strips of 1 × 3, 1 × 4, or 2 × 2 lumber or of metal units designed for the purpose. The strips are nailed diagonally between floor joists in both directions, forming an "X." An advantage of cross bridging is the openings through which pipes, ducts, and electrical wires can be run. Solid bridging consists of dimensioned lumber that spans the space between joists. Strap bridging is accomplished by nailing long boards beneath joists. See Figure 5.11.

Floor Trusses

Floor trusses may replace joists and are especially desirable when a long uninterrupted span is desired beneath them. Trusses can span long distances—up to 40 feet—without supporting beams, posts, or load-bearing walls. Like the wooden I-beam, a truss is a framework of chords, in this case, held together by fasteners called **gussets**—flat plates of wood or metal. The web is usually open because the parallel top and bottom chords are connected by diagonal bracing made of wood or tubular steel, forming triangular sections. See Figure 5.12.

When solid joists are used, pipes and ducts that run perpendicular to floor framing members must be placed beneath joists, effectively lowering the height

of the ceiling below. When trusses are used, plumbing pipes, wiring, and much of the ductwork can be installed within the open web, so the ceiling height may not be affected.

Truss spacing depends on the length of clear span and truss size. Floor trusses are often deeper than joists, with 16-, 20-, and 24-inch depths the most common. This added depth affects floor height and the amount of exterior surface that must be finished. Although bridging may be omitted, its use between trusses strengthens the floor and makes the floor act as a cohesive unit.

Planning Floor Construction for Noise Attenuation

Impact noise transmitted through floors is especially troublesome, as residents of multistory housing know. Footsteps, vacuuming, and furniture being moved cause vibrations. A standard wood floor beneath which drywall is attached has an approximate STC rating of 31—certainly insufficient to reduce sounds to acceptable levels, especially between separate living units such as apartments. Figure 5.13 illustrates various floor construction methods designed to reduce impact noises. See Box 5.2 for a further exploration of noise in a structure.

Openings in the Floor

Openings in the floor for stairwells or chimneys require special framing to ensure that the floor structure

Figure 5.11 Types of bridging.

strap bridging

solid bridging

cross bridging

Figure 5.12 A floor truss.

gusset   top chord

web

bottom chord

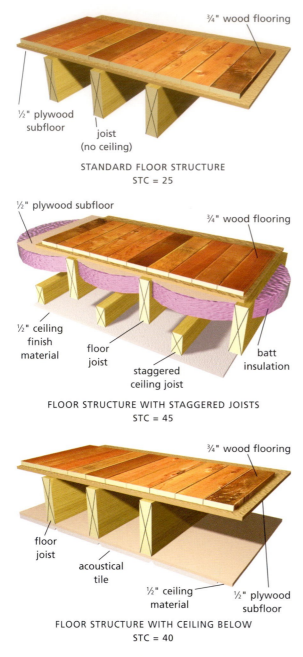

¾" wood flooring

½" plywood subfloor

joist (no ceiling)

STANDARD FLOOR STRUCTURE
STC = 25

½" plywood subfloor

¾" wood flooring

½" ceiling finish material

floor joist

staggered ceiling joist

batt insulation

FLOOR STRUCTURE WITH STAGGERED JOISTS
STC = 45

¾" wood flooring

floor joist

acoustical tile

½" ceiling material

½" plywood subfloor

FLOOR STRUCTURE WITH CEILING BELOW
STC = 40

Figure 5.13 A standard floor structure, a floor structure with staggered joists, and a floor structure with ceiling below each provide a different level of sound transmission.

Before planning for a new floor opening in existing spaces, ensure that the opening can be supported. This may require the addition of bearing structures in the space below.

is not weakened. An extra joist called a **trimmer** is placed at each side of the opening, and **headers** span each end. When the opening is longer than 32 inches, trimmers are doubled; if wider than 48 inches, headers are doubled. The short joists resulting from cutting around the opening are called **tail joists**. See Figure 5.14.

Subfloor and Underlayment

A **subfloor** is placed over the joists or floor trusses to create a solid, level surface and to add rigidity. In platform framing, the subfloor is laid before walls are constructed. In balloon framing, it is laid after the walls are erected.

The thickness of subflooring depends on the joist spacing and the type of material used: When 16-inch centers are used, the IRC requires a minimum thickness of panels such as plywood, waferboard, or OSB of ½ to ¾ inch, depending on species. Subflooring is laid perpendicular to the floor joists to encompass the greatest possible number of joists, resulting in better dimensional stability. Panel material is the most common and can be laid quickly. Boards can be laid either perpendicular to joists or diagonally. Diagonal construction improves the dimensional stability of corners but wastes material. Gluing the subfloor to the joists

Box 5.2 Noise and the Structural Envelope

In order to reduce construction costs, lighter-weight building materials have replaced heavier materials for the exterior of small and medium-sized buildings. As a result, sound is more easily transmitted through the structure. When building in a noisy environment or when a quiet space is highly desirable, the higher cost of heavier materials may be offset by acoustic isolation. Concrete, filled concrete block, well-sealed hard stone, or brick—preferably constructed in two layers that do not connect—will all attenuate sound very well.

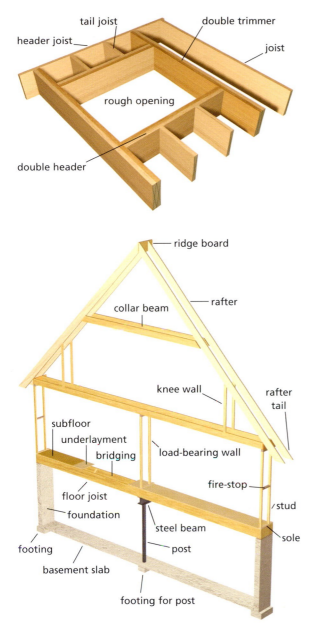

Figure 5.14 (TOP) Framing for a floor opening.
Figure 5.15 (BOTTOM) A building cross-section.

reduces floor vibrations and squeaks, but the greatest advantage of the use of glue is that it bonds the joists and subfloor together so they act as a single unit.

After the walls are erected, an additional layer called an **underlayment** is laid at right angles over the subfloor. Because it is laid between walls, the clear

Tongue and groove materials are preferred for subfloors because they fit together without open cracks that allow air to enter and they increase the stiffness of the floor. A layer of building paper between the subfloor and the underlayment further reduces air infiltration and squeaky floors. ❀

wall height is reduced by the thickness of the subfloor and later by the thickness of the finished flooring. Underlayment serves as a base for finish flooring. The choice of material used for underlayment depends on the type of finish flooring to be used. Smooth-surfaced materials such as particleboard, waferboard, or OSB are used under carpet and vinyl. If plywood is used, any cracks, checks, and knotholes must be filled prior to installing the finish flooring, otherwise normal wear will eventually damage the flooring. Cementitious tile backer board is the preferred underlayment for ceramic tile because moisture will not damage it. Plywood is preferred beneath hardwood flooring.

Wall Framing

In platform construction, the walls are framed after each floor is completed. Wall framing provides vertical support for the ceiling, any floors above, the roof, and interior and exterior wall coverings. See Figure 5.15.

Four-inch walls are used for interior partitions, with the exception of certain walls carrying drains and vents too large for a nominal 4-inch wall thickness. When 4-inch toilet drains and vents are used, the walls in which they are located must be a minimum of 6 inches.

Four-inch walls are allowed to support only one additional story and a roof, and then only when the wall height is limited to 12 feet or less and stud spacing is not less than 16 inches o.c. The IRC recommends

When energy-efficiency is a consideration, 6-inch ❀ walls should be used. However, these wider walls consume living space, making actual room dimensions smaller.

Any walls on stories above that must carry the 4-inch drain or vent must also be 6 inches.

Like floors, walls are constructed with framing members on 16-inch centers, although when 6-inch walls are used, this spacing requirement may differ. See Box 5.1.

6-inch exterior walls and 4-inch interior walls. See Box 5.1 for other specifications. In a recent survey,[9] the National Association of Home Builders (NAHB) found that respondents preferred higher than standard ceilings—9- or 10-foot ceilings were preferred by more than two-thirds for first-story rooms but 61 percent preferred 8-foot ceilings in rooms on the second story or above.

Wall Framing Members

Wall framing members include the sole, studs, header, and **top plate**. In platform framing, these members are laid out on the platform and nailed together before being erected. Once the wall is erected and made plumb, it is attached to the floor. The walls may be constructed of dimensioned lumber nominally 2 inches thick, engineered lumber, or light steel components. Vertical light steel framing members have precut holes for wiring and other components and are slightly wider than traditional wood components. Steel members are designed to be either load-bearing or non-load-bearing and must be used appropriately.

Sole. The sole provides a continuous base for the studs, ensuring they retain their correct position, pro-

When the on center spacing is known, it is a simple matter to determine where there is support for heavy objects. Finding the first vertical framing member is the key. Because boxes housing electrical outlets, switches, and telephone jacks are typically nailed to a stud, the first framing member should be relatively simple to locate. The next member can be located by measuring.

vides a surface to attach the wall to the floor, and distributes weight over a large area. The material used for the sole is laid on its side and is used as the bottom framing member for each wall. In balloon framing, the studs are attached to the sill and the joists, and no sole is used.

Studs. Studs are vertical wall framing members that support the roof, outline the positions of the walls, and support interior and exterior wall coverings. The IRC requires that studs be installed with their narrow face running the same direction as the wall to help resist lateral loads. The stud size and spacing are determined by expected loads. Single-story buildings may have studs placed either on 16- or 24-inch centers, although codes require that all stories be constructed on 16-inch centers in multistory homes. In addition, when three stories are built, the first story must have 6-inch walls; subsequent levels may be constructed of 4-inch material if desired.

Corners are weak points and require special attention to ensure their stability. Additional studs—called **corner posts**—are placed at building corners to strengthen them and to provide a stable base for the attachment of exterior finishing materials. Wood or metal diagonal braces are let into wall studs to provide dimensional stability, and walls are tied together at the top. Interior corners require additional studs to allow for attachment of interior finishing materials or adjacent walls. See Figure 5.16 for various corner plans.

Header and Top Plate. The wall header and top plate form a double layer of side-laid material located at the top of the studs, which are collectively known as the **double header**. The studs are attached to the header so that they stand erect and stay in place. The top plate is added to help support the weight of **rafters**—diagonal roof framing members—and ceiling joists resting on the walls, and to tie walls together at the top. The IRC allows the use of a single header for curtain walls. Steel straps may be required in seismic zones at joints in the top plate.

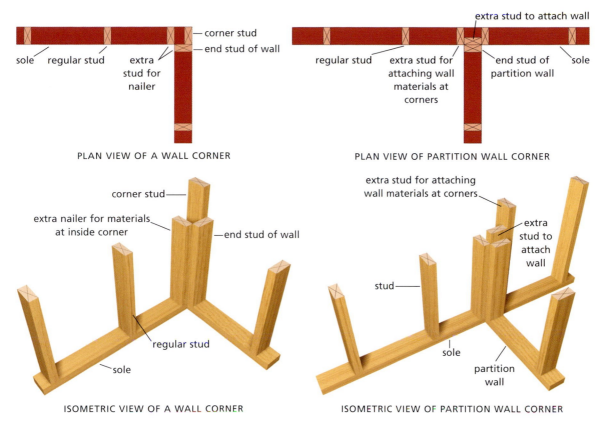

corner stud
end stud of wall
sole   regular stud   extra
stud for
nailer

PLAN VIEW OF A WALL CORNER

extra stud to attach wall
regular stud   extra stud for   end stud of   sole
attaching wall   partition wall
materials at
corners

PLAN VIEW OF PARTITION WALL CORNER

corner stud
extra nailer for materials
at inside corner
end stud of wall
regular stud
sole

ISOMETRIC VIEW OF A WALL CORNER

extra stud for attaching
wall materials at corners
extra
stud to
attach
wall
stud
sole
partition
wall

ISOMETRIC VIEW OF PARTITION WALL CORNER

Figure 5.16 Plan and isometric views of an outside corner and plan and isometric views of a partition corner.

Figure 5.17 Support for cabinets, grab bars, fixtures, and window treatments may be provided by structural lumber "let in" or installed in notches in vertical framing members.

When attaching objects, such as mirrors to a wall, it is necessary to ensure sufficient support. Objects can be attached directly to wall framing members, such as studs or trimmers, but this affects placement. When it is known during construction where heavy objects will most likely be hung, an additional structural support can be provided. See Figure 5.17.

Fire-Stops. Because of the way they are framed, completed walls contain hollow spaces between the studs. Contemporary building practices in most areas result in the filling of these spaces with insulation; however, older homes and buildings in warmer climates may not have insulation. In the event of fire, the hollow spaces act as flues, spreading heat and flame. The IRC requires that fire-stops be used between studs to break up the air spaces every 10 feet of vertical space, decreasing the hazards of fire. Small pieces of dimensioned lumber are nailed horizontally at intervals

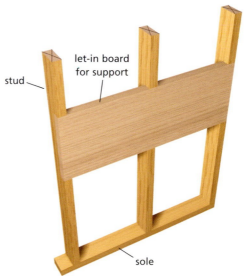

let-in board
for support
stud
sole

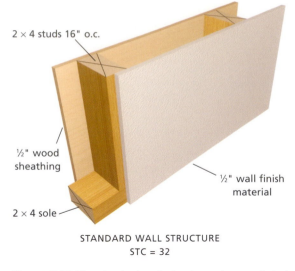

2 × 4 studs 16" o.c.

½" wood
sheathing

½" wall finish
material

2 × 4 sole

STANDARD WALL STRUCTURE
STC = 32

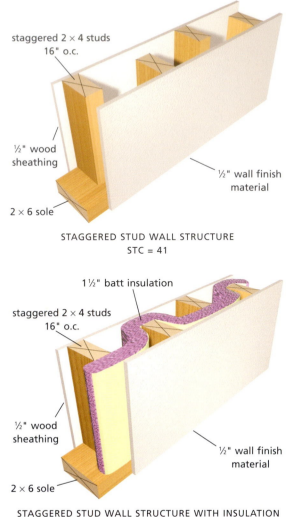

staggered 2 × 4 studs
16" o.c.

½" wood
sheathing

½" wall finish
material

2 × 6 sole

STAGGERED STUD WALL STRUCTURE
STC = 41

1½" batt insulation

staggered 2 × 4 studs
16" o.c.

½" wood
sheathing

½" wall finish
material

2 × 6 sole

STAGGERED STUD WALL STRUCTURE WITH INSULATION
STC = 45

Figure 5.18 The standard wall structure, staggered stud wall structure with insulation, and staggered stud wall structure each have a different sound transmission class.

between the studs for this purpose. When walls exceed 10 feet in height, fire-stops may be required for dimensional stability of the wall regardless of whether the cavity is filled. Fire-stops are always required at each level in balloon framing. Other types of fire-stops are used in multifamily dwellings and commercial construction, including masonry walls at specified intervals.

Wall Structure for Noise Control

The most effective way to control noise transmission through structural components is to interrupt the continuity of the structure, preventing the vibrations from being carried to the other side. This can be accomplished in a number of ways. Figure 5.18 illustrates the sound transmission class of various wall-construction techniques.

• Vertical slots can be cut in the studs of non-load-bearing partitions.

⊞ When double-wall construction is used, the size of the living space is reduced.

• Some manufacturers are now producing split single-wall framing systems connected with resilient clips to reduce sound transmission, although some are not recommended for load-bearing walls and would not then be suitable for most exterior walls.
• Double-wall construction with a separate set of studs and plates for each side prevents sound vibrations from being transmitted from one side of the wall to the other.
• Use of construction materials that have heavy mass and natural sound-deadening qualities

effectively reduces sound transmission but often increases costs significantly.

Vapor Barrier. Due to differences in exterior and interior temperatures, it is necessary to provide a vapor barrier to prevent condensation from building up within wall structures, which could damage wood framing members and cause exterior paint to crack and peel. The vapor barrier is installed on the inside or warm side of the building. Vapor barriers are inherent in faced batt insulation but a separate polyethylene barrier can be installed on the inside of the studs.

Sheathing. Sheathing is applied to the exterior of the frame to enclose the space. Sheathing forms the outside face of the wall, and finish materials are applied to it. The IRC requires wood panel sheathing, but standard practice in many places requires wood panel sheathing only at unbraced corners. In warm areas of the country, sheathing may be optional and finish materials are installed directly over the studs. Commonly used sheathing materials include plywood, waferboard, OSB, exterior-grade fiberboard or gypsum board, and rigid foam panels. As in floors, panels are installed perpendicular to the framing component (in this case, studs). The thickness of the sheathing depends on the type of material used and the spacing of the studs.

The use of wood panels improves the dimensional stability of the structure—especially at the corners. On center spacing is used for all framing members. The IRC specifies that plywood or OSB be used at all corners even if other materials are used on linear surfaces, eliminating the need for diagonal bracing of the walls at corners. In active seismic and hurricane areas, walls are fully sheathed with wood panels. These panels also provide a solid base to which finish materials can be nailed.

Gypsum board, fiberboard, and foam panels are inexpensive, making them suitable for low-cost housing. None provide additional dimensional stability nor backing sufficiently strong to attach exterior finishing materials. Rigid foam or fiberglass panels are often used for sheathing in energy-efficient homes because of their high insulative value. The panels may be faced with foil on both sides to further increase the insulative value and decrease air infiltration. The foil also minimizes moisture flow through the walls. When insulating panels are used, the minimum thickness is 1.5 inches unless they are applied over other sheathing.

To minimize air infiltration through structural components, building paper or a house wrap can be installed over the sheathing. Building paper or building felt is a heavy paper that has been saturated with asphalt or coated with paraffin; it comes in rolls and is installed in overlapping layers. House wraps are polymer membranes and come in wider rolls so that a single layer can cover the walls. On multiple-story buildings, it may be necessary to use additional overlapping layers.

Partial Walls

Partial walls are constructed in the same manner as other walls, although a single top plate is used. These shorter walls may be used as room dividers or guardrails around openings in the floor, and decorative devices such as spindles or lattice may connect them to the ceiling. Most codes require that partial walls have a minimum height of 3 feet. The height of these walls is indicated on floor plans.

Furred Walls

When masonry construction is used, it is often necessary to build non-load-bearing walls against masonry walls to provide space for insulation, a vapor barrier, wiring, and mechanical system components, and to provide a base for the attachment of traditional wall finishing materials. These **furred walls** support no weight but their own and may be 2 inches thick rather than 4 or 6 inches. Obviously, the thinner the furred wall, the more space remains for actual living area. Furred walls are also used around columns, plumbing pipes, and ductwork that intrude into living spaces.

Openings in Walls

Openings for windows and doors must be provided in the wall framing. These openings—called **rough openings**—are slightly larger than the size of the prefabricated windows and doors to be placed in them, ensuring that there is no pressure on the pre-assembled units that would force them out of alignment. Because openings weaken the structural integrity of walls, headers—also called **lintels**—are used to support the ceiling and roof structure above. Headers transfer the load horizontally across the opening to vertical supports, where it is then carried to the ground. The depth of the header depends on the load that must be supported—including additional stories and the roof. See Box 5.1 for specific details.

Headers may consist of edge-laid lumber flush with the inside and the outside of the wall, with shortened **jack studs** used between the opening's header and the double wall header for support. See Figure 5.19. **Box headers** made of plywood and smaller dimensioned lumber can be made in any depth, making it possible to eliminate the need for shortened studs between the opening header and top plates. When the top of the opening is sufficiently close to the top plate, the use of solid headers made of dimensioned lumber can also eliminate these extra studs. See Figure 5.20. Trussed headers can span longer distances and support greater weight than can other header types.

The studs at the sides of window and door openings are doubled to maintain structural strength and stability. The **king stud** runs from the sill (in balloon framing) or sole (in platform framing) to the wall header, and its attachment to the shortened trimmer or jack stud close to the opening ensures that the imposed load will be carried vertically.

The trimmer is cut to support the header. Single, double, or triple trimmers are used to support the

---

⊞ All wall openings must have headers for support. When planning for additional openings in existing load-bearing walls, make certain the load is supported during construction.

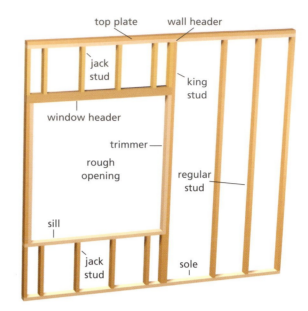

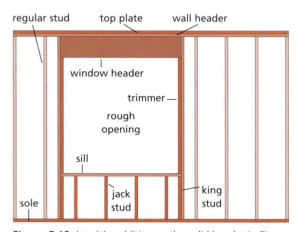

Figure 5.19 (TOP) In addition to the solid header in Figure 5.20, headers can be formed using smaller dimension lumber with jack studs. Jack studs may be used to fill in the space between wide headers and wall headers when walls are higher than 8 feet.

Figure 5.20 (BOTTOM) A window opening.

header, depending on the width of the opening. Double trimmers are most frequently used and suffice for openings less than 5 feet in width. Even when the king stud or trimmer is close to the on center spacing, regular studs should not be omitted. (Wall finishing materials are made in 2-foot modules—4 × 8, 4 × 10, or 4 × 12—and the centered spacing insures a stable base for attachment of the material.) The shortened studs beneath windowsills and above headers are called jack studs. The wall beneath a window is an **apron wall** and the wall above any opening is a **spandrel wall**. Door openings are constructed in the same manner as window openings, except that the opening extends to the floor.

Ceilings

Ceilings are constructed in the same manner as floors and, like floors, may be constructed of joists or trusses, both of which may incorporate bridging. Ceilings are often constructed of smaller framing members than are floors because they support less weight. When living areas are located above the ceiling, it is constructed as a floor, and the finish ceiling material for the room below is attached directly to the bottom of the floor joists. The roof may rest on the walls or on the ceiling, depending on the construction.

When the ceiling must support part of the roof load, the ceiling joist size is affected. The size of ceiling joists also depends on the materials used, the

Figure 5.21 A ceiling nailer board.

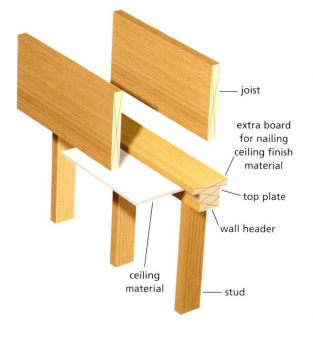

- joist
- extra board for nailing ceiling finish material
- top plate
- wall header
- ceiling material
- stud

spacing between framing members, and the **span**. Ceiling joists are typically installed to conform to rafter spacing in the roof—12, 16, or 24 inches on center. Ceiling joists are supported by load-bearing walls and beams, tying exterior walls together and counteracting some of the outward thrust of the rafters. Ceiling beams may be located below ceiling joists or flush with the bottom of the ceiling joists. Beams are supported by load-bearing walls or isolated posts.

In a structure with a flat roof, the ceiling is nailed to the underside of the joists. When a cathedral or angled ceiling is used, the ceiling finish materials may be attached to roof framing members and ceiling joists omitted. Special trusses are available that retain the angled ceiling but also provide space between the roof and the ceiling. Ceiling backing is used to provide a nailing surface for finish materials when ceiling edges are parallel to joists or trusses. See Figure 5.21.

When the ceiling or roof is constructed of flammable materials, the IRC requires a minimum access opening to the attic area above the ceiling of 22×30 inches. These openings, as well as those for stairways and chimneys, are framed in the same manner as those in floors. The access hatch is located in an inconspicuous but accessible area—frequently in a garage—and has some type of movable covering such as a trapdoor.

Roofs

The roof is one of the more complex parts of a structure. Roofs can be constructed in many different styles, each of which requires a different framing plan to outline its shape. The angle of the roof can vary from very shallow to very steep. Generally, flatter roofs are subjected to greater stresses than higher-pitched roofs and must be constructed of stronger materials. See Box 5.3 for an illustration of roof terminology. Terms specifically relating to roof construction, styles, coverings, and trim, measurement of roof angle, and so on are defined as those topics are discussed.

Box 5.3 Roof Terminology

- The ridge is the horizontal line at the highest point of the roof.
- The eave refers to the lower border of the roof where it meets or overhangs the wall.
- A gable is the vertical triangular face of a building formed by the angle of the roof. ("Gable" is also a term for a particular style of roof that has gables.)
- The **rake** is the inclined edge of the roof at the gable.
- A dormer is formed by a vertical wall projection through a sloping roof, providing a surface for a window for light and ventilation as well as additional floor space in the room beneath the roof. Dormers may be wide enough for only one window or as wide as the house. A dormer has its own roof.
- A **valley** is a place where two roof slopes meet to form a low point in the surface of a roof. For example, a valley is formed where a dormer intersects the main roof or where the footprint of the house changes direction.
- A hip runs from the corners of the building to the ends of the ridge. It is a place (other than a ridge) where two roof slopes meet to form a high point in the surface of a roof. It is also a term for a particular style of roof having four sloping sides.

Roof angle is described as both **pitch** and **slope**. Although the terms are not interchangeable, they are two ways of describing essentially the same thing. Both pitch and slope are ratios between the **rise** and either the span or the **run** of the structure.

- The span is the horizontal distance across the width of the house, measured at the horizontal point where the roof meets the walls.
- The run is the horizontal component of the distance from the edge of the roof to the **ridge**— the highest point on a roof segment. Except when irregularly pitched roofs are used, the run is half the span.
- The rise is the vertical distance from the top of the ceiling joists to the ridge. See Figure 5.22.
- Pitch is the ratio of total rise to span. It is always expressed as a fraction reduced to its lowest form. For example, when the rise is 9 feet and the span is 36 feet, the pitch is ¼.
- Slope is expressed as the number of inches of rise for every 12 inches of run (not span). It is usually written as "X" in 12.[10] The fraction is not reduced, as when expressing pitch. For instance, the roof in the previous example, with a 9-foot rise and 36-foot span, has an 18-foot run. It therefore has 6 inches of rise for every 12 inches of run, or a slope of 6 in 12. Most roofing materials are designed to protect roofs with a slope of 3 in 12 or greater. See Figure 5.23.

Roof Angle

The angle of the roof and its height are important considerations from the standpoint of cost, materials selection, and water-shedding capabilities, although climate is the major determinant. Where snow or rain is frequent, steeper slopes are necessary for efficient runoff. Roofs with a shallow slope require a more waterproof coverage than more steeply sloped roofs and are usually found in drier climates.

Figure 5.22 An illustration of roof slope ratios.

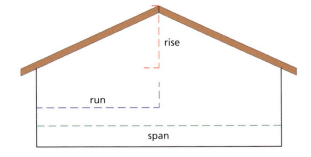

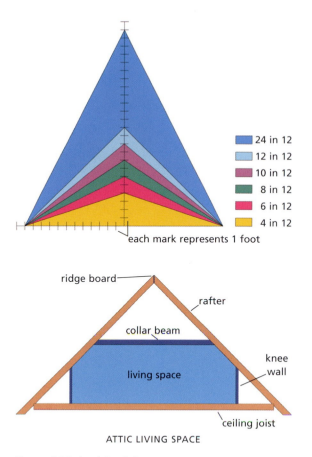

each mark represents 1 foot

▮	24 in 12
▮	12 in 12
▮	10 in 12
▮	8 in 12
▮	6 in 12
▮	4 in 12

ATTIC LIVING SPACE

Figure 5.23 (TOP) Roof slopes.
Figure 5.24 (BOTTOM) The amount of living space available beneath the angle of the roof depends on the steepness and width of the roof.

As the slope of the roof increases, the space beneath the roof becomes larger, making it possible to house living spaces between the top of the walls below and the ridge of the roof. Vertical knee walls are constructed to provide wall space for furnishings and eliminate the triangular-shaped space at the sides that are too short to use or maintain. Access to **eave** areas can be provided by a short opening in the knee wall. See Figure 5.24.

Roof Styles

The style of the roof, its finish material, and the finish of the roof at the eave line are important exterior details. Roof styles vary according to climate, although many styles are associated with specific styles of architecture. See Box 5.4 for roof style illustrations.

Flat. Flat roofs are best used in climates where rainfall is infrequent and where snow does not collect. Water standing on a flat roof would eventually seep through, causing leakage and damage to the interior. To prevent water buildup, most flat roofs are slightly sloped, with a rise of ⅛ to ¼ inch for every foot of run.

The horizontal members of flat roofs function as both ceiling joists and rafters. These structural members must be relatively wide to support the weight of both the ceiling and the roofing materials and greater stresses due to live loads.

Shed. Shed roofs may be constructed at any angle from nearly flat to very steep. Their distinguishing characteristic is a slope in a single direction. Shed roofs may be used for an entire house or only over a **dormer** or addition. In colonial America, shed roofs were used when kitchens were added to the back of the original one- or two-room homes, creating the characteristic saltbox roof. Dormers with shed roofs may extend along the entire length of the house.

Gable. In a gable roof, the two sides of the roof, usually (but not always) having equal slopes, meet at the ridge. In a simple gable roof, the ridge line runs the entire length of the building, but the **gable** is often used as a basic part of more complicated roof shapes. Gable end walls rise to meet the ridge at an angle equal to the angle of the roof. The gable end wall is finished with exterior finishing materials such as siding that are more expensive to purchase and maintain than are roofing materials.

Winged Gable. A variation of the gable roof is the **winged gable**. While the roof is configured in the same manner as a gable roof, the ridge projects farther beyond the house than it does at the eave.

Box 5.4 Roof Styles

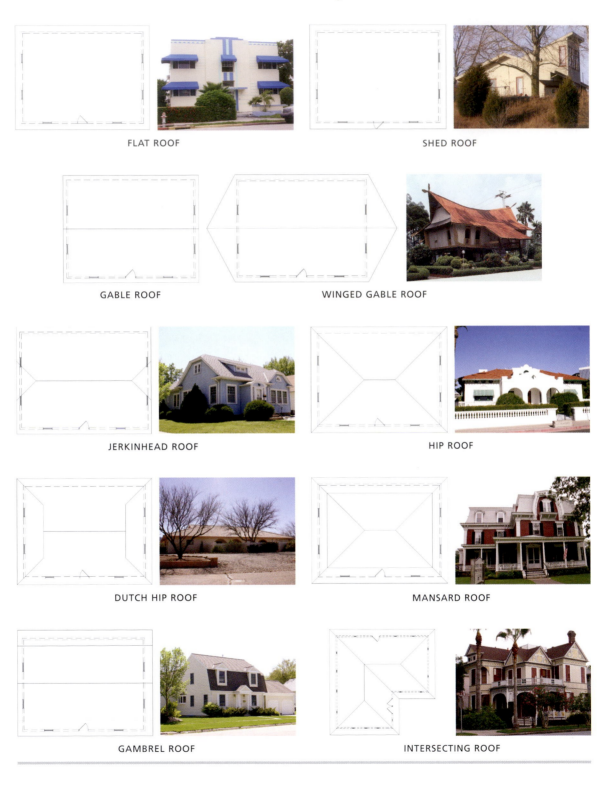

FLAT ROOF

SHED ROOF

GABLE ROOF

WINGED GABLE ROOF

JERKINHEAD ROOF

HIP ROOF

DUTCH HIP ROOF

MANSARD ROOF

GAMBREL ROOF

INTERSECTING ROOF

Jerkinhead. The **jerkinhead** or **clipped gable** roof is essentially a gable roof that has a short **hip** on one or more ends. Its original purpose was to reduce air turbulence at the gable end.

Hip. A **hip roof** slopes on all sides, creating a protective overhang. Since roofing materials are used to the eave line on all four sides, a hip roof eliminates the gable-end areas of exterior wall finish material, resulting in lower costs and less maintenance.

Dutch Hip. The **Dutch hip roof** is a combination of a gable and a hip roof. At the gable end walls, there is an additional roof called a **pent** that intersects the bottom part of the gable in a hip.

Mansard. The **mansard roof** is similar to the hip roof in that the roof slopes on all four sides of the building, but there are two slopes on each side rather than a single one. The part of the roof near the top is almost flat, while the section closest to the ground is very steep. Because of this, a second usable story can be tucked under the roof without adding height to the building.

Gambrel. The **gambrel roof** is similar to the gable roof and has gable end walls but, like the mansard, has two slopes. By minimizing the area of the roof that has a low pitch, the gambrel design also minimizes the area that can collect snow. It is therefore popular in cold climates. Like the mansard, the gambrel roof provides sufficient headroom for an additional story beneath the roof.

Intersecting. An **intersecting roof** is a roof of any type or combination of types that has a change in direction or level, requiring that at least two roof slopes intersect at one or more points. Each section of the roof has its own ridge. Valleys and hips are formed where roofs intersect.

Other Styles. Other traditional roof styles include round roofs, onion domes, bell roofs, domes, and vaults, among others. Round roofs of varying slopes are easier to construct than rectangular roofs. Onion domes are popular in Russia and the bell roof in Islamic architecture. Buildings with classical architectural styles often have domes or vaults, and modern structures may consist entirely of domes. Recent technological developments in methods and materials have led to the use of unusual roof styles. The butterfly roof, saddle roof, and hyperbolic paraboloid roof are examples.

Roof Construction

Although roof styles vary considerably, most roofs in Western cultures are constructed by one of two methods. The joist and rafter method utilizes individual framing members nailed into place on the site and lends itself to complicated roof styles. The truss method uses prefabricated triangular frameworks that are attached to the building as units—usually requiring heavy equipment such as a crane. Roof trusses speed up building construction but are limited to simple rooflines.

Joist and Rafter Construction. The most common roof construction type is the joist and rafter method, where roof components are cut, fit, and assembled on the site. Joist and rafter construction is versatile, making changes in roof direction simple. Joist and rafter construction is the method of choice when living spaces are located between the eave and ridge because it leaves the largest open spaces.

Rafters slope upward from exterior walls and individual rafter names designate where rafter ends are attached. The rafter dimensions depend on the load and the strength of the wood, and clear span is limited. Rafters may extend beyond the exterior wall at the eaves, forming a **rafter tail**. See Figure 5.25.

In most roof styles, some or all of the rafters meet at the **ridge board**. The ridge board provides little structural support, serving primarily as a surface to which rafters are attached, maintaining their spacing. In fact, the ridge board may be omitted, allowing

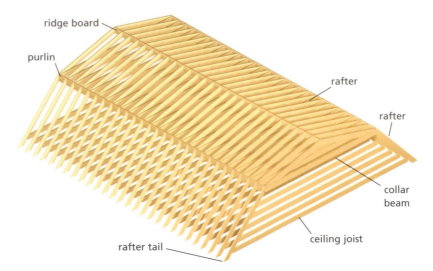

ridge board

purlin

rafter

rafter

collar
beam

ceiling joist

rafter tail

Figure 5.25 Roof framing.

rafters to push against one another to provide structural stability at the apex. After several years, however, the weight of roof finish materials may cause the ridge line to sag between rafter pairs when there is no ridge board.

When the roof slope is high or the rafters are long, **collar beams** (also **collar ties**) are used to help resist the outward thrust of the diagonal members. Collar beams are attached to pairs of rafters on opposite sides of a ridge, tying them together. It is not necessary that collar beams be used on every pair of rafters. When the attic space is finished, collar beams may also function as ceiling joints.

To further support rafters and maintain their spacing, **purlins** may be used. Purlins are horizontal members placed along the inside edges of rafters to tie them together—usually where there is a change in roof angle. Purlins may be braced for additional strength and they may be used with or without collar beams.

Roof trusses. The advantages of prefabricated roof trusses include savings of time, labor, and materials. Like floor trusses, roof trusses are prefabricated in a factory and are made of lumber of smaller dimensions than would otherwise be required for the span. The use of smaller wood members is possible because trusses are supported across their spans by various types of bracing. Trusses tie diagonal roof framing members together at the bottom with a horizontal chord and replace both joists and rafters. Trusses, then, inherently counteract the outward thrust of the diagonal members. The framework, however, precludes the use of the space beneath the roof for living areas.

Trusses are readily used on rectangular structures or on rectangular portions of buildings, such as both wings of an L-shaped house, but not every roof can be constructed using only trusses. Roofs that change direction or use combinations of styles require that some on-site fabrication be done where trusses cannot be used. While filler trusses can be purchased, the portions of a structure not easily adaptable for trusses are generally stick-built on site after trusses are installed. Trusses are usually placed on 24-inch centers.

Roof trusses can often span the entire width of a house without support other than that provided by the exterior walls, so interior partitions can be placed anywhere and need not be load-bearing. Generally, the greater the number of braces within the truss, the longer the truss will span without intermediate support. Of course, more material means more expense. See Figure 5.26.

Sheathing and Underlayment. Trusses or joists and rafters provide the framework for the roof, but the framework must be enclosed for the roof to function effectively. Sheathing and underlayment are the first steps in that enclosure and serve as a base for finish materials.

Figure 5.26 While the major function of roof trusses is structural, they can be exposed and become part of the decor on the interior of the structure.

Roof sheathing closes in the structure, provides support and backing for finishing materials, and increases the strength of the frame. Sheathing is not necessary with all types of roofs but does provide an extra measure of protection against moisture and air infiltration. Some roof finishing materials—clay or aluminum tiles and, sometimes, shakes—require **skip sheathing**. Rather than cover the entire roof surface with panels, individual boards are nailed horizontally across rafters with spaces between them to allow the hooks on the back of finish materials to be attached to them.

Roof underlayment, installed between sheathing and some finishing materials on roofs, consists of a layer of **roofing felt**—a heavier asphalt-saturated paper than that used on walls. Underlayment keeps the sheathing dry prior to the installation of finishing materials and also serves as a barrier between the two layers, preventing possible damage due to chemical incompatibility of sheathing and roof finishing materials. In addition, underlayment functions as added protection in the event that strong winds force water beneath the finish material or other seepage occurs.

Roof Openings. Openings in the roof for skylights and chimneys are constructed in the same manner as openings in floors. Skylights may require **wells**—finished vertical openings from the roof through the attic space and the ceiling.

Post and Beam Framing

Post and beam or timber framing began when large timbers were more easily acquired than boards and when nails had to be made by hand. Mortise and tenon joints are used in post and beam construction, requiring a high degree of skill. Until the development of balloon framing, this was the construction method of choice when wood was used. Today, much of the appeal of post and beam framing is in the exposed framing members on the interior, which add distinctive architectural detailing. Posts can take the place of interior load-bearing partitions, creating spacious interiors. Sloped ceilings are typical and wide roof overhangs are possible. Stud walls may be placed between the posts if conventional finishes are desired but serve no structural purpose, making large expanses of glass possible.

Post and beam construction incorporates posts, beams, and planks as framing members. These framing members are of greater size than those used in conventional construction and are spaced farther apart. The length of framing members, however, is limited due to the availability of large timbers. Even though it requires fewer framing members, post and beam framing is more expensive than contemporary conventional construction. Post and beam construction may utilize a poured foundation as in conventional construction, but often piers are used instead. Piers are vertical structures—usually concrete—that start below the frost line and are located beneath each post.

When a foundation is used, beams spaced 48, 72, or 96 inches apart—called **girts**—form the framework for the floor. Thick planks are laid across the girts to form the floor platform. A timber sill outlines the floor, and posts long enough to extend to the roofline are placed at the same space intervals as the floor girts. At the roofline, a timber top plate is attached to support the roof framing members. Because the posts are widely spaced, flame does not spread as rapidly between members, and because the timbers are thicker, there is a slow loss of strength once members do catch fire.

The roof consists of beams overlaid with planks. The beam at the ridge line may be supported by center posts placed at the same intervals as the posts in the walls, or the timber rafters can be tied together horizontally with collar beams and ceiling girts. The other roof beams may be transverse—running perpendicular to the ridge—or longitudinal—running parallel to the ridge. In either case, the planks are placed at right angles to the beams. Transverse beams may extend beyond the wall, forming large overhangs.

The structure of a post and beam house essentially consists of a number of individual frameworks—called **bents**—arranged in a row. Pairs of posts (one for each side of the structure) and their corresponding girt and rafters can be assembled on the ground and lifted into place by a crane.

Because interior partitions running perpendicular to the ridge need sloped tops, they are often built in two sections. The bottom section is constructed as a conventional stud wall. A triangular section is attached to the top once the wall is in place. Load-bearing interior walls are not necessary except under the ridge beam.

Full post and beam construction is most suitable for warmer climates but it can be used in combination with conventional framing methods. Post and beam framing is also called **plank and beam framing**, especially when it is used only for the roof or floor of a building. By using conventional framing for walls and plank and beam construction for the roof, the interior can feature insulated finished walls while retaining sloped ceilings with exposed beams.

There are certain limitations in post and beam construction that can be easily rectified. The floors, made of planks, will not hold up under heavy loads. Therefore, additional framing members are needed beneath bathtubs, refrigerators, pianos, and other heavy items. In addition, when post and beam construction is used for walls, there is no place to conceal ducts, wires, and pipes for the house systems and no spaces for insulation. Curtain stud walls can be attached to the outsides of the posts, leaving the posts exposed on the interior for aesthetic effects, or alternately constructed between the posts. Both methods provide space for insulation, wiring, pipes, and ductwork. Insulation can be incorporated if stressed skin panels are used for the walls but wiring, plumbing, and ductwork would have to be concealed in some other manner.

Pilotis

The twentieth-century architect Le Corbusier designed several structures using **pilotis**. Pilotis are posts that raise the structure off the ground—sometimes making the structure almost appear to float in the air. Piers or isolated footings are used beneath the pilotis to ensure their stability, and the structure is built on top of the poles. The space between the ground and the structure can be used for parking, gardens, or outdoor living. If a ground-floor structure is desired, it can be built anywhere within the open space beneath. Because the building is supported by the pilotis, ground-floor structures require only curtain walls.

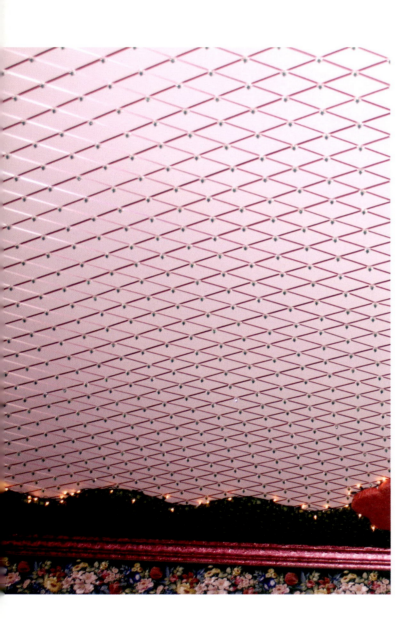

Finishing
the
Structure

Chapter 6

Aside from the basic framework of the house, there remain details of construction that help to enclose space. The finish of exterior surfaces and the number and type of windows and doors are affected by the architectural style of the structure and are often decorative. Gutters and downspouts direct water from roof runoff to appropriate drains or areas. On the interior, structural components such as floors, walls, and ceilings may be given special treatments and moldings to enhance decorative appeal.

Exterior Wall Finish Materials

Because walls are highly visible, the choice of an exterior wall finish is especially important. For the most part, exterior wall finishes are chosen for their appearance and to complement the architectural style of the home. Common finishes include **shingles**, **shakes**, horizontal and vertical siding, brick, stone, and stucco. See Table 6.1 for a percentage breakdown of the common finishes across the country, and Box 6.1 for IRC requirements.

Shingles and Shakes

Wood shingles, cement shingles, and wood shakes can be used to cover walls as well as roofs. Application begins at the bottom of the wall or roof, with succeeding rows overlapped, permitting water to drain freely. While shingles are uniform in size, shakes provide a more rustic appearance because their size differs.

Wood shingles and shakes can be given any of several types of finishes. Left unfinished, they will weather naturally to a soft gray color. Clear varnish prevents weathering while emphasizing the natural beauty of the wood. Penetrating preservatives or

---

Box 6.1 International Residential Code Requirements for Exterior Finishing Materials

EXTERIOR WALL COVERINGS

• The exterior wall covering must be weather-resistant.

• When using cement plaster on the exterior, a minimum of two coats is required over masonry and 3 coats over lath.

• Flashing is required beneath the first masonry course above grade level. The flashing must extend through to the outside of the wall.

• Weep holes must be installed in exterior masonry walls with a maximum spacing of 33 inches o.c. The minimum diameter of weep holes is 3/16 inches.

Source: International Code Council, *International Residential Code for One- and Two-Family Dwellings 2003* (Country Club Hills, IL: International Code Council, 2003).

Table 6.1 Principal Type of Exterior Wall Material of New Single-Family Dwellings in Percent

Location / year	Brick	Wood	Stucco	Vinyl Siding	Aluminum Siding	Other
Total U.S.						
1975	32	36	10	NA[a]	11	11
1980	28	42	13	NA	9	8
1985	22	42	14	NA	10	12
1990	18	39	18	NA	5	20
1995	20	25	16	30	3	6
2000	20	14	17	39	1	7
2004[b]	19	7	22	38	1	14
Northeast						
1975	8	44	S[c]	NA	20	27
1980	9	49	S	NA	26	14
1985	5	50	2	NA	20	22
1990	5	45	S	NA	10	39
1995	6	28	3	59	3	S
2000	4	19	2	73	1	1
2004	2	11	2	81	1	3
Midwest						
1975	16	54	S	NA	22	7
1980	13	62	S	NA	20	5
1985	15	55	S	NA	14	15
1990	16	45	S	NA	10	29
1995	12	23	S	53	7	3
2000	11	18	1	62	4	4
2004	11	8	1	70	1	8
South						
1975	61	20	3	NA	6	10
1980	49	32	6	NA	5	8
1985	38	36	6	NA	8	12
1990	34	33	9	NA	4	20
1995	37	17	7	33	1	11
2000	38	6	8	34	1	12
2004	36	4	9	32	Z[d]	19
West						
1975	8	41	40	NA	2	9
1980	6	46	40	NA	3	6
1985	3	43	46	NA	4	4
1990	2	41	52	NA	2	2
1995	2	39	50	5	2	2
2000	1	23	56	14	1	5
2004	1	11	65	11	Z	12

Source: www.census.gov/const/www/charindex.html#singlecomplete (9/18/05).

[a] NA = Not available

[b] From the information above, trends in exterior materials can easily be seen. Dramatic decreases in the use of brick and wood in most areas of the country since 1975 are coupled with rises in the use of stucco and vinyl siding.

[c] S = Estimate did not meet publication standards

[d] Z = Less than 0.5 percent or less than 500 total units

stains provide color with a rustic appearance. Wood shingles can also be given a coat of paint, as can asbestos cement shingles. All of these coatings must be periodically reapplied.

Siding

Siding is narrower than shingles and comes in longer strips. Horizontal siding is applied in overlapping layers, beginning at the bottom, and gives homes a long, low appearance. When applied vertically, siding makes homes appear taller. Both horizontal and vertical siding are available in wood, plywood, hardboard, aluminum, and vinyl.

Wood Board Siding

Because wood is so adaptable, wood siding comes in a variety of patterns, sizes, and colors. When properly maintained, it will retain its beauty for centuries. Some wood siding patterns are achieved by the method used to apply the siding. Board siding, with straight sides and squared edges, can be overlapped in a horizontal **clapboard** pattern. In the vertical **board-on-board** style, the boards alternate between those with both edges overlapping adjacent boards and those with both edges underlapping. When narrower strips of wood are alternated with boards, the result is the **board-and-batten** style.

Other siding patterns depend on the shape of the siding boards themselves. **Bevel** siding is thicker at the bottom edge than at the top, increasing the depth of the shadow line. A flat surface can be achieved by using shiplap or tongue and groove siding, the edges of which are notched to fit into succeeding rows. Log siding gives a structure a rustic appearance. See Figure 6.1 for different types of siding joints.

Plywood and Hardboard

Plywood and hardboard siding usually come in sheets that are 4 feet wide and up to 12 feet long. The sheets are manufactured to give the appearance of various styles of wood siding. They can be applied

The finish chosen for wood siding often depends on the texture of the siding. Smooth surfaces are generally painted, while rough ones are treated with preservatives or stains. Wood siding can also be treated with varnish. Redwood, cedar, and cypress siding can be allowed to weather naturally.

horizontally or vertically and can be nailed directly to studs without sheathing. Plywood and hardboard siding are also available in narrow strips to give shadow lines similar to other siding materials. Hardboard siding can be purchased prefinished or prepared for finishing. Plywood siding can be finished with the appearance of stucco or rough-sawn wood.

Aluminum and Vinyl

Aluminum and vinyl siding both have permanent finishes that can be cleaned with soapy water, and both are impervious to termites. Aluminum siding has a baked-on enamel finish or a factory-applied vinyl coating, and may be smooth or textured with a wood grain. Since it conducts electricity, aluminum siding needs to be grounded for protection against lightning. Aluminum siding is noisy, especially during rainy

Figure 6.1 Siding is installed so it overlaps to keep water from getting behind it. A variety of joints are used to achieve this.

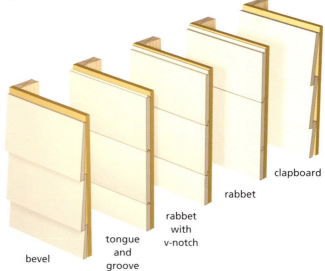

bevel

tongue and groove

rabbet with v-notch

rabbet

clapboard

weather, and hail or other hard substances may cause dents and subsequent corrosion.

The color in vinyl siding is added while the vinyl is in liquid form, making any chips or scratches almost undetectable. Although the vinyl material itself is not damaged by sunlight, some colors may fade over time. Most manufacturers offer a color warranty for a specified period of time. Vinyl siding doesn't dent, and it resists the effects of the sun, salt water, and acids. Vinyl does not retain moisture as wood does, nor does it sweat like metal. However, it may freeze and break in extremely cold weather, especially if improperly applied.

Brick and Stone

Brick or stone veneer can be used as a facade on frame construction. The higher initial cost of masonry veneer is offset by the low-maintenance cost. The veneer is not applied directly to the frame but approximately 1 inch away. See Figure 6.2. The brick or stone is tied to the frame with metal strips, and **flashing** is placed behind the veneer at the bottom of the wall to direct water away from the wood frame. **Weep holes** for the draining of any moisture condensation are provided through the masonry near the bottom.

Stucco

Stucco is a cementlike exterior finish that can be applied over masonry walls or over sheathing in frame construction. If used in frame construction, the stucco is held to the building face by a metal mesh backing called lath. Three coats of stucco are used. The first and second coats usually have some type of fiber or hair mixed with them for a binder. The final coat may be tinted, or color may be applied with paint.

Roof Finish Materials

The roof finish material must be fire-resistant, have good water-shedding capabilities, and be durable

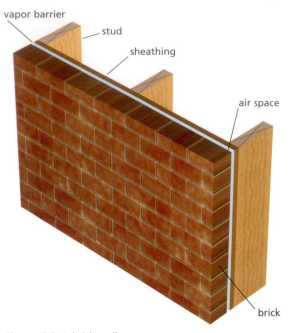

Figure 6.2 A brick wall.

enough to withstand long exposure to heat and cold. For further weather protection, roofing materials should have wind resistance. To obtain an Underwriters' Laboratories (UL) wind-resistant rating, roofing must remain entirely flat without a single member lifting during a two-hour test under high winds. Interlocking shingles or self-sealing thermoplastic strips on the back of some shingles increase wind resistance. The thermoplastic material becomes soft and forms a seal under the heat of the sun. Durability is generally determined by the roofing weight—the heavier the material, the longer it lasts. However, there are some lightweight materials, such as fiberglass and aluminum, that have long life expectancies.

Roof coverings can be divided into two categories: multiple unit and membrane. Multiple-unit coverings come in small pieces that are overlapped during installation. Such materials effectively shed water on sloped roofs, with the amount of overlap increasing as the slope decreases. Shingles are an example of a multiple-unit roofing material. Membrane roofing consists of sheets or layers of material such as metal, asphalt, and tar. Because the materials used are watertight, membrane roofing can be utilized on flat roofs and those with low slopes.

Multiple-unit roofing materials are purchased by the **square**. One square covers 100 square feet of roof with standard overlapping. The amount of weather protection of shingles and shakes is indicated by **coverage**, or the number of layers achieved by overlaps. Where shingles overlap once, there is double coverage. Decreasing the **exposure**, or distance from the bottom of one shingle to the next, provides triple coverage. Multiple-unit roofing materials are used on roofs with a minimum slope of 3 in 12, although individual materials may require greater slopes.

Shingles and Shakes

Shingles and shakes are commonly used multiple-unit roofing materials. Shingles may be made of asphalt-

Roofing materials are heavy: Aluminum roofing weighs between 40 and 60 pounds per square; composition shingles, 240 to 400 pounds; lightweight cement shingles or clay tiles, 500 to 800 pounds; regular-weight cement shingles or clay tiles, 900 to 1200 pounds; and slate, 700 to 800 pounds. For this reason, it is imperative to know which roofing material will be used when constructing a building. Heavier roofing materials require heavier construction. Before reroofing an existing structure with a different material, it is necessary to determine whether the structure can support the new material.

soaked paper or fiberglass, cement, or wood. Shakes are wood shingles with a hand-hewn appearance patterned after those used by American pioneers. Both shingles and shakes are applied beginning at the bottom so that they can be overlapped at the top to shed water. See Figure 6.3.

Figure 6.3 Because shakes emulate hand-hewn originals such as these, they are uneven in width and vary in length. Shakes have a deep shadow line.

Composition Shingles

Composition shingles have a base made of roofing felt or a fiberglass mat coated with asphalt to provide water-resistance. Fiberglass shingles are more fire-resistant than felt-based shingles are. A layer of small stone granules is then embedded in the asphalt. These granules increase fire-resistance, protect the shingle from damage by the sun, and provide color. Composition shingles are available as individual square units or as strips of two or three "tabs," which may be square or hexagonal in shape. Because they are relatively flexible, they should be interlocking, self-sealing, or secured with adhesives to keep them flat during high winds. Moderately priced and relatively durable, composition shingles are the most popular roofing material in the United States today.

Cement Shingles

Cement shingles are made of cement or concrete with embedded cellulose fibers.[1] During manufacture, the cement product is pressed or rolled, making it possible to provide any number of textures and to make the units resemble shingles. Color is added to the wet mix. Although durable, they will shatter if hit suddenly. They are used on roofs with a medium to steep slope and usually on moderately priced housing.

Wood Shingles

Wood shingles are prohibited by some building codes because of the fire hazard they create, although they can be treated to increase fire-resistance. Wood shingles are usually made of the heartwood (strong, dense wood from the center of the tree) of species that resist decay, including cypress, cedar, and redwood. Although durable, wood shingles may split or curl as they become weathered.

Recycled synthetic shingles with the appearance of more expensive slate or wood shakes are relatively new. The materials used for manufacture include recycled rubber and plastic. For the look of slate, a small percentage of slate powder is added to recycled tires to form individual units that weigh 25 to 33 percent as much as real slate. Wood-like shakes are made from recycled PVC and wood fibers. These recycled products are expected to have life expectancies greater than 3 times longer than composition shingles.

Slate

The stone used for roofs is slate. In its natural state, it is formed into thin layers that can be cut into rectangular shapes for shingles. Slate makes a durable roof, lasting 50 years or more, although individual stones may be broken with a blow. The two major drawbacks to the use of slate are its weight, requiring a strong structure for support, and its cost. Slate is very expensive and has been used in the past as a status symbol.

Tile

Baked clay tile, a form of masonry, is an attractive roofing material, providing deep shadow lines. Like slate, tile roofing materials are heavy, fragile but durable, and expensive. Because they are also fireproof, they are popular in areas such as California where brush and forest fires are frequent. Because of their weight, they are wind-resistant and decrease air infiltration.

Round Spanish tiles are still popular, but other styles include French, Greek, Roman, and Mission. Specially shaped tiles are used for corners and ridges. Unglazed tiles are usually an earthy red tone, while green is a popular color for glazed tiles. See Figure 6.4.

Individual tiles have a hook on the back for installation. This requires the use of skip sheathing on the roof rather than traditional sheathing. Skip sheathing is typically 1 × 4s laid perpendicular to the rafters, with approximately 4-inch spaces between individual boards. The hooks on the tiles can be seen beneath the roof structure unless the roof is insulated. Replacing broken tiles is a simple process.

Figure 6.4 Tile roofs have been used for centuries to minimize the danger of fire. In fact, tile roofs were used in medieval Europe after laws forbidding the use of thatch in cities were passed. Natural color variations in the material are characteristic.

Metal Roofing

Several metals and alloys can be used for roofing. Metal roofing is lightweight but durable and has a glossy appearance for aesthetic appeal. Metal roofing is also noisy, must be grounded for lightning protection, and is suitable only for roofs with a 4 in 12 slope or greater. Metal roofing is available as shingles, corrugated sheets, and sheet metal strips, some of which are embossed with decorative designs.

Copper is an expensive form of metal roofing that weathers to a soft green patina. It is rarely used over the entire roof of a residence but is occasionally used for roofs over bow or bay windows, porches, or cupolas. Gold leaf is infrequently used for roofing domes or other specific roof components on some public and religious structures, but its use on domestic structures is nil.

Other metal roofing materials include galvanized steel, aluminum, and steel coated with a tin alloy. Naturally finished aluminum roofs are most common in warm climates where their reflective surfaces resist the heat of the sun. Color can be introduced by adding an enamel coating to the aluminum. Galvanized steel roofs are corrugated for rigidity and must have a rust-protective coating for durability. They are most often used for utility buildings with medium to high slopes. **Terne** roofing consists of rolls of iron or steel coated with a tin alloy to make them rust-resistant. Terne roofing weathers to a gray patina but most types require painting every few years to retain rust-proofing characteristics.

Translucent panels—usually corrugated—of fiberglass or acrylic plastics allow some light transmission while providing protection from the weather. They are used over carports and patios and in utility buildings.

Built-up Roofing

Built-up roofing consists of alternate layers of asphalt and roofing felt with a final covering of gravel for color and heat reflection. It is used for flat roofs or those with low slopes because it is waterproof.

Cornice

The finish given to the roof at and just below the eaves forms the **cornice**. There are several styles of cornices. If there is no extension of the roofline beyond the wall, the cornice is a **close cornice**, and a **shingle molding** is used at the edge to finish the roofline. When there is an overhang, either an **open cornice** or a **box cornice** is used. In either case, a board called a fascia covers the exterior edge of the cornice where the rafters end. See Figure 6.5. Open cornices are not finished on the underneath side. Rafters are exposed and the bottom of the sheathing can be seen. Box cornices have a facing applied to the bottom of the rafters or horizontally from the bottom edge of the fascia to the wall. This bottom enclosure is called a **soffit**. Ventilation for the attic space is provided by vents in the soffit.

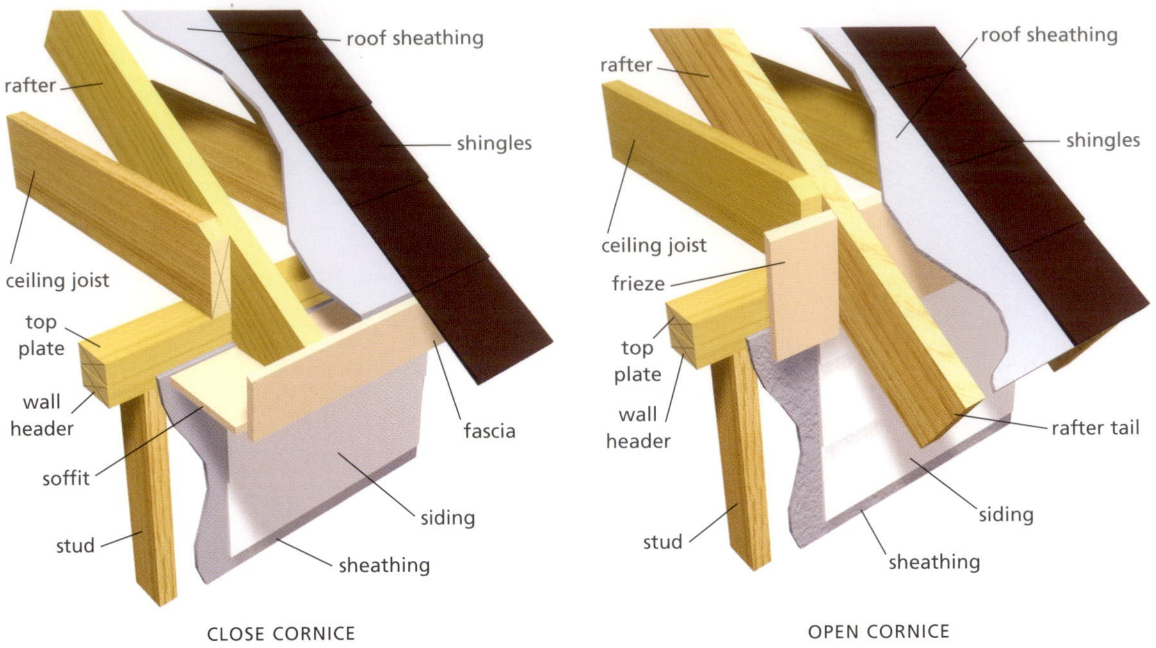

roof sheathing
rafter
shingles
ceiling joist
top plate
wall header
soffit
fascia
siding
stud
sheathing
CLOSE CORNICE
roof sheathing
rafter
shingles
ceiling joist
frieze
top plate
wall header
rafter tail
siding
stud
sheathing
OPEN CORNICE

Figure 6.5 The way the exterior cornice is treated depends on the architectural style.

Water-Carrying Components

Where dissimilar materials meet, where construction details may permit leakage, or where there is interruption of the regular placement of materials, flashing is necessary. Flashing insures that moisture runs off, rather than through, materials. Flashing usually consists of a strip of flexible sheet metal installed prior to the roof finish material. At the bottom of the wall frame behind a masonry veneer, flashing directs water toward the exterior, protecting the wooden frame from moisture. Flashing is also used where two roof slopes meet, as in valleys, and around openings in roofs through which chimneys and vents project. Flashing prevents water seepage beneath finishing materials at roof edges. See Figure 6.6.

Gutters and downspouts provide a system for the control of water distribution from roofs. Although roofs are designed to shed water, the water should not be allowed to run directly off the roof to the ground below, because water standing near the foundation could seep into the basement or crawl space. Soils that expand when wet may cause additional damage by increasing the pressure on foundation walls.

Gutters are channels installed along the eaves to catch runoff from the roof. They are suspended an inch or two below the eaves to prevent damage from the expansion of water as it freezes. Gutters are made of metal, vinyl, or, infrequently, wood. The size is determined by the area drained and the amount of rainfall anticipated. They should be sufficiently sized to carry water away quickly. Gutters should slope slightly downward so that water collected in them flows to downspouts. Gutter covers come in a variety of types and are used to prevent the buildup of leaves and debris that could stop up the gutter and cause it to overflow. If the structure has wide overhangs, there may be no need for a water-distribution system. In this case, care should be taken that water does not drain off over an entrance.

Downspouts are vertical channels running from the gutter to the ground or to a storm drain or well. Elbow joints allow the downspouts to rest inconspicuously next to the walls of the house while still leading water away from the structure. If metal gutters or downspouts are used, it is necessary to ground them to protect the house from lightning. An insulated wire connecting the metal to a pipe in the ground is sufficient. Vinyl and wood gutters and downspouts do not need to be grounded.

Windows

Windows may be simple openings or may be filled with glass or other material to shut out the elements of nature. In ancient Egypt, Greece, Assyria, and Crete, the glare of the Mediterranean sun made it necessary to use mats or other devices for shading what windows were used. In more northern areas, there was a need to allow smoke from indoor fires to escape and to permit as much light as possible to enter the house. Unfortunately, these openings provided no protection from inclement weather or from insects. Early windows were located high in a structure—either in the roof, as in the Indian tepee, or near the roof, as in Egyptian temples. Only small openings in walls were structurally feasible until the development of construction methods that did not require the outer covering of a house to bear a load.

Although glass was known in ancient Egypt, it was the Romans who first used glass in window openings

Figure 6.6 The flashing used at valleys and around the chimney are obvious in this home.

Secondary light sources such as reflection and glare affect interior light, requiring advance planning to achieve a desired uniformity of light across a room under normal environmental conditions.

in the baths of Pompeii. Roman domestic structures, however, did not boast glass but rather translucent sheets of mica, gypsum, or marble as window enclosures. It was not until the twelfth century that glass began to be used in homes. Then only small openings in shutters were glazed, permitting light to enter while window openings were closed. A development of the eleventh and twelfth centuries that had a greater effect was the emphasis given windows by framing them with molding. When glass was expensive, some countries even levied taxes on windows, and glass was removed from abandoned buildings to decrease tax loads.

Window Functions

Windows provide light, ventilation, and a means of egress, and it is these functions that are of concern in building regulations. Windows, however, can also frame a view and serve a decorative function, and

---

When energy efficiency is a primary concern, as little window area as possible should be used unless the home is designed to collect and store solar radiation.

To minimize heat gain through west-facing windows, awnings can be used over the windows, the windows can be shaded by low-growing trees or shrubs or by trellised plants, or fences or berms may be used to keep rays of the low-lying sun from reaching the windows.

In the winter in the Northern Hemisphere, south-facing windows receive sufficient sunlight to provide significant passive solar heat. Making use of this heat source can help reduce energy loads.

their location affects furniture placement. Each of these factors is of concern to designers, who must work within code parameters, meet the needs of clients, and achieve a pleasing living environment. See Box 6.2 for noise control guidelines.

Light

Careful planning is needed to achieve a balanced level of natural light throughout a room. The size, placement, time of day, current environmental factors, and type of window opening affect the amount and quality of available light.

The International Residential Code (IRC) requires glass areas in a room equal to a minimum of 8 percent of the floor area for light, although most rooms exceed this requirement. To ensure an adequate amount of natural light even on cloudy days, glass areas equal to 20 percent of the floor area may be needed. See Box 6.3 for IRC requirements.

The quality of light is just as significant as the quantity. Sunlight pours into east- and west-facing windows at certain times of the day, often producing glare and unwanted heat. North-facing windows receive no direct sunlight and provide light that is fairly uniform throughout the day. In the Northern Hemisphere, south-facing windows receive direct sunlight during winter months but are usually free of direct sunlight during the summer.

The size and configuration of both the windows and the room must also be considered when planning for natural light. Windows near the ceiling and large window areas are effective in distributing light. Small windows light a small area, resulting in sharp contrasts in light intensity; tall, narrow windows allow light to travel farther into the room; and wide windows spread light over a broad area. In general, light from windows penetrates a distance equal to one and a half to two times the height of the top of the window from the floor. Unless it is located on the east or west side, light from a window with a header located 84 inches from the floor reaches approximately 10 feet 6 inches to 12 feet 4 inches into the room.

Box 6.2 Noise Control for Windows and Doors

Windows and doors are the parts of the building envelope most vulnerable to noise transmission. For purposes of acoustic control, glass doors can be considered as windows. The following steps should be taken to ensure adequate noise control through these areas.

- Minimizing the number of doors and windows, locating as few openings as is feasible on walls exposed to high noise levels, and treating even small cracks and gaps for acoustic control can significantly decrease sound transmission through the units. Even a small opening can make a significant difference in sound transmission. "A hole representing less than 0.01 percent of total wall area can reduce the sound blocking ability of the wall from 50 dB to 22 dB or 56 percent reduction in performance."*

- Weather-stripping doors and windows, filling the space between the rough opening and the window or door frame with insulation, minimizing the gap between the bottom of a door and the floor, and sealing the unit into the opening with acoustic sealant can improve the STC rating. When interior doors are treated in this manner, however, it is necessary to ensure adequate air return for the HVAC system.

- Multiple-glazed windows—storm windows or thermal pane windows—with a minimum of a half inch of air space between glass panes provide better sound attenuation than do single-glazed units. Sound transmission through windows is further reduced if the layers of glass are of different thicknesses.

- Nonoperable windows are sealed, making them less vulnerable to noise transmission than operable units.

- To prevent sound reflection from one room to another when casement windows are used, all the windows along a side should face the same direction.

- In places where windows are located for light only, glass blocks can be used—increasing the STC to about 40.

- Exterior doors are usually 1⅜ to 1½ inch thick solid-core doors. The Canadian Wood Council reports that a well-sealed solid-core wood door with gaskets and weather-stripping can reach an STC of 27.

- Insulated steel doors with double seals have an STC of 30 or greater. Thicker doors—2¼ inches or more—provide STC ratings of 49 or greater. Recording studios use sound-rated door assemblies with even higher STC ratings. Special hardware is used on these doors to prevent sound from crossing the barrier through the doorknob.

- Storm doors provide a dead air space between them and the exterior door, adding to the STC of a doorway. Double doorways with a minimum of 6 inches of air space between doors provide even better sound conditioning and, when spaced sufficiently distant from each other, can provide an air-lock entry with the added advantage of energy-efficiency.

- Panel doors vary in thickness, and STC ratings are lower than those for solid-core flush doors.

- Hollow-core doors are often used on the interior of residential structures because they are less expensive than solid-core doors. However, STC ratings range in the low 20s or less even when well fitted. To reduce noise transmission within the home, use solid-core doors in the interior as well as on the exterior.

- When doorways are staggered rather than opposite one another, whether they are in a residence or between residences in apartment buildings, sound transmission is decreased.

* www.atlasblock.com/ocba_sound_transmission_class_rating.htm

Better distribution and uniformity of interior light are achieved if windows are located in more than one wall.

Successful experiments with controlled reflected light has led to the use of mirrorlike reflective adjustable blinds. With these devices, light can be directed to specific areas of a room. In conjunction with reflective ceilings, the depth of light can be extended, expanding daylight deep into rooms.

Light from east- and west-facing windows, of course, penetrates substantially farther in the early morning and late afternoon. If the room is wider than light penetrates, shadows form on the far side of the room and artificial light may be necessary even during daylight hours.

Reflections from water, sky, snow, and concrete as well as direct sun create glare. Glare can be controlled by:

- Placing windows high on walls
- Landscaping to shade openings
- Using translucent, tinted, or reflective glass
- Using small openings
- Providing interior shaded courtyards
- Using light-reducing screening devices that permit ventilation

Ventilation

If providing light inside a house were the only function of windows, they would all consist of fixed panes of glass. Windows, however, can be excellent sources of natural ventilation, helping to remove excess heat, moisture, and odors from the house. The IRC requires that the ventable portion of windows be equal to 4 percent of floor area. When operable windows will be used for ventilation (rather than relying on mechanical systems), it may be desirable to increase the ventilation area.

Windows are especially important in bathrooms and kitchens for the dispersal of odors and moisture.

Box 6.3 International Residential Code Requirements for Windows and Doors

WINDOWS

- Minimum window area in habitable rooms is equivalent to 8 percent of the floor area of the room.
- The minimum openable area for habitable rooms is 4 percent of the floor area of the space being vented.
- Light and ventilation for rooms without windows can be provided by an adjacent room if at least half of the common wall is open and the window area is a minimum of 10 percent of the floor area of the interior space. Window area must be equal to or greater than 25 square feet.
- Bathrooms must have a minimum of 3 square feet of exterior glazing, half of which must be openable unless there is sufficient artificial light and mechanical ventilation to circulate a minimum of 50 cubic feet per minute intermittently or 20 cfm continuously.

DOORS

- A minimum of one door that leads from the living area directly outdoors must be provided. This door must be a minimum of 3 feet 0 inches wide.

Source: International Code Council, *International Residential Code for One- and Two-Family Dwellings 2003* (Country Club Hills, IL: International Code Council, 2003).

Fans placed in these areas can speed up the ventilating process or take the place of windows, but ample window space is still desirable. To provide for maximum air flow, windows should be located to encourage cross-ventilation. Windows placed on opposite sides of a house are especially effective if one of the openings is located to take advantage of prevailing breezes. Windows high on walls are not especially effective unless air enters through a lower opening.

Box 6.4 Finishing the Structure for Accessibility

CHILDREN

- Children will appreciate windows they can see out of. If longer windows are used, standard head height can be retained and the windowsill made sufficiently low for children and seated adults. Windows located lower than 18 inches, however, must have tempered or safety glass.
- Windows on upper stories need to have safety locks to help prevent children from accidentally falling from them.

ACCESSIBILITY

- For wheelchair use, interior doors should be 36 inches. When a wheelchair width of up to 29 inches is added to the distance required for operation of the unit, there may be insufficient clear space in a 32- or 34-inch doorway, especially if there is a turn to get into the room.
- When a door swings toward a wheelchair, approximately 18 inches of clear wall space on the latch side is needed to approach the door.
- Pocket doors are easier to approach and operate from a seated position than are swinging doors.
- Lever-operated door hardware rather than knobs that must be turned are not only easier for individuals with limited mobility to operate but for everyone.
- Adding a kick plate near the bottom of a door will help prevent marring of the door by wheelchair footrests.
- Casement windows, awning windows, and sliding windows are easier to operate from a seated position than are double-hung windows.
- Window controls should not be higher than 4 feet 6 inches.

Windows should be located to take advantage of prevailing breezes in the summer which are generally from west to east in the Northern Hemisphere. In addition, winds from the south, which are often moist, combine with westerly winds to create southwesterly winds throughout much of the United States during the summer. Therefore windows placed facing south and west are usually more efficient for cooling than windows on the north and east. Variations occur in every locality, however, especially where topographic features such as lakes and mountains influence air patterns.

Although good air flow is achieved when inlets and outlets are approximately equal in size, better flow is generated when the opening through which air enters is smaller than the one through which air leaves the house. This is an application of the Venturi principle. In essence, this law of physics says that when the space through which a fluid—in this case, air—becomes smaller, the velocity of the fluid increases. See Box 6.4 for design guidelines for accessibility.

View

Windows are psychologically important: They expand the line of vision, provide for a view, and increase the relationship of the interior and exterior of the home. Large uninterrupted glass areas can make rooms appear larger. When glass areas face public spaces, however, the resulting lack of privacy may make it necessary to cover windows, shutting off a view. Privacy can be retained by facing most windows toward the interior of the lot rather than the street. Windows facing interior courtyards, landscaped backyards, and patio areas provide an alternative to undesirable natural views and also ensure privacy.

When windows are designed to take advantage of a view, they should be placed so people can see out whether they are seated or standing.

Windows also serve a decorative function on both the interior and the exterior. The shape, style, and size of windows should be in keeping with the architectural style of the house. Window location also affects furniture placement. Low windows effectively reduce the wall area and may preclude desirable interior arrangements. Windows located high on a wall affect furniture placement less drastically—usually making it possible to locate furniture beneath them.

Window Parts

Glazing is the term used by the industry for the glass in a window. Windows may be separated by wood or metal dividers called **muntins**, and each division is called a **light**. Muntins may hold individual lights together, or a snap-out muntin panel may be placed over a single pane to divide it into lights. The latter gives the illusion of a multipaned window without the nuisance of cleaning the panes individually and having to paint the muntins while they are in place. Removable muntins of wood or vinyl are available in various patterns, with rectangular and diamond shapes being most popular. A **mullion** is a vertical post that separates two windows in the same frame.

The **sash** is the framework that holds the glass. If the window is operable, it is the sash that moves. Sashes are made up of vertical **stiles** and horizontal **rails**. The window frame is built into the wall and holds the sash. See Figure 6.7. The sides of the window frame are called **jambs**; the top, the **head** or lintel; and the bottom, the sill. The outer sill projects from the wall surface to prevent water dripping onto the exterior surfaces and slopes away from the window to permit drainage. The interior sill is level and may also project from the wall surface. Because metal windows are generally attached directly to the exterior

---

Figure 6.7 Window parts.

---

surface of a building, most metal windows do not have an exterior sill.

To finish the window, trim is applied on both the interior and exterior surfaces. This **casing** seals off the space between the rough opening in the wall framing and the finish frame. The sill is finished with a molding known as the **stool**, and the horizontal casing beneath it is the **apron**. On the outside, a **drip cap** is installed over the casing to prevent moisture collection.

The materials most often used for the window sash and frames are wood, aluminum, and vinyl. Wood can be easily painted, stained, and repaired. Aluminum components weigh less, require less maintenance, and permit increased glass area because the sash and frames can be narrower. Solid vinyl windows require no painting and do not warp as easily as wood. Color choice, however, is very limited. Wood is a better insulator than aluminum and vinyl, although **thermal break construction** of aluminum components slows heat loss considerably. Thermal break construction consists of a layer of vinyl (or some other material that does not conduct heat well) sandwiched between the interior and exterior metal layers, interrupting the flow of heat to the exterior.

There is no "standard" window size. Prehung windows are available in predetermined sizes, although those sizes differ according to the manufacturer.

Most domestic structures make use of prehung windows—preassembled window units including frames that are ready to install in a rough opening. These windows are weather-stripped, may be prefinished, and are protected by a factory-applied water-repellent.

Types of Windows

While all windows perform similar functions, a variety of window styles have evolved over time. A major differentiation between window styles is whether they are stationary or operable.

Stationary Windows

Windows that are fixed in place are called **stationary windows**. Their function is to provide light and a view. Because they require no operating hardware, they are less expensive than operable windows of the same size, and because they are sealed into their frames, there are no cracks through which air can penetrate. In areas where dust storms are common or where central air-conditioning is installed, houses are built with a combination of fixed and operable windows. A common method used is to install a large fixed window with smaller movable windows at the sides to provide ventilation and meet egress codes.

Fixed windows can be made in larger sizes than can operable ones. A **picture window** has a large uninterrupted span of glass that frames a view. Plate glass is generally used to minimize distortion. Heat gain or loss through the large glass area may be excessive but can be offset with energy-saving measures such as storm windows and interior window treatments. Proper orientation can make picture windows even more efficient by allowing them to become passive solar energy collectors.

Sidelights are generally tall, narrow stationary windows placed at one or both sides of an exterior door. They may be transparent or translucent, providing light for the entry. When there is no glass in the door, sidelights serve a security function by providing

The IRC requires an exterior egress from every habitable sleeping room. This function is often fulfilled by one or more operable windows. In buildings up to three stories high, it is important that this egress not be blocked by decorative details such as wrought-iron railings on the exterior. Local codes, however, may require railings that block windows on upper stories of multi-unit dwellings. In this case, the railing prevents individuals from falling from windows.

a view of anyone at the door. In recent years, some operable sidelights have been installed.

A **fanlight** is a semicircular or elliptical fixed window placed over a door. It can be separated into lights in a variety of ways, often in shapes resembling a fan. The fanlight is a feature of several traditional architectural styles, including Georgian and Federal. See Figure 6.8.

Figure 6.8 This door has a fanlight and sidelights, both of which provide natural light to the interior of the home as well as providing architectural detailing on the front of the structure.

Glass blocks may be incorporated into a wall to admit light to the home. Interesting effects can be created with plain, swirled, fluted, or pebble-patterned blocks, and color blocks can be used to create unusual lighting effects. Glass blocks can also be used to construct non-load-bearing partitions, including shower walls.

Operable Windows

Windows that open and close are operable windows. In addition to providing light and a view, operable windows permit ventilation and egress.

Side-hinged windows hung to swing either inward or outward are **casement windows**. Casement windows open with a rotary crank, and up to 100 percent ventilation can be achieved (that is, it is possible for air to flow through all of the window area). Because those that open inward create a safety hazard, most casement windows open outward, although even then, they can obstruct pathways and present a danger. See Figure 6.9.

A variation of the casement window is the **pivot window**. Rather than being hinged at the side, this type of window rotates on pivots set in the top and bottom of the window at the center. Pivot windows are easy to clean on both sides but may create a safety hazard because they project beyond the wall on both the interior and exterior.

When developed in the eighteenth century, **double-hung windows** quickly replaced casement windows. Double-hung windows have been popular in America for almost 275 years and are the most common window used in homes today. A double-hung

---

Windows that swing inward—pivot, hopper, and some casements—interfere with window treatments. Window treatment design must take this factor into consideration. Windows that swing outward—most casements, awning, and jalousie windows—make it necessary to install storms and screens on the interior rather than the exterior.

Figure 6.9 A weather-tight seal is difficult to obtain on casement windows, making them less energy-efficient than other types.

window consists of two sashes that slide vertically on tracks or grooves in the side jambs, providing up to 50 percent ventilation.

Because they present two flat surfaces, double-hung windows do not interfere with window treatments, and storm windows and screens can be installed on the outside. Their major disadvantage is the difficulty of cleaning them from the inside. However, manufacturers produce spring releases, pivots, and other mechanisms that allow the removal of windows for cleaning.

Slip-head windows are windows that, when open, disappear into the wall. They are uncommon, occurring especially in older homes in the South. These windows may be as tall as doors or even higher; they raise completely into the wall above or lower into the ground, permitting the opening to be used as a doorway and opening up a large space for maximum ventilation. They are generally arranged in pairs or groups and placed to encourage cross-ventilation. Their use, however, requires that the structural system be modified to include pockets in the wall or foundation. In either case, the use of insulation in wall pocket areas is precluded, affecting the energy-efficiency of the structure.

Horizontal **sliding windows** are essentially double-hung windows turned sideways. Tracks for operating the window are located in the head and sill of the frame. The window can be opened from both the right and left sides or may be operable from one side only, depending on the manufacturer. As with double-hung windows, ventilation is limited to 50 percent of the window area and there is no interference with inside window treatments. Horizontal sliding windows are desirable in hard-to-reach areas or relatively high on the wall because it is easier to slide a window than to lift it. Horizontal windows may not blend with some traditional designs.

Awning windows are hinged at the top and swing outward at the bottom. As their name implies, they are awninglike in appearance when open. Awning windows provide both 100 percent ventilation and protection from rain when open. See Figure 6.10.

Hopper windows are awning windows turned upside down and backwards. Hinged at the bottom, they open inward at the top. This method of operation creates a safety hazard unless the windows are high on the wall, such as in a basement at the top of a foundation.

A **transom** is a horizontal window above an interior door, hinged at the bottom and swinging outward at the top. The Romans used transoms over their doors, but they were filled with a grille rather than with glass. Modern transoms may or may not be glazed. Because of their location, they are difficult to clean.

Jalousie windows consist of a series of movable, narrow horizontal panes. A cranking device adjusts these outward-opening windows. When closed, the bottom edge of each pane overlaps and fits snugly against the top of the next pane, although they are not weather-tight. Privacy can be increased by the use of translucent, rather than transparent, panes. Because they have many small panes, these windows are difficult to clean. In addition, if metal sashes are used,

Figure 6.10 Awning windows are operated by a push bar or a rotary crank and are often combined with stationary windows.

Figure 6.11 Because jalousie windows provide protection from rain and are adjustable to provide up to 100 percent ventilation, they are popular in warm climates.

condensation and frost may build up on the inside surfaces during cold weather. See Figure 6.11.

Special Window Styles

There are three types of windows that project outward from a house—**bow**, **bay**, and **oriel**. Bow windows project in a curve, while bay windows are angular. Bow and bay windows are often cantilevered so that additional support is not needed, although there may be a foundation beneath the window instead. An NAHB survey found that 50 percent of respondents desired a bay window. An oriel window is a bow or bay window on an upper story of a home that is supported by a bracket. Any of these projections may include stationary windows, operable windows, or both. See Figure 6.12.

A **Palladian window** is a combination of three windows, with the center one taller than the others and almost always curved at the top. See Figure 6.13.

Individual dormers, or projections of a wall through the roofline, may be placed along a roofline, or one long dormer can be constructed along an entire side of the roof. A dormer has its own roof, which may be of any style. Windows in dormers provide light and ventilation for attic spaces. See Figure 6.14.

Clerestory windows are located high along a wall, generally at the ceiling line, and may project upward from the roof plane on the exterior. They can be located in opposite walls projecting through the roof, they may project upward from the roof plane on one side only, or a series of vertical clerestories can be located in a sawtooth configuration above the roof. The primary function of clerestories is to provide diffused light. Maximum light can be gained when the adjacent roof plane is reflective. Although they may be stationary or movable, operable clerestory windows require special hardware. When operable, they also function as part of the ventilation system.

Skylights are windows in a roof and, depending on the location, can deliver daylight deep into the home. Skylights can present a problem with heat gain and glare and should have louvers or another type of luminance control to minimize both. If there is an attic space between the roof and the ceiling of the room lit by the skylight, a well, or enclosed tube, connects the roof opening with the ceiling opening. Splaying the well can increase the area over which light diffuses in the room.

Leakage around skylights may become a problem. Skylights on slanting surfaces can be flat, while those on flat surfaces are formed into bubbles to encourage drainage. Domed skylights help to mitigate the problems of dirt accumulation on the skylight itself and aid in drainage. While most skylights are stationary, they can be operable and may be electrically controlled. Forty-two percent of individuals responding to an NAHB survey wanted skylights in their new homes. See Figure 6.15.

Figure 6.12 (TOP LEFT) Oriel windows were popular in medieval England and remain popular today. Because they project outward from the wall surface, they provide a small amount of additional interior space and permit the installation of windows facing more than one direction in the room.

Figure 6.13 (BOTTOM LEFT) The Palladian window is used extensively in Georgian architecture.

Figure 6.14 (TOP RIGHT) Dormer windows were developed during the Renaissance in France, where steep roofs predominated. Without windows, the attic space was virtually unusable. To use this space for sleeping quarters, the French placed vertical windows in a pitched roof by constructing a separate framework with a roof of its own. Since the French word for sleep is *dormer,* the windows were called dormers.

Figure 6.15 (BOTTOM RIGHT) Because they are exposed to the elements more than windows in a wall, skylights are often made of tough plastic rather than glass. These skylights provide light for a room under the roof. (Source: Barbara Huffman)

Both clerestories and skylights have the distinct advantage of introducing natural light to spaces away from outside walls. However, this light is not always easily controlled. When heat sink materials are located where the sun strikes them through these windows, they provide some passive solar benefit. A disadvantage of both clerestory windows and skylights is the difficulty of cleaning them.

Doors

Windows are only one of the two major openings in homes. They let in light and air, but not people. Doorways fill that function. Entrances are often specially treated, providing architectural emphasis and serving as a focal point for the building. Doors affect the character of a house and of rooms and may serve as status symbols.

Entry doors protect the house and the entrance from the elements. Doors are also universally respected as the beginning of the private domain, where entry is by invitation only. They block or permit passage and can be made more secure by locks. Entry doors may also admit light or provide ventilation, but these are secondary functions. Inside the home, doors provide privacy, dictate traffic patterns, affect furniture placement, and influence climate control. Interesting are attitudes toward doors in various cultures. In America, people tend to leave interior doors open. When privacy is desired, the doors are closed. In Germany, interior doors remain closed, because open doors are considered disorderly.

Building codes specify the minimum door sizes for egress. The IRC specifies a minimum 3 feet 0 inch

---

✿ Exterior doors should have a door sweep or other sealing device attached to the bottom. This sweep contacts the threshold when the door is closed and seals the bottom of the door against air infiltration.

door for egress but does not stipulate door sizes for other areas. Bedroom doorways should be a minimum of 2 feet 6 inches in width for ease in moving furniture; 2 feet 8 inch doors are better options when there is a difficult turn required for entering. Bathroom doors may be 2 feet 4 inches or greater. Standard doors are 80 inches high. Doors should be located where they do not interfere with the swing of another door, where they do not cover light switches, or where they do not swing into a position where someone is likely to be sitting or standing.

A doorway includes an opening, a door, and a frame. A door is a relatively solid surface that closes to fill the entrance to an enclosed space.

Door Parts and Manufacture

The door frame fits inside the rough opening and supports the door. The frame consists of two vertical side jambs and a horizontal head or lintel at the top. In addition, exterior doors have a horizontal sill at the bottom that connects the two side jambs. The sill is sloped so that water drains away from the door. The threshold covers the joint between the sill and the floor. A **stop** extends about a half inch from the frame on the top and two sides and prevents the door from moving farther when it is being closed. See Figure 6.16.

As on windows, the casing around the interior and exterior of the doorway conceals the space between the frame and the rough opening. The design of the casing may be simple or elaborate but should be in keeping with the architectural style of the house.

Door frames are usually made of wood or aluminum. Although pine or fir is used for frame components, door sills are usually made of oak because it is more wear-resistant. If a softer wood is used for the sill, a metal **shoe** is attached to prevent wear. Thresholds can be made of oak, metal, or vinyl. Prehung doors can be purchased already assembled and in the

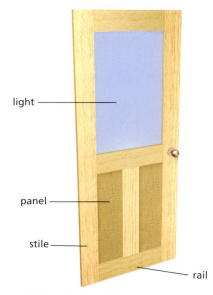

light

panel

stile

rail

Figure 6.16 A diagram of door parts.

frame, eliminating the often tricky task of hanging a door. Although doorknobs are usually placed 36 inches from the floor, prehung doors that include knobs may have them located at the halfway point, or 40 inches.

The doors themselves can be made of wood, aluminum and glass, or steel. Wood and steel doors can be easily painted, but only wood doors can be stained. Steel doors meet building code requirements for fire-resistant doors between houses and attached garages, and they resist intruders better than wood doors do. Steel doors are not solid but have a metal skin over a core of polyurethane. This thermal break construction not only increases energy-efficiency but also prevents the buildup of condensation on the inside of the door.

Door Types

The types of doors can be categorized in two ways: the type of operation—whether the door swings, slides, or folds to open and close—or according to the construction and stylistic details that affect their appearance.

For acoustic privacy, bathroom doors should be sealed as much as is feasible even if other interior doors are not. It may be desirable to treat bedroom, office, or other doors in the same manner.

Because of the difference in the type of glue used for assembly, doors are manufactured specifically for use on either the interior or the exterior. Exterior-grade doors may be used on the interior but interior-grade doors should not be used where they will be exposed to the elements.

Types of Operation

Swinging doors are hinged or pivoted at the side and swing in one or both directions. The most commonly used door is attached to the jamb with metal hinges and swings in one direction only. The hinges of a swinging door are on the inside, and therefore cannot be seen or removed from the outside. Because of this, hinged doors can be effectively secured. They can also be weatherproofed and soundproofed, making them ideal for exterior use. In residences, exterior doors open inward while in public buildings, they open outward to facilitate egress during emergencies.

All swinging doors require uninterrupted space for opening and closing. Doors that swing in one direction should open into rooms, although exceptions are

Although most house doors are of standard sizes and styles, specialty doors and those made to individual specifications are available. Specialty door manufacturers offer unusual stock designs, including hand-carved coats of arms, mythological characters, fraternal emblems, and professional insignia. Oversize doors, doors with arched tops, and doors with jade lights are "standard" with such companies but are, of course, more expensive than ordinary doors. Even more expensive are custom-designed doors. These are specifically created for individual customers, with an almost limitless range of design possibilities.

made for accessibility and other purposes. When located near a corner, doors should open on the side allowing the most free access to the room—generally on the side away from the perpendicular wall. Doors should be located sufficiently far away from the corner to allow for operation and a casing—2 inches is usually considered minimum, although that does not allow enough space for standard casing materials. Four inches or more will allow for wider casings. Hinged swinging doors are either right-hand or left-hand doors depending on which direction they swing. If the knob is on the right when the door is viewed from the inside (the side from which the hinges are visible when the door is closed), the door has a right-hand swing.

Less commonly used are **double-action swinging doors**. These doors are mounted on pivots rather than hinges, enabling them to swing through a 180-degree arc. Double-action doors are used between rooms to obtain visual privacy and for decorative purposes, and can easily be operated even when a person has both hands full. A common place for double-action doors is between the kitchen and dining room. When hung in pairs that open from the center, they are called **cafe doors**. Many double-action swinging doors operate with a spring-loaded pivot that automatically returns them to a closed position. When the doors are not full-length, it is easier to see when someone is approaching the opening from the other side, helping to prevent collisions. If full-length cafe doors are used, they should have a light (window) in them for viewing.

A **Dutch door** is a hinged swinging door that is divided horizontally, essentially forming two doors. Each portion can be opened independently, or the two can be latched together and treated as a single door. The upper portion of the door may contain a window. Dutch doors are still popular in European cottages because the top half can be opened for ventilation and light while the closed bottom half keeps small children and barnyard animals where they should be. It is difficult to seal Dutch doors against cold and moisture,

Figure 6.17 Dutch doors are excellent for keeping pets in designated areas and are now most frequently used as interior doors.

and they are not as common as other types of doors on the exterior. See Figure 6.17.

Sliding doors operate on an overhead track and remain parallel to the wall when opened. This requires that the wall space occupied by the open door remain barrier-free. They are ideal for closets because they don't use space in the room or the closet for swinging. When sliding doors are used for large openings, tracks or glides are usually provided on the floor to prevent the bottom edge from swinging in or out. Because they are not restrained by hinges, wooden sliding doors are subject to warping. Sliding doors may be flush, paneled, louvered, or glass. In fact, sliding glass doors are frequently used on the exterior of homes. A fixed pane and a movable door are combined with a screen, making 50 percent ventilation possible. Three- and four-panel units are sometimes used for larger areas. Muntins may be incorporated so the doors blend with specific architectural styles.

When two doors slide past each other, they are called **bypass sliding doors**. Door pulls must be recessed to permit operation. The major disadvantage of bypass doors is that only 50 percent of the opening is usable at any one time.

Pocket doors eliminate this problem. They disappear into an opening, or pocket, in the wall when open. However, this type of operation requires a different type of wall construction and may require that walls be thicker than normal. Manufacturers do produce steel pocket door frames that fit into or can be used with 4-inch or 6-inch wood frame walls, however. Pocket doors are less popular than other door types because they are unhandy to operate and, when they come off the track, may be difficult to rehang. Because they are difficult to lock securely, they are considered interior doors only. Since they slide into a wall, pocket door pulls must be recessed or flush. See Figure 6.18.

Folding doors operate on an overhead track and move on nylon rollers. A floor track may also be used, especially for larger doors. Because they must be lightweight to operate easily, they are not effective as sound insulators, so they function primarily as visual barriers. Folding doors require less space for operation than swinging doors and are efficient for closets, laundry and utility areas, and as room dividers.

There are two types of folding doors. **Accordion doors** have a metal skeleton to which is attached fabric, vinyl, thin wood slats, or other suitable material. Each fold is approximately the width of the door jamb. When open, no space is required in the room permitting furniture placement in close proximity. Because the folds themselves take up space, however, the actual size of the opening becomes smaller when the door is open.

Bifold doors are pairs of doors of equal width hinged to fold together. A single pair may be used for

Because one door of a pair of bypass sliding doors must be hung in front of the other, one edge of a door is always exposed. This edge should not be visible from the entry or the center of the room.

smaller openings or a pair can be attached to each side of a wider door frame. Room dividers can be made by attaching more panels, but these heavier doors may require electronically controlled operation. Because of their width, bifold doors project into the room when folded.

Figure 6.18 Pocket doors are particularly useful between kitchens and dining rooms, in compartmentalized bathrooms, and as closet doors.

Door Construction and Style

Flush doors present two flat surfaces. They are constructed with a plywood or veneer facing attached to both sides of a wood framework that surrounds a core material. Solid-core flush doors have cores of particleboard or lumber. Because they provide excellent protection from weather with minimal warping, solid-core doors make good exterior doors. They also provide security. A second type of flush door is the hollow-core door. The framework of a hollow-core door is a supporting grid made of wood, foam, cardboard, or other material. Since these doors are lightweight and less expensive than solid-core doors, they are used extensively as interior doors, providing visual privacy but little acoustic privacy. Hollow-core doors are sometimes used as exterior doors, but not in areas where temperature differences between the interior and exterior are likely to be great. Excessive differences in temperature and humidity on the two sides of hollow-core doors cause them to warp.

In an NAHB survey, only 19 percent of respondents desired flush doors, which are more contemporary in appearance than other doors. Although the distinguishing characteristic of a flush door is its flat surface, exterior flush doors often include one or more panes of glass for convenience and decoration. It is also possible for decorative panels to be mounted on the surface of the door, adding individuality and architectural interest.

Panel doors are made of vertical stiles and horizontal rails that frame thin panels of wood, metal, or glass, and are described by the number of panels they contain. During the Renaissance, the panels were extensively used as carving surfaces, and panel doors became highly decorative. The most popular panel doors today have six panels but a number of other varieties are readily available. See Figure 6.19. **Sash doors** result when a part of the space between stiles and rails is glazed. Other portions may be paneled, louvered, or flush. An NAHB survey found that 51 percent of individuals favored panel doors.

Louvered doors have narrow, angled wooden

Figure 6.19 Modern panel doors are popular as exterior doors, where decorative surfaces give added emphasis to the doorway, or the simplicity of flat panels enhances certain architectural styles.

slats in the spaces between the stiles and rails. Although they are not soundproof, they provide visual privacy and permit air to circulate through them. These characteristics make louvered doors ideal for use as closet doors and in laundry and utility areas.

French doors are completely glazed, permitting light to enter. Although classified as doors, they are really casement windows large enough to be used as doors. **Rim French doors** have one large piece of glass as a filler between stiles and rails, while **divided-light French doors** have muntins dividing the window area into smaller lights. Today, that muntin is usually separate and snaps in and out for ease of cleaning. As doors leading to a patio or porch, French doors are used singly or in groups of two or more. In

Europe, and increasingly in the United States, they are also popular as interior doors. An NAHB survey found that French doors were particularly desired by individuals expecting to purchase upscale homes.

Batten doors consist of one layer of boards nailed to a second layer. In one type, two complete layers are nailed to each other diagonally. Another type has a layer of vertical boards nailed to several horizontal ledge boards or to one or more diagonal brace boards. Batten doors lend themselves to medieval architectural styles, including Elizabethan and Tudor styles. Batten doors may also be used for cellars, sheds, and barns where appearance is not important.

Garage Doors

In older homes, the garage is located behind the house and often faces an alley. However, the garages of most newer houses face the street and are an im-

Because garage doors are so prominent when located on the front of a house, if there is sufficient space on the lot to do so, the garage can be turned so that the door is actually on the side of the house rather than the front. Some housing developments insist on this configuration.

portant part of the architectural styling of the front of the house. With an increasing number of families owning not one but two or more vehicles, the garage has been enlarged, emphasizing it more. As a result, garage doors have become increasingly important from an aesthetic standpoint. Garage doors can be trimmed to make them conform to the architectural style of the house or to make them more individual in appearance. See Figure 6.20.

A single door is used for a one-car garage. For a two-car garage, one large or two single doors may be selected. The larger door requires heavier framing

Figure 6.20 This three-car garage dominates the facade of the residence. The garage doors are batten doors.

for support but is less expensive than two separate doors. Standard single doors are 9 feet wide and 6 feet 6 inches or 7 feet high, while double doors are 15 or 16 feet wide. Garage doors are also manufactured in 10- and 18-foot widths and 8-foot heights. Garage doors are made of wood, fiberglass, or metal, and may include windows. Because most newer garages are attached to homes, energy-efficiency becomes a factor in their construction. A polystyrene or polyurethane core in a fiberglass or metal door prevents excessive heat loss. Weather-stripping seals the space between the bottom of the door and the garage floor and also acts as a cushion when the door is closed.

The earliest type of garage door is found infrequently today. It consists of a double door mounted on hinges to swing outward from the center. This type of garage door is the least expensive and the easiest to install. Its major disadvantage is that the doors are not protected from the weather when open.

A second type of garage door, also uncommon, is made up of several panels that slide horizontally on an overhead track. In some styles, the panels fold against one another when open. In other types, the track curves around the inside of the garage wall and the door panels fit side by side on the track. An inside track is preferable so that the doors are not exposed to the elements.

The most commonly used garage door in homes today is the **overhead door**. When open, this type of door rests just under the ceiling of the garage, where it is protected from the elements. A **single-section overhead door** swings up on a pivot. Tracks are mounted in the ceiling with rollers at the top of the door to keep it in place. A **sectional overhead door** consists of four or five hinged sections. Rollers on the sides of each section fit into tracks that run under the ceiling and down the sides of the opening. Overhead doors have a torsion spring or stretch spring counterbalance system that helps support the weight of the door. An under-ceiling clearance of about 12 inches is required for overhead doors, although special kits can

be purchased that decrease the amount of clearance needed. A 7-foot-high overhead door requires at least an 8-foot-high ceiling.

Garage doors are opened either manually or electronically. Working on a radio frequency or a magnetic principle, electronically operated doors can be opened or closed using a portable transmitter or wall-mounted button. A release switch permits manual operation in case of power failure. Most automatic garage door openers include a light that comes on when the door is opened and that remains on for several minutes. Some models also have a security switch that deactivates the unit when the house will be unoccupied for extended periods.

Details of Interior Finishing

On the interior of the structure, floors, walls, and ceilings may be treated to provide decorative effects. When they are used primarily to establish an architectural background, they should be unobtrusive. Each may, however, become a focal point in a room, contributing significantly to design.

Floors

Floors are subjected to the greatest amount of wear of any structural component in a building and receive the most dirt. The finish materials used for floors must be durable and, in areas where the most dirt collects, scratch-resistant. The finish flooring material affects comfort, maintenance characteristics, appearance, and noise levels in a home. A single flooring material can be used to make areas flow together, giving the illusion of greater space and creating unity. A change in flooring material can define traffic patterns or delimit space without the use of walls. A change in the level of the floor by one or two steps can establish boundaries between spaces. Flooring can be divided into two types: nonresilient and resilient.

Nonresilient Flooring

Nonresilient materials are hard and do not "give" when walked on, making them less comfortable than resilient flooring materials. In general, nonresilient floors are noisy when walked on and, because they are hard surfaces, tend to magnify sounds. This characteristic, however, makes nonresilient floors highly durable and ideal for high-traffic zones. These flooring materials are high in initial cost but are longer lasting and easier to clean than resilient materials. Nonresilient flooring materials include masonry, wood, and glass.

Masonry floors are made of stone, brick, concrete, or ceramic tile. Masonry flooring is cold, an advantage in warm climates but not in cold climates. Types of stone used for floors include marble, travertine, granite, slate, and flagstone. Maintenance characteristics vary, although most types are easily cared for. While many of these materials will take a high polish, this finish is not recommended for floors, as it can be slippery, and the abrasion caused by walking on the surface will scratch the gloss. All masonry materials are somewhat porous and, therefore, subject to staining by oil-based and sometimes water-based materials. A number of sealing compounds are available that make these materials impervious to most stains. Masonry floors can also serve as heat sinks in passive solar homes.

Resilient Flooring

Resilient flooring is more comfortable to walk on than nonresilient materials. Resilient flooring "gives" when a load is placed on it and usually springs back to the original shape once the load is removed. These flooring materials also absorb some noise. For the most part, resilient flooring is less expensive than nonresilient flooring but also less durable. Resilient flooring materials include linoleum, vinyl, rubber, cork, and carpet. Subfloors must be smooth and level to ensure a smooth-surfaced resilient floor. If plywood is used for the subfloor, any splits or knotholes must be filled and sanded smooth to prevent the flooring material—

The hardness of nonresilient flooring materials may cause physical problems for employees in hospitals, restaurants, and other commercial establishments who are on their feet much of the time while working. In homes, this factor may affect flooring choice in kitchens but rarely in other rooms.

resilient flooring or carpet—from wearing through at those points. Liquid underlayments are ideal for this purpose.

Walls

Walls define the shape and size of a space, enclose and protect it from the elements and from other spaces within the structure, and provide privacy. Walls may serve simply as a background, they may be constructed with openings that provide a view to a space beyond, or they may be architecturally interesting by themselves.

Wall Finishes

Wall and ceiling finishes need not be as durable as floors, nor do they as directly affect comfort. Appearance, maintenance characteristics, acoustics, and fire safety are among the criteria used in their selection. Any exterior material can be used for interior walls, as can flooring materials, but the most common materials for both walls and ceilings are plaster and gypsum wallboard that can be further finished and paneling that needs no further finishing.

Paint. Paint can be applied over textured or smooth walls. Paint gives a uniform surface appearance and is available in hundreds of colors. It is relatively inexpensive and can be applied quickly. Many paints are washable and thus easily maintained. Painted faux finishes can give the appearance of marble, leather, and other more expensive materials without the high cost.

It is not only the color of paint that affects the appearance of a room but also its sheen. As the amount

When thin panels of any material are applied to structural components on 24-inch centers without a backing of another material, the panels may eventually become concave over the openings between the structural members. Furring strips are used to apply the paneling over masonry walls or walls that are very uneven.

of sheen increases, the durability also increases. Surface imperfections are best hidden with low-sheen finishes. One paint manufacturer offers the following paint surfaces, beginning with the lowest sheen: flat, matte, eggshell, pearl, satin, semigloss, and gloss.

Wallpaper. Wallpaper is a flexible covering that comes in a variety of textures, colors, and printed designs. The surface material may be paper, vinyl, foil, or cloth, and paper or cloth is used for a backing. Wallpaper is applied with paste or by wetting prepasted paper. Removing wallpaper before painting or repapering may require the use of a steamer. Strippable wallpapers, however, peel off dry in large strips. Wallpaper can be used on ceilings as well as walls for unusual decorative effects.

Tiles. Ceramic, plastic, and metal tiles, as well as mirror tiles, can be applied as a finish over plaster or water-resistant gypsum board. Because they are impervious to water, tiles can be used in showers and around bathtubs and lavatories. Tile is easily maintained and provides a permanent finish. Because of its hard, smooth surface, tile reflects the noise in a room. Mirror tiles have the unique advantage of increasing apparent space and can be used on ceilings as well as walls.

When the color of the inside of a wall niche matches or approximates the color of the room, the items displayed in the niche become a focal point. When the niche color contrasts with the room, the niche itself is a focal point. Lighting, of course, influences this effect.

A number of other decorative wall coverings are possible. Felt, burlap, grass cloth, fabric, leather, cork, and other materials add imaginative touches to interiors.

Paneling. Paneling requires little maintenance and can be cleaned easily. Unlike paint and wallpaper, paneling does not need to be reapplied periodically. This feature, however, makes paneled rooms more difficult to redecorate. Materials used for paneling include wood planks, plywood, hardboard, or plastics.

Wood paneling consists of individual boards that can be applied vertically, horizontally, or diagonally. Horizontal boards can be nailed directly to the studs, while other patterns require furring strips or some other type of nailing support. Tongue-and-groove or shiplap boards fit snugly against one another, while plain boards can be applied in a board-and-batten pattern or other styles. The choice of wood species for paneling is wide, ranging from informal knotty pine to more formal walnut and mahogany. The wood can be stained or left with a natural finish. Although attractive, wood paneling is expensive and its application is time-consuming.

Wall Niches

A **niche** is a recessed architectural detail. A niche can be squared or rounded—most typically a semicircular headed opening with a half-domed shell in the recess. Niches are used in some Oriental structures and in churches for shrines; classical interiors used niches for the display of busts, and modern niches range from those with fountains to a shelf for displaying objects. A variety of prefabricated niches are available, including those designed for wet places such as showers.

Niches project only slightly from the wall, so they can be placed almost anywhere. Niches can often be installed between wall studs without additional framing. If the location of the niche requires it, however, and a stud must be cut, a header and sill must be added in non-load-bearing walls. In load-bearing

Figure 6.21 Lozenge shapes in this ceiling are defined by ribbon, with fabric-covered Styrofoam around the edges.

walls, structural framing is more critical. A wall **nook** differs from a niche in that the sides of the niche are curved, while the sides of the nook are straight. Nooks may have more than one shelf.

Ceilings

Ceilings are important because they affect acoustics, lighting, and energy-efficiency as well as appearance in a room. In a study, the NAHB found that 63 percent of individuals prefer higher ceilings on the first story, although 8-foot ceilings on subsequent stories were preferred by 61 percent.

The ceiling is the largest uninterrupted space in most rooms and, historically, has been highly decorative. Paintings and frescoes done by famous artists are found throughout the world on ceilings.[2] Renaissance painted ceilings were often vaulted, with intricate gilded wood and plaster designs surrounding the paintings. Today's ceilings are much less intricate. Typical ceilings are painted in light neutral colors to help reflect light, have horizontal surfaces, and are inexpensive. See Figure 6.21. Relatively few materials are used for ceilings and these do not need to be very durable.

Ceiling Materials

Most ceilings are covered with wallboard and may be textured to create interest, mask any unevenness,

The height of ceilings affects energy efficiency. Because heat rises, it is warmer near the ceiling than at floor level. The higher the ceiling, the more heat is wasted. Reversible ceiling fans alleviate this problem to some extent. These fans insure good circulation, pushing warm air downward in the winter. For the most part, however, in cold climates, ceilings should be the minimum 8 feet high required by the IRC and other codes to ease the heating load. In hot climates, higher ceilings will make the home cooler. Many older homes have high ceilings ranging up to 13 feet or more. Lowering the ceiling will increase energy efficiency.

and absorb some noise. Although most exterior, flooring, and wall materials may be used on ceilings, there are some materials that are designed especially for ceilings, such as stamped metal tiles and acoustic tiles. These materials may, of course, be used on walls as well. Ceiling materials, like wall materials, do not need to withstand as much wear as flooring and exterior materials do.

Changes in Ceiling Height

Ceiling height may be used to establish implied boundaries, make a space more intimate, or open space up.

Even when the plane does not change, ceilings may be made to appear higher by carrying the wall treatment onto the ceiling a short distance, increasing the number of vertical lines in the room that draw the eye upward, or installing a cove or curve between the wall and ceiling rather than treating this joint with a right angle. Horizontal lines in a room, a dark color on the ceiling, especially if the ceiling treatment extends downward onto the wall, or attaching a molding on the wall some distance below the ceiling all tend to lower the ceiling visually.

Figure 6.22 The central part of this ceiling is suspended and employs mirror tiles beneath painted plastic panels. The mirrors reflect light from the chandelier into the room. The supporting grid is exposed.

- A **dropped ceiling** may be used for an entire room or just a portion of a space. Although the lowest part of the ceiling is usually around the outside edges of a space, dropped ceilings can be used in the center of a room to great effect. Dropped ceilings provide ideal locations for recessed lights. Structurally, a dropped ceiling requires the addition of a soffit.

- Soffits are L-shaped frames built at the junction of a wall and ceiling and are usually covered with wallboard. Soffits may hide electrical wires, plumbing pipes, and HVAC ducts; enclose structural supports such as beams; house light fixtures; bridge the gap between a ceiling and a wall cabinet; or lower a ceiling. The IRC requires that blocking be used in soffits every 10 feet and between the joist or stud spaces and the soffit if wallboard does not separate the two. Lightweight steel framing may be better for framing soffits in which lights will be installed than is wood framing because of its greater resistance to fire.

- A suspended ceiling is a type of dropped ceiling that usually encompasses the entire ceiling area. The major difference between a suspended ceiling

and a dropped ceiling is that the suspended ceiling is installed on a lightweight metal track. The track is hung from wires attached to the ceiling or joists. Lightweight panels similar to ceiling tile are laid in the openings of the framework. The panels are usually 2 feet × 2 feet or 2 feet × 4 feet. Lighting fixtures can be hung from the track or recessed over a translucent panel. It is uncommon to use suspended ceilings with acoustic tile in upscale residences, although basement ceilings may incorporate them to provide access to pipes, ducts, and wiring. Tracks may be exposed or hidden by the tiles. Suspended ceilings of other materials can be used with good effect in any home. See Figure 6.22.

- A **tray ceiling** is raised in a portion of a space; it may be created by a soffit or may be framed into the ceiling. Installation of a tray ceiling in an existing room may require cutting out sections of existing joists, which is best accomplished in rooms without a living space above. The ends of the joists must be secured with headers. See Figure 6.23.

- Grand historical rooms may have a recessed ceiling dome made of plaster. Modern domes are typically one-piece polymer units. Some domes are flush-mounted and have no molding; others have molding around the rim. Like a tray ceiling, a structural recess must be provided into which the dome can be installed. It may be easier to lower the ceiling with a soffit around the room to install a dome without cutting joists.

- Ceilings may be slanted, often following the roof line and increasing apparent space. Ceilings beginning at the top of the wall and slanting upward are called **cathedral ceilings**.

Ceiling Decoration

Ceiling joists or beams can be left exposed, opening the ceiling up into the roof area or using the floor or roof above for the ceiling surface. To present an attractive appearance, the joists or beams may be cased with finish lumber. Laminated beams and beams made of lumber are other alternatives. The surfaces between the joists or beams may be covered with wood planks, wallboard, or other material. If beams are exposed, no intermediate insulation can be used. Exposed ceiling beams are often sloped, creating a spacious appearance in rooms.

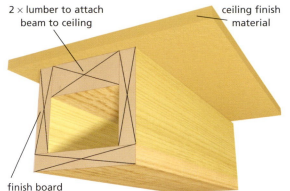

2 × lumber to attach beam to ceiling

ceiling finish material

finish board

Figure 6.24 This drawing illustrates only one of several ways to construct a box beam.

The impression of exposed beams can also be created by installing wood beams, imitation beams made of rigid foam, or built-up decorative boxes that appear to be beams after a ceiling of wallboard or plaster has been installed. See Figure 6.24. The advantage of faux beams is that insulation can be used between ceiling joists.

Coffered and caissoned[3] ceilings have been popular since Roman times. Generally, ancient and medieval coffered ceilings were composed of beams and cross-beams required for structure. Some, however, like Renaissance coffered ceilings, and those used today are constructed of moldings and are not structural in nature. Small rosettes or other types of moldings may be distributed over the ceiling to create interest as well. Generally, such a large amount of decoration is only suitable for high ceilings. See Figure 6.25.

Interior Trim

Interior trim includes decorative strips, panels, and other details used to give a room a finished appearance or for other reasons. Most trim is also referred to as molding. Molding includes strips of pattern lumber milled to specific shapes for their purposes. Molding made from wood is also called **millwork**. Molding

Figure 6.23 This tray ceiling houses two ceiling fans and recessed lighting. (Source: Barbara Huffman)

Figure 6.25 The panels in this coffered ceiling are highly decorated, as is typical of Oriental ceilings. In addition, the beams and brackets are also painted. The detail work makes the large span of space more interesting and more aesthetically pleasing.

includes decorative designs that are molded or cut in plaster, vinyl, plastic, or other materials.

Moldings were used before the time of the ancient Greeks, probably as a means of covering seams and corners. While they retained the original purposes of moldings, the Greeks also used them to decorate their structures. The Romans simplified many of the Greek designs for use on their buildings. Since that time, moldings based on the classical designs have alternately risen and fallen in popularity. After the Civil War, American homes relied heavily on moldings and other decorative details for their ornamentation. By the beginning of World War II, moldings had become streamlined and were used in fewer places.

Moldings can be used near the floor, on a wall, on the ceiling, and around openings. In addition to window and door casings, interior trim includes base trim, wall moldings, and ceiling moldings. Any of the molding types may have decorative carvings or pressed designs on their surfaces. Specially designed inside and outside corners facilitate the cutting of molding at corners, making it possible to butt molding to the corner piece rather than to miter the corners.

Traditional moldings are made of wood, which is difficult to bend. Flexible moldings made of polymer resins make it possible to install **base**, shoe, **chair rail**, and **crown moldings** on curved surfaces. Flat arched moldings of resin must usually be preformed at the factory unless the trim width is very small.

Base Trim

Base trim is installed where the floor and wall meet, covers the joint to provide a finished appearance, and protects the wall from accidental damage. Often, a single piece of base is used, but a second and third piece can be added for decoration or where joints are very uneven.

The base or **baseboard** may consist of a strip of molding or a plain board nailed to the wall at the junction with the floor. Either can be used alone or with a **base shoe**. A base shoe is a piece of molding with a convex outer edge that covers the joint between the floor and the base molding and protects the base molding from damage by cleaning tools and furniture. When a board is used for the base, a narrow strip of molding called a **base cap** or **cap molding** may be added at the top. See Figure 6.26.

Wall and Ceiling Moldings

A variety of trim is used for walls, often depending on the architectural style of the dwelling. Trim can be used to cover the joint between the wall and the ceiling, to provide protection, or to cover walls or parts of walls for decorative or functional purposes. Wall molding can be used to create a formal mood; to accentuate artwork, stairways, and other features; or simply to add interest to a room.

Crown Moldings. A crown molding covers the joint between the wall and the ceiling and serves a decorative function. It may also be used on the exterior between the wall and the soffit under the eave as well.

Because a crown molding lowers the apparent height of the ceiling, it is most often used in homes with high ceilings, so it is infrequently found in homes built during the last half of the twentieth century. In some architectural styles, several pieces of molding are used to create a crown and give a formal look to the room. Crown molding was preferred by 45 percent of NAHB survey respondents.

Picture Molding. Picture molding is installed around the perimeter of a room anywhere from only a fraction of an inch to several inches below the ceiling. Picture molding, too, lowers apparent ceiling height. Although decorative, the major purpose of picture molding is to provide a ledge from which objects can be suspended. Thus, pictures and other objects can be hung and moved without leaving unsightly holes, nails, or hooks in the wall. Many of the world's museums use picture molding for this reason.

Figure 6.26 Pattern lumber is shaped to fit into specific locations and to provide interest along the front. Crown molding, for example, is cut to fit at a 45-degree angle between the wall and the ceiling. Baseboard is plain near the bottom to allow users to install a shoe molding.

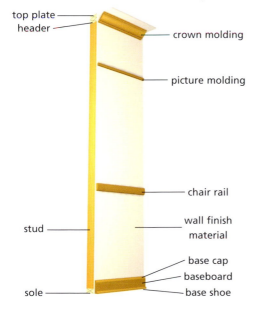

top plate
header
crown molding
picture molding
chair rail
stud
wall finish material
base cap
baseboard
sole
base shoe

Chair Rail. The original function of a chair rail was to protect plaster walls from damage by the backs of chairs. Base molding does not provide sufficient protection, since most chair backs are angled more than 90 degrees from the seat.[4] Because of their purpose, chair rails were originally installed at the height of chair backs. In contemporary homes, a chair rail often serves only a decorative function and can be placed at any height on the wall.

Wainscot and Dado. A **dado**[5] refers to any distinctive treatment on the lower portion of a wall. It originated as a covering of wood panels framed by stiles and rails and painted or stained. The paneling covered the portion of the wall that received the greatest wear, thus serving a protective as well as decorative function. This style of dado is still used with some formal architectural styles. A dado can also be created by papering a wall above a chair rail and painting it below, or simply painting the wall with two different colors. Since the contrasts of color and texture lower the apparent ceiling height, **wainscots** are most prevalent in high-ceilinged rooms. A cap molding may be used to finish the top edge and a decorative base to finish the bottom. The term *wainscot* is often used with the same meaning as dado. It may also refer to a wall covering of wood panels, stiles, and rails, whether it extends only to dado height or covers the entire wall. A **boiserie** is a type of wood wall panel designed as a unit and that has highly decorative details. Parts of the boiserie may be gilded.

Other Moldings. Decorative designs can be formed with molding on any wall or ceiling. A common wall treatment in traditional architecture calls for large squares or rectangles formed by strips of molding. The area inside the molding may be painted a contrasting color, covered with textured wallpaper, or decorated with applied moldings in almost any material.

A variety of moldings that emulate historical detailing are available. Medallions, rosettes, spandrels, banded moldings, and a variety of swags, urns, and animals are made in plaster, plastic, foam, and wood. These pieces can be used on any structural component as well as on furniture. Ceiling medallions were especially common in the nineteenth century and are often ornate. Usually a chandelier hangs from an opening in the center of the medallion.

Wall Backing

Although the studs in corners extend 1½ inches into the room, once wall finishing materials are attached, this distance is shortened to approximately 1 inch. This allows insufficient backing for the attachment of molding—crown, chair rail, and base—especially when trim blocks are used in the corners. Figure 6.27 illustrates a method to provide structural backing for the attachment of moldings.

Backing may also be necessary around windows and doors. In most instances, trim covers the space occupied by the trimmers and king studs. Often, there is no structural support for window treatments for this reason. One solution is to run longer headers across window openings—usually to and from regularly spaced studs will provide sufficient clearance beyond window trim for the attachment of window treatments. When the installation of a longer header is not viable or when it does not provide a complete solution, extra backing may be installed. See Figure 6.28.

Columns and Pilasters

Columns define space, serving as an implied barrier, and may or may not be structural. Columns are manufactured as complete columns or they may be split so that two halves can be wrapped around a support

---

If a load-bearing wall must be removed, it can be replaced with a beam supported by columns. In this case, structural columns must be used. Decorative hollow columns can be placed over the structural unit to enhance appearance.

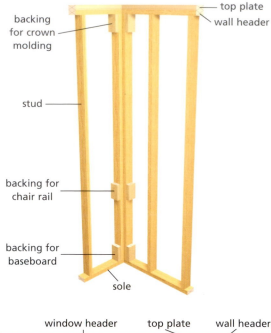

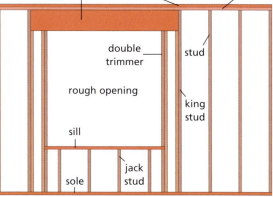

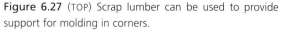

Figure 6.27 (TOP) Scrap lumber can be used to provide support for molding in corners.
Figure 6.28 (BOTTOM) Longer window headers will provide substantial support for future window treatments.

post. Manufacturers produce round and half-round hollow moldings in aluminum, resin, or wood along with a number of capital options for both round units and flat pilasters. Modern materials make it possible to produce capitals that are highly ornate and that have a hand-carved look.

A **pilaster** is a squared-off column surface that projects slightly from the wall. The base consists of a **plinth**—a flat block wider than the shaft with a band of molding between the plinth and the shaft that gives the appearance of a column base.

Trim Around Openings

Trim is needed around windows and doors to cover the space between the rough opening and the frame, and may be used around openings between rooms that have no doors or windows. The trim is called casing or **case molding**. When used for openings without windows or doors, the opening itself is termed a **cased opening**. Casing ranges from plain boards to decorative millwork. Casing is used on all four edges of window openings and around three edges of door openings. Flat corners can be treated in a variety of ways: They can be mitered or butted, a shouldered architrave can be used, or corner blocks can be used. See Figure 6.29.

Openings may also be trimmed with pilasters or engaged columns at the sides and a variety of pediments over the top. Pediments may be constructed on site, prefabricated, or purchased from a trim manufacturer.

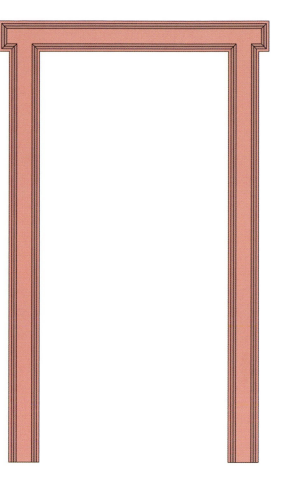

Figure 6.29 The header on a shouldered architrave extends beyond the vertical casing.

Part Three

The
Operation
of
Homes

The
Electrical
System

Chapter 7

In the past one hundred years, electricity has changed the American home more than any other single development. Electricity was not invented—it is a natural phenomenon. People observed the effects of static electricity for thousands of years, but it was not until the nineteenth century that methods were devised to control electricity and subsequently put it to practical use. While it is the electrician who is responsible for installing electrical outlets and switches and for ensuring that the electrical system complies with local codes, it is the designer who can ensure that the electrical system exceeds minimum specifications by locating extra switches and receptacles to fit client needs, identifying circuits that may supply motors, selecting appliances, specifying adequate lighting, recommending lamp types and sizes, and encouraging energy-efficient electrical use.

History of Electricity

During the nineteenth century, many advancements were made in the quest for a power source. Joseph Henry (1797–1878) improved the electromagnet[1] so it produced sufficient power for practical use. It is now used in telephones, doorbells, and other electronic devices. Michael Faraday (1791–1867) developed the process of producing a flow of electrical current by using a magnetic field. This process is now used to generate electricity.

Although Otto von Guericke demonstrated in 1650 that light could be produced by electricity and many of the principles were known, electricity was not applied to lighting before the latter part of the nineteenth century. Several individuals, from 1845 onward, developed electric lightbulbs (called **lamps**) but

Figure 7.1 Today, power lines carry electricity to homes, businesses, and commercial establishments across the world to provide light and power for a myriad of devices.

these all had at least one thing in common: They burned out quickly. The first really notable improvement in the electric lamp came in the last quarter of the century when Joseph Swan and Thomas Edison independently developed electric lamps that lasted about 150 hours—long enough to make electric lighting feasible.

The contribution of George Westinghouse in the field of electric current transmission completed the developments needed for widespread use of electricity. It was Edison, however, who built the first power plant in the United States[2]—Pearl Street Station in New York City—to furnish electricity for his lights. When this central power plant began generating electricity on September 4, 1882, it powered 800 lamps. By December of that year, Edison had 203 customers using more than 3100 lamps. By 1908, there were more than 3.5 million lights connected to Edison's power plant, in addition to the 54,000 streetlights in New York City. Twenty thousand Westinghouse lamps bathed the grounds in light at the 1893 World's Columbian Exposition in Chicago, and the American public became more fully aware of the virtues of electricity. After that, the demand increased rapidly.

Today, wires conduct electrical energy from power plants to homes, factories, and offices (see Figure 7.1), multiplying human physical capacity by performing work, lighting the environment, and carrying visual and auditory messages instantaneously. Electricity use has grown exponentially in the past 50 years. See Table 7.1. While electricity is always available in wealthy nations, it may be available only during certain hours in other areas. It is not uncommon for power to be supplied only during evening hours in developing nations. In many rural areas of the world, there is no access to electricity. More than 85,000 villages in India have no access to electrical power.[3]

Demand for electricity has increased to the point that if a power **blackout** or loss of power occurs, it shuts down everything from traffic lights to the kitchen stove, and **brownouts**—when there is insufficient pressure in electrical lines to properly operate

Table 7.1 Increase of Electricity Use in Residences in the United States

Year[a]	Percent All Dwellings With Electricity	Percent Farms With Electricity	Cents per Kilowatt-hour	Average kWh Used per Customer
1902	NA[b]		16.20	NA
1907	8.00		10.50	NA
1912	15.9		9.10	264
1917	24.3		7.52	268
1920	34.7	1.6	7.45	339
1925	53.2	3.9	7.30	396
1930	68.2	10.4	6.03	547
1935	68.0	12.6	5.01	677
1940	78.7	32.6	3.84	952
1945	85.0	48.0	3.41	1,229
1950[c]	94.0	77.7	2.88	1,845
1952	96.1	86.9	2.77	2,186
1955	98.4	94.4	2.65	2,773
1956	98.8	95.9	2.61	2,989
1960[d]			2.47	3,854
1965			2.25	4,933
1970[e]			2.10	7,066
1975			3.50	8,200
1980			5.40	8,900
1985			7.39	8,900
1990			7.83	9,500
1995			8.40	10,000
2000			8.24	10,700
2001			8.62	10,500
2002			8.46	10,900
2003			8.71	10,800

Sources: U.S. Census Bureau, "Growth of Residential Service, and Average Prices for Electric Energy: 1902 to 1970," *Historical Statistics of the United States: Colonial Times to 1970,* Part 2, Series S 108-119 (Washington, D.C.: U.S. Department of Commerce, 1975), 827. 1902–1970 Cost per kWh from U.S. Census Bureau, "Growth of Residential Service, and Average Prices for Electric Energy: 1902 to 1970," *Historical Statistics of the United States: Colonial Times to 1970,* Part 2, Series S 108-119 (Washington, D.C.: U.S. Department of Commerce, 1975), 827. 1971–2003 Cost per kWh from "Average Retail Prices of Electricity, 1960– 2003," *Annual Energy Review 2003*, Table 8.10 (Washington, D.C.: Energy Information Administration, 2003), 255. KWh used for 1975, 1985 from U.S. Census Bureau, "Electric Utilities—Generation, Sales, Revenue, and Customers: 1970 to 1988," *Statistical Abstract of the United States: 1990*, Table 971 (Washington, D.C.: U.S. Department of Commerce, 1990), 576. KWh used for 1990 from U.S. Census Bureau, "Electric Utilities—Generation, Sales, Revenue, and Customers: 1970 to 1993," *Statistical Abstract of the United States: 1995*, Table 970 (Washington, D.C.: U.S. Department of Commerce, 1995), 605. 1980, 1995, 2000 average kWh used from U.S. Census Bureau, "Electric Utilities—Generation, Sales, Revenue, and Customers: 1980 to 2002," *Statistical Abstract of the United States: 2003*, Table 922 (Washington, D.C.: U.S. Department of Commerce, 2003), 596. Number of kWh used 2000 to 2003 from "Electric Utilities—Generation, Sales, Revenue, and Customers: 1980 to 2004," *Statistical Abstract of the United States: 2006*, Table 909 (Washington, D.C.: U.S. Department of Commerce, Bureau of the Census, 2006), 604.

[a] In the 50 years from 1952 to 2002, electricity use in the average U.S. household increased by almost 500 percent, in large part due to the plethora of appliances and electronics that have been developed during that time.

[b] NA = Not available

[c] In 1950, the way data was organized was changed. Beginning in 1950, kWh cost and annual kWh usage data are not comparable with previous years.

[d] 1960 is the first year for which data from Alaska and Hawaii are included.

[e] Beginning with 1971, total kWh used are rounded to the nearest 100.

electrical devices—are almost expected during peak-demand periods. Blackouts are usually caused by a defect—damage to system components, a short circuit, or **overloads**. Hospitals, data centers, and telecommunications require emergency generators to provide power during these events.

Principles of Electricity

Electricity is a result of the movement of electrons from one atom to another within conductive materials. Atoms—the tiny particles of which all matter consists—are held together by the attraction between positively charged protons in the nucleus and negatively charged electrons that orbit the nucleus. Complete atoms have no charge because they have an equal number of protons and electrons. Electrons orbit the nucleus in concentric circles called shells. The first shell is completed with 2 electrons; subsequent shells hold up to 32 electrons, but the outer shell always has space for 8. The fewer electrons in the outer shell, the more easily those electrons can move from one atom to another. When electrons are detached from an atom, electrical equilibrium is lost and the atom becomes positively charged.

Materials in which electrons transfer easily are called **conductors**. Good conductors allow electrical energy to flow through them with little resistance. All metals are conductors, as is the human body. Most other materials are conductors to some extent, but their conductivity is rarely significant. The electrical conductivity of materials is noted in the Periodic Table of Elements. See Table 7.2 for a partial list of electrical conductors. See Figure 7.2 for a representation of the copper atom.

Atoms whose outer shells are full or almost full are resistant to the movement of electrons between atoms. **Insulators** are materials that resist the flow of electricity; they include plastic, air, ceramic, glass, and rubber.

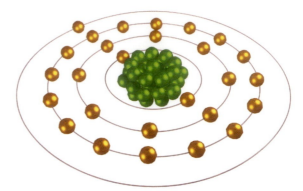

Figure 7.2 With a single electron in its outer shell, copper is an excellent conductor of electricity. Aluminum, with three electrons in its outer shell, is also sometimes used for electrical wiring.

A force must be applied to ensure that electron transfer between atoms is accomplished. In a power plant, electricity is produced by passing a conductor through a magnetic field in a generator—the force—which induces electron movement between atoms and creates an electrical **current**.

Electrons themselves are neither consumed nor destroyed in the process of producing a current but continue to seek a positive charge. Individual electrons

Table 7.2 Electrical Conductivity of Elements

Element*	Conductivity	Electrons in Outer Shell
Silver	62.9	1
Copper	60.7	1
Gold	48.8	1
Rubidium	47.8	1
Aluminum	37.7	3
Magnesium	22.4	2
Tungsten	18.2	2
Zinc	16.9	2
Nickel	14.6	2
Iron	11.2	2
Platinum	9.4	1
Mercury	1.0	2
Oxygen	—	6

Source: http://web.mit.edu/3.091/www/pt/pert7.html.

  * Silver is the best conductor of electricity, but it is too expensive to use for wiring. Copper has the best combination of conductivity and affordability.

move relatively slowly—less than an inch per second. The current is actually a result of the electrons jostling one another, much the way a row of falling dominoes transmits energy. Although the electrons do not move far, electric current travels through a wire at nearly the speed of light.

Even good conductors of electricity offer some resistance to electron flow. This resistance is measured in **ohms**.[4] The greater the resistance, the more energy is required to induce electrons to move from one atom to another. Low resistance is desirable in wires that carry current. When resistance increases, the flow of current is reduced unless there is also an increase in pressure. Resistance can be useful because its by-products include heat and light. Resistors are introduced into appliances such as hair dryers, clothes dryers, and ranges to produce heat and into lamps to produce light. The higher wattages of appliances that produce heat or light are a result of the necessity of increasing the pressure to force the current through the resistor. Fans, mixers, and other devices that use electrical current to drive a motor do not depend on resistors and therefore require less electricity.

Circuits

A **circuit** is the path taken by electric current as it travels through a conductor from the power source and back to the source. Along the way, the current may produce light, heat, or mechanical motion. A **closed circuit** is complete and may be doing work at some point during its flow, while an **open circuit** has a break—usually due to a switch that is turned off. When a switch is turned on, a piece of metal or a conducting fluid such as mercury moves into a closed position, completing the circuit. Electricity can then flow through the switch to the device controlled by it.

A **short circuit** is an open circuit that occurs when a connection is loose, a wire breaks, or the insulator around a wire becomes worn and the wire comes in contact with another conductor. Any of these conditions may result in current leaking from the circuit. Because electricity flows along the path of least resistance, if the wire that is leaking current comes in contact with any conductor or series of conductors offering a path back to the source or to the ground, the current will flow along that path. If the conductor it contacts has high resistance, the result can be overheating, which may cause a fire. If the conductor is a human body, the result is an electrical shock that can prove to be fatal. Another type of short circuit occurs when wires from two different parts of a circuit accidentally touch. The result is a surge of current, causing overheated wires and perhaps sparks, which may in turn start a fire.

Measuring Electric Current

Several units of measurement are used to describe varying aspects of an electric current. **Voltage**—measured in **volts**[5]—is the pressure provided by a power source or battery that forces electron movement through a circuit. The higher the voltage, the more ably a current flows.

The amount of flow of an electric current is called **amperage** and is measured in **amperes**. Amperage is affected by both pressure (volts) and resistance (ohms). The relationship of voltage (V), current in amperes (I), and resistance (R) is shown by the formula

$$\text{volts / amperes = resistance}$$
$$V / I = R$$

The rate at which work is done is called **power** whether the work done is mechanical or electrical. The unit of electrical power is the **watt**. The wattage of an electrical device is the rate at which the device converts electrical energy to heat, light, or motion. While power requirements for most electrical devices are given in volts, amperes, or watts, some devices are rated in either tons or horsepower. See Box 7.1 for converting horsepower or tons to watts.

Box 7.1 Electricity Ratings in Horsepower or Tons

Electric motors are often rated in horsepower (hp) rather than watts. One horsepower is equal to 746 watts. If a fan is rated at ⅓ hp, then it would consume 246 watts.

$$746 \times \text{number of horsepower} = \text{watts}$$
$$746 \times 0.33 = 246$$

Cooling equipment may be rated in tons, each of which is equal to approximately 352 watts.

With some exceptions, wattage (power) can be calculated using the following formula:

$$\text{volts (V)} \times \text{amperes (I)} = \text{power (P)}$$
$$V \times I = P$$

A watt is such a small unit that electricity consumption is commonly measured in **kilowatts**—each equal to 1000 watts. Utility companies charge customers in units of **kilowatt-hours (kWh)** each of which represents 1000 watts used for one hour. The wattage rating of any electrical apparatus can be multiplied by the number of hours the device has been used to determine the number of watts used. To convert watts to kWh, divide by 1000.

$$\text{watts} \times \text{hours} / 1000 = \text{number of kWh used}$$

When a 75-watt lamp burns for 13 hours and 20 minutes, it uses 1 kilowatt-hour of electricity.

$$75 \text{ watts} \times 13.33 \text{ hours} / 1000 = \text{kWh}$$
$$999.75 / 1000 = 1$$

Similarly, a 100-watt lamp lit for 10 hours uses 1 kWh.

$$100 \times 10 / 1000 = 1$$

To determine the cost of operating lights and appliances, multiply the number of kilowatt-hours used by the cost per kilowatt-hour.

Table 7.3 Typical Appliance Wattages

Appliance	Typical Wattage
Aquarium	50–1210
Clock radio	10
Coffeemaker	900–1200
Clothes washer	350–500
Clothes dryer	1800–5000
Dishwasher	1200–2400
Dehumidifier	785
Electric blanket (double)	100
Fans	
Ceiling	65–175
Window	55–250
Furnace	750
Whole house	240–750
Hair dryer	1200–1875
Heater (portable)	750–1500
Iron	1000–1800
Personal computer	
CPU—awake/asleep	120 / 30
Monitor—awake/asleep	150 / 30
Laptop	50
Radio (stereo)	70–400
Refrigerator (frost-free, 16 cu. ft.)	725
Television (color)	
19"	65–110
27"	113
36"	133
53"–61" Projection	170
Flat screen	120
Toaster	800–1400
Toaster oven	1225
VCR / DVD	17–21 / 20–25
Vacuum cleaner	1000–1440
Water heater (40 gallon)	4500–5500
Water pump (well)	250–1100
Waterbed heater	120–380

Source: www.eere.energy.gov/consumerinof/factsheets/ec7.html, 9/14/05.

$$\text{number of kWh} \times \text{cost per kWh} = \text{operating cost for specified period}$$

The average cost of electricity in America in 2003 was 8.71 cents per kilowatt-hour. (See Table 7.1.) It would then cost about 9 cents to operate each of the above lights for the time specified. See Table 7.3 for typical appliance wattages.

Some electronic devices have a **phantom load** or **standby loss**, which means that they consume a small amount of electricity even when turned off. Phantom loads occur in appliances that have "instant on" features, a remote, memory, or a timer. The only way to reduce this load is to disconnect the appliance from the power supply. It can be unplugged or, if the appliance is plugged into a strip outlet, the power supply to the strip can be turned off. See Table 7.4.

Some appliances do not draw electricity all of the time, even when operating. Air conditioners, water heaters, and refrigerators heat or cool to an appropriate temperature, cycle off until the temperature goes beyond acceptable limits, and then cycle on again. For example, although a refrigerator is plugged in and "operating" all the time, it typically consumes power only about a third of the time. To obtain a more accurate idea of operating costs, the percentage of "on" time should be considered. In this instance, actual operating cost is determined using the following formula. This example uses a refrigerator rated at 572 watts operating for one year.

$$\text{watts} \times (\text{hours} \times \text{percent "on" time}) /$$
$$1000 = \text{kWh}$$
$$572 \times (8760 \times 0.33) / 1000 = 1670 \text{ kWh per year}$$
$$\text{number of kWhs} \times \text{cost per kWh} = \text{total cost}$$
$$1654 \times \$0.0871 = \$145.46 \text{ annual}$$
$$\text{operating cost}$$

Producing and Distributing Electricity

Unlike other sources of energy, electricity cannot be stored easily. It must be constantly generated and transmitted as it is needed by end users. Electricity is generated at power plants located some distance from consumers—sometimes hundreds of miles. The electrical energy is transmitted over high-voltage power lines to specific areas where lower-voltage lines branch off to distribute power to individual neighborhoods.

When selecting appliances, determine phantom loads when possible. Calculating operating costs and comparing the life cost of two models may encourage clients to purchase more energy-efficient devices.

Table 7.4 Standby Power Usage

Appliance[a]	Average Standby Wattage	Annual kWh[b]	Annual cost[c]
Answering machine	3.0	26.280	2.29
Battery charger	0.9	7.884	0.69
Breadmaker	1.6	14.016	1.22
Cable box	10.8	94.608	8.24
Cordless phone	2.6	22.776	1.98
Clock radio	1.7	14.892	1.30
Computer	1.7	14.892	1.30
DVD player	4.2	36.792	3.20
Garage door opener	3.0	26.280	2.29
Internet terminal	10.6	92.856	8.09
Microwave	2.9	25.404	2.21
Phone/fax/copier	1.5	13.140	1.14
Power tool	2.0	17.520	1.53
Printer	5.0	43.800	3.81
Range	2.7	23.652	2.06
Satellite system	12.6	110.376	9.61
Security system	13.7	120.012	11.93
Stereo			
Portable	2.2	19.272	1.68
Compact	9.7	84.972	7.40
Component system	3.0	26.280	2.29
Television	5.0	43.800	3.81
TV/VCR	7.6	66.576	5.80
Vacuum cleaner	2.1	18.396	1.60
VCR	6.0	52.560	4.58
Video game	1.3	11.388	.9

Source: http://standby.lbl.gov/Data/SummaryTable.html

[a] While standby losses are minimal for individual appliances, it is estimated that these losses account for approximately 5 percent of the residential electrical power consumption in the United States (Source: http://eetd.lbl.gov/EA/Standby/DATA/International.html), about 20 percent of miscellaneous electricity use (Source: http://enduse.lbl.gov/Projects/ResMisc.html, p. 1), and about half of the energy used by electronics. When the number of units is considered, the total electricity use for standby losses is considerable. Worldwise.com estimates that standby losses for all American television sets require as much energy as a large power plant produces (Source: www.worldwise.com/energy.html, p. 2).

[b] Determined by multiplying standby loss wattage by 8760 hours then dividing by 1000.

[c] Using an average cost per kWh hour of $0.0871.

Types of Current

Static electricity is a form of **direct current (DC)**—current that flows in one direction. Batteries produce direct current, which flows from the negative pole to the positive pole through one wire and back to the negative pole through a second wire. Direct current is generated, transmitted, and used at the same voltage because there is no economically feasible method of raising and lowering voltage. Direct current is generated in voltages ranging from 6 to 550 volts. This type of current is used for automobiles, aircraft, ships, and devices that require unwavering power supplies, such as elevators and cranes.

Because the voltage in **alternating current (AC)** can be changed easily, making it possible to transport the current long distances, this type of current is used for most electrical devices. In an alternating current generator, voltage is induced at one magnetic pole in one direction at maximum value, and then midway to the opposite magnetic pole the voltage is reduced to zero, rising again to maximum value at the second pole, but in the opposite direction. The number of pairs of poles passed per second is the Hertz (Hz). In the United States and most of the Western Hemisphere, the standard number of cycles per second is 60, meaning that the pressure pushing the current through wires alternates approximately 60 times a second between zero and 170 volts. The average is usually between 110 and 120 volts. Most other countries, including those in Europe, use 50 Hz and 220 or 240 volts. Appliances are made to operate at a specific number of Hz, and the rated Hz of the appliance and the power supply must match for optimum performance. For example, a 60-Hz clock will not keep correct time when connected to a 50-Hz power supply.

Generating and Transmitting Electricity

The process of electricity generation begins with an energy source, which may be fossil fuel combustion, nuclear fission, the kinetic energy inherent in wind and water, or sunlight. This energy drives a prime mover—a gas or oil engine, a steam turbine, a windmill, a water wheel, or some other device—which in turn powers an electric generator. The generator converts mechanical power from the prime mover into electrical power, usually by revolving a magnetic field inside a coil of conductive wire (or vice versa).

A typical power plant generates electrical power at voltages up to 13,200. (See Figure 7.3 for an example of an early power plant.) Even higher voltages, however, are more efficient for transmitting electricity from the power plant to substations near the areas where power will be used. The device used to change the voltage of a current is a **transformer**. Step-up transformers increase voltage; step-down transformers decrease it. Step-up transformers are located near power plants to increase voltage before transmission —typically up to 287,500 volts. Approximately 1000 volts per mile[6] are consumed for the transmission of the current, so the greater the distance the electricity must be carried, the higher the voltage required. Intermediate step-up transformers may be necessary when the distance is long.

Figure 7.3 This is one of Thomas Edison's first electrical power plants. It is now housed in Greenfield Village in Dearborn, Michigan.

High-voltage lines carry electrical power to substations near where the power will be used. (See Figure 7.4.) At these substations, the voltage is decreased in step-down transformers and is then distributed to neighborhoods. The voltage is further stepped down by a smaller transformer before entering small-use areas or individual buildings. By the time the current reaches the typical consumer, the voltage has been reduced to 120 volts.

Current can be carried to consumers via overhead or underground wires. Overhead service is unsightly, gets in the way of tree growth, and is subject to damage by ice and windstorms. Although the installation of underground electrical service is significantly more expensive than overhead service,[7] many new subdivisions are incorporating it. Developers simply pass on the cost to those who purchase homes. Underground service may be from the street to the house or may be provided for entire neighborhoods.

Figure 7.4 At this substation near the edge of town, voltage is stepped down before it is carried to neighborhoods and other small-use areas. Voltage will be further stepped down as it reaches individual homes.

Electricity in the Home

Because electricity is potentially dangerous, local governments have recognized the need to set standards for its safe use. The **National Electrical Code (NEC)**, developed by the National Fire Protection Association, provides minimal guidelines for wiring design.[8] Although the code carries no enforcing power of its own, it is generally adopted by local authorities. Local codes may, of course, have different—usually more stringent—requirements than the national model. Insurance companies also use the NEC as a standard and may not insure buildings that do not meet these guidelines. See Box 7.2 for a summary of NEC requirements for residential electrical systems.

When electricity from the power plant reaches an individual home, it passes through a service entrance and a meter. It then flows to a distribution panel, where the current is divided into a number of branch circuits to carry electricity to different parts of the home. The end points of use are **outlets** and the switches controlling them. Outlets include not only **receptacles** to which portable appliances can be connected by plugs and cords but also light fixtures (called **luminaires**) and **hard-wired appliances**. Hard-wiring indicates that an appliance such as a fan, dishwasher, or water heater is permanently wired into the electrical system and requires no plug.

Electrical wire is encased in insulators such as vinyl or rubber to direct current along a path and preclude leakage. In the process, the insulators prevent electrical shocks to individuals handling the wire and minimize the possibility of fire that may be caused by heated wires in contact with flammable objects.

NEC guidelines are designed for safety and provide minimal services, so it is best to design electrical systems that exceed the guidelines. The number of electrical appliances continues to increase—often overtaxing electrical service. Planning for future uses will ensure that the electrical system provides good service for years to come.

Box 7.2 Summary of National Electrical Code Requirements for Residences

GENERAL-PURPOSE CIRCUITS

- A circuit designed for use with cords and plugs cannot exceed 80 percent of its rated amperage.
- Receptacles must be installed in living areas: kitchens, living rooms, dining rooms, dens, bedrooms, and other rooms in which general living activities occur.
- All newly installed receptacles must be grounded.
- No point along a wall can be more than 6 feet from a receptacle in living areas. Bathrooms are not considered living areas and need not meet these criteria.
- The maximum distance along a wall between receptacles is 12 feet.
- Any isolated wall space 24 inches wide or greater must have a receptacle.
- Fixed glass panels (as in patio doors) in exterior walls are considered wall space, although sliding panels are not.
- Fixed room dividers, including railings and counters, are considered wall space and must meet receptacle spacing requirements.
- Receptacles that are positioned more than 5 feet 6 inches from the floor do not count as required receptacles nor do receptacles located within cabinets.
- If a balcony handrail is more than 6 feet in length, a floor receptacle is required under certain circumstances.
- Circuits serving kitchens, pantries, and eating areas may not serve other spaces.
- Switches must be installed no more than 6 feet 7 inches from the floor to the center of the switch.
- Sensors may be used to control lighting outlets if they are equipped with a manual override switch.
- Luminaires must be UL listed.

- Outlet boxes designed for luminaires are permitted to support a light weighing up to 6 pounds. Outlet boxes specifically designed to support additional weight may be used for light fixtures weighing up to 23 pounds. Heavier luminaires must be supported independently.
- Only boxes specifically designed for the support of ceiling fans may serve that purpose. Other fans must be independently supported.
- The maximum temperature to which combustible materials near luminaires can be subjected is 194 degrees Fahrenheit.
- Lighting tracks may not be installed where they are concealed, where they extend through partitions, or less than 5 feet above floor level. Low-voltage track lights may be installed less than 5 feet high.

EXTERIOR RECEPTACLES

- There must be at least one exterior receptacle, but one for each 15 linear feet of wall bordering an outdoor living area is recommended.
- Exterior receptacles and those in damp locations must have a weatherproof receptacle enclosure that provides a watertight seal.
- At both the front and back of the structure, there must be a minimum of one receptacle located no more than 6 feet 6 inches above grade level. In two-family dwellings, each unit must have two exterior receptacles—one at the front and one at the back.
- The entry of a residence must be illuminated by a wall-switched luminaire.
- Exterior receptacles should be controlled by switches located inside the house or by photoelectric or timer switches.

Box 7.2 (continued)

SMALL-APPLIANCE CIRCUITS
- There can be no outdoor receptacles, hood fans, or lighting outlets on small-appliance circuits.

ALL HABITABLE ROOMS
- Each habitable room should have a minimum of two receptacles, although at least one on each wall is more convenient.
- Lighting should be provided over or beside mirrors, including full-length mirrors.
- If there is no central heating or air-conditioning system, a receptacle should be installed in each living area to accommodate a space heater or room air conditioner.
- Receptacles should be installed near spaces ideal for china cabinets, display cabinets, and other lighted furniture.
- If an overhead lighting fixture is not installed in a habitable room, at least one receptacle should be controlled by a switch so that portable lighting can be switched on or off from the entry to the room. In kitchens and bathrooms, the lighting unit itself must be controlled by the switch.

KITCHENS
- A minimum of two 20-ampere small-appliance circuits are required in the kitchen.
- All receptacles in kitchens and eating areas, with the exception of those used by refrigerators, must be on 20-ampere circuits.
- Receptacles serving countertop areas are required to be protected by a GFCI.
- Any point along a kitchen countertop must be within 2 feet of a receptacle. This is not necessary for peninsulas or islands.
- Each counter space 12 inches or more in width is required to have a receptacle. This is not required for peninsulas and islands.

- Island counters 24 inches or more in length and 12 inches or more in width require at least one receptacle.
- Isolated counters, including those on peninsulas that are 24 × 12 inches or more, require a receptacle. Isolated counters occur when a range top, sink, or other unit separates the counter from other areas.
- Receptacles serving countertop areas must be installed within 20 inches above the counter. In some instances, receptacles may be installed below the countertop. Islands and peninsulas are permitted to have receptacles located beneath them.
- Receptacles may not be installed horizontally in the countertop.
- A receptacle serving the refrigerator does not require GFCI protection unless the circuit also serves the countertop area.
- The placement of receptacles in the kitchen other than those serving a countertop is determined by wall space.

WET BARS
- Receptacles serving the countertop area and that are located within 6 feet of a sink edge must be protected by a GFCI.
- Receptacles not serving the counter area but which are within 6 feet of a sink edge do not require GFCI protection.

RECEPTACLES FOR ROOM AIR CONDITIONERS
- The receptacle installed for a 120-volt room air conditioner must be sufficiently near the window that it can be reached with a 10-foot power cord. For 240-volt air conditioners, cord length is restricted to 6 feet.

DINING ROOMS
- A dining table should be well lit. Usually this means a light is installed over the table.

(continued)

Box 7.2 (continued)

BEDROOMS

- All receptacles and luminaires in bedrooms must be protected by an AFCI.
- Once the probable bed location is established, receptacles should be installed on both sides of the bed centerline, enabling the use of clocks, lamps, radios, and electric blankets.
- There should be sufficient illumination around the bed for reading.

HALLWAYS AND STAIRS

- Each hallway and stairway must have a minimum of one luminaire. The lighting must be controlled by a switch or by a remote or central location or automatically.
- Stairs with six or more risers must have a wall switch for the luminaire at each floor. If there is an entryway at a landing, there must be an additional switch at that level.
- Hallways 10 feet or greater in length require a minimum of one receptacle. Length is measured down the center of the hall and around any corners.

CLOSETS

- Pendant luminaires and incandescent fixtures with bulbs that are partially or wholly exposed are not allowed in clothes closets.
- Surface-mounted incandescent luminaires must be a minimum of 12 inches from any storage space and surface-mounted fluorescent luminaires at least 6 inches away.
- No luminaires or receptacles are required in closets.
- No overcurrent devices such as GFCIs are allowed in clothes closets.

BATHROOMS

- There must be at least one 20-ampere circuit in a bathroom. That circuit can serve no additional areas.

- Each receptacle in a bathroom must be GFCI protected.
- Within 36 inches of the edge of each sink or lavatory in a bathroom, there must be at least one receptacle.
- A minimum of one switch-controlled luminaire is required in bathrooms.
- The bathing zone includes an area 3 feet horizontally from the tub or shower and 8 feet vertically from the bathtub rim or shower threshold. No hanging luminaires, those connected by a cord, track lighting, or suspended ceiling fans are permitted in the bathing zone. Recessed and surface-mounted luminaires are permitted.
- At least one receptacle should be located next to the mirror in a bathroom for use of shavers and hair care appliances. Lighting both sides is preferable.

GARAGES

- Receptacles in the garage must be protected by a GFCI unless designed for a specific appliance, such as a deep freezer, that would be difficult to move or located in the ceiling above 79 inches. These appliance receptacles do not count as required outlets.
- A minimum of one accessible (within 79 inches of the floor) receptacle is required in an attached garage, although its location is not determined by wall space.
- A minimum of one wall-switched lighting outlet is required in an attached garage. A light combined with a garage door opener does not meet this requirement.
- A luminaire must be located within any area that has equipment that may require servicing, such as a furnace or water heater. This luminaire may serve as the required lighting outlet.

Box 7.2 (continued)

- If a detached garage has electrical power, it must meet the requirements for an attached garage. There is no requirement, however, that a detached garage have electrical power.

BASEMENTS
- If a basement is divided into habitable rooms, each separate area (even though unfinished) must have at least one receptacle.
- At least one wall-switched luminaire is required for a basement.
- A luminaire must be located within any area that has equipment that may require servicing, such as a furnace or water heater. This luminaire may serve as the required lighting outlet.
- The lighting requirements for basement stairways are the same as those for living-level stairs.
- There must be at least one receptacle within 25 feet (and on the same level) as the heating and air-conditioning equipment.

LAUNDRIES
- At least one 20-ampere circuit is required in the laundry area. Multiple receptacles may be installed but the circuit may not serve other areas.
- The laundry areas must have at least one receptacle. A receptacle to be used by an appliance must be within 6 feet of the intended location.
- Receptacles to be used for the laundry cannot be located more than 5 feet 6 inches from the floor.
- There is no requirement for the presence of a 240-volt circuit for a clothes dryer.

UTILITY ROOMS
- A utility room must have a light fixture.

ATTICS
- Attic spaces that are not used for storage and that do not house equipment that may need servicing do not require receptacles or luminaires.
- If an attic space is used for storage or houses equipment that may need servicing, at least one light is required. The light must be capable of being controlled from the point of entry, although the control does not need to be a switch.

CRAWL SPACES
- At least one receptacle shall be located in a crawl space in which there is equipment that may need servicing. That receptacle must be located within 25 feet (and on the same level) as the equipment.
- If the crawl space is used for storage or contains equipment that may require servicing, it must have at least one light that can be controlled from the entry to the crawl space. The control does not need to be a switch.
- There must be at least one light near any equipment that may require servicing. If the light controlled at the entry illuminates the equipment area, an additional light is not necessary.

In addition to the items listed above, the National Electrical Code has a number of other requirements concerning wiring, wire size, service entrances, and other components.

Local codes, of course, may have additional requirements. Common local requirements include the following. This list is not comprehensive; none of these may be required and other requirements may be stipulated. Always check local codes when designing.

(continued)

191

Box 7.2 (continued)

- That a licensed electrician install electrical system components, including receptacles and luminaires
- Required grounding of lights and switches

- Bathroom heaters must be on a dedicated circuit.
- That large appliances such as dishwashers, refrigerators, microwave ovens, and food disposers be on dedicated circuits

Source: Adapted from National Fire Protection Association, *National Electrical Code 2002* (Quincy, MA: National Fire Protection Association, 2002).

Electrical power to residences is provided at 120 volts of pressure. As users along a power line turn on appliances, there is a slight drop in pressure in the line. Line voltage usually ranges between 110 and 120 volts, although slightly lower or higher voltages are not uncommon for short periods of time. For this reason, 120-volt service and equipment may be called 110, 120, or even 115 (the average of 110 and 120), and 240-volt service and equipment may be 220, 240, or 230. On hot summer days, the voltage may drop even more due to the number of appliances drawing power from the electric line. When this happens, a brownout may occur, causing lights to dim and heating appliances such as ranges to provide less heat.

Power may momentarily surge with a greater number of volts coming through the lines than the system can handle. These surges rarely damage most electrical components, but surge protectors are needed to shield electronic equipment, computers, modems, and other devices. Surge protectors (also called arresters or suppressors) can be installed in the distribution panel to protect the entire electrical system, but most are located on outlet strips plugged into receptacles. Surge protectors direct the power to the house ground. Lightning also causes surges of power. Lightning rods mounted on the roof have a wire that connects to the ground, but there is no guaranteed protection from lightning.

The Service Entrance

When overhead wires are used, a cable called the **service drop** carries current from the pole to the house. The service drop consists of two or three wires that lead to the **service entrance** where electricity enters the structure. If three wires enter a building, two of those each carry current at 120 volts and a specific number of amperes. Together, the two 120-volt wires provide 240-volt service for large appliances such as clothes dryers, central air conditioners, ranges, and water heaters. The third wire is a neutral wire that completes the circuit from the power plant to the home and back again. If only two wires come from the pole, one is a 120-volt wire and the second is a neutral wire providing only 120-volt service and precluding the use of 240-volt appliances.

Regardless of whether electrical service is underground or overhead, there is a main ground near the point where service enters the house. See Figure 7.5. This is usually a copper rod buried in the soil and connected to the service entrance by a wire.

The Electric Meter

The electric meter is located near the service entrance and measures the number of kilowatt-hours of electricity used. The meter is not turned back to zero each month, so two readings are needed to determine usage. The electric company subtracts the previous month's reading from the current one to determine the amount of electricity used during the billing period. In urban areas, the utility company generally reads electric meters; however, in rural areas, it is common for residents to read their own meters and report the reading each month to the utility company.

Some meters automatically transmit data back to the utility company office. See Box 7.3.

The Distribution Panel

After passing through the service entrance and the meter, the electric current is carried inside the house to the **distribution panel**.[9] The distribution panel houses a main switch and a main fuse or circuit breaker that controls the flow of current entering the structure. When the main switch is off, the service wires leading to the house are "hot" or "live," but no electricity flows through to the circuits in the house. Sometimes the main switch is located in a separate panel inside or outside the house. The NEC has

Figure 7.5 This home has underground electrical service. The **conduit** protrudes from the ground near the house, runs upward close to the wall, and connects directly to the meter, eliminating the service entrance as a separate entity. (Source: Heather Ireland-Weter)

Box 7.3 Reading an Electric Meter

The most common type of electric meter has four or five dials similar to one-handed clocks. The dials are connected by cogwheels, causing the pointers on adjacent dials to move in opposite directions. The pointer on the dial to the right makes one complete revolution before the pointer on the dial to its left moves one digit. Thus, each dial measures units ten times larger than the dial on its right. The digit read for each dial is one the pointer has passed. If the pointer appears to be exactly over a number, the dial to

the right should be consulted to see if a complete revolution has been made. The meter above reads 50573.

A second type of meter is the cyclometer. It operates much like the odometer of a car, providing a numerical readout. It is most often used in rural areas where customers read their own meters and mail the reading to the utility company. These meters result in fewer errors than the dial type when read by untrained people.

The distribution panel should be located where it is easily accessible so that the main switch can be turned off for repairs and maintenance and so that circuit breakers are accessible.

established a maximum height of 79 inches above the floor for any switch in the distribution panel. Beyond the main switch in the distribution panel, the electric current is distributed to specific paths or circuits, each providing electricity to a portion of the structure.

In addition to the wiring that divides the circuits, the distribution panel contains several safety devices. Each circuit is protected by a **fuse** or **circuit breaker**. (A distribution panel contains either fuses or circuit breakers, but not both.) Fuses and circuit breakers are rated by the number of amperes they can carry. When there is a short circuit or an overload—too many appliances in use on the circuit—the fuse or circuit breaker creates a gap in the circuit, preventing the flow of electricity. An overload or short in an individual circuit will break that circuit without shutting off power to the entire house. Fuses and circuit breakers—also called **overcurrent devices**—protect wiring from overheating. They do not protect against shocks, appliance malfunctions leading to overheating or fires, surges, or some ground faults.

Fuses

A fuse has a strip of metal inside an insulator such as glass. When too much electricity tries to flow through the fuse, the strip melts or "blows" to break the circuit. Fuses must be replaced once they have blown.

Ordinary fuses have very little time lag built into them, so they may blow easily when motor-driven appliances such as a vacuum cleaner are started. (Motors require additional current for a few seconds when they are started.) **Time-delay fuses** provide a momentary delay to allow for the start-up current required by motors. **Type S fuses** also have a time-delay feature but in addition help prevent overloads by ensuring that the proper-capacity fuse is used when a

Figure 7.6 The circuit breaker on the left is one type of protective device in the electrical system. The Edison-base fuse on the top right screws into an ordinary fuse socket, while the cartridge fuse at the bottom right is used for large-appliance circuits or the whole house.

fuse is replaced. In modern homes, fuses are used near equipment but circuit breakers are usually used in the distribution panel. See Figure 7.6.

Circuit Breakers

A circuit breaker is a switch that turns itself off automatically when too much electricity flows through it. Like time-delay fuses, circuit breakers provide a momentary delay before switching off, making them suitable for circuits to which motor-driven equipment will be connected. When the problem that caused a circuit breaker to trip has been resolved, a circuit breaker must be reset manually.

The Grounding System

The NEC requires that every home's electrical system be **grounded** to protect occupants from shock and the home from fire. The grounding system deliberately provides a path from the electrical system to the earth so any leaking current can be safely carried to the earth. If this safe path were not provided, stray current would try to reach the earth any way it could. The ground wire in each circuit is usually a bare copper wire. It does not carry current unless defective equipment is used or damaged wiring develops.

At the distribution box, the ground wires from all circuits are connected to a **buss** (or **bus**) **bar**, which is in turn connected to the main house ground. This main ground wire may be attached to a metal rod thrust into the earth, to a grounded metal cold water pipe, or both. In addition, the neutral wires from all the circuits and the neutral wire of the supply drop are also connected to the buss bar and thus to the ground. Grounding the system in this way prevents electrical current from causing injury, fire, and damage to motors when a circuit is not completed.

In order for the grounding system to be effective, it must be connected to every switch, luminaire, and receptacle. Appliances that are plugged into grounded receptacles are themselves grounded.

Ground-Fault Circuit Interrupters. Fuses, circuit breakers, and the grounding system are designed to protect wiring. Circuits do not trip until an overload is created—more than 15 or 20 amps. This is over 2500 times the amount of electricity required to fatally shock a person. **Ground-fault circuit interrupters**[10] (**GFCI**s) are designed to protect life. An individual can still be shocked by an appliance protected by a GFCI but the shock will feel more like a pinprick and will not be severe.

The NEC requires GFCI protection for newly installed receptacles in bathrooms, garages, crawl spaces, unfinished basements, countertop receptacles near a sink, and outdoor areas including porches, decks, pool areas, and outbuildings. GFCIs should not be used for circuits on which there are dryers, ranges, or ovens, because these appliances have internal grounding systems, nor on circuits where life or property will be jeopardized if the power is off. This includes deep freezers and medical equipment.

A GFCI can detect minute differences in the incoming and outgoing current flow through the hot and neutral wires of a circuit. Such a difference indicates that a fault in the grounding system is allowing current to leak out of the circuit—perhaps through a human body. If a fault as low as 0.006 amperes is de-

tected, the GFCI will break the circuit within a fraction of a second. Three types of GFCIs are available: those on circuit breakers, individual GFCI receptacles, and in-line.

GFCI circuit breakers installed in the distribution panel protect an entire circuit just as any other breaker but with the additional protection of tripping when there is a current difference anywhere in the circuit. To reset the circuit, users must switch the circuit breaker completely off and then on again. Individual GFCI receptacles have reset buttons, requiring no trip to the distribution panel to reset them. (See Figure 7.7.) When a GFCI receptacle is installed, every outlet beyond it in the circuit is protected by it but none of those in the circuit before the GFCI. In a circuit where the GFCI is in the third of eight receptacles, six receptacles are protected by the device—the GFCI receptacle and the five receptacles farther down the line from it. In-line GFCIs act as a short extension cord

Figure 7.7 This receptacle is a GFCI type, with the reset button located unobtrusively between the two outlets.

with ground-fault protection. They plug into a receptacle and then an appliance can be plugged into the in-line GFCI, protecting the appliance even if the receptacle or circuit is not protected. This type of GFCI is convenient for apartment dwellers because it can be easily removed.

Arc-Fault Circuit Interrupters. A relatively new type of circuit protection is the **arc-fault circuit interrupter (AFCI)**. Arcs are luminous discharges of electricity between conductors across an insulating medium such as air. Arcs can cause sparks and subsequent fires when there is combustible material nearby. Arcing frequently occurs and causes damage at levels too low to be detected by GFCIs. AFCIs detect this low-level activity in the circuit and trip before a fire can be started. The 2002 NEC requires that all bedroom receptacles and luminaires be protected by AFCIs.

Home Circuits

Electrical systems should be designed to meet two criteria: accessibility and capacity. Components such as switches and receptacles should be conveniently located and provided in sufficient numbers to ensure safe, easy operation. Circuits should be capable of operating at full capacity, although normal loads may not use more than 80 percent of maximum capacity. No circuit should have more than 10 outlets. Three types of circuits are used in homes: general-purpose circuits, small-appliance circuits, and special-purpose circuits.

General-Purpose Circuits

General-purpose circuits supply 120-volt power for receptacles, luminaires, and ventilating fans. They have 15-ampere capacity and a 15-ampere fuse or

---

■ Subsequent revisions of the NEC will probably require additional protection by AFCIs. It is necessary to check codes to ensure proper compliance.

circuit breaker. Since watts equals volts times amperes, a 15-ampere circuit provides up to 1800 watts.

$$\text{volts} \times \text{amperes} = \text{watts}$$
$$120 \times 15 = 1800 \text{ watts}$$

Normal load must not exceed 80 percent of capacity; hence, on this 15-ampere circuit, 1440 watts should be considered the maximum normal load.

$$\text{watts} \times \textbf{80 percent} = \textbf{normal load}$$
$$1800 \times .80 = 1440 \text{ watts}$$

The NEC requires a minimum provision of 3 watts per square foot of living area for general purposes, including lighting, although good design may dictate 4 or even 5 watts per square foot. This should be sufficient to ensure power for future electrical devices.

Small-Appliance Circuits

Small-appliance circuits also supply power at 120 volts but provide more amperage than general-purpose circuits. Appliances requiring 1000 watts or more are often used in kitchens, bathrooms, dining areas, family rooms, laundry areas, and workrooms, so these rooms need circuits that provide 20-ampere service or up to 2400 watts.

$$\text{volts} \times \text{amperes} = \text{watts}$$
$$120 \times 20 = 2400 \text{ watts}$$

The NEC requires a minimum of two 20-ampere circuits in a kitchen, one for the laundry, and at least one in a bathroom. The actual number needed in any home is determined by the number of appliances that would be operated simultaneously, the location of areas requiring them, and the number of receptacles installed on the circuits. According to the NEC, there should be no lighting fixtures on these appliance circuits.

Special-Purpose Circuits

Special-purpose circuits serve a single outlet and provide either 120 or 240 volts. Appliances such as

Figure 7.8 Plugs and receptacles for 240-volts circuits are specially designed so that amperage ratings of both must match. 240-volt receptacles will not accept 120-volt plugs nor will a 30-ampere dryer receptacle accept a 50-ampere range plug.

microwave ovens that use 1500 watts or more will be best served if they are on these dedicated circuits. In some localities, a dedicated circuit is required for room air conditioners and large appliances. Motor-driven appliances such as dishwashers, garbage disposals, refrigerators, and 120-volt room air conditioners should also be on special-purpose circuits to preclude the possibility of two motors starting simultaneously on the same circuit and tripping it.

All 240-volt circuits are special-purpose circuits and provide 30 to 60 amperes of current for appliances rated over 1650 watts. An electric range may consume up to 12,000 watts, requiring a 60-ampere circuit. A dryer rated at 5000 watts requires a 30-ampere circuit. See Figure 7.8.

Service Size

Service size, or the total number of amperes of electrical capacity required in a home, is based on the number of circuits and their capacities. The total number of amperes provided by the electrical system is stamped on the distribution box. Generally, 30- to 200-ampere service is provided. Each ampere provides approximately 240 watts of electricity. Older homes may still have 30-ampere service, which provides up to 7200 watts. This is sufficient for lighting

but very little additional service. Today, 100-ampere service is required even for small homes. That much current will operate some major appliances in addition to lighting and small appliances. However, if central air-conditioning or electric heat is used, minimum service size is 150 to 200 amperes. The demand for electrical power continues to increase, so it is important to design new service to accommodate additional requirements.

Receptacles and Switches

Circuits distribute electricity to outlets such as receptacles and luminaires, any of which can be controlled by a switch. Behind each outlet and switch is a metal or plastic box in which all wires are connected. The boxes prevent bare wires or sparks from contacting flammable materials and causing fires. Junction boxes are also used wherever a circuit branches off in two or more directions, protecting vulnerable connections.

Receptacles

Receptacles[11] supply electrical power to devices that are plugged into them. Two vertical slots in the receptacle accept the blades of a two-prong plug. One of the slots is slightly longer than the other. Certain appliances, such as some television sets, have plugs with one blade (the neutral) wider than the other. These **polarized plugs** can be inserted into a receptacle only when they are correctly oriented. This prevents reversing the hot and neutral sides of a circuit and at the same time grounds the appliance if the receptacle itself is grounded. Receptacles in older homes may have only these two slotted openings but those more recently installed have a third opening. When wired properly, these are grounded receptacles.

Grounded receptacles. Many appliances have a three-prong plug at the end of the cord, indicating that the appliance can be grounded for safety. Since the early 1960s, the NEC has required homes to have grounded receptacles that accept these three-prong plugs. Three-opening receptacles will also accept ordinary two-prong plugs found on lamps and small appliances.

If the system as a whole is properly grounded, three-prong plugs can be inserted into older two-slot receptacles by using an adapter. The adapter has a short green wire or a rigid tab that must be connected to the screw holding the receptacle's cover plate in place. If the entire electrical system is not properly grounded, the appliance plugged into the adapter will not be grounded.

Placement of receptacles. One-hundred-twenty-volt receptacles should be conveniently located in all areas of the house. The NEC requires that in living areas, no place along a wall should be more than 6 feet from a receptacle and that any isolated wall space 2 feet wide or greater should have a receptacle. See Box 7.4. For convenience, each wall of a room should have at least one 120-volt receptacle. Receptacles are usually installed so the tops are 12 inches from the floor, although the NEC only specifies maximum height above the floor for required receptacles. Receptacles located above countertops in kitchens and bathrooms are usually located at 48 inches from the floor. The receptacles in a room should not be on the same circuit as the lights.

■ Receptacles will be more accessible when furniture is placed in a room if they are located near the ends of walls.

Box 7.4 Noise and the Electrical System

Electrical outlets placed back-to-back and even boxes placed within the same stud space allow sound to travel between rooms with little attenuation. To avoid this possibility, electrical outlets should be offset—locating them in different stud spaces along common walls. The use of an **acoustic sealant** around the electrical boxes further reduces sound transmission. Acoustic sealants are nondrying, nonhardening, and form no skin; they maintain a tight seal because they remain flexible.

Split-wiring allows one half of a receptacle to be controlled by a switch while the other half remains "hot" all the time. When there are no permanent luminaires in a room, the NEC requires that at least one receptacle either be wholly operated by a switch or split-wired. This allows lights plugged into the receptacle to be activated by a wall switch, preventing the need for walking through a dark room.

Special Types of Receptacles. There are instances when a special type of receptacle will better meet requirements than a standard model. Some special receptacles are designed for safety, others for convenience. Each of these must be specified on the electrical plan.

- Receptacles placed within reach of young children present a safety hazard. Locking receptacles or covers have an additional plate that rotates a quarter turn to cover the slots when the receptacle is not in use. To insert a plug, the plate must be rotated to align the openings; when unused, the plate prevents children from poking objects into receptacles.
- Recessed receptacles are installed within the wall leaving space for a plug and cord so a clock or lighted picture can be placed flush against the wall.

- Weatherproof receptacles have hinged caps that cover the receptacles when they are not being used and form a protective "umbrella" when a plug is inserted. Other weatherproof receptacles have caps that cover a plug for a more permanent use, such as that for an electric fence.

Switches

Switches control appliances, receptacles, or luminaires. Switches are usually installed 48 inches above the floor, although those installed for children may be 36 inches from the floor and, for universal design, 24 inches. Most wall-mounted switches control overhead luminaires or split-wired receptacles, but not all. Switches are also installed to operate equipment located in hard-to-reach places: Garbage disposals are controlled by wall switches rather than from under the sink, and attic and ceiling fans by switches in a convenient location.

Location of Switches. Light switches should be installed at the latch side of the door in the same room where the light controlled by the switch is located. If the room has more than one entrance, a switch should be located at each for safety. Two types of specially wired switches—**three-way** and **four-way switches**—make it possible to control one or more luminaires from several locations. To determine whether a three- or four-way switch is needed, add the number of switch locations plus one. If there are two switches controlling the same light or lights, those switches are three-way. Four-way switches provide control from three locations. Both types look like ordinary lever-operated switches except that the handles are not marked "on" and "off." Changing the position of any one of the switches will open or close the circuit. The NEC requires that three-way switches be used for stairs so that lights can be operated from both the top and the bottom.

Types of Switches. The most common types of switches are operated by a small lever that projects

When possible, ensure that there are sufficient receptacles to meet user needs without the use of extension cords. When extension cords are necessary, the shortest possible ones should be used and then only temporarily. Cords should never be run under rugs or carpeting, as the friction caused by people walking over the cord can wear through its insulation. It is also important to use the proper size cord for the equipment. The use of heavy-duty cords on heat-producing appliances helps to prevent hot wires and the danger of fire. (To determine whether a cord is heavy duty, look at the rated wire size, not the apparent size of the insulated cord. Eighteen-gauge wire should be used only for lamps and other appliances that require little power. Sixteen- or fourteen-gauge wire are better options.)

from the wall. Quiet switches open and close with a soft click. Rocker switches have a large flat surface that can be easily tripped with the palm of the hand and are especially suitable for individuals who lack small-muscle coordination. All these switches are relatively inexpensive and last up to 20 years.

Mercury switches make no noise when operated. A small tube partially filled with liquid mercury, an excellent conductor of electricity, rotates to open or close the electrical circuit. Mercury switches are more expensive than other switches but last appreciably longer.

Equipment controlled by ordinary switches comes on and goes off immediately when the switch is operated. Delayed-action switches have an air cushion that delays electrical cutoff for 30 to 60 seconds after the lever is moved—allowing time to exit an area or cross a room before the lights go out. Delayed-action switches are useful when a bedroom light cannot be

---

To save energy, install three- and four-way switches to enable users to switch lights on and off when entering or leaving a room, regardless of the path taken.

It is difficult to quietly read in a room with an acoustic- or motion-sensing device because the lights may go off due to the lack of noise. Before specifying these switches, ensure that they will not interfere with normal client use of rooms.

operated from a switch near the bed or a garage light cannot be operated from the house.

Lights—but not appliances or receptacles—can be controlled by switches that change the flow of current and the amount of light. Incandescent lights can be easily dimmed; however, only special fluorescent fixtures have that capability.

- High-low switches provide two illumination levels. On the low setting, approximately half the electricity is used to provide 30 to 50 percent of normal light.
- Dimmer switches allow light to be adjusted to any desired level, usually by turning a dial. Modern dimmer switches interrupt the flow of current to the light, resulting in both dimmer illumination and energy savings. Dimming lights has the added advantage of increasing the life of the lamp. Dimmers produce radio-frequency interference that can be heard on other appliances on the same circuit—a radio, stereo, television, intercom, or cordless phone.

If a 60-watt lamp remains on all the time and electricity is 8.71 cents per kWh, the light uses 526 kWh per year.

$$60 \times 24 \text{ hours} \times 365 / 1000 = 526 \text{ kWh}$$

If a motion or sound sensor were installed to control the light and it operated only 5 hours per day, the light would use 110 kWh a year—a savings of $36.23.

$$60 \times 5 \text{ hours} \times 365 / 1000 = 110 \text{ kWh}$$
$$526 \text{ kWh} \times .0871 = \$45.81$$
$$110 \text{ kWh} \times .0871 = \$9.58$$
$$\$45.81 - \$9.58 = \$36.23$$

- When a switch operates a remote light or fan, users may not be aware that the device is turned on. A **pilot light switch** provides a reminder light either in or below the switch lever that glows when the circuit is closed.
- Night-light switches have a neon light in the lever that glows when the switch is off. These switches are easily located in the dark and are frequently used in bathrooms and in children's bedrooms.
- Timer switches are often used for ventilating fans or supplementary heaters in bathrooms. The switch dial can be rotated to the desired setting—usually between 5 and 60 minutes. After the user leaves the room, the appliance continues to operate for the specified time, then shuts off automatically. Timer switches that switch lights on and off once a day are commonly used for exterior lighting.
- Programmable switches turn lights on and off more than once a day and are frequently used to operate lights when users are away from home to fool potential burglars into believing someone is occupying the house.
- Motion- and acoustic-sensing devices turn lights on when they sense movement or sound. After a specified period of time, they turn the lights off. Motion-sensing devices are often used for exterior lights while acoustic-sensing devices are used for interior spaces.
- Photoelectric sensors are sensitive to light and are often used outdoors to turn lights on at dusk and off at dawn.

Low-voltage remote-control master switches make it possible to switch all lights and appliances attached to the master control from a single location. Small low-voltage wiring runs from each light to a master control box. Pilot lights indicate when a remote light is on so that the user can switch the light off from the master switch. If the coffeepot is plugged into a switched receptacle, it is even possible to make the coffee before getting out of bed.

Surface Wiring

Most of the wires carrying electricity in homes are concealed beneath floors, in ceilings, and in walls, so they must be installed during construction. Adding wires to existing service is often a difficult task, requiring that holes be made in finished surfaces and then repaired. Surface wiring simplifies the addition of receptacles and luminaires. Narrow metal or plastic channels—called **raceways**—are installed on the wall or ceiling surface. The raceways house wires leading to surface-mounted outlets. Depending on the type, the raceway either plugs into an existing receptacle or is wired into a wall box at the starting point. Adding outlets to any circuit should not result in exceeding code limits for the number of outlets on a circuit. It may be necessary to add a circuit for the new wiring.

Appliances

The number of electrical appliances in the typical American home has increased dramatically since 1940. Appliances are labor-saving devices but, at the same time, consume energy. In the past two decades, there has been a significant effort to design electrical devices that use less energy than previous models. In fact, large appliances may use as little as a third of the energy they used 20 years ago.[12]

The federal government requires that appliances using significant amounts of energy have energy usage labeled. Equipment, appliances, and lamps may have Energy Star ratings, indicating they use less energy than comparable products. The label is designed to enable consumers to identify energy-efficient products.

Information about appliances is usually provided on an inconspicuous label. This information includes the following:

- The manufacturer's name
- The voltage of the appliance. Most appliances accept a range of voltages—from 110 to 120 volts

or 220 to 240 volts. When the power fluctuates between those limits, the appliance will operate as designed.
- Either the maximum number of watts or amperes used by the appliance. If the label indicates amperage rather than watts, the number of watts used can be calculated by the formula

$$volts \times amps = watts$$

- The number of Hertz
- Whether the appliance is approved by the Underwriters Laboratories. If a UL symbol is shown on the label, the appliance has been tested by Underwriters Laboratories and has been judged safe for use. Local building codes may require that equipment installed in a home be UL listed.

Replacement of older equipment models may save significant amounts of energy. Calculations done for clients may demonstrate the desirability of new equipment. Following is an example: In 1990, the average 20.6-cubic-foot refrigerator used 955 watts; in 2001, 478 watts. (Remember, a refrigerator usually operates only a third of the time.)

$$955 \text{ watts} \times (24 \times .33) \times 365 / 1000 = kWh$$
$$955 \times 8 \times 365 = 2788.6 \text{ kWh}$$
$$2788.6 \times .0871 = \$242.61$$
$$478 \text{ watts} \times 8 \times 365 / 1000 = 1395.8$$
$$1395.8 \text{ kWh} \times .0871 = \$121.57$$
$$\$242.61 - \$121.57 = \$121.04$$

If a refrigerator lasts 20 years, total savings at current electric prices would be $1210.04—almost double the price of a new refrigerator. Of course, keeping the old refrigerator to store drinks in the garage negates any savings.

Because heat is produced as a by-product of electrical use in most appliances, some models can generate excessive heat, especially when in small, enclosed spaces. When there is insufficient space for air to circulate around appliances such as stereo systems and televisions, heat may rise to dangerous levels. When locating such appliances, ensure sufficient space for safe operation.

Smart House

Since 1976, when the first 150 personal computers were sold, computer technology has become a part of many objects, ranging from coffeepots to video games. The Internet has made it possible to connect to outside services. But the home can also be networked—making it a Smart House. With proper wiring, anything with a computer chip in it can be automatically controlled. Draperies can be opened and closed, appliances turned on or off, hot water temperatures set, and even a vehicle can be started. These tasks can be done automatically or by remote control. A user can set the controls in the coffeemaker to turn the unit on at a certain time each day or can access the controls remotely through any home network point or Internet connection (including one at the office or in a vehicle). Video monitors throughout the house and outdoors can be accessed from any point, allowing parents to monitor the activities of children,

Connecting the climate-control system and the hot water heater to the home network makes it possible for the temperatures of both air and water to be controlled automatically. Water can be heated at 7:00 a.m. to 115 degrees for showering, to 140 degrees at 7:00 p.m. for washing dishes, and to any other specific temperatures for other tasks. Connecting home lighting to the network can enable lights to come on automatically when someone enters the room and to go off when users leave. The result of automatic control can save significant amounts of energy.

check on the baby from any location, or see who has come to the door.

The home entertainment center in the Smart House is not a cabinet along one wall that houses all of the entertainment devices—DVD players, satellite TV boxes, television sets, and music CDs—but an area where all these devices throughout the home are interconnected. Because of this interconnection, the satellite TV connection can be distributed throughout the home and used where desired rather than only at one location. A DVD can be put into a player that distributes the signal to every television in the home or just to specific units. The room in which these devices are housed is different from the central wiring location.

While homes can use existing wiring to achieve some of this automation using wireless connectivity, more versatility and power can be given to the home Internet if new cables are installed. This is more economically feasible in new, rather than existing, homes. A room with a minimum area of about 32 square feet is needed to house wiring and connections. This wiring closet should be located on the main floor of the home on an exterior wall for ease of connection to incoming service feeds from cable, telephone, and satellite services. Moisture, extremes in temperature, and dust all affect the network wiring and equipment, so the room should be located where there will be minimal effects from these environmental factors. While the wiring room can be located in a basement, garage, or attic, these are not the best locations and should be avoided.

Artificial Lighting

The first electric light fixtures in homes had both gas and electric components, which could be used separately or together—necessary because the first electric bulbs were short-lived and the power supply was not always reliable.

The coming of electricity brought with it many advantages, not the least of which was the absence of smoke and odor from burning lamps. Electric bulbs were also free of fire hazards, unlike any previous light source in history. They could be operated in virtually any position—horizontal, vertical, even upside down —and they could be placed without concern for accessibility because they did not need to be snuffed or filled with oil.

The illuminative value of bulbs was gradually increased, the life of the average bulb was increased to 1000 hours, and the cost of fixtures and bulbs decreased considerably. These factors, coupled with the advantages of electricity, have made it the most common form of illumination in twenty-first-century America.

Lighting accounted for 8.8 percent of the electricity used in residences in 2001,[13] a much lower percentage than that used for climate control (26 percent) and refrigerators (14 percent).[14] But lighting was the first use of residential electricity and, if a choice had to be made, would probably be the last to go. Proper lighting serves several functions in the home: It increases safety, helps people perform tasks with greater accuracy, and prevents eyestrain.

Taking advantage of natural light by incorporating skylights, locating less frequently used spaces in areas without exterior walls, and minimizing window coverings can help reduce the energy required for artificial lighting. It is important, however, to balance the energy required for light with that needed for climate control. It may be less energy-intensive to cover windows, for example, than to cool an area that receives direct sunlight or to heat an area losing excessive heat through glass surfaces.

Natural light (see Figure 7.9) must be supplemented by artificial light for special tasks in parts of a structure located away from natural light sources and at night. Artificial light has an advantage over daylight in that it can be located exactly where it is needed. It is also an economical design tool: Lights can be used to create dramatic effects, minimize structural defects, accent desirable areas, and create moods. In addition, while natural light is not always available, artificial light is available on demand.

Planning Interior Lighting

Lighting a room is more complicated than turning on a lamp. **Reflectance**, **brightness**, and the effect of light on color all affect the quality of light in a room.

Reflectance is the percentage of light that is reflected from a surface. If a material is transparent, most of the light passes through it. Most of the light bounces off the surface of reflective materials. Light that is not reflected and that does not pass through the surface is absorbed by it.

Reflection and absorption are affected by surface texture and color. Smooth and polished surfaces are highly reflective—polished metal, satin, and mirrors are examples. Light colors also reflect light. White walls reflect approximately 90 percent of the light that strikes them, while light pink or blue walls reflect 55 to 65 percent. Brown and olive green walls reflect only 5 to 15 percent. Rough-textured surfaces

Figure 7.9 Natural light is the standard by which artificial light is measured. Light from windows, skylights, and atria is the best-quality light but is not always available.

create tiny pockets of shadow that reflect light unevenly and make it more diffuse, presenting a duller appearance.

Brightness is the intensity of light. Perceived brightness is relative: The darker the surroundings, the brighter an object appears. A certain level of brightness is desirable, but too much can cause visual discomfort. Uncomfortable levels of brightness also occur when there are sharp contrasts between light and dark areas in a room. Although equal brightness throughout a room can be monotonous, no area in a room should be more than ten times brighter than any other portion. Brightness can be controlled by covering light sources with a diffuser such as a shade.

Concentrated light, or an excessive amount emanating from the same source, results in glare. Bare lamps, clustered fixtures, lights in the line of vision, and reflective surfaces are often causes of glare. Glare can be controlled by changing the location of the light source, diffusing the light over a greater area, or redirecting the light in a different direction using reflectors.

The desirability of a lamp is partially determined by how the light affects colored objects and by the color of light it produces. Color is totally dependent on light. Most colors look different in artificial light than in daylight. The various types of artificial light also affect color perception differently, causing colors to seem to be different when in fact only the light is varied.

When colored lamps are used, light is further affected. Some of the light is absorbed by the lamp, so colored lamps produce less effective light than white or clear lamps while using the same amount of energy. When compared with a clear lamp at 100 percent light output, light output from a white lamp is 85 percent and from a blue lamp 3 percent. Colored lamps are often used for insect control: yellow lamps to keep insects away, bluish light to attract insects to insect traps.

The Color Rendering Index (CRI) uses a scale from 1 to 100 to represent how the color of an object appears under a light source as compared with daylight. The higher the CRI, the more accurately a color is rendered. A CRI of 70 is minimally acceptable indoors; a CRI of 80 or above is considered satisfactory.

The color of the light produced by an artificial lamp is indicated by its temperature (Correlated Color Temperature, or CCT), which is measured on the Kelvin (K) scale. On this scale, 3500 K is neutral, lights with a warm cast have temperatures below 3100 K, and cool-colored lights have temperatures over 4000 K. North sky light has been assigned a color temperature of 10,400 K.

Light for Different Purposes

Lighting needs for specific areas are based on the activities that take place there. Some light is needed for safety and general purposes. More concentrated light is needed for close visual activities. Light may also be decorative rather than purely functional.

General Lighting. General lighting is low-level lighting that illuminates uniformly, eliminating shadows and strong contrasts, and provides light for safety and for general household activities. The best general lighting comes from overhead and is usually built in. Although it may not provide sufficient light for close work, general light creates a comfortable visual background.

Task Lighting. Task lighting, or specific lighting, illuminates a relatively small area. The amount of light needed depends on the activities in which people are engaged. Detail work such as reading or sewing, fast-paced action such as playing Ping-Pong, and using mirrors require more light than activities such as conversation or dining. Task lighting should be sufficient to prevent eyestrain but illuminate the work area without creating glare. Task lighting in one area may simultaneously function as general lighting in another.

Accent Lighting. **Accent lighting** is designed for decorative purposes, drawing attention to focal points and creating dramatic effects. Inside the home, accent lighting can be used to highlight a sculpture, a painting, or even an interesting wall treatment. Lights can be recessed, placed behind or under important objects, or hung in view. Exterior lighting can be used for accents to illuminate trees and shrubbery, statuary, and dramatic or interesting details of the house.

Ways of Casting Light

There are a variety of placement alternatives for any type of light. Lighting designers can follow nature's example and direct light rays directly, indirectly, or semidirectly.

Direct lighting furnishes light in a small area because it shines directly toward the place where it is used, with little reflectance. For this reason, it is often used for task lighting.

Indirect lighting is usually concealed by fixtures or structural details. The light shines toward reflective surfaces, such as ceilings or walls, and is then reflected into the room, resulting in soft, relatively shadow-free light. Indirect light is used in most homes for general illumination but can be monotonous when used in this way. When used as accent lighting, indirect light can produce dramatic effects.

Semidirect lighting is a combination of direct and indirect light. A portion of the light shines directly on a surface while the remainder is directed toward a reflective surface. Many portable lamps furnish semidirect light.

Measuring light

The amount of light emitted by a source is measured in **lumens**. A candle provides 10 to 15 lumens. **Illuminance** is the amount of light that actually reaches a surface and is measured in terms of the number of lumens striking a given amount of surface area. In the English system of measurement, illuminance is measured in **footcandles**. One footcandle

equals one lumen per square foot. In the metric system, illuminance is measured in **lux** or lumens per square meter.[15] One footcandle is equal to 10.76 lux. Lighting recommendations are inexact, however, and illuminating engineers use a value of 10 lux as equivalent to one footcandle when writing recommendations. Each of the types of artificial light provides different amounts of lumens and, thus, illuminance but typically the number of lumens decreases with the usage of lamps. The desired illuminance varies according to the task and the room and is measured at the work surface, which is defined as a horizontal plane 30 inches above the floor. Even where there is no horizontal plane present above the floor and the space is empty, illuminance is still measured in this manner.

The illuminance necessary for tasks varies according to the visual difficulty of the task and the age and visual acuity of the user. The Illuminating Engineering Society of North America (IENSA) has established recommended illuminance levels for a variety of tasks. These recommendations are designed for a person between the ages of 40 and 55. Illuminance levels can be decreased for individuals under this range and

Table 7.5 Illumination Categories

Category	Visual Performance	Footcandles
	Occasional visual tasks where performance is not important	
A	Public spaces	3
	Conversation, relaxation, entertainment	
	General lighting for movement through passageways	
B	Simple orientation for short visits	5
	General lighting in residences and stairways	
	Dining	
	Some ordinary tasks such as crafts	
	Toilets and washrooms	
C	Working spaces for performance of simple visual tasks	10
	Simple sewing tasks	
	Common visual tasks where performance is important	
D	Performance of visual tasks of high contrast and large size	30
	Applying makeup	
	Shaving	
	Critical tasks such as workbench tasks and fine crafts	
	Easel work	
	Cleanup tasks	
	Laundry tasks	
	Reading music	
	Casual reading	
	Table games	
E	Performance of visual tasks of high contrast and small size or low contrast and large size	50
	Difficult tasks such as fine sewing	
	Critical tasks such as cutting in kitchens	
	Serious reading or study	
F	Performance of visual tasks of low contrast and small size	100
	Visual tasks of critical importance	
G	Performance of visual tasks near threshold	300–1000

Source: Excerpted from the *IESNA Lighting Handbook, 9th Edition,* with permission from the Illuminating Engineering Society of North America.

should be increased for individuals above this range. See Table 7.5 for recommended illumination levels and Box 7.5 for determining lighting needs.

Required Labeling

By the end of 1995, in an effort to encourage consumers to purchase more energy-efficient lamps, lamp manufacturers were required to label certain types of lamps, providing:

- Light output in lumens
- Energy used in watts
- Expected lamp life in hours

In addition, lamp packaging must carry the following message: "To save energy costs, find the bulbs with the light output you need, and then choose the one with the lowest watts."

Artificial Light Sources

Today's homes commonly use two types of interior lights: **incandescent** and **fluorescent**. Both types have characteristics that make them more or less suitable for general purposes, specific tasks, and decorative effects. **High-intensity discharge** (**HID**) lights are often used for outdoor lighting because their color

Box 7.5 Calculating Lighting Needs

The following process is used to determine lighting requirements for a specific area. This example uses a 120-square-foot room for which 50 lumens per square foot is recommended.

1. Multiply the number of square feet by the number of lumens per square foot recommended for the specific room.

area × lumens per square foot = total lumens

Example:

Room that requires 50 lumens per square foot

120 × 50 = 6000 total lumens

2. For incandescent lamps, divide the total number of lumens by 16 (the approximate efficacy of a 75-watt lamp that produces 1200 lumens).

total lumens / 16 = number of incandescent watts

Example:

6000 / 16 = 375 watts of incandescent light

3. For fluorescent lamps, divide the total lumens needed by 63.2 (the approximate efficacy of a 19-watt lamp that produces 1200 lumens).

total lumens / 63.2 = number of watts of fluorescent light

Example:

6000 / 63.2 = 95 watts

In this example, approximately 95 watts of fluorescent light would be sufficient. This is considerably less than the 375 watts required when incandescent light is used. Operating cost is also affected.

Cost of Using Incandescent Lamps 5 Hours per Day for One Year

number of watts × (hours used per day × number of days) / 1000 = kWh

375 watts × (5 × 365) / 1000 = kWh

375 × 1825 / 1000 = 684 kWh

number of kWh × cost per kWh = operating cost

684 × $0.0871 = $59.58

Cost of Using Fluorescent Lamps 5 Hours per Day for One Year

number of watts × (hours used per day × number of days) / 1000 = kWh

95 watts × (5 × 365) / 1000 = kWh

95 × 1825 / 1000 = 173 kWh

number of kWh × cost per kWh = operating cost

173 × $0.0871 = $15.07

annual savings = $44.51

rendition is generally poor. The number of lumens per watt varies considerably with lighting type. The **efficacy** or efficiency of a light source is determined by the following formula.

total number of lumens / number of
watts used = lumens per watt

See Table 7.6 for the number of lumens per watt of various light sources. Although the widespread use of fluorescent lamps would result in significant energy savings, only a small proportion of lamps used in the United States are of this type.

Depending on the manufacturer, a new 60-watt incandescent lamp yields approximately 14.2 lumens per watt. Therefore, a 60-watt lamp emits up to 852 lumens.

lumens per watt × number of watts =
total lumens

14.2 × 60 = 852 lumens

A 13-watt fluorescent lamp will furnish almost as many lumens as a 60-watt incandescent lamp.

lumens per watt × number of watts =
total lumens

61.5 × 13 = 800 lumens

If a 60-watt incandescent lamp is lit 5 hours each day when electrical power costs 8.71 cents per kilowatt-hour, the annual operating cost would be $9.54.

watts × hours / 1000 = kWh

60 × (5 × 365) / 1000

60 × 1825 / 1000 = 109.5 kWh

number of kWh × cost per kWh = total cost

109.5 × 0.0871 = $9.54

On the other hand, a 13-watt fluorescent fixture providing approximately the same amount of light would cost only $2.06 to operate for the same number of hours.

watts × hours / 1000 = kWh

13 × 1825 / 1000 = 23.7 kWh

number of kWh × cost per kWh = total cost

23.7 × 0.0871 = $2.06

Table 7.6 Typical Efficacies and Life of Lamp Types

Type of Lamp	Efficacy (Lumens/watt)	Lumens per watt*	Rated Life In Hours
Incandescent			
15 watt	110	7.3	2500
25 watt clear	215	8.6	2500
40 watt clear	480	12.0	1500
40 watt daylight	350	8.75	1500
52 watt long life	720	13.8	2500
60 watt	800	13.3	1000
60 watt soft	850	14.2	1000
67 watt long life	940	14.0	2500
75 watt	1200	16.0	750
100 watt clear	1730	17.3	750
100 watt frosted	1690	16.9	750
100 watt daylight	1270	12.7	750
200 watt clear	3980	19.9	750
300 watt clear	6200	20.1	750
Fluorescent			
18 watt	950	52.8	15,000
20 watt sunshine	875	43.8	9000
22 watt	1400	63.6	12,000
30 watt cool white	2250	75.0	18,000
32 watt	2400	75.0	12,000
Compact Fluorescent			
11 watt	600	54.5	8000
13 watt	800	61.5	8000
19 watt	1200	63.2	8000
23 watt	1600	69.6	8000

Source: Lamp packaging and promotional materials. Source for rated life: Lamp packaging.

* The type of lamp, the wattage, and whether the lamp is frosted, clear, or treated for improved color rendition, such as in daylight and cool white lamps, all affect the number of lumens per watt.

Incandescent Lamps

With a CCT between 2700 K and 3100 K and a CRI of 95 or better, incandescent lamps produce light that is slightly yellowish. This light grays blue and green objects. Incandescent light is usually produced by tungsten filaments. Electric current passes through the filament, causing it to heat up and glow. Incandescent lamps are preferred for domestic use because their warm golden light enhances skin color. The most common sizes—40, 60, 75, and 100 watts—are relatively inexpensive and can burn for 750 to 1500 hours. Life expectancy is not significantly affected by repeatedly switching the lamp on and off.

Incandescent lamps used in homes range from 7 to 350 watts. The higher the wattage, the more light produced per watt. See Table 7.7. Because less heat is produced during operation, smaller-wattage lamps last longer than higher-wattage lamps. A 40-watt lamp, for example, has a rated life of 1500 hours, while standard 75-watt and larger lamps have a rated life of 750 hours. Actual available light depreciates gradually over the life of the lamp. When the lamp burns out, it may be giving off only 85 percent of its original light.

Less than 10 percent of the energy consumed by incandescent lamps is converted to light. The other 90 percent[16] produces heat, and the need for dissipation of this heat affects the placement of incandescent luminaires. In closed spaces, improperly sized lamps may soon produce so much heat that they burn out prematurely. Therefore, lamps of lower wattage must be used even though they may not provide the desired level of illumination. Because of the high heat produced during operation, incandescent lamps will shatter from thermal shock if splashed with water. Special shatter-proof lamps are available for use in steamy or wet places.

Table 7.7 Percentage of Lamp Use in Residences

Type of Lamp*	Percent of Electricity Used for Lighting
Incandescent	
Standard	87
Halogen	3
Fluorescent	
Compact	1
Miscellaneous	9

Source: "2001 Total Lighting Technology Electricity Consumption, by Sector (10^9 kWh/year)," *Buildings Energy Databook: 5.9 Lighting.* Figures not available for metal halide or low-pressure sodium lamps.

* Most of the lamps used in residences are either incandescent or fluorescent. High-Intensity Discharge (HID) lamps are infrequently used in rural areas in exterior settings but there are fewer than half a billion HID lamps used in this way in the United States.

Specifying the most energy-efficient lamp that will function appropriately will help reduce energy costs. In many cases, the most energy-efficient lamp is fluorescent. A number of utility companies offer rebates on energy-efficient lamp purchases.

If four 100-watt lamps operating 8 hours a day were replaced with 19-watt compact fluorescent lamps (with approximately the same number of lumens), the annual savings would be $82.39 when electricity costs 8.71 cents per kWh.

$$(4 \times 100 \text{ watts}) \times 8 \text{ hours} \times 365 / 1000 = 1168 \text{ kWh}$$
$$1168 \text{ kWh} \times .0871 = \$101.73$$
$$(4 \times 19) \times 8 \text{ hours} \times 365 / 1000 = 222 \text{ kWh}$$
$$222 \times .0871 = \$19.34$$
$$\$101.73 - \$19.34 = \$82.39 \text{ savings}$$

When possible, specify larger-wattage lamps rather than multiple smaller lamps. A single 100-watt lamp (1730 lumens) yields almost twice as much light as four 25-watt lamps ($4 \times 215 = 860$ lumens).

Long-life incandescent lamps last approximately 2500 hours because they operate at cooler temperatures than ordinary lamps. For this reason, while consuming as much electricity as other incandescent lamps of the same wattage, they generate less light—often just 80 percent as much light. Long-life lamps, however, are the best choice for inaccessible fixtures such as those in high ceilings and over stairs.

Reflector lamps have an aluminum coating that permits light to shine through only a small portion of the lamp so the light can be directed to a small area.

Because incandescent lamps produce significant amounts of heat, luminaires using incandescent lamps require clearance from flammable materials. Luminaire packaging or instructions should be consulted to determine whether a fixture is appropriate for a specific location.

Because they produce less light per watt, the use of long-life lamps should be minimized.

These lamps must be kept away from flammable materials because they generate high heat. Reflector bulbs are suitable only for interior purposes. PAR (parabolic aluminized reflector) lamps offer good beam control and are suitable for exterior purposes.

Three-way lamps contain two filaments that operate separately or together to provide different levels of light. For example, when a 50/100/150-watt lamp is used, the first switch position activates the 50-watt filament; the second switch position, the 100-watt filament; and the third switch position, both filaments. Three-way lamps do not operate correctly unless the switch is designed for three settings.

Halogen lights are a type of incandescent lamp that lasts up to 3500 hours. Their color temperature is approximately 3000 K, producing a bluer light than do standard incandescent lamps, which results in a whiter appearance. Unlike incandescent lamps, the number of lumens per watt does not significantly depreciate over the life of halogen lamps. The major concern with halogen lamps is that they create more heat than other bulbs—often reaching temperatures up to 1200 degrees Fahrenheit. Such heat creates a serious fire hazard. The 1992 fire at England's Windsor Castle, which caused $90 million in damage, was caused by a halogen lamp. Low-voltage halogen lamps are not so heat-intensive.

Fluorescent Lamps

Fluorescent lamps are made of translucent glass filled with mercury and other gases: Light color varies according to the specific mixture of gases. When electricity passes through the gases, ultraviolet rays are created. These are then converted to visible light by a phosphor coating in the tube. Since the light is not produced by heat, fluorescent tubes operate at cooler temperatures than incandescent lamps. For this reason, they can be used in enclosed areas, such as in suspended ceilings and recessed areas. In addition, their cooler operating temperatures result in an effective life of approximately 12,000 to 20,000 hours, making them cost-efficient even though their initial cost is higher than incandescent lamps. Frequent switching shortens their life, so fluorescent lamps last significantly longer when they are left on for long periods.

Because about four times as many lumens per watt are produced by fluorescent lamps than by incandescent ones, smaller-wattage lamps can be used, resulting in lower operating costs. It is for this reason that most commercial, industrial, and institutional lighting is fluorescent.

Three types of fluorescent lamps are available: standard, deluxe, and rare earth. Standard fluorescent lamps produce a relatively "cool" illumination due to the lack of red and yellow light rays. For this reason, they tend to distort colors and are not flattering to skin tones. Deluxe lamps improve color rendition but produce fewer lumens per watt than do standard lamps. New-generation fluorescents use rare-earth phosphors that result in even better color rendition and higher efficacy. The industry uses an RE followed by a number to designate these rare-earth lamps. The number indicates both color rendition and color temperature. For example, a lamp labeled RE830 has a color rendition index in the 80s and a color temperature of 3000 K. Pink, green, yellow, and other colored fluorescents can be used to create dramatic decorative effects. Fluorescent lamps have a CRI between 49 and 92 depending on the type, with a CCT ranging from 3000 K to 5000 K. Germ-killing fluorescent lamps and those that stimulate plant growth are also available.

All fluorescent lamps require a ballast in order to operate. Magnetic ballasts are the least expensive but produce the flicker and buzz associated with standard fluorescent lamps. Translucent shades or panels mini-

Fluorescent lamps containing mercury must be properly disposed of. Mercury is highly toxic and builds up in the tissues of living organisms.

Figure 7.10 These CFLs have an integral ballast. The three on the left are designed to fit a standard Edison-base socket while the one on the right is a pin-base lamp.

mize this effect and at the same time further diffuse the light. More modern electronic ballasts reduce both flicker and noise and increase the energy-efficiency of the lamp.

Compact fluorescent lamps (CFLs) (see Figure 7.10) are designed to fit ordinary fixtures. Some have integral ballasts and screw into typical light sockets; others have pins and fit into ballasts that are either a part of a light fixture or are screwed into a socket. Pin-based CFLs are less expensive than CFLs that have an integral ballast. Some are shaped of convoluted tubes to make them approximately the size of incandescent lamps although not all sizes will fit some fixtures. The flicker and hum associated with tubular fluorescent lights is absent in CFLs.

High-Intensity Discharge Lights

High-intensity discharge lights include mercury vapor, metal halide, and high-pressure sodium lamps. Low-intensity sodium lamps are classified as miscellaneous-discharge sources but share most of the characteristics of HID lights. These lamps produce light by sending an arc through a gas-filled tube. HID lamps are small but have high pressures inside them. A common feature of all four types of lamps is that once they are turned off (or the power is interrupted), they must cool off before being restarted. Although some low-pressure sodium lamps will restart almost immediately, others require more time. High-pressure sodium lamps require a cooling period of about a minute, mercury vapor about 3 to 5 minutes, and metal halide

Specify fluorescent fixtures in garages, laundries, and kitchens when possible to decrease energy requirements. Even changing a 4-watt incandescent night-light to a 1.5-watt mini fluorescent or electron luminescent lamp can save energy.

Magnetic ballasts require more energy for operation: The ballast on an 80-watt lamp may use an additional 16 watts of power. When specifying fluorescent lamps, select more energy-efficient electronic ballasts.

The use of compact fluorescent lamps (CFLs) helps to conserve energy while maintaining desirable light levels. Replacing a single 75-watt incandescent lamp (800 lumens) with a 13-watt CFL (800 lumens) saves approximately 550 kWh over the life of the CFL. In a coal-fired power plant, it requires about 1 pound of coal to produce one kWh. Replacing the lamp, then, conserves coal, reduces the amount of carbon dioxide released by a coal-powered electric plant by 2 pounds, and reduces the heat produced in a room (influencing the amount of cooling required). Both foreign and American governments are encouraging the use of CFLs to decrease total energy consumption. ❀

15 to 20 minutes. HID lamps are commonly used in rural areas and outside commercial establishments as security lights. They are ideal for mounting in high places because they have a long life expectancy—an average of 18,000 hours. When mercury vapor, metal halide, and sodium lamps are broken, they may still continue to operate. Broken lamps should be removed to prevent harmful ultraviolet light that may cause damage to eyesight. The major difference in the

In order to function properly, fluorescent lamps require temperatures of 50 degrees Fahrenheit or greater. Special fixtures can be installed to use fluorescent lamps in unheated areas such as garages or basements.

appearance of the light produced by these lamps is in color.

- Mercury-vapor lamps emit a blue-green color that enhances landscaping, but their strobe effect can be objectionable. Their poor color rendition (22–52 CRI) results in blues that appear purple and in ghostly skin tones.
- Metal halide lamps produce a slightly blue light, although some newer lamps may provide good color rendition. CRIs for metal halide lamps range from 65 to 92. These lamps are frequently used for lighting sports events because the light color matches that of television cameras. The expected life of metal halide lamps is affected by the position of the lamp. Metal halide lamps are significantly affected by the number of hours they are left on each time they are started, and they are designed to be operated in a vertical position.
- High-pressure sodium lamps operate at extremely high temperatures and produce a yellow light that has a poor color temperature—around 2100 K—and often a poor CRI—between 21 and 80. Even higher-pressure sodium lamps have a color temperature of about 2700 K—more like incandescent—and provide better color rendition. High-pressure sodium lamps are often used for street and area lighting outdoors.
- Low-pressure sodium lamps produce yellow light with a CRI between 0 and 18, making everything appear gray except some shades of yellow. They are used for exterior lighting where color rendition is not important and are especially good where black-and-white surveillance systems are used.

Neon and Cold Cathode Lamps

Neon and cold cathode lamps are made of glass tubes that can be formed into an unlimited number of shapes. Cold cathode lamps offer several shades of white and a limited number of colors, but neon lamps can be made in a large variety of colors. The color is dependent on the type of gas used inside the tube.

Both of these types of lamps require a transformer for use but that transformer is often a part of the lamp itself. Decorative neon lamps in a number of shapes and colors are readily available for use in standard luminaires—usually portable lamps.

Other Types of Lighting

Two types of light are becoming increasingly feasible for use in residences: **fiber optics** and light-emitting diodes (LEDs). Fiber optics use glass or plastic fibers to transmit light from a remote source—usually a halogen or metal halide lamp, although LEDs may also be used. Each fiber is clad with a material that reflects light, resulting in total reflection of the light in a zigzag pattern along the length of the fiber. A third layer protects the fibers from damage and moisture.

Light is emitted at the end of the fiber, where there may or may not be a fixture. Fiber-optic systems can filter out infrared and ultraviolet wavelengths and require no wiring other than a connection at the light source. Fiber optics are being used in commercial settings with good results. In residences, fiber optics are used in some lamps and decorative lighting, but rarely for other purposes.

LEDs convert electricity to light without generating much heat. Colored LEDs—green, red, and yellow—were produced in the early 1990s. Watches, clocks, and other devices use LEDs to provide points of light. At present, LEDs can produce white light at the rate of about 24 lumens per watt. Manufacturers are concentrating on producing LEDs that will be competitive with fluorescent lamps in the number of lumens per watt. LEDs have a life of 50,000 hours or more and are very tough but currently are not economical enough for residential use.

Lighting Installation

Planning for lighting is often done haphazardly, but good planning that considers lighting principles, fixture type, and functionality can result in attractive, comfortable, and healthful homes. A wide variety of lighting fixtures and designs can be used to fulfill lighting requirements and create special effects. Luminaires can be stationary or portable, they can be attached to a surface or be recessed beneath it, and they can be completely visible or hidden behind structural elements.

Luminaires

One of the most popular lighting choices is a **surface-mounted ceiling luminaire** designed to supply general lighting. These fixtures are usually shielded with glass or plastic diffusers, spreading light over a large area and reflecting some from the ceiling.

Surface-mounted wall luminaires share the

Figure 7.11 A chandelier is a pendant luminaire that uses a number of low-wattage lamps to reduce glare, permitting light to diffuse in all directions.

Wall fixtures should be located approximately 66 inches from the floor and far enough from corners to prevent the heat from the light from creating hot spots.

characteristics of surface-mounted ceiling fixtures but are usually smaller and are not expected to diffuse light over as large an area. Wall-mounted luminaires, such as sconces, usually include a shade or a glass diffuser, and both the luminaire and the shade are visible from the room. Wall luminaires can also be a part of special lighting designs in which the luminaire is entirely concealed.

Pendant luminaires are those that are suspended from a ceiling mount or chain. Chandeliers, the most common form of pendant lighting, serve as decorative focal points and provide low-level general lighting. See Figure 7.11.

Drop luminaires are pendant luminaires that can be adjusted to any height. These lights serve as general lighting when located near the ceiling but can be pulled down for task lighting. Most frequently, drop luminaires have an opaque shade at the top so they do not lose light upward, while a diffusing shade at the bottom prevents their becoming a source of glare.

Downlights are tubular fixtures that surround lamps on all sides except the bottom, preventing light from being diffused in all directions. A reflective surface on the interior of the luminaire increases the amount of light that is directed downward. Downlights concentrate light in a small area, so they are most frequently used either for task lighting or as accent lighting. Several downlights used together, however, can function as general lighting. See Figure 7.12.

Downlights can be recessed or surface-mounted. One way to install surface-mounted downlights is as **track lighting**, which consists of a track or channel into which the lights are placed. The position of the

Chandeliers can be heavy and it is important to ensure that adequate support exists before specifying them.

Figure 7.12 This kitchen has downlights in the ceiling, pendant lights over the island, under-counter lights, and cabinet (furniture) lighting.

lights along the track can easily be altered, as can the direction in which individual lights are aimed, providing flexibility.

Downlights can be used to create interesting effects. Several located close to a wall can not only supply general lighting but also emphasize the texture of the wall surface and create a scalloped pattern of light. When a more even illumination is desired, a special type of downlight, called a **wall washer**, can be used. Wall washers have an angled reflective surface inside the canister that causes the light shining on the wall to be diffused slightly upward as well as downward, washing the entire wall with light and eliminating the scalloped pattern of ordinary downlights.

Luminous panels are a form of recessed lighting used in walls, ceilings (see Figure 7.13), and other locations. The luminaire is concealed by a glass or plastic panel that diffuses the light. A luminous panel constructed of sturdier materials can be used in a floor for special effects. Used in walls, luminous panels can make narrow areas appear larger.

Special Lighting Designs

Lighting design depends not only on the type of luminaire but where and how it is used. Luminaires can be concealed in a trough or behind a bracket, placed on the underside of cabinets or other surfaces, and even hidden in furniture.

Cove lighting consists of lights placed in a trough several inches beneath the ceiling, where fluorescent tubes are usually used. Light is directed upward to reflect from the ceiling, creating the illusion of added height in the room.

Cornice lighting is also concealed behind structural features near the ceiling but shines downward. Cornice lighting can be used for an entire wall or over a window or door, supplying direct light for a wall or to accent window treatments.

Valance lighting is used over windows with the light source concealed by structural features or by fabric on a rod or frame. Light is directed both upward for indirect light and downward for direct light.

Wall bracket lighting is similar to valance lighting but it can be located anywhere in a room. A series of lights are mounted on the wall and hidden by a continuous bracket. Light can be directed upward, downward, or both. Wall bracket lighting is used effectively as accent lighting over pictures. Over a bed, wall bracket lighting can provide task lighting for reading.

Soffit lighting is direct overhead light recessed in or attached to a **soffit**, the underside of a cabinet or other structural element. In kitchens, for example, downlights or luminous panels may be recessed beneath upper cabinets to provide task lighting for the countertops beneath. Soffit lighting is also effective in laundry areas, bathrooms, and workshops.

Furniture lighting is usually used as accent lighting, although general lighting is provided as well.

Figure 7.14 Portable lamps usually have a shade that permits the light to shine upward and downward, with some filtered through the shade itself. This semidirect lighting creates soft illumination without glare and provides both general and task lighting.

Lights can be installed in bookcases, in cabinets with glass doors and shelves, and in wall niches. When used in these areas, the light is generally directed toward the back. Lights can even be placed around the bottoms of chairs and sofas to create the illusion of floating seating and under tabletops fitted with luminous panels.

Portable Lighting

Portable lamps of all types and sizes provide supplementary light where it is needed. They are the most flexible of all lighting types because they can be moved easily. Some portable lamps stand on the floor; others are placed on tables or other furniture. See Figure 7.14.

Canister lights can be set on the floor to direct light upward. These uplights are used for accent lighting, although general lighting is also provided. Uplights are usually hidden from view behind plants, sculpture, or furniture.

Figure 7.13 Because of the enclosed nature of luminous panels, cool-burning fluorescent lamps are often used.

Communication Devices

While building codes do not regulate the location of telephones in residences, good planning includes providing for telephone access in each habitable sleeping room as well as in living areas. Although telephones can be permanently wired, more commonly telephone jacks are installed that permit easy installation and removal of the telephone itself. Since telephone systems use electrical current, it is not a good idea to locate telephones near locations where water is used. Telephone jacks should be located to provide quiet and privacy for conversations and, in bedrooms, ease of using the telephone in a darkened room. There should be at least one telephone access in an appropriate space for casual use by guests. This location should be accessible without going into or through private areas of the residence.

An intercom system facilitates communication between rooms in a structure. The master unit may include a radio and/or a CD player so that music can be broadcast to one or more remote units throughout the building. Interior remote units allow for two-way conversations—to another remote or only to the master. Door speakers are designed for wet areas and allow occupants to converse with people outside. Door units have no volume control. A chime module that broadcasts the doorbell to the entire system allows the doorbell to be heard at every location. Both of these types of communication systems use low-voltage wiring.

Electronic Security Systems

In recent years, increasing concern with high crime rates has prompted many households to replace the family dog with electronic security systems. The simplest and most inexpensive type of alarm is a self-contained unit that combines a power source, intrusion sensor, and alarm. One type is mounted on the inside of a door and sounds an alarm when the attached door chain is pulled taut, as when someone tries to enter. Another self-contained alarm is a compact unit that detects motion using ultrasonic waves. The unit sounds a horn and turns on a lamp if someone moves through the room in which it is placed. Self-contained alarms are easily installed but also easy for an intruder to locate and disable.

More complex, but more effective, are central alarm systems. Several sensors at various locations in the house are wired to a central control panel, which is often placed in the basement. This type of system can be used to sound an alarm in a police station or private security company instead of, or in addition to, the home itself. An alarm can also sound outside as well as inside the house, alerting neighbors and police. Fire alarms, smoke detectors, flood sensors, and emergency call buttons may be included in central alarm systems.

Unlike self-contained units, central systems have alarms and control panels widely separated from each other and from the intrusion sensor: An intruder cannot easily track down the sound of the alarm to a nearby "off" switch. In many cases, a central system can be designed to trigger the alarm when any of the wires in the system are cut. For the convenience of residents, central systems can be disarmed by switches at the entrances and bypass switches at windows.

A variety of sensing devices can be connected to a central alarm system. The most thorough systems use a combination of types to cover all entrance and exit points and to detect any intruder who gets inside the house. Perimeter sensors can be magnetic, push-button, or mercury switches that open or close a circuit if the door or window is opened. For sliding glass doors or fixed picture windows, strips of metallic tape can be placed on the glass so that the alarm sounds if the glass is broken. Just inside entrances, pressure-sensitive floor mats can sound an alarm when stepped on. One type of system can detect changes in air pressure caused by opening a door or window. An intruder who is already in the house can be detected by motion sensors, which may be heat-sensitive or use infrared or ultrasonic waves.

Unless very valuable items are kept at home, electronic security systems may present too many problems for most families. Although most types of systems have adjustable sensitivity, false alarms are frequent. Perimeter systems must be disarmed before family members can enter during the day. At night, motion sensors may set off an alarm when a pet roams through the house or when a family member goes for a midnight snack. If electric power is interrupted, systems without auxiliary battery power are useless.

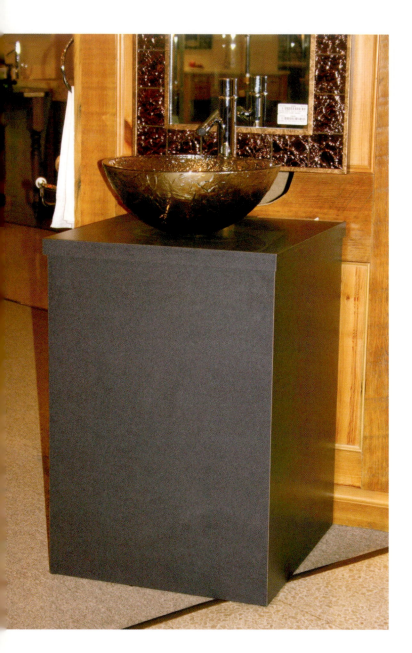

The
Plumbing
System

Chapter 8

Technically, plumbing systems include both water and gas lines, but it is water with which this chapter is concerned. Much of the plumbing system and the processes involved in obtaining, distributing, and treating water and sewage are hidden. The water source may be miles from the cities where it is used, and pipes run beneath the earth to homes and sewage-treatment plants and through walls and floors inside of homes. Sewage-treatment facilities are located where their appearance does not offend. Safe and efficient plumbing systems are attributable to these hidden parts of the system.

Designers need to be familiar with plumbing systems not only to communicate with plumbing contractors but to specify appropriate fixtures, fittings, and water-treatment devices such as water heaters

Figure 8.1 Approximately 40 percent of the water used in the United States is for irrigation. Brita reports that it requires approximately 1700 gallons of water to produce the food required by an American each day (http://ga.water.usgs.gov/edu/qausage.html, p. 1 and www.brita.com).

and softeners. Recommendations to clients may include the use of rainwater, recycled water, and water-efficient appliances. See the appendix for plumbing and sanitary plans.

Uses of Water

In addition to the water required to maintain homeostasis in the human body, humans use water in a variety of other ways:

- Water is necessary for the production, preparation, and cooking of food. See Figure 8.1.
- Sprinklers are used to water lawns.
- Water is used for cleaning utensils, surfaces such as walls and floors, and for washing clothing, vehicles, and other products.
- Bathing requires copious amounts of both hot and cold water.
- Disposal of both food and human waste products is facilitated by the use of water.
- Water is necessary for fire-suppression devices, including sprinkler systems.

- Water is used for ceremonial purposes and plays a role in many of the world's religions.
- Water is used for recreation—boating, swimming, fishing—often contributing to the pollution of reservoir areas.
- Water is used during manufacturing processes and for the generation of electricity.
- Water may be used for cooling. Some amusement parks spray a mist of water in areas where people are waiting, children play in sprinklers, and convection currents provide cooling around bodies of water. See Figure 8.2.
- Water is used for waterfalls, fountains, and aquariums.

Figure 8.2 In arid areas, narrow channels help to minimize water loss due to evaporation, although the evaporation that does occur provides cooling. At the same time, the water provides beauty and serenity to the garden.

Water Supplies

The amount of water on planet Earth is relatively static: Its form changes from ice to liquid to vapor, but the amount does not change significantly. Figure 8.3 shows one natural source of water. Water is so essential to sustain life that its availability has been a major determinant in the siting of human settlements and a growth-limiting factor. Ancient cities developed along natural watercourses and around springs and lakes. See Figure 8.4. A number of Greek cities, and even Rome itself, were located near natural springs. Entire civilizations developed along major rivers: the Indus in India, the Nile in Egypt, the Yellow in China, and the Tigris-Euphrates in Mesopotamia. Often, entire cities or civilizations were dependent on a single water supply. In Egypt, the Nile was the only natural source of water for the entire nation. Early wells—although shallow by modern standards—made it feasible for people to live in places farther from natural sources and provided supplementary sources in other areas.

Availability of Water

As populations grew and water supplies became inadequate or polluted, ancient cities found other ways to provide water to their citizens. By 2900 B.C., the water supply for Mohenjo-daro[1] was conducted from reservoirs through brick channels into the city. In ancient Assyria,[2] Greece,[3] and Rome,[4] **aqueducts** channeled water from distant sources.[5] Modern cities often store water in remote reservoirs and employ this ancient principle to transport water to their citizens.

Where supplies are limited, individuals may devise methods of providing water to ensure adequate reserves for their own use. On the island of Bermuda, there is no natural freshwater source. Rainwater is collected in reservoirs (called *lenses*) and houses have roofs designed to catch and drain water into private **cisterns**.[6] Although some individuals have wells, most

Figure 8.3 (TOP) More than 92 percent of the total volume of water on Earth is seawater and more than 2 percent is frozen in glaciers and polar ice caps. Most of the remaining water is atmospheric moisture, in the bodies of living organisms, and in inaccessible underground locations. Only about 1 percent of Earth's water supply is actually available for consumption (www.nps.gov/rivers/waterfacts.html, p. 1 and www.pbs.org/now/science/unwater.html, p. 2).

Figure 8.4 (BOTTOM) Cities have developed along most of the world's rivers not only because there is a reliable water supply but because goods can be more easily transported along waterways than overland. The city of Suzhou, China, was established along the Yangtze River in 514 B.C. and thrives today.

are controlled by the government. Well water in Bermuda is unsafe and requires treatment, although private citizens may use well water for flushing wastes, for bathing, and for doing laundry. In the United States, the annual per capita water usage is 45,977 gallons, while the annual per capita water usage in the world is 16,555 gallons.[7] In developing countries, the average distance a person must walk to obtain water is 3.7 miles[8]—and the water may not be clean.

Water Quality

It is not simply the presence of water that is critical but its quality as well. Water purity is at least implied when water is supplied by a municipal source. For those with independent systems such as wells, springs, and cisterns, standards are prescribed by health officials to ensure safety. Historically, if water supplies became polluted, dwindled to the point where they were no longer sufficient to meet needs, or were captured and controlled by others, people were forced to move or to surrender their rights. Poisoning the water supply of an enemy was an accepted warfare technique during ancient times, and there is concern in modern cities about this same technique being used by terrorists. Ancient city walls often encompassed either the water supply itself or entrances to underground sources to prevent the capture or pollution of its water by enemies. At Mycenae, city walls were expanded in the late thirteenth century B.C. to include the entrance to the major water supply, located 59 feet underground.

At an early time, people found that the disposal of wastes was facilitated by water, but rarely did cultures associate pollution of the water supply with disease until the scientific developments of the nineteenth century. Cholera and typhoid, both diseases carried by unsafe water, are still endemic in some areas of the world. In 1861, Queen Victoria's husband, Prince Albert, was the victim of typhoid, and their son, Albert Edward, Prince of Wales (the future Edward VII), nearly lost his life[9] to the same malady.

The development of modern sewage treatment has helped to alleviate the problem of pollution, although in much of the industrialized world, water supplies are polluted for at least short periods of time by industrial wastes or inadequate sewage treatment. Clean drinking water is almost always readily available to Americans. Short-term boil orders may be implemented when a public water supply has been found to harbor contaminants, and periodic rationing may be imposed to ensure that all will have adequate water supplies to meet basic needs during periods of drought.

In less-developed areas, water supplies may be more critical and more polluted. The 2003 International Year of Freshwater report published by the United Nations estimates that 1.1 billion people do not have safe drinking water, that 80 percent of disease in developing countries is the result of unsafe water and sanitation, and that up to 6,000 children die each day due to unsafe water or poor sanitation conditions.[10] The report also highlights the abundance of water in technologically sophisticated cultures, indicating that the amount of water individuals in developing nations have daily for drinking, cooking, and cleaning is about the same amount as is used when a toilet is flushed.[11]

Sources of Water

In the United States, the average indoor daily water use per person is about 74 gallons.[12] When outdoor uses such as watering lawns and gardens and filling swimming pools and hot tubs are added, this amount rises significantly. See Table 8.1. The water people use comes from three sources—rainfall, surface lakes and streams, and underground aquifers, wells, and springs.

Rainfall

Typically, people depend on the water source most readily available to them. Although in Bermuda that source is rainfall, that is rarely the case in the United

Table 8.1 Daily Indoor Water Use per Person in the United States in Gallons

Use	Without Water-Saving Features	With Water-Saving Features*
Showers	12.6	10.0
Washing clothes	15.1	10.6
Dishwashing	1.0	1.0
Toilets	20.1	9.6
Baths	1.2	1.2
Leaks	10.0	5.0
Faucets	11.1	10.8
Other uses	1.5	1.5
Total	72.6	49.7

Source: American Water Works Association Web site, www.awwa .org. Note: This chart shows only indoor water usage. The AWWA estimates that 50 to 70 percent of the water used in residences is used outdoors.

* By installing water-saving fixtures and fittings and correcting leaky ones, Americans could decrease water usage significantly, conserving not only water but financial resources as well.

States. Individual users in rural areas may catch rainwater and roof drainage in cisterns to use as their major water supply or to supplement public supplies. Rainwater is unreliable and often contains contaminants from the air, requiring that it be treated prior to human consumption.

Surface Water

Approximately 85 percent of water used in the United States is provided by public systems.[13] Public water supplies are drawn from lakes and rivers or from underground sources. More than 79 percent of the water used in the United States is surface water.[14] Public water systems using surface supplies generally store water in reservoirs prior to treatment and distribution, sometimes creating artificial lakes by damming rivers. See Figure 8.5. When water is needed, it

Figure 8.5 This dam holds back water in a lake that is used for recreation. The water is also used to generate electricity.

Individuals can improve the use of rainwater in their homes, which subsequently decreases the amount of water used from water supply systems and conserves freshwater supplies. Individuals, however, must pay for the additional systems needed to use rainwater. Most of the rain that falls in urban areas drains away.

- Limiting the amount of concrete and asphalt-covered surface can increase the amount of rainfall that enters the water table.
- Berms only a few inches high around lawns help retain rainwater until it has a chance to soak into the soil, reducing the amount of water required for watering lawns.
- Although rainwater may contain contaminants, cisterns can be built to collect rainwater, which can then be used for flushing, washing, and watering lawns.

---

is drawn from the reservoir and treated. New York City depends on reservoirs in the Catskills for much of its water supply.

Underground Water

Surface water may not be located in rural areas or sufficiently near small towns to be considered a major water source, nor may these areas have the financial resources to treat water prior to distribution. Large municipal areas may use some groundwater, but it is in small towns and rural areas that the largest percentage of wells is located. About 21 percent of the water used in the United States comes from underground sources. Wells must reach the **water table**, or the depth at which underground water supplies begin. The water table rises and falls according to the

---

If collecting rainwater is a priority, individuals may desire a steeply pitched roof because rainwater draining from steep roofs has fewer contaminants than water drained from lower-pitched roofs.

---

amount of rainfall and varies significantly from one area to another.

Wells. Early **wells** and those in developing nations today are typically dug by hand at topographical low points to minimize the distance to the water table. Water enters wells through the bottom. Wells are considered shallow if they are 25 feet or less in depth and their water source is from a layer of water-bearing rocks located above the first layer of impermeable material. When the water table is less than 10 feet below the surface, water may not have filtered far enough to be rid of impurities. Shallow wells are also subject to surface contamination and subsurface seepage, may not yield water suitable for drinking, and often dry up during prolonged dry periods or when they are overused.

Deep wells sunk below a layer of impermeable material may reach **aquifers** (water-bearing layers of rock, sand, or gravel) that cross hundreds of miles, providing water that is more reliable and safer than surface water. Rainwater that reaches the aquifers has been filtered through hundreds of feet of soil, gravel, sand, and sandstone, removing most bacteria and contaminants. For this reason, no pretreatment reservoirs are necessary when groundwater sources are used. In fact, water from underground supplies may require little purification other than final treatment processes in municipalities and often may be used without treatment by individual well owners. Digging wells makes it possible for individuals to possess safe water supplies without depending on municipal systems. For people who live in rural areas, this is often the only viable option.

Modern wells are narrow and closed, preventing surface contamination. The upper part of these wells is cased in pipe that extends above the surface, forming a stand pipe. Unless it becomes cracked or rusts through, this **casing** prevents both surface and subsurface water from entering the well. The casing must be sufficiently deep to ensure that water entering below it is pure, and it must be sufficiently strong to

Figure 8.6 In areas where there is no electricity, hand pumps are still used to force water through pipes to the surface.

Figure 8.7 Windmills are most often used to pump water to feed livestock or for other agricultural purposes. (Source: Heather Ireland-Weter)

bacterial and chemical content to ensure water safety prior to the first use of the well.

Well water is almost always acidic because it absorbs carbon dioxide from organic materials through which it passes. This acidic pH results in the corrosion of metals with which the water comes into contact—including well parts, the pump, storage tanks, and water heaters. Well casings and pipes made of PVC (polyvinyl chloride) are not affected. Because the water filters through the ground, well water also contains dissolved minerals such as iron, magnesium, calcium, sulfur, copper, lead, and arsenic.[16] While most of these minerals are harmless, their presence affects the hardness of the water.

A pipe located inside the casing and that has one end in the water provides the channel for moving water. The power to pump the water may be manual, wind, or electrical. See Figures 8.6 and 8.7.

prevent the sides of the well from caving in. A concrete collar serves the same purpose but in this case, it is important that the well opening be covered to keep out rain, runoff, and other water that has not been filtered through soil.

The International Plumbing Code[15] stipulates that the distance between wells and sewer lines be a minimum of 10 feet; between wells and septic tanks, a minimum of 25 feet; and between a water line and a sewer line, a minimum of 5 feet, with a few exceptions. Distances are longer and locally specified if there is limestone or shale. Local codes specify minimum distances between wells and septic tanks, sewer components, and property lines to assure that seepage from sewage does not penetrate wells. Codes may also require that water samples be checked for

When water is supplied by a well, it may be necessary to provide a water-softening device.

Electric pumps provide sufficient pressure for water use but intermediate pressurized storage tanks are generally used to store 40 to 50 gallons of water. Pressure in the tank moves the water through the system, making it unnecessary for the electric pump to cycle on every time a toilet is flushed or water is run from a faucet. After leaving the storage tank, the water can be filtered or treated with chlorine if desired.

Springs and Artesian Wells. Water from **springs** and **artesian wells** flows to the surface without the aid of pumps, although pumps may be needed to increase the water pressure for use. Artesian wells are formed when aquifers slope downward with impermeable layers both above and beneath. The force of the water from the source exerts pressure on that in lower portions of the aquifer, forcing water upward through openings in the surface. Although natural artesian wells are situated in low-lying areas, these wells may also be drilled. Springs flow from groundwater sources at low places where the water table is close to the surface. In rural areas, springs are an important source of drinking water. Because the water originates deep beneath the surface, it is generally safe but should be tested prior to use. Figure 8.8 illustrates these types of water supplies.

Figure 8.8 A cross-section view of water supplies in the earth.

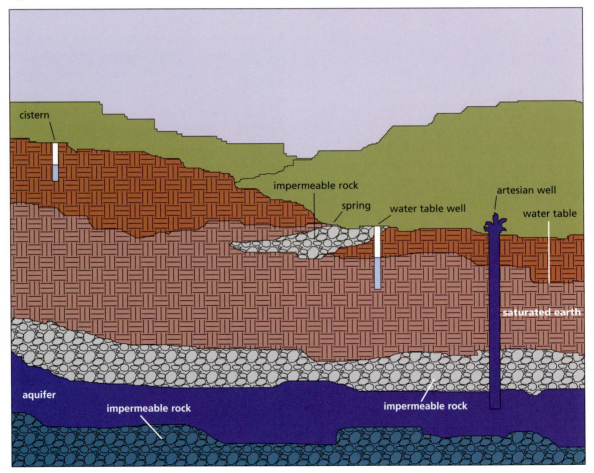

Figure 8.9 Water towers dot the American landscape, providing water to residents in both rural and urban areas. Such reservoirs store water at a higher altitude than homes to be supplied in order to provide adequate and equalized pressure for use.

Cisterns

Unlike wells, cisterns are not sufficiently deep to penetrate the water table because they are designed to store, not catch, water. Cisterns have impermeable walls, ensuring that groundwater does not seep in, nor can stored water leak out. Roof runoff may be channeled through a simple filtering system into cisterns to provide water for purposes other than drinking. In some rural areas, water is hauled in tank trucks to be stored in cisterns as the only water supply. Because it must be hauled, this water is more expensive than that from other sources. Cisterns must be periodically cleaned to prevent contamination of the water supply.

Pretreatment of Water

Water from surface sources requires thorough treatment prior to use to ensure safety. Water suppliers test for more than 100 contaminants and use some or all of the following processes during treatment.

- Removal of leaves, trash, and other solid matter in settling basins and through sand filters or screens
- Addition of coagulants to cause impurities such as iron and lead to sink to the bottom
- Filtration to remove dissolved gases
- Addition of chlorine or other chemicals to eliminate harmful microorganisms. Where it is practiced, chlorination of the water has almost eliminated the outbreak of diseases such as typhoid and cholera.[17]
- Aeration or use of a material such as activated carbon to absorb odors

Water Delivery

Treated water may go directly to a network of water mains for delivery to users or it may be stored in closed reservoirs such as vertical **standpipes**, water towers, and storage tanks located on high ground. Figure 8.9 illustrates one type of municipal water storage tank.

Pumps are used to lift water to the reservoirs. These steel tanks lined with corrosion-resistant substances are usually filled during low-use hours—at night and during the middle of the day. The static pressure of water in pipes leading from reservoirs increases at the rate of 0.433 pounds per square inch (psi) for every vertical foot of fall. (Conversely, water loses 0.433 psi for every foot of vertical rise.) If adequate water pressure cannot be attained by the reservoir, pumps must be used. Pumps are also often required to deliver water to buildings higher than six stories. If water were delivered to the base of a 60-foot-high building at 40 psi, by the time it reached the top (not taking into account friction and other factors), there would be only 14 psi of pressure in the

> When rooftop reservoirs are used, it is necessary to provide sufficient structural support for the weight of the tank and the water.

pipes. In some areas of the United States and in other areas of the world, rooftop reservoirs are used either to provide sufficient pressure for use or to ensure that water is available when public supplies are inadequate. This is often the case in high-rise buildings. In modern Nairobi, Kenya, city water supplies are frequently interrupted—generally on weekends; consequently, in new areas of the city, plastic storage tanks are positioned on residential roofs. When city water supplies are available, water is pumped to these tanks for use during shutoff hours. Their rooftop location allows water to flow by gravity into the homes, providing the necessary pressure for use. Pumps may be necessary to supplement the pressure.

Plumbing Codes

Plumbing codes are designed to protect the health of the public by ensuring clean water supplies, safe gas connections, and sanitary sewage removal. A number of model plumbing codes have been developed by different groups that state or local governments may adopt or adapt. Like all building codes, when a state adopts a code, municipalities within that state may have stricter requirements but must minimally meet state codes. The International Plumbing Code is a model code written by the International Code Council. Like other plumbing codes, this one establishes

> Plumbing permits may be required when installing a new plumbing system, adding on to existing systems, or altering a system—sometimes due to repair work. Sometimes a permit is required even to install a new dishwasher. Permits are also required when adding new gas appliances, water heaters, or fireplaces. Permit fees vary according to the size of the job.

standards for water supply, drainage, and vent systems for both residential and commercial structures.

In general, plumbing codes:

- Determine whether licensed plumbers must install system components
- Require inspections
- Specify pipe sizes and materials
- Require vents
- Specify distances between plumbing fixtures
- Ensure that the installation of plumbing fixtures and pipes does not weaken the structure
- Specify the minimum slope of drain and vent pipes
- Specify how pipes are supported
- Specify when permits are needed and establish fees

See Box 8. 1 for specific requirements for residential plumbing systems of particular concern to designers.

Delivery Pressure

Normal home water pressure ranges between 40 and 55 pounds per square inch. A minimum water pressure of 20 psi is necessary for most plumbing components to operate properly, but damage can be caused if pressures rise above 85 psi. Too little water pressure results in slowly running water, while too much pressure causes splashing.

Distribution

Water mains are large pipes made of corrosion-resistant materials. They run under or near streets or alleys, supplying water to homes. Owners must install and pay for pipes running from the water main to the house. When a municipal supply is available, all residences and commercial and public establishments are required to connect to the system, although in rural areas where hookups may cost thousands of dollars, it may be optional.

Box 8.1 Plumbing Code Requirements

- Toilets, bidets, urinals, and lavatories must not be closer than 15 inches from any obstruction at the side (including a wall, cabinet, door, or adjacent fixture) when measured from the centerline of the fixture. Adjacent fixtures must be a minimum of 30 inches apart from centerline to centerline.
- A minimum of 21 inches of clear space in front of toilets, urinals, bidets, and lavatories is required.
- Shower compartments must be a minimum of 900 square inches, with no side less than 30 inches in length. Soap dishes, folding seats, and other accessories are allowed to project into the 30 inches of clear space.
- A waterproof wall surround must be installed to a height of 6 feet from the room floor or 70 inches from the drain of a bathtub that has a showerhead.
- A smooth, readily cleanable, nonabsorbent material must be used for 2 feet on each side of a urinal to a height of 4 feet above the floor.
- There must be access to a pump on a whirlpool tub.
- Maximum fixture flow rates are as follows.
  - Lavatory: 2.2 gallons per minute (gpm) at 60 pounds per square inch (psi)
- Showerhead: 2.5 gpm at 80 psi
- Sink faucet: 2.2 gpm at 60 psi
- Urinal: 1 gallon per flush
- Toilet: 1.6 gallons per flush
- Shutoff valves are needed for each fixture other than bathtubs or showers, for each hose bibb, and for each appliance or piece of mechanical equipment that uses water. All valves need to be accessible.
- Circulating hot water pipes must be insulated.
- The hot water faucet supply must be on the left when there are two knobs.
- The minimum distance between the well and a septic tank is 25 feet and the minimum distance between a well and a sewer pipe is 10 feet. If shale or limestone are present, distances must be greater.
- Traps and vents are required for each plumbing fixture.
- Soil stacks must rise without decreasing in size and route as directly as possible to an outdoor terminal.
- If the outside design temperature is 0 degrees Fahrenheit or less, every vent through the roof must be a minimum of 3 inches in diameter.

Source: International Code Council, *International Plumbing Code 2003* (Country Club Hills, IL: International Code Council, 2003).

In municipal systems, there must be provisions for controlling water flow and metering the amount used. A branch line—usually 1-inch pipe—may enter the property from the municipal system through a **buffalo box** located near the property line and sufficiently beneath the ground to ensure that water in the pipes does not freeze. At this point, there is a shutoff valve that requires a special tool to operate. In older

Before scheduling plumbing contractors, designers should ascertain whether the shut-off valve in the buffalo box is the only means of turning off the water to a structure. If so, it may be necessary for utility company personnel to turn off the water to repair or replace plumbing pipes or fixtures. When the job is completed, utility workers must return to restore water service.

The Plumbing System   229

homes, this may be the only shutoff valve. The repair and installation of plumbing pipes beyond the shutoff valve are the responsibility of property owners.

The Water Meter

A water meter is installed where water enters the home from a municipal system. The meter may be in the buffalo box, it may be located next to the structure, or it may be inside the structure. The meter is used to determine the amount of water used by each customer. It may measure:

- The number of cubic feet of water that flows through it
- Only a portion of the water that enters the home
- The rate of flow rather than the amount of water

The water meter is owned by the utility company. The meter may be read by utility workers or it may be computer-controlled so that it can be read from the utility company office. Many areas still have dial-style water meters. When there is no buffalo box, the main shutoff valve may be located on the street side of the meter, where it can be easily accessed by the utility company.

Shutoff Valves

Inside the home, whether water is supplied by a municipal system or through a privately owned water supply, there should be a main shutoff valve controlled by property owners. This allows owners to turn off all water to the structure for repair or replacement of parts of the plumbing system. Many older homes do not have main shutoff valves. A **stop-and-waste valve** allows users not only to turn off the water but

---

■ When a building owner is planning to replace, repair, or add new plumbing pipes or fixtures and there is no main shutoff valve within the structure, the plan should include a new shutoff valve to enable owners to control water flow when necessary without calling the utility company.

Figure 8.10 Installing a shutoff valve at each plumbing fixture simplifies turning off water for repair and maintenance.

to drain the water out of the pipes—necessary when the structure will be left unheated during freezing weather. Stop-and-waste valves must be aboveground. Additional shutoff valves are needed for each branch in the system so that the water supply to individual fixtures or groups of fixtures can be interrupted while maintaining supply to other parts of the system. See Figure 8.10.

Supply Pipes

Water delivered to the home is carried to fixtures through a system of supply pipes. Because water in the pipes is under pressure, pipe runs can be in any direction although turns and offsets retard the flow of water—a factor to be considered when water is delivered at a relatively low pressure. Most homes require 300 feet or more of supply pipes ranging in size from ¾ to 1½ inches in diameter. A **branch pipe** close to the water meter goes to the water heater. From this point, two pipes—a cold and a hot water pipe—run in parallel branches to each fixture requiring both. In addition, cold water pipes run to toilets and ice makers, and hot water pipes to built-in dishwashers. Water pipes are usually installed beneath the first floor or slab, then run through interior walls to fixtures. Pipes may be routed near or through exterior walls if there is no danger of freezing or if they are well insulated.

Distribution pipes channel water from the main supply line at the point of entry to general locations of plumbing fixtures while branch pipes run from the distribution pipes to individual fixtures such as toilets and sinks. Water velocity is increased each time pipe diameter is decreased. Most fixtures require only ½-inch-diameter pipes for individual water supply, although water heaters and exterior hose bibbs should be supplied by ¾-inch pipe. **Supply tubes** run from local fixture shutoff valves to the fixture itself. Supply tubes are usually made of flexible materials, making them easier to install and remove. Supply tubes to toilets and lavatories may be decreased to ⅜ inch in diameter although other fixtures should be supplied with ½-inch tubes. Local codes, of course, dictate minimum pipe sizes. Where pipes enter a wall or floor, the hole should be sealed and an **escutcheon plate** used to cover the hole.

Plumbing pipes lead not only to interior fixtures but also to exterior **hose bibbs**, which have threaded ends to accept garden hoses. They are used for watering lawns and other outdoor purposes. Local codes may or may not stipulate the number or location of hose bibbs. A minimum of one is essential, and two or more will facilitate the use of hoses. Hose bibbs may have stop-and-waste valves, permitting them to be drained prior to freezing weather. Frost-proof hose bibbs are self-draining and eliminate this problem.

Preparation of Water for Use

Although much of the water used in American homes goes directly from public water systems to fixtures, some is further prepared for use by heating, softening, or filtering. Hot water is used for bathing, laundry, and washing dishes. When water contains an abundance of minerals, it may be desirable for it to be

When a leak occurs in a buried water line, especially one covered by concrete, it can require extensive digging to locate. The use of a stethoscope to pinpoint the location of the leak will minimize damage and costs.

softened prior to heating and use. Filters increase water purity.

Water Heaters

The International Residential Code requires that each dwelling unit have some type of water heating system. On the average, Americans use about 17 to 23 gallons of hot water a day, although in single-person households, this may rise to about 35 gallons per day. More energy is used for water heaters than any other single home appliance, excluding heating and air-conditioning systems. In fact, the Department of Energy estimates that 20 percent of an average household's annual energy expenditure is for heating water.[18] Much of that is wasted because water is heated 24 hours a day, 365 days a year, and rarely does a family use hot water more than a few hours a day. Meanwhile, the water heater radiates heat through its walls, its top, and through flues in gas

All water pipes benefit from being insulated. Insulation minimizes heat loss in hot water pipes, reducing energy use and costs. Insulating cold water pipes prevents moisture condensation or "sweating." Fiberglass strips spiraled around pipes and sealed with vapor-proof tape can serve as insulation for an entire system or for pipe angles. Cylindrical vinyl-covered foam strips purchased according to pipe size may be used to insulate straight pipe runs. Vapor-proof tape is used to hold the strips in place and to seal joints. To further conserve energy, hot water pipes should be as short as possible, requiring that water-heating devices be located in close proximity to major points of use.

Like other equipment, water heaters need to be located where they can be repaired and maintained. A small space usually suffices for the water heater. The heating element must be at least 18 inches from the floor.

Gas-fired water heaters require a flue that runs through the roof. (Side-venting water heaters are also available but are infrequently used.) Local codes may require that the flue and gas lines be exposed rather than enclosed in walls. Locating a gas water heater so the piping and flue can rise through a closet, pantry, or utility area may be necessary, especially if there are living areas on the story above the water heater.

systems. These losses, known as **standby losses**, account for up to 20 percent of the annual cost of heating water.[19]

Most homes rely on a large, centrally located water heater consisting of a tank with either a gas-fired combustion chamber or electric heating coils. The tank is insulated and covered with enameled sheet metal. Generally, hot water tanks are lined with glass to prevent rust from entering the water and discoloring it.

For energy-efficiency, hot water tanks can be further insulated using a special blanket of fiberglass.

Electric water heaters and electronically controlled gas heaters can be programmed to heat water to any temperature at a desired time. Thus, water heated to 110 degrees Fahrenheit could be ready at 7 a.m. for bathing and 140 degrees at 6 p.m. for dishwashing, and remain unheated during the night. Water is heated only as high as necessary for the purpose intended. The drawback to this system is that families must maintain regular schedules to minimize frustration.

Water is typically delivered to the water heater at about 50 degrees Fahrenheit, requiring that it be heated 70 degrees to bring it up to 120 degrees Fahrenheit. Water that is drawn off is replaced by cold water, which affects the temperature of the water in the heater after approximately 75 percent of the heated water has been used. When the water reaches a preselected temperature, the water heater shuts off automatically. A pressure and thermal relief valve in the tank—required by the IRC and other codes—opens automatically when heat or pressure builds above safe levels, preventing the tank from exploding.

The water heater must be properly sized so that energy is not wasted heating water unnecessarily, yet sufficient hot water is provided for periods of peak use. A 40-gallon tank is the minimum size even for small families. Homes with two bathrooms need more capacity, and large homes need at least a 100-gallon tank. The water heater should be located as close to the points of use as possible to conserve water and heating fuel.

For most purposes, water temperature should be between 114 and 120 degrees Fahrenheit, with a maximum of 140 degrees Fahrenheit. Maintaining the lowest acceptable temperature minimizes mineral deposits and tank damage from corrosion. For automatic dishwashers, water at 160 degrees Fahrenheit provides more sanitary dishes, although dishwashers themselves may have boosters to raise the temperature of incoming water.

Water heaters have a **recovery rate** that dictates to some extent the tank size needed. The recovery rate is expressed by the amount of water that, in one hour, the tank can heat sufficiently to raise the temperature by 100 degrees Fahrenheit. Gas water heaters recover relatively quickly; electric water heaters recover more slowly and are therefore more suited for heating large amounts during off-peak hours. Because they do not require venting, electric tanks may be located almost anywhere. Gas water heaters, however, require venting to the exterior.

Tankless Water Heaters

An alternative to traditional water heaters is the **tankless water heater**, also known as an instantaneous, point-of-use, and on-demand water heater. Tankless water heaters are common in the Middle East, Europe, and Japan. Although some models are automatic, others require that the user initiate water heating by pushing a button or lighting a pilot. While a standard water heater heats water 24 hours a day, the tankless model only heats water while it is being used. Automatic tankless heaters are activated by the flow

Figure 8.11 Tankless water heaters are small enough to fit under a cabinet and are available in both gas and electric models. Gas models require venting.

Gas water heaters—whether tank or tankless models—with an intermittent ignition device eliminate the need for a constantly burning pilot, saving energy. ❀

of water and begin to heat when a hot water faucet is opened. Water flows through heating coils, and by the time it reaches the outlet, the temperature has been raised sufficiently for use. Because the units continue to heat as long as water flows through the coils, hot water flows constantly, there is no recovery lag, and very little water is heated and left unused. See Figure 8.11.

Tankless units are available in a variety of sizes—from small units designed to supply a single fixture or room to whole-house units. They may be mounted in cabinets or on the wall, or they may be centrally located in a utility area, requiring less space than do conventional heaters. Currently, tankless water heaters cost significantly more to purchase than do conventional units but they have a longer life expectancy—about 20 years—because they do not heat water constantly. Additionally, most of the parts of tankless heaters are easily replaceable.

The use of several small tankless water heaters permits water temperature to be set at the levels needed at each point, resulting in energy savings. These water heaters are especially useful in areas with very corrosive water or in vacation homes.

Gas models have higher output ratings than do electric models but gas units must be vented. Tankless heaters are rated by the number of gallons per minute they can produce. Small units deliver 1 to 2 gallons per minute while larger units can produce 3 to 5 gallons per minute. Most tankless heaters cannot heat water quickly enough to supply simultaneous multiple outlets, although the use of water-conserving showerheads and faucets can help.

Solar Water Heaters

Solar water heaters gather heat from the sun in collector panels to heat water. To ensure adequate hot water during extended cloudy periods, solar water heaters should be backed up by a conventional water heating system; indeed, local codes may require it. Some solar water heaters are designed only to preheat water before it enters a conventional system. Solar water heaters are expensive to install and are currently cost-efficient in relatively few areas.

Circulating Hot Water

Circulating hot water provides the luxury of instant hot water from any outlet. Water constantly circulates in a closed loop from the water heater to fixtures and back. These systems are expensive to operate and consume energy unnecessarily.

Hot Water Dispensers

The hot water dispenser attaches to the kitchen sink and provides water at temperatures up to 190 degrees Fahrenheit for beverages and soups. A small half-gallon tank is located beneath the sink, and water is delivered through a tap at one side of the sink faucet. To prevent splashing, water in the hot water dispenser is not under pressure.

Hot water dispensers can boost the temperature of approximately 60 cups of water per hour. Although hot water dispensers use electricity to heat the water, model electric codes do not require that they be connected to a ground-fault circuit interrupter because they are fastened in place. Because they use electricity and heat water constantly, it may be more economical to heat water in the microwave unless the dispenser is frequently used.

Water Softeners

Water is either hard or soft, depending on mineral content. **Hard water** has a high mineral content that inhibits the formation of lather and reacts with soap

Automatic water-softener systems that have separate tanks require twice the space. Both tanks are approximately the same size.

to form a precipitate. This precipitate leaves a ring of scum in lavatories and bathtubs and remains on laundry washed with soap. (Detergents are less affected by hard water.) Heating hard water causes the minerals to leave the water and cling to pipes, teakettles, and water heaters, building up scaly deposits. These deposits decrease the effective diameter of pipes and the usable capacity of water heaters.

Water hardness is expressed by the proportion of minerals in the water. The number of grams or molecules of minerals per million grams or molecules of water is the parts per million (ppm). Soft water has a mineral content of less than 140 ppm and needs no treatment. When water hardness is 140 to 350 ppm, any water to be heated should first be softened to minimize scale deposits in pipes and in the water heater. Water with hardness over 350 ppm should be softened prior to any use. Water hardness of at least 50 ppm should be maintained because softer water lathers too well, making soap removal difficult, and because water with little mineral content corrodes metal pipes.

Minerals are removed by passing water through an ion exchanger called a water softener. The calcium and magnesium ions in hard water are exchanged for sodium ions in the zeolite beads contained in the softener. Eventually, the zeolite beads will have picked up too many calcium and magnesium ions to continue the softening process. The water softener must then be regenerated by washing away the calcium and magnesium ions and bringing in fresh sodium ions. This is done by flushing the system with brine, a solution of common table salt and water. The magnesium and calcium are sent into a drain along with the excess brine. In automatic systems, a separate tank stores brine and a timer controls the cycle of operation and regeneration. Manually operated softeners require not only the addition of salt but frequent manual flushing.

Water softeners may be rented or purchased and may be used for any portion of the water supply. Efficiently operated systems do not soften water used outdoors. Water used for toilets is not usually softened; however, using soft water in toilets minimizes mineral deposits and makes them easier to clean. Packaged water softeners for use only in the laundry or bathtub may be purchased.

Filters

Because water softeners do not remove other minerals, an additional tank containing filters designed for removing iron, sulfur, and other common minerals and for neutralizing acids may be necessary. In addition, undesirable chemicals, sediments, tastes, and odors may be present in tap water. Filtering devices partially remove these impurities. Central filtering units installed in the cold water supply line filter water for the entire system, while smaller units installed under a sink or attached to a faucet filter only the water used in that fixture.

Fittings and Fixtures

Fittings are the hardware associated with fixtures that control the flow of water—faucets, drain fittings,

shower heads and controls, and spray attachments. Most have interior parts made of coated or uncoated brass, which resists rust. The most common external coating material is chrome.

Fittings

A faucet consists of at least one outlet for water and one or two valves operated by a lever or knob to control the flow of water. Single-control valve faucets are the easiest to operate, mix hot and cold water, and have a single outlet. When two separate valves are used, the water may flow from both or converge into a single outlet. See Figure 8.12.

Faucets may have an aerator, or fine mesh screen disk, installed in the end of the spout to prevent splashing. The screen produces a slight vacuum, drawing air in and mixing it with the water to produce a controlled stream. Pop-up drain fittings have largely replaced rubber stoppers for holding water in lavatories, bathtubs, and sinks and are usually lever-operated from the faucet location.

The design of fittings includes features to ensure safe operation of the plumbing system. Supply pipes are never directly connected to waste lines through

Figure 8.12 European faucets typically use two separate outlets providing hot and cold water separately. If water is to be mixed in the basin, this arrangement is satisfactory. However, in the United States, when separate valves are used, water is typically mixed and comes from a single outlet.

Most faucets sold in the United States require holes in the sink or lavatory 8 inches on center. Faucets for bar sinks typically have 4-inch centers. When ordering a countertop with an integral sink or lavatory, this spacing must be specified so the holes can be located appropriately. Manufacturers also need to know if there will be a spray attachment, soap dispenser, or hot water dispenser so openings for those can be located as well. In some instances, the holes can be drilled on site.

fixtures or otherwise. This prevents the possibility of wastewater being siphoned into the pure water supply in the event of a drop in pressure in the supply lines. Faucets are rim-mounted on lavatories so that a connection between supply and waste lines cannot be made. An additional safety measure is the overflow, an opening below the rim through which water drains when it reaches that level. Overflows prevent water from reaching the level of the faucet and from spilling onto the floor below. Overflow drains are connected to drains beneath the fixtures or to waste pipe systems in the walls.

Fixtures

Plumbing fixtures include sinks, lavatories, bathtubs, showers, toilets, and bidets. A variety of fixture styles is available to enhance almost any decor—from Victorian motifs to ultramodern designs. Because most people are concerned about the resale value of their homes and will not purchase plumbing fixtures with an exotic appearance, there are fewer options in the United States than in some other countries. Fixture colors range from white and pastels to deep earth tones and bright hues. Hand-painted and patterned sinks and lavatories are readily available for high-end markets.

Low-flow aerators can help reduce the flow of water from 3 to 7 gallons per minute to as little as 1.5 gallons per minute.

Lavatories

Lavatories are relatively small basins that have rounded bottoms. Lavatories come in round, oval, rectangular, and triangular as well as other shapes. Some lavatories have a soap ledge, which may be perforated for water drainage. See Figure 8.13.

Lavatories in cabinet assemblies can be installed flush with the counter and held by a metal anchoring ring; they may have self-rims and be held to the counter using clips; they may be installed beneath the counter; or they may be mounted on top of the counter. Each of these installations requires one or more seams that collect dirt and are difficult to clean. A more satisfactory lavatory is one that is cast as an integral part of the counter, requiring no joints. Fittings for a lavatory include a faucet and a drain assembly. **Vessel lavatories** rest on the countertop. See Figure 8.14.

Sinks and Laundry Tubs

Sinks, like lavatories, are designed to hold water. Unlike the rounded bottom of the lavatory, sinks have flat bottoms. **Shampoo sinks**, kitchen sinks, and bar sinks are used in homes.

Figure 8.13 Drain pipes and supply lines are visible when freestanding lavatories are used.

Figure 8.14 Vessel lavatories require only a small opening in the countertop for the drain and others as appropriate for the faucet. Because they sit on top of the counter, vessel lavatories may be more comfortable for some individuals to use.

Kitchen sinks are generally installed as an integral part of a long counter. They consist of one or two bowls and sometimes an additional smaller, separate bowl with a garbage disposal.

Laundry tubs are deeper than kitchen sinks. A combination sink/laundry tub has two bowls, with the laundry tub deeper than the sink. The laundry tub may be covered with a removable drain board if it is located in the kitchen.

The distinguishing characteristic of shampoo sinks is the spray attachment. Some of these sinks also have faucets but others do not. Shampoo sinks are shallower than kitchen sinks and are usually installed in bathrooms.

In a small kitchen when a dishwasher is installed, a single-bowl sink may suffice, but double- or even triple-bowl sinks are preferred. The use of a dishwasher can save a significant amount of water. A dishwasher uses between 9 and 12 gallons of water per load; hand washing dishes requires about 20 gallons if the water is left running.

Bathtubs

Since water was not brought into most individual homes in ancient cultures, early Egyptians, Babylonians, Greeks, and Romans all developed some form of group bathing. The famous Roman public baths were large buildings that accommodated thousands of people at a time. However, a few Romans enjoyed private baths with hot running water in their homes.

After the fall of the Roman Empire, bathing fell into disrepute in most Western cultures. Perfume, toilet water, and pomades replaced bathing in elite social circles. Baths for rich and poor alike were events for birth, marriage, and death. It wasn't until the seventeenth century that the nobility in several European countries began to bathe frequently. They entertained visitors while they bathed, and it was fashionable to have their portraits painted while bathing. Their bathtubs were not mere open tubs but pieces of furniture and works of art. Although they were sometimes located in separate bathing rooms, these tubs were often part of the furniture arrangement of bedrooms or were carried in when they were to be used. Those who did not own a bathtub could wait for a wagon that came through city streets. When requested, a bathtub was brought into the client's home, then removed and carted down the street to the next client. The same water was used all day.

The modern bathtub did not appear until 1911, when the Kohler Company cast a tub in a single piece

For clients who like to wash their hair in the bathtub, a spray arm can be supplied with the bathtub faucet.

for scalding hogs and in its advertising indicated that when legs were added, it could be used as a bathtub. Most bathtubs are 5 feet long and 14 or 15 inches deep, although larger and deeper tubs are also available.

In 1968, Roy Jacuzzi introduced the whirlpool tub —a bathtub with an electric pump, piping to circulate water, and a number of underwater jets. Each jet featured a constriction near its opening that allowed air to be injected into the water. Today, whirlpool tubs offer luxurious bathing experiences but they are more expensive to purchase and noisy to operate. These tubs come in corner units, ovals, and rectangles in either cast iron or acrylic.

Showers

Showers can be combined with bathtubs. A showerhead is attached to an arm extending from the wall, and a handle diverts the water flow to either the showerhead or the bathtub faucet.

A pressure-balance mixing valve can be used to ensure that the temperature of the shower water

remains constant even when other fixtures are used intermittently while the shower is running. The IRC requires that a showerhead have a maximum flow of 2.5 gallons per minute although there is no limit on the number of showerheads that can be installed.

In order to meet IRC standards, a shower must have a minimum of 900 square inches of floor space —equivalent to 30 × 30 inches. In fact, 30 inches is the minimum interior length of each side of a shower. Minimum height for any wall in the shower is 70 inches above the drain. Soap dishes, fittings, and grab bars may intrude into the shower space, and fold-down seats are permitted.

Toilets

The use of indoor toilets, like that of bathing facilities, has a history reaching back to ancient times. Flush toilets were found in the fourteenth-century B.C. Minoan palace of Knossus, complete with vents, **traps**, and wooden seats. The Romans had the *sella pertusa*, consisting of a seat with a hole in it and fixed or movable containers beneath. Through the Middle Ages, however, outdoor latrines were most commonly used. Later, toilets in European countries were similar to the Roman sella pertusa but were highly decorated. Those who did not enjoy the accoutrements of wealth used the simple chamber pot, usually in the relative comfort and warmth of the bedroom. Louis XIV had a *chaise d'affaires* at Versailles and 274 additional *close stools*. These ornate pieces of furniture made it possible for their owners to perform necessary functions without leaving good company and the warmth of the room.

Flush toilets began to reappear around the seventeenth century. In 1596, Queen Elizabeth I was the first English monarch to have an indoor flush toilet— called a water closet. These were not common, however, until the late nineteenth century. A number of individuals worked on the development of the toilet. Between 1900 and 1932, more than 350 new water closet designs were submitted to the U.S. Patent Office. Today's toilets use many of the same principles and components of these early models. When the first housing census was done in 1940, more than 35 percent of American homes still lacked a flush toilet; in 1950, that figure was almost 25 percent. By 1970, however, only 10 percent of American homes lacked a flush toilet.[20] Some states, of course, had a much higher percentage of homes without this facility—up to 81 percent in 1940. In 2003, only 1.3 percent of occupied American homes did not have flush toilets.

It is the flush toilet coupled with sewage systems that has made high-density urban living possible. A toilet uses clean water to carry wastes into the sewage system, cleans itself each time it is flushed, and refills to a predetermined level before turning itself off.

In the United States, approximately 4.8 billion gallons of water per day are used to carry wastes away from toilets—40 percent of the water used inside of urban residences.[21] Depending on the toilet type, 1.6 to 7 gallons of water are used for each flush. In the mid-twentieth century, a typical toilet required 7 gallons of water to flush. This amount was reduced first to 5.5 gallons, then in the 1980s to 3.5 gallons (water-saver toilets) and in 1997, to 1.6 gallons.[22] Because few changes were made in toilet design as the amount of water used was reduced, some of these toilets performed inefficiently. It was not until engineers redesigned the toilet itself that low-water-consumption toilets became effective. Engineers continue to improve toilet efficiency and a number of new products have been introduced, including pressure-assisted toilets, vacuum-assisted, and electro-hydraulic units.

The type of toilet used in most residential design is the tank toilet. A tank behind and above the toilet bowl stores sufficient water to cleanse the bowl and replace the bowl water when flushed. A flush lever or button is attached to a valve in the tank that lets water out of the tank and into the bowl. Water is replaced in the tank, which contains a float that turns off the water supply when the water reaches the proper level. In tank toilets, temperature differences

Replacing 3.5-gallon toilets with 1.6-gallon-per-flush toilets saves the average person (who flushes 5 times) 9.5 gallons per day or 3468 gallons a year. A family of four could save almost 14,000 gallons of water a year. Some local water suppliers will provide rebates for users who replace older-model toilets with 1.6-gallon models.

---

between the water and the room may cause condensation to form on the tank on hot, humid days. The tank has a flat-surfaced, removable lid that allows access for maintenance. The tank and bowl may be a single unit or in two pieces. One-piece toilets have the advantage of quiet operation and a lower profile. The center of the toilet opening is located 12 inches from the wall behind it.

When the toilet is flushed, water enters the bowl through holes or slots on the underside of the rim, through a jet at the bottom of the bowl, or both. The rim holes are located around the circumference of the bowl, causing water to flow down the inside of the bowl to cleanse it. When water enters the bowl through the jet, its action helps to push wastes through the **trapway**—the passageway between the toilet bowl and the sewer pipe. Improvements in the shape of the trapway have caused it to create a suction or siphon action, making waste removal more efficient. Like all traps, some water is retained in the toilet bowl, preventing sewer gases from entering the living area.

All toilet bowls are designed to flush out wastes, but there are differences in the types of action—**wash down**, **reverse trap**, and **siphon jet**—that make each more or less desirable. Recent innovations have led to changes in the tank that result in other actions. Most toilets have a gravity feed, meaning that water pours into the bowl by gravity. As a general rule, the greater the size of the **water spot**—the amount of

---

Older homes may have toilets centered 10 inches from the wall, which could make it difficult to modernize the toilet.

area in the bowl covered with water—the better the cleansing action of the toilet.

Wash-down toilets are the least expensive but the noisiest to operate. They require more water for operation than other types, often fail to remove heavy waste products, and are less sanitary than other types because the water level in the bowl is low, resulting in a small water spot, and the self-cleansing action is poor. Although new models are difficult to find in the United States, they are still common in other countries and older homes may still have them.

Reverse-trap toilets are the most commonly used today, although their small siphonic trapways make them noisy. They have a flushing rim and good self-cleansing properties, since about two-thirds of the bowl is covered with water. The trap is at the rear of the bowl.

Siphon-jet toilets are quieter because they have larger trapways. Most of the bowl interior is covered with water, making the self-cleansing action of these toilets excellent. The action of the siphonic trapway is assisted by the jet.

Siphon-vortex or **siphon-action toilets** have a larger water spot than any of the above models. Because they are only available in one-piece models, they operate almost silently. These toilets use rim holes and may or may not feature a jet. Siphon-vortex toilets are more expensive than most other gravity toilets.

Pressure- or **power-assisted toilets** have a container in the tank—called an **accumulator**—that is filled with air. Rather than water entering the tank itself, it enters the container, compressing the air already there. When the toilet is flushed, the compressed air forces water out of the container and into the bowl in a powerful surge that creates a vortex, resulting in a stronger siphon for waste removal. Moving wastes does not depend on siphoning in the trapway, and the force of the action thoroughly cleanses the bowl. The action of the pressure-assisted toilet is very loud, although engineers are working to make it quieter. These toilets require a minimum of 25 psi of water pressure to operate properly and may even re-

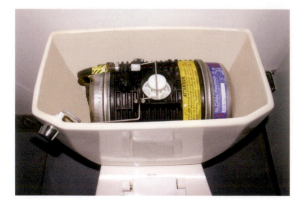

Figure 8.15 Pressure-assisted toilets hold no water in the porcelain tank itself but rather in a plastic container.

quire a compressor. Some models have a button on the top of the tank rather than the traditional flush lever. Because the water is contained in a plastic tank located inside the china tank, little or no condensation forms on the tank during hot, humid weather. See Figure 8.15.

Vacuum-assisted toilets have specialized tank components and a redesigned trapway, forming an interconnection between the tank and the trapway. Two plastic containers are housed within the tank, although their combined capacity is no greater than 1.6 gallons. (As with the pressure-assisted model, condensation does not form on the tank.) When the toilet is flushed, a vacuum is created, powering water into the bowl through the rim holes. No jet hole is necessary, nor is the siphon action of most trapways.

Electrohydraulic toilets are the newest models on the market. These toilets make use of motors and pumps. In one model, a tiny 0.2-horsepower electric pump is incorporated in the tank to add power to the flush, and steeper bowl sides improve the flow of wastes and water. The combination allows the wastes to be carried away with less water. Another model locates a pump and motor in the pipes under the toilet, where waste products are chopped until they are liquefied, and then pushed through the pipes.

Flush-valve-operated toilets are used in commercial settings. The tank is omitted and the valve is connected directly to the water supply. Because these toilets rely on the pressure in the water supply system and not gravity for the force of their flush, they have excellent cleansing action. With few exceptions, these toilets are not used in homes. See Box 8.2 for design concerns about noise and the plumbing system.

Bidets

The **bidet** is a plumbing fixture designed for cleansing the genital and perineal areas after using the toilet, eliminating the need for toilet paper. Because the intensity of the water spray can be controlled, the bidet provides hands-free cleaning—advantageous for individuals with impaired motor functions, including the disabled and the elderly. Stand-alone bidets resemble tankless toilets without seats, and some have heated rims. Figure 8.16 shows a bidet.

Hot and cold water faucets are located on the back or wall side of the bidet to give the user control of water temperature and flow intensity. Two types of

---

Box 8.2 Noise and the Plumbing System

Plumbing is a potential source of unwanted noise in the home. For quiet operation, water pipes and drains should be as straight as possible. Turns result in increased noise, as do pipes that are not large enough. Adding just four elbows to pipes increases noise in the pipes by 10 decibels. Using oversized pipes for both water supply and drains reduces pressure, flow, and noise, although care should be taken to ensure that adequate pressure remains for fixture use. When plumbing vents must traverse upper stories, they should not be installed in the walls of quiet areas. Cast-iron drains and vents are much heavier than PVC pipes and reduce sound levels significantly. Insulating the walls in which plumbing supply pipes and drains run not only helps to reduce noise from pipes but also improves the acoustic privacy of the bathroom.

When faucets are opened, water flows from them with pressure behind it. The water in the pipes continues to move from the main water supply pipe to the fixture until the faucet is shut off. If the faucet is rapidly closed, momentum causes the water to continue to move, increasing the pressure in the pipes. When the water is not released, it bangs against the valve and the pipes, resulting in a noise commonly known as **water hammer**. If the situation is not corrected, the pipes may be damaged as well.

To prevent the noise, air pockets are created to act as shock absorbers and help take strain off the piping system. Extra pipes are installed vertically on supply pipes near fixtures. Air chambers range from a few inches in length up to 2 feet or more. They are constructed of pipe at least as large as the supply pipes and

AIR CHAMBER FOR WATER HAMMER

(continued)

Box 8.2 (continued)

sometimes larger and are capped at the top. The extra pressure created when the faucets are shut off can then be expended, compressing air in the chambers.

Water striking the surface of plumbing fixtures and toilets flushing generate noise. In general, heavier fixture materials such as cast iron make less noise than do lighter-weight fixtures, although they are usually more expensive to purchase. Selecting quiet-operating fixtures (especially toilets), caulking around fixtures and around pipes where they penetrate structural components, and isolating tub and shower units on resilient bases to reduce impact noise all help to sound-condition bathrooms. To ensure the structural integrity of floors beneath plumbing fixtures, a concrete-based backer board is preferred. The installation of a resilient foam base between the backer board

and a tub or shower provides a solution to both problems. Although it is common practice to install shower and tub units directly against stud walls, extending the wall finish material behind these units will provide some measure of sound-conditioning; insulating the walls increases the sound transmission class further. To ensure that plumbing noises are dampened in walls, make certain that the insulation is installed between the pipes and the adjacent room.

Toilets can also be noisy. A typical flush in a reverse-trap toilet produces approximately 75 decibels; the flush of a pressure-assisted toilet is even noisier, at about 90 decibels. Where noise may be an issue—as in a bathroom in a public zone of a residence—clients may spend additional funds to purchase a more quietly operating toilet.

spray action are available—vertical and horizontal. A vertical spray is directed upward from the center of the bowl, while a horizontal spray comes over the rim of the bidet. A pop-up drain allows the user to fill the bowl for foot washing, sitz baths, or laundry. Doctors may recommend the use of bidets to ease the symptoms of certain medical conditions such as hemorrhoids, prostate infections, and vaginal cramps. Clearances and space requirements for bidets are the same as they are for toilets.

The bidet is a common feature in Latin America, Europe, the Middle East, and Japan, but relatively few homes in America have one. Originating in France, the bidet became common in eighteenth-century Europe when whole-body bathing was an infrequent,

Figure 8.16 The bidet is designed to facilitate cleanliness and is a standard feature of homes in many parts of the world.

rather than daily, event. To use bidets until the last few decades, it was necessary to straddle the unit.[23] This made it difficult to use when wearing undergarments or trousers. Most contemporary bidets are still used in the same manner, although alternatives are now available.

The Drainage System

Water and waste leaving the points of use—lavatories, tubs, showers, toilets, bidets, sinks, appliances, and floor drains—enter the drainage system, which is commonly known as the DWV or drain-waste-vent system. Its function is to carry water and waste products from the house to the sewer system. Special designs such as traps and vents protect the house from sewer gas and allow for the efficient carrying away of water and waste.

Traps

Sewer gases and odors are prevented from entering the house by traps located within or beneath plumbing fixtures. Traps are an integral part of toilets; drains from other fixtures have S- or J-shaped traps beneath them. See Figure 8.17. At the lowest point, many traps have a cleanout to permit access if the drain becomes clogged. If a drain is not used for a period of time, the water in the trap may evaporate, allowing sewer gases into the structure. This problem usually occurs in unused laundry and basement sinks. To solve the problem, it is only necessary to run some water through the drain, filling the trap.

Vents

Vents are empty pipes that channel rising sewer gases from each fixture through the roof, where they are dissipated. Vents also admit air from the atmosphere into the plumbing system, equalizing the pressure in

Figure 8.17 Plumbing traps work by retaining sufficient water to seal off the pipe and, consequently, the entry of gases and odors from beyond it. Trap water is replaced every time fixtures are used, keeping it fresh.

the drainage system with that of the outside atmosphere to ensure that drain pipes do not run slowly. Too much pressure buildup in the drainage system can cause siphonage or blow out the water seal in plumbing traps, allowing sewer gases to enter the structure.

Codes stipulate a maximum distance from fixtures to the vent and from one vent to another. Little slope is necessary for horizontal portions of vent pipes because gases rise. If the size of the vent pipe is too small, the vent may become clogged, allowing sewer gases to escape into the home.

Large vents carry gases from toilets directly to the roof. Smaller vents from lavatories, sinks, and bathing units may lead straight to the roof or be channeled into a larger vent. Small vents are usually directed into larger vents or increased in size before penetrating the roof, to prevent clogging with ice or snow in the

Because vents must run from each fixture to the roof, their location requires planning when upper stories are to be used for living spaces. Otherwise, owners may end up with a vent passing through a room.

winter. Vents that are not a part of the drainage system are covered on the outside with an umbrellalike hood to prevent moisture from entering.

Gray Water

Water from toilets is considered **black water** and must be treated before any additional use. In some areas, codes define effluent from dishwashers and garbage disposals as black water; in others, it is considered **gray water** that is difficult to handle. Water drained from showers, bathtubs, lavatories, washers, and some sinks that contains no solid or hazardous waste products is considered gray water. In Australia, the law allows residents to water lawns with gray water as long as the water is thrown at least six feet.

In order to make use of gray water, it is necessary to have two separate drainage systems—requiring additional pipes and storage areas. In most places, a separate tank is required to store gray water. In urban areas, buildings are connected to a municipal sewage system. Because municipal systems are not usually designed to handle gray water separately, residents who desire to separate gray water from black water must install a tank in addition to their municipal hookup. There is no reason to add to the expense by having two systems unless the gray water will be used. In order to use the gray water for watering the lawn, a pump must also be installed, increasing the cost of the system. At present, only the most ecologically sensitive individuals go to the extra expense. In rural areas, a separate gray water system significantly slows the rate at which the black water **septic tank** is filled and decreases the frequency of pumping it out.

❀ Modern homes constructed with water conservation as an objective recycle wastewater. Gray water is collected, filtered, and chemically treated, then used for greenhouses, watering lawns, or flushing toilets. This practice not only conserves water but decreases the load on municipal sewage-treatment plants.

Drains

Wastes and water leave fixtures through the trap and enter the drain pipes. The pipes that actually carry water and waste to the sewage system have specific names depending on their function. Drainage pipes that carry only water from fixtures such as sinks, lavatories, bathtubs, and floor drains are called **waste pipes**. Those connected to toilets (and sometimes dishwashers or garbage disposals) carry solid wastes, which are called **soil**; the pipes that carry this waste are known as **soil pipes**. Because of the materials they carry, soil pipes must be larger in diameter than waste pipes. In most systems, waste pipes empty into soil pipes; however, if a separate gray water system is to be used, the contents of waste and soil pipes must be kept separated. Pipes are sized according to fixture type and the volume of waste expected.

Drainage is accomplished by gravity rather than pressure, requiring that all drain lines are at least slightly sloped. A quarter of an inch per foot is the minimum slope or **fall**, but almost any slope will result in free-flowing waste. When pipes are installed horizontally with only a slight slope, they are called **runs**. When installed vertically, they are called **stacks**. Thus, the vertical drain pipe that is connected to a toilet is called a soil stack. Soil stacks are always installed near toilets to offer the least resistance to the removal of soil into the sewage system. Stacks may also be installed adjacent to other fixtures, or the discharge from those fixtures may be directed to the main soil stack. The path that waste products must travel to reach the sewer system should be as straight as possible with a minimum of curves or angles. These precautions will also help to minimize clogs in the system.

Pipe Materials

Pipes must carry water to and from fixtures without leaking, making unnecessary noise, or imparting taste or color to water. Supply pipes should also carry water with minimal friction that would reduce water pressure. While all pipes should resist corrosion, it is drain pipes that are subjected to the most corrosive gases and materials. Selecting a pipe material is not as simple as choosing any one on the market that has proven effective. The temperature, hardness, acidity, and water pressure affect its reaction with various materials, making materials more or less suitable for individual applications. Copper, PVC, CPVC, steel, and iron are used for plumbing pipes.

Delivery to the Sewer System

Discharge from soil and waste pipes is carried to the sewer system. When the sewer system is not below the lowest drainage point, a **sump** and pump are employed. A sump is a large concrete, fiberglass, or cast-iron underground tank into which wastes flow by gravity. In the tank is a float switch that activates the pump when a certain capacity has been reached. The pump lifts wastes to a point above the sewage line where they can flow into the sewer system by gravity. Larger pipes and an ejector pump are used when sewage as well as wastewater is collected in sumps. Some sumps are used only as collection points for rainwater, which may include roof runoff. These prevent water from standing in basements during wet weather.

Waste Treatment

Once wastes from the plumbing system leave the house, they flow either to a municipal sewage system leading to a water-treatment plant or to a privately owned sewage-handling system. In both cases, wastes are removed and the water is at least partially purified before it is released into the environment.

Municipal Sewage Systems

In areas where roof drainage and storm water from streets, walks, and driveways are carried by separate

A stack or vent pipe must have a diameter at least as large as the diameter of the drain for the fixture it serves. When a 3-inch inside diameter stack is used behind a toilet, the outside diameter is 3½ inches and that pipe will fit into a standard 4-inch interior wall. A 4-inch-diameter stack requires 4½ inches of space. Since a 4-inch wall is actually only 3½ inches, the 4-inch stack will not fit and a 6-inch wall must be used. Cast-iron stacks always require 6-inch walls.

storm sewers, two hookups are necessary. When storm sewers are used, they carry runoff water directly to a natural watercourse without treatment. Some municipalities offer storm sewers for street runoff but not for roof drainage. In these areas, roof drainage is channeled to the ground away from the house and released to be soaked up by the soil. If this is the method by which roof drainage is disposed, municipal ordinances may require minimum unpaved yard areas around residences in proportion to the roof area drained.

The second hookup connects the house drainage system to the municipal sanitary sewer system that carries waste to treatment plants. In areas where the two distinctly different types of wastewater are carried away in a single system, only one hookup is needed. In that case, both storm runoff and house drainage are carried into the sanitary sewers to treatment plants. During rainy periods, this may overload municipal systems and cause treatment tanks to overflow before water has been sufficiently treated for release.

Sewer systems must be of sufficient size to carry the maximum expected volume, but rarely will they need that capacity. Because of this, sewer pipes are empty, or nearly so, most of the time. The resulting channel from the end of the system to individual homes is then open to carry sewer gases and their noxious odors back to homes. Traps and vents prevent these odors from entering homes.

Any system of pipes is subject to periodic clogging by dirt, leaves, or other materials. Access must therefore be provided for cleanout. In municipal sewage systems, manholes cover openings leading directly into the system. Less satisfactory are small pipe cleanouts leading from the sewers to the surface.

Sewage Treatment

The purpose of sanitary disposal is to separate toxic and offensive materials from the water carrying them. This is done in waste-treatment plants. Here, most cities subject sewage to two steps: **primary** and **secondary treatment**. Some use an additional **tertiary treatment** before releasing water to natural waterways.

Primary treatment removes heavy solid material from sewage. Screens first trap large pieces of matter, then sewage flows through grit chambers, where heavy inorganic materials such as sand are removed. The primary sedimentation tank is where other suspended solids settle out. **Sludge** forms at the bottom and lighter materials, such as grease, float to the surface where they can be skimmed. The effectiveness of primary treatment is limited. Only about 50 percent of the suspended solids and bacteria and 30 percent of the organic wastes are removed, making secondary treatment necessary.

Secondary treatment removes about 90 percent of the solids and organic wastes remaining after primary treatment by filtering sewage through rock containing bacteria that decompose organic matter or by moving bacteria through the sewage by bubbling air through it. Afterward, sewage flows to a final sedimentation tank where suspended and decomposed matter settles to the bottom. Sludge from primary and secondary treatment is further treated and burned or used as fertilizer. Tertiary treatment produces cleaner water by chemical treatment, microscopic screening, or radiation.

Clean water is released into natural watercourses from treatment plants. Government regulations determine how clean the water must be prior to dumping. They also regulate private disposal systems through minimum standards and periodic inspections. These private systems include septic tanks and **cesspools**.

Septic Tanks

Authorities consider septic tanks the most effective alternative to municipal sewage systems. They are used in rural areas where municipal sewage systems are unavailable. A septic tank system consists of the tank itself, in which wastes are broken down by bacteria, and an area for drainage. The underground tank is made of concrete or steel. It has inlet and outlet pipes near the top, a cleanout opening in the top, and sometimes an opening for inspection. The house drain is connected to the septic tank just as it would be to a municipal sewer. See Table 8.2.

Properly sized tanks are large enough for the sewage to flow through them slowly. Bacteria decompose the sewage, feeding on materials that are toxic to higher life-forms and breaking down organic wastes. In the process, they produce gases that must be carried through a vent in the tank or through the house roof vent. Bacteria do not decompose all matter in the tank. Eventually, sludge builds up and must be pumped out through the cleanout opening by a special truck. If roof drainage is channeled through septic tanks, the large volume prevents solids from settling out and they are washed into drain fields, clogging the system.

The water that carried the sewage is almost clear by the time it leaves the septic tank and flows into the drainage system. Drainage can be accomplished in a seepage pit or a **leach field**. Either spreads the liquid out over a wide area for absorption, preventing odor and contamination.

A leach field consists of a number of perforated clay or concrete tiles or perforated plastic pipes located 2 ½ to 3 feet beneath the surface through which the water seeps into the soil. The size of the drainage field is determined by local health authorities based on the septic tank size and the results of soil percolation tests. These tests determine the speed

Table 8.2 Accessibility to Water and Sewage in the United States (2003)

(Total Number of Units 120,777,000)

Feature	Number	Percent
Plumbing facilities		
Lacking some or all plumbing facilities*	2,597,000	2.2
No piped hot water	1,247,000	1.0
No tub or shower	587,000	0.5
No flush toilet	522,000	0.4
Lack of exclusive use of plumbing facilities	1,204,000	1.0
Water supply		
Public system or private company	104,567,000	86.5
Well serving 1 to 5 units	15,426,000	12.8
Drilled well	13,116,000	10.9
Dug well	1,081,000	0.9
Other or not reported	2,013,000	1.7
Safety of primary water source		
Safe to drink	107,082,000	88.7
Not safe to drink	10,389,000	8.6
Safety not reported	3,234,000	2.7
Means of sewage disposal		
Public sewer	94,618,000	78.3
Septic tank, cesspool, chemical toilet	25,741,000	21.3
Other	417,000	0.3

Source: American Housing Survey for the United States: 2003, Table 1A-4 "Selected Equipment and Plumbing—All Housing Units," www.census.gov/hhes/www/housing/ahs/ahs03/tab1a4.htm. Figures may not total 100 percent because more than one category may apply to a unit.

* Plumbing facilities include hot and cold piped water, a flush toilet, and either a shower or bathtub. More than 2.5 million households in the United States still lack complete plumbing facilities and more than 10 million households lack a safe water supply.

with which water is absorbed into the drainage field. Smaller drainage fields are adequate in sandy soil and gravel because water quickly filters, or leaches, through these materials. Clay soil requires a much larger drainage field.

The soil acts as a filter, helping to complete the purification process. By the time the water reaches natural watercourses or underground supplies, it is no longer contaminated. Some of the water seeps upward by capillary action, and a lush green patch of lawn usually reveals the location of the drainage area.

Septic tanks are sized according to home size, with a minimum of 500 gallons or an amount equal to a four-hour sewage discharge, whichever is greater. Because of the greater number of people expected to use the facilities, the recommended tank size increases with the number of bedrooms.

Cesspools

Cesspools are similar to septic tanks but do not work as effectively and are therefore much less satisfactory systems. A cesspool is a covered tank made of brick, stone, or concrete into which sewage is drained. It differs from a septic tank in that it is deeper and is constructed of porous materials, permitting liquids to seep through all along its walls. Solids sink to the bottom, and the resulting sludge must be pumped out frequently. Wastes are not as thoroughly decomposed in a cesspool as in a septic tank. Drainage is in a limited area which may become saturated.

Alternative Systems

Concern for the conservation of one of the earth's most precious resources—clean water—has led some people to not only decrease household consumption of water but also make use of alternatives to traditional waste disposal. Flush toilets can be exchanged for less wasteful and more environmentally compatible toilet types. The composting toilet is a Swedish innovation that organically breaks down human waste and kitchen scraps without the use of water. The system is safe, odorless, and reduces wastes to a small amount of compost that can be used as fertilizer.

Air-Quality
Control

Chapter 9

Although the body maintains a
constant temperature through metabolic processes,
humans function well only in a narrow temperature
range. The human body produces heat as a result of
metabolic functions and carries it to the skin, where it
is then lost to the surroundings.[1] When there is a balance between the generation of heat and its dissipation, humans are comfortable. It is not, however, just
temperature that affects thermal comfort.

The velocity of moving air affects the speed with
which heat is carried away, resulting in the perception that temperatures are lower. **Windchill** compares
temperature and air currents and indicates the rate
at which heat is carried away from the body. When
the air temperature is 20 degrees Fahrenheit and
there is a 15-mile-per-hour wind, body heat is carried

Figure 9.1 Even a simple shelter such as a windbreak can slow the rate of heat loss.

away as rapidly as if the temperature were 0 degrees Fahrenheit. See Figure 9.1. Table 9.1 details windchill figures.

The human body also loses moisture to the atmosphere. The rate of evaporation is affected by the percentage of moisture present in the air. The evaporation of 1 pound of water carries away 1000 Btus of heat.[2] Body moisture evaporates more rapidly when the humidity of the air is low—rapidly lowering perceived temperature. Thus, in winter, higher air temperatures will be required to maintain comfort levels.

❋ Modern commercial buildings are often constructed with inoperable windows, even in hot climates. Their designers believed that climate control would be simplified if nothing but mechanical systems were used. In hot parts of the United States, residences may be constructed with the minimum number of operable windows to meet building codes, while using stationary windows in other places. This philosophy was more appropriate when energy was plentiful and inexpensive and there seemed to be little need for using natural processes efficiently.

If the human body were always able to adjust adequately to changing temperatures, humidity, and wind velocity, there would be little need for climate control in buildings. Technological improvements through the centuries have resulted in the ability to control environmental factors through mechanical means—making it possible to ignore natural phenomena. Instead of building to take advantage of natural cooling and solar radiation, today's homes are constructed without regard for solar or wind orientation. See Figure 9.2. Modern air-quality-control systems are termed **HVAC** (heating, ventilating, and air-conditioning).

In addition to controlling temperature and humidity within structures, modern technology has made it possible to minimize the presence of indoor air contaminants such as dust, pollen, and other allergens. Sociological factors, economics, and technological availability affect the desired near environment between and within cultures. Recognizing that no single environment would be suitable for every individual, American Society of Heating, Refrigeration and Air-Conditioning Engineers (ASHRAE) standards are designed to satisfy at least 80 percent of individuals

Figure 9.2 New homes are often constructed without regard for solar orientation or site characteristics. Instead of leaving mature trees on a building site, builders often clear the site completely, planting new trees that will require years before providing shade for the structure.

Table 9.1 Windchill Chart*

Wind Velocity (miles per hour)	Temperature (° Fahrenheit)												
	−30°	−25°	−20°	−15°	−10°	−5°	0°	5°	10°	15°	20°	25°	30°
5	−46	−40	−34	−28	−22	−16	−11	−5	1	7	13	19	25
10	−53	−47	−41	−35	−28	−22	−16	−10	−4	3	9	15	21
15	−58	−51	−45	−39	−32	−26	−19	−13	−7	0	6	13	19
20	−61	−55	−48	−42	−35	−29	−22	−15	−9	−2	4	11	17
25	−64	−58	−51	−44	−37	−31	−24	−17	−11	−4	3	9	16
30	−67	−60	−53	−46	−39	−33	−26	−19	−12	−5	1	8	15
35	−69	−62	−55	−48	−41	−34	−27	−21	−14	−7	0	7	14
40	−71	−64	−57	−50	−43	−36	−29	−22	−15	−8	−1	6	13
45	−72	−65	−58	−51	−44	−37	−30	−23	−16	−9	−2	5	12
50	−74	−67	−60	−52	−45	−38	−31	−24	−17	−10	−3	4	12

Source: Office of Climate, Water, and Weather Services, National Weather Service, http://www.nws.noaa.gov/om/windchill/index.shtml, 2001.

* As the wind speed increases, the apparent temperature decreases, making air seem colder than it actually is because body heat is carried away more rapidly. The National Weather Service defines windchills for temperatures of 50 degrees Fahrenheit or less with wind velocity greater than 3 miles per hour. In 2001, the National Weather Service updated the method used to determine windchill factors. This windchill chart is based on that method.

living in the United States.[3] These standards are based on 60 percent relative humidity in a draft-free environment. Preferred temperatures range between 68 and 79 degrees Fahrenheit, depending on the type of clothing worn.

Heating

Fortunately, people can compensate for extreme conditions to some extent through simple protective measures, enabling them to live in areas otherwise unsuitable for habitation. It is, however, heating technology—beginning with fire—that has enabled humans to spread throughout most of the world. People do live in extreme climates without the benefit of sophisticated climate-control systems but the comfort levels achieved are not acceptable to a majority of individuals living in modern industrial cultures.

Fireplaces

Of the heating technologies common in modern buildings, the fireplace is one of the older innovations. Its invention and the subsequent development of the chimney brought the first measure of thermal comfort to buildings after the loss of ancient heating technologies. Today, fireplaces are a desirable feature in homes. In 2003, almost 32 percent of existing homes had a usable fireplace.[4] That same year, 59 percent of new homes constructed had fireplaces, down from the 66 percent of new homes in 1990.[5] An NAHB survey, however, found that 73 percent wanted either a gas- or wood-burning fireplace in their new home.[6] In 2004, only 4 percent of the homes in the United States had more than one fireplace.

Parts of a Fireplace

Fireplaces consist of several parts, all of which must be fireproof for safety. See Figure 9.3. See Box 9.1 for fireplace design code requirements.

The **hearth** is the bottom of the fireplace on which the fire is built. Fireplaces that are frequently used should have a hearth made of firebrick to withstand the intense heat generated by combustion. The **extended hearth** is the portion of the hearth that extends into the room. While it must also be constructed of fireproof materials to a thickness of at least 2 inches, it is not necessary that the materials be capable of withstanding extreme heat; thus, brick, stone, ceramic tile, or other materials can be used, depending on the desired effect. When the bottom of the **firebox** is located at least 8 inches above the extended hearth, the thickness of fireproof materials can reduced to ⅜ inch (IRC).

For a fireplace with an opening of less than 6 square feet, the IRC requires that fireproof materials extend a minimum of 16 inches beyond the front of the fireplace opening and 8 inches on each side. When the firebox opening is larger, the hearth must extend a minimum of 20 inches in front and 12 inches on each side.

The firebox is constructed around the hearth, forming the walls that enclose the fire. Built of firebrick, the firebox is generally splayed outward—the front opening larger than the rear of the enclosure. The upper portion of the back of the firebox slopes toward the front, directing heat into the room.

The **ash dump**, a small trapdoor located in the hearth, provides access to the **ash chamber,** or ash pit, beneath. Ashes from previous fires are swept into the ash chamber and removed through the **cleanout** door. This door is usually accessible from outdoors or from a basement, keeping living areas free of the mess. When minimal space is allotted for the fireplace and there is no room for an ash chamber, a small recess in the hearth floor serves the same function. In that case, the fireplace must first be emptied and ashes removed through the living area.

An opening called the **throat** directs the flow of smoke from the firebox into the **smoke chamber.** Generally triangular-shaped, the smoke chamber funnels smoke upward into the **flue** opening. The **smoke shelf** is a flat horizontal surface in the smoke chamber designed to divert downdrafts that would block the upward flow of smoke and to catch any soot and other particles that fall from above.

Individual flues for more than one fireplace can be offset in the same chimney, but each fireplace must have a separate flue. The flue runs from the fireplace to a point 3 feet above the roof, affecting the placement of rooms on upper stories.

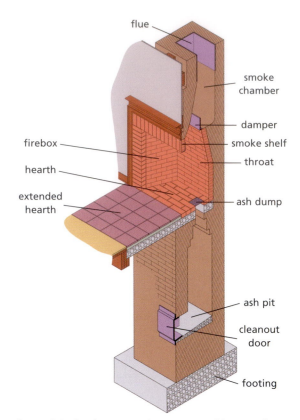

Figure 9.3 Fireplaces must be constructed in accordance with thermodynamic standards established by combustion engineers. These standards, which establish size ratios between the parts of a fireplace, have proven effective for providing adequate draft and minimizing smoke in rooms. Designers should understand these relationships before designing a fireplace surround or determining the size of a fireplace opening.

The flue is a hollow vent rising from the fireplace to the roof and beyond. Flue size is important because it governs the amount of smoke that is directed upward. If the flue is too small, smoke enters the room instead of going up the chimney. Flue height affects the strength of the draft, or pull of air, which is necessary for proper combustion. A chimney cap provides a covering for the chimney to prevent rain and snow from entering, while its open sides allow smoke to dissipate.

The IRC also requires that a **damper** be located inside the flue to regulate the flow of air into and out of

FOOTINGS

- Footings for masonry fireplaces and chimneys must be a minimum of 12 inches thick and extend at least 6 inches on all sides of the fireplace.

HEARTH

- The hearth must be a minimum of 4 inches thick.
- Fireproof materials must be installed within 8 inches on each side of fireplace openings and 16 inches in front of them when the opening is 6 square feet or less. If the opening is greater than 6 square feet, side extensions must be a minimum of 12 inches and front extensions 20 inches. Extended hearths must have a minimum thickness of 2 inches unless the bottom of the firebox is at least 8 inches above the extended hearth.

MANTEL AND SURROUND

- Combustible materials must be placed at least 6 inches from the fireplace opening. Any combustible materials within 12 inches must not project more than $\frac{1}{8}$ inch for every inch from the opening.

FIREPLACE SIZE

- Minimum firebox depth is 20 inches.

DAMPER

- Masonry fireplaces must have a damper that is operable from the room in which the fireplace is located.

CHIMNEYS

- A minimum of 2 inches of clearance is required between the portions of a chimney located within a structure or wall. Chimneys in exterior walls require only 1 inch of clearance.
- The chimney must rise a minimum of 3 feet at the roofline. Two feet is acceptable if there is nothing within 10 feet of the top of the chimney.

Source: International Code Council, *International Residential Code for One- and Two-Family Dwellings 2003* (Country Club Hills, IL: 2003).

the chimney, helping to control the rate of burning. Dampers also help prevent downdrafts and minimize the amount of heated air that escapes when no fire is burning.

The **surround** is a facing for the fireplace opening. Its design, in part, determines fireplace style. Because it is close to the fire, it must be constructed of fireproof materials. The IRC requires fireproof material a minimum of 6 inches on each side of the firebox opening, including the top. In addition, any combustible materials within 12 inches cannot project more than $\frac{1}{8}$ inch for each inch of distance from the opening. Thus, a combustible column placed 8 inches from the side of the opening cannot project more than 1 inch. See Figure 9.4.

Other style considerations include the level of the hearth and the type of **mantel**, if any. A mantel may be either a decorative frame around the fireplace, including a shelf above it, or simply the shelf alone. It may be made of any material, but mantels of flammable materials must be positioned beyond the fireplace opening far enough to meet the minimum distance requirements for the surround. Mantels over 18 inches deep must be located a minimum of 12 inches above the fireplace opening.

An **inglenook** is a small semi-enclosed space in

Automatic fireplace dampers are thermally controlled, closing when there is no fire burning and requiring no action on the part of users. Specifying an automatic damper can help improve the energy-efficiency in a home.

From a construction standpoint, the most practical location for a fireplace is on an outside wall. There, it is close to the foundation and requires little additional structural support. However, an outside location is the least energy-efficient. In any fireplace, the walls of the firebox and the flue act as heat sinks, absorbing heat and dissipating it to colder surfaces. This is true whether the heat source is a fire in the fireplace or, when there is no fire, heated room air. When the fireplace is located on an exterior wall, the absorbed heat is dissipated to the atmosphere outside. A fireplace and chimney built in an interior location dissipate heat to the interior of the house, where it can decrease the load of the primary heating system.

Figure 9.4 Fireproof materials extend past the fireplace opening, ensuring that the surround is safe from combustion. The mantle on this fireplace projects very little. (Source: Barbara Huffman)

front of or beside the fireplace. Its proximity to the fireplace and protection from most of the drafts make it warmer than the rest of the room. Inglenooks are often found in colonial-style homes.

Because of its weight, a masonry fireplace requires additional structural support, including a heavy footing and foundation. Because they weigh less than masonry units, prefabricated fireplaces require no special foundation or footing and can be installed anywhere without structural changes.

Prefabricated Fireplaces

Prefabricated fireplaces are factory-made units built according to established dimensional relationships, minimizing the chance of smoky fires or those that do not burn correctly. Insulation and fireproof materials used in their construction allow some prefabricated fireplaces to be placed close to any surface, including flammable ones (called **zero clearance**). The initial cost is much lower than for masonry fireplaces.

Gas and electric fireplaces use no wood for fuel, so they burn cleaner than conventional fireplaces. Their major function is aesthetic, although heaters and fans can be concealed in them to provide some warmth

and they may be thermostatically controlled. Gas fireplaces must be connected to a gas line and have a vent (flue) to allow noxious gases to escape through the roof. Electric fireplaces require no vent, and because they can be plugged in anywhere, they are easily relocated. This feature makes them popular with renters as well as homeowners.

Fireplace Efficiency

Most fireplaces are only 5 to 10 percent efficient and may even be less than zero percent when used only occasionally. Efficiency improves to 15 to 40 percent when used almost continuously, partly because the chimney warms up and stores heat, reradiating some to living areas. Low fireplace efficiency means that only a small proportion of the heat capacity of the fuel is actually converted to useful heat. Fireplaces do consume wood—a renewable resource—and they can provide heat during emergencies when power failures disable other heating systems, but it is their aesthetic appeal that makes them popular. Attempts have therefore been made to improve the efficiency of fireplaces with a modicum of success.

To support combustion, fireplaces draw room air, which may have already been warmed by the primary heating system. The majority of heat produced by the fire is channeled up the chimney, as is heated room air. The rising heat creates a suction, causing cold outside air to pour through cracks and crevices into the room. If there is insufficient air for draw, smoke enters the room instead of rising through the chimney. In tight houses, it may be necessary to open a window to provide sufficient air flow for smoke-free combustion.

A good fire in a medium-sized fireplace requires more than 20,000 cubic feet of air per hour. An average-sized house (2250 square feet with 8-foot ceilings) contains about 18,000 cubic feet of air. Thus, the fire itself would require more than one entire air exchange per hour and return little heat to the room. As the fire dies down, heat is still removed from the room, further decreasing fireplace efficiency.

Efficiency can be improved by bringing air in from outside to support combustion rather than using room air. Air-intake systems include special ducts leading directly from outside to the fireplace, vents leading from a basement window to the fireplace, or ventilating bricks in the fireplace foundation.

Heat-circulating devices also increase fireplace efficiency. The simplest is a curved tube convection heater, which can be installed in any wood-burning fireplace. The fire grate (which supports the wood) is replaced by one made of C-shaped tubes. Room air is sucked into the bottom of the tubes, then warmed as it is drawn through the tubes under and around the fire. Rising by natural convection, the warmed air returns to the room through the top of the tubes. Blowers can be attached to increase the volume and speed of air being returned to the room. Because both ends must be where room air can be easily withdrawn and replaced without losing it through the chimney, the grate must be placed forward in the fireplace. These devices increase fireplace efficiency only slightly and are of questionable value.

Other circulating fireplaces have double-wall con-

Regardless of whether there is a fire in the fireplace, the natural drafts created by the chimney pull room air through the chimney and out the roof—even during the cooling season. Fireplace efficiency can be improved by reducing the amount of conditioned room air pulled through the chimney and by directing more of the heat produced in the fireplace into the room.

struction with a metal hearth, under which is an air space, and a metal **fireback**, behind which is a connecting air space. Air is heated as it passes beneath the fire, rises through natural convection behind the back, and is sent back into the room through registers at the top of the fireplace. Blowers and thermostats provide thermal control. See Figure 9.5.

Figure 9.5 One way to minimize room air loss through a fireplace is to use tempered glass doors such as these. These doors also reduce the amount of conditioned room air escaping up the chimney when the fire becomes low or goes out. Adding hearth-level louvers to limit the amount of room air supplied to the fire would improve the efficiency further.

Table 9.2 Percent Primary Heating System Types in the United States in 2003

Type of Heating System[a]	U.S. Total[b]	Northeast	Midwest	South	West
Forced warm air	61.80	40.42	80.81	59.24	64.55
Steam or hot water system	12.5	47.84	8.78	1.70	3.48
Electric heat pump	10.72	2.79	2.40	24.12	5.58
Built-in electric units	4.50	11.70	4.35	2.28	0.71
Gravity warm air	5.00	4.23	1.72	3.72	13.14
Room heaters with flue	1.34	1.74	0.85	1.89	1.37
Room heaters without flue	1.41	0.29	0.13	3.61	0.24
Portable electric heater	0.69	0.13	0.07	1.33	0.85
Stoves	0.99	1.56	0.66	0.98	1.52
Fireplaces	0.18	0.10	0.13	0.17	0.37
Cooking stoves	0.14	0.45	—	0.16	0.17
Other	0.27	0.28	—	0.45	0.29
None	0.42	0.02	0.02	0.35	1.30

Source: U.S. Census Bureau, "Housing Units—Characteristics by Tenure and Region: 2003," *Statistical Abstract of the United States: 2004–2005,* Table 947 (Washington, D.C.: Department of Commerce, 2005), 609.

[a] The type of primary heating system varies with the region of the country, although forced warm air predominates everywhere except in the Northeast. Steam or hot water systems, on the other hand, are prevalent only in the Northeast.

[b] Totals may not equal 100 percent due to rounding.

Even with these devices, fireplace efficiency remains low. Thus, fireplaces function best as auxiliary heat sources. In 2003, less than 0.2 percent of homes in the United States used fireplaces as a primary heating system. See Table 9.2.

Stoves

Although fireplaces are familiar, much of the world, including rural America, makes considerable use of various types of stoves. In general, stoves are more efficient, require less fuel, and provide more satisfactory thermal comfort than fireplaces.

Masonry Stoves

Masonry stoves were developed in Europe several centuries ago and remain common, especially in rural areas. See Figure 9.6. Designed to burn almost any solid fuel, the most frequently used fuel is wood. The stoves consist of a small firebox lined with firebrick or other materials that can handle extremely high temperatures, channels through which smoke and hot gases travel to the chimney, and a large masonry mass

Figure 9.6 The secret of masonry stoves is the long, convoluted smoke channels. As the smoke and hot gases pass through the channels, they constantly lose heat to the masonry mass enclosing the passages. By the time the heated substances have been exhausted through the chimney, most of the heat has been transferred to the masonry mass. Heat travels slowly through this heat sink, finally reaching the surface where it radiates heat into the room. A single fire can provide heat for as long as 20 hours.

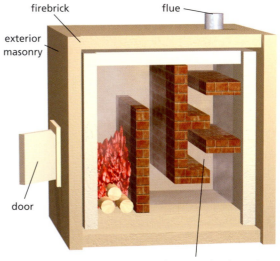

that serves as a heat sink. A small fire can be built once or twice a day. Because the fire burns at extremely hot temperatures—2000 degrees Fahrenheit—almost complete combustion occurs, creating few, if any, pollutants escaping through the chimney, leaving minimal deposits of creosote and soot inside the stove or chimney, and resulting in efficiency ratings as high as 90 percent.

Because of the mass of the masonry, exterior surfaces are warm but not dangerously so—typically about 120 degrees Fahrenheit. Sleeping shelves, ovens, cooking surfaces, and small niches for drying gloves or heating water are often integral parts of these stoves. Although surface temperatures rarely reach 150 degrees Fahrenheit, masonry stoves should not be closer than 1 foot from combustible materials.

Although expensive to install, these stoves are popular in the American Northwest. Due to their interior complexity, their construction is a task for professionals. Unlike other stoves, masonry units may heat an entire structure when correctly designed. Masonry stoves are often called Russian, Siberian, or Finnish stoves.

The **kachelöfen**,[7] or tile stove, is a type of masonry stove. See Figure 9.7. Glazed earthenware tiles are used on the outside surfaces, making the stoves highly decorative. To provide extra surface area for dissipating heat, the tiles are often curved or decorated with raised or recessed designs. Because tiles can be made in any shape, these stoves may be disguised as urns, model buildings, or even statues. Because the kachelöfen is located completely within a room with all sides exposed, there is little loss of heat. Modern versions may burn wood, gas, oil, or other fuels. While there are a few companies building these stoves in the United States and Canada, their high cost limits their popularity. They are still popular in Europe, however, where design choices are extensive.

Metal Stoves

Metal stoves are made of cast iron or welded steel and lined with firebrick. The firebrick prevents metal surfaces from becoming excessively hot. Doors of

Figure 9.7 The kachelöfen is decorative as well as functional. Usually, fuel is added through a door in an adjacent room, eliminating the need for carrying wood into the living area.

metal, glass, or ceramic seal the firebox, allowing air intake to be controlled with vents on the front of the stove. Providing an outside air intake limits the amount of heated room air used for combustion. Airtight stoves may reach efficiencies as high as 80 percent. Blowers increase the circulation of the heated air.

Metal stoves may be freestanding or inserted into a fireplace. See Figure 9.8. Freestanding units must be a minimum of 36 inches from combustible materials and 18 inches from noncombustible heat shields, but all sides are within a room, limiting heat loss. Flues may lead into a chimney or directly through the roof to vent gases, smoke, and particles outdoors. Although most burn wood, pellet stoves are popular in areas where wood is expensive.

Figure 9.8 Metal stoves must be kept away from combustible surfaces. Note the metal-covered asbestos pad beneath the stove to protect the floor from heat. When stoves are completely within a room, the flue is exposed.

Disadvantages of stoves include:

- Freestanding stoves require significant space within a room.
- Space is needed for storing wood close to the stove.
- The fire must be tended.
- Local codes may not permit their installation or may require traditional backup systems, increasing costs.
- Insurance companies may charge higher premiums when these stoves serve as the primary heating system.

Any unit that consumes combustible fuel must have a vent going to the outside—usually through the roof. Space for these vents must be provided in each succeeding level of the structure. In some instances, codes do not allow the vents to be enclosed, limiting the design of the space.

Central Heating Systems

Unlike **space heaters** such as fireplaces and stoves that heat one area, central heating systems distribute heat to all parts of a structure. A central heating unit is located out of sight, usually in a basement, crawl space, or utility area, where it produces sufficient heat for an entire building. This heat is then distributed through a series of ducts or pipes. See Box 9.2 for IRC requirements for furnaces.

Types of Central Heating Systems

Several types of central heating systems exist, depending on two major variables. First, the fuel used to provide heat may be wood, oil, coal, natural gas, liquid petroleum gas, solar energy, or electricity. Some systems are capable of using more than one fuel. Most

---

Box 9.2 Code Requirements for Furnaces

HEATING

- Every dwelling located where the winter temperature is lower than 60 degrees Fahrenheit must have a heating system capable of maintaining a minimum temperature of 68 degrees Fahrenheit in the living space.

FURNACE CLEARANCE

- The furnace in a central heating system must be located where there is a minimum of 30 inches of space in front of the unit for access. Room heaters require only 18 inches of space in front.
- Central furnaces must have a minimum of 3 inches of working space at the sides, back, and top of the unit. The enclosing space must be at least 12 inches wider than the furnace.
- The passageway leading to the furnace must be a minimum of 24 inches wide.

Source: International Code Council, *International Residential Code for One- and Two-Family Dwellings 2003* (Country Club Hills, IL: 2003).

---

multifuel systems are designed to burn wood and a more conventional fuel. Second, the heat distribution medium may be by air, water, or steam. Warm air systems rely on convective air currents for heat exchange. Steam and hot water systems use a liquid medium (water or an antifreeze solution) for heat exchange.

Heating units located in basements or crawl spaces take advantage of the natural tendency of heat to rise. A central location is desirable to minimize heat loss. Houses built on slabs require furnaces located on the same level as the living space, and when more than one heating unit is required in a multistory home, one of them may be located in an attic. In these cases, **counterflow**[8] **furnaces** may be installed. These furnaces force warmed air downward to direct it through the distribution system. In large homes— more than 3500 square feet—it is more efficient to have two separate climate-control systems than a single one. The installation of multiple units may also be necessary when air-conditioning is a part of the climate-control system. It is more difficult to push cold air than warm air; thus, cold air travels at a lower velocity. In addition, pushing cold air upward is inefficient. The obvious advantage of having separate units is that zoned heating and cooling can be easily accomplished. Disadvantages include:

- Initial cost of the equipment
- Increased amount of space that must be assigned to equipment

System Components

A central heating system is divided into four major components:

- The **heat producer**
- The **heat exchanger**
- The distribution system
- The controls. See Figure 9.9.

The Heat Producer. The heat producer is a fireproof combustion chamber within a furnace where wood,

oil, coal, gas, or other fuel is burned to produce heat. The gases that result from combustion are directed into a flue and vented through the roof.

Electric furnaces produce heat by the flow of current through coil heating elements. The resistance of

Figure 9.9 In this warm air furnace, the heat producer burns gas. The heat produced warms the air in the tubes in the heat exchanger located above the burners and sealed from them to prevent noxious gases from intermingling with the warmed air. When the heated air leaves the heat exchanger, it enters the plenum, from which it is distributed to all parts of the system. The noxious gases that are a by-product of combustion are carried away through the flues. Controls are located in the living space.

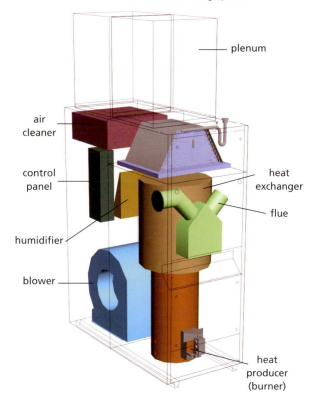

plenum

air cleaner

control panel

humidifier

blower

heat exchanger

flue

heat producer (burner)

the metal coils to the flow of electricity causes them to heat. No chimney or flue is needed for the escape of combustion gases, and the furnace can generally be placed in a confined space without a fire hazard.

The Heat Exchanger. The heat exchanger transfers the heat from combustion into a form that can be carried through the house. A system of sealed convoluted tubes containing air or water is located in a chamber heated by the burner or by electric resistance coils. Electric heating coils may be located in the chamber itself; when using other fuels, the chamber is separated from the burner to prevent the heating medium from being contaminated by combustion gases. In warm air systems, once heated air leaves the heat exchangers, it is channeled into the **plenum**, a large **duct** that supplies individual ducts in the system.

The Distribution System. The distribution system is distinctive to the system type—ducts and registers, grilles, or diffusers[9] for warm air; pipes and convectors or baseboard units for hot water; and pipes and radiators for steam systems. Pipes carry water or steam to closed heat outlets where convection currents distribute the heat.

Ducts are hollow tubes leading from the heat exchanger to registers in each room. Both the distance and the direction traveled by warmed or cooled air affect air velocity and system efficiency. Changes in direction and vertical travel slow velocity rapidly. When ducts run from one room to another, as they frequently do—especially in multiple-story homes—noises may be carried through them from one living area to another, affecting privacy. The IRC and other building codes specify duct size, allowable ducting materials, mounting requirements, and required clearances.

Regardless of the type of system used, heat outlets should be located for maximum efficiency and even distribution. If heating has higher priority than cooling, the registers, radiators, or convectors should be close to floor level, preferably on outside walls. Locating the supply outlets beneath windows where sinking cold air is concentrated, will help minimize drafts.

Warm air systems require additional return air ducts to direct cooled room air back to the furnace. Because they carry cool air, return inlets are most efficient when located in or near the floor. To ensure that conditioned air circulates throughout a space, returns should be located as far as possible from supply registers, while remaining within the area of air circulation for the same space. Return air inlets are not necessary in each room if room air can circulate to a central area. In small homes, a single large return air inlet may be all that is necessary, although multistoried structures require a minimum of one return air inlet on each story. However, even in small homes, additional return air inlets are required when there are major directional changes, such as an L-shape. Insufficient draft for circulation caused by the lack of access to a return air inlet will result in spaces that are not heated evenly or effectively.

The Controls. Climate-control systems are controlled by **thermostats**. The thermostat switches the heating system on when the ambient temperature is lower than the temperature at which it has been set. When the appropriate temperature is reached, the thermostat signals the system to cycle off.

A single thermostat may control an entire house, but more efficient systems have two or more thermostats, permitting individual temperature control of separate zones. Multiple thermostats, however, can only be used if the entire system, including the ductwork, is designed for zoned heating. Separate thermostats are required for each zone or furnace when multiple climate-control devices are used or when the distribution system is divided into zones. Thermostats must be installed within the area they control.

The location of the thermostat is critical because the temperature of the air where it is located controls the operation of the entire system.

- Placing the thermostat on an inside wall protects it from temperature fluctuations on exterior walls due to solar radiation and wind.
- Extraneous heat sources, such as direct sunlight, lighting fixtures, and heat-producing activities such as cooking, raise the temperature in the immediate area, so these locations should be avoided.
- The thermostat should be positioned in a place free of drafts—both cold and warm—precluding areas near supply or return vents, exterior doors, or near vertical openings such as stairways.

Automatic set-back thermostats can be set for different temperatures during the day and at the time specified. Thus, if residents prefer cooler temperatures for sleeping but want to wake to a warm room, they may set the thermostat to turn up the heat prior to their waking time. One-day and seven-day programmable thermostats are available. Seven-day thermostats allow for changes in schedule on different days of the week.

A damper is a circular metal plate that fits inside the flue. In an automatic damper, an electric motor rotates the damper to the open position when the thermostat signals the burner to cycle on. When the burner is off, the damper rotates to close. With some automatic flue dampers, the electric motor operates continuously and opens the damper in the event of a

Locating supply registers beneath windows limits the design of window treatments. Treatments that extend almost to floor level will impede the flow of warmed or cooled air, affecting heating and cooling efficiency and air circulation. Furniture placed in front of supply registers will also impede air flow. During the heating season, such furniture may also suffer adverse effects from dry heated air, which may cause joints to loosen and cracking to occur in wood members. Designers may be consulted by engineers and HVAC contractors prior to finalizing the placement of supply registers and return inlets.

power failure. Others use the motor only for opening and closing, requiring no electricity otherwise.

Systems Used for Heat Delivery

Each heating system component operates in the same way, regardless of the type of heating system used: warm air, hot water, or steam.

Warm Air Heat. Warm air heating systems distribute heated air to the entire home, usually through a series of ducts. Two types of warm air systems are generally available: gravity and forced air.

Lamps, television sets, VCRs, and DVD players generate heat while operating. None of these should be placed near a thermostat. In winter, the heating system could cycle off prematurely. In summer, the cooling system will cycle on more frequently, using energy unnecessarily.

Even after the burner cycles off, warm air continues to rise through the flue and is dissipated outside. The thermostat can activate an automatic damper to prevent the loss of warm air through the flue connected to the heat producer when the burner is not operating. Flue dampers improve the energy-efficiency of climate-control systems and can be added to existing systems.

GRAVITY WARM AIR SYSTEMS. The movement of air in gravity warm air systems depends on the tiny difference in density between warm and cool air. Gravity warm air systems are designed so that heated air rises naturally through the ducts or, in the case of a ductless system, through a central floor register—a **floor furnace**. No mechanical assistance is used to move the heated air, so these systems operate relatively quietly. Cool air sinks and returns to the furnace by gravity.

Because there is no blower to move the air, the ducts should not be longer than 15 feet. This typically requires that heat supply registers be located on inside walls and return air ducts on outside walls. With the ducts arranged in this manner, the slow-moving warmed air loses heat before it reaches the colder outside walls, often causing the perimeter of the house to be significantly cooler than the center. Since warm air cools relatively quickly, it may be several degrees cooler by the time it reaches rooms located away from the furnace, so temperature differences between rooms are also large.

Gravity warm air systems are best used in homes under 1000 square feet, and the furnace must be located below the level of the registers. In a home without a basement or crawl space, the furnace can be located on the first floor. In this case, registers must be installed high on the wall—an arrangement that creates a large temperature difference between floors and ceilings, as well as pockets of uncirculated stale air.

An additional problem associated with gravity warm air systems is that other climate-control systems cannot be combined with them. The air flow in a gravity system does not have sufficient force to go through an air-filtration device, furnace-mounted humidifier, or air-conditioning system.

⊞ Even when a heating system alone is initially installed, it is often a good idea to size ducts for the eventual addition of air-conditioning. Then when the cooling system is installed, it will be unnecessary to tear out finish materials to install new ducts.

Figure 9.10 Forced air furnaces have sufficient power to force air through supply vents located on exterior walls.

FORCED WARM AIR SYSTEMS. While a gravity warm air system depends on natural convection currents to distribute heat, a forced warm air system has a blower that forces heated air rapidly through the system. See Figure 9.10. Less heat is lost during distribution, so the air does not need to be heated to the higher temperatures required by gravity systems; more usable heat can be obtained from an identically sized furnace than when a gravity system is used. Forced warm air heat is the system of choice in more than 60 percent of modern American homes. (See Table 9.2.)

Forced air systems can also support other climate-control devices. Both the heating and cooling systems can use the same blower and the same distribution system. In this case, the ducts are sized for the larger capacity required by air conditioners. Initial installation of the air-conditioning system thus costs much less than would a separate installation. Forced warm air systems also operate with sufficient force behind the circulating air to allow humidifiers and air filters to be installed.

Forced air systems cause drafts near registers, but the greatest disadvantages of forced air systems are associated with the blower. Although air filters help, the blower causes circulating air to stir up existing dust; thus, household tasks are increased. The noise made by the blower during operation is carried through the ducts into living areas. See Box 9.3 for a discussion of noise control in the HVAC system.

Hot Water Heat. Hot water heating systems use water rather than air for heat storage and distribution.

Box 9.3 Noise and Air-Quality Control

The HVAC system is a major source of noise in most buildings: Forced air systems require a fan to circulate the air, and pipes in hydronic systems ping and pop as they heat and cool. To minimize the noises associated with HVAC systems, purchase models designed for quiet, vibration-free operation, locate the equipment in an isolated area, and sound-condition ducts or pipes. Equipment noise should also be considered when choosing or designing a location where it will be housed.

It may be possible to locate the furnace or boiler in a basement away from living areas, but when that is not feasible, isolate the equipment in a closet that has walls with a high STC rating. Further, use a well-sealed solid-core wood or insulated metal door and omit any louvers through walls or doors. Combustion air for forced air systems can be obtained through the attic, crawl space, or basement rather than from the living area. Set the equipment on isolating pads to reduce vibration as well as noise.

Both supply and return ducts should be lined with acoustic material and have as few turns as possible (angled turns create more air turbulence and, thus, more noise than do radial turns or curves in HVAC ducts). Use flexible connectors and couplings where ducts pass through walls, ensure that duct hangers are lined with resilient material, seal openings around ducts, and size ducts so that air velocity does not exceed 1000 cubic feet per minute. (Ducts leading to and from kitchens should not be lined with acoustic material because grease could accumulate.) Because ducts act as megaphones and carry sounds from one outlet to another, the system design should be well thought out. In addition, lining the plenum with sound-absorbing materials can reduce noise significantly. The decibel level in an average-sized plenum chamber lined with 2-inch-thick fiberglass panels can be reduced as much as 20 decibels at most frequencies.

Hydronic systems should be similarly treated: Wrap pipes to reduce vibration, provide flexible couplings, seal around openings to isolate the pipes from framing members, size pipes so flow velocity is limited, and support pipe runs with resilient hangers.

The burner (heat producer) heats water in a boiler (heat exchanger). The hot water is then carried to radiators, convectors, or baseboard units through a network of concealed pipes (usually copper). Baseboard convectors are the least conspicuous. Larger models can be freestanding, wall-mounted, or recessed.

A convector consists of a hot water pipe and a system of metal fins. The fins increase the surface area over which the room air flows. Cold air near the floor is warmed as it moves through the fins, creating gentle convection currents. As the warmed air rises, it pulls cool air up into the convector, where it passes over the fins.

A radiator consists of loops of pipe through which hot water flows. Like convectors, radiators create nat- ural convection currents that rise through the spaces between the pipes. It also radiates heat from its cast-iron surface. Radiators are larger than convectors and therefore more conspicuous. People sometimes attempt to disguise radiators with a shelf or enclosure, but this decreases the efficiency of the heating system.

The gentle air flow of hot water heating systems is less disturbing than the drafts created by forced warm air systems. Because no mechanical force is needed to circulate air, hot water heating systems operate silently. Hot water heating systems can be easily installed in separate zones; thus, portions of a home can be efficiently shut off and left unheated, or some parts kept warmer than others.

Water heats slowly but retains heat for a long

period of time. Thus, hot water systems are slow to respond to sudden temperature changes, but for the same reason, pipe runs can be sufficiently long to place the heating units on outside walls. Unlike forced air systems, hot water heating systems cannot be used for air-conditioning, air filtration, or humidity control.

Hot water heating systems have certain other disadvantages that have diminished their popularity. Equipment is expensive to purchase and install, maintenance costs may be high, and corrosive water may harm boilers and pipes. Preventative maintenance calls for treating water with chemicals to minimize corrosion. If homes are left unheated during cold weather, pipes may freeze and burst, causing damage to the structure, finishes, and contents.

As with warm air heating systems, there are two types of hot water heating systems: gravity and forced hot water.

GRAVITY HOT WATER SYSTEMS. Like gravity warm air systems, gravity hot water systems operate on the principle that a warm fluid is less dense than a cool fluid. The boiler is located beneath the room heat outlets, and hot water rises through gently sloping pipes

to convectors or radiators in the spaces above. This process is relatively slow when compared with other systems. The heat from the water is transferred to the metal surfaces of convectors or radiators, and as the water cools, it sinks and returns to the boiler via a second pipe. This two-pipe distribution system (supply and return) makes gravity systems expensive to install, and they are no longer common, although older homes may still have them.

FORCED HOT WATER SYSTEMS. A pump circulates water through a forced hot water or **hydronic** system, carrying water quickly through the distribution system, providing more usable heat, and making it possible to use a smaller boiler and pipes than those required by gravity systems. Because water is pumped through the distribution network, the boiler can be located anywhere.

Two pipes, like those in a gravity hot water heating system, provide the most efficient heat distribution for forced hot water heating. However, because two-pipe systems are expensive, they are rarely used in residences. One-pipe systems have a single pipe that carries hot water from the boiler to all outlets. As the pipe nears the outlet, a branch circuit carries part of the water into the heating unit. The rest remains in the original pipe, bypassing the unit. The cooled water from the radiator or convector is released back into the hot water pipe by a second branch beyond the heating unit. The mixed water is then carried to the next outlet. Newer systems use a special fitting that minimizes the problem associated with older systems—the diminishing temperature at outlets farther away from the central heating unit. Because of the amount of plumbing required, one-pipe systems are still relatively expensive to install.

A less expensive method of hot water distribution is the **series loop** system. All radiators are connected in series so that the hot water must go through every heating unit in the line. Since water cools relatively rapidly under these circumstances, heating units toward the end of the line receive much cooler water and provide less heat. Reverse flow systems carry water directly from the boiler to the heating unit farthest away to begin the circuit. In a series loop system, no heating unit can be turned off without cutting off distribution to others farther along the line, but two or more series loops can be installed for zoned heating. A single circulating pump can force water through the different loops or separate pumps can be used.

INDIVIDUAL BASEBOARD SYSTEMS. Individual baseboard systems are self-contained hot water baseboard units designed to heat a single room. The burner, boiler, **expansion tank**, and heat distributor are integral parts of the small heating unit. Most are electric, but gas units are used in some areas. These systems are inexpensive to install because there is no central boiler and no piping system. Because each unit is complete, zoned heating is automatically accomplished.

Steam Heat. Steam heating systems, found mostly in older homes, use boilers to boil water to generate steam. The steam rises of its own accord, requiring no pump for distribution. It is routed to radiators or convectors, where it transfers its heat to the metal surfaces, causing it to condense. Convection currents warm the room air, although a significant amount of heat is radiated from the radiators. The condensed steam (water) flows by gravity through the same valve it entered and returns to the furnace. Two-pipe systems provide separate returns to the boiler.

Because it requires extensive plumbing, steam heat is expensive to install. Steam heating systems are also noisy, hissing and banging as the metal radiators or convectors expand and contract. However, the heat is distributed relatively quickly after the initial vaporization of the water. Since the temperature is higher than that used in hot water heating systems, more usable heat reaches the radiators or convectors.

Radiant Systems. Modern radiant heating system are reminiscent of ancient heating systems. Today, the centuries-old Korean *ondol*[10] and Chinese *k'ang*,[11] similar to the ancient Roman **hypocaust**, are still used. Hot gases from the cooking fire are channeled be-

Disguising hot water or steam radiators by installing decorative devices over them—even those with perforated surfaces—decreases the air flow necessary to maintain comfortable temperatures and increases operation costs.

---

neath a floor or platform through supports similar to those used in the early Roman hypocaust. The ondol warms the floor, while the k'ang warms a platform used as a bed and a sitting area by all family members. While the traditional system is still used in rural areas, homes in urban areas have hot water pipes channeled through concrete floors to warm the living space.

In contemporary structures, radiant heating systems first heat a surface or mass. This heat is then passed to the air by conduction and convection. Because these systems heat objects rather than air, the thermostat can often be set 6 to 8 degrees lower than with forced air systems to maintain the same comfort level. No blowers are used, so radiant systems do not disturb dust, reducing household tasks, and noise is not a problem.

There are two types of radiant systems—hot water and electric. Radiant systems do not affect furniture placement. Concealed pipes or coils take the place of the convectors or radiators that are found in other systems. Pipes or coils are embedded in floors, walls, or ceilings, or in panels that may double as artwork. Because radiant systems are hidden from view, the system components are inaccessible for maintenance.

The wall, floor, or ceiling structural materials—often concrete or plaster—must be heated before the room can be warmed, creating a significant time lag when low temperatures call for heat. This time lag is also evident when heat is no longer needed. Although

---

Because system components in radiant systems loop through structural members, their specific location may not be known. Therefore, adding light fixtures and fans or attaching decorative items to walls or ceilings requires care so that fasteners do not penetrate components.

extremely expensive to operate, radiant systems can also be used in concrete driveways and sidewalks as a snow- and ice-melting system.

When a radiant system is embedded in a floor slab, the slab must be insulated to prevent heat from escaping into the ground. Floor insulation is also imperative when radiant systems are embedded between structural members in framed floors. System temperatures of approximately 85 degrees Fahrenheit are maintained, because higher temperatures would cause discomfort when walking on the floor.

Higher temperatures can be maintained in radiant systems in ceilings and walls. However, care should be taken that draperies do not decrease the amount of usable heat from wall units and that fasteners for decorative items do not pierce the pipes or coils.

Because they require loops of pipes or coils, radiant systems are expensive to install. System components are embedded in or sandwiched between structural materials and are difficult to service or change. As with any heating system through which liquids flow, pipes may eventually corrode or freeze and leak. Because the pipes are embedded in structural components, damage caused by leakage can be extensive. Electric systems, of course, are immune to leakage.

Heat Pumps. Heat pumps move heat from one place to another. They work on four principles:

- Matter has heat until its temperature reaches absolute zero[12] (−460 degrees Fahrenheit). Thus, even cold winter air contains some heat.
- Heat flows from warmer to cooler matter.
- When matter changes form, heat is absorbed or given off. For example, when water is precisely at its boiling point, it absorbs heat in the process of changing to steam, although the temperature remains at 212 degrees Fahrenheit.
- When a liquid is under pressure, its temperature and its boiling point are both raised.

A heat pump removes heat from the outside air and moves it indoors in the winter, and reverses the process in the summer. Because heat pumps can serve a dual purpose, the installation of climate-control systems is simplified. See Box 9.4.

The efficiency of heat pumps varies considerably with outside temperatures, decreasing drastically at temperatures below 30 degrees Fahrenheit. They function most efficiently in climates with mild winters and hot summers. Connection to solar panels can make heat pumps efficient to 0 degrees Fahrenheit or below.

Air-to-air heat pumps extract heat from air and add it to air. Liquid-to-air heat pumps remove heat from and transfer heat to a liquid, then use that heat to warm the air. While most heat pumps transfer heat to and from outside air, better efficiency can be achieved if the heat pump absorbs heat from water or air beneath the surface, because it remains above the temperature necessary for efficient heat transfer all year. At 30 feet below the surface, year-round soil temperatures remain at the average annual temperature for an area—near 50 degrees Fahrenheit in much of the United States. Soil temperatures at shallower depths are more moderate as well and are not subject to extreme daily fluctuations.

Ground source heat pumps take advantage of these more constant underground temperatures. Pipes beneath the surface carry warmer underground air to the heat pump in a ground source system.

Because water holds more heat than air, it can be a better source for heat transfer. Either groundwater or well water can be used; the pipes for both are deeper than those carrying air in ground source systems. Because well water is more reliable, it is more frequently used for heat extraction than is groundwater. To use the heat in water, pipes carry antifreeze solutions from the heat pump to the water source, where its temperature is raised.

Heat pumps are often chosen primarily for their

Box 9.4 Heat Pump Operation

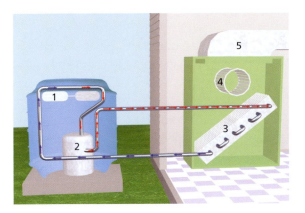

The medium used to exchange heat, called the refrigerant, has a low boiling point under normal pressure. As it flows through the various parts of the heat pump, it changes from a liquid to a gas and back again, exchanging heat with each cycle. The liquid refrigerant is pumped outside, where it is colder than the ambient temperature. There a fan (1) circulates outside air over the coils. The refrigerant absorbs heat from the air, which is then amplified by a compressor (2), causing the liquid to change to a gas. The hot refrigerant flows to the indoor coils (3), where heat is absorbed by the cool room air and condenses into liquid form. A blower (4) moves the heated air into the ductwork (5) and it is distributed to all parts of the house. The system can be reversed to provide cooling in the summer.

cooling efficiency. In cold climates, this may mean that the unit selected does not have sufficient heating capacity, and either a backup system or a supplementary heat source may be required. Heat pumps may have electric heating coils to provide a backup without an additional system, or they may be connected to an existing furnace. The problem with using an existing distribution system, however, is that heat pumps deliver air at lower temperatures than conventional furnaces, so larger ducts are required.

Because heat pumps use electric power, they are

Because ground source heat pumps use air beneath the surface, the air supplied to the interior of a structure has fewer pollutants and allergens.

clean heat sources. As air conditioners, they use about the same amount of energy as conventional models, although ground and water source heat pumps can significantly reduce the amount of energy used for air-conditioning. Because they move heat around rather than generate it, heat pumps require less energy for heating than do conventional units. In fact, ground source heat pumps can operate at up to 400 percent efficiency and conventional ones at 300 percent—a significant improvement from high-efficiency furnaces in the 90 percent range.

Space Heaters. While a majority of Americans depend on central heating, some use space heaters—self-contained units that include all the components necessary for producing and distributing heat. Space heaters require no network of pipes or ducts, and there is no large central unit, making the initial cost low and installation simple. Temperatures in each room or area can be individually controlled, resulting in fuel savings. Units in different rooms may even use different fuels and be of different types. Space heaters, for these reasons, are excellent for additions to homes.

ELECTRIC SPACE HEATERS. Space heaters include a variety of built-in and portable devices. Among the most common are those that produce heat from electricity. Although electric resistance can be used to provide heat in a furnace, it is particularly well suited to space heating. The various types of electric space heating can function as the only system for the entire house or as an auxiliary system in one room.

Room-sized electric heaters can be recessed in a wall or ceiling to provide supplemental warmth where needed. Their most frequent use is in bathrooms. These units may consist of a heating element backed by a metal reflector, or a panel with a blower and louvered grille to supply warm air. Portable electric space heaters are freestanding units that can be plugged

Electric units are almost 100 percent efficient as heat producers because none of the heat produced is vented up a flue. However, the electricity is generated by power plants using fossil fuels, hydropower, nuclear energy, or bioconversion at much less than 100 percent efficiency, making these furnaces more inefficient overall than those that consume other fuels. In most areas of the country, electricity is the least cost-efficient heating source.

into any outlet, offering radiant heat, forced warm air, or a combination of the two.

The type of electric space heating most frequently used as a primary system for the whole house is baseboard heating. The small units are similar to the baseboard convectors used in hot water heating systems, except that they contain wire heating coils instead of hot water pipes. The units are wired directly into the home's electrical system. Air is pulled up through the heating element, setting up convection currents that distribute the heat.

Each unit is controlled by a separate thermostat, increasing efficiency and making electric resistance heat an excellent backup system for wood-burning stoves and furnaces. Because these heaters need no blowers or pumps, no large central furnace or boiler, and no extensive distribution network, they are initially inexpensive and easy to install. Furthermore, little or no maintenance is necessary.

Electric heat is clean because no fuel is burned on-site but the heated air cools rapidly and electric units

---

❀ While the heat generated by clothes dryers, hot water heaters, ranges, dishwashers, and refrigerators adds to ambient heat, it is lighting that is the most significant factor. Incandescent bulbs convert approximately 90 percent of the electricity they use to heat—a 100-watt bulb transmits over 300 Btus per hour to room air. Keeping lights off or using cooler-operating fluorescent bulbs will help maintain cooler air temperatures.

will not support additional climate-control systems, so it is necessary to provide other means of air circulation, air filtration, humidity control, and air-conditioning.

COMBUSTION SPACE HEATERS. While electric space heaters are the most common, there are other types that operate by the combustion of wood or fossil fuels. Permanently installed gas and oil units are connected to a separate fuel source by supply pipes. Portable gas, oil, and kerosene heaters store the fuel as well as burn it, so they must be refilled as the fuel is used. Fireplaces and wood- or coal stoves are other familiar forms of space heating. All of these types of heaters produce fumes when burning and should be used in ventilated areas or be vented to the outdoors.

Cooling

In most areas of the world, certain parts of the year are uncomfortably warm. Although the human body can tolerate the heat of most climates, a majority of people in industrialized nations are concerned with keeping cool in hot weather.

Because in the summer months the interior of homes is generally cooler than outdoor temperatures, heat flow is from outside to inside. The rate of flow depends on insulation features that slow down the flow of heat and the difference between outside and inside temperatures. The greater the temperature difference, the faster the heat flow.

In addition, heat is generated by living in a house, reducing the winter heating load but increasing the summer cooling load. An average person gives off 400 Btus per hour during sedentary activities. With strenuous exercise, this figure may climb to 2000 Btus per hour. The greater the number of occupants, then, the greater the heat transmitted to the rooms.

Keeping cool is accomplished in a variety of ways. The methods requiring the least energy are natural or mechanical ventilation. Forms of air-conditioning require more energy but may control humidity as well.

Natural Ventilation

The term *ventilation* implies not simply control of air movement but the delivery of clean outdoor air to dilute room air and its contaminants. Natural ventilation is the movement of air without mechanical assistance.

Ventilation of Living Areas

For summer comfort, windows should be located to take advantage of cooling breezes. Throughout much of the United States, moist winds from the south combine with prevailing westerly winds to create southwesterly winds during the summer. Generally, then, windows placed on the south and west will be more efficient for cooling than windows on the north and east. Variations occur in every locality, however, especially where topographical features such as lakes and mountains influence air patterns.

Air can be directed through openings in the house by creating a path for its travel. An open window on the windward side of the house allows air to enter. However, little air will enter if an exit is not provided on another side of the house. Opening a few well-positioned windows causes a faster rate of air flow than opening all the windows. To provide for maximum air flow, windows should be located to encourage cross-ventilation. Windows placed on opposite sides of a house are especially effective if one of the openings is located to take advantage of prevailing breezes. Windows high on walls are not especially effective for cooling the home unless air enters through lower openings.

Good air flow is achieved when inlets and outlets are approximately equal in size, but better flow occurs when the opening through which air enters is smaller than the one through which air leaves the house or vice versa. This is an application of the Venturi principle. In essence, this principle states that when the space through which a fluid (in this case, air) flows becomes smaller, the velocity of the fluid increases. Thomas Jefferson utilized this principle when building his bedroom at Monticello by placing his bed in a small space between two larger areas, each with windows. The breeze flowed in one window, increased its velocity as it flowed through the bed area, and eventually went out a window on the other side. All the while, Jefferson was enjoying a free natural cooling system.

Attic Ventilation

The sun beating down on the rooftop and hot air rising from the home's interior make attics notoriously hot in the summer. In fact, attics can reach temperatures over 160 degrees Fahrenheit. Insulation beneath the roof helps, but most homes without livable attic space have insulation in the attic floor instead.

Ventilating the attic can keep it from getting more than 10 degrees hotter than the outdoor temperature. Several vent types are used: gable-end vents, soffit vents, ridge vents, and **turbine ventilators**. Turbine ventilators are activated by slight breezes. When a breeze spins the blades, a low pressure area is created, sucking attic air through the turbine. Inlet vents in the soffit or elsewhere are necessary for proper ventilation with turbine vents. Turbines should be located on the highest portion of the roof to catch breezes from every direction. They should be covered during the heating season to minimize heat loss.

For gable roofs, louvered vents installed in the gable ends provide for cross-ventilation. They are often triangular but can be square, rectangular, semicircular, or polygonal. These vents are not large enough to do an adequate cooling job without added mechanical ventilation. For better and more effective ventilation, louvered or screened vents can be placed in the soffit for air intake and in higher openings at the roof peak for exhaust. The combination of gable-end vents and soffit vents ensures a natural flow of air beneath the slope of the roof, carrying hot air up and out. The outlet can also be a continuous ridge vent, a series of separate ventilators just below the ridge, a cupola, or a turbine ventilator. Outside breezes that blow over vents reduce air pressure, creating a suction that pulls cooler air in through soffit vents. See Figure 9.11.

A single turbine ventilator can adequately vent 600

Figure 9.11 The row of square ventilators on this roof vent the attic space.

square feet of attic space. For other types of attic vents, approximately 1 square foot of vent area is needed for each 300 square feet of ceiling when vapor barriers are used. In homes without vapor barriers, approximately twice as much vent area is needed. Since screens, louvers, and other coverings reduce the actual ventilation area, vents should be slightly oversized. Vents should be sized for summer efficiency because summer requirements are greater than those for winter.

Mechanical Ventilation

Window fans may be portable or permanently installed. Portable fans can easily be moved to positions where they are needed for added circulation. All fans placed in windows can draw fresh air into rooms or remove room air, depending on the direction the blades are rotating. Some permanently installed fans have a switch that reverses air flow direction.

Decorative ceiling fans may also be reversible. See Figure 9.12. In the summer, they draw air upward, circulating cool floor-level air. During the winter, they reverse, forcing warm air at the ceiling level downward into the room.

Larger **whole-house fans** (often inappropriately called attic fans) are installed horizontally in the ceiling

---

▦ Because whole-house fans are noisy and cause vibrations, they are best located away from sleeping areas. In addition, because they bring in dust, pollen, and other allergens with outside air, their use may be precluded if residents have certain allergies.

between the attic and living areas. They can cool an entire structure by drawing in outside air to replace hot, stuffy indoor air.

In order for a whole-house fan to work, some windows must be opened and the attic must be well-ventilated. A whole-house fan should be selected according to the volume of air it will move per minute—even small models will move 5000 cubic feet of air in that amount of time. Generally, it is best to purchase a fan that will move 50 to 100 percent of the volume of air in a house in one minute.

Louvers that open automatically when the fan is turned on and close when the fan is turned off close off the attic, preventing excessive heat loss in winter and heat gain in summer. Because the louvers do not seal, a fan cover is recommended during the winter.

Figure 9.12 The fan located over the table in this dining room is an example of an early form of ventilation in the American South. Called a "shoo-fly" fan, this **punka** was operated by pulling a rope. The movement of the air helped to cool individuals at the table and, as the name implies, helped to reduce the number of insects in the area.

Temperature-Cooling Devices

During hot weather, ventilation alone cannot compensate for the amount of heat present in room air. Units that not only circulate air but also cool it are necessary to maintain thermal comfort levels on many summer days. See Table 9.3 for statistics on the popularity of air-conditioning. Two types of cooling devices accomplish this: **evaporative coolers** and air-conditioners.

Evaporative Coolers

Evaporative coolers[13] move air and lower its temperature. The unit, usually installed on a rooftop, consists of a fan that forces air through a water-soaked filter pad. As the air travels through, its heat evaporates the water, which absorbs the heat, cooling the air. The cooled air is then circulated through the house below, where it raises the humidity and reduces the ambient temperature.

Evaporative coolers work well only in dry climates, operating efficiently only if the relative humidity is at 40 percent or below. For this reason, in the United States, evaporative coolers are found mostly in the Southwest, where the air is dry. See Figure 9.13. Evaporative coolers can cool the air only a modest amount, reducing their efficiency when temperatures reach 90 degrees Fahrenheit and above. However, evaporative coolers require significantly less energy for operation than do air-conditioning units.

Figure 9.13 In the United States, evaporative coolers are found mostly in the Southwest, where the air is dry.

Air-Conditioning

Where heat and humidity are both high, air-conditioning creates more comfortable homes because they cool, dehumidify, filter, and circulate air. The development of air-conditioning has had a substantial effect on building design in the past century. Buildings constructed prior to the advent of air-conditioning often had multiple stories to take advantage of cooler breezes higher off the ground and operable windows to allow for natural ventilation. Structures were sited to take advantage of solar radiation, shade, and prevailing breezes. Modern buildings can be enclosed in glass—often sealed—and located without regard to the advantages or disadvantages offered by a site. The obvious result is an increase in energy usage.

Air conditioners work on the same principle as heat pumps—moving heat around—in this case from indoors to outdoors. Like heat pumps, air conditioners use a refrigerant,[14] which changes from a liquid to a gas and back again, exchanging heat with each cycle. A compressor increases the pressure of the refrigerant, raising its temperature. The gas is then moved to a condenser located outdoors, where it releases its heat and condenses back into a liquid. The liquid is pumped indoors to an evaporator, where it absorbs heat, vaporizing again and completing the cycle. Cool air is produced by means of a fan that circulates air over the cold surfaces of the evaporator. The cool air is then cleaned by a filter and circulated through the living space.

Colder air holds less moisture than warmer air; therefore, when the temperature is lowered, the relative humidity is also decreased. Because air conditioners

Table 9.3 Percent of New Single-Family Dwellings with Air-Conditioning*

Year	U.S.	Northeast	Midwest	South	West
1975	46	13	35	71	29
1980	63	29	45	84	47
1985	70	43	59	92	51
1990	76	50	75	95	60
1995	80	64	80	98	52
2000	85	76	89	99	60
2004	90	82	93	100	74

Source: www.census.gov/const/www/charindex.html#singlecomplete.
* Air-conditioning became popular more quickly in some regions of the country than in others. In warmer areas, it is an essential component of new dwellings.

remove moisture from the air (sometimes as much as 25 gallons a day!), it is necessary that they have drain lines leading either to a drain or outdoors. If an air-conditioning unit is located below grade, it may be necessary to provide a condensate pump to lift the water removed to a place where it can be drained.

Room Air Conditioners. Air conditioners can be room models (also called **packaged terminal air conditioners**) or central units. A room air conditioner is installed in a window, while a through-the-wall unit is installed in an opening in the wall. Each type is sized to handle a small volume of air. These units are self-contained and include the compressor, condenser, and refrigeration unit. They are easy to install, require no duct work, and are therefore ideal for room additions or adding air-conditioning to an existing home. Zoned cooling is simplified and the units are accessible for repair and maintenance.

A room air conditioner circulates air directly into the room where it is located. The flow of air from the air conditioner should be directed upward to encourage convection currents so the cooled air is circulated throughout the space. This air flow, however, also causes cold drafts that may be uncomfortable. There are other disadvantages to be considered when selecting a room air conditioner.

- Because the unit is located in the room, it is noisy.
- The use of multiple units requires repair and maintenance of several units rather than one.
- Operating costs are higher for several small motors than for a single larger one.

Central Air-Conditioning. A central air conditioner is sized to cool an entire home. It may be installed separately or combined with a central forced air heat-

---

✿ Because the air-conditioning condenser gives off heat collected from indoors, it is more efficient if it is located in a relatively cool outdoor area—in the shade or on the north side of a building.

ing system. When the system is combined with a forced air furnace, the initial cost of total climate control is lowered. The cooling coils are installed with the furnace, and both furnace and air conditioner share the same plenum and distribution system. The condenser must be located outside.

Separate central air-conditioning units are generally placed in the attic, and the ducts are placed high on the walls or in the ceilings, because cooler air sinks. When a warm air heating system is combined with a central air-conditioning system, the same ducts may be used for both. Cold air moves more slowly than warm air; therefore, ducts used for air-conditioning need to be larger than those for heating. In fact, efficient cooling requires twice as much air circulation as does heating. For combined heating and air-conditioning systems in warm climates, supply ducts and registers can be located overhead, where they function most efficiently for air-conditioning. In colder climates, where demand for heating is greater than for air-conditioning, ducts are placed in or near the floor.

Removable baffles can be added to floor registers during the cooling season to direct the air upward, increasing air-conditioning efficiency. The best location for return air ducts for air-conditioning is near the ceiling, where the warmest air is. Return air ducts for heating, however, are near the floor. Some central systems have two complete sets of ducts, while some have two sets of return air ducts. When there are two return air systems, a damper permits easy switching from one to the other. Generally, however, a single distribution system is installed, and the location of supply and return ducts and registers is determined by the system used the most.

Air conditioner cooling capacity is stated in either Btus per hour or tons per day. In the past, air conditioners have been rated in tons, and many contractors still use this system. A one-ton air conditioner absorbs the same amount of heat as one ton of ice melting in 24 hours. This figure is approximately 12,000 Btus. In 1956, the major manufacturers agreed to standardize air conditioner ratings using Btus per hour based on a standard testing method. Since a Btu is the amount of heat required to raise the temperature of one pound of water 1 degree Fahrenheit, lowering its temperature one degree will remove the same number of Btus. A 6000 Btu air conditioner will remove 6000 Btus of heat per hour, cooling an area of approximately 220 square feet.

The law requires that new air conditioners have an **energy-efficiency rating** (EER).[15] This rating compares the amount of electricity used with the amount of heat removed under test conditions and is calculated using the following formula:

$$\text{Btus of heat removed per hour} / \text{watts used} = \text{EER}$$

Example:
$$14{,}000 \text{ Btus} / 2000 \text{ watts} = 7$$

As the efficiency rises, the EER also rises, and operating costs decrease. The size of the unit affects the EER—better efficiencies are achieved when larger units are used. Thus, equivalent-size units should be compared when determining which systems to purchase. A window air conditioner with an EER of 7.5 or better, or a central unit with a minimum EER of 10, is preferable. The law requires that each air-conditioning unit sold also has a **seasonal energy-efficiency ratio** (**SEER**)—the seasonal equivalent of the EER. As of January 2006, newly manufactured central air conditioners must have a minimum SEER of 13.[16]

Innovative Air-Conditioning. Engineers are seeking ways to improve the efficiency of air-conditioning systems, which would result in energy savings and lower operating costs. Two systems present promising possibilities: chilled water air-conditioning, currently used mostly in commercial applications, and ice air-conditioning.

CHILLED WATER AIR-CONDITIONING. Chilled water air-conditioning is similar to hot water heating systems, except that water cooled by a refrigeration unit is carried through pipes to convectors or coils, where fans may circulate air over them. Pipes should be well insulated to prevent condensation, as the water in the system is cooled to 40 to 45 degrees Fahrenheit. The major components, including the compressor and heat exchanger, are located outside, often on the roof. Chilled water air conditioners may be combined with hydronic heating systems, using the same pump and distribution network. The fact that liquid responds more slowly to temperature changes than air makes this delivery system especially useful for large-scale climate-control systems, such as those in commercial and manufacturing structures.

ICE AIR-CONDITIONING. Ice air-conditioning is a relatively new system still in the developmental stage. The University of Minnesota, Kansas City Power and Light, and the Salt River Project in Phoenix are leaders in the research and development of this air-conditioning type.

The concept is simple. In temperate zones, the amount of extra heat in the summer is approximately equal to the amount needed during the winter. An underground water tank and a heat pump make it possible to store summer heat for winter use, and winter coolness for summer air-conditioning. A network of coiled pipes circulates a refrigerant through the water tank. During the winter, heat is moved from the water to the house. As heat is removed from the water, it becomes colder and eventually turns to ice. During the summer, the process is reversed. Heat is removed from living areas and carried to the water tank. There, the refrigerant releases heat, melting the ice and becoming cooler. Oklahoma City and Nashville, Tennessee, located at 36 degrees north latitude, have ideal climates for ice air-conditioning. In colder areas, outdoor heat may need to be channeled through the ice during the summer to insure that the water holds sufficient heat for winter use. Conversely, in warmer areas, additional cold air must be circulated during the winter to insure that sufficient ice is formed for summer air-conditioning.

Predicted operating costs for ice air-conditioning are considerably lower than for a traditional air-conditioning system, although initial costs will probably be higher.

Air Filtration

Air movement causes dust particles and other contaminants such as pollen to be carried throughout the house. Odors are common air pollutants in kitchens and bathrooms, and smoke adds other particles to the air that eventually settle, increasing household cleaning tasks.

The most common method used to control air quality is a filter installed in a heating or air-conditioning system. These filters may be disposable, in which case they need to be replaced periodically, or they may be of more durable materials (for example, aluminum mesh) that can be washed and replaced. Filters remove some of the dust particles from the air but are generally rated at about 15 percent efficiency.

A more efficient method of removing dust particles is the installation of an electrostatic air cleaner. These units may also be installed in central heating and air-conditioning systems, establishing electrical fields that cause the particulates in the air to become positively charged. As the particles move through a series of metal plates in the filter, they stick to negatively charged surfaces. Such air cleaners can remove up to 90 percent of the dust, pollen, and other particles in the air. The result is fewer allergens and pollutants in the air. In addition, because there are fewer particles in the conditioned air to settle out, household tasks are reduced and fabrics, carpets, wallpaper, and paint look better for a longer period of time. Electrostatic air cleaners are relatively expensive to install and consume electricity for operation. They must also be washed periodically to remove particles adhering to the surfaces.

Odors are more effectively removed by adding a charcoal filter either after air has been filtered in a central heating or air-conditioning system or at the point of use. Typically, charcoal filters are used in kitchens and bathrooms in conjunction with exhaust fans. These fans are required by the IRC to move a minimum of 50 cubic feet per minute in bathrooms and 100 cubic feet per minute in kitchens. There are two types of exhaust fans.

- Circulating fans move air through the filter and return it to the room. Thus, odors are removed but moisture and heat are not.
- Venting fans exhaust air to the outside, removing heat and moisture as well as odors.

Controlling Humidity

Since comfort is affected by humidity as well as by temperature, it is often desirable for climate-control systems to increase or decrease the moisture content of room air. The moisture content of inside air is usually not the same as that of outside air, because climate-control systems affect the relative humidity—usually reducing it. Humidity is also constantly added to the home. Cooking, plants, bathing, laundry, and human occupancy add up to an average of 4 ½ gallons of moisture per week per person.

The ideal humidity level depends on the season. In summer, people tend to be most comfortable at 75 to 78 degrees Fahrenheit and 40 to 60 percent relative humidity. In winter, the ideal interior conditions are 72 to 75 degrees Fahrenheit and 30 to 35 percent relative humidity. If dehumidification is needed, it is usually in the summer. Air must be humidified in the winter.

Humidifying the Air

Insufficient humidity during the winter months causes dry skin, cracks in wood floors and furniture, loose wood joints, and static electricity. Inside air is dry in the winter for several reasons. First, the outside air contains little moisture, even when relative humidity is high, because it is cold. When this air is heated to 70 degrees Fahrenheit, the relative humidity of the air at this higher temperature is lower. It is not uncommon for the interior relative humidity to be between 5 and 10 percent. Even the Sahara desert averages 20 percent. This does not mean that the outside air contains a great deal more moisture but simply reflects the fact that it takes less moisture to saturate cold air than warm air. In homes without vapor barriers, heated air escaping through cracks and crevices carries moisture with it, lowering relative humidity further.

Humidity can be added to interior air by connecting a humidifier to the heating system or by installing self-contained units. Humidifiers have a water reservoir through which a pad rotates to pick up moisture. When a humidifier is combined with a forced warm air heating system, water is automatically added to the reservoir and the treated air is forced into the distribution system. Self-contained humidifiers have a blower to force room air through the pad, and their reservoirs must be periodically filled.

Humidifier capacity is rated in gallons per day. The capacity needed depends on the amount of air infiltration and the size of the home. For a 1500-square-foot house with insulation, vapor barriers, and storm windows, 7 to 8 gallons per day is recommended during winter months. For the same size house with no insulation or storm windows, the recommended capacity is 11 to 12 gallons per day.

When warm, moist air strikes cooler surfaces, the air cools. If it can no longer hold all the moisture as water vapor, the water condenses on the cold surface. When interior air escapes through cracks and crevices in walls, water may condense on the inside of colder sheathing, where it may run down harmlessly or it may soak through the wood and cause exterior paint to blister and, over time, cause the wood to rot. Vapor barriers and ventilation help solve this problem.

Condensation on cold window panes is a common problem, especially if the interior humidity has been increased. Excess moisture on the window glass can seep down into the window frame or structural members. If this happens frequently, wood frames will eventually rot, but solid vinyl windows are not affected. Using storm windows or insulating glass helps prevent condensation, as does blowing warm air over the inside surface of the window glass—an added benefit of locating heat supply registers beneath windows.

Condensation can also be a problem in the sum-mer, especially when homes are insulated or air-conditioned. Warm, humid outside air leaks into the cooler house. As the moist air strikes cooler surfaces, it condenses. This condensation may not be noticed, however, because it may be between structural members in the roof or walls and the insulation. The effectiveness of insulation is decreased if the insulation absorbs significant moisture. In homes without air-conditioning, humid air may condense on cooler basement walls and pipes. Ventilating the area and insulating pipes will help solve this problem.

Dehumidifying the Air

In some climates, dry air is a problem year-round, but in others, the summer months are not only hot but uncomfortably humid. Air-conditioning removes much of the humidity from the air inside the house but dehumidifiers may also be used to reduce humidity—sometimes negating the need for air-conditioning.

Dehumidifiers operate much like air conditioners and heat pumps. A refrigerant flows through an evaporator, where it absorbs heat and is vaporized. As it absorbs heat, the metal tubes of the evaporator are cooled. The refrigerant is then compressed or pressurized and pumped to the condenser, where it releases its heat and reliquifies. Since both the condenser and evaporator are located indoors, no heat is moved from one place to another. A fan blows air over the cold surface of the evaporator coil, causing water to condense on it. The water drips into a collection reservoir. If the reservoir is not connected to a drain, it must be periodically emptied.

Dehumidifiers are rated according to the amount of water they remove from the air during a day when the temperature is 80 degrees Fahrenheit and the relative humidity is 60 percent. The size of the dehumidifier is dictated by the area of the house and its interior moisture condition. A house that has 1500 square feet of floor space may require a dehumidifier with a capacity ranging from 18 to 26 pints per day, depending on the amount of moisture in the house.

Green
Design:
Energy-
Efficiency

Chapter 10

The Department of Energy has

established recommendations for energy-efficient housing but it is state and local building codes that can require energy-conservation strategies in building design. Individuals may be sufficiently concerned with energy costs that they desire energy-efficient features even if local codes do not require them. Most new homes are constructed using traditional designs with energy-efficient features, although an NAHB survey found that only 30 percent of respondents were willing to pay an additional $5000 for energy-efficient housing that would save them $1000 per year in energy costs. See Figure 10.1.

Truly energy-efficient homes make use of technology and materials demanding the least energy before, during, and after construction, even when initial costs are higher. Most existing energy-efficient homes, however, are designed to obtain a reasonable balance

Figure 10.1 In some areas of the world, housing materials and forms reflect an understanding of and willingness to cooperate with climatic factors. Such shelters respond to climatic conditions peculiar to their locations, utilizing nonmechanical means to modify interior environments—often without the use of supplementary heating or cooling systems.

between construction and operating cost and energy-efficient performance after completion. Because it is climate-control systems that use the most energy in a home, many of the energy-efficient design features focus on lowering the amount of energy required for this purpose.

Thermal Energy

Heat—thermal energy—is produced when molecules move. Even in solid materials, there is molecular

---

Designers can encourage clients to opt for energy-efficient features that result in lower energy costs. A few calculations may be necessary to demonstrate the cost-effectiveness of energy features.

movement until the temperature reaches absolute zero (-460 degrees Fahrenheit). Heat is always present in materials above that temperature. Heat is measured in British thermal units (Btus), explained in Chapter 2.

Principles of Heat Transfer

Heat flows from objects with higher temperatures to those with lower temperatures. In homes, this means that during the winter, heat flows from inside the home to the exterior, causing heat loss; during the summer, heat flows from outside to inside, causing heat gain. The environment is constantly seeking thermal equalization through **conduction**, **convection**, and **radiation**.

Conduction is the flow of thermal energy within a material or between two substances having physical contact. Much of the heat transfer in homes is due to conduction through the materials used in walls, floors, ceilings, windows, and doors. During the winter, when heat reaches the exterior surface, it is carried away by convection.

Convection is the transfer of heat from the surface of a material to an adjacent fluid (liquid or gas) or from one part of a fluid to another. When air molecules are cooler than the surface of building materials, heat is transferred from the materials to the air, removing heat from the building. Because moving air carries heat away at a faster rate than still air, wind speed affects the amount of heat lost by convection.

Radiation is the transfer of thermal energy through waves of varying lengths or frequencies. Infrared (heat) waves are emitted in all directions by substances that have heat (anything at temperatures above absolute zero). Infrared waves are but one example of radiant energy. Dark colors absorb radiant energy, while light colors reflect it, changing the direction of the rays. Unique to radiant energy is that the medium through which it passes is not appreciably heated. On a winter day when the air temperature is freezing (32 degrees Fahrenheit), the temperature of a dark-colored surface, such as a solar collector, may be over 150 degrees Fahrenheit.

Energy Conversion

One of the most important characteristics of energy is its ability to change form. Two laws of physics govern energy transformations.

- The total amount of energy is constant. Energy can be changed from one form to another but it cannot be created or destroyed (First Law of Thermodynamics).
- When energy changes form, there is always energy loss, causing an increase in the randomness of the universe (Second Law of Thermodynamics).

When energy is converted from one form to another, some energy is made less useful. For example: Chemical energy in oil can be burned to run turbines that produce electrical energy, which is then used to produce radiant energy in homes in the form of light. Not all of the energy released from the oil is used to operate the turbine, nor is it transformed into electrical energy. Some of the oil is converted to thermal energy, heating the room in which the turbine is located. It would be difficult to collect that thermal energy and make it useful for other work; therefore, this energy is released to the randomness of the universe.

Efficiency is the ratio of output energy to input energy and is expressed as a percentage. The more efficient an energy system is, the less energy is lost when it is transformed, but the efficiency of an energy system is always less than 100 percent. A machine that is 80 percent efficient puts out 80 units of energy for every 100 units it consumes. Overall effciency may be reduced by other factors. The efficiency of a home heating system, for example, is reduced by air infiltration and the conduction of heat to the outside.

Energy Use in the Building Industry

How a particular home affects energy consumption is not just a question of the energy that is used while it is occupied. The extraction, refining, processing, transportation, and installation of building materials accounts for a significant percentage of total energy use in the United States.

The amount of energy used for construction is affected by the relatively short life span of homes. Historically, many homes have been constructed to last for generations, but this is not true of new housing in many cultures. As populations become more mobile, there is less incentive to build homes that will last for centuries. Because building materials are generally not reused, the replacement of homes lost to the market through abandonment, deterioration, fire, and natural disasters consumes additional energy.

Contemporary homes are often rambling and spread out in plan, requiring increasing amounts of materials for construction of the shell and for plumbing, electrical wiring, and climate-control systems. In addition, newer materials used in homes may require more energy for their production than the older materials they replace, their manufacture may emit pollutants, and their disposal may result in additional pollution. For example, vinyl has almost replaced linoleum in flooring and paper in wall coverings. In this case, the extra energy expenditure is offset by the fact that vinyl lasts longer, performs better, and is easier to care for. On the other hand, carpeting made of acrylic, nylon, or polyester does not wear as well as wool carpeting, nor does it have the rich appearance of wool. Synthetic carpeting is popular because it is less

Figure 10.2 The proximity of water affects ambient temperatures, humidity, and air movement, changing the microclimate of a building site.

expensive than wool but its manufacture depletes petroleum reserves.

The Building Site

Characteristics of the building site greatly affect energy consumption. The orientation of the building on

Generally, south-facing homes designed to take advantage of winter sunlight are located in northern climates where heating costs more than cooling. In areas where cooling costs are higher than heating costs, this orientation is unsuitable.

If the home is placed in the northern portion of the lot, the possibility of later buildings blocking the sun from the structure is minimized. This placement also ensures that usable outdoor spaces on the south, such as patios and gardens, will have adequate sunlight.

the site, landscaping, and air movement all affect heat gain and loss. See Figure 10.2.

Orientation

As a south-facing slope nears an angle perpendicular to the sun, the amount of heat it absorbs increases. Placement of the home on a south-facing slope ensures direct sunlight from 9 a.m. to 3 p.m. on winter days—the hours during which 90 percent of the solar energy that strikes an area is received. Aligning the structure on an east-west axis with the longest wall facing south will ensure that winter sunlight is admitted to help heat the home. Homes built on south-facing slopes require shading or ground cover on the south to prevent overheating during summer months. Shade keeps the air cool by preventing about 70 percent of the radiant energy striking the area from being absorbed by the ground. In fact, the temperature under a tree may be almost 20 degrees less than in the sun.[1]

The darkest, coldest, and usually least used space in and around the home is the north side, which does not receive direct sun at any time during the year. Because prevailing winter winds are from a northerly direction during the winter in most areas in the Northern Hemisphere, heat loss on the north is excessive.

Landscaping

Landscaping includes not only the arrangement of plantings but the location of other buildings, pavement, and fences. The goal for energy-efficient landscaping is to improve heat gain during winter months while providing cooling during the summer. If prevailing winds are from different directions during the two seasons, landscaping for both will be simplified. When winds during both seasons are from the same direction, it is most appropriate to design for the season with the highest energy bills.

Energy can be saved when few openings are located on the north side of a structure. Energy consumption can be further reduced by locating spaces with lower heating and illumination requirements, such as garages, storage areas, and laundry rooms, on the north side of the building. These areas will then protect warmer rooms from the northern exterior.

Landscaping changes the microclimate of the building and thus can reduce heating and cooling costs. See Figure 10.3. Deciduous trees should be located where they will shade windows from summer sun, but permit sun to penetrate during winter months. This is especially true of homes utilizing passive solar heating.

Ground cover is also an important consideration in energy-efficient housing. Vegetation absorbs less heat

Figure 10.3 Mature trees located where they shade a house can block up to 70 percent of the sun and lower cooling costs by as much as 25 percent (http://earthshare.org/tips/trees.html and http://montgomerycountymd.gov/deptmpl.asp?url=/content/dep/greenman/shady.asp).

Unfortunately, it is common practice to remove mature trees at a site prior to construction; thus, occupants must wait years for the benefits from such trees. With planning, however, this could be avoided and mature trees left in appropriate places.

than bare earth, masonry, wood, and other materials. In fact, temperatures at ground level can be as much as 10 degrees less when the surface is covered by grass than when bare earth is exposed.[2] Vegetation also reflects less heat, helping to maintain cooler temperatures within nearby structures.

The color of pavement for a driveway or patio affects the way it reacts to heat. Lighter-colored pavements such as concrete reflect much of the heat away from it—often right into windows in the structure. In the process, glare may also be created. Dark-colored pavements such as blacktop and brick absorb heat, which is reradiated when temperatures drop at night. Urban areas are always a few degrees warmer than surrounding rural areas partly due to the amount of pavement. Even along highways, the warmer temperatures of the roadway are evident when plants in the warmer soil along pavement edges become green in the spring before those in other areas.

The purpose of energy-efficient landscaping is to protect a structure from winter winds and to funnel breezes toward it during the summer. Adjacent structures such as fences or buildings must be considered. Buildings should be located to provide shade during the summer or a windbreak during the winter. When possible, add structures on the north side of a house to provide a windbreak, moderating the air flow, which results in less heat being carried away by convection currents. Fences, **berms** (artificial hills), and

To minimize the impact of a home on the natural environment, use as few impervious surfaces on the ground as possible. A brick sidewalk laid in sand, for example, allows water to drain through to the soil beneath.

walls may be used for the same purpose. These solid windbreaks deflect wind over them, but some of the wind returns to the ground on the leeward side due to the change in air pressure on the two sides of the windbreak. A better solution is a penetrable windbreak such as trees or a louvered fence. Solid windbreaks may be used as a temporary solution until plants mature.

Planted perpendicular to the direction of the prevailing wind, a windbreak of trees can be used to lessen air infiltration in a home during the winter. Trees used as windbreaks should be dense and retain their foliage in the winter—usually evergreen species. Trees with foliage that reaches the ground are best because even air moving close to the ground is slowed or deflected. Multiple rows of trees work even better. Trees will deflect wind over a structure within a distance equal to approximately five times their mature height. A windbreak 35 feet high can slow a 35-mile-per-hour wind to 10 miles per hour 100 feet in its lee.[3] The wind that comes through the trees is slowed by the foliage, resulting in slower convection currents around the home.

To ensure that the structure receives winter sunlight on the south, deciduous trees should be used. If winter winds come from the south, a row of trees with sparse foliage planted a distance equal to 10 to 15 times their height away from the house will temper the winds. At maturity, the height of the trees should not obstruct the winter sun.

Landscaping can reduce cooling costs during summer months by funneling breezes to the structure. Rows of tall hedges angled toward the house from the direction of the prevailing summer breeze will not only channel the breezes but, as the path narrows, the speed of the air increases—the Venturi effect.

Air Movement

In the United States, prevailing winds typically come from southerly directions during the summer and from northerly directions during the winter. However, localized patterns may exist at a site because of nearby topographical features.

As wind blows across the warm exterior surface of a home, it carries away heat by convection. The greater the wind velocity, the more rapid the heat loss. Wind velocity can be lowered by barriers such as fences or windbreaks. Because evergreens retain thick foliage all year, closely planted rows can buffer homes from prevailing winds, minimizing their effect. It is also important to have plants close to exposed foundation walls to slow winds and minimize heat loss and gain. The windward side of a structure can also be protected by building it into a slope. On the sides with earth contact, this method not only minimizes air infiltration but helps to moderate temperature differentials between the outside and inside air.

At the same time that winter wind is being guarded against, the need for good ventilation during the summer must not be forgotten. Dense plantings should be kept away from the side of the house where summer breezes prevail. Because wind blowing directly through living areas does not provide ventilation as effective as that passing through at an angle, ventilation areas should not be perpendicular to the direction of the summer breeze but at a 20- to 70-degree angle from it.

Building Design

Awareness of conservation strategies makes it possible to select or plan a home with design features that minimize energy consumption. The type of residential unit, its shape, the colors used on the interior and exterior, and special energy features all affect the energy-efficiency of the structure.

Type of Home

Single-family detached dwellings lose heat in winter and gain it in summer at a more rapid rate than

The wind patterns on a site should be identified prior to construction so that the structure, orientation, and landscaping can be designed for maximum efficiency.

Because windows and entrances are particularly vulnerable to heat loss, it is especially important to protect them from wind. They can be recessed from the exterior surface, oriented away from prevailing winds, and protected by windbreaks, improving the energy-efficiency of the entire structure. ❀

dwellings that share common walls. Row houses with only two exposed walls exhibit a 15 to 20 percent energy savings over detached homes of the same size. Apartments realize further reductions in energy consumption—in some cases approaching 50 percent—because they have a smaller area for heat loss or gain through roofs and floors.

Shape

Since most heat is gained and lost through walls and ceilings, the shape of a home affects its energy-efficiency by affecting the amount of exposed surface area through which heat can flow. A dome-shaped structure encloses the greatest amount of space with the least exposed surface. The very efficient Eskimo igloo utilizes this form. The geodesic dome is the most familiar building alternative with a circular plan. It is difficult, however, to work with circular plans in arranging both living and work areas.

Space can generally be used more efficiently when the plan is square or rectangular. The square has a better ratio than the rectangle of enclosed space to surface area. As a square becomes larger, however, passageways require a greater percentage of space and decrease living areas significantly. This problem can be somewhat alleviated by the use of two-story square plans—with an even lower ratio of exposed surface to interior space than a single-story square

Because heat rises, the ceiling height affects energy-efficiency. For the most part, homes in cold climates should have ceilings no more than 8 feet high to ease heating loads, although reversible ceiling fans can help reduce wasted heat by pushing warm air downward in winter. In hot climates, higher ceilings may reduce air-conditioning loads during the summer. High ceilings also increase the volume of air within the structure that must be heated and cooled.

plan. Other factors may outweigh surface-to-space ratios, however. When buildings are designed to take advantage of solar energy, for example, a rectangular form on an east-west axis is the most efficient.

Color

The color of both the interior and exterior surfaces of buildings affects energy-efficiency. Light colors tend to reflect radiant energy and light, resulting in lower illumination requirements when they are used on interior surfaces. Dark colors absorb both radiant energy and light. Exterior surface colors may affect energy-efficiency significantly, although because the roof is exposed to direct sunlight all day, it is the surface where color can be most important. For cooling during the summer, light-colored roofs are most desirable; dark-colored roofs absorb heat, making attic spaces excessively hot. In cold climates, dark roofs may be desirable for winter heat gain if the attic floor is uninsulated. Color has a decreasing effect on heat loss or gain as insulation is increased.

Special Energy Features

Double walls or roofs have traditionally been used to retain cool interior temperatures in the summer, although they are almost as effective in reducing heat

⊞ In extreme hot or cold climate areas, double roof or wall construction may be cost-effective.

loss during winter months. Before the widespread use of refrigeration in America, underground ice houses made use of double roofs—two roofs with a 3- to 4-inch air space between them. This air space interrupted the flow of heat to maintain cooler temperatures. See Figure 10.4.

Double entries[4] significantly reduce the amount of heat that escapes when exterior doors open directly into living spaces. These entries have two doors, one opening to the exterior and one to the interior, with a small corridor between. The space between the doors may be unheated or heated to a lower temperature than the home itself. See Figure 10.5. Double entries

Figure 10.4 The double dome of the Taj Mahal allows the heat absorbed through the exterior surface to be dissipated by air currents before it penetrates the interior dome. (Source: © Jeremy Horner/CORBIS.)

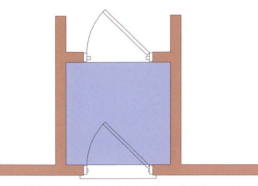

Figure 10.5 Heat loss is reduced when double entries are used because when one door is opened, the other remains closed. When both doors are closed, air infiltration around the doors is also reduced.

can project from or be enclosed within the basic shape of the home. Either method is effective in reducing energy consumption, but entries that do not project are most efficient because less wall area is exposed.

Efficiency of the Building Envelope

To maintain thermal comfort, heat must be replaced in winter and extracted in summer as rapidly as interior thermal conditions are altered. Heat loss or gain can be reduced by making the building envelope more airtight and controlling heat transfer from its surfaces. **Caulking** and **weather-stripping** are used to seal small cracks between the various parts of the structure, helping to minimize air infiltration. Insulation is necessary to protect the interior from extreme temperature fluctuations. **Vapor barriers** are needed to protect against dampness and condensation.

Infiltration

Although some air exchange is necessary to maintain a healthy interior environment, much of the energy used for heating and cooling homes is wasted due to

Maximizing the energy-efficiency of the building envelope, using special energy features, and working with the site are green design precepts that should be followed to improve the relationship between the environment and the structure. ✿

air infiltration. Infiltration is heat loss or gain due to air leakage around windows and doors and through chimneys and cracks. The amount of air infiltration is also affected by the number of times doors are opened—small children and pets that frequently go in and out will increase air infiltration levels.

Blowing wind has a higher air pressure than the still air inside homes, causing air to infiltrate on the windward side. On the leeward side of the home, there is an area of lower pressure, resulting from the wind's deflection over the structure. The low pressure creates suction, drawing warm air from the home, while the higher pressure on the other side pushes cold air in.

The **chimney effect** also affects the amount of air infiltration. Warm interior air rises and leaks from the ceiling and roof. At the same time, suction is created that causes cold air to filter through lower cracks and gaps. The building itself thus serves as a chimney for the air that has been warmed by the climate-control system.

Air exchange through the building surface can be reduced by a layer of building paper or house wrap between the exterior siding and the house sheathing. Cracks and gaps can be sealed with caulking and weather-stripping, both of which are relatively inexpensive and usually have short payback periods. Building codes may require that caulking and weather-stripping be used in the appropriate places in residences, stipulating the maximum amount of air flow allowable around openings. Figure 10.6 shows the sources of air leaks in a typical home.

Caulking

Caulking is done where a permanent seal is desirable. Caulk is a pliable substance used where two

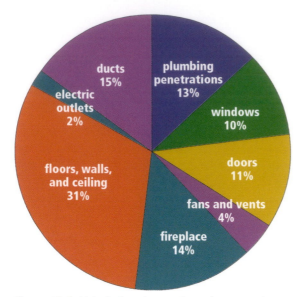

Figure 10.6 Air leaks from homes through structural components such as walls and windows, as well as through cracks around openings such as vents that penetrate the roof. Improving the energy-efficiency of a home requires attention to each source of air infiltration. (Source: U.S. Department of Energy, www.eere.energy.gov/consumer/tips/air_leaks.html)

parts of a structure meet or where two different materials come together. These places typically include:

- Where siding meets the foundation
- Where pipes and vents penetrate exterior surfaces
- Around door and window frames
- At corners formed by siding
- Where chimneys meet siding
- Around chimneys at the roofline

Caulking comes in various forms differing in cost and life expectancy. Some types of caulk are appropriate for joints of dissimilar materials, while others are unsuitable in such places; some are more durable if they are painted, others cannot be painted over; some adhere well to almost any surface, others can be used only on specific materials. For optimum performance, directions on the caulking itself should be followed.

Weather-stripping

In contrast to the permanent seal provided by caulk, weather-stripping is used around operable openings. Weather-stripping is necessary around the outside edges of doors, including beneath them, between window frames and sash, and between sashes in operable windows. When properly installed, weather-stripping creates a tight seal, preventing drafts and reducing energy requirements.

Metal door sweeps are applied to the bottom edge of doors and may be edged with felt, vinyl, or other flexible material. They hang below the edge of the door, sweeping the floor as the door opens and closes and sealing the gap against air infiltration. Door sweeps are effective when first installed, but friction from the floor and threshold quickly wears them down.

Thresholds are a type of weather-stripping installed on the floor beneath exterior doors to keep out moisture and air. Metal thresholds with an inserted vinyl strip are easy to install and create a good seal when the door is closed. Interlocking thresholds are made of two pieces of metal or vinyl, one of which is attached as a threshold and the other to the bottom of the door. When the door is closed, the two pieces interlock, forming a tight seal.

Insulation

Decreasing air infiltration effectively decreases heat loss and the introduction of cold air into homes, resulting in more uniform room-to-room and floor-to-ceiling temperatures. However, heat is also gained or lost due to conduction through roofs, walls, and floors. If these components are uninsulated, their inside surfaces may be 8 to 14 degrees colder than those that are insulated. In addition, air adjacent to cold structural components becomes chilled and is pulled downward, while warmer air rises, causing drafts.

In order to effectively impede the flow of heat through structural materials, it is necessary to insulate buildings. In some cultures, people take advantage of natural insulative materials. Snow is an excellent insulator because it has millions of tiny dead air spaces that resist the transfer of heat. See Figure 10.7. In Scandinavia, steeply pitched roofs will not hold the snow, which slides off onto the ground below. In fact, many homes have a main entry on the second level because the snow piles up against the sides of the house, insulating the walls but precluding exterior access to lower-level spaces during the winter. These techniques are effective where snow remains throughout the heating season.

R-values

The insulative properties of materials are expressed as **R-values**. An R-value is a measure of the thermal resistance of a given thickness (usually an inch) of a material. The greater the resistance a material has, the higher the R-value per inch of thickness. All building materials have an R-value because they impede the flow of heat to some degree, but the insulative qualities of most building materials are minimal. Only materials with an R-value of two or more per inch are considered **insulators**.

As the thickness of the material increases, the R-value also increases, but the relationship is not directly proportional. The first inch of thickness reduces heat transfer more than subsequent inches. For example, fiberglass insulation has an R-value rating of 3.7 per inch but 3½-inch-thick fiberglass has an insulative value of R-11, not R-12.95 (3.7 × 3.5 = 12.95).

To determine the approximate thermal resistance of walls, ceilings, or floors, the R-values of each material within the structure are added together.

R1 + R2 + R3 . . . = Total R-value

To determine the exact R-value of a structural component, it is necessary to test an identical component in the laboratory. Charts that list accurate R-values for some common wall, floor, and ceiling types are available, but on-site variables make it difficult to determine exact R-values. The formula above results in a reasonable approximation.

In contrast to R-values, which are a measure of the *resistance* of a material to the flow of heat, **U-values** measure actual heat flow through the material. "U" is short for Btu, and a U-value of one indicates that one Btu per square foot per hour is lost through the material or structural component for each degree of difference between inside and outside temperature. Low U-values and high R-values correspond with each other—each indicating little heat flow. When calculating heat loss or gain, it is U-values that are used.

Government-recommended R-values are based on climate and are shown in Figure 10.8. The IRC stipulates minimum R-values for structural components in residences according to climate. See Box 10.1. Insulating homes to recommended R-values can save a significant percentage of the energy used for heating and cooling the home. The cost-effectiveness of insulation depends on climate, present and future fuel prices, and initial cost. Payback periods usually range from two to five years. At that point, the insulation has saved enough money on fuel bills to pay for itself and further savings can be banked.

Figure 10.7 The Swiss take advantage of snow as an insulator by constructing low-pitched roofs to prevent snow from sliding off. They add wood or metal bars or small stones to act as snow fences, ensuring that the snow will remain on the roof throughout the winter.

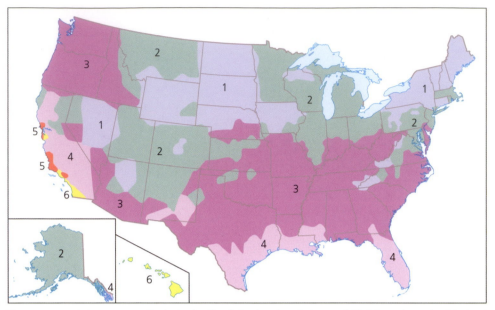

These recommendations are cost-effective levels of insulation based on the best available information on local fuel and materials costs and weather conditions. Consequently, the levels may differ from current local building codes. In addition, the apparent fragmentation of the recommendations is an artifact of these data and should not be considered absolute minimum requirements.

Zone	Gas	Heat pump	Fuel oil	Electric furnace	Ceiling Attic	Ceiling Cathedral	Wall[a]	Floor	Crawl space[b]	Slab edge	Basement Interior	Basement Exterior
1	✔	✔	✔		R-49	R-38	R-18	R-25	R-19	R-8	R-11	R-10
1				✔	R-49	R-60	R-28	R-25	R-19	R-8	R-19	R-15
2	✔	✔	✔		R-49	R-38	R-18	R-25	R-19	R-8	R-11	R-10
2				✔	R-49	R-38	R-22	R-25	R-19	R-8	R-19	R-15
3	✔	✔	✔	✔	R-49	R-38	R-18	R-25	R-19	R-8	R-11	R-10
4	✔	✔	✔		R-38	R-38	R-13	R-13	R-19	R-4	R-11	R-4
4				✔	R-49	R-38	R-18	R-25	R-19	R-8	R-11	R-10
5	✔				R-38	R-30	R-13	R-11	R-13	R-4	R-11	R-4
5		✔	✔		R-38	R-38	R-13	R-13	R-19	R-4	R-11	R-4
5				✔	R-49	R-38	R-18	R-25	R-19	R-8	R-11	R-10
6	✔				R-22	R-22	R-11	R-11	R-11	[c]	R-11	R-4
6		✔	✔		R-38	R-30	R-13	R-11	R-13	R-4	R-11	R-4
6				✔	R-49	R-38	R-18	R-25	R-19	R-8	R-11	R-10

[a] R-18, R-22, and R-28 exterior wall systems can be achieved by either cavity insulation or cavity insulation with insulating sheathing.
  For 2 in. × 4 in. walls, use 3 ½ in. thick R-15 or 3 ½ in. thick R-13 fiberglass insulation with insulating sheathing.
  For 2 in. × 6 in. walls, use either 5 ½ in. thick R-21 or 6 ¼ in. thick R-19 fiberglass insulation.
[b] Insulate crawl space walls only if the crawl space is dry all year, the floor above is not insulated, and all ventilation to the crawl space is blocked.
  A vapor retarder (e.g., 4- or 6-mil polyethylene film) should be installed on the ground to reduce moisture migration into the crawl space.
[c] No slab edge insulation is recommended.

Figure 10.8 Recommended R-values depend on climate. This map shows R-values that are considered cost-effective for six zones in the United States. (Source: U.S. Department of Energy, www.eere.energy.gov/consumer/tips/insulation.html)

Types of Insulation

Five types of insulation are used in buildings—batts, blankets, loose fill, foam, and reflective. Most insulation is made in such a way as to leave tiny pockets of trapped air to reduce the transfer of heat.

Box 10.1 International Residential Code Requirements for Energy-Efficiency

FENESTRATION

- The window area should not exceed 15 percent of the gross area of exterior walls. Town houses may have glazing area up to 25 percent.
- The U-values of glazing depend on climate zone. See the chart below.

INSULATION

- Insulation R-values for ceilings, walls, floors, basements, crawl spaces, and slab perimeters are also variable and depend on the number of heating degree days. The minimum and maximum required R-values are listed below, as well as R-values for an area with the median number of heating degree days (HDD). If the basement has no living area, the floor between the basement and the first story may be insulated to the recommended basement R-value rather than insulating the basement walls.

Component	500–999 HDD	4,500–4,999 HDD	9,000–12,000 HDD
Window U-value	0.90	0.45	0.35
Ceiling R-value	R-19	R-38	R-49
Wall R-value	R-11	R-16	R-21
Floor R-value	R-11	R-16	R-21
Basement wall R-value	R-0	R-19	R-19
Crawl space wall R-value	R-4	R-17	R-20

Source: International Code Council, "Simplified Prescriptive Building Envelope Thermal Component Criteria: Minimum Required Thermal Performance (U-Factor and R-Value)," *International Residential Code for One- and Two-Family Dwellings 2003*, Table N1102.1 (Country Club Hills, IL: 2003), 287.

Insulative materials that are compressed lose their pockets of air and much of their insulative value in the process. It is important, then, that insulated spaces not be overfilled or insulation compressed. The R-values of insulation depend on the type of material used and the thickness of the insulation. Each type of insulation has characteristics that make it suitable for specific purposes and locations. Some insulative materials deteriorate when exposed to ultraviolet light (daylight); most require fire-resistant coverings where they are exposed; some are not suitable for exterior or underground use; and some will compress under the weight of a concrete slab. It is necessary, therefore, to understand the individual characteristics of insulative materials and to use them appropriately. Insulative materials may be faced with paper, plastic, or foil to provide a vapor barrier.

Batts and blankets made of fiberglass or mineral wool fit between or over structural framing members. Blanket insulation comes in long rolls and is often used over ceiling joists to minimize the amount of heat lost through the wood framing members of the ceiling. Batts are rectangular segments of blanket insulation that fit between framing members in walls, ceilings, and floors.

Loose fill insulation is made of cellulose, mineral wool, fiberglass, perlite (formed from volcanic glass), and vermiculite (formed from mica). Cellulose must be treated to be fire-retardant. These materials are poured into ceilings in both new construction and existing buildings and blown into walls of existing buildings. Loose fill insulation is subject to settling, which results in lower R-values over a period of time and spaces without any insulation. Special adhesives sprayed at the same time as the loose fill insulation help resist settling.

Rigid foam boards are made of polyisocyanurate, extruded polystyrene, expanded polystyrene, and fiberglass. These boards typically have higher initial per inch R-values than fiber-based insulations used in batts and rolls. Over time, however, some rigid foam can lose as much as 20 percent of its R-value. Foam boards may be used to insulate foundations either inside or outside the structure, cathedral ceilings, beneath concrete slabs, and beneath siding. When rigid foam insulation is used as sheathing to improve the R-value of walls, additional diagonal bracing is needed to maintain the dimensional stability of the structure.

Foamed-in-place insulation is installed by professionals as a liquid that expands, much like shaving cream, to fill wall cavities and to form a tight seal around openings. Foam may shrink up to 10 percent as it cures, pulling away from studs and decreasing effective R-value.

Box 10.2 Insulation Locations in Residences

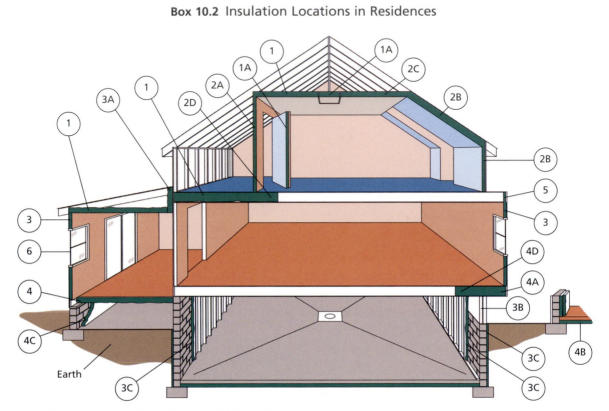

1	Between and over floor joists in unfinished attic spaces.
1A	Attic access door
2A	Between studs of knee walls in finished attic rooms
2B	Between studs and rafters of exterior walls and roof in finished attic rooms
2C	Ceilings in finished attic rooms with cold spaces above them
2D	Extend insulation in joist spaces in unheated spaces past knee walls in finished attic rooms
3	All exterior walls
3A	Walls between living spaces and unheated garages, shed roofs, or storage areas
3B	Foundation walls above grade level
3C	Foundation walls in heated basements
4	Floors above cold spaces
4A	Portions of a floor cantilevered beyond the exterior wall
4B	Beneath slab floors
4C	Foundation walls of unvented crawl spaces (as alternative to insulating the floor above in the same area)
4D	Extend insulation between floor joists beyond exterior walls on the interior side
5	Between joists around the perimeter at each story
6	Replacement or storm windows and caulk and seal around all windows and doors

Source: Oak Ridge National Laboratory (www.ornl.gov/sci/roofs+walls/insulation/fig1.html)

Some insulation materials have one or more foil faces that reflect heat when there is a minimum of ¾ inch of air space in front of them. Reflective insulation uses the same principle but adds multiple layers, each with an inherent air space. A reflective material such as foil may be corrugated or accordion folded and supported on a thin backing—usually paper.

Insulation Locations

Insulation for energy-efficiency is needed in every part of the structure that interfaces with the exterior. The amount of insulation recommended as well as the type of insulation used, however, differs with location. See Box 10.2 for a diagram of where to insulate.

Ceilings. Because heat rises, the ceiling has the greatest potential per square foot for heat loss. Heat loss through uninsulated ceilings is often more than ten times as great as through one with R-19 (6 inches) insulation.

The value of insulation becomes evident when it snows. Heat from a home with a poorly insulated ceiling will melt the snow on the roof while snow remains on the roofs of homes with good insulation. In single-story buildings, the roof also often exposes the greatest area to exterior climatic factors. For example, a 30 by 40-foot house with 8-feet walls has a total gross wall area of 1120 square feet, a ceiling area of 1200 square feet, and a roof area even greater, depending on the slope.

Not only does ceiling insulation yield high energy savings but ceilings are the easiest places to insulate in an existing building. Unless a heated attic is located over the ceiling, insulation should be installed in the attic floor. In heated attics, insulation is placed under the roof. When insulating the attic space, an air space between the roof sheathing and the insulation is necessary to permit ventilation and prevent damage due to trapped moisture.

Walls. Exterior walls and walls between heated and unheated spaces should be insulated. See Box 10.3 for

Box 10.3 Noise and Energy-Efficiency

Insulation within the wall cavity, even in interior walls, reduces the effect of airborne sounds. Blanket insulation woven through the staggered studs of a double wall serves to further decrease noise transmission. Fiberglass insulation not only absorbs sound but, when placed in the wall cavity, reduces resonance as well. When both factors are considered, however, 3½ inches of fiberglass insulation decreases the decibel level only about 7 decibels. In a double wall with 9 inches of insulation, the decibel level is reduced by about 15 decibels. Glass fiber boards are more dense and, therefore, more sound-absorbing.

the noise implications of insulation. Energy-efficient homes are often built using a combination of batts between studs and rigid board insulation on the exterior surface. When siding is replaced on existing homes, rigid board insulation can be applied as sheathing under the siding or can be purchased to fit under individual siding members.

Floors. Insulating floors will help keep them warm. Floors over unheated basements and crawl spaces should be insulated using batts between floor joists. It is unnecessary to insulate floors over heated basement spaces and between two stories of heated living area. It is necessary, however, to insulate between the floor joists at the perimeter of the building in these floors.

Basements. Basement walls should be insulated either on the exterior, on the interior, or both. Interior basement insulation requires the addition of wood furring strips or studs inside masonry construction to facilitate the installation of rigid board or batt insulation. Both should be covered with fire-resistant materials.

Insulation can be installed around the outside perimeter of basements or foundation walls and under concrete slab floors. Homes that have slab floors also lose heat through uninsulated perimeters. Current recommendations include the use of 2 to 3 inches of rigid board insulation around perimeters all the way to the base of the foundation. An additional strip of insulation between the foundation wall and concrete slab will reduce heat losses through the floor to the foundation, but this must be installed before the slab is poured.

Superinsulated homes use double-wall construction with a second non-load-bearing wall built an inch or two inside the exterior wall. See Figure 10.9. A minimum of 18 inches of insulation is used in ceilings, making it necessary to construct a platform above the insulation if attic space is to be used. Because heat losses through openings are significant, superinsulated homes have few windows and doors, and those are often foamed in place to prevent air infiltration. The goal of superinsulated homes is to make use of internal heat gains from light fixtures, appliances, and people, requiring little additional heat.

Vapor Barriers

In the average home, humidity is generated by cooking, dishwashing, bathing, doing laundry, houseplants, humidifiers, and people. Problems arise because heat and moisture from the interior move outward during cold weather. Because water is a good conductor of heat, many insulation materials lose effectiveness when they absorb moisture. For this reason, it is necessary to protect them with vapor barriers—materials through which moisture does not readily pass. Vapor barriers are placed between the warm air of the interior and the insulation, reducing moisture flow. The colder side of insulation should be properly ventilated to dissipate any moisture that does collect. When two or more layers of insulation are used, there should be no vapor barrier between them, and when insulation is used in interior walls for sound dampening, no

---

■ Because they have few windows, the site location and orientation of the superinsulated house on a site are less relevant.

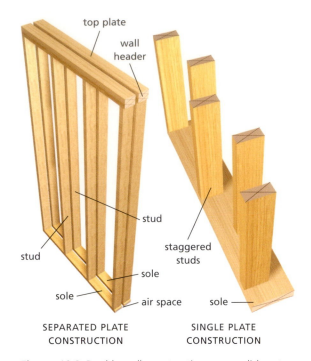

Figure 10.9 Double-wall construction accomplishes two things: Additional insulation can be used in walls, and heat loss through framing members is minimized because no framing member (other than plates in some walls) goes all the way through the wall.

vapor barrier should be used. A second purpose of vapor barriers is to prevent moisture from getting through to exterior walls, where it can condense and freeze, causing paint to peel and cracks to form.

Vapor barriers may be separate or combined with building materials. Polyethylene film is an effective separate barrier and is used especially under and around masonry slabs and walls, on the ground under unheated crawl spaces, and under loose fill insulation. Foil forms effective vapor barriers on the back of gypsum wallboard or when attached to insulative batts, blankets, and rigid foam board. An added advantage of foil is its reflective quality, which reflects radiant energy back through walls. To be effective for this purpose, however, foil requires a dead air space of ¾ inch in front of it. Kraft paper is a less expensive vapor barrier attached to insulation materials. Some paints also exhibit qualities inherent in vapor barriers.

Windows

Maximizing the efficiency of windows is crucial. Heat is lost around windows by convection and is gained or lost through the glass by conduction and radiation. Heat loss through a single glass pane is more than 20 times as much as through a well-insulated 6-inch wall. While the IRC requires that the window area be equal to a minimum of 8 percent of the total heated floor space, many homes have window areas totaling 20 to 25 percent. The maximum glazed area recommended by the IRC is 15 percent, except in town houses, where it is 25 percent of the gross exterior wall area (not square feet of structure).

Glazing That Improves Cooling

Environmental control glass is used primarily in the Sun Belt because it reduces heat gain. It also diminishes glare, making it preferred for homes around large bodies of water or where the sun is especially bright. Environmental control glass, however, reduces the amount of visible light transmitted and increases lighting requirements within a building. There are two types of environmental control glass: tinted and reflective.

Tinted glass absorbs some heat and reradiates it to the outside, reducing heat gain through glass by up to 25 percent. The darker the tint, the greater the reduction in heat gain and glare and the more light is blocked. Tinted glass also helps to preserve the colors of carpet, upholstery, and draperies by blocking ultraviolet rays—a major cause of fabric fading.

Reflective glass is even more effective, cutting heat gain to almost half that of standard window glass. Reflective glass is also capable of controlling up to 65 percent of glare and 80 percent of ultraviolet light. In manufacturing reflective glass, a metallic coating is applied on or fired into tinted glass. Viewed from the exterior, reflective glass is mirrorlike as long as light levels are higher outside than inside. This characteristic ensures indoor privacy during the daytime. At night when light levels are greater inside than outside, light

Minimal window area will reduce energy requirements but decrease natural light in the structure. To improve the efficiency of the building envelope, use environmental control glass, spectrally selective glazing, or low-emissivity glass to prevent heat gain. Use low-emissivity glass, multiple glazing, or gas-filled glass to prevent heat loss.

---

is reflected back into the building. Thus, users on the interior cannot see out the windows.

Low-e (low-emissivity) windows have a microscopically thin metallic coating between two panes of glass. The specific location of the coating depends on whether heating or air-conditioning is most important. The metallic coating reflects infrared waves reducing heat transmission through the glass.

Spectrally selective glass uses low-e technology to filter up to 70 percent of infrared rays but transmits almost all of the natural light, which results in lower illumination requirements on the interior. Because spectrally selective glass does not allow for solar gain during the winter, it is most used where air-conditioning is a primary consideration.

Glazing That Improves Heating Efficiency

Heat loss can be reduced by using multiple glazing: storm windows, insulating glass, or both. Each of these methods utilizes a dead air space for insulation.

When using reflective glass, it is important for clients to understand that at night when light levels are higher inside a structure than outside, objects on the inside are visible as if through uncoated glass.

Because reflective glass may present driving hazards due to reflection onto the highway, local codes may limit the use of these surfaces. It is also necessary to ensure that new construction using reflective glass will not inflict greater heat gains on existing buildings nearby.

Storm windows are separate entities installed inside or outside existing windows, depending on the type of window. The air space between the window and the storm window is approximately 4 inches. Storm windows used with casement, awning, and hopper windows and often on storm doors must be exchanged with separate screen units in the spring and fall. These are often heavy, clumsy, and difficult to install on second-story windows and in hard-to-reach places. Double-hung and horizontal sliding windows have double or triple tracks to permit the storage of storm windows when not in use. Screens are an inherent part of these windows. One disadvantage of storm windows is that there are two units to clean. It is usually less expensive to add storm windows to existing buildings than to change the windows themselves. In new construction, costs should be compared before making decisions about window type.

Insulating glass consists of two layers of glass separated by a ½ to 1-inch air space. This space is dehydrated and sealed to prevent condensation and collection of dust between the panes. Condensation on the inside pane is also virtually eliminated.

Organically sealed glass uses spacers at the edges of the glass to maintain a specified distance between panes. The glass is sealed to these spacers. Large fixed windows, sliding glass doors, and operating windows can all be constructed of organically sealed insulating glass. Movement, however, can break the seal over time. When this occurs, moisture and dust may get between the panes and the unit will need to be replaced. Welded-edge glass consists of two panes of glass with the edges fused together in a U shape. Most welded-edge insulating glass used in homes is found in operable windows.

Whether employing insulating glass or storm windows, double glazing reduces heat loss through windows by about one-half, and triple glazing provides even more thermal protection. Although it is possible to install triple-glazed units in single frames, triple glazing is normally achieved by adding storm windows to insulated glass areas. The three panes of glass, with two air spaces between them, cut heat loss by about two-thirds. Triple glazing is cost-effective in very cold climates.

Gas-filled windows have double panes and the space between the panes is filled with a gas (usually argon or krypton) that reduces the thermal air currents between the panes, adding to the insulative qualities of the unit.

Determining Energy Use

The amount of heat lost through the building envelope depends a great deal on the climate. Two identical houses with the same energy features in dissimilar climates gain or lose heat at different rates.

Degree Days

Climates in different areas of the country are compared using **degree days**. Degree days are the units that show the relative amount of energy needed for heating or cooling in a certain climate. During each season, degree days are added together in order to determine the heating or cooling energy necessary to maintain thermal comfort. As the number of degree days increases, energy requirements also increase.

Degree days are calculated differently in the heating and cooling seasons. Each heating degree day is a unit representing a one degree Fahrenheit difference between the mean temperature for the day and 65 degrees Fahrenheit, the lowest outdoor temperature at which homes need no heating. See Box 10.4. When added together, the median number of heating degree days during the heating season in the United States is 4500. A cooling degree day is a one degree Fahrenheit difference between the mean temperature

Box 10.4 Determining Degree Days

Degree days are used to determine the severity of climate and compare areas with varying climates on an equal basis; for calculating heating and cooling loads; and for sizing the mechanical systems. Heating and air-conditioning engineers have calculated that if the average temperature for a day is 65 degrees Fahrenheit or above, no supplemental heating is necessary. If the average temperature for a day is 65 degrees Fahrenheit or below, no cooling is necessary. Therefore, it is usually necessary to calculate two types of degree days: heating degree days and cooling degree days. Obviously, some climates remain either below 65 degrees Fahrenheit most of the year or above 65 degrees Fahrenheit most of the year. For these climates, only a single type of degree day must be calculated.

During the entire heating or cooling season, the number of degree days accumulated in each 24-hour period is added to determine the total number of degree days for the season. For example, Louisville, Kentucky, has an average of 4514 heating degree days per year. The average number of heating degree days per year for American households is 4500. Energy requirements for operating heating and air-conditioning systems increase as the number of heating or cooling degree days rises.

CALCULATING THE AVERAGE TEMPERATURE

The day's average temperature is determined by summing the high and low temperatures for a 24-hour period and dividing by two. For example, on a day during which the high temperature is 54 degrees Fahrenheit and the low temperature, 22 degrees Fahrenheit, the average temperature is 38 degrees Fahrenheit.

**high temperature + low temperature / 2 =
average temperature**
54 + 22 / 2 = 38 degrees

HEATING DEGREE DAYS

Each heating degree day is one degree Fahrenheit difference between 65 degrees Fahrenheit and the average temperature on any given day. In the example above, 38 degrees Fahrenheit is the average temperature for the day. The average temperature is subtracted from 65 degrees to determine the number of heating degree days for that 24-hour period. In this case, the number of heating degree days is 27.

**65° F − average temperature =
heating degree days**
65 − 38 = 27 heating degree days

COOLING DEGREE DAYS

Cooling degree days are used to calculate air-conditioning needs. The number of cooling degree days in a 24-hour period is the difference between 65 degrees Fahrenheit and the daily average temperature. For example, on a day when temperatures soar to 100 degrees Fahrenheit and drop only to 80 degrees Fahrenheit, the number of cooling degree days is 25.

**mean temperature − 65 degrees =
cooling degree days**
90 − 65 = 25 cooling degree days

The average number of cooling degree days per year for American households is 1000 when using 65 degrees Fahrenheit as a base.* In Louisville, Kentucky, the number of cooling degree days is 1342.

* U.S. Government tables use 65 degrees Fahrenheit as the base temperature for both heating and cooling degree days. Users can, however, determine degree days using any desired base temperature. When using published tables rather than determining degree days using local mean temperatures, the results may be high.

Table 10.1 Heating and Cooling Degree Days for Selected U.S. Cities

City	Heating Degree Days	Cooling Degree Days	City	Heating Degree Days	Cooling Degree Days
Albuquerque, New Mexico	4425	1244	Los Angeles, California	1458	727
Atlanta, Georgia	2991	1667	Louisville, Kentucky	4514	1288
Atlantic City, New Jersey	5196	826	Memphis, Tennessee	3082	2118
Baltimore, Maryland	4707	1137	Miami, Florida	200	4198
Bismarck, North Dakota	8968	488	Milwaukee, Wisconsin	7324	479
Boise, Idaho	5861	754	Minneapolis, Minnesota	7981	682
Boston, Massachusetts	5641	678	Mobile, Alabama	1702	2627
Burlington, Vermont	7771	388	New Orleans, Louisiana	1513	2655
Charleston, West Virginia	4646	1031	New York City, New York	4805	1096
Cheyenne, Wyoming	7326	285	Oklahoma City, Oklahoma	3659	1859
Chicago, Illinois	6536	752	Omaha, Nebraska	6300	1072
Cleveland, Ohio	6201	621	Phoenix, Arizona	1350	4162
Columbia, South Carolina	2649	1966	Pittsburgh, Pennsylvania	5968	654
Concord, New Hampshire	7554	328	Portland, Maine	7378	268
Dallas, Texas	2407	2603	Portland, Oregon	4522	371
Denver, Colorado	6020	679	Providence, Rhode Island	5884	606
Des Moines, Iowa	6497	1036	Raleigh, North Carolina	3457	1417
Detroit, Michigan	6569	626	Reno, Nevada	5674	508
Great Falls, Montana	7741	388	Richmond, Virginia	3963	1348
Hartford, Connecticut	6151	677	St. Louis, Missouri	4758	1534
Honolulu, Hawaii	0	4474	Salt Lake City, Utah	2765	1047
Houston, Texas	1599	2700	San Diego, California	1256	984
Indianapolis, Indiana	5615	1014	Seattle, Washington	4908	190
Jackson, Mississippi	2467	2215	Sioux Falls, South Dakota	7809	744
Jacksonville, Florida	1434	2551	Washington, D.C.	4047	1549
Juneau, Alaska	8897	0	Wichita, Kansas	4791	1628
Little Rock, Arkansas	3155	2005	Wilmington, Delaware	4937	1047

Source: U.S. Census Bureau, "Sunshine, Average Wind Speed, Heating and Cooling Degree Days, and Average Relative Humidity—Selected Cities," *Statistical Abstract of the United States: 2001 (121st Edition)* Table 377 (Washington, D.C., 2001), 230.

and 65, 70, or 75 degrees Fahrenheit. The choice depends on the climate and the desired level of cooling in the home. Government-prepared charts showing cooling degree days use 65 degrees but users can prepare calculations based on any desired temperature if the charts are not used for the number of cooling degree days. This text uses 65 degrees. To determine cooling degree days, subtract the desired temperature, in this case 65 degrees from the mean temperature in degrees Fahrenheit. The median number of cooling degree days per year for American households is 1000 (based on 65 degrees). See Table 10.1 for average heating and cooling degree days for some American cities.

Calculating Energy Requirements in a Residence

Determining heat loss or gain in a structure is imperative for sizing mechanical systems and is useful for determining energy usage in a home. While there are a number of formulas used for these calculations,[5] regardless of the complexity of the formula used, the result is still an approximation. There are too many variables involved to obtain extremely accurate results. Such variables include not only climatic factors but the age and condition of the structure, variations in thermal characteristics of different samples of the same material, quality of construction, and living habits of the occupants. For large buildings or in buildings for commercial use, it is important to take as many variables into account as possible and to use the most sophisticated methods of arriving at energy use estimations. When calculating energy use in residences, it is common practice to simplify the process. The resulting figures are within acceptable parameters from a practical standpoint.

When calculating heat loss and gain for sizing mechanical systems, each room is calculated separately to ensure proper sizing of the system for each area. When calculating heat loss or gain to determine annual energy requirements, however, calculations are generally done for the entire structure as a unit. See Box 10.5 for specific directions and an example.

To calculate energy requirements for a building, it is first necessary to determine the net area of structural components, including walls, floors, ceilings, windows, and doors. Because the R-values of windows and doors are not the same as the R-values of walls in which they are located, the total area of windows and doors must be subtracted from the gross wall area. To determine air infiltration, it is necessary to calculate the volume of the structure. The volume will be multiplied by an air infiltration factor—the number of times per hour the total volume of air is exchanged with unheated outdoor air.

Box 10.5 Calculating Heat Loss in a Structure

EXAMPLE STRUCTURE
- Length: 60 feet
- Width: 30 feet
- Wall height: 8 feet
- Single-story building
- Unheated full basement
- Framework on 16-inch centers
- Doors
  2 exterior doors (36" × 80")

  $2 \times 3' \times 6'8" = 40$ square feet
- Windows
  6 windows @ 3' × 4'

  $6 \times 3' \times 4' = 72$ square feet

  1 window 2' × 2'

  $1 \times 2' \times 2' = 4$ square feet

  1 window 6' × 5'

  $1 \times 6' \times 5' = 30$ square feet

1. Determine the area of like structural components. The formula for area is

   Length × width = area

a. Example: Walls

   Add the length of all walls together.
   Length side A + length side B + length side C + length side D = total length
   $30' + 60' + 30' + 60' = 180$ feet

   In the case of walls, to find the area, multiply total length by the height of the walls.

   Total wall length × wall height = gross wall area
   $180' \times 8' = 1440$ square feet

b. Example: Floors and ceilings
   Length × width = area
   $60' \times 30' = 1800$ square feet

2. Because windows and doors do not have the same R- and U-values as the structural components they are a part of, they must be calculated separately. To do so, the area of windows and doors must be subtracted from the area of the structural component in which they are located.

(continued)

Box 10.5 (continued)

3. Determine the wall area without openings.

   a. Add the area of windows and doors in walls together.

   Door 1 + door 2 + window 1 + window 2 + window 3 = total opening area

   40' + 72' + 4' + 30' = 146 square feet

   Total window area = 106 square feet

   Total door area = 40 square feet

   b. Subtract the total opening area from the gross wall area to determine net wall area.

   Gross wall area – total opening area = net wall area

   1440 square feet – 146 square feet = 1294 square feet

4. For residences, it is generally acceptable to estimate the number of times the volume of interior air is exchanged per hour. Use the following to determine the air infiltration factor.

Homes without caulking and weather-stripping	5 or 6
Older homes with poor caulking and weather-stripping	1.5 to 2
Average homes built since 1980	1
Energy-efficient homes	0.5

   Since a volume of air is exchanged, first calculate the volume of the structure.

   a. Determine the volume of the structure.

   Length × width × height = volume

   60' × 30' × 8' = 14,400 cubic feet

   b. To calculate air infiltration, multiply the air infiltration factor by the volume of the structure. For the example structure, which is an energy-efficient home, use 0.5 air exchanges per hour to allow for children, pets, and other factors affecting air infiltration.

   Air infiltration factor × volume = air exchanged

   0.5 × 14,400' = 7,200 cubic feet

5. Record net area (in the case of air infiltration, volume) for all components.

   Example:

Component	Net area
Walls	1294
Floors	1800
Ceilings	1800
Windows	106
Doors	40
Air exchange (cubic feet)	7200

6. Determine the amount of heat that flows through each of the structural components. This is done by summing the R-values of all materials used for each component. In addition to R-values of building materials, there is an R-value for the air film that exists on both the interior and exterior of a structure. Charts showing the R-value of exterior air films are based on an average wind speed of 15 miles per hour. The R-values used in the following calculations are obtained from Table 10.2. Once R-values are obtained, they can be converted to U-values by using the following formula:

   1/R-value = U-value

   a. Walls, floors, and ceilings are composed of a framework and the spaces between the framework. While differences in R-values between these two areas may be ignored, better accuracy is obtained if the two areas are calculated separately.

Box 10.5 (continued)

Between framing members		Framework	
Wall	R-value	Wall	R-value
Exterior air film (vertical)	0.17	Exterior air film (vertical)	0.17
½" × 8" wood bevel siding	0.81	½" × 8" wood bevel siding	0.81
Building paper	0.06	Building paper	0.06
⅝" plywood sheathing	0.77	⅝" plywood sheathing	0.77
3½" fiberglass	11.00	3½" wood framing member	4.35
½" drywall	0.45	½" drywall	0.45
Interior air film	0.68	Interior air film	0.68
Total R-value	**13.94**	**Total R-value**	**7.29**
U-value (1/13.94)	**0.0717**	**U-value (1/7.29)**	**0.1372**

Floor (heat flow down)	R-value	Floor (heat flow down)	R-value
Interior air film	0.92	Interior air film	0.92
Carpet with pad	0.48	Carpet with pad	0.48
⅝" plywood underlayment	0.78	⅝" plywood underlayment	0.78
Building paper	0.06	Building paper	0.06
¾" plywood subfloor	0.94	¾" plywood subfloor	0.94
6" fiberglass	19.00	12" softwood framing member	15.00
Airspace (3.5" or more)	0.93	Airspace (3.5" or more)	0.93
Interior air film	0.61	Interior air film	0.61
Total R-value	**23.72**	**Total R-value**	**19.72**
U-value (1/23.72)	**0.0422**	**U-value (1/19.72)**	**0.0507**

Ceiling	R-value	Ceiling	R-value
Horizontal air film	0.61	Horizontal air film	0.61
½" drywall	0.45	½" drywall	0.45
6" fiberglass	19.00	8" framing member	9.06
Airspace (3.5" or more)	1.00	Airspace (3.5" or more)	1.00
Total R-value	**21.06**	**Total R-value**	**11.12**
U-value (1/21.06)	**0.0475**	**U-value (1/11.12)**	**0.0899**

Doors	U-value
1.25" thick solid wood with wood storm door	0.28

Windows	U-value
Double insulating glass with 0.1875" air space	0.62

Air	U-value
It requires 0.018 Btus of heat to heat one cubic foot of air.	0.018

b. Determine the average U-value for structural components such as walls, floors, and ceilings that have both frame-backed portions and sections between the framework. For framing on 16-inch centers, use 20 percent of the total wall area. For framing on 24-inch centers, use 15 percent. For floors and ceilings, use 10 percent. The formula used to determine the average U-value is

Percent of framed area / 100 × U-value of framed area + percent of between frame area / 100 × U-value of between frame area = Average U-value

Example: Walls
20 percent / 100 × 0.1372 + 80 percent / 100 × 0.0717 = Average U-value
0.20 × 0.1372 + 0.80 × 0.0717 = Average U-value
0.02744 + 0.05736 = Average U-value
0.0848 = Average U-value

Example: Floors
10 percent / 100 × 0.0507 + 90 percent / 100 × 0.0422 = Average U-value
0.10 × 0.0507 + 0.90 × 0.0422 = Average U-value
0.0051 + 0.0380 = Average U-value
0.0431 = Average U-value

Example: Ceilings
10 percent / 100 × 0.0899 + 90 percent / 100 × 0.0475 = Average U-value
0.10 × 0.0899 + 0.90 × 0.0475 = Average U-value
0.00899 + 0.04275 = Average U-value
0.0517 = Average U-value

Example:

Component	Net area	U-value
Walls	1294	0.0848
Floors	1800	0.0431
Ceilings	1800	0.0517
Windows	106	0.6200
Doors	40	0.2800
Air exchange (cu. ft.)	7200	0.0180

(continued)

Box 10.5 (continued)

7. Determine the number of Btus of heat lost or gained per hour. Multiply net area by U-value for each component and record the results. Total the number of Btus.

Example Problem:

Component	Net area	U-value	Btu loss per hour
Wall	1294	0.0848	109.73
Floors	1800	0.0431	77.58
Ceilings	1800	0.0517	93.06
Windows	106	0.6200	65.72
Doors	40	0.2800	11.20
Air exchange	7200	0.0180	129.60
Total			**486.89**

8. Determine annual heat loss.

a. Multiply the number of Btus lost per hour by 24 to determine daily Btu loss. This number can be rounded off to the nearest Btu.

Btus per hour × 24 = Daily Btu loss
486.89 × 24 = 11,685

b. Multiply daily heat loss by the number of heating degree days to determine annual heat loss. For this example, use 4500—the median number of heating degree days for the United States.

Daily Btu loss × heating degree days = Annual Btu loss
11,685 × 4,500 = 58,582,500 Btus

While it is possible to measure every crack length and width to determine air infiltration, there are still so many variables, such as the number of times doors are opened, that the result is approximate. For purposes of calculation, an air infiltration factor of 0.5 is used for new, tightly sealed homes, a factor of 1 for most homes built within the past 25 years, a factor of 1.5 to 2 for older homes with caulking and weather-stripping, and up to 5 or 6 for older homes without caulking or weather-stripping. Although it is possible to reduce the air infiltration factor to less than 0.5, more tightly sealed homes are not desirable. Some air exchange is necessary to allow harmful substances to dissipate.

The second step in calculating heat loss (or gain) is to determine the amount of heat that flows through each of the structural components, including doors and windows. This is done by summing the R-values of all materials used for each component. In addition to the R-values of building materials, there is an R-value for the air film that exists on both the interior and exterior of a structure. Walls, floors, and ceilings are composed of a framework and the spaces between the framework. While differences in the R-values between these two areas may be ignored, better accuracy is obtained if the two areas are calculated separately. See Table 10.2 for the typical R-values of various building materials. See Figure 10.10 for typical cross-sections of structural components. Once the R-values have been determined, they can be converted to U-values by using the following formula:

1 / R-value = U-value

After determining the U-values of individual sections of building components, it is necessary to determine the average U-value for each. While it is possible to count boards used and determine this percentage very accurately, for practical purposes, if framing is on 16-inch centers, it generally comprises approximately 20 percent of the total wall area. If framing is on 24-inch centers, the figure is 15 percent. For floors and ceilings, the framed area is considered to be 10 percent. The formula used to determine the average U-value is:

Percent of framed area / 100 × U-value of framed area + percent between framed area / 100 + U-value of between framed area = average U-value

Table 10.2 R- or U-values of Building Materials and Components

	R-value		U-value Winter	U-value Summer
Boards and Panels		**Glass (Vertical)**		
Drywall (½")	0.45	Single pane	1.10	1.04
Drywall (⅝")	0.56	Insulating glass (double)		
Plywood (Douglas fir ⅜")	0.47	¼" air space	0.58	0.61
Plywood (Douglas fir ½")	0.62	½" air space, 0.40 low-e coating	0.38	0.45
Plywood (Douglas fir ⅝")	0.77	Storm windows (1"–4" air space)	0.50	0.50
Plywood (Douglas fir ¾")	0.93	Glass block 6" × 6" × 4" thick	0.60	0.57
Particleboard (⅝")	0.82			
Building Membrane		**Glass (horizontal as in skylights or domes)**		
Building paper/felt	0.06	Single pane (winter)	1.23	0.83
House wrap	Negligible	Insulating glass (double)		
Finish Flooring		¼" air space	0.65	0.54
Carpet with fibrous pad	2.08	½" air space	0.59	0.49
Carpet with rubber pad	1.23	½" air space 0.40 low-e coating	0.52	0.42
Vinyl	0.05	Plastic dome—single wall	1.15	0.80
Hardwood (¾")	0.68	**Doors**		
Insulation		Solid wood, no storm door (1.5")	0.49	0.47
Fiber batts and blankets		Solid wood 1.5", wood storm door	0.27	0.47
3.5"	11.00	Solid wood 1.5", metal storm door	0.33	0.47
5.5"–6.5"	19.00	Steel door 1.75"	0.59	0.58
8.5"	30	**R-values**		
Panels		Exterior air film	0.17	0.17
Expanded polystyrene extruded	4.00–5.00 per inch	Interior air film	0.68	0.68
Expanded polyurethane	6.25 per inch	Heat flow up (as from ceiling to attic)	0.61	
Loose fill				
Cellulose	3.13–3.70 per inch	Heat flow horizontal (as through walls)	0.68	
Perlite, expanded	2.70 per inch			
Vermiculite, exfoliated	2.27 per inch	Heat flow down (as through floors to basement)	0.92	
Masonry Materials		Air space 1"–4" (approximately)	1.00	
Brick, face	0.11 per inch			
Concrete block (3 oval core sand and gravel aggregate 8")	0.71			
Stone	0.08 per inch			
Roofing				
Asphalt shingles	0.44			
Slate	0.05			
Wood shingles	0.94			
Siding Materials				
Wood shingles 16" with 7.5" exposure	0.87			
Wood siding, bevel ½" thick	0.81			
Wood				
Hardwoods	0.91 per inch			
Fir, pine, other softwoods	1.25 per inch			

Source: Based on *ASHRAE Handbook* © American Society of Heating, Refrigerating and Air Conditioning Engineers, Inc., www.ashrae.org

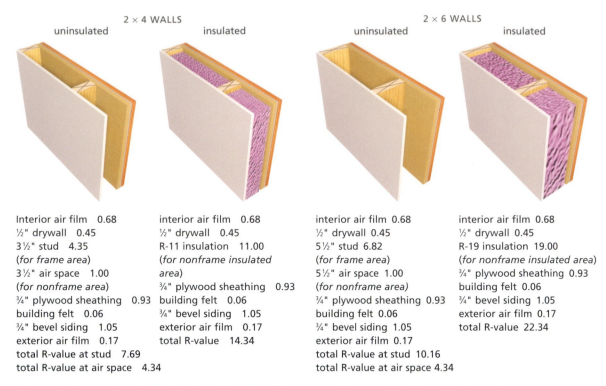

Interior air film   0.68
½" drywall   0.45
3½" stud   4.35
(for frame area)
3½" air space   1.00
(for nonframe area)
¾" plywood sheathing   0.93
building felt   0.06
¾" bevel siding   1.05
exterior air film   0.17
total R-value at stud   7.69
total R-value at air space   4.34

interior air film   0.68
½" drywall   0.45
R-11 insulation   11.00
(for nonframe insulated area)
¾" plywood sheathing   0.93
building felt   0.06
¾" bevel siding   1.05
exterior air film   0.17
total R-value   14.34

interior air film 0.68
½" drywall 0.45
5½" stud 6.82
(for frame area)
5½" air space 1.00
(for nonframe area)
¾" plywood sheathing 0.93
building felt 0.06
¾" bevel siding 1.05
exterior air film 0.17
total R-value at stud 10.16
total R-value at air space 4.34

interior air film 0.68
½" drywall 0.45
R-19 insulation 19.00
(for nonframe insulated area)
¾" plywood sheathing 0.93
building felt 0.06
¾" bevel siding 1.05
exterior air film 0.17
total R-value 22.34

Figure 10.10 Improving the total R-value of a structural component is accomplished by adding insulation.

To determine the number of Btus of heat lost or gained for each component:

$$\text{Net area} \times \text{U-value} \times 24 \text{ (hours in a day)} \times$$
$$\text{heating or cooling degree days} =$$
$$\text{total Btu loss or gain}$$

Add the Btus lost for all components to get the total number of Btus lost for the structure. To determine the cost of heating or cooling with a specific fuel, see Box 10.6. A comparison of heating costs in different climates is shown in Table 10.3.

Energy-Efficient Homes

While many mid-twentieth-century buildings depended on mechanical systems for heating and cooling, the high cost of fuel during the last few decades has resulted in an effort to lower energy requirements for a structure while maintaining thermal comfort. Most new homes have insulation, weather-stripping, and caulking and may have minimal window area. Homes designed specifically for their energy-efficient qualities include solar designs and earth contact structures.

Solar Homes

Solar homes are designed to collect, store, and redistribute solar energy to heat water or living spaces. Such homes not only utilize special devices to capture and use energy from the sun but by necessity are energy-efficient in design, including insulative properties, compatibility with natural features, and orientation. Both active and passive solar systems can be used for space heating—the residential system most adaptable to solar use.

Box 10.6 Estimating Annual Fuel Costs

To determine the amount of fuel needed to heat a home for a year, determine the cost of fuel per unit. The following chart shows projected national average costs for 2005 and the number of Btus per unit. Costs change frequently and local costs may be different from national averages. For accurate calculations in a specific area, it is necessary to look at a recent utility bill or call utility companies.

1. Determine the annual number of Btus required by doing heat loss calculations for a structure.
2. Because the efficiency of fuel-consuming units except for electric units is less than 100 percent, divide the total number of Btus required by the efficiency of the heating unit in decimal percentages. This results in the total number of Btus required. See the chart to the right for typical unit efficiencies.

   In this example, a total of 53,613,000 Btus is required, using a 100 percent efficient unit.

Heat producers starred are used in the example. Wood and pellet stove efficiency used is the average of the high and low efficiencies.

3. Divide the total number of Btus required by the number of Btus produced by one unit of fuel.
4. To determine the cost of the fuel, multiply the number of units of fuel by the cost per unit.

Heating Equipment Type	Typical Efficiency in Percent
High-efficiency oil-burning*	89.0
Typical oil-burning central unit*	80.0
High-efficiency gas central unit*	97.0
Minimum-efficiency gas central unit*	78.0
Central gas boiler	85.0
Vented gas room heater	65.0
Electric baseboard unit	99.0
Electric forced air central unit*	97.0
Heat pump central unit*	200.0
Ground-source heat pump	300.0
Woodstove with fan*	40.0–70.0
Pellet stoves*	85.0–90.0

Fuel	Unit	Btus Required	/	Percent unit efficiency	=	Total Btus	/	Btus per unit	=	Number of units	×	Unit cost	=	Annual cost
Electricity	Kilowatt hour	53,613,000		97.0		55,271,134		3412		16,199		0.0906		$1467.63
Natural gas	Therm	53,613,000		78.0		68,734,615		102,500		671		1.09		731.39
		53,613,000		97.0		55,271,134		102,500		539		1.09		587.51
LP gas	Gallon	53,613,000		78.0		68,734,615		91,330		753		1.55		1167.15
Oil	Gallon	53,613,000		80.0		67,016,250		140,000		479		1.76		843.04
		53,613,000		89.0		60,239,326		140,000		430		1.76		756.80
Wood	Cord	53,613,000		55.0		97,478,181		20,000,000		4.87		$175.00		852.25
Pellets	Ton	53,613,000		87.5		61,272,000		16,500,000		3.71		$165.00		612.15

Sources: Source for national average cost per fuel unit except wood: www.npga.org/i4a/pages/index.cfm?pageid=914. Source for national average cost per cord of wood and for pellet fuel: www.pelletheat.org/3/residential/compareFuel.cfm. Source for heat-producing unit efficiencies: www.eere.energy.gov/consumerinfo/factsheets/cb5.html.

   *As the efficiency of a furnace increases, the amount of fuel required decreases but greater differences are found between fuels. It costs more to heat a home using electricity than any other fuel even though the efficiency is high.

Table 10.3 Comparison of Heat Loss for Identical Homes in Varying Climates[a]

Location	Heating Degree Days[b]	Annual Btu loss	Number Therms Gas	Annual Gas Cost[c]	Number Gallons Oil	Annual Oil Cost[d]	Number KWh	Annual Electric Cost[e]
Atlanta, GA	2991	36,352,614	355	$386.95	260	$457.60	10,654	$965.25
Chicago, IL	6536	79,438,544	775	844.75	567	997.92	23,282	2109.35
Denver, CO	6020	73,167,080	714	778.26	523	920.48	21,444	1942.83
Juneau, AK	8897	108,134,138	1055	1149.95	722	1270.72	31,692	2871.30
Los Angeles, CA	1458	17,720,532	173	188.57	127	223.52	5,194	470.58
Phoenix, AZ	1350	16,407,900	160	174.40	117	205.92	4,809	435.70
Portland, ME	7378	89,672,212	875	953.75	641	1128.16	26,281	2381.06
Seattle, WA	4908	59,651,832	582	634.38	426	749.76	17,483	1583.96
St. Louis, MO	4758	57,828,732	564	614.76	413	726.88	16,949	1535.58

[a] The Btu loss per day in the example is 12,154 Btus. Efficiency of furnaces is not considered in this example because it is for comparison only.

[b] The number of heating degree days used in this chart is from Table 10.1.

[c] Projected average cost of natural gas in the United States in 2005 was $1.09 per therm. Source: www.npga.org/i4a/pages/index.cfm?pageid=914.

[d] Projected average cost of oil in the United States in 2005 was $1.76 per gallon. Source: www.npga.org/i4a/pages/index.cfm?pageid=914.

[e] Projected average cost of electricity in the United States in 2005 was $0.0906 per KWh. Source: www.npga.org/i4a/pages/index.cfm?pageid=914.

Principles of Solar Heating

When radiant energy from the sun strikes a material, three things can happen: It can be transmitted through the material, reflected off its surface, or absorbed by it. An opaque material is only capable of reflection or absorption, while transparent and translucent materials can also transmit radiation. A transparent material transmits most of the radiation that strikes it; a shiny or light-colored material is best at reflecting; a dark matte finish maximizes absorption.

When solar radiation is absorbed by a material, the various wavelengths are changed to long wave heat energy. This absorbed heat raises the temperature of the object. Some of the energy is reradiated to the surroundings still in the form of heat.

These properties of radiation and materials make possible the **greenhouse effect**, an important principle of solar heating. Glass has the property of transmitting most of the short wave radiation present in sunlight, but it is nearly opaque to long wave radiation. When a dark-colored radiation-absorbing material is placed in a glass enclosure, it is possible for sunlight to pass through the glass, then strike and

be absorbed by the dark mass. The reradiated heat cannot return through the glass, and so remains trapped inside. Some, but not all, plastics have properties similar to glass and can be used for the same purpose. The greenhouse effect is used to capture heat for both passive solar heating, such as with window walls, and active solar heating, where it is the principle behind **flat-plate collectors**.

Passive Systems

Passive solar heating systems use nonmechanical means to collect heat and disperse it to the interior of the home. The building itself is designed to collect and store solar energy. Because of this, the use of passive solar systems is generally limited to new homes designed specifically for the purpose. Homes using passive solar energy are designed to admit the sun's useful energy during sunny periods, and then close tightly to prevent heat loss when sunlight is not available.

Passive solar heating systems are often heavily constructed using masonry walls and floors, which form **thermal masses** that absorb heat—**direct gain** systems. The mass gives off stored thermal energy to the surrounding area when the room air becomes cooler than the mass.

Some passive systems use water as a heat storage medium. Plastic or metal containers or hollow concrete walls with waterproof lining may be used but must be placed in direct sunlight. When the exterior face is painted a dark color, thermal collection is improved. Because the sun heats the water and then the water reradiates heat to the interior, this type of system is **indirect gain**. A common type of indirect system is the **Trombe wall**.[6] A masonry thermal storage wall or water storage device is located 2 to 5 inches from south-facing glass. Heat is trapped by the glass due to the greenhouse effect and transmitted through the storage unit by conduction. Heat can also be supplied to the interior by the process known as **thermosiphoning**. When vents are placed in the thermal mass near the floor and ceiling, the rising warm air in the space between the windows and the thermal mass can be directed through the upper vents to the

When floors are used as heat-collecting devices, they must be left uncovered. This precludes the use of carpeting where sunlight strikes the floor. Furniture arrangement is also affected.

living area. Cooler room air is pulled through the lower vents. These convection currents function effectively only while the space inside the windows is still warm. See Figure 10.11.

A third type of passive system, **isolated gain**, uses solar collection and thermal storage areas that are not part of the house but are attached to it. The most prevalent type of isolated gain system, the natural convective loop, uses components similar to those of active systems, but without any mechanical assistance from pumps or blowers. Air in one or more solar collectors is heated and rises naturally to an outlet near the top of the collector. The air flows to a storage mass of rock or earth located beneath the house. A vent permits warmed air to rise from the storage area into the house and can be closed when heat is not

Figure 10.11 The sun's rays pass through glass and strike heat sink materials used on interior surfaces. When the inside temperature falls below the temperature of the heat sinks, heat is radiated into the air. In rooms where the sun does not directly strike heat sink materials, vents can be installed to allow natural air currents to move warm air to cooler areas (thermosiphoning).

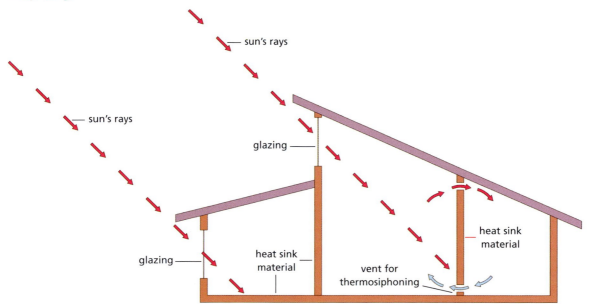

Even an existing home can employ some of the principles of passive solar design, although it may require the active participation of residents. When planning a new conventional structure, use as many passive solar design concepts as possible—facing most windows south, providing thermal masses in areas where sunlight strikes the surface, making use of reflectors and overhangs, and ensuring that warmed air can circulate throughout the structure.

needed. A return vent in or near the floor brings cool air through ducts to the bottom of the collector.

The initial costs of passive solar homes may be higher than for conventional construction. Because they require no mechanical devices for efficient operation, passive systems generate little if any noise, nor do they break down or require extensive maintenance. Overhangs, reflectors, movable insulation, and shades are used to help control the amount of sun entering, although overheating may still occur. Conventional backup systems are usually necessary because

passive systems do not readily respond to sudden temperature changes, nor can they store sufficient heat for use during several sequential days of cloudy weather.

Active Systems

Active solar heating systems convert sunlight into heat by the use of solar panels or collectors installed on the roof or walls or in close proximity to the home. These panels convert visible light energy from the sun to thermal energy. Heat exchangers in solar units transfer the heat derived from solar energy to heat storage units—liquid or rock. From these storage systems, heat can be extracted as needed to warm living areas or to heat water. See Figure 10.12. Active solar systems are initially expensive but have the capability of collecting and storing more thermal energy than passive systems.

Collectors. The collector most commonly used is the flat-plate collector—a well insulated box containing an absorptive surface beneath a transparent cover.

Figure 10.12 Like refrigerators, air conditioners, and heating units, solar units use heat exchangers—collectors—that transfer heat from one fluid to another even though the fluids do not come in direct contact with each other. The fluid used can be air or a liquid.

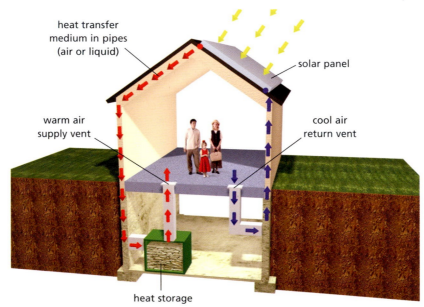

heat transfer medium in pipes (air or liquid)

solar panel

warm air supply vent

cool air return vent

heat storage

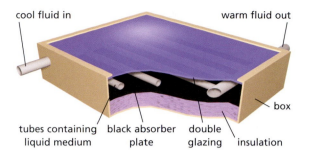

cool fluid in   warm fluid out

box

tubes containing   black absorber   double
liquid medium   plate   glazing   insulation

Figure 10.13 Although single glazing may be used, collectors often have two or more layers of glazing. The use of multiple glazing reduces reradiation of heat to the atmosphere and improves the overall efficiency of the system, although it cuts down the percentage of light rays that pass through the cover.

The glass or plastic cover not only serves to trap heat inside but protects the collector from the effects of inclement weather. See Figure 10.13.

Located about 1 inch beneath the glass is the most important component of solar collectors: the **absorber plate**. The plate is constructed of a highly conductive metal, usually copper, although aluminum and steel are also used. The top surface is painted black, maximizing energy absorption. The absorber plate absorbs light energy, changes it to thermal energy, and transfers the heat to a fluid. Hydronic (liquid) systems require plumbing, with the accompanying possibility of frozen pipes, leakage, and subsequent damage to the home. Air systems require less maintenance because there is no corrosion and any leaks that occur are not as potentially damaging as those of hydronic systems. However, because air is a much less efficient heat transfer medium than water, the ducts necessary for moving air take up more space than the pipes used with hydronic systems. Although collectors using air are less complex than hydronic collectors, more collectors are needed when air is used.

To prevent heat from being lost through the back of the collector, thermal insulation is located beneath the absorber plate. Fiberglass insulation is preferred because it is not affected by the high temperatures in solar panels. A dead air space is provided between the insulation and the absorber plate, and a foil surface on the insulation serves to reflect escaping heat back into the collector.

Solar collectors range widely in efficiency, depending on the outside temperature, wind velocity, and materials used in the collector. On average, each square foot of collector area produces usable heat equivalent to 300 to 350 Btus per day. The collector area should be equal to approximately one-half of the floor area that is to be heated, although many variables can affect this ratio. See Figure 10.14.

A thermostatically controlled pump or blower moves the fluid from the collector to the storage area. Sensors measure temperatures at the storage area and the collector absorber plate. When the absorber plate is 10 to 18 degrees Fahrenheit warmer than the storage area, the pump or blower is automatically activated. When the absorber is only a few degrees warmer, the system is deactivated.

To prevent freezing in cold climates, a hydronic system should be filled with an antifreeze solution rather than pure water. An alternative method is to use

Figure 10.14 Solar collectors must face true (not magnetic) south, although there is relatively little loss of efficiency within a 10 degree range on either side of true south. To be effective, collectors should be exposed to direct sunlight from 9 a.m. to 3 p.m.

pure water in a **drain-down system**. When sensors detect a temperature on the absorber plate of 35 degrees Fahrenheit or below, the water is automatically pumped into a reservoir located where it cannot freeze.

Heat Storage. Separate heat storage areas are used with active systems. When possible, these storage areas should be within the heated space of the house so that heat loss through the storage tank or bin will become heat gain in living areas. Nevertheless, storage areas must be well insulated to prevent excessive heat loss. Three storage methods are currently used: **phase-changing materials**, water, and rock.

Phase-changing materials (pcms) are chemical substances that absorb and release heat as they change from solid to liquid and back again. Once pcms absorb sufficient heat to change phase (melt), they continue to absorb heat without significant temperature increases. This heat is released when cool air is blown over the substance, crystallizing it. A small volume of phase-changing materials can store considerably more energy than the same volume of other mediums.

Hydronic systems usually employ water as the heat storage medium. Water is more efficient than air in transferring, storing, and maintaining heat. However, the **down point temperature**, or the minimum temperature at which it is possible to extract useful heat from storage, is a relatively high 100 degrees Fahrenheit. Water is stored in well-insulated plastic, concrete, or steel tanks.

When a rock storage system is used, heated air is blown through bins filled with 1 to 3 inch rocks. Heat from the air is transferred to the surface area of the rocks and then conducted throughout each rock. The use of larger rocks would decrease the exposed surface area, while the use of smaller ones would restrict air flow. Rocks store heat at temperatures over 212 degrees Fahrenheit, an advantage over water storage. At the same time, the down point temperature of rock is 75 degrees Fahrenheit. Therefore, heat can be extracted when the system is operating at a lower temperature than is possible with a water storage system.

A combination of hydronic and rock systems may be used by placing a water storage tank in a rock bed. Heated water is stored in an uninsulated tank. Heat lost through the tank subsequently heats the rock. Cool room air can be drawn across the warm rock and heated before rising back into living spaces. Louvers or movable insulating panels are necessary to prevent overheating during warm weather.

Extracting Usable Heat. The end use heating system for active solar panels can be hot water heat using baseboard units or radiant panels, or a forced air heating system. For a warm air collector, the most common heating system is forced air.

When active or passive solar systems are used in homes, energy consumption is greatly decreased. Further reductions in energy use can be realized with the second type of home built specifically for energy-efficiency: **earth-contact homes**. Many of these homes utilize the extra benefits of solar heating.

Earth-Contact Homes

A major disadvantage of surface structures is that they are plagued by weather—storms, wind, sun, and extremes in temperature. Energy is wasted by inadvertently heating or cooling the surrounding air. Although much of this loss may be due to the inefficiency of the building envelope, much is also due to temperature differentials between the inside and outside air. An earth-contact home is surrounded by earth on one or more sides and may even have an earth-covered roof, protecting it from the extremes of temperature of the surrounding air. By reducing the amount of the home's surface that is exposed to air, the earth covering minimizes temperature differentials and increases energy-efficiency. See Figure 10.15.

Modern earth-contact homes may be completely underground with only entrances and utilities protruding; have an atrium open to the sky with under-

Figure 10.15 For maximum efficiency, it is not necessary for an earth-contact home to be located completely beneath the surface. For aesthetic appeal and elimination of potentially adverse psychological effects, earth-contact structures open to a view function better as residences. In fact, most existing examples are not completely underground, but rather are open to the outside on one or more sides.

ground rooms arranged around it; or have one or more sides exposed to the environment.

The amount of earth cover on the roofs of earth-contact homes varies from none to several feet. Conventional roofs without earth cover are often used in warm climates. The exposed roof permits natural ventilation and presents a more conventional appearance. In cold climates, earth covering on the roof is more common than not. Because of the heavier roof loads an earth-contact home must bear, adequate structural support must be provided, which may affect other design aspects, including the floor plan.

For earth-covered roofs, a flat concrete roof is the most prevalent form and permits the use of almost any type of floor plan. Flat roofs may be constructed of precast concrete slabs or may be poured in place. Less commonly found are roof systems of wood, although these have been successfully used. A disadvantage of the flat roof system is that if several feet of earth are to be used, the roof itself must be comparatively thick.

Although soil is not a good insulator, it is an effective temperature moderator. On the surface, seasonal temperatures may vary by 100 degrees Fahrenheit or more. Just a few feet below the surface, the temperatures in summer and winter vary by as little as 10 degrees Fahrenheit. At 15 feet below the surface, the temperature remains almost constant through the year at or near the average annual temperature on

Although energy conservation is a major advantage of earth-contact homes, they also serve to conserve land and the natural environment. During the last few decades, pressure has been exerted by population growth, industrial expansion, and suburban sprawl for the use of the limited quantities of land available. In addition, the demand for recreational areas has increased as people have gained more leisure time. The use of earth-contact structures for both residential and public purposes would free more land for recreational areas and agriculture.

> With decreased background noises, common household noises become more apparent. It may be necessary to add white noise.

the surface. In most parts of the United States, that temperature is between 54 and 60 degrees Fahrenheit. Earth-contact buildings take advantage of the temperature of the earth mass, reducing heating loads during the winter and cooling loads during the summer. This means that less fuel energy is required to maintain normal interior thermal comfort levels. Many earth-contact homes can be kept cool during hot summer months simply by circulating the air with fans or with natural ventilation. In the winter, the earth blanket not only moderates temperatures but also helps to prevent air infiltration.

Because earth-contact homes are typically energy-efficient, alternative energy systems such as solar collectors and ice air-conditioning are more cost-effective than in conventional homes. Passive solar energy systems may be sufficient to provide both heat and hot water. When active solar energy systems are used, the decreased energy requirement can be met with fewer solar collectors than are necessary for above-grade residences.

Earth contact homes are safer during tornadoes and high winds than conventional structures. They also have unique acoustical qualities that result in freedom from surrounding sounds such as traffic, industry, and aircraft. The more completely surrounded by earth the home is, the more acoustic isolation will occur. When noise control is considered, earth-contact homes may be built on less expensive or less desirable lots in urban areas without the disadvantages of urban noise.

Part Four

Designing
Interior
and
Exterior
Spaces

Housing Styles

Chapter 11

The development of an architec-

tural style is influenced by available materials and their characteristics, the current limits of technology, and social factors such as philosophy, politics, economics, and religion. Once they originate, architectural styles often become widespread because of the desire—on the part of both those who build homes and those who live in them—to follow currently popular trends. Most architectural styles are closely identified with a particular period and geographical area.

Overlapping of styles is common even within a geographic region, so time lines are indistinct, structures built during transition periods between two styles often have features of both, and buildings geographically removed from style origins may reflect unsophisticated interpretations of the style. The function of the structure does not necessarily affect its style —any architectural style can be used for residences,

313

religious structures, or public buildings. Building styles are often based on earlier styles, some are designed purely for whimsy or eccentricity, and some are produced by builders to be functional without regard for style. Most homes, however, are at least loosely based on previous architectural styles, so it is helpful to look at architectural traditions of the past that have reverberated through history.

Ancient and Classical Architecture

Ancient architectural styles include those of Egypt, Mesopotamia, Greece, and Rome. Each of these has had a significant effect on building construction and design—partially a result of technological developments that have continued in use throughout the centuries. Some of the building types and styles of these ancient cultures have been revived—often when there was some other interest in the culture.

- Features of the ancient Egyptian style were revived by Napoleon as a part of the Empire style in France. Elements of the style gained popularity in America during the nineteenth-century Egyptian Revival style, and during the first decade of the twenty-first century, architectural elements of ancient Egypt are being revived again.
- Fired brick, a contribution of the ancient Mesopotamian cultures, has been used in every style since that time because of its durability, widespread availability, and ease of use. During the last quarter of the twentieth century, molded brick—another Mesopotamian feature—again became popular.

No past styles, however, have had a greater effect on building design and ornament throughout history than the classical architecture of ancient Greece and Rome.

Greece (7th century B.C.–146 B.C.)[1]

Greek architectural forms reflect the quest for aesthetic perfection in the use of formal balance and symmetry. Two features are characteristic of Greek architecture: the use of **fluted** columns for support and the triangular truss for roof structures. Columns had been used by the Egyptians, Minoans, Persians, and others, but it was the Greeks who refined them and elevated them to their highest beauty. Over a period of time, the Greeks developed three architectural styles: **Doric**, **Ionic**, and **Corinthian**—known as classical orders of architecture. Although the differences in these styles are reflected in several ways, it is the style of the columns that is most distinctive.

Columns consist of three parts: an enlarged **base**, a vertical post called a **shaft**, and a decorative **capital**. The capital itself is made of two parts: a plain square block at the top—an **abacus**—that may be very small and a more decorative portion.

In addition to the columns themselves, several other features are characteristic of Greek architecture. At the top of a row of columns is a horizontal **entablature** consisting of several parts: a lower molding known as the **architrave**, a decorative **frieze**, and a projecting **cornice**. Above the entablature, at each end of the building, the triangular face of the roof structure forms the pediment. The exact configuration and decoration of the entablature and pediment depend on the particular order of architecture.

- Doric columns have a prominent square abacus at the top, with a round, flat cushion devoid of ornamentation beneath. Unlike the other styles of columns, Doric columns have no base at the bottom of the shaft. Greek Doric columns were designed to be fluted. Because the fluting was done after the column was erected, there are examples of unfinished, unfluted columns. See Figure 11.1.
- The capital of Ionic columns has two **volutes** or spirals, which are a result of Oriental influences.

Figure 11.1 (ABOVE) The Greek Doric order features columns that have a relatively large diameter for their height, flutings along the shaft of the column, no base, and a simple capital.

Figure 11.2 (ABOVE RIGHT) The volutes of the Greek Ionic order are on two faces only, except at corners. Roman and later Ionic capitals often have volutes on all four faces.

Figure 11.3 (RIGHT) The rows of acanthus leaves on the capitals of these Corinthian columns are characteristic of this classical order.

The fluted shafts of Ionic columns are more slender in relation to their height than those of Doric columns. See Figure 11.2.

- Corinthian columns are more ornate, with two rows of acanthus leaves carved around the capital. The slender fluted shaft is similar to the Ionic shaft. The Greeks used the Corinthian style only infrequently and then on the interior rather than the exterior of structures. See Figure 11.3.

Rome (146 B.C.–476 A.D.)

When the Romans conquered Greece in 146 B.C., they adapted Greek architectural forms for their own use and subsequently carried them throughout their empire. The Romans added the **Tuscan** and **Composite** orders of architecture to Greek models and used the Corinthian order extensively on both the interior and the exterior of buildings. The shafts of Roman columns, especially in the far-flung reaches of the empire, were sometimes left unfluted.

- In the Tuscan order, the capital is similar to the Greek Doric capital, the shaft is unfluted, and a base is present. See Figure 11.4.

Figure 11.4 (BELOW) The Tuscan order is simpler than any of the other classical orders of architecture because it has no fluting.

Figure 11.5 (RIGHT) The pilasters on this modern building in Greece have Ionic capitals painted much like the originals would have been.

Figure 11.6 (BELOW RIGHT) Engaged Ionic columns finish the curve of this porch.

- The Composite order combines the volutes of the Ionic with the acanthus leaf decoration of the Corinthian and is infrequently found.

Romans also used architectural forms for nonstructural purposes, serving only a decorative function.

- The pilaster is a decorative, square-shafted column applied to a wall that projects only about one-fourth of its width. See Figure 11.5.
- The **engaged column** is a curved portion of a column that is attached directly to a wall and projects up to half its width. See Figure 11.6.

Figure 11.7 (TOP) Medieval castles were designed for protection and their walls were difficult to scale. Windows are a much later addition to castle walls.

Figure 11.8 (BOTTOM) A pendentive curved horizontally to fit a quarter of the bottom of the dome then traveled downward in a vertical curve, decreasing in width so that at the bottom, the pendentive could rest on a corner. The pendentive in this baroque structure is covered with mosaics just as those in Byzantine structures were.

Pilasters and engaged columns recur in later architectural styles both on the interior and the exterior of buildings and are often used to flank an entry. Other characteristics of Roman architecture include the use of arches, vaults, and domes. The Roman architectural style has reappeared a number of times.

Medieval Styles

Medieval styles include the Byzantine, Romanesque, and Gothic. When the Roman Empire fell, much of the government had already been moved to Constantinople. Here, the Byzantine Empire grew to power. The Byzantines combined the architectural technology of the Romans with the delicacy and refinement of the Oriental arts. While the Byzantine style remained popular for almost a thousand years in Eastern Europe and Asia Minor, it reached only a few cities in Western Europe.

During the medieval period in Western Europe, it was the Romanesque and Gothic styles that were popular. It was also during this period that the castle, with its towers and battlements, was widely used in Western Europe. The castle provided a home for wealthy individuals and served as protection during troubled times for townspeople as well. Towers and battlements are not uncommon on nineteenth-century revivals of both styles. See Figure 11.7.

Byzantine (320–1453)

The magnitude of the wealth of the Byzantine Empire is reflected in the opulence of their structures. Roman structural forms and techniques continued in use, although decorative detailing changed significantly over time. It was the builders of the Byzantine Empire who developed a method of using a dome to roof a square structure, making more feasible the widespread use of the Roman dome. The Romans usually used domes on circular structures. Byzantine builders discovered that by filling the corners between the dome and a square building with triangular **pendentives**, they could provide support for the roof. This method is still the predominant method used for supporting a dome. See Figure 11.8.

Byzantine builders also positioned half domes against a higher central one to help counteract the thrust of the larger dome. From the exterior, Byzantine

structures were impressive, but under the influence of Oriental cultures, the primary emphasis was given to aesthetically pleasing interiors. See Figure 11.9.

Romanesque (7th century–12th century)

The Romanesque style was a revival of one element of the ancient Roman style—the vault and its associated semicircular arch. Roman remains were scattered throughout Europe and, during the Romanesque period, builders copied and adapted the style for more contemporary use—often incorporating parts of ancient structures in their own buildings. Roman building technologies, including the making of concrete, had been lost or forgotten, and medieval builders did not have the skills nor the desire to construct exact reproductions. Security was of primary importance and all buildings were to some extent at least semidefensive. Romanesque buildings were often massive ashlar stone structures. Massive buttresses counteracted the thrust of barrel vaults. See Figure 11.10.

Gothic (12th century–16th century)

Romanesque architecture gave way to lightness and delicacy in the Gothic style, especially in Northern Europe, where the dark, heavy Romanesque style was unsuitable for capturing sunlight. The pointed arch predominated, and structures soared to almost unimaginable heights for the time. Towers and spires added to the sense of verticality. It was, however, a development in building technology that most affected architecture and, indeed, made towering vaults possible. The Romanesque style used bearing wall construction; the Gothic style used skeleton construction. The outward thrust of roof vaults was counteracted with **flying buttresses**—a major architectural innovation of the Gothic period. See Figure 11.11. Flying buttresses maintained the lightness of the structural appearance and made high vaults possible. Walls between the supports had only to support their own weight, making it possible to incorporate large

Figure 11.9 (TOP) Intricate mosaics of glass, gold, semi-precious stones, marble, and other materials covered large areas of walls and ceilings in Byzantine buildings.
Figure 11.10 (BOTTOM) Round towers were frequently used in Romanesque castles, probably because square corners provided less protection against undermining—a typical medieval warfare technique.

Figure 11.11 The structural support provided by flying buttresses was the first major technical advance in building since Roman times. Although flying buttresses are not used in residential construction, the development of this technique is important because it made it unnecessary to use bearing wall construction for support and subsequently led to skeleton construction.

stained glass windows to light the interiors. Stained glass also filled intricate stone **tracery**—a term used to describe pierced designs executed in stone.

Other architecturally significant developments of the medieval period were the chimney and the cannon. The chimney made heating more efficient and provided a means for smoke to escape from hearth fires. The cannon negated the invincibility of medieval castles, thereby eliminating their protective function. For the wealthy, palaces replaced castles, and the emphasis shifted from protection to comfort and luxury.

It was during the medieval period that homes began to take on a character that is familiar. Half-timbering was used in many areas because large forests had been burned in an effort to halt the spread of the plague. A framework of vertical, horizontal, and diagonal timbers was used for structural support, while walls were filled in with brick (**nogging**) or woven branches covered with clay (wattle and daub). The timbers were exposed on both the interior and the exterior of the building. The patterns resulting from the contrast of dark timber and lighter daub or stucco became a decorative element. These patterns, which often varied on each story of the structure, ranged from simple rectangles to extremely complicated designs. See Figure 11.12. Steeply pitched thatched roofs were most common. It was typical to add on to these buildings using whatever materials were available or affordable at the time. An addition to a stone house might be made in brick, for example.

Cities burgeoned with population increases outpacing physical growth. To combat the scarcity of land, people built upward. Cantilevered second-story projections provided additional space in upper stories but soon grew to proportions that cut light from the narrow streets below.

In England, the Gothic style was known as Tudor, after the ruling family; hence, later adaptations of the half-timbered buildings were known as Tudor. However, there is a second group of buildings also called Tudor that are reminiscent of the homes of the wealthy in Renaissance England. Medieval features of

Figure 11.12 It was not uncommon for a half-timbered structure to make use of different materials in different parts of the structure. This medieval house exhibits both nogging and wattle and daub with half-timbering.

domestic buildings of the common people persisted for several centuries, and it was these building traditions that were first brought to America.

Renaissance (1420–1600), Baroque (1600–1720), and Rococo (1720–1750)

The Renaissance began in Italy, where the Gothic style had never been particularly popular. The many large windows of Gothic buildings allowed too much heat into the buildings for the hot climate in the south. The style was also associated with the so-called barbarian tribes who had settled in central Europe. During the Renaissance, which began in fifteenth-century Italy, people rediscovered and adopted classical philosophy, art, and architecture. Large numbers of standing Roman ruins in Italy provided design inspiration.

Formal balance and symmetry were important, so openings were confined to where they were most appropriate for the exterior facade. Centered doorways under triangular or curved pediments were a dominant feature. Rounded arches predominated, and classical cornices and moldings were used at roof edges. **Rustication**—emphasis of masonry joints— was popular, although not a classical characteristic. See Figure 11.13. **Belt courses** (also called **string courses**), or rows of masonry that projected beyond the facade or that were of a different material, drew the eye horizontally. Glazed double-hung windows admitted natural light and fresh air, and large fireplaces with chimneys increased the comfort and safety of Renaissance homes. The wealthy of Italy, France, and later of England constructed palaces with greater opulence than had been seen in the West. It was Renaissance homes that were first planned for convenience and privacy, with separate rooms for eating, sleeping, and living.

As with other architectural styles, Renaissance ar-

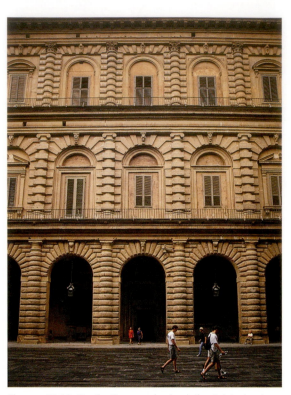

Figure 11.13 Rustication emphasized the joints in stone buildings, calling attention to the strength and stability inherent in the construction.

chitecture took on regional characteristics. The most influential of these various styles has been that of Elizabethan England—the second type of Tudor architecture. Brick was the most popular building material in England, and masons developed individual brickwork bonds for use especially in the predominant chimneys and chimney pots of the period. The Tudor arch is pointed at the apex but otherwise is relatively flat. Tall, narrow casement windows were popular, although because only small panes of glass were available, each window was necessarily divided into a number of individual panes.

A number of architects had a significant impact on Renaissance design, among them Michelangelo, who used **giant order** columns—those that extended more than a single story and often all the way to the roof. Andrea Palladio (1508–1580) was also influential, in part due to his architectural treatise *The Four*

Books of Architecture, published in 1570. This was the first of many architectural books published during the Renaissance that affected design in many countries. The portability of a book made it possible to accurately copy designs or to use elements in buildings a great distance from the originals.

Both the Baroque and Rococo styles were elaborations of Renaissance forms. Large-scale ornamentation is featured in the Baroque, smaller-scale ornamentation in the Rococo. The cost of these structures was prohibitive for all but public buildings, religious structures, and palaces. In the Western Hemisphere, some churches were built by the Spanish that included Baroque features, but these styles were only rarely used in the growing nation to the north.

It was during the Renaissance that the great voyages of exploration occurred that eventually resulted in the colonization of the two continents of the New World. Colonists came for a variety of reasons, but it was the English who were most successful in developing a self-sufficient group of colonies that resulted in the United States.

Colonial American House Styles

For the most part, American housing forms were adaptations of those of the middle class in Europe. Colonists from many parts of Europe used familiar building techniques from their countries of origin, adapting the styles to the materials available and to the climate. During the early colonial era, the regions in which colonists from different nations settled in effect formed separate pockets of architectural styles. As the colonies prospered, the trend began to shift toward the adoption, over a wide area, of one architectural fashion at a time. By the end of the nineteenth century, the pattern had shifted again. Numerous architectural styles enjoyed periods of overlapping popularity, setting the scene for the endless variety of modern homes.

English Colonial Styles (1607–1780)

Many of the examples of English Colonial houses in America were similar to medieval English houses of the yeomanry—the common people. This was especially true in New England, where settlers were for the most part members of that social stratum in England. In the American South, English Colonial homes reflected English buildings of a wealthier class of people: Many of the colonists who settled in the South were second or third sons of English nobility who received large land grants from the British monarchy. These wealthier individuals built larger homes in styles more consistent with those of the English nobility.

In general, the English Colonial styles that are most familiar to present-day Americans are those that originated in the New England area. Early homes in this region were built in several forms, but all shared a number of characteristics.

The first New England homes necessarily reflected the primitive and arduous lifestyle of establishing a new colony. Colonists quickly learned that not all of the building methods they had used in England were suited to the more rigorous American climate. The stuccoed brick or wattle and daub that they used as filler between timber framing members quickly cracked, so the colonists turned to the abundant wood of New England and covered their homes with clapboards. Later, they abandoned brick or wattle and daub fillers altogether and built their homes entirely of wood. Wood on the exterior was often left unpainted and weathered to a gray color.

The torrential rains and heavy snows of New England also made thatched roofs unsuitable for the American climate. Wood shakes were substituted, but the traditional steep roof pitch required by thatch remained. There was very little roof overhang. In later colonial homes, this steep pitch provided approximately half as much living space beneath the roof as there was on the ground floor. Adding windows in the gable ends and sometimes fenestrated dormers on the sides made this space suitable for sleeping.

A massive chimney was located in the center of the home to conserve heat. Early colonial homes had little or no decorative trim. In very early examples, windows and doors were placed where needed, without regard to exterior appearance, but later examples follow contemporary English trends and are symmetrical. The earliest windows were very small, with fixed or casement sashes and small square or diamond-shaped panes. Later, these were replaced with single- or double-hung windows. Shutters covered the windows in inclement weather. Doors were most often of the board-and-batten type.

Several structural forms of English Colonial homes have become well known as individual styles. The Cape Cod, the Saltbox, and the Garrison are widely recognized because of their distinctive characteristics and, in modified form, have been used for many homes built in the last 100 years.

Cape Cod (1750–1850, 1940–1950s)

Cape Cod houses are two rooms deep, have a central chimney, and have little roof overhang. They are side-gabled one-and-a-half-story houses with the entry centered in a symmetrical facade. One or two windows are located on each side of the door. Gable end windows provide light and ventilation in the attic space, making it functional. Modern examples usually have windowed dormers as well.

In addition to the wood-frame version, very similar masonry homes were built, primarily in the southern colonies, where masonry construction was much more common than in New England. Like most southern examples, these homes had a chimney on each end wall rather than a single interior chimney. The exterior fireplace placement provided sufficient heat during the mild winters and helped to prevent heat from the cooking fires from building up in the home during the hot summers. Modern versions of the Cape Cod include both wood and masonry examples, usually have double-hung windows, and wood versions are usually painted white. See Figure 11.14.

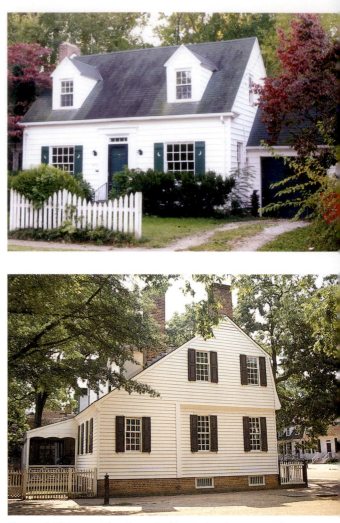

Figure 11.14 (TOP) The Cape Cod home has been one of the most persistent house forms in American history. After the colonial period, similar homes continued to be built as the nation expanded westward. In the mid-twentieth century, the Cape Cod, along with other colonial styles, underwent a widespread revival of popularity. This modern example adds dormers, decorative headers, and a transom to the simple style.

Figure 11.15 (BOTTOM) The saltbox house was named for its similarity in shape to the box in which salt was kept in the home.

Figure 11.16 (OPPOSITE) This style is popularly known as Garrison because it is similar to the style of early defensive outposts. However, the colonial home builders adopted the overhanging second story from the Elizabethan architecture they had been familiar with in England, not from the need for defense.

Saltbox (1650–1830)

Saltbox houses differ from Cape Cod models in that they have two or two-and-a-half stories with a lean-to kitchen at the rear. The result was a roofline longer in the rear than in the front, creating the characteristic saltbox shape. Often there was less than one full story of wall height beneath the roof at the rear of the house. Early saltbox homes showed a change in the roof slope where the kitchen had been added to the original structure, but later homes had a single roof slope due to the construction of the kitchen at the same time as the house. In southern regions, the uneven gabled roof is called a **catslide**. See Figure 11.15.

Garrison

In the northern colonies, some side-gabled homes were built with a second story cantilevered over the first to create a slight overhang known as a jetty. Usually, only the front was cantilevered, although there are examples of Garrison houses with the gable ends cantilevered as well. Some Garrison houses had an additional jetty at the eave line. The corners of the overhang were decorated with carved **drops** in the form of pineapples or acorns. The front jetty provided some protection at the central side entry. Other than the jetties, the Garrison house is the same as the saltbox

house and, indeed, there are examples of Garrison houses with and without the saltbox roofline. See Figure 11.16.

Dutch Colonial (1626–1664)

Colonists from Holland and Flanders settled primarily in the Middle Atlantic States—along the Hudson River Valley and in New Jersey and New York. There are several types of Dutch Colonial houses, usually depending on the area in which they are built. Rural Dutch houses were largely story-and-a-half side-entry structures. Unlike contemporary English Colonial homes, the fireplaces in Dutch houses were on the ends and built within the structure rather than protruding from the wall. Only the chimney could be seen above the roof. On the inside, these fireplaces had no side jambs, but most of them have now been replaced.

Seventeenth-century rural Dutch Colonial homes had gable roofs with a curved flare at the eave—known as a **Dutch kick** or **Flemish kick**. Later homes retained the flare on a gambrel roof, which was also used by English colonists in the area. In New Jersey and southern New York, the Dutch kick extended beyond the eave line on the sides to cover a porch, although the overhang at the building ends was very slight. A few examples made use of the hip roof—a type of roof unused by the British before that time.

It was not the type of roof that distinguished the Dutch Colonial home from those of their contemporaries but the method of construction. The Dutch used structural framing members in the form of the letter H known as **anchor bents**. The cross bar served as the ceiling of the rooms on the lower story, while the extension of the vertical posts created short vertical walls in the upper story. The roof rested on top of those raised walls rather than just above the ceiling level of the first floor. When these buildings were constructed of stone, that material usually ended at the top of the anchor bents, and the gable end was completed with wood.

Dutch colonial houses had a **stoop**[2]—a raised platform at the entry that featured a Dutch door. The stoop often had railings and benches at either side and most frequently a roof supported by two posts or columns at the outer corners. See Figure 11.17. In some areas along the Hudson River Valley, stone was

Figure 11.17 (TOP) Even on this modern version of the Dutch Colonial house, there are slightly flared eaves. The stoop is typical of Dutch Colonial houses but the shed-roofed dormer is not.

Figure 11.18 (BOTTOM) Crow-stepped gables on parapet walls are typical of Belgium and the Netherlands and were brought to America by colonists from those countries.

used for walls, although the more expensive brick was much preferred. Openings often had segmental relieving arches above them, and diamond-paned casement windows were typical.

In the cities,[3] Dutch Colonial homes were significantly different. Houses were built of timber, stone, or brick[4] with steep gable roofs hidden by a **crow-** or **corbie-stepped**[5] **parapet** wall. This type of gable has a profile similar to a stairway. As in the Netherlands, these urban houses had a gable end entrance. A projecting bracket near the roof was used for hoisting furnishings to upper stories. Similar homes were occasionally built in the countryside but with the entrance on the long side. See Figure 11.18.

French Colonial (1615–1763)

The French established trading posts and forts from Labrador to the Gulf of Mexico but they built few towns. It was the French gallery[6] house of Louisiana that had a subsequent impact on American architecture. The French who settled in the swampy Louisiana area and along the lower Mississippi River valley built to suit the hot, damp climate. Cedar and cypress native to the area were cut into posts and partly buried in the ground. The spaces between posts were filled with a mixture of clay and either grass, Spanish moss, or deer hair. The floor of the home was elevated so that air could circulate beneath, preventing excessive dampness. Later, homes of timber construction were elevated on stone foundations or brick pillars. In this way, the vulnerable wooden members were protected from dampness and insect damage.

The typical French Colonial home in Louisiana had a pavilion or hip roof, which extended beyond the structure's walls to cover a gallery, or porch that ran the full length of one or more sides of the home. See Figure 11.19. Slender wooden posts supported the roof at its edges. Frequently, the roof had an outward change in pitch at the location of the walls—an architectural style that was reminiscent of that found by the French in the West Indies.

The gallery roof shaded the home, provided protection from rain, and allowed the porch to serve as an outdoor sitting room as well as an exterior hallway. Doors allowed access to the gallery from each room and also permitted much of the wall area to be opened. The floor plan was one room deep, and each room had openings on both sides, permitting maximum ventilation. The kitchen was often separated from the main structure so the heat from cooking did not add to ambient temperatures in the house.

Later examples followed the same plan but had two stories. The brick first story housed the kitchen and sometimes servants' quarters. Exterior stairs led to the second-story family living and sleeping quarters. The raised second story was better able to capture breezes than the area near the ground.

Spanish Styles (1525–1821)

The Spanish came to the Western Hemisphere searching for riches, settled in Florida across to the Southwest and in California, and established missions and forts but few civilian settlements. Three types of houses were prevalent in the Southwest and California: the early Pueblo style, the Territorial style, and the Spanish Colonial style. An additional style used in early missions resulted in a later adaptation for domestic use.

Pueblo Style

The original Pueblo-style structure was typical of existing Native American structures of the Southwest. The Spanish were familiar with the adobe construction used for these buildings because there were Moorish examples in Spain. While the material was the same, the method of construction differed. Native Americans daubed mud for walls; the Spanish brought the brick form typical of Moorish structures.

The flat roofs of the Pueblo style were appropriate for the arid climate of the American Southwest. Heavy timbers called **vigas** spanned the roof and projected beyond the wall. See Figure 11.20. These long timbers

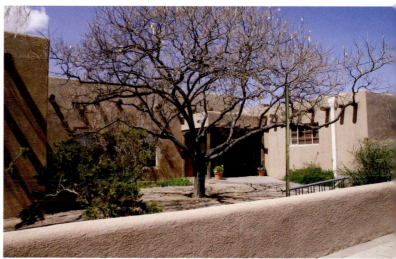

Figure 11.19 (TOP) One of the few surviving original French Colonial houses in the United States, this structure has the typical gallery and is raised off the ground.

Figure 11.20 (BOTTOM) This remodeled Spanish Colonial Pueblo-style structure retains the exposed vigas and the placita, but the openings have been enlarged and modernized and a porch has been added. Inside, the original lateral branches of the roof structure can be seen above the vigas.

were usually obtained in the mountains and had to be hauled great distances to the building site. Cutting the timbers was difficult with the stone tools used by Native Americans, so their structures had uneven viga projections. The Spanish brought metal tools, making it easier to cut the timbers to length, so the viga projections on their buildings were more uniform. Smaller branches were laid across the vigas to form a base for the adobe roof. Parapet walls extended beyond the roofline and drainage was provided by rainspouts made of wood, tin, or fired clay tile.

Territorial Style

The Spanish Territorial style was a continuation of the Pueblo style. Adobe construction with flat roofs constructed with vigas and smaller branches were typical. Influence of the concurrent Greek Revival style is found in the wood trim around openings and, infrequently, brick **dentil** molding at the top of adobe walls. Dentil molding has toothlike projections. An attached covered porch, or **corredor**, faced the courtyard, serving as a circulation zone to provide access to all interior rooms. Posts supported the corredor roof and often had simple back-to-back brackets at the top known as **zapatas**. See Figure 11.21.

Spanish Colonial Style

Spanish Colonial–style homes were constructed of adobe brick covered with stucco, lime wash, or plaster for protection. Many originally had flat roofs, but these were later replaced with low-pitched shed, gable, or hip roofs covered with tiles. The windows were small, set deep into the wall, and were initially covered with wooden grilles and interior shutters. These were later replaced when multipaned glass windows became more widely available.

These long, low residences were often built in an L- or U-shape to provide a courtyard, or **placita**. Sides of the placita not enclosed by the structure itself were walled to provide shade, protect residents from the wind, and keep animals out of living areas. It was the Spanish Colonial house that was the forerunner of the twentieth-century ranch-style house. See Figure 11.22.

Mission Style

Among the first architectural contributions of the Spanish to the New World were the missions established by Dominican and Franciscan missionaries. The architectural style of these Southwest missions was a mixture of Spanish, Moorish, and Mexican Baroque influences. Typically, missions had a curvilinear parapet wall on the facade that covered the gable end, towers with or without domed roofs, stuccoed exterior walls, and arcades in front of covered porches. Although the original Spanish Mission style was not used for homes, the style was adapted for domestic use around the turn of the twentieth century.

Monterey Style (1830–1955)

The Monterey style originated in California in the 1830s. It was a blending of indigenous Spanish architecture and the spreading Greek Revival. These rectangular two-story homes had thick walls and small windows, as did most Spanish architecture. The distinguishing feature was a second-story balcony that ran across the front that had delicate railings and was sheltered by the roof overhang. Some variations use first-floor porch posts to support the balcony thus creating a covered walkway on both levels; some have cantilevered balconies. Latticework was sometimes used at the ends of the veranda and balcony to provide privacy. Greek Revival details were evident in the door and window surrounds and other wooden trim.

Figure 11.21 The porch roof on this Territorial-style house is supported by posts with paired zapatas. Original Territorial-style structures usually had exposed vigas.

Figure 11.22 This modern version of the Spanish Colonial–style house is typical of the style, with the exception of larger windows and an extended, rather than separate, roofline over the porch.

Swedish Colonial (1638–1655)

A few Swedish immigrants settled along the Delaware River in 1638, bringing with them the round log construction with which they were familiar. A log structure could be quickly constructed from available materials, and the collection of the materials—stone and timber—helped to clear the land for growing crops. Notching of the logs at corners made it unnecessary for these structures to have an extra framework. Early log structures had a single door and few windows, which were covered with oiled paper. Stone fireplaces with mud-lined wood chimneys completed the structure. Original Swedish fireplaces were located in the corner; later German examples had the fireplace centered on the short wall.

The use of round logs resulted in large cracks between the logs, which were filled with mud chinking. Later, German immigrants used squared-off logs that fit together more tightly and required less chinking. By the time of the American Revolution, the log cabin was used by immigrants of all nationalities—especially those moving westward. See Figure 11.23.

Today's log homes often employ wood or synthetic log siding that is attached to a frame structure. When it is desirable for logs to appear on the interior as well, log siding may also be used. This allows wiring, pipes, and ducts to be carried through walls, and for walls to be insulated for energy-efficiency while retaining the rustic appearance of the log house.

Era of Consolidation and Expansion

In the eighteenth and early nineteenth centuries, the settled areas of the eastern seaboard underwent the transition from English colonies to an independent nation. During the latter part of the period, the new nation quickly expanded westward to the Mississippi River and beyond. Architectural styles popular during this period of consolidation and expansion include Georgian, Federal, and Greek Revival.

Figure 11.23 Log houses range in size from single-room cabins to modern multistoried structures with complicated footprints. In this log house, the chinking between the logs is quite evident. Like other early-nineteenth-century structures, this one has double-hung windows.

Georgian (1700–1780)

From the beginning of the eighteenth century until the American Revolution, the predominant architectural fashion in the English colonies was the Georgian style. This style, named for the four King Georges who ruled during the era, originated in England and was the first Renaissance style to reach American shores. A number of English architectural style books were published and brought to America during this period, resulting in consistency of design even in different regions of the country.

Georgian homes were typically two or two and a half stories and rectangular in form. Residents of the northern colonies built wood-frame Georgian homes with clapboard siding; those in the middle and southern colonies more frequently used brick or stone. A string course usually identified the vertical limits of each level. Georgian homes had gable, gambrel, or hip roofs with very little overhang. The lower edge of the roof was trimmed with a cornice that often featured a series of dentils. Formally symmetrical, the centered doorway was flanked by an equal number of windows on each side. Second-story windows were located directly above openings on the first floor. See Figure 11.24.

The doorway was treated as an important feature. The **surround** or decorative treatment around the doorway most commonly consisted of pilasters that supported a classical entablature or pediment. Pediment styles varied and could be triangular or curved. **Broken pediments** on which the upper extreme of the diagonal lines did not meet were also common. Some masonry examples highlight the door with a change in brick pattern rather than an elaborate surround. The doorway frequently included a row of small square or rectangular glass panes just above the door itself. Infrequently, a semicircular window was installed over the door. The door itself was generally paneled.

In late Georgian examples, elements of Palladian

Figure 11.24 The Georgian-style house had formal symmetry with a centered entry.

design are evident: giant order pilasters rising the full height of the building at corners, a two-story entry **portico**, and a five-part plan consisting of a tall central block with smaller dependencies on each side connected by **hyphens** or symmetrical extensions stepped back from the central facade. The portico at the entry often rose to the eave, was capped by a pediment, and had decorative pilasters or columns at the sides. A Palladian window was often located on the second floor just above the entry. This type of window, named for Andrea Palladio, has a central arch-topped window flanked on both sides by shorter square-headed windows. Palladio also used the dome on domestic structures and infrequently, it was incorporated in American Georgian designs.

Multipaned double-hung windows were also frequently topped with a classical entablature or pediment in wood-frame houses, and exterior shutters are often present. Pedimented dormers, when present, usually have rectangular windows in homes dating from the early part of the period. Arched dormer windows became more common during the late Georgian era. Window and door trim, cornices, and moldings were often painted white, especially on brick homes. Like their earlier counterparts, Georgian homes in southern areas had paired end chimneys, while northern examples had interior chimneys.

The corners of many Georgian homes were decorated with **quoins**, or areas of contrasting materials. In brick homes, quoins consisted of large stone blocks or raised brickwork. Carved wooden blocks were sometimes used as quoins on wood-frame buildings. Other decorative elements found on later Georgian homes included a centered front gable and a balustrade near the top of the roof.

Federal (1780–1820)

In America, the Neoclassical style popular in Europe at the time of the Revolutionary War was called Federal, after the new government, or Adam, after the English architects who influenced the development of the style. The Federal style had its roots in ancient Rome, and classical details are often used. The two- or three-story Federal homes are symmetrical. The central entry is flanked by sidelights, with a semicircular or elliptical fanlight surmounting the whole. A small single-story portico supported by columns and with a pedimented

Figure 11.25 Federal style-houses are similar to Georgian models but may have more prominent structural details, such as windows and doorways, and more delicate ornamentation.

roof or classical entablature may be featured. Flat-roofed porticoes formed by the entablature feature a railing and become a balcony accessed through the Palladian window on the second floor over the entry. Polygonal or bowed window bays are common, as were polygonal and oval-shaped rooms. The surface of the home is sometimes embellished with pilasters, quoins, slightly recessed arches, decorative swags, or other ornament; however, the overall impression is one of delicacy and relative simplicity. See Figure 11.25. Columns and pilasters on Federal architecture are elongated—more slender and delicate than the Roman models they emulated.

The low-pitched hip or gable roof sometimes has a balustrade around the edge. The balustrade may be closer to the top of the roof, where a flat portion is enclosed. Originally, this area was called a widow's walk for those who watched in vain for their husbands to return from sea voyages. Belvederes—small rooms that served as lookouts—might be located at the roof ridge.

The multipaned windows have square heads and on the first story are often triple-hung and have low sills—almost to the floor. In masonry homes, the windows are topped with stone lintels, frequently with an emphasized keystone. Often, a Palladian window is placed on the second floor above the doorway. Arched dormer windows are another common feature. Windows often decreased in height from the first story to the second and third stories.

Although the exterior was relatively simple, interiors were often lavishly decorated and included open curved staircases. The simple exteriors made Federal homes popular as row houses in urban areas.

Jeffersonian[7] architecture was a type of Federal architecture, but instead of deriving his designs from the houses and villas of ancient Rome, Thomas Jefferson used Roman public structures as models. Jeffersonian architecture follows Roman models closely, and columns, entablatures, and cornices have classical proportions rather than the attenuated proportions of other Federal architecture. The resulting buildings are heavier and more masculine in appearance. The buildings themselves are raised off the ground, as were Roman temples. Jeffersonian porticoes were usually supported by four classical columns and surmounted by a pediment in which a segmentally curved window, a semicircular window, or a round window was located. Part of the roof may form a dome. Jeffersonian architecture originated in Virginia and is rarely seen outside the South.

Greek Revival (1818–1870)

Archaeological discoveries, a desire to break away from English influence, and sympathy with the Greek War for Independence spurred American interest in ancient Greek architecture during the early nineteenth century. The resulting Greek Revival style was based on the Greek temple, which used neither arches nor domes. See Figure 11.26.

The appearance of a Greek temple was suggested in several ways. Most often, the entire house was oriented with the narrow end toward the street and the gable exposed, suggesting a classical pediment. The

Figure 11.26 Greek Revival homes are designed to give the illusion of an ancient Greek temple. This example exhibits the classic facade and has pilasters at the corners and engaged columns flanking the door.

gable end sometimes extended to form a large portico supported by classical columns—most frequently Doric. Wings could be added to either or both sides of the main structure. When the long side of the home formed the front facade, a centered two-story portico with a triangular pediment and classical columns typically projected. Some Greek Revival entrances are located near one corner on the front or side of the home.

Greek Revival homes had a low-pitched gable or hip roof with a wide band of trim at the cornice, reminiscent of the ancient Greek roofline. Small horizontal rectangular windows were sometimes set below the cornice line to light the attic and to suggest a classical frieze. Pilasters often flanked the squared doorway, which typically had sidelights and a rectangular transom. Opening surrounds frequently featured a **shouldered architrave. Corner boards** or pilasters were often used on wood-frame examples. Window trim was usually simple and flat. The chimneys—not a feature of ancient Greek architecture—were de-emphasized by making them plain. Flat exterior surfaces were achieved by butting siding boards rather than overlapping them, and the structure was usually painted white. Some examples exhibit a **colonnade**, or row of columns, across the front or around the entire house. Southern plantations often used the side entry form with a colonnade.

What today is known as Southern Colonial was a variation of the Greek Revival style in combination with the French Colonial form already familiar in the South. The result was a large plantation home in which the two-story gallery of the French Colonial became a classical colonnade. Other details, such as fanlights and Palladian windows, were borrowed from the Georgian and Federal styles.

Exotic Revivals

Nineteenth-century revival styles included three that are considered exotic: the Egyptian Revival, the Moorish Revival, and the Swiss Chalet style.

Egyptian Revival (1830–1850, 1922–1930)

During his Egyptian campaigns, Napoleon's soldiers found the Rosetta Stone, which was translated in the early decades of the nineteenth century. That translation was a significant factor in the fostering of widespread interest in the ancient Egyptian civilization. The resulting Egyptian Revival architectural style was most frequently used for public buildings and cemeteries. Features of this style included massive gateways reminiscent of Egyptian pylons, smooth wall surfaces, Egyptian column types, a concave curved cavetto molding at the top of a structure, and spread falcon wings centered on a sun disk. See Figure 11.27.

In 1922, King Tut's tomb was discovered in Egypt, which resulted in another Egyptian Revival, frequently

Figure 11.27 (LEFT) The Egyptian Revival style was typically used on commercial structures such as this one. Here, the columns are most prominent, although there are a few Egyptian motifs used on the building front above the columns.

Figure 11.28 (ABOVE) This Moorish Revival structure features onion domes.

used for movie theaters. Most of the extant Egyptian Revival homes are from this period and often have only the Egyptian column, with its characteristic inward curvature at the bottom.

Moorish Revival (1850s–1860s)

Late eighteenth- and early nineteenth-century trade with the Orient and with India resulted in the use of certain architectural features. The ogee arch (with a double curve terminating in a point), the horseshoe arch, and the onion dome were sometimes used on American homes as decorative details. The style may be called Moorish Revival, Turkish Revival, or Oriental Revival. See Figure 11.28.

Swiss Chalet (1840–1860)

A third exotic style of the nineteenth century was the Swiss chalet. See Figure 11.29. This style was popularized by Andrew Jackson Downing in his book

The Architecture of Country Homes (1850) and was frequently used in the Adirondack Mountains for resorts. A few other homes were constructed in this style, which featured heavy exposed timbers, low-pitched front gable roofs with wide overhangs supported by brackets, large windows, and second-story balconies. Shaped wood balusters and patterned wood trim were characteristic. Often, the decorative details were simply superimposed on Greek Revival or other style homes.

Victorian and Late-Nineteenth-Century Styles

The Victorian era was named for Queen Victoria, who ruled England from 1837 to 1901. During that time, the Industrial Revolution had a profound effect on home styles in America. The invention of the jigsaw made intricately patterned millwork possible. Turned pieces—round posts shaped with grooves and curves—were accomplished on a lathe. These innovations of the machine age made architectural embellishments more affordable, and the growth of the railroads made tools and materials more widely available. Houses were decorated with wood **gingerbread** trim in every place imaginable. Applied ornament was more important than structure, and architectural embellishments announced social prominence. In addition to the confusion produced by the proliferation of ornament, structural elements were combined without thought for balance, proportion, or harmony in design. Turrets and towers projected from irregular masses, and lines were further broken by bay windows, gables, porches, and balconies.

The architecture of the Victorian era offered people a choice. Previously, American home styles were dominated by one architectural fashion at a time—first Georgian, then Federal, then Greek Revival. But in the middle and late nineteenth century, several

Figure 11.29 (ABOVE) The Swiss chalet style in America is reminiscent of typical Swiss mountain homes like this one. Balconies with sawn wood balustrades and turned posts are typical of the style, as is the large roof overhang.
Figure 11.30 (OPPOSITE, TOP) Where walls project upward from the top edge of the wall, wall gables are formed. These gables can be found on a number of house styles.
Figure 11.31 (OPPOSITE, BOTTOM) This Gothic Revival house features a bargeboard along gable edges, a complicated roofline, diamond pane windows, and drip molds over windows. The battlements over the bay window are typical of large Gothic Revival structures.

popular architectural styles existed concurrently. These styles were often lumped together as Victorian, but in fact there was no one style by that name.

Gothic Revival[8] (1840–1870)

As the popularity of the Greek Revival began to wane, another revival took its place. It was patterned after the Gothic architecture that developed in Europe between the twelfth and sixteenth centuries. Proponents of the Gothic Revival style expounded the virtues of original Gothic Christian architecture as opposed to pagan Greek influences. The Gothic Revival brought back characteristics of the original style: asymmetry, pointed arches, wood tracery in windows, and an emphasis on vertical lines.

The development of balloon framing in 1845 made it simpler to build structures with irregular shapes, and houses expanded outward as a result of function. Rooms were no longer squeezed into a plan based on exterior form: Exterior form was subjugated to interior planning.

Large Gothic Revival homes with elaborate details were constructed of stone, wood, or stucco over brick. These homes had steeply pitched gable roofs as well as towers and pinnacles to emphasize verticality. Complicated rooflines formed by cross gables,

Designing a successful home for individuals still requires an understanding of their needs. Because modern homes typically have an informal style, it is more feasible to design these structures from the inside out.

wall gables (vertical extensions of the wall through the roofline), pointed windows, high massive chimneys, finials at gable peaks, and full-length vertical board and batten siding contributed to the effect. See Figure 11.30.

Intricately cut wood was not only substituted for stone tracery in windows but was used in every place imaginable. A fanciful wood edging at the rake called a **bargeboard**, or **vergeboard**, was typical. In fact, this was often the only distinguishing feature of small Gothic Revival homes. Decorative trusses or cross bracing were sometimes seen on later examples. Walls of Gothic Revival homes were made of a single material and were one color. See Figure 11.31.

Other homes mimicked medieval castles with **battlements**—notched parapets—extending above the edge of the flat roof. Pointed and rounded arches or square-headed openings were used for doors and windows. Bay and oriel windows, stained glass, and stone window tracery added special charm.

Italianate (1840–1885)

The Italianate style, like the Gothic Revival, represented a break from the formalism of the Greek Revival. Unlike the Gothic Revival, Italianate homes were typically symmetrical and nearly square or cubical in form, although asymmetrical examples were not unusual. Two or three stories high, Italianate homes were constructed of brick, stone, and wood, which were often combined on the same building. The low-pitched hip or gable roof had a wide overhang supported by large brackets—often in pairs—at the cornice. These brackets were subject to the scrolls and fanciful cuts of other styles of the era.

A square cupola reached by a trapdoor might be placed on the rooftop, and a square tower was a common feature.

The heads of the windows were often rounded, segmented, or flattened arches, although square-headed windows were also common and, indeed, all could be used in the same building. Two-story bay windows—often symmetrical—were common. Doors could be doubled and might have large glazed sections. A centered or full-width covered porch was typical, although porches within spaces formed by L's in the floor plan were also common. See Figure 11.32.

Italian Villa

The Italian villa form was less formal and often found in the countryside. Usually, the Italian villa had one or more square or octagonal towers, a smooth exterior finish such as stucco, arched openings along porches, and decorative ironwork on balconies. Quoins were used at corners.

The Octagon House (1850–1870)

The octagon house was not a style but rather a floor plan. The book *A Home for All*, written by Orson Squire Fowler, popularized the octagon form, promoting its geometric shape as efficient, practical, and healthy. An octagonal perimeter encloses 20 percent more area than a rectangular perimeter of the same length. The octagonal form also permitted more light to enter. Fowler advocated a cupola for ventilation on the roof. The octagon could be built in any style, but most frequently the exterior decoration was Italianate or Gothic Revival. See Figure 11.33.

⊞ Octagonal structures resulted in rooms with angled walls. Care should be exercised when designing any space with angled walls because it may not be possible to arrange furnishings in a functional and pleasing manner in such rooms.

Figure 11.32 (TOP) Italianate-style houses almost always have predominant brackets at the cornice line, either singly or in pairs. The jigsaw made it possible for these brackets to have almost infinite variety.

Figure 11.33 (BOTTOM) The Octagon-style house may be round or have 6, 8, 10, 12, or 16 sides. Central cupolas are common, as are porches. This example features Italianate details, although Octagon-style houses may have stylistic details from Greek Revival or Gothic Revival styles as well, or they may lack detailing.

Figure 11.34 (OPPOSITE) Frequently, Second Empire houses have a centered tower flanked by dormers. Typical is the Italianate detailing seen here in the paired brackets beneath the eave. In Second Empire examples, however, the eave overhang is generally less than that on Italianate homes.

Second Empire (1855–1880)

Another of the Victorian styles had its beginnings in France, where Napoleon III and Empress Eugenie ruled over a short-lived second French empire from 1853 to 1871. Americans were exposed to the French influence at the International Expositions of 1855 and 1867 and carried the seeds of the style home from Paris. The Second Empire style in America was also called the General Grant style.

The two-, three-, or four-story symmetrical Second Empire home had a mansard roof, which usually had a very steep lower slope and a nearly flat upper slope. Multiple pedimented dormers pierced the roof. Ironwork cresting was sometimes located at the change in roof slope. Square towers were common, as were central projections in the front facade. See Figure 11.34.

Second Empire homes were built of wood or brick, and stone was sometimes used for quoins and trim. Large bracketed cornices were common, although they were generally smaller than those on Italianate examples. Windows, too, were often similar to Italianate examples in shape and trim. Contrasting colors set off the moldings, roof, and wall surfaces.

Figure 11.35 Stick-style houses are distinguished by their detailing, which is reminiscent of medieval half-timbering. In half-timbering, however, it is structural components that are exposed; in the Stick style, these elements are purely decorative.

Stick Style (1855–1875)

The Stick style house was asymmetrical and had multiple stories. Steep gable roofs with multiple intersections for projecting gables were typical. Jerkinhead gables and flared eaves were found on some examples. The most characteristic feature of Stick style houses was flat, straight-edged wood trim that projected from wall surfaces to outline vertical, horizontal, and diagonal lines tying together structural elements such as corners, windows, and dormers. See Figure 11.35.

Romanesque Revival (1840–1900)

The Romanesque Revival was a revolt against the more flamboyant styles of the nineteenth century. Its use in domestic architecture was pioneered by Boston architect Henry Hobson Richardson. For this reason, some examples of the style are also known as Richardsonian Romanesque.

The Romanesque style that served as Richardson's inspiration was itself a revival of Roman forms of architecture characterized by the use of round arches, arcades, and thick ashlar or rubble stone walls. See Figure 11.36. The two- or three-story Romanesque Revival buildings shared these characteristics and were typically constructed of ashlar stonework or brick trimmed with stone. The heavy appearance was emphasized by thick walls, evident in the deeply recessed windows and doors. Offsets in the footprint provided spaces for deep porches. Wide round arches often sprang directly from the ground or from a porch floor rather than from piers or columns. Rhythmic arches might be used beneath the eaves of large structures. Corner buttresses—often with pinnacles—or round corner towers with conical roofs had dissimilar features. The roof was often hipped or gabled, although other styles were also used. Dormers and wall gables were common.

Squared or arched window openings were used. Both types were frequently found on the same house—the style changing on different stories of the building. Some windows were grouped and headed with a single arch or blind arch.

Chateauesque (1860–1890)

The most distinguishing feature of Chateauesque structures was their immense size and most were designed by architects. Inspiration for early models came from sixteenth-century French chateaus, pictures of which were published in magazines during the 1880s. Steeply pitched roofs in any style, Gothic roof cresting, stone walls, basket-handle arches, and tracery all occurred.

Queen Anne (1880–1900)

The Queen Anne house had multiple stories and was asymmetrical. Steeply pitched, irregular roofs, round or octagonal towers with domed or conical roofs, and

Figure 11.36 This Romanesque Revival house features two towers that are typical of the style, ashlar stone walls, and a semicircular arch that forms the entry for the porch.

large chimneys reached for the sky. The surface of the structure was broken up by projections, bay and oriel windows, brackets, and horizontal bands of trim. Brick, stone, wood siding, and variously shaped shingles were used, with each story often finished in a different material. Gables, in particular, were frequently decorated with patterned shingles.

Porches often extended across the front and around the sides of these homes, and recessed porches on the upper stories were common. The porches were enclosed by turned posts and balustrades of turned spindles or jigsawed patterns. Across the tops of the porch posts, on gables, and on balconies, spindles or intricately patterned wood grillwork created a lacy appearance. The trim and the rest of the house were frequently painted in contrasting colors. See Figure 11.37.

Palladian windows were often located in gable ends at the attic level. The front surface of bay windows in Queen Anne homes was frequently flush with the wall or gable above, so the bay appears to be cut into the wall surface rather than to project from it. Although window frames were usually simple, small colored glass panes and leaded glass used in some of the windows added to the overall decorative effect.

Simplified versions of the Queen Anne style were sometimes called Princess Anne. These homes usually lacked much of the ornamentation of the Queen Anne but retained the steeply pitched irregular roofs, asymmetrical design, and large porches.

Eastlake (1870–1890)

As the highly ornamented Queen Anne style rose in popularity, many existing homes were brought into fashion by the addition of spindle work or jigsawed trim at porches and gables. These homes were generally simple and symmetrical in form, without the complex roof shapes and wall surfaces of the true Queen Anne.

Shingle Style (1880–1900)

The distinguishing feature of the Shingle-style house was the uniform covering of unpainted wood shin-

Figure 11.38 The Shingle-style house relies on its shape rather than decorative detailing around openings and on wall surfaces for its design. Half towers whose roofline blends into the main roof structure are common.

gles on exterior walls and the roof. See Figure 11.38. Other materials were sometimes incorporated on the first story, however. Shingle-style houses were asymmetrical and two to three stories in height. Windows were small, simply trimmed, and grouped in pairs or threes. The roof might slope from a third-story ridge to a first-story wall at the sides, making the amount of floor space in each story different and providing a roof for porches. Otherwise, the roof had little overhang. Multiple intersecting gables and pent roofs were common. Towers or projections often had conical roofs that extended to intersect with a gable or side gable.

Figure 11.37 The Queen Anne style often has a tower on the front, or within an L of the structure, and a variety of shingle types. Complicated rooflines and decorative wall surfaces—often shingles of different shapes and colors—are characteristic.

Mission Revival Style (1890–1920)

Homes patterned after the Spanish missions began to be built in the late nineteenth century in California, and the style spread eastward. Mission Revival–style homes were two stories, with a low-pitched hip roof finished with tile. Deep roof overhangs were common and often covered an arcaded corridor. Stucco walls had little ornamentation other than curvilinear para-pets covering the gable and sometimes dormers. Large examples often had balconies and towers with or without domed roofs.

Mission Revival-style houses have low-pitched hip roofs with deep overhangs. The predominant roofing material is terra-cotta tile. Curvilinear dormers and parapets project above the roof. A porch is usually present, often with arched openings. The walls are typically covered with stucco and usually have little ornamentation. See Figure 11.39.

Beaux Arts (1885–1930)

The Beaux Arts style is named for the French Ecole des Beaux Arts, which influenced the style. Beaux Arts homes were massive structures based on Renaissance models. Wall surfaces were typically elaborately de-tailed—garlands, shields, and floral motifs were com-mon. See Figure 11.40. Paired columns or pilasters of the Ionic or Corinthian order, quoins, stone construc-tion (often rusticated on the first story), elaborate win-dow surrounds, and window balconies were reflective of the taste of the wealthy patrons.

Twentieth-Century Styles

More than any other period of American history, the period from 1900 on has been an era of almost unlim-ited choice in housing styles. In general, the styles of the twentieth century fall into two categories: con-scious attempts to develop new forms of architecture and reworkings of past styles with a wide range of ori-gins from colonial America to seventeenth-century France. Both trends existed simultaneously to produce a wealth of house styles.

At the 1876 Centennial Fair in Philadelphia, the elegant Japanese pavilion, so different from the Vic-torian styles, exposed the general public to a sim-

Figure 11.39 (ABOVE) Large, flat wall surfaces are typical of the Spanish Mission style. On this house, as on many Mission-style homes, some walls terminate in parapeted complex curved gables. Although not all Mission-style houses have tile roofs, they are very common.

Figure 11.40 (OPPOSITE, TOP) The Elms was a summer res-idence modeled after the French Chateau d'Asnieres. As with most of the Beaux Arts homes, this one was designed by an architect—Horace Trumbauer. Most houses in this style are concentrated in areas that were populated by the wealthy in the late nineteenth and early twentieth centuries.

Figure 11.41 (OPPOSITE, BOTTOM) The use of contrasting materials emphasizes the horizontal line of this Prairie-style house. Although the principal mass of the house is two stories, single-story porches were common. Prairie houses may be symmetrical or asymmetrical, and the front entry is generally inconspicuous.

pler architectural style. At the same time, there were the beginnings of a trend away from elaboration and decoration in architecture. These factors were par-tially responsible for some twentieth-century styles that exhibited an almost complete absence of details. Other twentieth-century styles used ornament in orig-inal ways.

Prairie (1900–1920)

The Prairie style was developed by Frank Lloyd Wright. Prairie-style homes were low and wide, emphasizing horizontal lines that represented the line where earth and sky meet. Although low in profile, Prairie homes almost always had two stories. The flattened hip roof sloped gently and had deep overhangs that resulted in deep recesses and shadowing for porches and balconies. Outside, low walls enclosed porches and terraces and helped to merge the house with the natural landscape. Windows were grouped into long bands that further emphasized horizontal lines. Leaded glass windows were often used or simulated with wood muntins. See Figure 11.41.

Brick, stone, concrete block, stucco, and wood were used alone or in combination to create the Prairie facade. Chimneys were typically wide rectangular masses with a low profile in the center of the house. Inside Prairie-style houses, spaces were more open than in previous styles.

Art Nouveau (1890–1910)

The Art Nouveau style was the result of an attempt to create a new form of art. Historic forms were avoided and anything novel was embraced. Most Art Nouveau designs were based on natural forms such as flowers, grapevines, and trees.

The Art Nouveau movement primarily influenced interior decoration, having little architectural effect. However, some homes were built in the Art Nouveau style. The balanced, willowy curves characteristic of the style were most frequently found on the front of the house at the roofline, although some curved rooms were included. The exterior finish was often stucco, and wrought iron in the form of grapevines, flowers, and leaves provided decorative detail. Stained and leaded glass featured the same flowing forms.

Art Deco (1920–1940) and Art Moderne (1930–1949)

The term *Art Deco* was coined in 1966 after a Paris exhibition that commemorated the 1925 *Exposition Internationale des Arts Décoratifs et Industriels Modernes*, where modern decorative and applied arts were emphasized. Art Deco design was a marriage of style interpretations from a number of periods (French Neoclassic, ancient Egypt, Mayan structures, Japanese art, and modern art styles including Cubism) with the materials of the machine age.

The style affected everything from ocean liners to toasters. Long lines and curved surfaces predominated. Art Deco buildings featured smooth wall surfaces—often stucco—small vertical "towers" projecting through the roofline, stepped window and door surrounds, and highly stylized doorways. Decorative details included **reeding**—a series of convex curves,

sunbursts, floral designs, and geometric motifs such as chevrons and zigzags. Detailing was frequently painted in striking colors. The style was used for office buildings (such as the Empire State Building), theaters, and apartment buildings but rarely on single-family residences. See Figure 11.42.

Art Moderne closely followed Art Deco and had many of the same features. Art Moderne structures often had curved building corners—a result of stream-lining—windows on both sides of corners, and **eye-brows**, or flat horizontal projecting surfaces over windows and doors. Glass block windows were common. Art Moderne was more horizontal than Art Deco, had flat roofs, and possessed little of the decorative detailing typical of Art Deco. Art Moderne structures were usually white.

International (1920–1945)

The International style originated in Europe during the first quarter of the twentieth century. Homes in this style were cube-shaped structures with flat roofs. See Figure 11.43. Concrete was the most popular building material for International-style homes, although they were occasionally built of wood and covered with stucco or even siding. The predominant color was white, in keeping with the simplicity of the architecture. No moldings, trim, or decorative details were used. Large windows or horizontal bands of glass were used in conjunction with open interior plans to create the illusion of space.

Twentieth-Century Revival Styles

Although the twentieth century saw the development of original architectural styles, not all new homes built during the period drew upon these innovations. Features of previously popular architectural styles were revived, especially in the 1920s and 1930s and, in modified form, continue to influence homes built today.

Figure 11.42 (ABOVE) The Art Deco style in residential architecture is most prevalent on multifamily dwellings.

Figure 11.43 (OPPOSITE, TOP) The International style was a result of a rejection of most traditional house designs in favor of buildings that were designed to incorporate modern technologies and materials. The resulting building is usually a simple geometric structure with little ornamentation. (Source: © Angelo Hornak/CORBIS)

Figure 11.44 (OPPOSITE, BOTTOM) The half-timbering on Tudor Revival homes is not structural but merely a decorative addition designed to give the appearance of a Tudor structure.

Colonial Revival (1880–1955)

One of the most continuously popular of the period styles has been the Colonial style. The Colonial Revival style was based on the Colonial, Georgian, and Federal houses of American history. Renewed interest in these early architectural styles began with the nation's centennial in 1876 and gained momentum by the turn of the century.

Some Colonial Revival homes were nearly exact replicas of Georgian, Federal, or English Colonial homes. Others simply adopted modified versions of some of the details of those styles—such as dentils, pilasters, pediments, or fanlights—without attempting historical accuracy. Often, the result was a mixture of details from more than one early style or a combination of period details with more recent ones. Because of the stylistic mixing and adaptation that occurred, Colonial Revival homes were found in a wide variety of forms.

Tudor Revival (1890–1940)

The Tudor style, very popular in the 1920s and 1930s, was used for all types of homes ranging from modest one-story dwellings to large mansions. The style was based on English architecture of the Tudor period. The revival style was known variously as Elizabethan, Tudor, and Jacobean.

One of the most recognizable characteristics of Tudor structures was the use of half-timbering, and many Tudor-style homes built in the twentieth century made apparent use of this feature. See Figure 11.44. Usually, only a portion of the home, such as a gable or

the upper floors, was half-timbered. Whether or not the home featured half-timbering, the surface materials might include brick, stone, stucco, wood siding, or a combination of these.

Tudor-style residences were almost always asymmetrical. An identifying feature was a steeply pitched roof with prominent gables. Door and window openings and porch supports often featured the wide, slightly pointed Tudor arch. Tall, narrow casement windows made up of small panes and bay and oriel windows were popular. One or more tall chimneys were usually incorporated in the design. In large or highly detailed Tudor-style brick or stone homes, the chimneys often had paired or triple shafts decorated with spirals or other molded designs.

Another distinct type of Tudor-style home suggested the appearance of a large Tudor hall or castle rather than a small rural dwelling. The design featured parapeted gables, either angular or curved. Pinnacles and battlements were sometimes included as well. Homes in this style were usually constructed of stone or brick and did not include half-timbering.

Cotswold Cottage (1890–1940)

This style is closely related to the Tudor and was popular at the same time during the twentieth century. Its origins, however, extended as far back as the Norman Conquest in the eleventh century. The cottages that began to be built around that time in the Cotswold district of rural England were handed down from generation to generation. Many of the features of the style that evolved are also found in its more modern descendant.

Like the Tudor style, the Cotswold Cottage was characterized by a steeply pitched gable roof. Most of these homes had one and a half stories, a roofline that extended down to the tops of the windows, and a low appearance. A front gable might be curved and roof edges were sometimes curved to suggest thatch. New examples may feature artificial thatch. Dormers and extra gables gave the roof an irregular shape.

Some twentieth-century revival styles loosely based on original models may feature only a single true stylistic characteristic. Simply adding different decorative details to the facades of identically planned houses results in the appearance of architectural style differences.

Modern examples sometimes have faux projecting vigas on all sides. In designing Pueblo-style structures, it should be remembered that the vigas were actually structural members and only showed on the front and back of the structure.

The walls were often a combination of materials, brick with stone being very common. Massive chimneys were a dominant feature of these homes. The windows were usually small, multipaned casements. Cotswold cottages were asymmetrical, echoing the original examples that were often added on to over a period of years. See Figure 11.45.

Pueblo Revival Style (1910–present)

The Pueblo Revival style was a mixture of Native American and Spanish pueblo influences. See Figure 11.46. Most were built of concrete with a stucco finish, and had projecting vigas, a flat roof, and parapet walls. Like Native American pueblos, they often had multiple stories, and upper floors might be stepped back, forming complicated footprints and facades.

French-Influenced Designs

Norman French architectural features were found on a number of large homes. Norman French–style homes were generally asymmetrical two-story structures built of brick or stone. The steep hip or gable roof was usually broken by dormers and turrets. A round tower, which usually housed the entrance and a winding stairway, was a typical feature. The doorway was often arched. See Figure 11.47.

French Provincial homes were based on French architecture of the seventeenth century. These two- or two-and-a-half-story homes were symmetrical, with steeply pitched hip roofs. French doors were often used on the first floor, and upper-story windows often

Figure 11.45 (TOP) The Cotswold Cottage style is one of the Tudor styles. A steep front-facing gable usually houses the entry and often exhibits the use of multiple materials— usually stone with brick or stone with wood. The Tudor arch and diamond pane windows are common.
Figure 11.46 (BOTTOM) This Pueblo Revival style–house mixes the Spanish single-story adobe brick style with the Native American stacked and stepped-back multifamily dwellings.

broke through the eave line. Shutters were a common feature. Brick was typically used for an exterior finish, although some examples had a stone or stucco facade.

Late-Twentieth-Century and Contemporary Styles

During the last few decades of the twentieth century, there was no predominant architectural style, and this tendency continues. Contemporary homes often integrate indoors and outdoors, minimizing the home's impact on the natural environment. Wood siding or shakes may be left to weather naturally, or be painted or stained in colors that help the house blend into the environment. Rubble stone is another favored building material. Window walls, skylights, and clerestories bring the outdoors into the living space. Living areas may face patios, atria, and other private outdoor areas. The interior plan is open and informal, often with large spaces designed for recreational purposes.

Some homes are constructed using elements from historic precedents, others employ energy-efficient features such as solar panels or earth sheltering that dictate to some extent the appearance of the structure, and other homes make use of innovative technologies or elements such as sprayed foam structures or unusual rooflines.

Neoeclectic and Postmodern (1965–present)

The Neoeclectic style began as a rebellion against modernism. It was most popular in modest homes during the 1960s but, as it has continued, the style has affected not only homes in all sizes and price ranges but commercial structures as well.

Neoeclectic designs are loose adaptations of Colonial, French, Spanish, Tudor, and even Victorian styles.

Figure 11.47 A round tower with a conical roof housing the entry is a characteristic feature of French Norman houses. Some examples feature half-timbering or quoins, others do not.

In fact, a single structure may exhibit features characteristic of several historic styles. The builders of such homes are in this way meeting the increasing desire of home buyers for familiar architectural styles of the past.

Postmodern homes are similar to Neoeclectic structures, and either term may be used to describe both. There is, however, a difference. Postmodern homes use the same mixture of style precedents as does Neoeclectic but added to the mixture are familiar forms used in surprising ways, completely new forms, and a sense of contradiction.

Vernacular Forms

Throughout each period of American history, a great number of homes have been built that do not belong to any identifiable style classification. While architectural styles have come and gone, these simple home designs have remained essentially unchanged. Such homes must, of course, utilize some roof type, some wall covering, and so on. They are, however, without any of the particular combinations of shape, roof form, materials, and ornamentation that mark the various architectural styles. They are often called folk houses or vernacular houses.

Although vernacular houses do not conform to any style, they are by no means all alike. Since these houses cannot be differentiated from one another by the presence of stylistic details, they are usually described in terms of their structural form. For example, a house may be described as front-gabled, side-gabled, or L-shaped. Indeed, distinctive house forms often come to be considered styles in themselves.

In discussing twentieth- and twenty-first-century homes, the line between styles and forms becomes even more difficult to draw. Many times, homes are

grouped together because they share the same form. Yet within that grouping, some homes may be ornamented with details reminiscent of one style or another; other homes may have no style details at all. Nevertheless, the grouping as a whole is readily recognizable.

The more familiar of these twentieth-century housing forms include the American Foursquare, the bungalow, the ranch, the geodesic dome, and the A-frame. In one sense, these terms describe a home's shape rather than its architectural style. Yet in another sense, especially when the home displays little ornament, the shape is itself the style.

American Foursquare (1890–1930s)

Popular during the first two decades of the twentieth century was a boxlike form known as American Foursquare. It was a two- or two-and-a-half-story home with a pyramidal hip roof and, frequently, dormers. See Figure 11.48. When there was a porch, its roof was supported by columns or piers. Usually, the houses were symmetrical, although the entry door might be offset. Many examples of the American Foursquare were simple and unembellished, in keeping with other styles that followed the ornate ones of the Victorian era. Others borrowed moderate amounts of decorative details from the Colonial Revival, Prairie, or even Mission styles. American Foursquare homes were available through mail-order.

Bungalow (1910–1930)

Bungalows had a single story and a relatively low-pitched gable roof with wide overhanging eaves. Some were side-facing, some front-facing. A porch often extended across all or part of the facade and usually had a separate gabled roof. The porch roof was typically supported by masonry piers or by squared **battered** columns set on piers. See Figure 11.49. Battered columns had slanted sides that de-

Figure 11.48 The American Foursquare home has a pyramid roof and almost cubical shape.

Figure 11.49 Sloped or battered sides on columns or piers on bungalows often extend without a break from the ground to a point above the porch floor, sometimes forming a low porch wall enclosure.

creased in size as they increased in height. The porch itself might be enclosed by low walls. Many bungalows followed the Craftsman style. Other bungalows were simple and unadorned. In these small homes, large windows created the illusion of added space. A semi-bungalow sheltered an extra half-story under a side-gabled roof. Exterior materials included stucco, stone, brick, shingles, or siding.

The Craftsman style[9] itself originated in California, although it was greatly influenced by the European Arts and Crafts movement. The dominant characteristic of the style was a low-pitched gable roof with a wide overhanging open cornice. In the cornice, exposed rafters might be structural components or merely decorative additions.

In shape, Craftsman homes ranged from a simple rectangle to rambling forms. The uppers sashes of the double-hung windows were often separated by wood muntins into rectangles, diamonds, or squares. Inside, Craftsman-style houses often had built-in furniture and natural materials and finishes.

Ranch (1940–present)

Ranch homes are single-story rectangular or L-shaped houses spread out over a relatively large area. The roof is low-pitched and may be gabled or hipped. Ranch homes often have large expanses of glass shielded from direct sun by wide roof overhangs. Sliding glass doors opening onto outdoor living areas are a common feature. Siding, brick, or other materials cover the exterior and are often combined. When decorative details are added, they are usually of English Colonial or Mediterranean inspiration. The ranch style became popular in the 1940s, dominated the succeeding decades, and is still commonly built today.

Geodesic Dome (1954–present)

The sphere encloses a greater volume per unit of surface area than any other form. The dome, as part of a sphere, requires fewer materials for construction, while providing more floor space. A 30 x 40 foot rectangular structure has 140 linear feet of wall and encloses 1200 square feet. A dome with 140 linear feet of wall encloses approximately 1560 square feet—an increase of 30 percent. A dome is aerodynamic and withstands high winds better than structures with vertical walls, has a low center of gravity and moves with the earth during earthquakes, and will carry greater loads than conventional roofs.

The geodesic dome is a product of the age of technology after World War II, when manufacturing processes began to expand into the housing market. Geo-desic domes are constructed of circles of triangles. Each triangular section creates local rigidity and distributes stress. Geodesic domes are light in weight and actually become proportionally stronger as they increase in size. The use of the geodesic dome in the 1967 World's Fair in Montreal helped to popularize them. R. Buckminster Fuller used the geodesic dome for large sports arenas and other buildings as well as homes.[10]

Triangular sections of rigid or flexible panels of wood, glass, plastic, or other material are framed by equal lengths of steel, wood, aluminum, or plastic struts. The panels are arranged to form a domed structure. See Figure 11.50. The design allows the stresses of the structure to be carried by the relatively lightweight struts, giving strength and stability with little expenditure of material. Several domes are often

Figure 11.50 The geodesic dome employs multiple triangular sections to create its form. Some of the domes have few vertical walls; others use the dome basically as a roof structure. In this example located on the beach, the structure is raised off the ground to minimize water damage.

combined in one structure. Inside, the dome requires no bearing walls making large open spaces and soaring ceilings feasible.

Geodesic dome homes, however, have a number of drawbacks. Exterior walls are composed of angles, making space planning and furniture arrangement difficult, partition walls may be difficult to construct for privacy, and there is significant material waste during construction. The large volume of air in the structure must be heated and cooled even though much of the space above 8 feet is unusable.

A-Frame

The A-frame design, like the geodesic dome, appeared in America after World War II and is easily rec-

The geodesic dome results in angled walls—in this case relatively short—that may be difficult to work with when arranging furniture and designing spaces.

ognized by the steeply pitched gable that serves as both roof and side walls extending to floor level. Because of the angle of the roof, space in the upper story is considerably less than that on the lower floor. Some A-frame houses have two full floors, with one located below grade level. Maintenance is low due to the extended use of roofing material and the large expanses of glass in the end walls. Balconies and surrounding decks are frequent additions. A-frames are most frequently used as vacation or retirement homes.

Planning
Space
Use

Chapter 12

Planning is essential for every stage of the development of housing. Good planning takes into account the functions of the various rooms and areas of the home, and the relationships between those areas. When the potential use of space is planned prior to construction, the resulting housing can be more efficient and land can be more effectively used. Both of these characteristics significantly affect final costs. Good planning also results in a home environment that is pleasant and that allows the occupants to make efficient use of time and human energy. These benefits apply equally to existing housing. Efficient use of the spaces that are available can prevent or postpone the need for costly new construction or a move to other quarters. Space planning must consider acoustic features to maximize privacy.

Planning for Acoustic Privacy

Achieving visual privacy is simple: Doors that close and walls between spaces accomplish this easily. Acoustic privacy is more difficult to achieve. Consideration must be given to space planning and the relative locations of noisy and quiet spaces, to the treatment of structural components, and to the appliances and equipment selected for the home. An NAHB survey found that 53 percent of respondents wanted acoustic control[1] features in their homes.

Space Planning

When planning space use, locate infrequently used or noisy areas closest to the major sound source (such as a street), with quiet areas farthest away. Group noisy spaces such as family rooms, passageways, kitchens, laundry rooms, bathrooms, and utility areas together, and acoustically isolate them from quiet areas. Locate closets between rooms in quiet zones and between quiet and noisy areas: The clothing absorbs much of the sound transmitted through walls, but doors must be kept closed for the full acoustic benefit. Back-to-back closets provide even better acoustic isolation. Filled bookcases or cabinets serve the same function when placed on shared walls. However, unless these units are tall, sound will still be transmitted through the free wall area.

Structural Components and Their Treatments

The use of double wall or floor construction discussed in Chapter 5 will greatly reduce sound transmission between rooms or areas, although there should be no rigid mechanical connections (such as HVAC duct-work) or structural blocking connecting the two components. It is especially important to treat floors or ceilings for acoustic control if there are multiple living levels. Impact sounds are by far the most difficult to control. Carpeting with padding can reduce sound transmission significantly but will not be sufficient to control it in all cases.

Sound is absorbed by soft surfaces and reflected by hard ones, so the absorption value of a structural component depends on the surface porosity and subsequent vibration of the material. The sound waves enter tiny pores in materials and are dissipated as low-level heat energy. Thus, designing rooms to include fabrics in draperies, upholstery, and wall coverings; floor coverings of carpet, cork, vinyl, or rubber; and acoustic ceiling tiles can help reduce sound. See Figure 12.1.

Figure 12.1 Soft materials such as draperies, upholstery, and carpeting will absorb sounds in a room.

When planning space for acoustic privacy, consider both the horizontal and vertical orientation of rooms.

Because sound absorption depends partially on the thickness of the material, draperies provide only a small amount of acoustic control. Using heavy, textured fabrics, lining the draperies, and increasing fullness results in greater absorption, but the amount is still not significant. These soft surfaces, however, do not reflect sound as do walls, floors, ceiling surfaces, and glass, thus reducing potential noise. Large fiber wall hangings such as quilts, tapestries, and rugs have the same characteristics.

The materials used to finish structural components affect the amount of sound transmitted. Traditional acoustic treatments—acoustic tiles and fiberboard—have little aesthetic appeal, but panels made of the same materials including mineral fibers may be covered with almost any material, including decorative metal. The perforations, striations, or etched surfaces of the material still trap and absorb as much as 70 percent of the sound striking them. Not only do all of these materials help to quiet the space in which they are located but they also reduce the noise escaping to other areas. Fabric-covered ceilings, false fiberglass beams, and melamine acoustical foam ceiling tile are other alternatives.

Appliances and Equipment

Most appliances used in American homes are noisy—some even operate at decibel levels sufficiently high to cause hearing loss. Although the technology exists to create more quietly operating appliances and equipment, it is usually more expensive to do so. Quiet units may require better design, sometimes reduced power, and acoustic mountings for which consumers may not be willing to pay. In addition, consumers often associate power with noise in appliances such as vacuum cleaners and garbage disposals. Some manufacturers are producing more quietly operating appliances and equipment, as evidenced by advertisements for products such as dishwashers, air conditioners, and automobiles. These advertisements focus on assuring consumers that quiet opera-

Fabrics attached directly to hard surfaces are not effective sound absorbers, but those attached to fiberglass panels or other sound-absorbing materials not only absorb sound but also provide pleasing surfaces and textures.

tion is indicative of added quality rather than reduced power.

Acceptable noise levels depend on the frequency and length of operation of an appliance as well as its location in the home. Appliances and equipment such as refrigeration units and HVAC components that operate for lengthy periods of time are typically designed for quieter operation than those that are used for shorter periods. Consumers may tolerate noisy appliances located in remote areas—laundry equipment is an example. The noise of convection ovens and dishwashers is more annoying due to their more central location. Placing foam pads beneath small appliances and vibration mounts beneath large appliances will decrease decibel levels during operation.

Space Requirements in the Home

An important consideration in planning how space will be used is, of course, how much space is needed. To a great extent, family size dictates minimum floor space requirements. Approximately 200 square feet of finished floor area per person is the recommended minimum home size. However, this amount of space does not provide needed privacy for individual family members unless the home is carefully designed to furnish it. Five hundred square feet per person

Equipment and appliances are only infrequently sold with noise ratings. When selecting these units for the home, consumers should be aware of typical decibel levels and encouraged to make choices suitable for their lifestyles.

provides adequate privacy as well as space for social interaction.

Although these figures provide some guidelines, they do not always reflect actual space needs. It must be remembered that some of the space in the home is shared by all family members. As a result, space needs do not continue to increase at a constant rate as more family members are added. For example, the recommended size of a home that will provide adequate space for four people is 2000 square feet. However, because the kitchen, bathrooms, and living areas are shared, a total of 1500 square feet, or 75 percent of the recommended size, would probably be sufficient. Of course, families differ in their space needs due to differing activities, lifestyles, values, and other factors. However, if the minimum number of square feet per person is used, a greater percentage must be provided for even minimal privacy. Thus, while a minimum of 800 square feet is needed for four people, it will probably require all of that. Average home sizes have increased dramatically in the past 35 years. See Table 12.1

Overall Space Use

Houses are usually made up of individual rooms or areas, but it is the way in which these separate entities are put together that has the greatest effect on the home's usefulness. In a well-planned home, rooms with similar functions or design needs are grouped together into zones. Good design also provides for efficient traffic patterns between and within areas. The size of the home and whether rooms are separate or open to one another are other factors to consider in the overall plan for space use.

Zones

The space inside and outside a home can typically be divided into three zones according to function: the service zone, the social zone, and the private zone. These zones should be separated to prevent interference from activities in other zones. Related indoor and

Table 12.1 Average Square Feet of New One-Family Homes 1975 to 2004

Year	U.S.	Northeast	Midwest	South	West
1975	1645	1575	1580	1705	1635
1980	1740	1770	1685	1750	1735
1985	1785	1830	1820	1765	1770
1986	1825	1850	1855	1825	1800
1987	1905	1955	1890	1915	1870
1988	1995	2005	2015	1985	1995
1989	2035	2075	1970	2030	2065
1990	2080	2105	2005	2055	2160
1995	2095	2240	2020	2125	2045
1996	2120	2280	2025	2160	2070
1997	2150	2265	2065	2175	2135
1998	2190	2270	2125	2200	2200
1999	2223	2298	2135	2244	2234
2000	2266	2435	2170	2287	2244
2001	2324	2466	2209	2351	2317
2002	2320	2516	2209	2317	2350
2004	2349	2543	2222	2368	2352
Difference (1975–2004)	704	968	642	663	719
Percent Difference*	43	61	41	39	44

Source: http://www.census.gov/const/C25Ann/sftotalmedavgsqft.pdf (9/19/05).

* New homes have steadily increased in size since 1970. In fact, the average home size has increased by 43 percent in that time. Homes in the Northeast increased significantly more than those in the rest of the nation.

outdoor zones should be easily accessed from one another. These zones are discussed in the following three chapters.

In most homes, the three zones overlap to some degree. Certain guests may be entertained in the kitchen. Overnight guests may use private zones. Visual isolation between traditional social and service zones may be eliminated, as when a kitchen is open to the living area.

The design and use of each zone depend on family needs and values. The most important guideline is that housing be functional for families. Getting from one zone to another is a function of circulation areas. While not a separate zone, circulation areas often serve as dividing lines between zones. Although the zones are individually identified, there is usually little if any actual separation between zones within the home.

Open and Closed Plans

The design of a home's floor plan can be characterized as open or closed. **Open plans** feature spaces that flow into one another, enhancing spaciousness and flexibility. Rooms in **closed plans** are separated by walls and offer privacy. Most homes provide a combination of open and closed plans.

Housing has become less formal as lifestyles have become more casual. This informality has led to home interiors that are more open, using fewer walls than traditional closed designs. Today, most homes are built with a combination of open and closed spaces to allow for both flexibility and privacy.

In an open plan, areas for different purposes are visually and acoustically connected. Spaces for specific functions may be defined by screens, dividers, furniture arrangements, or changes in level rather than by walls. An open plan creates large open spaces designed for group living. Such spaces flow visually from one area to another and even to the outdoors. Several activities can occur simultaneously, allowing participants to interact with one another. Thus, a person preparing a meal is not segregated from family members and activities if the kitchen and family room flow together. This freedom from isolation may, however, interfere with privacy. See Figure 12.2.

Openness may be horizontal, vertical, or both. Vertically open spaces can create a special sense of excitement and elegance. See Figure 12.3. High ceilings, skylights, and balconies add to the overall spaciousness of the home. However, windows located in soaring spaces are difficult to clean and maintain. Horizontally open areas also create a sense of spaciousness. In plans where living and dining areas are visually connected, for instance, each area appears larger than if it were defined by walls.

Lighting is more efficient in an open plan, with fewer fixtures needed for general illumination. Noise,

Figure 12.2 (TOP) This dining room is open on two sides. On this side, it is open to the entry and the living room. Both of these social areas are located conveniently for guests.

Figure 12.3 (BOTTOM) Opening up a space vertically can be very dramatic. In this case, the verticality is emphasized by the windows.

Open plans may also waste energy if not correctly designed. Individual rooms cannot be shut off and left unheated. In vertically open plans, heat rises and is lost to the space near the floor where it is most needed. On the other hand, homes with passive solar heating systems need open plans for efficient heat distribution.

---

however, often creates problems. Spaces that are visually connected are also acoustically connected, making it difficult to design areas for quiet activities.

A closed plan uses walls to separate spaces, creating visual and acoustic privacy for activities taking place in individual rooms. This makes it possible to obtain privacy for conflicting activities or those of different age groups. Bedrooms, bathrooms, and utility areas generally utilize closed plans, even if other areas in the home have open plans.

Although closed planning does not lend itself well to flexibility and multiple uses of space, it does allow a certain degree of freedom in decorating and maintenance. In a closed plan, rooms decorated in different styles and colors are not as distracting as in an open plan, where decor of all spaces should blend well. A closed plan also makes it possible to have some casual and some more formal rooms. Messy children's rooms and informal family rooms can be shut off from view.

Because closed plans are made up of separate, clearly defined areas, traffic patterns are rather rigidly controlled. Space limitations are more apparent because lines of sight are restricted.

Rarely would a single type of plan be best for residences. Most families need some open space for family activities and social functions as well as closed space for privacy. While houses are separated into zones and rooms, it is the way in which these separate entities are put together that affects its usefulness for a family.

❀ Closed plans are generally more energy-efficient. Individual areas can be closed off and left unheated or uncooled when not in use.

Rooms and Areas of the Home

In most cultures and time periods, spaces have served multiple functions. Ancient Greeks used movable screens and partitions to create private areas in large rooms. Today, multipurpose space may be treated similarly in small apartments. The Japanese may roll out mats for sleeping in a common space used for other activities during the day.

More commonly in most Western cultures, homes are divided into areas designed for specific uses. Most modern homes include an entry, a living room, one or more dining areas, a kitchen, at least one bathroom, and one or more bedrooms. Other spaces often found in housing include the family room or den and the garage or carport. Special consideration should be given not only to these specific areas but to storage facilities throughout the home.

Family Size and Number of Rooms

The average American family size has decreased consistently since 1940. In 2003, the number of persons per household was 2.57, down from 3.67 persons in 1940. See Table 12.2. Homes, however, have

Table 12.2 Average Household Size*

Year	Number of Persons
1940	3.67
1950	3.37
1955	3.33
1960	3.33
1965	3.29
1970	3.14
1975	2.94
1980	2.76
1985	2.69
1990	2.63
2000	2.62
2002	2.58
2003	2.57

Source: "Total Number of Households and Buildings, Floorspace, and Household Size, by Year," *Buildings Energy Databook: 2.1 Residential Sector Characteristics,* Table 2.1.1 (2004).

* The size of the average household has decreased in the last 65 years even though floor space in homes has increased.

Table 12.3 Number of Rooms in Percent*

	1 Room	2 Rooms	3 Rooms	4 Rooms	5 Rooms	6 Rooms	7 Rooms	8+ Rooms	Median #
1960			19.5	21.3	24.5	19.1	15.5		4.9
1970			16.1	20.6	24.8	19.8	17.4		5.0
1979			14.6	19.3	23.3	19.9	19.7		5.1
1995	0.8	1.3	9.3	19.0	22.2	20.2	13.0	14.2	
1997	0.4	1.3	10.4	20.9	21.8	19.0	12.3	13.9	
1999	0.5	1.2	9.6	20.4	23.0	20.2	12.3	12.8	
2001	0.5	1.2	9.0	19.4	23.4	20.7	12.3	13.5	
2003	0.4	1.2	9.1	19.3	23.2	20.4	12.1	14.3	

Sources: Source for 1960, 1970, 1979 figures from U.S. Census Bureau, "Housing Units—Summary of Characteristics: 1960 to 1979," *Statistical Abstract of the United States: 2000*, Table 1372 (Washington, D.C.: Department of Commerce, 2000), 760. In these sets of figures, 1–3 rooms are grouped and the maximum is 7 or more rooms. Source for 1995 figures from U.S. Census Bureau, "Housing Units—Size of Units and Lot: 1995," *Statistical Abstract of the United States: 2000*, Table 1213 (Washington, D.C.: Department of Commerce, 2005), 725. Source for 1997 from U.S. Census Bureau, "Housing Units—Size of Units and Lot: 1997," *Statistical Abstract of the United States: 2000*, Table 1211 (Washington, D.C.: Department of Commerce, 2000), 721. Source for 1999 from U.S. Census Bureau, "Housing Units—Size of Units and Lot: 1999," *Statistical Abstract of the United States: 2001*, Table 954 (Washington, D.C.: Department of Commerce, 2001), 606. Source for 2001 from U.S. Census Bureau, "Housing Units—Size of Units and Lot: 2001," *Statistical Abstract of the United States: 2004–2005*, Table 961 (Washington, D.C.: Department of Commerce, 2005), 621. Source for 2003 from U.S. Census Bureau, "Housing Units—Size of Units and Lot: 2003," *Statistical Abstract of the United States: 2004–2005*, Table 949 (Washington, D.C.: Department of Commerce, 2005), 611.

* The number of rooms in homes has steadily increased since 1960. In 1960, the percentage of homes with one to three rooms was 19.5; in 2003, it was 9.7—about half of the 1960 percentage. In 1960, the upper limit for the Census Bureau questionnaire was 7 or more rooms and 15.5 percent of homes had this number. In 2003, 26.4 percent of homes had 7 or more.

shown a marked increase in the number of rooms present. While only 15.5 percent of homes in 1960 had 7 or more rooms, more than 26 percent of homes had 7 or more rooms in 2003. See Table 12.3. Most American homes are designed with families in mind: The larger the number of bedrooms, the larger the living spaces. An NAHB survey, however, found that most of the size increase in homes is due to larger rooms, additional bathrooms, more family rooms, and separate entries rather than an increase in the number of bedrooms. This is consistent, of course, with the decrease in the number of people in the household.

While averages look at the overall picture, it is important to understand that some homes, regardless of the number of rooms, are overcrowded. The U.S. Census Bureau defines crowded homes as having more than one person per room and severely crowded homes as having more than 1.5 persons per room. Using these definitions, in 2000, 5.7 percent of homes in the United States were overcrowded, while 2.7 percent were severely crowded. Like other conditions, crowding depends on geographic location, among other factors. In 2000, California had a crowding rate of 15 percent—more than double the national average with 9.1 percent of homes severely overcrowded —more than three times the national average.

Room Size

Although the number of rooms is significant, other factors determine how functional and satisfactory those rooms are. Rooms must be sufficiently large to accept the furniture needed for activities that take place in them and to allow circulation around furnishings. The IRC stipulates that no dimension in a habitable room other than a kitchen be less than 7 feet, with a minimum of 70 square feet in the room. Bathrooms, laundry rooms, utility areas, and closets are not considered habitable rooms and do not need to meet these minimums. A room of this size is very small. In fact, if either the length or width is less than 10 feet, the room is considered small.

Small rooms may create a sense of overcrowding, but they are more intimate in nature and encourage interaction. Small rooms require fewer and smaller pieces of furniture. Changing the decor of a small room does not usually entail a great deal of expense, so the space can be changed more frequently to fit family needs. Individuals may spend a significant amount of money on a single piece, such as an Oriental rug, without making changes to the entire house.

A few techniques can be used to make small rooms appear larger.

- Locate the focal point near the center of a wall to draw the eye away from perpendicular wall limits.
- Match the color of the bottom part of the wall with the floor color.
- Use a few small furniture pieces rather than many pieces or large items.
- Multiple-purpose furniture has been used for centuries and should be considered for small rooms—foldout couches, tables that convert to chairs, and tables that fold into smaller units are

examples. A foldout sofa takes up less space during the day, leaving open space in the room during waking hours.

- Transparent tabletops, open chair backs, and armless chairs are less visually limiting than other types of furnishings, resulting in the illusion of more open space.
- Raise furniture, cabinets, and appliances slightly off the floor on legs, extending the view of the floor.
- Use mirrors to give the illusion of more space.
- Use the same flooring material in the entire room, such as wall-to-wall carpeting, hardwood, or tile. See Figure 12.4. The use of area rugs provides visual boundaries and results in limiting the space.
- Use unobtrusive patterns and colors for furnishings, window treatments, and finishes for structural components.
- Make good use of windows. Glass areas visually expand space. If the view is appropriate, minimize window treatments to take advantage of the expansiveness of glass. If the view is inappropriate, use floor-to-ceiling window treatments so the edges are not visually limiting.
- Open up the walls to share space with other rooms.

Large rooms lend themselves to social interaction and are generally perceived to be better for entertaining. Monumental furnishings can be used with good effect, but small-scale furniture can become "lost" in the space. Large rooms require more furnishings than do small rooms, as well as a greater number of accessories such as lamps and artwork. The initial design and any modifications require a greater expenditure of funds to ensure that each item complements the space. Larger expanses of windows can be used in these rooms allowing more natural light into the space. Screens and furniture can be strategically placed to create a feeling of intimacy, changes in

Figure 12.4 Using the same flooring throughout a room can create an expansive sense of space. (Source: Barbara Huffman)

floor level within the space can create the suggestion of separate rooms, and furniture can be arranged into mini rooms within the space.

A room's functionality is not totally dependent on its size but on how well the space is actually used. Room size and functionality are affected by the number and size of openings. Even in large rooms, glass can decrease usable space significantly and dictate furniture placement. Usable space is also diminished when several entrances take up wall space needed for furniture arrangement. The functionality of rooms is further affected by their arrangement in the structure and their relationships to exterior and interior zones.

Openings in Rooms

The IRC requires a minimum of one emergency egress from each habitable room—a window or door directly to the exterior. If there is no exterior door, one of the windows must open far enough to permit an emergency exit. In addition, there will usually be a door or opening into the room from the interior of the space. Each door or window in a room affects the usable wall space and, thus, furniture placement.

A minimum of 3 feet of closet rod and shelf space per person in each bedroom is needed. In many homes, closets are larger. If closets have sliding doors, much of the wall space on that side is eliminated. Walk-in closets are popular because they offer a large amount of storage space but require little wall space for an opening.

Doors. In residences, both interior and exterior doors swing in; in commercial applications, exterior and some interior doors swing out. Residential doors that swing or fold require space in the room, and furniture should be arranged so that the sweep is unimpeded. The use of sliding doors and pocket doors eliminates these problems. The guidelines below should be followed when planning door locations.

- No door—whether to a room or closet or cabinet doors—should interfere with the swing of another door.
- Doors should not open in front of light switches, making it necessary to close the door to operate the switch.
- Doors shouldn't open into an area where someone may be standing, sitting, or accessing cabinets and furniture doors or drawers.
- If a door will remain open much of the time, it should not be in the way.

The location of doors affects furniture placement. Locating doors near corners will leave long unimpeded wall spaces for placing furniture. When possible, walk-in closets should be used not only for the extra storage space but to minimize the wall space required for doors in the room. In fact, as few doors as possible should be used.

Windows. Windows, too, are architectural features that reduce the usable wall area. Windows placed low on a wall may interfere with furniture placement, but they do provide an emergency egress if they are operable. It is important to provide for privacy near windows using window treatments, screens, or other devices. Standard head height for windows is 84 inches when 8-feet walls are used. When long windows are used, they will intrude upon space that might be needed for furniture. If the walls are higher than 8 feet, the windows could be located higher.

A good option is to use ribbon windows just below the ceiling, although there should be at least one window positioned for egress if there is no exterior door in the room. Ribbon windows do not restrict furniture placement, they allow light farther into the room than do windows with an 84-inch head height, and they ensure privacy for occupants. The obvious disadvantage, however, is the lack of a view through the window—not always desirable, especially if the view is less than pleasing.

Windows on the north side of a structure never receive any direct sun but lose a great deal of heat during winter months in most climates. For energy-efficiency, north-facing windows should be minimized. South-facing windows that are well shaded with overhangs during summer months can provide much-needed passive solar heat during winter months without significant heat gain during the summer.

Large windows should face east or south in most climates. West-facing windows should be avoided when possible, unless there is shade to reduce heat gain in the afternoons and evenings.

Designing Individual Rooms

While the architectural features of a home and of each room certainly affect the use and design, there are certain techniques to enhance the aesthetic quality of living spaces that designers should use. Each room or area needs a focal point or center of interest around which the room design revolves. Spaces may need to be subdivided either permanently or temporarily to ensure visual privacy. Furnishings must be appropriately arranged for use as well as for aesthetic purposes.

Focal Points

Most rooms have a focal point—a pleasing space or object that draws the eye—whether or not it is intentional. Strong colors, unusual shapes, graphic patterns, and spotlighted objects are visually powerful. Each room should have one major focal point. See Figure 12.5. There may be some additional smaller minor focal points, but too many visually powerful objects can be confusing.

The view from a window can be a focal point. To reinforce it, place visually powerful objects in front of it. The fireplace, too, may be a focal point, and it can be reinforced by placing a mirror above it. The fireplace may, however, lose its appeal when there is no fire. Often, a television is the focal point because furnishings are arranged for viewing and the eye is drawn in that direction. This technique can be used to reinforce any focal point. Because of their size, large-screen televisions may dominate a room even when they are not operating. Their appeal can be improved by projecting a still of a piece of art or other object. A number of objects can be rotated to ensure that no image is burned into the display, which would affect the viewing quality.

Subdividing Space

Areas can be subdivided to improve functionality, increase visual privacy, and provide dramatic effects. Large rooms, multifunction spaces, or rooms with open planning may all benefit from being subdivided.

Temporary space division can be accomplished in a variety of ways. Furniture can be arranged into a number of different groupings within a space to define areas for specific activities. A seating unit in a bedroom—especially when a small table and a lamp

Figure 12.5 As in most bedrooms, this bed is the focal point of the room, with furnishings grouped around it and the most striking colors used at that point.

are provided—identifies a quiet reading area within a room designed for sleeping. **Boundary furniture** can be used within a room to establish limits as well. Boundary furniture is often used to define traffic routes, especially in open planned spaces. The use of boundary furniture can also delineate an entry if there is insufficient space for a separate entry. When visual privacy is desired, tall enclosed furniture can be used. It may, however, be necessary to provide some treatment for the back of the furniture, as most furniture is not designed to be viewed from all sides. A faux wall can be attached to the back of furniture—even low furniture—to provide visual space separation. If the purpose is to divide the space and visual privacy is not an issue, open shelving or low furnishings such as benches can be used effectively.

A variety of types of screens are available that can be used to temporarily subdivide space. **Shoji screens** have panels filled with rice paper, which is translucent. Oriental fretwork screens allow some light to filter through but may not provide sufficient visual privacy. Fabric-covered and solid wood screens block the transmission of light but provide excellent visual privacy. All of these screens have multiple panels hinged together so they can be stored in a small space when not in use. Some are very decorative and can become a focal point in the space.

Architectural features such as fireplaces, stairs, closets, or **floating walls** permanently divide spaces that are otherwise open to one another. A floating wall is less than full height and does not extend to the ceiling. A planter, latticework, or turned posts or columns can effectively divide space as well. Archways create a dramatic division of space. A glass block wall may be floating or full height and will transmit most of the light striking it through to the opposite side. Such transparent barriers are not as visually limiting as are more solid-appearing objects.

Varying the treatment of structural components can also subdivide the space. Area rugs placed over wall-to-wall carpeting, hardwood, or other flooring define space by creating "islands." Changes in floor

Using blinds, shades, or curtains hung from the ceiling to subdivide space can decrease energy use by reducing drafts.

or ceiling levels or a change of materials in the wall, floor, or ceiling can also limit space.

The appropriate arrangement of furnishings within a space depends not only on the room size but on the functions for which the room will be used. When a room or open area will serve multiple functions, it may be important to visually separate the areas or to disguise some functions. For example, if a home office is incorporated in a family room, it will probably be more aesthetically pleasing to be able to minimize the visual effects of "work" or "business" when the room is being used for other activities.

Arranging Furniture

Furniture arrangement in a space can enhance or detract from the functionality of a room. The location of doors and windows will significantly affect the furniture placement, as will traffic patterns. There should be no obstructions in the traffic path not only into the room but into groupings of furniture. An individual should be able to access a conversational grouping, for example, without the necessity of walking around it before entering. It is also necessary to consider the view from the entrance to a space. Furniture arrangements that align objects so backs face the entry are less appealing and welcoming than those with furnishings that appear ready to receive guests.

When defining minor traffic patterns, ensure ease of access to the most frequently used items, such as the television, a bookcase, or a quiet reading corner. It is also important to be able to use each of the features of furniture pieces. There should be sufficient space in front of doors or drawers to access them without colliding with objects across from them. A minimum use area of 42 to 48 inches in front of each will suffice, although in smaller rooms it may be necessary to decrease the space to as little as 36 inches.

It is best to place large pieces first and to provide

each with a surrounding space without crowding pieces together. Large objects need more open space around them than do smaller objects. Positioning furniture away from walls may make the space appear larger because more floor area is visible. In fact, lining furniture up against walls is uninviting. Angling furniture in a space provides a dramatic flair and is more dynamic but requires more space than arranging furniture parallel to or perpendicular to walls.

Circulation Areas

It is the entry door that serves as the dividing line between public and private space in most homes. Those who pass beyond the door enter the home—often through a space designed to provide a buffer. Circulation routes flow to both the exterior and the interior from the entry, providing access to spaces in and around the home, including social areas (Chapter 13), service areas (Chapter 14), and private areas (Chapter 15). Getting from one zone to another is a function of circulation areas.

Entries

There is often more than one entry for a home: one used by family members, another by guests. Both guest and family entries should be planned to correspond with the major mode of transportation. If the automobile will be used most often, a path leading from the driveway to the entries is important. If public sidewalks in front of the home will be used frequently, a path from the sidewalk to the entry is needed. See Figure 12.6.

Outside the home, a number or other identification highly visible from the street assures visitors that they are in the right place. An exterior light helps identify the exact location of the entrance, illuminates steps and porch areas for safety, and helps residents identify visitors. When there are long walkways leading to the entrance or several flights of steps, additional lighting of the walkway is desirable. All of the exterior lights should be weatherproof fixtures and should be switched from an interior location, preferably near the entrance they serve. Covered entries furnish protection from inclement weather.

Entry space should be in proportion to the rest of the house: Small homes may have no separate entry, with the door opening into a living area. Furniture can be arranged to ensure that traffic flows efficiently from the entry into public areas. In larger homes, the entry may be a separate area of the house screened with walls or dividers.

Most families find a separate entry area or foyer more desirable because it provides a place for guests to be received and to remove outer garments, it serves as a buffer zone in which deliveries can be received and uninvited guests detained without disturbing activities in living areas, and it ensures the privacy of individuals within the home. A minimum of a 3 × 3 foot area should be allowed for an entry, although unless the entry is open to another space, this may be insufficient for the door to be fully opened. A better minimum entry size is 3 × 5 feet, although this may still be insufficient for accessibility and may inhibit the entry of equipment and furnishings. Realistically, the entry should be wide enough to approach the door from one side with sufficient space in which to move while opening the door. An entry 5 × 7 feet will provide the necessary space.

An entry used by guests should lead into the social zone. If outdoor living areas are to be used for entertaining, an additional entry—sometimes called a special-purpose entry—should be provided for guests that leads from the interior social zone to patios, decks, pools, and other outdoor areas. For the

Figure 12.6 The entry to this home is well defined, with a sidewalk leading to it from the street.

Figure 12.7 This shelving is located just inside the family entry. Each child has a separate space for belongings, making them easy to find.

convenience of guests, a closet should be located in or near the main entry. The closet should be located within 5 feet of the latch side of the door but not behind the door. This configuration allows guests to use the closet without closing the door—especially important when multiple guests are expected. The guest closet should have a minimum width of 3 feet. If there is no closet at the entry, a coatrack or hooks on the wall can provide a place for outer garments.

A service entrance is needed for carrying in groceries, taking out refuse, transporting laundry, and as a family entrance. It should be convenient to the kitchen and the garage, carport, or driveway and lead into the service area of the home. There should also be a closet or other facilities for storing garments at the family entry. Additional family entries may lead from an individual room to private outdoor living areas. See Figure 12.7.

Because of the heavy traffic flow, entry floors should be hard-surfaced and easy to clean. Although the entry should not be crowded with furnishings, providing a seating unit in the entry will facilitate the

The entrance to the guest bathroom should not be visible from the social zone.

removal of boots, and a small table or shelf will allow family and guests to lay carried items down while removing outer garments. A mirror hung in the entry will allow guests to check their appearance before entering a social zone. A half-bath should be located either in the main entry or within a short distance of the entry to allow guests to freshen up before entering social spaces.

A **mudroom**—a combination entry and laundry—located at the family entrance will be welcome especially when children may be muddy or when family

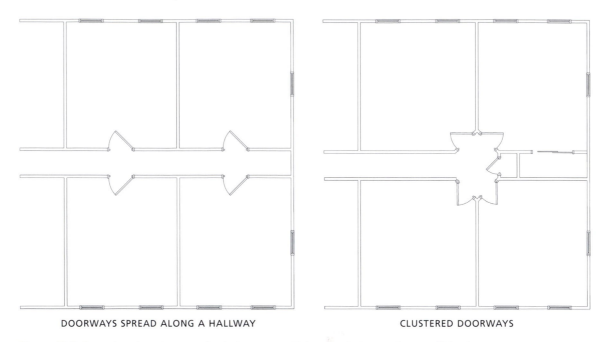

DOORWAYS SPREAD ALONG A HALLWAY   CLUSTERED DOORWAYS

Figure 12.8 Arranging doors to rooms in clusters can result in space being used more efficiently.

members are employed in occupations in which they can expect to become dirty. The mudroom makes it possible to enter the home, remove soiled clothing, and sometimes shower before entering the living area.

Circulation

Circulation areas are transitional spaces that connect the zones and each of the rooms in them. Halls and stairs are a part of the circulation system and lead from entrances to other areas of the home, from one level to another, and through rooms. In addition to major circulation areas between zones, minor circulation patterns direct the flow of traffic within each room or area.

The IRC requires a minimum hallway width of 3 feet. Wider halls may be necessary for moving furniture when there are sharp corners or when doors are located near the ends of halls where there is little room for maneuvering furniture and equipment. In hallways where individuals will be expected to pass one another frequently, 42 inches is a better width.

Because hallways require costly floor space, they are often eliminated in favor of directing traffic through rooms.

In general, hallways and traffic routes should be as short and direct as possible. One approach is to arrange room entrances in clusters around a central hall area rather than being widely spaced along a narrow corridor. See Figure 12.8. When a route leads from one level of the home to another, both the top and the bottom of the stairs or ramp should lead directly into circulation areas that provide access to any zone on that level. With certain exceptions, it should be unnecessary to pass through a room to reach another. Thus, activities are not interrupted or privacy lost. Guests should not need to move through rooms to access a closet or bathroom.

Paths within rooms are outlined primarily by boundary furniture and the location of entrances. Locating doors near the corners of rooms frees up wall space in the room and makes it possible to avoid traffic patterns that cut through quiet, conversation, or work areas within rooms.

Level Changes

Stairs facilitate the transition from one level to another and make it possible to use vertical space. In addition to being functional, stairways may be a major architectural feature of the home. Residential elevators have now become economically feasible and provide access to multiple levels for individuals with limited mobility. Ramps on both the interior and exterior ensure accessibility.

One or two steps may be used to define a space without the use of barriers—leaving the space open. A step down into a dining room, up to a platform on which a bed is located, or down into a conversation area can provide a dramatic line of demarcation between areas with different uses. There should be a walkway a minimum width of 3 feet around any furnishings or objects on a raised platform.

Other stairways connect levels in a home that are separated by half a story or more. Split-level houses have an entry on one level and require that users go up or down half a story to reach any living level. Two- or three-story homes and homes with basements have full-height stairs running from one level to the next. While stairs are usually a dominant feature in homes, if they do not lead to social spaces, it is not necessary that they be visible. Stairs leading from an area near the family entry to bedrooms located on the living level above or below the entry level may be concealed from public view.

Stairway Parts

Although there are different types of stairways, most consist of multiple **stringers** or **carriages** made of heavy materials—usually 2 × 12 or 2 × 14—that support the individual stairs. Stringers are installed diagonally and support the **treads** and **risers**. A stairway must have a stringer on each side and may include a third stringer in the middle. There are two kinds of stringers. **Plain stringers** have saw-toothed edges to

Space must always be allowed for doors to swing, which affects furniture placement and traffic patterns. The use of sliding doors, including pocket doors, frees up this space.

follow the lines of the treads and risers. They are used in the center of most stairways to support weight across the span and are often used at the side as well. **Housed stringers** are straight boards that have grooves cut into their sides into which the treads and risers fit. They can only be used for the side of a stair that is against a wall. Plain stringers are easier to construct and must be used where there is no wall to support the stringer, but housed stringers are more stable and minimize squeaks. Often, stairways are built with a plain stringer on one side and a housed stringer on the other side.

If a plain stringer is used for the side of a stairway that is exposed, a **finish stringer** is added for appearance. The finish stringer does not provide support but simply enhances the design of the stairway. If a housed stringer is used, a finish stringer is not necessary because the visible part of the housed stringer takes its place. See Figure 12.9.

Figure 12.9 Stair parts.

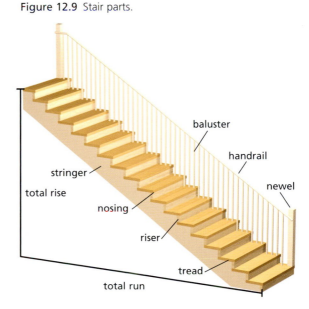

When determining head height beneath stairs, it is necessary to deduct the depth of the stringer. This distance can be determined from an elevation drawing. Once the staircase is drawn, the vertical distance from the bottom of a riser to the bottom of the stringer is the amount to be subtracted from clear space.

The riser fills in the vertical space between the levels of two treads, hiding the space beyond the stairs from view and preventing users from slipping through the space between stairs. Stairways located in places where appearance is not of primary concern, such as basements and attics, may not have risers, and exterior staircases usually do not have risers, either. The IRC, however, requires that the space occupied by risers be too small for a 4-inch sphere to pass through on stairs more than 30 inches in total height. While risers are not required, some space infill is necessary to comply with this code requirement. See Box 12.1. The IRC stipulates a maximum of 7¾ inches for riser height.

The tread is the horizontal part of each step and must be constructed of strong materials for support and to minimize wear. Hardwood is preferable, although softwood is often used for basement and attic stairs. Because the tread supports individuals walking on the stairs, it is necessary for the tread to be of sufficient depth to provide support for most of a person's foot. The IRC requires a minimum tread depth of 10 inches for staircases. Maximum tread depth for comfort is 12 inches, and local codes may preclude deeper treads. The total horizontal distance from one end of the stairs to the other is the **run**. The run is determined using the following formula.

Number of treads × tread depth = run
Example:
14 treads × 10 inches depth = 140 inches

Typically, a straight run staircase in a space with an 8-foot ceiling height (plus the thickness of the floor above) requires approximately 12 feet of run not including required landings. In a typical staircase, there is one less tread than the number of risers.

The shaped front portion of the tread is called the **nosing**. The IRC requires nosing on treads less than 11 inches deep. The nosing extends beyond the riser a minimum of ¾ inch but the projection should be less than 1¼ inches to avoid a safety hazard. The nosing is not included when measuring tread depth.

The floor at the top or bottom of a flight of stairs is called a **landing**. Minimum landing width must be equal to the width of the stairs; landing depth must be a minimum of 36 inches in the direction of travel. Some stairways also include one or more **platforms** between flights of stairs. A platform breaks up the stairway, making it easier to climb, and may also provide a place for a change in direction. The IRC requires that stairways greater than 12 feet in total rise have intermediate platforms.

The IRC requires a railing on at least one side of a flight of stairs if there are three or more treads, even when enclosed by walls. The railing may consist of a handrail attached to a wall or a handrail supported by a series of posts or **balusters**. The handrail is rounded for ease in grasping, helping to steady individuals as they ascend or descend the stairway. The IRC stipulates that the height of the handrail above the nosing of the treads be between 30 inches and 38 inches. If the handrail is attached directly to the wall, there must be additional support in the wall to withstand the expected forces.

A row of balusters topped by a handrail is called a **balustrade**. The balusters may extend to the treads or may be supported by a **shoe** or rail located a few inches above the treads. **Newel posts**, located at the beginning and often the end of the stairway and at platforms, are larger than balusters and may be highly decorative. A **guardrail** is the level railing around an opening, including one for a stairway. Minimum guardrail height is 36 inches. The IRC requires that all usable space beneath the stairs be enclosed with Type X gypsum board with a one-hour fire rating.

Box 12.1 International Residential Code Requirements for Stairs and Ramps

STAIRS

- Stairways must be a minimum of 36 inches wide and above handrail height, which must be clear width.
- Handrails may project 4½ inches on either side, reducing the stairway width at and below handrail height to 31½ inches if there is a single handrail; 27 inches if there is a handrail on both sides.
- Minimum headroom height is 6 feet 8 inches above the stairs.
- The maximum allowable riser height is 7¾ inches, and differences between any two risers in a stairway may not exceed ⅜ inch.
- A minimum tread depth of 10 inches is required with differences between any two treads no more than ⅜ inch. Winders must meet the minimum depth requirement at a point 12 inches from the narrow side. The minimum tread depth of winders at the narrow side is 6 inches.
- Nosing is required for treads having less than 11 inches of depth. Nosing must project a minimum of ¾ inch but no more than 1¼ inches. Variations between treads may not exceed ⅜ inch.
- Where open risers are used, they must be designed so a 4-inch sphere cannot pass through. When the total rise does not exceed 30 inches, opening size is not limited.
- There must be a landing at both the top and bottom of each flight of stairs.
- When the vertical rise of a stairway exceeds 12 feet, there must be intermittent level platforms or landings for each 12 feet of rise.

- Landing width must be a minimum of the width of the stairway and no less than 36 inches in the direction of travel.
- When more than three risers are present, a handrail must be present on at least one side.
- Handrail height must be between 34 and 38 inches from the treads and must be continuous except where connected by a newel post at a turn or at the bottom, where a turnout is permitted.
- When a circular handrail is used, its diameter must be between 1¼ and 2 inches. When a noncircular handrail is used, the perimeter dimension must be between 4 and 6¼ inches with a maximum diameter of 2¼ inches.
- Spiral stairs must have a minimum width of 26 inches, a tread depth of at least 7½ inches at a point 12 inches from the narrow edge, and a riser height that does not exceed 9½ inches.
- Minimum headroom for spiral stairs is 6 feet 6 inches.

RAMPS

- Maximum ramp slope is one unit of vertical rise for every eight units of horizontal dimension.
- Ramps that exceed a slope of 1 unit of vertical rise for every 12 units of horizontal run must have a handrail that meets stair handrail criteria.
- A minimum 3 × 3 feet landing must be provided at both the top and bottom of a ramp and at any change in direction.

Source: International Code Council, *International Residential Code for One- and Two-Family Dwellings 2003* (Country Club Hills, IL: International Code Council, 2003).

Local building codes may stipulate either maximum distance between baluster centers or the maximum size object that can pass between balusters. A 5-inch maximum size object is typical. This size opening should preclude the head of a child from passing through.

Types of Stairways

Stairways may be open, half-open, or closed. Closed stairways have walls on each side. Such stairways do not have balustrades, although a handrail may be attached directly to the wall. Half-open stairways are exposed on one side for part of their length. Generally, this is a bottom portion of the stairway. Open stairways either have a wall for support on only one side or are open on both sides. Open stairways are the most decorative, giving prominence to the stairway itself.

Straight Run Stairs

Stairway design is often dictated by the space allotted in the home, although appearance may be considered first. **Straight run stairways** have no change in direction but may include one or more platforms. They are the most easily constructed stairways but require a long floor space. It is easier to move furniture up or down a straight stairway than one that changes direction. Figure 12.10 illustrates the types of stairways.

L-shaped stairways, which make a 90-degree turn, are used where length is a problem. If the turn is near the top or the bottom, the stairway may be called a long L or dog-legged stairs. If there is a 90-degree

Figure 12.10 Types of stairs.

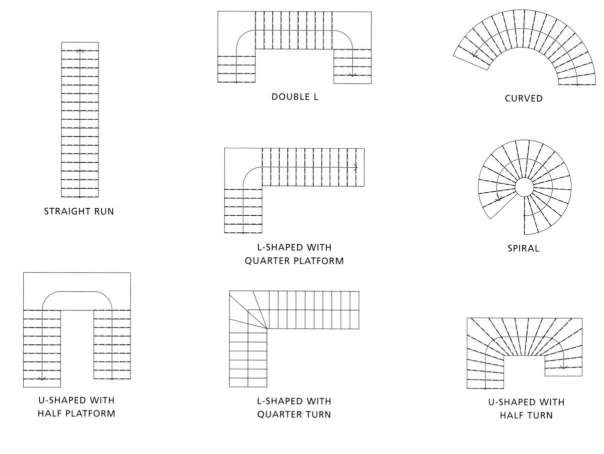

STRAIGHT RUN

DOUBLE L

CURVED

L-SHAPED WITH QUARTER PLATFORM

SPIRAL

U-SHAPED WITH HALF PLATFORM

L-SHAPED WITH QUARTER TURN

U-SHAPED WITH HALF TURN

turn near the top and another near the bottom, the stairway is a double L.

U-shaped stairways are used where space is limited in both length and width. The stairs turn back on themselves so that the first and last flights face in opposite directions. A narrow U stairway has one level platform at the change in direction, while a wide U has two platforms with a few stairs between. In addition to conserving space, U-shaped stairways add to privacy because the top and bottom of the stairs can be concealed from each other.

Cleat stairs are used where beauty is not important, as in basements and attics, but only when local building codes allow them. They are built much like angled ladders and have no risers. Local codes may require that the open riser spaces meet the IRC 4 inch maximum. The treads are supported by **cleats**, or small wood pieces, nailed to the inside of the stringers. Cleat stairways are often more steep than other stairways and may have narrower treads. This can make cleat stairways more difficult and dangerous to traverse.

Disappearing stairs are used where space is at a premium and where the stairway is infrequently used. When not in use, these stairs fold up to ceiling level, where they are concealed by a panel. Access to attic space is often provided with disappearing stairs.

Curved Stairs

In addition to platforms, **winders** can be used to change the direction of stairs. Winders are treads that are angled, with the outer edge wider than the inner corner. The IRC stipulates that the tread depth at the narrowest part of a winder be a minimum of 6 inches. Because the tread depth is often very narrow on the inner side, winders are hazardous. They do, however, permit a change of direction in a small space. Winders may make it difficult to carry furniture and equipment from one level to another.

Tread depth stipulations in building codes affect curved stairs as well as straight stairs. When stairs have winders, the tread depth is measured at a point 12 inches from the inside edge. For example, if the staircase is 36 inches wide, the tread depth is measured at a point 12 inches in from the inside edge of the free space. Curved stairs include spiral, angel, circular, and elliptical.

Spiral stairways require little floor space and may be a focal point because of their unusual design. Spiral stairs are not supported by stringers but rather by a center post or column that usually makes the stairway entirely open. Spiral stairs are often made of metal and come in kits for easy assembly. Most do not have risers. All of the steps are winders and are narrow at the interior corner, making spiral stairs hazardous and difficult to climb or descend. In addition, it may be impossible to move furniture up and down spiral stairways. The IRC stipulates that the minimum width of spiral stairs be 26 inches, with a minimum tread depth of 7 ½ inches at a point 12 inches from the inside edge. The riser height may not exceed 9 ½ inches. Local building codes may stipulate the maximum floor area served by a spiral staircase. Usually, when the floor area served is greater than 400 square feet, an alternative egress must be provided. **Angel stairs** are similar to spiral stairs except there is no center post. See Figure 12.11.

Circular and elliptical stairways are similar to spiral stairways but use more space. Although winders are used throughout the stairway, they are usually wider than treads on spiral stairs, presenting little difficulty to the user. Circular and elliptical stairways are often used as a striking architectural feature and are usually completely open. **Horseshoe stairs** are double curved stairs going in opposite directions and ending at the same platform.

Safe Stairway Design

Before calculating stair dimensions, it is necessary to determine the **total rise**, or the vertical distance between finished floor levels. For estimation purposes, when 12-inch floor joists are used, 12 inches can be added to wall height. While it may be possible

Figure 12.11 These angel stairs spiral tightly about a center but there is no apparent support.

Head height is the vertical distance from the nosing to any obstruction overhead. The IRC requires a minimum head height of 6 feet 8 inches for stairways, although stairs with a head height of 7 feet 0 inches are preferred. This same code allows head height for spiral stairways to be 6 feet 6 inches. In most cases, sufficient head height is allowed when stairways from the first to the second floor are located over stairways from the basement to the first floor. This configuration saves space in the home but may not always be feasible or desirable.

The relationship of the height of the risers and the depth of the treads is important. Risers that are too short or too tall are uncomfortable to traverse, and either may present a safety hazard. Tread depth should be sufficient to support the length of the entire foot. In addition to following these guidelines, architects and others who design stairways make use of formulas to determine proper ratios between riser height and tread depth. While the maximum riser height allowed by the IRC is 7¾ inches, most typically, riser height is between 6½ and 7½ inches. A safety hazard presents itself when all risers in a flight of stairs are not the same height. The IRC allows a maximum riser height variation of ⅜ inch; variation between the tread depths of two steps of ⅜ inch; and the variation between nosing projections of ⅜ inch.

Stairway width is calculated as the free step area between railings. The IRC stipulates that stairways in the main portion of the house be a minimum of 36 inches wide, although 42 or 48 inches allow greater ease in passing on the stairs and in carrying furniture up and down. If the stairway is closed, has winders, or turns, a minimum of 42 inches is recommended. Stairs to a basement or attic can be steeper and more narrow than the principal stairs. See Box 12.2 for calculating staircases.

To further enhance the safety of stairways, mini lights can be installed beneath the nosing to ensure that the edge of the tread is highly visible. Another alternative for lighting treads is to provide wall panel lights near the tread level. Lighting the stairs in this

to estimate the total rise for stairways for drawings, it is imperative that actual measurements be taken on the site from finished floor to finished floor before the stair calculations are finalized. It is possible to measure from subfloor to subfloor if the actual materials for finish flooring are known and their thickness measured. The measurement should then be corrected for finish flooring materials.

When designing stairways for people of short stature or limited mobility, it may be desirable to adjust the riser height downward. In any case, the riser height must meet local code requirements.

Box 12.2 Calculating Stairs

Before doing final calculating stairs for a home, get the actual measurement from finished floor to finished floor. During early planning stages, estimates can help ensure there is sufficient space for the stairs. The following steps are used to calculate stairs whether using actual measurements or estimates. The example uses a measurement of 120 inches from finished floor to finished floor.

1. Find the total rise from finished floor to finished floor levels in inches.   120"
2. Divide total rise by 7 to obtain the number of risers required. Ignore any remaining fractions.   120 / 7 = 17
3. Divide the total rise by the number of risers needed. This gives you the exact height of each riser.   120 / 17 = 7.0588
4. Divide the decimal fraction by 0.0625 (1/16") to convert the decimal to the nearest 16th.   0.0588 / 0.0625 = 1
5. Add the number of 16ths from step 4 to the whole number.   7 + 1/16
6. Subtract 1 from the total number of risers to obtain the number of treads needed. For each intermediate platform, subtract one more.   17 – 1 = 16
    (If the stairway in the example had a platform within its run, 2 would have been subtracted from the number of risers.)
7. Multiply the number of treads needed by the depth of each tread (10" is the minimum). This is the total run.   10" × 16 = 160"
8. Convert inches to feet.   160 / 12 = 13' 4"

CALCULATING CURVED STAIRS

Follow steps 1 through 7 above. Continue as follows.

8. Determine the portion of a circle to be used for the stairs. This is a design decision. The example uses 1/2 of a circle.
9. Multiply the portion of a circle used by 360 degrees.   0.5 × 360 = 180
10. Divide the total run from Step 7 by the portion of a circle to be used. The result is the perimeter of the circle on which the tread depth must be measured. (The IRC requires that tread depth be a minimum of 10 inches at a point 12 inches in from the inside corner of the tread.)   160 / 0.5 = 320
11. Divide the perimeter of the tread depth circle by *pi* (3.14). The result is the diameter of the tread depth circle.   320 / 3.14 = 101.91
12. Round the diameter of the tread depth circle up (not down) to the next inch.   101.91 = 102
13. Divide the diameter of the tread depth circle by 2 to get the radius.   102 / 2 = 51
14. Subtract 12 inches from the radius of the tread depth circle. The result is the radius of the circle on the inner edge of the treads.   51 – 12 = 39
15. Determine the desired width of the treads. The minimum width is 36 inches. This is a design decision. The example uses 42 inches.
16. Add the width of the treads to the radius of the circle on the inner edge of the treads. The result is the radius of the circle at the outer edge of the treads.   42 + 39 = 81
17. Divide the number of degrees of a circle used by the number of treads to determine the number of degrees in the angle of each tread.   180° / 16 = 11.25°

manner will be especially helpful for individuals with limited visual acuity.

Stairs Leading to Basements

Basements are typically part of the service zone, although finishing a basement to provide additional living area is relatively inexpensive. Regardless of use, a separate entry into the basement can ease traffic on stairways, facilitate the moving of lawn equipment, and provide access for the installation and repair of mechanical equipment. Stairways leading to basements should be located to provide the shortest route possible from the living areas most closely associated with basement functions. If the basement, for example, is unfinished, stairs leading from the kitchen, garage, or family entry provide access to freezers and extra storage. If the laundry is located in the basement, the stairway should lead to bedroom areas, where most of the laundry is generated. If the basement includes finished living space used for entertaining, a more appropriate location for the stairway would be from the social zone on the main living level.

Many stairways leading to basements are narrow and steep to conserve space; however, a 36-inch-wide stairway is recommended if there is no exterior entry to the basement and it will be necessary to carry equipment and furniture down the stairs, or when there is finished living area located there. The IRC requires this minimum width for all stairways, although local building codes may require it only for main staircases.

Heating ducts and plumbing pipes are often run beneath the ceiling in basements, decreasing the height of the space. When planning stairways to basements in new homes, it is necessary to ensure that HVAC and plumbing contractors know to route mechanical systems in locations that will not interfere with headroom for stairways, including at the bottom of the stairs.

Elevators

Elisha Graves Otis was the inventor of the first safety elevator in 1852. It was the elevator and the braking system devised by Otis that made skyscrapers feasible. Modern elevators are direct descendants of these nineteenth-century models.

Residential elevators have become more popular in recent years. The type of elevator required depends on the number of stops required, whether entry and exit will be from the same side, and travel height. Most elevators require a shaft and, in order that the elevator floor can be level with the first floor, there must be a pit beneath it. Residential elevators usually have a vertical travel limit of about 23 feet and a weight limit up to 1000 pounds, depending on the model. Some models can have as many as 4 stops. The platform size ranges from 3 × 4 to 3 × 5 feet. A shaft, or **hoistway**, that has smooth interior surfaces is required. Guide rails direct the **cab** or moving portion of the elevator through the hoistway. A motor is required for lifting the device, and overhead clearances must comply with the manufacturer's specifications. An elevator uses 240-volt electrical service.

Stair lifts are a type of elevator but are installed on the stairway itself. The maximum capacity is 500 pounds, depending on the model selected. An electronically operated seat is attached to the treads of the stairs, which must be sufficiently stable and strong to support the weight. Most models have a maximum vertical travel distance of about 17 feet 6 inches. Because the track projects into the free stairway width, the effective width is decreased. The folded seat projects about 13 inches, while the track projects about 9 inches. Stair lifts can turn corners, so they can be installed on any type of stairway—there are even models designed for curved stairs. A stair wheelchair lift has a platform rather than a seat. There must be a minimum 3 foot by 6 foot area at the bottom of the stairs on which the platform can rest when the unit is not in use. Because they are mounted to the wall, a load-bearing wall is required. Additionally, wheelchair platform lifts only operate on straight run stairs. Lifts usually operate on 120-volt power.

A **dumbwaiter** is a small elevator designed to move materials and objects—not people—vertically. Clothing, laundry, groceries, and firewood are commonly moved from one story to another, and the dumbwaiter is ideal for this purpose. The weight capacity ranges from 50 to 500 pounds, depending on the model. Dumbwaiters may be operable from more than one side. Most have a maximum travel distance of about 35 feet. Like elevators, dumbwaiters require an enclosed shaft, a motor, and rails on which the cab rides. Dumbwaiters require 240-volt service.

Ramps

Replacing stairs with ramps, or providing ramps in addition to stairs, increases accessibility for individuals with limited mobility, including those in wheelchairs. Ramps at curbs and building entrances are provided in many urban areas. **Universal designed** or accessible homes should have entrances at grade level or ramps for ease of access. The IRC requires that ramps have a maximum of 1 foot of rise for every 8 feet of length. However, 1 foot of rise for each 12 feet of length is better.

The IRC requires a handrail on at least one side when the rise of the ramp exceeds 1 in 12. Handrails on one or both sides permit users to pull themselves along. Handrails must meet stairway handrail criteria. An additional middle rail may be located between 18

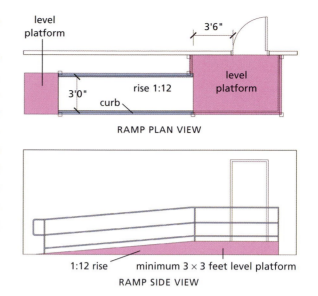

RAMP PLAN VIEW

1:12 rise   minimum 3 × 3 feet level platform
RAMP SIDE VIEW

Figure 12.12 Views of a ramp.

and 20 inches above the ramp. Handrails should extend 12 to 18 inches beyond the end of the incline at the bottom. The maximum length of the incline on a ramp is 30 feet; longer ramps require an intermediate-level platform. A level platform should extend a minimum of 42 inches on the latch side of any door. See Figure 12.12 for two views of a ramp.

A raised edge along at least one side of the ramp helps to prevent accidents due to running over the edge and provides a convenient surface against which to brake when traveling down slope. Covered ramps permit access during inclement weather and prevent ice and snow from collecting.

Designing
Public
Areas

Chapter 13

Housing serves as a background

for social interaction, affects relationships, and is, in turn, influenced by those relationships. Socialization may be among family members or with individuals outside the family group. Family members who participate in social activities at home may require large or small, formal or informal, indoor or outdoor spaces, depending on the type of entertaining most prevalent in their social groups. Extra bedrooms, dining rooms, formal living areas, game rooms, and media rooms may be necessary for entertaining. Social areas are not always for entertaining, however. It is frequently necessary to design the home office so that clients can enter, conduct business, and leave without disturbing family activities or entering family living areas.

People who desire socialization with family members may seek housing that encourages family members to spend time together. The Chinese *kang* is a

Figure 13.1 Social relationships outside the home are affected by site or community plans. Houses lined up in rows do not encourage social interaction among neighbors. Psychologists have found that houses arranged on cul-de-sacs are more amenable to social interaction. Much of that interaction is with neighbors across the street. (Source: © Royalty-Free/Corbis)

large raised platform covered with straw mats that sometimes occupies a third of the floor area. In the winter, ducts going through the kang receive heat from a small stove in an adjacent area, making the kang the warmest place in the house. Family members sit on the kang to eat, they sleep together on the kang, and elderly family members often stay on the kang all day, making it possible to participate in family activities. In Japan, family members gather around the hibachi for warmth; both the hibachi and the people are covered by a common quilt. There, the family socializes during the evening hours until it is time to unroll sleeping mats side by side on the floor. See Figure 13.1.

Socialization with other individuals has been so important to people throughout history that specific areas have been designed for entertaining. During the Baroque period, the residences of the wealthy pro-

vided a social stage where individuals could see and be seen, engage in the fine art of conversation, and indulge in cultural enrichment through music, dance, and theater. Rooms were necessarily large to accommodate vast assemblages. In the following Rococo period, rooms became smaller, more numerous, and increasingly specialized, because entertainment was more intimate. In the pre-Civil War American South, plantation houses were large partly in order to accommodate guests. Because land holdings were large, the distances between plantations were necessarily long, making it necessary to spend the night or even several days when attending a gala event such as a ball.

Homes in ancient Mediterranean countries were arranged around a **courtyard** that served as the major living area. This practice was also typical of most ancient cultures in semitropical and tropical areas such as India, Egypt, and Colombia. Other cultures in warm climates had no indoor living room but used shelters only for sleeping, eating, and food preparation. This practice continues in many areas of the world today. Living rooms evolved from these open spaces used by families. In the Middle Ages, upper rooms in watchtowers were converted to family living areas. These rooms were generally multifunctional, serving as living room, dining room, and sometimes kitchen and bedroom. In colonial America, a main "great room" sheltered all living activities because the hearth was located there.

As the new country became well established, the formality of lifestyles increased. The development of the Franklin stove and later heating systems made rooms more comfortable. This gave rise to further divisions of the house into space set aside for specific purposes. The parlor became the room where guests were entertained. A separate living room was established for family use. Less affluent families used the kitchen for family activities. As lifestyles decreased in formality, the parlor disappeared. Once again, the living room functioned for both family activities and entertainment of guests.

Indoors, spaces composing the social zone vary but usually include living rooms, dining areas, dens, and recreation rooms. Social spaces are frequently larger than others, to accommodate group activities. Families use these rooms on a daily basis. Because the social zone is also where guests are received, it is here that others form many of their impressions of the occupants.

Outdoor spaces designed for entertainment may also be included in the social zone. **Patios**, picnic areas, play yards, and swimming pools should be located adjacent to indoor social zones if they are to be used for this purpose. Outside the home—especially in the front—the social zone becomes more public. It includes everything seen by the people who pass by.

Although a private space, a bathroom for use by guests should be located in or near the social zone. It should not be necessary for guests to go through private or service areas to access a bathroom.

A swimming pool or other body of water may be designed for public or private use, but if it is within public view—sometimes from any side of the structure—codes may require that it be fenced to prevent accidents that may be caused when unauthorized individuals trespass.

Living Areas

In the mid-twentieth century, leisure time and affluence increased, and entertainment became more important. A family room or den began to appear in many homes, and the living room again became more formal. Today, homes may have one or more living areas: living rooms, family rooms, **hearth rooms**, or **great rooms**. In fact, in 2001, 28.7 percent of American homes had multiple living areas. Depending on the lifestyle of the occupants, other rooms may become living areas as well—a dining room, den, recreation room, or even a porch or patio. The living area size depends on the activities that take place there. If the living room serves for receiving guests and for family activities, it is generally larger than when there are other rooms with similar functions. Even if other spaces are used, the functions of a living area are varied and often vague. Therefore, living areas should be flexible spaces.

Living Rooms

Most of the functions of the living room have been moved to other living areas. In homes with two or more living areas, the living room is a more formal area—a place for conversation or possibly music. See Figure 13.2. Formal living rooms receive as little use as formal dining areas in some homes. In homes with a single living area, the room must accommodate both family and guests. An NAHB survey found that 46 percent of respondents would opt for a larger family room and omit the living room

The major criterion used to determine the living

Figure 13.2 When there are multiple living areas, the living room may be the most formal and may be used only occasionally.

room size is the number of bedrooms in the home. The recommended size increases with the number of bedrooms since it is assumed that a greater number of people will be occupying the home and using the living room. With changing household styles, this method of determining the living area size may no longer be appropriate.

The living room should be near the entry and directly connected with it, but it should not serve as a circulation area for reaching other areas of the home. If the entry opens into the living room, a traffic path that does not run through the conversation areas should be defined. If there is a pleasant view on one side of the building, the living room should be located so that it looks out onto that vista.

There should be at least one conversational grouping where seated individuals will be 8 to 10 feet from one another—approximately 10 to 14 feet in diam-

▦ The sunken conversation pit does not allow changes in furniture arrangement, nor does it offer extra space for enlarging the conversation area when necessary.

eter. At this distance, people can not only hear well but also distinguish facial expressions and body language. If the room is large enough, an additional grouping can be arranged. Usually, the conversation area is combined with a focal point such as a fireplace or piano. There should not be a traffic pattern that crosses between the focal point and the conversational grouping. For times when the living room is used by larger groups than normal, it should be possible to rearrange seating units so that additional people can be involved in activities. This requires movable furnishings: Built-in furniture is not as flexible nor usually as comfortable as movable pieces. See Table 13.1 for typical living area furniture sizes.

Ideally, a living room should have sufficient space for an additional area, providing an intimate setting where individuals can read, relax, or perform quiet tasks. Individuals occupying this space can participate in group activities as desired.

Because the sofa is generally the largest single piece of furniture in a living room, it should be placed first. Sofas often accommodate three people, but unless all other seats are taken, the center seat may remain unoccupied. Some individuals choose to stand or sit on the floor rather than occupy the center seat. It may be more desirable and functional to use a love seat and an extra chair rather than a sofa. Task light-

Table 13.1 Typical Living Room Furniture Sizes (in Inches)

Furniture	Height	Width	Depth or Length
Bookcase	60, 66, 72	33, 36	12
Entertainment wall	76, 80, 96	96, 106, 142	26, 28
Grandfather clock	77	18	10
Sofa (19" seat height)	36, 38	88, 95	33, 37
Sleeper chair	30	40	33
Loveseat	36	62	33
Chair	38	36	33
Ottoman	18	32	26
Recliner		31	31
Cocktail table	20	52	30
End table	25	28	24

ing should be provided beside each seating unit including the sofa for reading, sewing, or other activities. When the light is adjustable, it allows for changing the mood of the room.

Furniture lined up against a wall is not conducive to conversation. More conversation takes place between individuals at right angles to one another than those in any other position, followed by those across from one another. People sitting next to each other tend to converse the least. Any furniture arrangement should have one or more ways to enter the grouping through a minimal 32-inch opening, although a larger opening is needed for accessibility. There should also be 18 to 30 inches in front of each seating unit for access. In a typical living room, the coffee table is placed in front of a long sofa, making access to the center seat difficult. A minimum of 12 to 15 inches between the sofa and the coffee table or other obstruction will provide space for a seated individual's legs and feet but does not provide good access. Using end tables in lieu of a coffee table will free up space.

Family Rooms

The family room is an American innovation developed since World War II. A family room may serve as a second living area that is more flexible and less formal than a living room. A number of terms are used to describe the family room—recreation room, multipurpose room, playroom, hearth room (if there is a fireplace), or great room.

The family room can be designed for both active and passive leisure activities, ranging from table tennis and electronic games to watching television or listening to music. Generally, the family room is both visually and acoustically isolated from the living room. Family rooms allow social interaction with family members and close friends yet privacy from less intimate guests. This privacy eliminates the need for putting partly finished craft and hobby projects away and hiding toys and games from view. See Figure 13.3.

When the family entertaining style is casual, the family room may be the only living area. If it is located near a separate living room, the family room can become overflow space when needed for entertaining. Family room size depends on the activities expected to take place there. Sufficient space should be allowed around equipment for active participation. Playing Ping-Pong, for example, requires more space around the table than playing board games.

The family room may be located adjacent to or near the kitchen for ease of access. The advantage of this location is that family members can communicate easily even when one or more is preparing a meal. When a living area connects to and is open to the kitchen, that entire area is called a great room. The area may also flow to exterior family activity areas. The family room should have comfortable furnishings and be easy to maintain. Because of the variety of activities taking place there, the family room and its furnishings should be flexible. For example, if a convertible sofa is used, the family room can even serve as a guest bedroom on occasion.

Figure 13.3 A family room or game room is a place where family members can gather to participate in activities they enjoy and to socialize not only with family members but with informal guests. (Source: Barbara Huffman)

The family room may be separated from the rest of the house in a basement or attic space. A remote location helps to isolate the noise associated with spirited activities. Additionally, there may be a larger free space in a remote location. If the kitchen is some distance from the family room, a mini-kitchen or wet bar in or adjacent to the family room will provide access to snacks and drinks. When there is a pool or outdoor area used for recreation, the family room should be located in an adjacent space.

Outdoor Living Areas

Appropriate play areas in and around the home are needed so that children will have a safe place for activities and for socialization with others. In crowded urban areas, the outdoor living area may actually be a park or greenbelt rather than a space adjacent to the

Figure 13.4 This is a typical gallery on an old plantation home of the South that provides shade and sufficiently wide space for people to relax. Shuttered doorways permit the home to be opened up to catch cooling breezes.

home. In suburban and rural areas, having a play area close to home is more feasible. For safety, the area should be fenced. Glass areas opening onto play yards will facilitate parental watchfulness. Children's play areas may include equipment such as a swing set, sandbox, or climbing apparatus.

Outdoor areas are not just for children, however. Adults use outdoor areas for private or social enjoyment as well. In 2003, 84.6 percent of American homes had an outdoor living area such as a porch, deck, balcony, or patio.[1] Courtyards also provide additional living area outdoors.

When people took the time to walk rather than jog and when a major social activity was conversation, the front porch was a favorite spot for relaxation. Neighbors stopped by to chat, and families spent evenings cooling off in the porch swing. Today, the automobile makes it unnecessary to walk by neighbors' homes and itself provides a place for socialization. The faster pace of society, the need for two incomes, television and a multiplicity of other entertainment alternatives, and climate-control systems making homes more comfortable and, therefore, more appealing all affect socialization. Consequently, the large front porch has almost disappeared from modern American homes.

Porches are raised off the ground and may be enclosed with screens, glass, railings, or short walls. The IRC requires that any area raised off the ground 30 inches or more have a wall or railing to prevent accidental falls. The porch forms an entrance to the building and may be extended from the structure or recessed into it. A porch may also be called a stoop. A roof provides protection from the elements for individuals, and it also minimizes the amount of snow and ice that collect, making access safer. The roof also shades the walls of the house, cooling the air several degrees before it reaches the structure. Twenty-six percent of the individuals responding to an NAHB survey indicated that a front porch was essential.

A **gallery** runs along one or more sides of a structure and is also roofed. See Figure 13.4. In some areas of the country, a gallery is called a **veranda**, in others, a **loggia**. The roof is often supported by columns or posts, forming a colonnade. Galleries are very common in warm-climate areas and were used on colonial French and Spanish[2] homes. Galleries may have multiple stories with a second level above the first.

An unroofed porch is a **deck**. Decks may, however, have some type of structural shading over them—narrowly spaced edge-laid boards, a lattice, or a framework that supports vegetation. Deck railings are typically open.

Balconies are usually on upper stories; first-story balconies are rare. A balcony projects from the structure and has a railing or short wall for safety. A balcony may have a protective covering such as a roof or an extension of the house above but it is not necessary.

A courtyard is an enclosed yard at grade level that has either a wall partially surrounding it and at least one side adjacent to the structure or that has buildings on more than one side. Courtyards are frequently found in warm climates where they are protected by the walls of the home. Family and friends can gather outdoors in privacy. Originally, a patio was a courtyard, but contemporary usage includes an area surrounded by short walls or a simple grade-level surface of a material other than that surrounding it.

Outdoor living areas may be located in public view, located in a more private setting but used for social activities, or located in private areas and used for private activities. Their location and access to them from the interior of the home should coincide with their uses. A back deck used for entertaining should have a door leading from a social area in the home. A private deck off a master bedroom should be accessed through that room and be screened from the remainder of the yard to ensure privacy.

Outdoor living areas can extend indoor space, especially when the living area is well landscaped and a large quantity of glass is used in the walls facing them. The size of the living area depends on the activities that will take place. Some individuals may desire a cooking appliance such as a smoker, barbeque pit,

or grill. If food is to be consumed in the outdoor area, a mini refrigerator and a seating area would make it more usable. Sufficient space is needed at the cooking surface for one or more people to work. A minimum area 30 inches deep, preferably 42 or 48 inches, and the width of the cooking surface plus any work surfaces on either side should be free of traffic. Bars or tables should have the same clearances as for dining room tables. When the outdoor living area is used for conversation, the criteria for designing indoor conversation areas should be followed.

Dining Areas

Eating satisfies a basic physiological need, but how and where that need is fulfilled varies according to the culture and historic era. Historically, people with wealth and status have established dining customs that emphasized the individual's status. In ancient Greece and Rome, guests were seated in order of their importance—a practice that continues in formal settings. In medieval England, the table for the host and hostess, their family, and honored guests was placed on a raised dais—a subtle indication of elevated social status. The host and hostess were served first and were the first to taste the food. This assured guests that they were not to be poisoned. A saltbox was placed at the center of each table. Guests seated "below the salt" were considered inferior.

In colonial America, the kitchen, dining room, and living room were combined in a single room where the hearth was located. In fact, with few exceptions, dining was one of the last activities to be assigned a separate room. By the Victorian era, the dining room had become the family social center, and servants prepared and served meals. By the end of the nineteenth century, the dining room was often the largest room in the house. Because it was heated for meals and therefore more comfortable than other rooms in the home, the family stayed after meals to sew, read, or play.

Figure 13.5 (TOP) An eating area in the kitchen encourages socialization while food is being prepared and provides an informal gathering place for family and friends.
Figure 13.6 (BOTTOM) The formal dining room is an ideal place to entertain guests; the ambience of the room makes it inviting for extended dinner conversations.

With the decline in domestic help in the 1920s, meal service was simplified, and the size of the dining room decreased. As the living room developed into an informal living area, the dining room became more formal. By 1960, most family meals were served in the kitchen. See Figure 13.5. The infrequent use of dining rooms and increasing building costs led to the disappearance of dining rooms in many homes.

One of the reasons for the demise of the formal dining room in low- and mid-priced housing is its cost per use. The lives of Americans have become increasingly informal, families and individuals are eating out more often, and busy schedules have precluded the family dinner in many homes. Many families rarely eat a relaxed meal together and, when they do, it is often informal. If the cost for a 12-by-14-foot room is $120 per square foot, the room, without furnishings, costs $20,160. The average mortgage rarely exceeds 6 years. Therefore, if a dining room is used only for formal occasions and holidays, it may be used as few as 4 times a year—24 times during the 6 years a family occupies the home, making the room itself cost $840 per use. Bedrooms, on the other hand, may be used daily—351 days per year when a two-week vacation is considered. Over 6 years, the same 12 by 14 foot room then costs $9.57 per use. Obviously, when the home is sold, much of the construction cost will be recouped; however, monthly mortgage payments reflect interest as well as principal. Whether to save the cost of the extra room needed for dining or to use the same amount of space more frequently is a choice based on values.

Today's homes may have two or three eating areas, some of which are more formal than others. In 2001, slightly more than 47 percent of American homes had a separate dining room. When a separate dining room is present, it is generally reserved for special occasions or formal entertaining, with other areas used for most family meals. See Figure 13.6. In that case, the dining room may be infrequently used unless the family entertains often. Some families, however, prefer to use the dining room for all their evening meals. Less

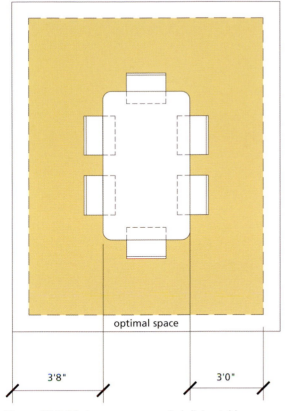

optimal space

3'8"   3'0"

Figure 13.7 Minimum recommended dining table space

formal eating areas may then be used for breakfasts, lunches, and snacks. Eating areas should be near the kitchen to decrease the number of steps required for moving food, dishes, and utensils. Separate dining rooms should be located near the living area used by guests and should be accessible from the living area without going through service or private areas. The dining area can be an extension of the living room or the kitchen. When combined with the living area, it may be possible to entertain a larger number of guests by extending the table into the living area.

When there is a separate dining room, it should be large enough to accommodate a full-size table and chairs. Many builders include a dining room that is too small to provide space for furniture as well as space for actually using the furniture. Dining rooms separated from the kitchen are made more convenient if they include storage space for dishes and a surface on

Round or oval tables seat more people than rectangular tables of the same size.

which food can be placed for serving. A dining room table is usually centered in the room, although when additional furniture such as a sideboard, buffet, or china cabinet is included, the table itself may be off center.

If there is a chandelier in the dining room, it should be centered over the table. If the dining room is large enough in one dimension to accommodate a china cabinet or other piece of furniture, the location of that piece of furniture needs to be determined before placing the chandelier. The same care should be taken when designing a visually interesting ceiling. A tray ceiling, a dropped ceiling, or a ceiling with a strong pattern should be arranged so it, too, is centered over the table. The window should also be visually centered with the chandelier, the table, and the ceiling.

A typical dining room table is 42 × 72 inches and seats 6 people comfortably. Two feet of table length is required for each seated individual. See Figure 13.7. It is easier to arrange chairs around tables with pedestals rather than legs, especially if trying to add one more person to the table than it is designed for. Drop leaf tables may be used in small eating areas.

The minimum distance between the edge of the table and any obstruction depends on chair size but is usually 32 inches. This may not allow sufficient space for passage behind an occupied chair without turning

While American dining rooms usually include a table approximately 28 inches high with chairs arranged around it, individuals in the Middle East and in Asia often sit on floor cushions at a low table. These furnishings are arranged in the center of a room for eating, then moved away so the room can be used for other purposes when the meal is finished. Such furnishings might be appropriate for individuals with global sensitivity or where it is desirable for rooms to serve a variety of functions.

Table 13.2 Typical Dining Room Furniture Sizes (in Inches)

Furniture	Height	Width	Depth or Length
Chair	36	18	20
China/curio	80	18	48
Buffet/hutch	85	18	48
Hutch	90	18	66
Pub set table	42	36 round	
Stool	30	17	24
Sideboard	40	18	56
Table w/20" leaf	30	46	86, 92, 106
Round	30	42, 48, 52	
Informal	30	48	30

sideways. A better distance between the table and an obstruction is 36 to 44 inches, which allows space for serving. See Table 13.2 for typical dining room furniture sizes. When a hutch, china cabinet, or buffet is desired, additional space should be allowed in the room.

When a dining room is enclosed with walls, it should be sufficiently large to enable users to extend tables to their full length and still allow space for seating. If one or more walls is open to another room or area, the table may be extended into that area when necessary for entertaining.

Many homes have no separate dining room but rather a dining area that is part of the living room, family room, or kitchen. Because eating areas in the kitchen are not separated from the food preparation area, they are the most convenient but the least formal. Large or extended kitchens provide space for a table and chairs. For even more informal dining, a portion of a kitchen counter or other surface can serve as an eating bar. Often, an eating bar forms an open divider between the kitchen and family room, providing a handy serving area for meals and snacks. Outdoor spaces may also serve as dining areas, depending on the climate and the season of the year.

Changes in floor level may preclude extending a dining room table into another area.

Regardless of the location of the dining area, there should be sufficient knee space for seating and sufficient space for passage behind occupied seating units as follows.

- At least 19 inches of clear knee space depth
- For each user, 24 inches of width that is a minimum of 15 inches deep
- A minimum of 32 inches between the edge of the counter or table and any obstruction behind it

Entertainment Areas Requiring Attention to Sound Control

There are certain areas of the home designed specifically for listening to music or for watching video projections. Typically, these areas are part of the social zone of the home and are used not only for family activities but for entertainment of guests. Before designing these spaces, it is necessary to have a basic understanding of sound and its properties. The principles used when designing spaces specifically for listening and viewing can be used in designing other spaces as well.

Sound

Sound is a response of the brain caused by sensory inputs to the inner ear. Sound travels in waves from a source: The wave shape depends on the type of source and can be spherical, cylindrical, or flat. Like waves in water, sound waves have peaks and valleys, resulting in vibrations. The distance between peaks is the wavelength. Humans respond to sounds waves from 0.67 inch to 56 feet in length.[3]

The speed of sound is affected by the density of the material through which it travels, the temperature, and the atmospheric pressure. At sea level when the temperature is 68 degrees Fahrenheit, sound travels approximately 1125 feet per second through air

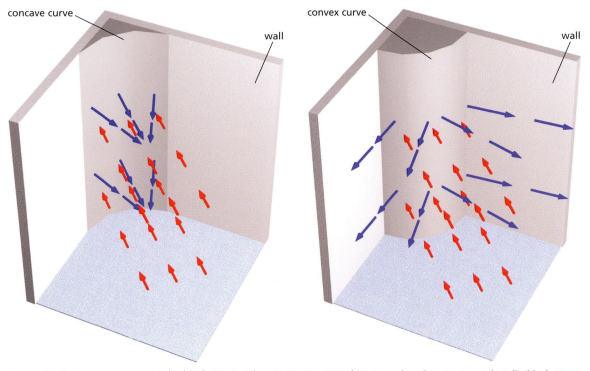

concave curve | wall

convex curve | wall

Figure 13.8 Concave curves in cylindrical corner units concentrate sound at one point. Convex curves in cylindrical corner units help to diffuse sound in all directions.

(767 miles per hour), 4862 feet per second through freshwater (3315 miles per hour), and 19,554 feet per second (13,332 miles per hour) through steel.

Characteristics of Sound

When sound waves encounter an obstacle, they may pass through, be reflected, be absorbed, or a combination of these effects. Even small openings and cracks allow sound to pass through unobstructed. Sound also flanks objects, unless the barriers are of sufficient length to prevent sound waves from wrapping around.

The amount of reflection, or return of sound waves, depends on the characteristics of the medium struck by the sound wave. Hard, smooth surfaces reflect most of the waves, mixing sounds together and affecting the intelligibility of speech. Smooth surfaces direct sound waves in a single direction, resulting in sound reaching a listener from a seemingly single

location. Rough textures diffuse sounds in a number of directions, so listeners receive sound from many locations. Soft, textured materials absorb sounds. In rooms designed for quiet speech, many absorptive materials are used.

The size of a surface affects the behavior of sound waves striking it: When the surface size is a minimum of four times the wavelength of the sound striking it, the angle of reflection equals the angle of incidence. Diffusion of sound occurs when sound strikes small surfaces compared with wavelength, or when the texture of a surface is about the same as the wavelength of the sound.

The reflection of sound also depends on the shape of the surface. Flat surfaces reflect sounds at the angle of incidence. Curved surfaces, however, do one of two things. The reflections from concave surfaces tend to focus sound energy at a single point. Convex surfaces diffuse sound. See Figure 13.8.

The reflection of the sound wave leads either to an **echo** or to **reverberation**—the bouncing or reflection of sound from a secondary source once the original sound has ceased. The effect of any sound on a human endures about $1/10$ of a second. When multiple sounds reach the ear within that time, the original sound seems prolonged. At room temperature, it requires about $1/10$ of a second for a sound to travel 56 feet and back; therefore, reverberations are common in rooms with dimensions of less than 28 feet. Reverberation depends on the dimensions and volume of the space as well as the absorption properties within the space. Reverberation is necessary for music to sound good but interferes with the intelligibility of human speech.

An echo results when a reflected sound comes more than $1/10$ of a second after the direct sound. In this case, the human ear has perceived that the first sound has died out, and the second, reflected, sound is perceived as a new sound. For this to occur, the path of the reflected sound must be a minimum of 70 feet longer than the path traveled by the first sound.

Designing Spaces for Listening

Designing spaces with the acoustic qualities conducive to listening to music is a challenge. The serious enthusiast may desire to consult an acoustical engineer, as should anyone designing a large commercial or public space or recording studio. The guidelines that follow should produce an environment of superior quality for the enjoyment of music in a residence.

The sound quality within a room depends on the room size and configuration, room surfaces, and equipment location. Some of the techniques employed for sound-conditioning a listening room can also be beneficial when designing spaces for other uses. These techniques result in lower noise levels within the space and little leakage of sound from the room. The resulting acoustics lend themselves to intimate settings where multiple simultaneous conversations can occur with little aural competition.

Room Size and Configuration

Small rooms with less than 1500 cubic feet are impractical for sound reproduction due to the response of the room itself to music. When wavelengths are close to the room dimensions, those frequencies cause the room to resonate. Cube-shaped rooms and rectangular rooms may doubly or triply reinforce these natural frequencies, but most researchers specify rectangular rooms. Specific room dimension ratios have been shown to be effective. Table 13.3 shows those ratios identified by Sepmeyer[4] as suitable for residential listening rooms. Using these ratios, the room sizes in Table 13.4 would be appropriate.

As an alternative to the rectangular room, and to provide less reinforcement of natural frequencies, room corners can be constructed at angles other than 90 degrees. Irregularly shaped rooms such as trapezoids are used for recording studios but rarely lend

Table 13.3 Ratios Identified by Sepmeyer as Suitable for Residential Listening Rooms

Alternative	Suitable Dimension Ratios for Residential Listening Rooms		
	Height	Width	Length
A	1.00	1.14	1.39
B	1.00	1.28	1.54
C	1.00	1.60	2.33

Source: L. W. Sepmeyer, *Computer Frequencies and Angular Distribution of the Normal Modes of Vibration in Recording Rooms,* Journal of the Acoustical Society of America, Vol. 37, No. 3, March 1965, 413–423.

Table 13.4 Room Sizes Appropriate for Sepmeyer's Ratios

Suitable Dimension for Residential Listening Rooms (in Inches)		
Height	Width	Length
96	109.4	133.4
96	122.9	147.8
96	153.6	223.68
108	123.12	150.12
108	138.24	166.32
108	172.8	251.64

themselves to residential application. Splaying one or two walls improves the diffusion of sound in a room. A ratio of 1:10 to 1:20 can be used to determine the minimum amount of splaying required. A wall 10 feet long, then, should be splayed outward 6 inches to 1 foot. Rather than splaying walls, the corners of the room can be chamfered. The use of convex curves is generally limited to isolated cylindrical units either positioned along walls or in corners.

Room Surfaces

It is the proportion of absorptive to reflective materials that affects the sound quality in a room most significantly. Higher-frequency sounds are readily absorbed by the soft materials used for upholstery, draperies, carpets, and acoustic panels. These absorbing materials, however, should be randomly distributed throughout the room to help diffuse sound. While symmetrically or rhythmically placed absorbent materials are aesthetically pleasing, they are not as effective for diffusing the sound so that it comes from all directions approximately equally. The disadvantage of the use of absorptive materials is that sounds are not as loud and may require further amplification.

Wall treatment should include at least one wall covered with absorptive material, such as fiberglass or soundproofing polyurethane foam panels. The absorptive wall should be opposite the speakers.

Equipment

Placing speakers on the floor improves the apparent bass output but can cause the vibration of bass frequencies to transfer to the floor. At some frequencies, this not only causes the floor itself to vibrate but for the sounds to be carried through the floor to other living spaces. Placing the speakers on carpet or on a special sound-dampening material can help tame these resonances. Elevating the speakers on a shelf or rack, mounting the speakers on a wall, or suspending them from the ceiling are possible solutions.

Locating speakers near multiple hard surfaces—floors or walls—increases the bass performance. Plac-

When speakers are placed on a shelf, the front speaker edge should not extend beyond the shelf front, there should be no free space between the top of the speaker and the shelf above, and the sides of the speaker should be flanked by solid objects such as books to prevent resonance around the speaker.

ing the speakers in a corner near the floor provides three reflective surfaces. It is common practice to position pairs of speakers symmetrically near the corner at the same ends of a room. When speakers are located away from a corner and not directly opposite one another, the bass sound is cleaner.

The optimal vertical placement of speakers is at the level of the ears of seated listeners—approximately 4 feet from the floor, with all speakers at the same height. There should be no objects between the listener's ear and the speaker to impede the sound although because the bass unit is located at the bottom of the speaker, some screening of this area does not present a significant problem. Speakers should be located equidistant from the listener—ideally forming an equilateral triangle.

At a decibel level of 0, the minimum frequency sound humans hear is about 1000 Hz. For this reason, it is usually necessary to amplify low-decibel bass sounds. The amplifier must have sufficient power to ensure full enjoyment of the music.

Home Theater Design

The function of the home theater is to provide a comfortable place for viewing that has excellent sound characteristics. The selection of equipment affects the quality of sound and video and must be carefully considered. The number of wires used to connect equipment increases dramatically as the number of pieces of equipment increases. There are technical considerations for which accommodation must be made to ensure operation of the equipment, including concealing the wires. It is not enough, however, to have excellent equipment. The room itself must be functional for the purpose, which means control of lighting, and the selection and location of seating units.

Equipment Selection

The equipment needed for a home theater includes a large-screen display, a video source, and excellent sound characteristics to ensure the impact of the theater experience. A viewing room for a television can benefit from the same features. A number of other components are necessary, including VCRs, DVD players, gaming devices, amplifiers, receivers, and other equipment as desired, but discussion of these devices is beyond the purview of this text. Each of these units should be selected with the end use in mind.

Displays

There are two types of displays: televisions and projection devices. One of the most important considerations is the size of the viewing area. The smaller the viewing area, the closer individuals must be to the screen to fully enjoy the video experience. When watching a 27-inch television, the ideal viewing distance is 6 feet 9 inches for most people.[5] The viewing distance for high-definition television is slightly less—about 6 feet 3 inches for a 30-inch screen. A 60-inch display can easily be viewed from about 15 feet. Because display equipment shows images in lines or pixels, it is possible to get too close to the screen and to see these individual units.

Television sets have a relatively small viewing area—up to 40 inches, measured diagonally. **Direct-view television** has either a curved (traditional) or flat screen surface. Flat screens are less susceptible to stray light than are curved screens. **Flat-panel televisions** (not flat screens) are thin televisions with a flat screen that use a different type of technology to project an image. Flat-panel televisions can be mounted almost anywhere without being obtrusive (unless the size of

Figure 13.9 This illustration compares the aspect ratios of the various display types.

the screen is objectionable when the set is not turned on). Some flat-panel televisions are monitors only, meaning that they must be connected to additional equipment to provide any type of image.

An important consideration for any display device is the **aspect ratio**. This is the relationship between the screen width and height. See Figure 13.9. The aspect ratio of standard television broadcasts is 1.33:1 (commonly known as 4:3). High-definition television signals are broadcast with an aspect ratio of 1.78:1. Both of these differ from movie standards. Wide-screen movies have an aspect ratio of 1.85:1, while Panavision and other super-widescreen movies have an aspect ratio of 2.35:1. Display devices should be selected based on the aspect ratio of the most-watched type of video.

Direct-view televisions are heavy and bulky, and the larger the screen, the more bulk behind the screen and the more room required for the set itself. Televisions can provide excellent picture quality, although by comparison with other display devices, the resolution is not as good. High-definition televisions have better resolution. Televisions provide good quality video when ambient light levels are relatively high. Most televisions suffer from **burn-in** (as do computer monitors) when the image is static, such as with video games. Burn-in permanently burns in an image so that even when viewing something else, the image remains. This can be very distracting.

Depending on the technology, flat-panel televisions may preclude burn-in, may or may not have good brightness characteristics, and may not have sufficient resolution for viewing high-definition images. Some flat-panel televisions have more limited viewing angles than others.

Projection systems make it possible to view images on a much larger display. Some front-projection systems have displays that measure 10 feet horizontally (not diagonally, as with televisions). Both front- and rear-projection devices are available. Rear-projection systems are the most popular. They are simple to install because all of the components are located in one unit. The unit, however, requires more floor space than a direct-view television and their bulk may be objectionable. The projector is behind the screen and the image is projected from behind the screen. For best viewing, individuals need to sit directly in front of the display. Rear-projection devices have fixed aspect ratios, so they cannot be adjusted according to the type of video being viewed.

Front-projection units provide an even larger viewing area because the projector is a separate unit from the screen. The projector can be inconspicuously mounted on the ceiling, in the rear wall, or on a mount or piece of furniture. The image is projected onto a separate screen.

Projection systems require darker spaces for quality viewing—especially front-projection devices. They may also be subject to burn-in, depending on the type selected, and they wear out relatively quickly. Some also perform poorly when projecting black tints. The technology is rapidly changing but the considerations discussed are likely to remain the same.

Screens

Projection devices need a screen on which to project images. There are two realistic choices for home theaters: retractable screens and fixed screens. Retractable screens roll into a metal cylinder when not in use and can be operated either manually or electronically. For viewing quality, it is essential that these screens be flat when used. Fixed screens can be mounted almost anywhere but usually are mounted on walls or ceilings (for viewing from a reclined position). For a dedicated home theater, the fixed screen will probably be the choice of most individuals, but the screen is difficult to conceal if the room is used for other purposes. Draperies or movable partitions can be used for this purpose, however.

There are other factors to consider when selecting a screen. A measure of the reflective characteristics of a screen is **gain**. This is essentially how much of the light projected onto the screen is reflected back for viewing. Desired gain depends on the type of system used for projection. Manufacturers' recommendations should be followed. In general, low-gain screens can be used with brighter projection systems and vice versa.

> **Designers should be careful in specifying large-screen projection devices for small rooms because viewers may not be able to sit sufficiently far from the screen to see the entire image.**

Screens also have a limited angle of view, which affects the furniture placement. When high-gain screens are used, the viewing angle is less than the angle appropriate for low-gain screens. Selecting the lowest gain screen appropriate for the equipment will provide the greatest viewing angle. The listed viewing angles in screen specifications include the entire range of view. When seated in the center of the room directly in front of the screen, the actual viewing angle is half the rated angle on either side. For example, for a screen with a rated viewing angle of 80 degrees, viewers see a high-quality picture 40 degrees left and 40 degrees right of their position. When arranging seating in the room, it is critical that all seats be within the viewing angle range of the screen. The screen selection should also consider the aspect ratio of the projection device.

Surround Sound

While the display is the focus of the room, the audio system creates the ambience. The sound system of a home theater must go beyond that of the listening room to provide the sound necessary for full enjoyment of video. Speaker type and location are even more important in the video environment because the sound must project from a specific location. Most of the action and, thus, the sound must appear to be coming directly from the front. It is possible to design a video system using only front speakers, as with a television, but if viewers want to experience a movie the way it was intended, they must actually be surrounded by sound. Surround sound enables viewers to become a part of what is happening on the screen. When a jet flies by, it can be heard approaching from one direction and leaving from another. It is not difficult to plan for side-to-side sounds. Three speakers at the front—right, center, and left—will be sufficient. Speakers should be identical, so sound progression across the room is consistent. The center speaker, however, may of necessity be smaller because it may need to be above or below the screen, while tower speakers can be used at the sides. If the speakers are

not identical, they should be from the same manufacturer and have the same performance characteristics. Front speakers are designed to localize sounds so audio appears to emanate from the action on the viewing screen.

These speakers should be at ear level if possible—about 4 feet above the floor for a seated viewer. Those near any direct-view television should be **video shielded**—designed so they do not create interference with the video display. The same type of speakers should be used near any device that has cathode ray tubes (as do most televisions).

Surround speakers are designed to diffuse sound to make the viewer a part of the fantasy on the screen. The sounds of a storm, of raindrops, or of traffic help to set the stage and immerse the individual in the action. The sounds reaching the viewer's ear from surround speakers most often is reflected sound rather than the direct sound associated with front speakers. Some direction-specific sounds come from surround speakers. Since the surround speakers are located higher on the wall and behind viewers, they can be used for sounds associated with back-to-front movement—a jet or a siren screaming by, for example.

When two surround speakers are used, they should be located on side walls; when four are used, two should be mounted on the sides and two along the back wall. The final speaker in the home theater is the subwoofer—the speaker that provides the low sounds. This speaker is fairly large and can be individually controlled. It should be located in the back of the room relative to the viewing screen. It is the subwoofer that will produce most of the vibrations that are carried through the floor to other rooms.

Housing the Wiring

Like the Smart Home, the home theater employs a number of wires, many of which terminate at a central location—in this case known as a **hub**. The hub for an audio/visual system is one of the system components (the A/V receiver). The Smart Home central wiring panel and the wires and hub for a home theater can be connected in such a way as to allow video to be carried throughout the house. The wiring for a video system will probably require telephone connections, cable or satellite connections, and, if video games are to be played online, an Internet connection.

The large number of wires required and the utilitarian appearance of system components present a design challenge. Most of the components need to be accessed only infrequently once they are set up, and in most systems, all the components will fit into one shelving unit. If there is sufficient space to house these components and the wiring in a remote location, designing the home theater space itself will be easier. Locating the equipment behind the screen, putting it in a basement or garage, or providing a separate closet will hide it from view. It will be necessary to provide access for periodic changes, maintenance, or the addition of new equipment. Locating the video equipment closet with the central wiring location for a Smart Home, or providing sufficient space for the addition of Smart Home components, would facilitate connections between the two systems.

Most of the equipment used in home theaters requires that minimum temperatures do not go below 55 degrees Fahrenheit, so climate-control systems should be designed in a way that will ensure this minimum temperature in the equipment enclosure. This is usually an issue only when the equipment is in a remote location such as a garage or basement.

Designing the Home Theater Environment

Like the listening room, the home theater (see Figure 13.10) should be well controlled acoustically to filter out stray sounds and to prevent internal sounds from being carried through the rest of the home. Depending on the location, the theater may require double wall or floor construction, mounting of finishing ma-

Figure 13.10 This home theater has tiered seats, with each individual enjoying a comfortable viewing position. Components and the wiring hub are behind the screen.

terials with clips, and sound-absorbing materials in structural components. The room in which the home theater is housed should meet the structural and design criteria of the listening room.

The amount of light in a room designed for video display is affected by the type of equipment selected. Television sets work well in bright rooms. When large-screen formats are used, in most cases it is essential to be able to darken the room. Light is most easily controlled in a room without windows, which means that an interior room or a space in a basement would be ideal. At the same time, these spaces would not be as suitable for other functions. In rooms with windows, it may be necessary to provide heavy draperies or other light-blocking window treatments. If the area used for video display is open to another area of the home, the same type of treatments can be used to eliminate any light from that source. The goal is to make the room itself disappear. To that end, muted colors or objects should be used in the rooms—anything that will absorb stray light. Light-reflecting objects will create light ghosts at the sides of the screen, as will mirrors and glass in picture frames.

Stray sounds will interfere with the sound qualities of the viewing room—a ticking clock, operating refrigerator or laundry equipment, HVAC equipment, any fans on projection devices, and aquarium pumps are examples. Sound-absorption techniques can be used to minimize external sounds but it is important to have as few noise-producing objects in the space itself as possible.

Seating is an important consideration for the viewing area as well. A variety of specialized seating, as well as more traditional pieces, is available for home theaters. Couches and chairs may have storage compartments, speakers, control panels, or motorized adjustments for comfort. High-back seats may block sounds from behind. In addition, when seating is arranged in rows, high backs may intrude on the view of those seated behind. Changes in the floor level can accommodate the latter.

The arrangement of the furniture is critical so that each viewer can enjoy the sound effects equally. Because ideally sounds should come from all sides of the viewer, seating units should not be aligned against a wall but away from walls with sufficient distance from speaker locations. Attention should be paid to the viewing angle limitations of the equipment selected when locating seating.

Home Offices

Every home functions as an office, although all of the activities may be carried out from a single drawer: paying bills, maintaining tax records, and ordering materials. There is an increasing number of people earning a living from a home office, however. In fact, the number of home offices is increasing at a rapid rate. Provisions of the Clean Air Act and California

---

⊞ When a space within the home is to be used for an occasional office, the use of typical office furniture should be avoided.

Regulation 15 are encouraging companies with high numbers of employees to allow some employees to telecommute. The regulations are designed to decrease air pollution caused by automobile emissions, but companies are finding that home offices reduce costs, improve profits, and help them to retain valued employees. Employers often find that productivity increases substantially when employees work from home offices. (Time saved from commutes is often significant and can be channeled into productive work.) Some home offices are actually designed and furnished by employers; others are underwritten by home owners themselves.

As employers are downsizing to cut costs, they often convert permanent employees to contractors or outsource jobs. Many home office workers are self-employed—often working in technical and creative fields such as software developers, writers, editors, designers, and architects. Professional fields in which home offices play a major role include psychologists, psychiatrists, attorneys, consultants, and salespeople.

Locating the Home Office

The design of the home office depends on the type of work to be done in the office, whether clients are to be expected, and required equipment. Small office spaces may be redeemed from existing spaces—under stairs, in an unused nook, or a single wall in another room. Other offices may require substantial space. An office located within a room or space in the home should be visually isolated as much as possible from the rest of the room. Doors or dividers can be closed to hide office clutter when not in use, to shield the office area from view, and to prevent disturbing non-working individuals in the room.

The serious home office should be located away from the activities and distractions of the home. A remote location provides a place where work in progress will be untouched by children, where family members understand that a work environment needs to be maintained, and where noises and smells from the home will not disturb workers. If the home office space is to be deducted on income taxes, the Internal Revenue Service requires that it be a separate space, has a door, and is furnished exclusively for working at home. Shared spaces will not qualify for this deduction. Offices need to meet the requirements for the Americans with Disabilities Act if more than five people are employed in the office. It is prudent, however, if a client base is expected to visit the office, to plan for accessibility.

If clients or guests are expected at the office, there should be a separate outside entrance with direct access to the driveway or parking area. The entrance should be easily identified and well lit at night. If the office is located within the family area, it should be located as near the entry as possible so that guests need not pass through rooms in the home.

Guests and clients will need somewhere to hang outer garments and a place to sit while waiting. The number of chairs provided for guests depends on the number of guests expected at any given time. If guests may be expected to wait, a small table may be provided on which to place reading materials and a lamp. If guests will not be waiting, no special area is required. A conference area can double as a waiting area if necessary.

It may be desirable to provide a half bath for workers or guests so that no one needs to enter the family living area during work hours. If guests will be served coffee or other refreshments, a minikitchen or wet bar is appropriate in the office space.

Designing the Home Office

Equipment needs vary according to the activities that take place in the home office. The first piece of equipment required is usually a telephone with a separate line. Planning in advance for wiring of a second or third telephone line will allow the wires to be concealed in the structure. In fact, a line dedicated for conversion, an additional line for a fax, and another for Internet access may be prudent. Planning for

future needs will make the home office more functional for a longer period of time without major remodeling.

Every office needs a primary work surface. This can be a desk or table with a minimum surface area of 24 × 42 inches. A larger area will allow space for more than a telephone and a writing surface, space for reference materials, and additional drawers for storage. See Figure 13.11. A standard office desk is 30 × 60 inches and has two pedestals with drawers. See Table 13.5 for typical office equipment sizes. Standard desktop height is 28 to 29 inches, although if there is no lowered area for a computer keyboard, the desk height should be at 28 inches maximum. A corner work surface provides more depth but little area to the sides for needed items.

Traditional front-opening file cabinets require less space than do side-opening file cabinets, although side-opening cabinets provide better access to files. Both types require space in front for opening drawers and accessing files. Designers should allow for full drawer extension plus a minimum of 24 inches of additional space for optimal use.

Figure 13.11 This home office provides a comfortable place to work and blends well with the decor of the home. Plenty of storage conceals needed items.

Table 13.5 Home Office Equipment and Furniture Sizes in Inches

Equipment	Height	Width	Depth
Computer desk	30	56	25
Copier	17	17	25
	34	27	26
	46	32	23
Credenza for computer	90	81	24
Desk	30, 31	45, 60, 72	25, 30, 36
Fax/copier	8	13	16
	13	15	16
Open file shelving	65–97	30, 36, 42, 48	12 or 15
Printer	19	27	24
	14	17	23
Shredder	22	15	13
	34	23	14
Vertical files—2 drawer	29, 42, 52, 62	15 letter, 18 legal	24
3 drawer	42		
4 drawer	52		
5 drawer	62		
Lateral file cabinet	28, 40, 53, 65	30, 36, 42	20, 25, 28

A computer requires a surface area of 30 × 44 inches, including minimal space for disks, pens, and other small items. To incorporate a printer, additional space is necessary—60 inches in length. Computer components may be spread through the room, with just the keyboard and monitor requiring surface space. Planning for computers, however, is difficult because the technology changes rapidly. The keyboard surface height should be between 24½ and 28 inches.

Desktop copy machines and fax machines should be located at work height and should have sufficient clearance for access to both the paper supply and paper product. A minimum clear area of 24 × 24 inches should be provided in front of both machines. Equipment specifications list the size of copy machines without paper trays extended. When locating copy machines, designers should allow for additional space for paper storage and feed and receiving tray extensions. The fax machine may be a separate unit, or the copier may serve both functions. Both functions may also be a part of a printer. The fewer the number of units required, the less space is needed. In 2001, the Department of Energy reported that more than 20 million U.S. households had photocopy machines and 23.6 million households had fax machines.[6] It is important to remember the cords and plugs associated with office equipment and to plan for rear clearances for use of electrical outlets.

Drawing surfaces are required by graphic designers, interior designers, architects, engineers, and others. The size of the drawing surface depends on the size of the product, but a 30 × 42 inch surface is minimal. The drawing surface may be portable (in which case a place for storage is needed) or freestanding.

In small offices, it is essential to use vertical space. Freestanding shelving units, wall-hung shelves, and bookcases can be used to store equipment and supplies. The space above and beneath work surfaces can be utilized for additional storage.

Counter surfaces at which most of the work done will be accomplished while standing, or which is designed to provide separation between public and more private areas of the office, are usually 39 to 43 inches high. Seating units for counters should have a seat height of 27 to 30 inches.

Power Supply

It may be necessary to provide additional wiring for a home office. High-tech equipment is sensitive to voltage irregularities, and power outages may cause additional problems. Surge protectors can help protect expensive equipment from power spikes but they do not provide emergency battery power. Data may be lost on a computer when power outages—even momentary ones—occur. Power companies can provide an uninterrupted power supply (UPS) device for each computer that will provide about 15 minutes of battery backup. This is sufficient time to save any data. The cost is based on the number of amperes needed by the equipment. Computers require little power; faxes and copiers that rely on high-intensity light for operation require more current. A medium-

A refrigerator or other motor-driven appliance should not be on the same electrical circuit as a computer because the startup of the motor may lead to voltage fluctuations.

sized copier may require 1500 watts of electricity during operation and may require a dedicated circuit.

Air Quality

Some office equipment uses chemicals that should be vented to the outdoors. Humidity may condense on electronic parts, so it may be necessary to provide humidity control through a dehumidifier or air conditioner. A humidifier may be necessary during dry periods, as static electricity can build up, causing data to be lost. Typical airborne debris from a home, such as smoke from a fireplace, grease from cooking, and pet dander, can negatively affect high-tech equipment, hindering its performance.

Designing
Service
Areas

Chapter 14

Most of the work in the home is done in the service zone, which includes the kitchen, laundry area, workshop, and utility areas. Outside, the service zone includes sidewalks, driveways, garages, storage facilities, and trash receptacles. Guests are not normally expected to enter the service zone, except by invitation. Service zones should be designed primarily for efficiency and practicality. See Box 14.1 for IRC code requirements for service areas. Outside service areas may be screened from view to present a better appearance. In some developments, it may be against the rules to leave a garage door open or for trash containers to be located within view of the street.

Kitchens

Much of the expense of kitchens is due to cabinetry and appliances. In homes where large commercial appliances are used, the initial cost may be even higher. Kitchen size is generally proportional to the total floor area of the home. According to the National Kitchen and Bath Association (**NKBA**), a small kitchen has 150 square feet or less, a medium kitchen 151 to 350 square feet, and a large kitchen more than 350 square feet. A kitchen may have space only for food preparation, it may have an adjacent dining area, or it may be part of a family room or great room, becoming a family living center. While some kitchens retain the traditional role of food preparation, including the canning of produce, others are rarely used for cooking. One family may use a kitchen infrequently; another may want it to be family-friendly and a center for family togetherness. See Box 14.2 for suggestions for designing kitchens for families with children. See Box 14.3 for accessibility requirements.

The kitchen should be located where there is easy access to the garage, carport, or family entrance, and it should be adjacent to all dining areas.

Basic Principles of Kitchen Design

The kitchen is considered a work area and should be designed for efficiency. The first kitchen standards were established in the 1950s as a result of a 1948 study by Mary Koll Heiner and Helen McCullough.[1] Subsequent standards were based on their results until the 1990s, even though family needs had changed significantly. Current standards published by NKBA are partially the result of research carried out in the late

---

Box 14.1 International Residential Code Requirements for Service Areas

KITCHEN

- Each dwelling unit must have a kitchen with a sink supplied with both hot and cold water.

RANGE HOOD VENT

- Unless an approved ductless vent fan is installed, the vent fan above the range must vent through the wall or the roof and terminate outdoors.

LAUNDRY

- The maximum length of a clothes dryer vent is 25 feet. For each 45-degree turn, 2 feet 6 inches is subtracted from the maximum allowable length. For each 90-degree turn, 5 feet is subtracted.
- The dryer vent must lead through the wall or roof and terminate outdoors.

GARAGES AND CARPORTS

- Any door leading from the garage into the living area must be a solid wood door or a solid- or honeycomb-core steel door with minimum thicknesses of $1\frac{3}{8}$ inches.
- Openings from a garage may not lead directly into sleeping rooms.
- The wall between the living space and the garage must have a minimum of $\frac{1}{2}$ inch of gypsum wallboard on the garage side.
- Between a garage ceiling and a living space above, there must be a minimum of $\frac{5}{8}$ inch thick Type X gypsum board.
- Garage floors must be of noncombustible materials.
- Carports must be open on at least two sides. If open on only one side, they are considered garages.

Source: International Code Council, *International Residential Code for One- and Two-Family Dwellings 2003* (Country Club Hills, IL: International Code Council, 2003).

Box 14.2 Designing Kitchens for Children

- A natural barrier, such as an island or peninsula, can help keep young children away from the cooking area while maintaining a sense of inclusion. A pass-through or viewing opening through a kitchen wall to an adjoining room serves the same purpose, allows children more room to play, and may even keep toys out of the kitchen. Folding shutters, a tambour door, or sliding doors can close off the opening when it isn't being used for supervision.
- If children are going to help with cooking, a lower counter surface or table can be included where children can sit on a low stool or chair.
- Kitchens should have locking or inaccessible storage areas for potentially harmful cleaning supplies, especially when children are present in the home. Cupboard doors and drawers should have childproof latches on them. It is a good idea, however, to provide one floor-level cupboard or drawer for plastic and wooden utensils for very young children to play with.

- Range controls should be on the top rather than in front of the cooktop or oven.
- Chest freezers should be kept locked even if they are located in a utility room, basement, or garage.
- When cooking, turn the handles of saucepans inward to guard against children pulling pans with hot contents onto themselves.
- Breakable items such as glassware and china should be stored out of reach of children or in a cupboard with childproof latches or locks.
- Raised rims on countertops prevent spilt liquids from running over the edge.
- A clock in the kitchen is a good place for children to practice telling the time. An analog clock is better than a digital clock for this purpose and numbers should be clear. Roman numerals on a clock face may confuse a child who is learning to tell time.
- If there is a telephone in the kitchen, it should be wall-mounted and the cord should be kept out of reach of small children.

1980s by the University of Minnesota.[2] These standards take into account social changes that occurred in the last part of the twentieth century.

- In many families, more than one person cooks.
- The average family has fewer children now than did a family in the mid-twentieth century.

The guidelines published by the NKBA are listed in Box 14.4. For the most part, these standards are *minimal*. See Figure 14.1 for a well-designed kitchen.

Figure 14.1 This kitchen is an inviting space for family and friends. Commercial appliances have been well integrated, the work triangle is efficient, and there is a space for informal dining.

Box 14.3 Designing Kitchens for Accessibility

Certain guidelines are designed for accessibility and may not be necessary in all kitchens. Affected criteria include the following:

- Make kitchen passageways a minimum of 4 feet wide.
- When possible, countertops and sinks should have a height of 30 inches, although up to 34 inches is allowable.
- Knee space should be included at or adjacent to major work areas including sinks, dishwashers, cooktops, ovens, and refrigerators. These knee spaces should have a minimum depth of 19 inches and a minimum width of 30 inches. At the front of the obstruction, the knee space should be at least 27 inches high, although the height may decrease progressively as the depth increases.
- Surfaces within knee spaces should be finished. In some instances, such as in a sink area, this hides the pipes, making the knee space more pleasing, but the major purpose of finishing knee spaces is for safety. Users are protected from rough or hot surfaces and working parts of appliances. In addition, the hidden units are protected from repeated impact.
- When calculating clear floor space at a work area, if the toe space is 9 inches high or greater (which allows clearance for wheelchair footrests), the depth of the toe space can be included in the dimensions.
- Clear floor space may include up to 19 inches of knee space.
- If there is a knee space at one side, a tall cabinet may be installed in a corner between work centers in the work triangle as long as the cabinet is recessed.
- Wall cabinets are rarely usable and may be omitted. When used, they should be installed no more than 15 inches above the countertop.

- Pullout shelves, lazy Susans, and drawers are the most convenient storage devices for base cabinets. All storage spaces should be located between 16 and 48 inches from the floor for accessibility.
- Front-loading dishwashers, oven doors hinged at the side, range controls located at the front, and pullout shelves in refrigerators help make kitchens more usable.
- Locating the dishwasher and oven up to 18 inches off the floor makes them more accessible.
- When accessibility is a priority and the microwave is to be used by a seated person, the microwave may be installed lower than 24 inches.
- Controls for lighting, thermostats, intercoms, and appliances should be operable with one hand, requiring minimal strength for operation. Entry and exit door handles, cabinet doors, and drawer pulls should follow the same guidelines.
- Handles and drawer pulls should require minimal strength for operation, be operable with one hand, and not require pinching, grasping, or wrist-twisting motions. C- or D-shaped handles are easier to use than knobs.
- Arranging the cooktop and sink with 12 inches of countertop between the centers makes it easier to move pots and pans between them. An extra-long hose on a spray attachment would make it possible to fill pans with water without moving them to the sink.
- Lever-operated faucets are easier to use than are faucets with handles that turn.

Box 14.4 National Kitchen and Bathroom Association Guidelines for Kitchens

1. Door/Entry

   The clear opening of a doorway should be at least 32" wide. This would require a minimum 2'-10" door.

2. Door Interference

   No entry door should interfere with the safe operation of appliances, nor should appliance doors interfere with one another.

3. Distance Between Work Centers

   In a kitchen with three work centers* the sum of the three traveled distances should total no more than 26' with no single leg of the triangle measuring less than 4' nor more than 9'.

   When the kitchen plan includes more than three primary appliance/work centers, each additional travel distance to another appliance/work center should measure no less than 4' nor more than 9'.

   No work triangle leg intersects an island/peninsula or other obstacle by more than 12".

4. Separating Work Centers

   A full-height, full-depth, tall obstacle† should not separate two primary work centers.

   A properly recessed tall corner unit will not interrupt the workflow and is acceptable.

5. Work Triangle Traffic

   No major traffic patterns should cross through the basic work triangle.

6. Work Aisle

   The width of a work aisle should be at least 42" for one cook and at least 48" for multiple cooks. Measure between the counter frontage, tall cabinets and/or appliances.

7. Walkway

   The width of a walkway should be at least 36".

8. Traffic Clearance at Seating

   In a seating area where no traffic passes behind a seated diner allow 32" of clearance from the counter/table edge to any wall or other obstruction behind the seating area.

   a. If any traffic passes behind the seated diner, allow at least 36" to edge past.

   b. If traffic passes behind the seated diner, allow at least 44" to walk past.

9. Seating Clearance

   Kitchen seating areas should incorporate at least the following clearances:

   a. 30" high tables/counters:
      Allow a 24" wide and 18" deep counter/table space for each seated diner.

   b. 36" high counters:
      Allow a 24" wide by 15" deep counter space for each seated diner and at least 15" of clear knee space.

   c. 42" high counters:
      Allow a 24" wide by 12" deep counter space for each seated diner and 12" of clear knee space.

10. Clean-up/Prep Sink Placement

    If a kitchen has only one sink, locate it adjacent to or across from the cooking surface and refrigerator.

11. Clean-up/Prep Sink Landing Area

    Include at least a 24" wide landing area‡ to one side of the sink and at least an 18" wide landing area on the other side.

    If all of the countertop at the sink is not at the same height, then plan a 24" landing

---

* A major appliance and its surrounding landing/work area form a work center. The distances between the three primary work centers (cooking surface, cleanup/prep primary sink, and refrigeration storage) form a work triangle.

† Examples of a full-height obstacle are a tall oven cabinet, tall pantry cabinet, or refrigerator.

‡ Landing area is measured as countertop frontage adjacent to a sink and/or an appliance. The countertop must be at least 16" deep and must be 28" to 45" above the finished floor to qualify.

(continued)

Box 14.4 (continued)

area on one side of the sink and 3" of countertop frontage on the other side, both at the same height as the sink.

The 24" of recommended landing area can be met by 3" of countertop frontage from the edge of the sink to the inside corner of the countertop if more than 21" of countertop frontage is available on the return.

12. Preparation/Work Area

Include a section of continuous countertop at least 36" wide and 24" deep immediately next to a sink for a primary preparation/work area.

13. Dishwasher Placement

Locate nearest edge of the primary dishwasher within 36" of the nearest edge of a clean-up/prep sink.

Provide at least 21"* of standing space between the edge of the dishwasher and countertop frontage, appliances and/or cabinets, which are placed at a right angle to the dishwasher.

14. Waste Receptacles

Include at least two waste receptacles. Locate one near each of the clean-up/prep sink(s) and a second for recycling either in the kitchen or nearby.

15. Auxiliary Sink

At least 3" countertop frontage should be provided on one side of the auxiliary sink, and 18" of countertop frontage on the other side, both at the same height as the sink.

16. Refrigerator Landing Area

Include at least

a. 15" of landing area on the handle side of the refrigerator, or

b. 15" of landing area on either side of a side-by-side refrigerator, or

c. 15" of landing area which is no more than 48" across from the front of the refrigerator or,

d. 15" of landing area above or adjacent to any under counter-style refrigeration appliance.

17. Cooking Surface Landing Area

Include a minimum of 12" of landing area on one side of a cooking surface and 15" on the other side.

If the cooking surface is at a different countertop height than the rest of the kitchen then the 12" and 15" landing areas must be at the same height as the cooking surface.

For safety reasons, in an island or peninsula situation, the countertop should also extend a minimum of 9" behind the cooking surface if the counter height is the same as the surface-cooking appliance.

For an enclosed configuration, a reduction of clearances shall be in accordance with the appliance manufacturers' instructions or per local codes. (This may not provide adequate landing area.)

18. Cooking Surface Clearance

Allow 24" of clearance between the cooking surface and a protected noncombustible surface above it.

19. Cooking Surface Ventilation

Provide a correctly sized, ducted ventilation system for all cooking surface appliances. The recommended minimum is 150 CFM.

20. Cooking Surface Safety

a. Do not locate the cooking surface under an operable window.

b. Window treatments above the cooking surface should not use flammable materials.

---

* In a diagonal installation, the 21" is measured from the center of the sink to the edge of the dishwasher door in an open position.

Box 14.4 (continued)

c. A fire extinguisher should be located near the exit of the kitchen away from cooking equipment.

21. Microwave Oven Placement

Locate the microwave oven after considering the user's height and abilities. The ideal location for the bottom of the microwave is 3" below the principle user's shoulder but no more than 54" from the floor.

If the microwave oven is placed below the countertop the oven bottom must be at least 15" off the finished floor.

22. Microwave Landing Area

Provide at least a 15" landing area above, below or adjacent to the handle side of a microwave oven.

23. Oven Landing Area

Include at least a 15" landing area next to or above the oven.

At least a 15" landing area that is not more than 48" across from the oven is acceptable if the appliance does not open into a walkway.

24. Combining Landing Areas

If two landing areas are adjacent to one another, determine the new minimum for the two adjoining spaces by taking the longer of the two landing area requirements and adding 12".

25. Countertop Space

A total of 158" of countertop frontage, 24" deep, with at least 15" of clearance above, is needed to accommodate all uses, including landing area, preparation/work area, and storage.

Built-in appliance garages extending to the countertop can be counted toward the total countertop frontage recommendation, but they may interfere with the landing areas.

26. Countertop Edges

Specify clipped or round corners rather than sharp edges on all counters.

27. Storage

The total shelf/drawer frontage* is

a. 1400" for a small kitchen (less than 150 square feet);

b. 1700" for a medium kitchen (151 to 350 square feet); and

c. 2000" for a large kitchen (greater than 350 square feet).

	Small	Medium	Large
Wall	300"	360"	360"
Base	520"	615"	660"
Drawer	360"	400"	525"
Pantry	180"	230"	310"
Misc.	40"	95"	145"

The totals for wall, base, drawer, and pantry shelf/drawer frontage can be adjusted upward or downward as long as the recommended total stays the same.

Do not apply more than the recommended amount of storage in the miscellaneous category to meet the total frontage recommendation.

Storage areas that are more than 84" above the floor must be counted in the miscellaneous category.

28. Storage at Clean-up/Prep Sink

Of the total recommended wall, base, drawer, and pantry shelf/drawer frontage, the following should be located within 72"

* Shelf and drawer frontage is determined by multiplying the cabinet size by the number and depth of the shelf or drawer in the cabinet, using the following formula:

Cabinet width in inches × number of shelf/drawers × cabinet depth in feet (or fraction thereof) = Shelf/Drawer Frontage

Storage/organizing items can enhance the functional capacity of wall, base, drawer, and pantry storage and should be selected to meet user needs.

(continued)

Box 14.4 (continued)

of the centerline of the main clean-up/prep sink:

a. at least 400" for a small kitchen;

b. at least 480" for a medium kitchen,

c. at least 560" for a large kitchen.

29. Corner Cabinet Storage

At least one corner cabinet should include a functional storage device.

This guideline does not apply if there are no corner cabinets.

30. Electrical Receptacles

Code Requirements: GFCI (Ground-fault circuit interrupter) protection is required on all receptacles servicing countertop surfaces within the kitchen.

31. Lighting

In addition to general lighting required by code, every work surface should be well illuminated by appropriate task lighting.

Source: © 2005 by the National Kitchen & Bath Association. Reprinted with permission.

Traffic Control

A major concern in kitchens and other spaces where work is being done is the control of traffic. Because food preparation involves the use of sharp objects and the handling of hot substances, traffic control is as much a safety issue in the kitchen as it is a convenience. Traffic pathways should be a minimum of 36 inches wide. Clearances between cabinets and appliances in one-cook kitchens should be at least 42 inches, in multiple-cook kitchens, a minimum of 48 inches, although 60 inches provides a better measure of safety. These clearances allow others to pass behind without interrupting work flow. They also allow users to open drawers and doors to access storage areas without bumping into opposite surfaces. Doorways in kitchens should have a minimum *clear* width of 32 inches, which would require a minimum door size of 2 feet 10 inches. Doors—whether they are entry, cabinet, or appliance doors—should not interfere with one another.

Ventilation and Natural Lighting

The International Residential Code (IRC) stipulates a minimum window area equivalent to 8 percent of the floor area. Windows provide some of the general lighting needed in the kitchen, but supplementary lighting may be needed even during the day. Task lighting is especially important in the kitchen because workers often stand between the general lighting source and the work surface. In addition, many of the tasks completed in the kitchen require attention to detail—reading recipes, measuring ingredients, and chopping vegetables to name a few. NKBA recommendations suggest that every work surface be provided with task lighting. Task lighting is often provided by installing fluorescent fixtures beneath the wall cabinets to light the counter surface. Recessed lighting installed in soffits projecting outward above the wall cabinets is another way to light kitchen work areas.

Work Centers

Kitchens need adequate counter space, plenty of storage, room for major appliances, and sufficient space in which to move about while working. The three main work centers are designed around the major items of equipment: the range, refrigerator, and sink. Work centers should have sufficient storage for all equipment and supplies normally associated with their functions.

Clear floor space a minimum of 30 inches wide should be provided at all work areas, including the sink, dishwasher, cooktop, separate ovens, and refrigerator. This space is measured from the face of the cabinet or appliance. Work areas within the **work triangle** should flow smoothly from one to another without tall separations such as refrigerators, tall cabinets, pantries, or other obstructions. The NKBA indicates that a properly recessed tall corner cabinet is acceptable.

Cooking Center

The cooking center is designed around the range. The cooking surface should not be placed beneath an operable window, and flammable window treatments should not be used for any window over a cooking surface.

A ventilating fan that moves a minimum of 150 cubic feet per minute is needed for all cooking surfaces. This fan directs heat, grease particles, and odors to the outside. A filter in the system removes grease and dirt particles and can be removed for cleaning. Some vent fans do not exhaust air to the outside but only filter and recirculate it. Usually, the vent is located in an overhead hood, although some range tops have integral proximity or down-draft ventilation systems. **Proximity ventilation** requires no overhead unit, permitting greater design freedom. For venting outdoors, however, they do require an under-floor passage.

A minimum of 24 inches of clearance between the cooking surface and any obstruction above is required, although if the range hood is combined with a microwave, manufacturers' specifications may stipulate a minimum distance less than 24 inches. If the surface above the cooktop is unprotected—such as the underside of a cabinet—at least 30 inches of clearance is necessary between the cooktop and the cabinet.

Ranges. Basic range styles include freestanding ranges with one or more ovens and a cooktop, drop-in ranges that fit between counters and appear to be built-in, and separate built-in cooktops and wall ovens. Some offer features such as automatic timers,

clocks, broilers, rotisseries, grills, griddles, or deep fryers. For typical sizes, see Table 14.1. When possible during construction, both gas and electric hookups should be provided for the range so subsequent residents may install the type of range they prefer without having to remodel.

Work Areas. A minimum of 15 inches of counter space should be provided on one side of a cooktop, with an additional 12 inches on the other side. These surfaces should be at the same level as the cooktop so that hot pans do not have to be lifted. Sliding a pan off the burner onto an adjacent countertop is the technique used by individuals with limited strength or balance. Heat-resistant counter surfaces will increase safety and minimize damage in this instance. It is a good idea to provide a heat-resistant surface with a minimum width of 15 inches on at least one side of a cooking surface in any kitchen. On a peninsula or island with a cooktop, a same-height counter surface should extend behind the cooking surface a minimum of 9 inches.

Additional Cooking Facilities. It is not necessary to locate separate ovens in close proximity to the cooking surface. In fact, when two or more cooks will be using a kitchen, the oven may be a part of a second work triangle. Regardless of the location, a landing surface with a minimum width of 15 inches and depth of 16 inches should be provided next to or above the oven. If there is no major traffic pattern between the oven and a surface within 48 inches across from it, the landing space may be on that surface. A heat-resistant landing surface may be desirable.

Microwave ovens are available in a variety of models. Some are freestanding and placed on a countertop. Others are combined with conventional ovens, combined with a range hood, or built into the wall.

Traditionally, the cooking center has been located closest to the most frequently used eating area.

Regardless of the type of installation, microwave ovens should be installed so their base is 3 inches below the user's shoulder. In no case, however, should the bottom of the microwave be more than 54 inches from the floor. A horizontal surface with a minimum width of 15 inches and a depth of at least 16 inches should be located adjacent to, above, or below a microwave oven on the handle side to provide a landing space. Because adjacent counter space is needed, separate cooking appliances should not be located in close proximity to one another.

Cleanup Center

The cleanup center is arranged around the sink, where water is available for washing fruits, vegetables, dishes, and utensils. Traditionally, the sink has been located under a window. From this vantage point, outdoor play areas can be supervised and the tedium of washing dishes relieved. When an automatic dishwasher is incorporated in the kitchen, users may spend less time at the sink, and a window might be better located elsewhere.

Sinks and Faucets. Kitchen sinks are generally installed as an integral part of a long counter. They consist of one or two bowls and sometimes an additional smaller bowl with a garbage disposal. Bowl-and-a-half sinks have one large and one small compartment and are used when two bowls are desired and there is insufficient space for a standard double-bowl sink. Double- and triple-bowl sinks require larger cabinets and more space—a minimum 36-inch-wide cabinet. They may also have an attached drain board that slants toward the sink. Small kitchens often have a single bowl sink that fits into a 27-inch-wide cabinet. When there is only one sink in a kitchen, it should be located between or across from the cooking surface and the refrigerator. In kitchens designed for multiple

---

When a dishwasher is installed, a single-bowl sink may suffice, although double-bowl sinks are preferred.

Table 14.1 Typical Appliance Sizes*

Appliance	Width	Depth	Height	Capacity
Beverage center	28	33	55	16 gallon
Deep freeze				
Chest	24	26	35	5.3 cu. ft.
	46	30	35	14.8 cu. ft.
	65	30	35	21.6 cu. ft.
Upright	30	32	67	16.7 cu. ft.
	33	30	67	19.6 cu. ft.
Large capacity	32	27	65	
Dishwasher				
Portable	24	37	36	
Under counter	24	25	34	
Ice maker	15	23	34	50 lb.
Microwave	30	16	18	1.7 cu. ft.
	18	13	11	0.7 cu. ft.
With hood	30	14	16	1.1 cu. ft.
Oven—Built in				
Single	30	23	29	
Double	27	23	57	
	30	23	51	
With microwave	30	23	43	
Range				
Commercial	48	26	36	
Home				
Drop in	30	25	32	
Freestanding	20, 24, 30, 36, 40	26	46	
Slide in	30	24	36	
Range hood				
Slide out	36	13	15	
Standard	30, 36	20	5	
Telescopic down-draft	30	2.25	27	
Refrigerator				
Commercial	40	30	79	
Counter depth	36	24	70	
2-drawer unit	27	24	35	5.3 cu. ft.
Home				
Side by side	36	30	72	24.5 cu. ft.
Freezer on bottom	30	33	67	18.6 cu. ft.
Freezer on top	33	33	67	21.7 cu. ft.
Compact	17	21	19	1.8 cu. ft.
	19	21	34	4.3 cu. ft.
Trash compactor	12, 15	24	34	
Warming drawer	30	24	10	
Wine chiller	16	14	34, 35	

* All dimensions are in inches. The dimensions given are typical and can be used for planning purposes. Actual dimensions of appliances selected should be used during final planning stages.

cooks, a second single-bowl sink is often included. Small bar sinks, round and oval-shaped sinks, or decorative sinks may be used for this purpose.

The bowl depth is an important consideration when selecting a kitchen sink. When large items are used consistently, a sink with deeper bowls will be appropriate. Sinks may come with colanders, cutting boards, and other accessories. Hospitals have been using sinks with an inherent antibacterial agent (Microban) for more than 25 years. These sinks are available for residential use in stainless steel and some composite materials. The Microban protection should last as long as the sink. Sinks for both kitchens and bathrooms come in a variety of styles, materials, and colors.

- Self-rimming sinks fit into an opening in the countertop but have a flat lip that sits on top of the counter.
- Under-counter sinks are installed beneath the countertop. Because the edge of the opening is exposed, these sinks work well with solid countertops. If used with laminated counters, the underside of the counter should be sealed to prevent water damage.
- Flush-mounted sinks are recessed into the counter substrate so that the tops of the two surfaces are at equal heights. Flush-mounted sinks designed for use with ceramic tile countertops have square ledges around them to accept the thickness of the tile.
- Rimmed sinks project slightly above the countertop when installed, and the joint between the sink and the counter may be concealed by a metal rim.
- Integral sinks are made with the countertop and are not separate entities. There is no joint between two components to collect dirt, making this the most sanitary and easily maintained type of sink. Integral sinks are usually made of stainless steel or of solid surfacing materials. A drain board can be easily included.

Although round sinks are popular as second sinks in kitchens, they do provide less interior space than square or rectangular units using the same counter width.

The materials used for kitchen sinks include enameled steel or cast iron, stainless steel, man-made composites, and stone. In general, heavier materials move less due to expansion and contraction with changes in temperature.

- Steel sinks tend to flex easily, making enameled steel units subject to chipping. Stainless steel sinks may have a brushed or mirror finish. Abrasive cleaners and everyday use scratch mirror finishes, while brushed steel resists water spots and conceals fine scratches.
- Cast-iron sinks are thicker, resulting in less movement, and the enamel used to finish cast-iron sinks is also thicker and, therefore, more chip-resistant.
- Composite materials are very durable, withstanding hard wear and damage due to utensils and pans. Any chips that do occur do not show because the material is solid. Solid surfacing materials are made of acrylic, although quartz or granite may be combined with resin for a faux stone appearance.
- Stone sinks are usually granite.
- Hand-painted and silk-screened sinks are less durable than other finishes.

Kitchen faucets generally have a swing spout so that water can be used in both bowls of a double

An undercoating applied to the relatively thin steel used for sinks helps to control noise and should be specified when possible.

Cast-iron and stone sinks are heavy and may require additional support or heavier cabinet construction.

sink. Most also have aerators. Faucets with two handles minimize the risk of burns from water that is too hot. Cross handles are difficult to grasp, but bar handles can be easily operated by most individuals, including children. Single-handle faucets are easier for individuals with stiff fingers or minimal small-muscle coordination. Spray attachments with a hose concealed beneath the sink lift out easily for operation. A lever on the spray attachment redirects the water from faucet to spray. Kitchen sink drains usually have a combination stopper and strainer.

Work Areas. Because the sink is the most frequently used of the three work centers, the primary sink should be located between the cooking surface and the refrigerator, or across from them. A minimum of 24 inches of counter frontage is recommended on one side of the sink, with a minimum of 18 inches on the other side. The 24 inches of counter space should be at the same height as the sink, and it is desirable that the counter on the other side of the sink be at the same height as well. The front edge of the sink should be a maximum of 3 inches from the counter front to ensure easy access to the water supply.

If there is at least 3 inches of counter space between the sink and a corner, the counter frontage on the return (around the corner) can be included, but only if the total distance is 24 inches or more. Secondary sinks do not require as much counter space: a minimum of 18 inches of counter frontage on one side and 3 inches on the other.

The food preparation area[3] should be located adjacent to a water source, whether that source is the primary or secondary sink. The minimum continuous counter space width for a preparation area is 36 inches and the minimum depth is 24 inches.

It may be desirable to have the work surface lower in the preparation area than in the remainder of the kitchen. Since many small appliances will be used here, they should be stored in nearby locations. They are more convenient if they can be stored on top of the counter and screened from view. A swing-up shelf is especially convenient for a stand mixer. It can then be easily hidden from view but ready for immediate use.

Dishwashers. The dishwasher should be located adjacent to the sink to preclude the necessity of running drain pipes through cabinets to the garbage disposer.[4] NKBA guidelines stipulate that the edge of the primary dishwasher should be within 36 inches of the sink. A minimum 30 × 48 inch clear floor area on both sides of the dishwasher ensures access from either side. If the dishwasher is located near a corner, at least 21 inches of clear floor area should be provided between the corner and the dishwasher to allow access on that side.

Food Storage Center

The food storage center, designed around the refrigerator, is where much of the food used by the household is stored. This center should be located near the service entrance for convenience in putting away groceries.

Refrigerators. Refrigerators come in single-door, double-door, and triple-door models. Double-door styles are more efficient since the freezer door is not opened nearly as often as the refrigerator door. The freezer may be beside the refrigerator section, above it, or below it. Three-door models in some side-by-side refrigerators keep more frequently used frozen items separated from others for increased operating efficiency. Refrigerators may also have automatic ice makers and cold drink dispensers. For typical sizes, see Table 14.1. The refrigerator should be situated away from heat sources, including direct sunlight, ranges, ovens, dishwashers, and heating ducts.

Work Areas. There should be at least 15 inches of counter space next to the latch side of the refrigerator or not more than 48 inches across from the refrigerator. When a side-by-side refrigerator is used, the countertop should be most accessible when using the fresh food section. When an under-counter refrigerator is used, the landing surface may be on the counter above the refrigerator.

The Work Triangle

The work centers should be organized so that tasks flow naturally from one to the other. The shortest paths between the center fronts of the primary sink, the cooking surface, and the refrigerator form a work triangle. For safety as well as efficiency, traffic should not be routed through the work triangle. Because food preparation has become a shared or even social experience, it may be desirable to have more than one work triangle. Two work triangles should not cross each other, although one leg may be shared.

Work Triangle Distances

The total length of the sides of the work triangle should be between 12 and 26 feet in an efficiently designed kitchen. Less distance does not provide sufficient space for moving about, and a greater distance results in wasted steps. The minimum distance between any two centers in the work triangle is 4 feet; the maximum is 9 feet. The path should not have any obstructions greater than 12 inches, although even that distance may result in collisions.

Work Center Configuration

There are five basic kitchen floor plans: one-wall, corridor, L-shaped, U-shaped, and G-shaped. See Figure 14.2 for an example of each. An island can be added to some of these plans. Both one-wall and corridor kitchens are best used by one cook. L-shaped, U-shaped, and G-shaped kitchens, or any kitchen with an island, may be designed for two cooks. The work triangle considers only the three major work centers. It is this configuration that gives kitchen shapes their names, not the configuration of the cabinets. Cabi-

netry may be arranged in a U-shape, for example, in an L-shaped kitchen.

One-wall kitchens are often found in small homes and apartments because they require little space. All work centers are arranged along a single wall. Although the work flow from one center to another is simple, little room remains for storage or counter space. However, there is little traffic through the work triangle and there are no "dead" corners.

In corridor or galley kitchens, the major work centers are arranged on two parallel walls. Corridor kitchens can be very efficient if the space between the counters is not a major traffic lane. The space between opposite work surfaces should be a minimum of 48 inches to allow traffic behind an individual working in the area. To limit traffic, one end of the kitchen may be closed off, and the refrigerator can be located near the entrance. If space is limited, 36 inches is allowed between opposite surfaces, although appliance doors may collide. In corridor kitchens, the work centers can be distributed evenly, and there are usually no "dead" corners. While storage space is limited, additional storage can be located outside the work triangle.

L-shaped kitchens have the major work centers along two adjacent walls. Through traffic does not disrupt the work triangle, and the ease of traffic flow within the kitchen permits more than one cook to work at the same time. Storage space and counter areas are continuous and generally ample. Usually there is enough space in the kitchen for a dining area or an island. The one "dead" corner requires planning if it is to be used efficiently.

U-shaped kitchens are generally regarded as the most efficient. The three major work centers are located on three adjacent walls or counters. An unbroken U shape prevents circulation patterns from crossing the kitchen, making work easier. U-shaped kitchens contain more storage facilities than other plans because the work centers are more spread out. They also have more counter space and, thus, more continuous work space. With a U-shaped plan, the

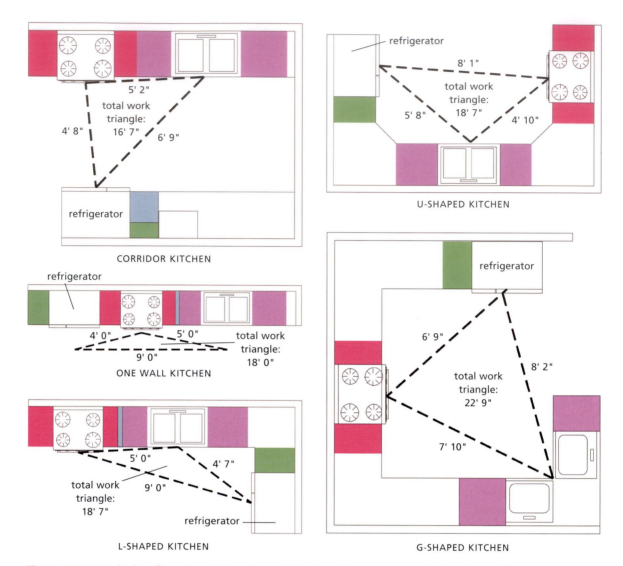

Figure 14.2 Basic kitchen floor plans. Colored areas indicate minimum recommended work area. Blue area represents shared space.

work triangle can be distributed more evenly than with other plans. The major problem encountered is the two "dead" corners. U-shaped kitchens do require more floor space, however.

G-shaped kitchens are a variation of the U-shaped kitchen and are fairly rare. G-shaped kitchens add a peninsula and a third corner to a U-shaped kitchen. Because kitchen shape is determined by the location of work centers, a G-shaped kitchen is possible only if dual centers are present or if a sink or cooktop extends around a corner. Because of the additional space, G-shaped kitchens can accommodate additional work centers and work triangles, and there is often space for an island. G-shaped kitchens, however, may make individuals feel enclosed, especially if wall cabinets are used on all sides. If one or more sides is open to adjacent rooms above the counter space, the enclosed feeling is relieved.

Islands and peninsulas add visual interest, extra work surfaces, access for multiple cooks, and more storage space; may incorporate additional features such as wet bars, warming drawers, and grills; and may provide a serving or eating surface for informal meals. See Figure 14.3. Often, the sink or range is incorporated into the island, thus improving the relationship between work centers. One advantage of islands and peninsulas is that access can be provided on two or more sides to cabinets beneath the countertop. Such access makes the corner formed by the peninsula more accessible as well. If a sink is to be installed on an island, pipes must run through the floor. When it includes a major work center, the island must be large enough to provide sufficient adjacent counter space. It is difficult to incorporate an island in a kitchen and still maintain appropriate clearances for proper use of all surfaces. When an eating surface is designed, the top usually overhangs the base area to allow seated users to comfortably access the counter.

It is unsafe to incorporate an eating area across the counter from a cooktop on an island or peninsula.

Islands can serve as partial partitions between kitchens and living areas, they may be on casters if there are no plumbing pipes or range vents to consider, and they may "float" or be suspended from the ceiling, although strong ceiling support is necessary. If possible, electrical receptacles should be installed on one or more sides of the island to facilitate the use of electrical appliances.

Kitchen Design Preferences

The kitchen can be isolated from the remainder of the home or it can be open to other areas. An NAHB reports that 63 percent of individuals prefer that the kitchen be visually open but separated by a short wall or have a completely open arrangement to the family

Figure 14.3 An eating area in the kitchen provides an informal space to gather where the cook can be included in the socializing of family and friends.

room. That same study found that the overwhelming majority preferred a walk-in pantry in or near the kitchen. Islands, too, were preferred by more than 70 percent of the individuals surveyed.[5]

Cabinets

Until relatively recently, cabinets were custom-built in each home. Cabinets are used in kitchens, bathrooms, laundry rooms, and other areas of the home. Most cabinet manufacturers offer a variety of basic styles, plus special cabinets and accessories. Desirable features include adjustable shelves, self-closing doors, turntables in corner cabinets, door storage, sliding shelves, and vertical tray storage.

Cabinetry sets the style for a kitchen. Modern cabinets may have a streamlined appearance or may look like furniture with crown moldings, valances, cabinet legs, and matching panels for appliances. The addition of pilasters, moldings, applied carvings, turnings, corbels, and gingerbread trim can change the appearance of the room significantly. Cabinet quality varies widely, but high-quality cabinets should meet the same standards of construction as does high-end

The typical kitchen makes use of a variety of cabinets, giving kitchens everywhere the same basic appearance. Because cabinets are permanently installed, it is not feasible to move them to a new home, nor would it be desirable for resale value to remove them. Cabinets organize space efficiently and present an uncluttered appearance. An alternative to the formulaic kitchen is an eclectic kitchen, which makes use of freestanding appliances and furniture used for food storage and preparation. Eclectic kitchens are less utilitarian in appearance than typical kitchens, present a personal look that is unique, make good use of awkwardly shaped rooms, and the furnishings can be moved to a new location.

furniture. An NAHB survey found that the preference for traditional cabinets, as opposed to contemporary models, has increased since 1995, with light-colored cabinets the most popular.[6]

Although most cabinets are wood or wood covered with a laminate, metal cabinets are available. They may give a kitchen an industrial look, they simplify the use of vertical curved surfaces, they may reflect light, helping to maximize natural light sources, and they are extremely durable and hygienic. Metal cabinets are usually more expensive than wood and show smudges readily. Punched or embossed surfaces change the look.

Types of Cabinet Manufacture

Regardless of the type of cabinets selected for a home, their cost is largely dependent on the type of manufacture.

- **Knockdown cabinetry** is shipped in precut flat pieces that are ready to assemble. The pieces may be finished or unfinished but the choice is relatively limited. Cabinet widths are based on stock cabinet sizes, but not all sizes are available as knockdown units, nor are high-end cabinets. The quality of construction depends on the skills of the consumer who assembles the units. Cabinets come in standard widths, making it difficult to fit them into individual kitchens, and spacers are often necessary. When using standard-sized cabinets, individual units are butted against one another, making an obvious joint.
- Stock cabinets are readily available at local home improvement stores, allowing quick delivery. Both finished and unfinished units are available, although styles and finishes are limited. Cabinet width is based on a 3-inch module, beginning at 9 inches with some manufacturers, 12 inches with others, and going to 48 inches. Cabinets up to 21 inches in width have a single door, 24-inch-wide cabinets may have one or two doors, and wider

cabinets usually have 2 doors. Some manufacturers also produce cabinets wider than 48 inches, in 1 foot increments—5, 6, 7, and 8 feet. For larger spaces, multiple cabinets must be used.

- **Semi-custom cabinets** are usually stock cabinets for which the consumer may select the door style, wood species, finish, and interior options. Some manufacturers offer custom size options. Semi-custom cabinets must be manufactured after the customer has submitted the specifications, requiring weeks or even months.

- Custom cabinets are designed specifically for individual customers. These cabinets are built for a specific location with exact measurements and may be constructed in continuous units, eliminating the awkward joint between two units: An entire wall of cabinets may be constructed as one unit. Drawers are located exactly as requested by the customer, all dimensions can be adjusted, and customers may opt for specialized features not available in stock cabinets. Custom cabinets are made by a local craftsperson, and delivery time depends on that individual's schedule.

Types of Cabinets

Most of the cabinetry in the home is in the kitchen, and there are four types of cabinets designed especially for that room: base units, wall units, tall cabinets, and special-purpose units. Each of these cabinets, however, can be used in other areas, including laundry rooms, bathrooms, and storage rooms. The vanity, linen closet, and 4-inch-deep wall cabinet are designed for use in bathrooms.

Base Cabinets. Base cabinets are installed on the floor, either freestanding or against a wall to which they are permanently attached. Standard-sized base units are 24 inches deep and 34½ inches high. The depth is measured from the wall to the cabinet face. The height is measured from the floor to the top of the cabinet. The top of base cabinets is typically covered with a 1½-inch-thick counter, providing a hori-

Cabinets on legs expose the floor beneath, giving the space a more expansive appearance. However, cleaning beneath the cabinets will be somewhat impeded, and the area will quickly become dusty.

The base cabinet height may be adjusted when custom cabinetry is specified. The standard 36-inch height with countertop is the same as a freestanding range, and dishwashers are designed to fit beneath this height. Adjusting the height downward may result in varying counter heights, affecting work efficiency. Where there is a long counter surface uninterrupted by major appliances, it is feasible to raise or lower just this section.

zontal work surface with a total height of 36 inches. A toe space at the bottom of the cabinet enables users to get closer to the cabinet than would otherwise be possible. The standard depth of the toe space is 3 inches and the height is 3½ inches. See Figure 14.4.

Figure 14.4 Standard dimensions of kitchen wall and base cabinets.

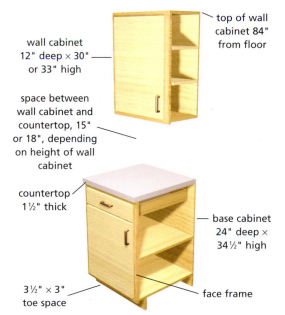

wall cabinet 12" deep × 30" or 33" high

top of wall cabinet 84" from floor

space between wall cabinet and countertop, 15" or 18", depending on height of wall cabinet

countertop 1½" thick

base cabinet 24" deep × 34½" high

3½" × 3" toe space

face frame

Most standard base cabinets have a single drawer above a door that opens into storage space, although vertical storage units have no drawer. Some units, known as **drawer bases** (see Figure 14.5), have multiple drawers—the number depending on the depth of individual drawers. When drawers are in cabinets

Figure 14.5 Drawer bases provide organized storage space in several areas of the home; they are critical in kitchens.

that are a minimum of 15 inches wide and 21 inches deep, the drawer frontage is calculated by multiplying the cabinet width by the number of drawers or rollout shelves.

The usable frontage of cabinets and countertops is measured across the face of the unit—counting only accessible space and leaving out blind portions of cabinets, such as those in corners. The NKBA calculates shelf frontage in the same manner as drawer frontage. The NKBA recommends that combined drawer and shelf frontage for small kitchens be a minimum of 1400 inches, in medium kitchens 1700 inches, and in large kitchens 2000 inches, divided among base and wall cabinets, pantry space, and drawer space. See Box 14.3 for specific requirements. Drop-in range tops and sinks take up some of the space in base cabinet units, and these units are not included in the minimum frontage for that reason.

Where cabinets turn corners, presenting "dead" space, three options provide efficient accessibility: the **lazy Susan**, **carousel shelves**, and the angled cabinet. Lazy Susans rotate 360 degrees and provide shelves attached to a center post. See Figure 14.6. Carousel shelves usually rotate 270 degrees, with a pie-cut formed by two doors attached to the shelves and which rotate with the shelves. Lazy Susans and carousel shelves in base cabinets count as a total of 30 inches of frontage. Lazy Susans and carousel shelves may be installed in base cabinets, walls cabinets, and tall cabinets. The NKBA recommends that at least one corner cabinet have a functional storage device. If the opposite side of the corner is accessible, a door may be placed in that side, although it does not count as usable frontage. Angled cabinet frontage is measured across the angle.

In order to ensure that cabinet doors can be completely opened, that any rollout units are fully accessible, and that handles do not interfere with one another, spacers may be necessary between a cabinet and a corner or between a cabinet and a wall. Four inches is considered the minimum distance between any door and a corner or a wall. It may be necessary

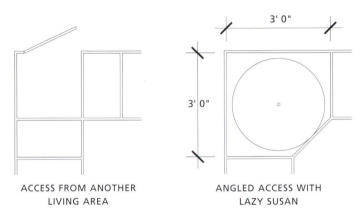

CAROUSEL SHELF WITH
PIE-SHAPED DOOR

ACCESS FROM ANOTHER
LIVING AREA

ANGLED ACCESS WITH
LAZY SUSAN

Figure 14.6 Corner access alternatives.

to add a filler piece to ensure proper operation while achieving a pleasing appearance. Fillers may also be needed between cabinets and appliances.

Because base cabinets are deep, not all of the counter area is usually used. Midway cabinets may be installed between base and wall cabinets to efficiently use this space and provide storage for frequently used items. See Figure 14.7. The most popular midway cabinets are designed for corners where adjacent counters meet. They often have **tambour** (roll-up) doors and are large enough to store small appliances.[7] Along straight walls, a minimum of 16 inches of usable counter space should remain in front of midway cabinets. This will require custom cabinetry with an increased depth. Receptacles located within the cabinets ensure ease of use of the appliances.

Wall Cabinets. Wall cabinets are installed above base cabinets to provide extra storage. Wall cabinets are hung on the wall, and the weight of the cabinet and its contents make it necessary to provide bracing in the wall to ensure stability. See Figure 5.17. These cabinets have a minimum depth of 12 inches, and 15-inch depths are available from some manufacturers.

Standard wall cabinets come in both 30- and 33-inch heights. Both are installed with their tops at 84 inches from the floor. If 30-inch cabinets are used, there is 18 inches between the top of a standard base unit and the bottom of the wall unit; 33-inch

wall cabinets leave 15 inches of space, which is the minimum distance necessary above a countertop for working and storage of appliances. A minimum of 4 inches of clearance is needed between a refrigerator and a wall cabinet above it, and 24 inches between a range top or a sink and any cabinet.

Wall cabinets should have adjustable shelving. Corners are treated in the same manner as base cabinet

Figure 14.7 These custom-built cabinets are 30 inches deep rather than the standard 24 inches, providing greater storage beneath. A 12-inch-deep row of appliance garages designed specifically to fit the appliances owned by the customer sits on the back of the countertop, leaving 18 inches of work surface.

corners. At least 60 inches of this frontage—whether in a tall cabinet or wall cabinets—should be located within 72 inches of the centerline of the primary sink.

There is little space between the top of wall cabinets and the ceiling when 8- or 9-foot ceilings are used. This area can be treated in a variety of ways.

• The top of the wall cabinets may serve as a shelf on which to display items.
• Small cabinets with separate doors can be installed to provide storage space for infrequently used items.
• A soffit may be installed above the cabinets, which may or may not house pipes, wiring, or ductwork. The use of a soffit ensures that dirt and dust do not collect on the top of cabinets. The soffit may project beyond wall cabinets, providing an ideal location for task lighting.

Tall Cabinets. Tall cabinets are usually 84 inches high and either 12, 14, 18, 21, or 24 inches deep. They may be designed to house appliances—microwave ovens, wall ovens, or steam ovens. Cabinet doors or drawers may be located both above and below the appliance opening. **Utility cabinets** are a type of tall cabinet used for storage and are often called pantries. Inside there may be stationary or adjustable shelves,

---

Because tall cabinets can be counted as wall cabinet frontage, it is not essential that wall cabinets be installed. In fact, small kitchens will feel less enclosed if wall units are omitted. In addition, when wall units are absent, the number of design possibilities broadens considerably, leaving space for decorative items, mirrors, and windows.

Bathroom vanities may be made of pieces of furniture rather than standard cabinetry, giving the bathroom a less utilitarian appearance. Wood tops must be sealed well to prevent water damage.

revolving shelves, or hinged shelf sections. There may also be space designed for broom and mop storage. Some of these units are narrow, have storage shelves on both sides, and slide out for access. Others have foldout doors with shelves and additional in-cabinet shelving. Shelves in tall cabinets are included when calculating frontage.

Special-Purpose Cabinets. Special-purpose cabinets include units designed to accept built-in ranges, cooktops, and sinks; desk units; trash receptacle units; pullout tables; and medicine cabinets.

Bathroom Cabinets. Vanities are often similar to base cabinets, with a drawer blank on the face that covers the area taken up by the lavatory. A major function of the vanity is to conceal the pipes necessary for the lavatory. Stylish vanities may look like furniture and have drawers and enclosed shelving for storage. The depth of vanities is usually 21 inches, although 18-inch units are available. Like base cabinets, widths begin at 18 inches and increase in 3-inch increments to 48 inches.

Toilet cabinets are designed to hang above the toilet tank and are 8 inches deep; linen closets for bathrooms may be 8 inches deep or more and 84 inches high; and 4-inch-deep wall cabinets with heights from 24 to 30 inches and widths in 3-inch increments from 18 to 48 inches are designed to be installed above a vanity to hold toiletries.

Organizing Options

Good planning should provide storage for items at the point where they are most frequently used. Seldom-used items can be stored in cabinets above eye level or below 15 inches. In addition to cabinets, kitchen storage can include open shelves, closets, carts, pegboard, overhead racks, cabinet doors, and countertops. Organizing options for cabinets are designed for making much of this space more usable. Organizing options include but are not limited to the following:

- Vertical dividers for storage of trays and cookie sheets
- Racks for pans and lids
- Bins for vegetable storage
- Trash receptacle holders
- Drawer dividers
- Tilt-out trays in front of the sink
- Towel racks

Cabinet and Drawer Construction

Most cabinetry is made of two pieces: a box and a **face frame**. The box itself may be constructed in one of two ways: with or without a frame. When frame construction is used for the cabinet box, the solid wood frame is built first and provides the support for thin panels that enclose the box. Panel construction is used when there is no frame for the box. In this case, thicker panels of plywood, hardboard, or particle board form the box and serve as the support. See Figure 14.8.

The front of the box may be covered with a face frame made of boards that frame the openings that are enclosed by doors and drawers. Part of the face frame may be exposed between doors and drawers and around the edges, although some door and drawer front styles cover the face frame. A face frame with a center vertical rail helps to strengthen wide cabinet boxes. Hinges may or may not be visible. European-style cabinets omit the face frame and attach doors and drawers directly to the cabinet box, providing a smooth line from one side to the other. European-style cabinets have hidden hinges, and because no space is consumed by a face frame, the interior of drawers can be as much as 20 percent larger than drawers in the same size unit with a face frame.

Doors

In addition to the cabinet itself having a framed or unframed face, cabinet doors may be framed or unframed. Either style door can be used with either cabinet face style.

Slab doors (called **unframed**) present the appearance of a solid piece of material and have a face in a single plane. They may, however, actually be made of solid wood planks joined together. Wood planks may be grouped together using one or more battens, instead giving the appearance of a board and batten door.

Plywood panels may have grooves emulating board construction. Laminated slab doors consist of a

Figure 14.8 Cabinets may be constructed with or without a face frame. Face frames use stile and rail construction similar to that used for doors.

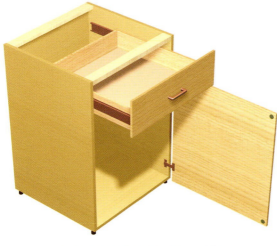

CABINET WITHOUT FACE FRAME

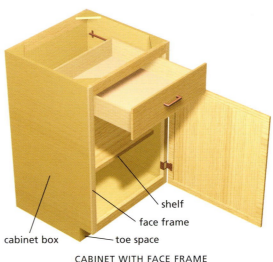

shelf
face frame
cabinet box — toe space

CABINET WITH FACE FRAME

substrate such as particleboard covered on all sides with any type of laminate material—most commonly plastic. Slab doors of any type may have plain or detailed edges.

A panel door (also called a **framed door**) has a center panel supported by stiles and rails and is constructed like a panel door. See Figure 14.9. The panel may be of any material, although wood, fiberboard, or engineered wood are usually used. Both raised and recessed wood panels are available. A recessed panel is a flat piece of material with a frame around it. A stile down the center of the door may be used to give the door an Arts and Crafts or Shaker appearance, or the panels may be grooved. Recessed panels are usually more contemporary in appearance than are raised panels.

Raised panels are made of thicker materials than are recessed panels. The edges of the panels are trimmed so that they are thin enough to fit into the grooves in the frame but the center of the panel remains at the original thickness. Raised panels may be square-headed, although common designs include cathedral and arched designs.

Panels may also be made of etched or stained glass panels, wired glass, ribbed glass, or clear glass. Glass is easy to maintain, presents a contemporary appearance, and gives the space a more open feel than do other materials. Perforated metal panels were often used on food storage cupboard doors before refrigerators became common and are seen in rustic decor today. Pull-down tambour doors or shutters are found on some contemporary cabinets.

Care should be taken when finishing objects using panel construction. Because panels are loose in the frame and can freely expand and contract, the edges of the panel may miss being stained, varnished, or painted. If the panel shrinks (usually during the winter), these unfinished edges may be exposed, marring the appearance of the door.

Figure 14.9 Raised panel doors provide surface interest without being visually overpowering.

In all types of panel doors, the stiles and rails are joined and glued together. Miter joints, mortise and tenon joints, and cope and pattern joints are common. This framework surrounds the panel, which is slipped into a groove in the frame. The panel is not glued or attached in any other manner to the frame because expansion and contraction of the panel due to temperature changes and moisture could result in its splitting.

Interiors may be surfaced with plastic or vinyl laminates for easy cleaning. Wood cabinets may have interior veneered surfaces, especially if particleboard or hardboard is used for the sides and back. Painting, staining, and varnishing help protect these surfaces and facilitate maintenance and cleaning.

Drawers

Drawers receive frequent pushing and pulling, causing stress on their joints, so they must be solidly constructed. Drawers can house dividers to better organize contents, they hide items from view, and they keep contents clean and relatively dust-free when they are closed. Drawers should slide easily and pull out far enough for use without tipping or falling from the cabinet. Drawers must fit well to operate properly; consequently, the drawer construction is an indication of the quality of the cabinets. Drawers can be made not only from wood but from metal or plastic. Strong joints and a thick bottom are signs of a well constructed drawer.

Drawers consist of a front, two sides, a back, and a bottom. The front is made of the same material used for the doors, of solid wood, or of plywood. Drawer fronts are usually between ¾ and 1⅛ inches thick. Drawer sides are usually constructed of ½-inch-thick material, although ⅜-inch material is sufficient for small drawers. Drawer sides may be of any material, including metal, plywood, hardboard, particleboard, or solid wood. When the sides of the drawer extend beyond the back, the extensions act as a stop when closing the drawer and help to prevent the drawer from tipping forward or falling out when it is fully extended.

Drawer sides and fronts usually have a groove slightly above the bottom into which the drawer bottom fits. The drawer back may be made of thinner material than the sides. In medium- and lower-quality drawers, the drawer back rests on the drawer bottom and may be attached with nails or staples. Higher-quality drawers have a groove in the back just as in the sides and front to receive the drawer bottom. Drawer bottoms are made of thin material—usually ¼-inch plywood or hardboard, although ⅛-inch bottoms are often used for inexpensive cabinetry. Figure 14.10 illustrates the joints used in the construction of drawers.

The drawer front may be **flush** so it fits into an opening in the cabinet and does not project from the cabinet front. Flush drawers require precise clearances and are difficult to make. A **lipped** drawer has a **rabbet** cut around the back side of the drawer front. The rabbet forms a recess, allowing the drawer to fit into the opening, but the drawer face is larger, fitting over the face of the frame. **Flush overlay** drawer fronts overlap the frame to the side of the cabinet, eliminating the need for a face frame. A **reveal overlay**

Figure 14.10 Types of joints used for drawer construction.

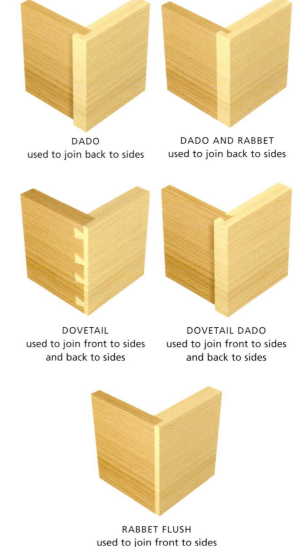

DADO
used to join back to sides

DADO AND RABBET
used to join back to sides

DOVETAIL
used to join front to sides
and back to sides

DOVETAIL DADO
used to join front to sides
and back to sides

RABBET FLUSH
used to join front to sides

drawer front has the appearance of a lipped drawer but there is no rabbet joint on the back side of the drawer front. The drawer front overlaps part of the cabinet face. See Figure 14.11 for examples of the different drawer fronts.

Countertops

Countertops overhang base cabinet edges to protect cabinet fronts from spills and to give a more finished appearance. For safety, countertop corners should be angled or curved, and edges should be rounded or beveled to eliminate sharp edges. Pullout countertops can provide work space in front of microwaves and other appliances placed on counter surfaces.

Materials

Countertops are made of various materials, including stainless steel, solid surfacing, ceramic tile, metal tile, vinyl tile, vinyl, masonry, resin composites, and wood. Masonry products, including concrete and stone, should be sealed to prevent staining, and wood should be sealed to prevent water damage. Most materials used for countertops are not easily damaged by scratching or denting. Most are easy to clean, and their smooth surfaces make them easy to keep sanitary. Some counters have metal edges that trap dirt. The edges of most newer countertops have no separate rims and may be rounded upward to prevent spills.

Plastic laminates are popular countertop materials made of layers of paper, melamine, and plastic resin that are bonded together. The finished material is

Because the color does not go all the way through plastic laminates, edges are obvious. The laminates can, however, be formed over curves, and most manufactured countertops of plastic laminate have a curve at the back to form a backsplash, a curve at the top of the backsplash, and a curved lip at the front of the counter. This formation eliminates edges that show.

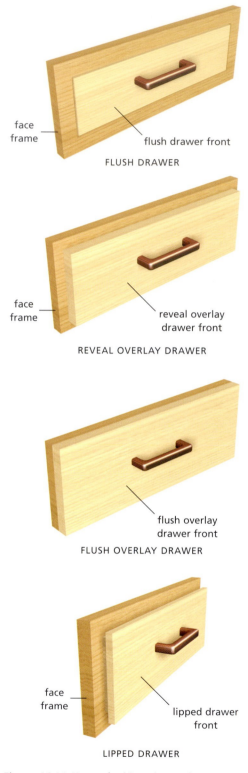

FLUSH DRAWER

face frame — flush drawer front

REVEAL OVERLAY DRAWER

face frame — reveal overlay drawer front

FLUSH OVERLAY DRAWER

flush overlay drawer front

LIPPED DRAWER

face frame — lipped drawer front

Figure 14.11 Types of cabinet drawer fronts.

glued to a smooth wood surface—usually plywood or particleboard—to form the countertop. This type of countertop is usually used in moderately priced homes. Plastic laminates can be chipped or scratched easily and can scorch when a hot pot is set on them. Damage to the laminate cannot be repaired.

Solid surfacing materials made of polyester or acrylic are extremely durable, have color through the material, and can be repaired by sanding. Solid surfacing materials are available with Microban protection from some manufacturers.

Masonry materials include concrete, brick, and stone. Marble, granite, slate, limestone, and sandstone are frequently used. Concrete, brick, marble, and limestone are fairly porous and absorb stains readily. For this reason, they should be protected with several coats of sealer. Slate scratches easily and should be used with care. Terrazzo can be used as a solid countertop or poured into tiles. Masonry countertops are cool to the touch and ideal for rolling out pastry, they have a luxurious appearance, require little maintenance, and are extremely durable, but their surfaces may be uneven and their weight may require additional support. Fragile items usually break when dropped on these hard surfaces.

Wood countertops provide a good cutting surface that can be refinished if necessary. A variety of wood species can be used, although hardwoods are preferred because they scratch less easily than softwoods. Wood counters must be sealed to protect them from moisture and humidity. They may be varnished or lacquered, or they may be oiled. Both finishes require renewing: Varnish or lacquer should be reapplied annually, while oil should be reapplied every few months. Oiled wood is more resistant to damage due to heat, although all woods will scratch, stain, and scorch. Teak is an excellent choice for counters because of its durability and resistance to moisture. All solid woods, however, are subject to warping. For this reason, laminated wood products are often used to make butcher block countertops. Wood is more difficult to sanitize than are other countertop materials

When using countertop materials that can be damaged by heat, it is advisable to install inlaid heat-resistant surfaces near cooktops and ovens. A minimum 15 × 15 inch surface is desirable.

because the pores may harbor bacteria that are difficult to remove.

Ceramic, porcelain, and glass tile countertops are heat-resistant, require little maintenance, are available in a large variety of sizes, shapes, and colors, and can be laid in an almost infinite variety of patterns. Ceramic wall tile is not sufficiently durable for use on countertops and a heavier grade should be selected. Unglazed tiles, including porcelain, should be sealed semiannually, as should the grout between tiles. If the grout is not flush with the tile surface, dirt and germs collect in the grout lines, which are difficult to clean. Large tiles are difficult to cut for fitting around sinks and pipes. Tile can chip when objects are dropped on it.

A glass counter is expensive but provides a durable, heat-resistant surface that is easily maintained. Its cool surface is ideal for rolling out pastry, and its reflective surface makes the area appear larger. Glass can be scratched, so it is not suitable for a cutting surface, and it can be broken if a heavy object is dropped on it. To ensure safety, a curved edge can be cut on glass. Like masonry products, glass counters may be sufficiently heavy to require additional structural support.

Stainless steel and zinc are also used as countertop surfaces. Stainless steel is easily cleaned and is often used in industrial kitchens and dairies because it can easily be sanitized. Zinc is more porous and stains easily. A variety of textures and finishes are available

Color can be mixed into concrete, ensuring that concrete countertops are the same color throughout their thickness. Because concrete is a plastic material when wet, countertops can be poured on site in any desirable shape and cast without seams.

for metal countertops, including matte, mirror, and ridged surfaces. Thin metal can be applied to curved surfaces.

Although all of these countertop materials are relatively heat-resistant, ceramic tile and masonry materials can withstand the highest heat. If a less heat-resistant material is used for the rest of the counter, an inset of ceramic tile or masonry is desirable near cooking surfaces and ovens. A hardwood inset is often used for a cutting surface, reducing the chance that the rest of the counter will be marred. The wood can be refinished if it becomes damaged.

Counter Recommendations

Countertops extend beyond the cabinet face 1½ inches, and distances to opposite surfaces are measured from the front of the countertop. Counter frontage is measured at the front edge of the countertop and may be continuous around corners. Countertops that are not usable counter surfaces, such as the space taken up by sinks and cooktops, is not considered part of counter frontage when calculating counter area. The NKBA recommends a minimum of 158 inches of countertop frontage on cabinets at least 24 inches deep for all kitchens. Overlapping of counters is allowed when work centers are adjacent. When calculating these overlapping counter surfaces, add 12 inches to the longest recommended dimension to determine the minimum counter space shared by the two work centers.

❀ Recycling is an important part of green design. A recycling center may be in the kitchen, although more frequently, it is in a garage or storage area. Separate containers for glass, recyclable plastic, aluminum, and paper provide temporary storage of the materials. Some municipalities have refuse service that separates recyclable materials, facilitating disposal of the items. In other areas, it may be desirable to have larger containers to minimize the number of trips to recycling centers.

Waste Receptacles

At least two waste receptacles should be included in a kitchen so that garbage can be separated from recyclables. The NKBA recommends that one of the waste receptacles be located near the sink. It is a good idea to locate waste receptacles out of eyesight. In many homes, the waste receptacle is kept in a cabinet under the sink. If the receptacle is emptied frequently, this location may be suitable; however, to preclude garbage and waste products from spilling into the cabinet, good kitchen design offers a better alternative. Enclosing waste receptacles in a pantry or broom closet, in pullout drawers that hold one or more waste receptacles, or installing a trash compactor provide some solutions.

Trash compactors are motor-driven electric appliances that compact trash to reduce volume by as much as 75 percent. They are designed to fit beneath a standard-height counter, they can be freestanding, or they can be convertible (installed either as freestanding or under the counter). During operation, they are noisy, although most models have some insulation designed to attenuate noise. A tilt-out trash container is a feature on some models. Because they may have up to 5000 pounds of compacting force, they have a key control to prevent accidental operation.

A home recycling center provides a place to temporarily store recyclable items. The recycling center can be located in the kitchen, in a closet, in the laundry, in the garage, or another location. Basements may have more available space, and a trash chute leading from the story above will simplify the immediate disposal of items. The number of containers required depends on the number of categories into which solid wastes are sorted. The number should comply with local recycling center requirements for sorting. Locating containers on carts will simplify moving them when they are full.

Electrical Requirements for Kitchens

The National Electrical Code (NEC) requires that kitchen receptacles be protected by a GFCI. In the kitchen, a receptacle is needed for every 4 feet of counter frontage, and there should be at least one receptacle at each separate counter area. Each counter space wider than 12 inches is required by the NEC to have a receptacle. Kitchens with a gas supply tube for a range also need a 120-volt receptacle near the range for a clock, timer, and fan that are part of some ranges. If planning for use of an electric range, a 240-volt circuit and receptacle should be located in the appropriate position.

Laundry Facilities

It was not until water was piped into homes that washing was brought inside. Today, automatic equipment makes a variety of laundry locations possible. An automatic washer requires a drain line, plumbing hookups for hot and cold water, and a 20-ampere, 120-volt circuit. A dryer requires either a gas supply and a 120-volt circuit or a 240-volt current. The National Electrical Code requires that a minimum of one receptacle be provided in the laundry area within 6 feet of the location of the washer. Because dryers need to be vented to the outdoors, the best location is near an exterior wall. The IRC requires that dryers be located so the maximum length of the vent is 25 feet or less. The NAHB reports that a separate laundry room was the top-rated essential feature of a home.[8]

In addition to the washer and dryer, other equipment located in the laundry area may include the following. See Table 14.2 for typical laundry equipment sizes.

- Pedestals beneath the washer and dryer raise the height of the equipment as much as 15 inches. Some models have drawers for the storage of laundry supplies. See Figure 14.12.
- A drying cabinet is designed to dry items that should not be put into the dryer. Pullout shelves are designed for drying flat items such as sweaters. These units also have hanging racks for drying clothing and other items. A 120-volt receptacle is needed.
- A fabric freshener is a collapsible electrical unit (120-volt) that uses steam to remove odors and wrinkles from clothing. The attached bag is much like a garment bag, and clothing can be hung inside. The collapsed size of the unit makes it portable.
- An ironing station fits between standardly spaced studs in a wall, although it projects into the room. A side-hinged door opens to reveal a fold-down ironing board, often with shelving behind it for the iron and other supplies.

Table 14.2 Typical Laundry Equipment Sizes*

Appliance	Width	Depth	Height
Fabric freshener	33	12	10
Ironing station	14.5	12	48
Washer			
Front load	27	32	38
Top load	27	27	44
Large capacity	27	26	43
Compact	24	22	34
Dryer			
Front load	27	32	38
Large capacity	29	29	43
Compact	29	28	36
Stacked washer and dryer	28	33	73
	24	28	72
Washer / dryer pedestal with drawer	30	27	13, 15
Drying cabinet	24	24	68
Jetted laundry tub	25	22	12

* All dimensions are in inches. The dimensions given are typical and can be used for planning purposes. Actual dimensions of appliances selected should be used during final planning stages.

Figure 14.12 The washer and dryer in this laundry have been mounted on pedestals, making them more accessible.

Laundry facilities should be placed so they are convenient, requiring as little relocation of laundry as possible. Basement locations may use otherwise wasted space but are not as efficient because people must climb up and down stairs to do laundry. A laundry chute makes it easier to get the clothes downstairs, but they must still be carried upstairs after they are laundered.

Where local codes permit, laundry equipment can be located in the kitchen if it is away from food preparation areas. Tasks of the kitchen and laundry can then be efficiently dove-tailed. Plumbing facilities are generally close at hand, so installation expense can be minimized. Separate laundry rooms are most often located near the kitchen for the same reasons. When placed in the kitchen itself, laundry equipment can be concealed behind folding doors or selected to coordinate with kitchen appliances.

A mudroom near the family entry is also a good place to locate laundry facilities, especially in rural areas and in homes with children at the age of rough-and-tumble play. Even a remodeled closet or pantry

can serve as a laundry area, especially when a compact, stackable washer and dryer are purchased.

In warm climates, the laundry center can be located in a carport, garage, enclosed porch, or breezeway. However, these areas should be avoided if freezing weather is expected. Water in pipes expands when frozen and may crack certain washer parts.

Since most dirty laundry is accumulated in bathrooms and bedrooms, a laundry center in this zone would seem ideal. Plumbing facilities are close and installation is inexpensive. However, the noise of equipment operation and the humidity and odors associated with laundry may preclude this placement. Sound conditioning in walls can help alleviate the problem of noise.

Laundry tubs are deeper than kitchen sinks and are used for hand-washing, pretreating stains, and diluting laundry additives. A combination sink/laundry tub has two bowls, with the laundry tub deeper than the sink, and is usually installed in the kitchen where the laundry tub may be covered with a removable drain board. A laundry sink may be a simple deep sink or a model with whirlpool jets. The jetted variety requires a 120-volt receptacle for operation. The jets are powered by a motor that forces water into the sink. This type of sink is designed for delicate items.

Storage facilities for laundry supplies should be handy to the washer and dryer location. Other desirable additions to the laundry area, depending on available space, are:

- A storage area for accumulated dirty laundry
- A work surface for sorting and folding
- A place to hang permanent-press garments as they come from the dryer
- A space for the iron and ironing board

These facilities should be arranged so that work flows smoothly through collection, sorting, pretreating and hand-washing, washing, drying, hanging and folding, ironing, and returning clothing to individuals for use. See Box 14.5 for accessibility guidelines.

Storage Areas

When people owned only what they could carry with them, storage was much simpler. As people acquired more possessions, the demand for permanent storage space in homes increased. Today, a significant portion of the housing dollar is spent on closets, cabinets, drawers, and shelves. Up to 10 percent of the floor space in a home may be allotted to storage. Built-in storage consists of permanently attached storage units, closets, and racks. Built-in storage more efficiently organizes space but it cannot be easily moved and it may interfere with furniture arrangement. Freestanding storage generally requires greater floor area but is more flexible. Major advantages of temporary storage units are that they can be moved within the house, taken along when the family leaves, or disposed of if no longer needed. Freestanding storage includes wardrobes, cabinets, and trunks. Open storage includes bookcases and display shelves and can be used in almost any room in the home. See Figure 14.13. Full bookcases are excellent sound and heat insulators.

Obviously, the number of items to be stored affects the amount of storage needed. Where and how items are stored is also important.

- Items should be stored where they will be used.
- Those items used together should be stored together.
- Frequently used garments and supplies should be stored where they are easy to reach without first removing other items.

Pegboards and narrow shelves help make stored items easy to locate at a glance. Heavy or bulky items

Box 14.5 Designing Laundries for Accessibility

- A front-loading washer is best for accessibility. The openings of both washer and dryer should be slightly higher than the armrests of a wheelchair.
- A stacked washer and dryer may be more accessible for individuals with walkers or crutches.
- All appliance controls should be accessible—on the appliance front is most appropriate.

should be stored near the floor. Factors such as the need for coolness or darkness also affect storage location.

Closets provide storage space in bedrooms, entries, and other places throughout the house. They usually have a rod for hanging clothes and may have shelves and drawers for other items. The available

Figure 14.13 Bookcases serve as storage not only for books but for other objects and take up little space in a room.

As the size of the home increases, the closet size should increase proportionately. While a minimum of 3 feet of closet rod per person may be sufficient in very small homes, 10 feet of closet rod per person may not be sufficient in larger homes. Individuals who can afford the luxury of a larger home will, in all likelihood, have more clothing and more nonessential items that must be stored.

If the attic has no floor, ensure that the joists are a minimum of 8 inches wide or more before using the area for storage. Often, smaller-dimension lumber is used for ceiling joists to minimize costs, and they may have insufficient strength to support additional loads.

rod space can be doubled by providing two rods at different heights. Short items such as jackets, shirts, blouses, and skirts can then be hung in layers. Each closet should, however, have some full-length rod space for longer garments.

Generally, a minimum of 3 feet of rod space per person is needed in bedroom closets. Closets may be long and narrow with doors along the entire length, but this configuration decreases wall space considerably and affects the furniture placement. Walk-in closets provide more storage space. They have rods on each side for hanging clothes and may also have shelves and drawers. Heavy garments on hangers require approximately 22 inches of space. Closets, then, should have a minimum clear depth of 24 inches. If clothing is hung on both sides of a walk-in closet, 24 inches should be allowed on each side, with a minimum of 22 inches and preferably 30 inches or more for a walkway, resulting in a minimum overall clear width of 5 feet 10 inches to 6 feet 6 inches. A 7-foot-wide closet will have approximately 6 feet 6 inches of clear space when wall thickness is subtracted.

When located on outside walls, closets help to insulate against heat loss or gain.

Closets should be lighted, preferably with an automatic switch that activates when the door is opened or closed, or with a switch located on the latch side of the door outside the closet. Closets are ideal as acoustic insulators and can be placed between rooms for this purpose.

In addition to clothes closets, homes need a linen closet with a minimum dimension of 2 feet wide and 18 inches deep near bedrooms. An NAHB reports that 88 percent of individuals prefer a linen closet in the bathroom as well.[9]

Basements and attics provide storage space for items that are seldom used. The high humidity of some basements, however, may lead to the damage of stored items. Attic storage is often limited by the height of the rafters and the size of the attic opening, especially when a small ceiling panel provides the only access. If there is no attic floor, boards may be laid at right angles to the joists to provide support for stored items.

Most people feel they do not have enough storage space. While this may be due to an excess of accumulated possessions, the storage space in many homes, especially in multifamily housing, is truly inadequate. Considerable ingenuity may be required to overcome this problem, but it can be done. The construction of bins or shelves in formerly wasted space, such as under stairways or in recesses, is an inexpensive way to increase the efficiency of the home. A small outdoor shed can relieve crowding in a garage or basement. When planning a new home, it is best to include enough space for not only present but future storage needs, although this consideration must be balanced with construction costs. In general, well-organized storage space means less space is required.

Garages and Carports

A garage is an enclosed unit, whereas a carport is open on at least two sides (as per the IRC definition).

Both are designed to protect the automobile from cold, rain, snow, and other outdoor hazards. A garage or carport may be a separate structure or attached to the house. Attached garages and carports are more desirable because they provide protection from inclement weather for the family. They should be directly connected to the family entrance or lead to it through a breezeway, porch, or covered walk. A 3-foot doorway between the garage and the living space is desirable but a 2-foot-8-inch or 2-foot-6-inch door may be allowable by local building codes. This door may not lead directly into sleeping areas due to the potential hazards of carbon monoxide. Usually, this doorway leads into a service zone in the home.

Single-car garages should be a minimum of 11 × 20 feet; two-car garages, a minimum of 21 × 20 feet. Minimum sizes, however, allow little space for walking around a vehicle and may not be large enough for some vehicles. A typical extended-cab pickup truck, for example, is 21 feet 4 inches long and 6 feet 8 inches wide, sports utility vehicles are often as long or longer, and recreational vehicles extend even further. See Table 14.3 for typical vehicle sizes. A minimum

Table 14.3 Typical Vehicle Sizes*

Vehicle type	Length	Width	Height
Compact car	181	69	53
	169	67	57
Midsize car	198	73	56
Luxury car	212	78	57
Sports car	187	72	53
Pickup truck			
Regular cab	225	78.5	74
Extended cab	249	79	74
Dual rear wheels		96	77
Sport utility vehicle	187	74	69
	204	82	80
	220	79	74
Van	212	80	82
Minivan	201	77	71

* All figures in inches are rounded to the next highest number. These figures are typical examples and do not represent specific vehicles.

Box 14.6 Designing Garages for Accessibility

- Minimum garage length for accessibility is 24 feet. Additional space may be needed depending on the vehicle length. A walkway of at least 3 feet should be provided.
- A minimum of 5 feet should be allowed between vehicles and between vehicles and other obstructions for a fully open vehicle door and an adjacent wheelchair. This increases the minimum garage width to 12 to 14 feet 6 inches, depending on the vehicle width.

---

additional length of 22 inches is needed to ensure adequate space for walking around the front or back of a vehicle to reach an entry; a more comfortable distance is 30 inches or more, which allows space for carrying packages. Opening a vehicle door may require as much as 4 feet of space, which should be allowed on both sides between a vehicle and a wall or between two vehicles. See Box 14.6 for accessibility guidelines.

A National Highway Traffic Safety Administration survey found that only 12 percent of the people who had three-car garages used them for parking. Most used them for storage. Three-car garages, however, require more space, which often means larger lots. It may be difficult to add a garage space for an

---

In determining the space needed in a garage, it is important to remember that all dimensions include the thickness of exterior walls and half the thickness of interior walls. Thus, a 20-foot-long garage does not have 20 feet of clear space but 20 feet minus wall thicknesses. In addition, an overhead garage door is installed on the inside of the garage, requiring approximately 4 inches of space.

Both garages and carports may also serve a storage function but additional length or width should be planned. Often, one side of a carport is enclosed and shelves or cabinets are added as storage space for lawn care equipment, tools, and outdoor recreation equipment. Storage in carports should be lockable.

additional vehicle and meet setback requirements in many urban areas.

Standard garage door sizes are 9 feet wide and 7 feet high for single doors and 15 or 16 feet wide and 7 feet high for double doors. Due to the size of SUVs owned by many clients, some are opting for larger doors—8 feet high and 10 feet wide for single doors. Double doors 18 feet in width should be used when the approach to the garage is not straight. A room above a three-car garage is an option, especially in upscale homes. The room can be used for any purpose, but there should be no connection between the garage and the living space. The IRC requires that when living areas are located above garages, ⅝ inch type X drywall must be used on the garage ceiling. The wall between the garage and living space must have at least ½ inch of drywall. Even climate-control vents should be adequately sealed to prevent noxious fumes from entering living spaces above. Siting the garage to the side reduces the impact of the large expanse of doors. See Table 14.4 for the percentages of different garage sizes.

Because they are enclosed, garages are more expensive to construct than are carports. In cold climates, however, they provide extra protection for family vehicles. Even though garages are not heated, cars protected by them start better in winter. A garage can additionally serve as a workshop. Each garage should have at least one standard-sized

---

The garage can serve as a buffer zone, insulating the house from winds and decreasing heat loss, especially when it is located on either the windward side of the house or on the north.

Table 14.4 Parking Facilities in New One-Family Houses by Percent*

Year	1-car garage	2-car garage	3-car garage	Carport	No facility
1975					
U.S.	14	53	NA	10	22
Northeast	28	41	NA	S	30
Midwest	11	64	NA	2	24
South	14	41	NA	16	30
West	9	72	NA	12	8
1980					
U.S.	13	56	NA	7	24
Northeast	29	42	NA	S	28
Midwest	12	66	NA	2	20
South	12	66	NA	2	20
West	10	71	NA	8	10
1985					
U.S.	15	55	NA	5	25
Northeast	30	40	NA	S	29
Midwest	13	73	NA	S	13
South	13	73	NA	S	13
West	10	77	NA	5	8
1990					
U.S.	10	72	NA	2	16
Northeast	22	59	NA	S	19
Midwest	8	83	NA	S	9
South	11	58	NA	4	26
West	3	91	NA	2	4
1995					
U.S.	8	63	13	2	14
Northeast	17	57	8	S	18
Midwest	6	64	20	S	10
South	9	63	5	3	20
West	4	65	24	1	5
2000					
U.S.	7	65	17	1	11
Northeast	16	59	10	Z	15
Midwest	4	63	25	Z	7
South	8	67	7	2	16
West	3	62	30	1	3
2004					
U.S.	7	64	19	1	9
Northeast	14	63	10	Z	12
Midwest	5	57	32	Z	5
South	8	68	9	1	13
West	3	61	31	2	2

Source: http://www.census.gov/const/C25Ann/parkingfacility.pdf (9/25/05).

* The NAHB reports that 54 percent of individuals surveyed desired a two-car garage, which is fewer than those who have them. Three-car garages are becoming more popular and 19 percent of newly constructed homes in 2004 had three-car garages. Source for the NAHB statistic: National Association of Home Builders, *What 21st Century Home Buyers Want: A Survey of Customer Preferences* (Washington, D.C.: Home Builder Press, 2001), 33.

door—preferably 3 feet—that opens to the outdoors to ensure that users need not open the large vehicle door in order to enter or leave the space.

Mechanical Space

Every home requires space for mechanical equipment, including heating and air-conditioning units, air-filtration devices, water heaters, and water softeners. The efficiency of air-quality control usually demands a central location within the home. Water heaters should be located as close to points of use

as possible and often this, too, requires a central location because wa-ter use is spread through various areas of the home. When a basement is present, the mechanical space may be located there, freeing up space on the main levels of the home for other uses. A 4 × 5 foot space is usually sufficient for mechanical equipment. In large homes (3500 square feet and over), it may be necessary to provide two mechanical spaces—one for each living story.

Designing
Private
Areas

Chapter 15

People's shelters may provide a home space where there is privacy and freedom from intrusion, a place where individuals make their own rules, a refuge where people can revive their spirits, and a place for intimacy and companionship. The need for such a refuge of peace and security is intensified by societal demands. The amount and type of privacy offered to individuals depends on both cultural attitudes and individual needs.

The front door marks the beginning of private family territory in a house; fences around the yard visibly extend that territory. Inside the home, the private zone is designed for use by family members rather than guests, although some overlapping occurs. Rooms in the private zone provide visual and acoustic seclusion and usually include bedrooms, bathrooms, and specialized areas such as libraries, darkrooms, and studios.

Privacy

The desire for privacy—the freedom from interaction with others—is not standard in all cultures and, in fact, is a relatively modern phenomenon. It was only in the seventeenth century that rooms were provided where people could get away from public view. These rooms were called *privacies*. In the Chinese language, the word for *privacy* has connotations of shady dealings indicative of their cultural attitudes concerning privacy. The Japanese language had no word for privacy until they had extended contact with Western cultures. They have added a word to their vocabulary—*praibashii*—an obvious reference to the English term.

Visual and acoustic isolation from outsiders can be effectively gained through the choice of site, the location of the house on the site, and such additions as fences and shrubbery. See Figure 15.1. Dwellings can offer extra privacy when some areas face a patio, garden area, or backyard rather than the street. In Mediterranean areas, homes are often built around courtyards, which are themselves not visible from the exterior. Exterior walls have few, if any, openings—most of which face the courtyard. Thus, families can congregate in outdoor areas while still maintaining privacy.

In most cultures, visual privacy is achieved through the use of walls and closed doors. Where climate demands open structures, other ways of achieving privacy must be found. **Jali**—openwork screens around courtyards—provide visual privacy for women in Muslim cultures in hot climates. These women wear veils in public to further protect their privacy. The Yagua of Peru[1] obtain privacy simply by turning away from the center of their open-walled multifamily houses. Among Northwest Coast Indian tribes, privacy is often associated with status. The chief has a private apartment that is screened by boards painted with totemic

Figure 15.1 A fence helps to establish the boundary between public and private spaces and often provides additional privacy for family members.

symbols in the extreme rear within the house. These quarters are off-limits to other occupants except by invitation. Acoustic privacy is more difficult to obtain than is visual privacy.

Even within American society, privacy values depend on status, family size, and individual attitudes. However, any space planned for two or more people should provide some areas for privacy. If it is not possible for each family member to have a private bedroom, the arrangement of furniture can still give a sense of privacy and personal territory. Extra bathrooms and locks on interior doors also help ensure privacy.

The private zone should be located in a quiet part of the house away from outside street traffic and noisy indoor activity areas. Outside, decks, patios, and yard areas designed for the family need to be visually isolated from the general public unless the residence is located in an isolated area. Even when exterior spaces are used as social zones, this visual isolation is an asset. Fences, walls, and hedges can screen outdoor zones.

Territoriality

Territoriality is a characteristic humans have in common with other animals. Animals stake out territory that other members of the same species do not violate or intrude upon. Marking is the first step to defending territory, and to feel safe, people need defensible spaces. Any area that cannot be defended is not private territory or domain.

Typically, the territory people are most willing to defend is their home space, which may include a shelter. The necessity for defending the shelter is obvious. The single-family dwelling in itself establishes a recognizable territory. Individual spaces within multiple-unit structures, however, are more difficult to define.

People in almost every culture use recognizable territorial markers to separate the private dwelling space from public areas. Some of these markers are symbolic in that while they define the space, they provide no

real defense against invasion of the territory; some provide real barriers. Symbolic barriers may include a few steps, an open gateway, or a row of shrubs, trees, flowers, or even a change from a concrete sidewalk to grass. Obviously, these barriers are not designed to bar individuals from entering but to create a distinction between the public and the more private space beyond. Beyond the barrier, an individual's presence requires justification. Real barriers differ from symbolic barriers in that they require some proof of belonging in order to enter. Locked or guarded doors, barrier walls, and electronic interview systems provide this type of barrier.

These barriers are effective because certain behaviors are expected of people who enter. Individuals whose behavior is outside the expected norm can be immediately recognized as strangers. In order to defend the space, it is necessary for residents to identify individuals who belong, be able to see what's going on, and know who is entering the semiprivate spaces such as yards and hallways. This means they must know their neighbors at least in passing. For effective surveillance, occupants of buildings must know one another by sight. They must also be able to see those who enter the semipublic spaces—video cameras and alarms are one way, but windows facing exterior parking lots, grassy areas, and playgrounds would be helpful.

High-rise apartment houses with long, double-loaded[2] hallways often fail because residents do not know who belongs and who does not and, therefore, take no action against invaders. Grouping small numbers of dwelling units on a short hallway with a separate entry limits the number of people officially using the semipublic space of the hall and enables residents to visually recognize one another. This makes it easier to challenge intruders.

Large homogeneous spaces and those that orient everyone toward the center lack lines of demarcation or internal barriers, making it difficult to establish and defend a small territory or to retreat from contact with others in the space. In some cultures, homes

built around a central hearth or that present a circular
footprint almost require that inhabitants acknowledge
and communicate with one another. Japanese huts
and American Indian tepees and hogans are examples. Small, well-articulated spaces generally make it
easier to establish and defend individual territories.

Within the home, it is necessary for individuals to
have a place to call their own. See Figure 15.2. Psychologists have found that when people have a specific space of their own in the home, there is greater
harmony and peace in relationships than when they

do not. When the territory of individuals overlaps, as
when two people share a bedroom, fighting to protect the territory can result. When individuals are located in a remote position, such as in a corner, alcove,
or other small space, it is less likely that another family member will invade the space.

Shelter is commonly used for sleeping. In this case,
the shelter itself may not be as important as the fact
that a territorial claim has been made and is respected
by others. Among the nomadic Basuto in Lesotho, single men and older individuals who lack women to
build a shelter for them simply push a stick into the
ground, claiming that territory for themselves for the
one night they will use the space. They arrange their
few possessions around the stick and stretch out on
the ground beside them to sleep, knowing that their
territorial claim will be respected. Other Basuto sleep
under arches of grass to protect their heads. These
temporary shelters will be blown away by the next
strong breeze, but the Basuto will have already left on
their endless trek for food. Modern campers may simply climb into a sleeping bag under the stars.

Figure 15.2 This study area is arranged so that both children in the family can work at the same time. Both have
their own spaces for filing and for storage of books and
materials, as well as their own computer stations.

Bedrooms

Beds began as straw laid on the floor to make people
more comfortable when they slept. Early civilizations
raised the straw off the floor onto simple frames.
Eventually, the wealthy had beds of ivory, precious
metals, and ornately carved wood. Rather than straw,
their mattresses were filled with feathers and down.

The space where beds are placed has varied according to the culture. Homer wrote of soft Greek
couches placed in recesses around rooms. These provided protection from cold, drafty air. In the four-
teenth century, curtains around European beds accomplished the same thing. In addition, they increased
privacy, especially in households where personal servants slept in the same room as masters. Since it was
warmer in bed than anywhere else in the house, the

bedroom became the place where guests were received. The bed and its hangings were often the most expensive furnishings in the home.

Today, in most parts of American society, the bedroom is the most personal room of the home. Parents occupy a separate bedroom, and children of opposite sexes do not share a bedroom beyond the age of five or six. A maximum of two persons per bedroom is recommended. Therefore, the number of family members determines to a great extent the number of bedrooms needed.

In an NAHB survey, 49 percent of respondents preferred 3 bedrooms but 33 percent preferred 4 bedrooms and 6 percent preferred 5 or more bedrooms. Of all respondents, however, only 67 percent said they would actually use three or more bedrooms for sleeping. These individuals preferred extra bedrooms in order to use them for other purposes—guest rooms, home offices, hobby rooms, exercise rooms, and for storage.[3] See Table 15.1.

Location of Bedrooms

Bedrooms provide personal space for individual activities, sleeping space, and storage areas for personal items. Bedrooms should be located together in the quiet part of the home, away from outdoor traffic noise, noisy indoor areas, and high-traffic areas within the home. For acoustic privacy, bedrooms should be separated from one another and from other parts of the house by closets, circulation areas, bathrooms, utility rooms, or chimneys. This isolation ensures periods of unbroken rest. Bedrooms should also be located where they can be reached directly from a hall without crossing another room. They should have their own bathroom or be near a bathroom, and the path from the bedrooms to the bathroom should not be visible from other zones in the home. In some homes, the master bedroom is separated from other bedrooms by some distance. Guest bedrooms, employee bedrooms, and in-law suites may also be separated from other bedrooms in the home.

Table 15.1 Number of Bedrooms in New One-Family Houses by Percent

Year	2 or fewer bedrooms	3 bedrooms	4 or more bedrooms
1975			
U.S.	14	65	21
Northeast	16	60	24
Midwest	17	65	19
South	10	71	19
West	16	57	27
1980			
U.S.	17	63	20
Northeast	25	53	22
Midwest	20	62	18
South	12	70	18
West	21	55	25
1985			
U.S.	25	57	18
Northeast	35	44	21
Midwest	24	55	20
South	22	63	15
West	23	55	21
1990			
U.S.	15	57	29
Northeast	23	47	30
Midwest	15	57	27
South	13	62	25
West	13	53	34
1995			
U.S.	13	57	30
Northeast	18	49	33
Midwest	17	54	28
South	9	62	29
West	13	54	32
2000			
U.S.	11	54	35
Northeast	18	44	38
Midwest	17	53	31
South	8	58	34
West	11	50	39
2004			
U.S.	11	51	37
Northeast	17	44	39
Midwest	20	51	29
South	8	56	36
West	9	45	45

Source: http://www.census.gov/const/C25Ann/bedrooms.pdf.

Given the fact that consumers plan to use bedrooms for other purposes than sleeping, designers should consider alternate uses for one or more bedrooms in homes and provide features to make the rooms functional for multiple activities.

Bedrooms should be designed for both visual and acoustic privacy and have sufficient floor space for furniture and circulation. There should be more than one spot to place the bed to allow for change and for individual taste. Bedroom suites may have linked spaces designed for separate uses: a sleeping area, exercise area, bathroom, dressing area, sitting area, or home office.

Beds

Although uncommon in America, there are a number of sleeping alternatives. In modern Japan, sleeping mats or futons for the whole family are folded out in a room that serves other functions during the day. In China, northern Europe, and other places, the mattress may be encased in a wooden box with sliding or folding doors to keep warm air in during the winter.

The International Residential Code (IRC) stipulates that a bedroom be a minimum of 70 square feet with no directional dimension less than 7 feet. However, it would take more floor space to accommodate a bed larger than twin size and still leave space for other furniture. See Figure 15.3. See Table 15.2 for mattress sizes.

Beds with headboards, footboards, or both require more space than a mattress on a frame. Beds themselves vary significantly in size even when using the same size mattress. If the actual size of the bed is not known, adding 6 inches of length each for a headboard and a footboard and 6 inches on each side of the mattress for the bed will usually be sufficient.

Table 15.2 Mattress Sizes

Mattress	Width in inches	Length in inches
Crib	28	52
Twin / single	39	75
X-long twin	39	80
Double	54	75
X-long double	54	80
Queen	60	80
Olympic queen	66	79 ½
Standard / eastern king	76	78 or 80
California / western king	72	84
Split king	78	80

Types of Beds

Beds may be freestanding, built-in, hidden from view, or stacked. Freestanding beds may be positioned in the center of a room, with one end against the wall, one side against the wall, in a corner with two sides against a wall, or angled. When more than one person will use a bed, a minimum passage of 22 inches for access should be provided from both long

Figure 15.3 Ideally, the room should be large enough that the bed can be placed to be easily made, with only one end against a wall and with 32 inches of clearance on the other sides.

sides. When two beds are separated only by a passage, a minimum of 22 inches is necessary. Better passageway widths would be 32 to 36 inches. When placed with one long side against a wall, 6 inches of clearance should be provided for the bedding.

Freestanding beds include **hammocks** and suspended beds. Hammocks are made of canvas or rope, with or without frames. Hammocks are often used for sleeping in hot climates because they allow air to circulate beneath the individual. In India, swinging beds suspended from the ceiling on chains are popular. The mattress is suspended on a metal frame and the bed rocks slightly. Swinging cribs are becoming more common in nurseries. **Captain's beds** have drawers for storage beneath them. To provide extra storage, the mattress may be higher than on a standard bed.

Built-in beds provide less flexibility than freestanding beds but are often located in a niche or specially built area. This location may make it difficult to make the bed. In many cultures, built-in beds are common, with the surface used during the day for sitting, eating, and other activities. An elderly or infirm person may occupy the bed during the day. In most instances, blankets and sleeping mats are rolled or folded into a corner during waking hours.

Sometimes, the headboard of a bed is attached to the wall and not to the bed itself. A common arrangement in motels, hotels, and apartments, this precludes moving the bed. Although platform beds are not actually built-in themselves, the bed sits on a raised platform, requiring one or more steps to reach it. The platform may incorporate storage beneath it. It is essential that there be sufficient circulation area on the same level of the platform as the bed for safety—a minimum of 32 to 36 inches on exposed sides of the bed.

Beds require a great deal of space. When the space is needed for other activities, hidden beds can provide extra room. The **Murphy bed**, invented in 1905, folds into a cabinet, closet, or bookcase when it is not being used. It may be hinged at the top or at one side. A **trundle bed** rolls beneath another bed.

Bunk beds are stacked to release living space. Bunks may be single beds, double beds, or a combination using a double bed at the bottom and a single bed at the top. **Loft beds** are located sufficiently far above the floor to allow standing headroom beneath them. Loft beds are usually mattresses on platforms and do not have springs. Both bunk beds and loft beds require a ledge or rail on all open sides to prevent falls. Ladders provide access. Bunks and loft beds are best used in high-ceilinged rooms because a minimum of 4 feet of headroom is needed for sitting up in the bed.

Location of the Bed

The bed should be placed where early morning sun will not shine directly on it, where circulating air does not draft across it, and where it does not become an obstruction when opening doors or drawers. A light switch should be located where it can be reached from the bed. This may be a switch for room lights or a switch on a bedside lamp. There should also be a direct path from the bed to the bathroom.

Because most of the time people spend in bedrooms is actually on the bed, the view from the bed is as important (or even more important) than any view in the room.

In order to provide as much uninterrupted wall space as possible, bedroom doors should be located close to a corner of the room. This includes doors within the bedroom that lead to patios, closets, and bathrooms. Bedroom furniture should not block passageways to closets, bathrooms, or to the bed itself. Case furniture with drawers should have sufficient clear space in front for pulling out the drawers—40 inches is the minimum, although following the recommendation for space between opposite surfaces in kitchens of 48 inches would facilitate use. Nightstands should be approximately the same height as the mattress. A minimum 42-inch diameter dressing

Table 15.3 Typical Bedroom Furniture Sizes[a]

Furniture Piece	Width	Depth	Height
Nightstand	34	19	30
	30	17	31
	26	17	22
Chest of drawers—3 drawers	37	22	31
	46	21	35
Chest of drawers—5 drawers	31	21	46
Chest of drawers—6 drawers	42	19	57
Armoire base and top	50	25	83
	59	27	86
	46	24	78
Double dresser	60	18	30
	68	20	40
Triple dresser	72	20	39
	68	20	44
	68	20	40
	69	20	42
Entertainment center	34	30	88
	94	26	74
	52	26	74
Beds			
California king	84	100	
King—4 poster	84	89	80
King	84	96	
	83	91[b]	
Queen—4 poster	68	89	80
Queen	67	96	
	69	90	
Full	57	92	
Twin	41		
Crib	54	33	41
Semanier—7 drawer	26	17	61
Vanity bench	20	16	18
End-of-bed bench	40	17	18
Toy box	36	20	21
Bookcase	30	12	30

[a] Furniture sizes are typical pieces and vary by manufacturer and type.

[b] Bed height depends on the height of the headboard and footboard and on the depth of the mattress and springs.

Figure 15.4 This tray ceiling has a television set in the angled wall to enable users to watch comfortably from the bed.

area should be provided in the room. See Table 15.3 for typical furniture sizes.

The Master Bedroom

The master bedroom is often located away from other bedrooms to ensure privacy and may, indeed, become a haven for its occupants. A master bedroom suite includes not only sleeping space but areas for other activities, either in the room itself or in adjoining spaces. The bedroom may be open to adjoining areas, including parts of the master bathroom. Other areas may include an exercise room, a sitting room, or a home office. The master bedroom area is a good place to incorporate high ceilings, domes, or cathedral ceilings to create the impression of greater space.

A seating area located within the space provides a quiet location for reading or conversation. Space for end tables and lamps will make the area more inviting and functional. An additional seating unit located at a vanity in the master bathroom ensures comfort while carrying out certain grooming activities. The vanity, of course, could be located within the bedroom space as well.

Providing space and appropriate wiring for an entertainment center in the master bedroom area brings some of the entertainment devices into the room. Some clients may desire to watch television while relaxing in bed or listen to music while in the room. A television can be concealed in an armoire or cabinet, decreasing its visual impact on the room. The ceiling in Figure 15.4 is located above a bed.

Walk-in closets in the master bedroom area provide room for the storage of clothing. Two separate closets not only provide additional storage but facilitate the separation of personal items. Built-in shelving and drawer units within the closets improve storage capacity even in a small space.

Children's Bedrooms

As children grow, they become involved in more social activities with their peers, and their need for space in which to entertain friends is increased. In addition, older children become more independent and need more privacy. Extra storage space for clothing and personal belongings is also important. Private bedrooms and large closets become priorities, but few modifications need to be made in the living space itself. See Figure 15.5.

Children change as they grow, so it is essential to consider not only present but future needs when

Figure 15.5 This bedroom is child-friendly and even has a stepstool to help the child get into the bed. Favorite things are part of the decor.

Providing an adult-sized chair in a child's room may not only invite parents to spend time in the room but assure the children that parents want to be there.

designing a bedroom for children. If two or more children share a bedroom, it is also necessary to ensure that each child has an individual space. This may be accomplished by a room divider, whether it is a screen, a low wall, or a piece of furniture, or by using an L-shaped room. Space should be provided for a bed, a storage chest, a child-sized chair, a nightstand or bedside table, and sufficient storage for toys and other paraphernalia.

To encourage creative activities and play, a child's room may have a specialized play area, such as a climbing device, a fantasy play area complete with spaceship or castle, or a stage on which children can become stars. When there are extra bedrooms, it may be desirable to use a space between two occupied bedrooms as a play space. A separate room for play makes it easier to keep bedrooms organized and removes the temptations of playing with toys during hours children are supposed to be sleeping. Plenty of shelving will also help children keep their play spaces organized. As children grow, the playroom can be converted to a room designed for study.

Because children will probably climb up to be able to see out of a window, it may be desirable to have windows with a lower sill height. The IRC requires that glazing lower than 18 inches be of safety glass or tempered glass. An alternative to a low window is a safe platform in front of the window that the child can use for viewing, but for safety, the window should be of safety glass.

Closet rods in children's rooms may need to be adjusted. In some instances, an additional lower rod can be installed for the child's use. Adjustable rods are also available, making it possible to move the rod upward as the child grows.

As children grow older, they may need additional storage space, a desk for studying, and extra space for entertaining friends. Teenagers may appreciate a mattress on a frame covered with pillows or bolsters in lieu of a bed frame. The bed can then serve as a couch during the day and a bed at night.

Guest Rooms

Guests may be accommodated in a separate room, an elaborate suite, or in a room used for other purposes. A convertible sofa in a family room, living room, or even a home office may house guests. Regardless of where guests are located, there should be a full-length mirror, a switchable night-light, and a bathroom that is easily accessible and that has either a counter space or a table near the lavatory for toiletries. Within the space, there should be a flat space for luggage located somewhat off the floor. A separate thermostat control in the guest area indicates a concern for the guest's comfort. If the guest room is to be frequently used, a private bathroom adjacent to the bedroom would be most welcoming.

Rooms Designed for Special Purposes

Because individual lifestyles vary significantly, the rooms within a home may differ. In some instances, space requirements are specific; in others, almost any type of space can be adapted. In many instances, it is a bedroom that is adapted for other uses. Hobbies, modes of entertainment, or collections may dictate how some spaces are used. Access to materials or the weight of objects may influence the location of the space. See Figure 15.6 for an example of an alternate use.

If a number of bookcases are to be used for storing books, they should be located perpendicular to joists or near walls that have sufficient support beneath them.

Figure 15.6 An exercise room may be located anywhere. An NAHB survey found that 29 percent of respondents would like an exercise room in their homes. This one has plenty of natural light, which helps make it an inviting space.

As the availability of leisure time increases, the number of avocational interests also rises. In fact, leisure activities may become an end in themselves. Americans typically have hobbies, some of which require a considerable amount of space in the home or a location near facilities such as a golf course. When people value their avocational interests highly, they select housing that will make it easier to pursue their hobbies. An extra room or specially designed corner may be necessary for working on hobbies or displaying collections. Additional space may be required for the storage of supplies and partially finished projects. The living space should also include provisions for more passive uses of leisure time, such as enjoying music, DVDs, conversation, and nature.

Libraries

An in-home library may be used for storing books, as an office, for reading, or for displaying collections of books. A 3-foot-wide bookcase that is eight feet tall can hold up to 700 pounds of books. If there are children in the home, bookcases should be attached to the floor or wall to prevent their falling over if they are climbed upon. A lighted slanted shelf, either free-standing or within a bookcase, can display a special book or allow users to peruse a volume while standing. The shelf should have a lip at the bottom so the contents do not slip off. If books are located more than 6 feet from the floor, a rolling ladder on a track provides access. NAHB survey results indicate that 54 percent of individuals prefer to have a den or library in their homes (the survey did not differentiate between the two).

Darkrooms

The serious pursuit of photography requires a darkroom. The room may be located almost anywhere and may not require a large space. It is important that the room be capable of being totally dark to avoid fogging undeveloped film. Windows can be covered with black adhesive film, painted black, or temporarily covered with photographic cloth. If possible, a darkroom should have a water supply, although prints could be carried elsewhere for washing. It is best if wet processes can be on opposite sides of the room from dry processes, although a screen could be installed between the two areas if necessary. A darkroom requires an air exchange approximately every six minutes to vent fumes from chemicals. A special light-proof vent may be necessary to ensure that light does not enter. Since most chemicals are used during wet processes, air should exit on that side to minimize the spread of chemical fumes through the room. A receptacle is needed for the enlarger and should be above the work area. The room may have a standard light as well as a red safelight. A place for hanging prints for drying is also needed.

Studios

Artists, draftspersons, architects, graphic designers, engineers, and others may desire a studio in their

Locating a studio on the north side of a structure helps to provide consistent diffuse light throughout the day, as well as throughout the year, and that creates no glare on surfaces.

homes. A major requirement for a studio is adequate lighting—preferably natural light from the north. A drawing board may be required for efficient work: A minimum surface of 30 × 42 inches and usually more is desirable. Adequate space for the storage of products should be provided. The type of storage desirable depends on the medium used and the size of the products. Storage for drawings or paintings includes the following.

- Work mounted on boards such as artists' canvases may be stored in vertical slots.
- Plan racks store drawings in vertical space.
- Flat files are composed of shallow drawers used for storing drawings horizontally. See Table 15.4 for flat file sizes.
- Pigeonholes store drawings that are rolled.

In all instances, sufficient space in front of the storage units is necessary for pulling out drawers or boards.

In some instances, special utilities need to be provided. A potter, for example, may require both a wheel and a kiln. Depending on the size, either may require 240-volt electrical service, and a gas kiln requires a gas line and an associated gas vent. The intense heat associated with firing makes good ventilation imperative—a fan or open window may serve the purpose.

Table 15.4 Flat File Sizes

Sheet Size	Width	Depth	Height*
24 × 36	41	29	20
30 × 42	47	36	20
36 × 48	54	42	20

* The dimensions above are exterior. Interior drawer sizes are approximately 1 inch larger than the sheet size. Height varies considerably depending on the number of drawers and whether there is a base beneath.

Dyes, glazes, and chemicals used by ceramists and fiber artists also require good ventilation. If a kiln is used, the floor may require protection with firebrick. Storage for pottery and other products may require open shelving.

Bathrooms

Puritans believed that bathing was not only unhealthy but immoral because it promoted nudity and promiscuity. In some states, it was illegal to bathe. However, by the nineteenth century, more than 1500 bathtubs had been sold and were in use in Philadelphia.

The bathroom in modern American homes serves two basic functions: bathing and the elimination of body wastes. Only relatively recently have facilities for these two functions been combined in a single room.

In fact, only recently has either been brought into the house. By the mid-nineteenth century, separate rooms were being built in finer new homes to house the bathtub. (See Figure 15.7.) The bathroom became the place for bathing. Heated water was carried in to fill the tub until running water was available. In the early part of the twentieth century, bathrooms as small separate rooms began to be included in most urban homes. Many rural homes did not have running water and, thus, bathrooms until after World War II.

Bathrooms range in size from tiny closets to large airy rooms with skylights and greenhouses. Most homes have at least one full bath with a toilet, lavatory, and bathtub. New homes with three or more bedrooms usually have at least two bathrooms, one of which may be a three-quarter bath and house a shower stall rather than a bathtub. See Table 15.5. A second bathroom off the master bedroom is very popular. In multistory homes, a bathroom on each

Figure 15.7 Victorian bathtubs were made of cast iron and raised on legs. This antique has been faux finished to match the walls. (Source: Heather Ireland-Weter)

floor is becoming more of a necessity than a luxury. A half bath (sometimes called a powder room)—consisting of only a toilet and a lavatory—is often located near the guest entrance, especially when all other bathrooms are located on another level. See Box 15.1 for suggestions for designing bathrooms with children in mind.

Bathroom Design Criteria

Because bathrooms are relatively small, their arrangement for maximum convenience, privacy, and comfort is important. The entrance to a bathroom should be visually isolated from living areas in the home, and the toilet in any bathroom should not be visible when the door is open. The bathroom may be located on an outside wall where it can be ventilated by a window in the summer. However, since a fan is needed in any case for cool-weather venting, interior bathrooms are becoming more common. Because bathers must disrobe, the bathroom also requires additional heat. A common solution is to install a separate heating unit or infrared bulb controlled by a switch. When windows are present, their location should be carefully considered. Windows inevitably create drafts and, thus, are least desirable over a shower or bathtub. Their placement over toilets is also questionable for this reason.

Although a bathroom is often a single room, compartmentalization increases its efficiency. Bathing facilities, the toilet, or both may be enclosed in an area separate from the lavatories. See Figure 15.8. Compartmentalization makes it possible for two activities to be carried out simultaneously while ensuring privacy for everyone. Because compartmentalization divides the room into smaller areas, each compartment may appear cramped. The use of pocket doors between areas eliminates the need for space for a door swing. Providing natural light in each area visually enlarges the space. This can be done with skylights, windows, or by using translucent materials such as glass blocks, obscure glass, or frosted glass for partitions

Table 15.5 Number of Bathrooms in New One-Family Houses by Percent

Year	1 ½ or less baths	2 baths	2 ½ baths	3 or more baths
1975				
U.S.	41	40	20	NA
Northeast	62	17	20	NA
Midwest	54	28	18	NA
South	34	47	19	NA
West	26	53	21	NA
1980				
U.S.	28	48	25	NA
Northeast	47	24	30	NA
Midwest	41	33	26	NA
South	22	55	23	NA
West	20	55	24	NA
1985				
U.S.	24	48	29	NA
Northeast	39	26	35	NA
Midwest	33	36	31	NA
South	20	54	26	NA
West	16	56	28	NA
1990				
U.S.	13	42	27	18
Northeast	24	23	42	11
Midwest	18	36	29	16
South	11	50	24	15
West	5	44	24	27
1995				
U.S.	11	41	33	15
Northeast	23	18	48	11
Midwest	18	31	38	13
South	8	49	28	15
West	6	45	29	19
2000				
U.S.	7	39	34	20
Northeast	13	19	53	14
Midwest	11	33	40	16
South	5	56	29	20
West	5	38	31	26
2004				
U.S.	5	39	33	24
Northeast	8	19	56	18
Midwest	11	33	35	21
South	3	45	30	22
West	3	37	31	29

Source: http://www.census.gov/const/C25Ann/sftotalbaths.pdf.

Box 15.1 Designing Bathrooms for Children

- Compartmented baths are particularly suitable for homes with children, providing each child privacy. At least the toilet should be in a separate compartment if there is insufficient space for compartmentalizing the bathing unit and the lavatories.
- Ideally, each child should have a separate lavatory. If there is more than one child in a family, at least two lavatories should be provided.
- Mirrors installed above the lavatory should extend to about 6 inches above the splashback to enable children to see themselves while brushing their teeth.
- Vanity and lavatory height can be lowered 6 inches so that it rises just 30 inches above the floor and is accessible for older children without being unduly uncomfortable for average adults. If the bathroom is to be used primarily by children, this is a good alternative. A stable stepstool that can be tucked beneath the lavatory will facilitate use by children.
- The faucet handles of a bathtub or combination tub and shower are usually easier for children to reach than shower controls. If accessible controls are not available, an adult should operate out-of-reach handles rather than providing a step for children.
- All bathroom faucets should have temperature-limiting devices if the temperature of the water heater is set above 105 degrees Fahrenheit. This will ensure that children do not burn themselves when using the facilities unsupervised or when washing their favorite toys.
- Faucets located where children could fall into them, such as in a shower or bathtub, may be protected with soft covers.
- Children can more easily access a bathtub if there is a step that runs the full length of the tub. Such a step also makes it easier for adults to help children bathe. The step should be a minimum of 12 inches deep.
- Install a ledge around the bathtub for resting bath toys.
- Even bathing units with nonslip surfaces on the bottom should have an additional slip-proof mat.
- A showerhead with an adjustable height will facilitate bathing for older children bringing the water down to a more comfortable height.
- Shower controls should be sufficiently low so that older children can reach them.
- Grab bars near showers and bathtubs should be located at an appropriate height for children in the family. It may be necessary to adjust the height as the children grow.
- Children are very territorial; when there is more than one child in a family, a shelf, drawer, or cupboard should be provided for each child in the bathroom where they can keep personal items.
- Towels and washcloths of different colors for each child can be hung on lowered towel racks for easy accessibility.
- Bleach-based additives should not be used in toilets until children are old enough not to be tempted by water in an accessible toilet bowl. Locks can be purchased for the toilet lid to prevent children from flushing away toys and other objects that might clog the pipes.
- Bathrooms should have a lockable cupboard for toiletries and cleaning products.
- Locks on bathroom doors should be capable of being opened from outside in case children lock themselves into the room.

442

Figure 15.8 The toilet compartment requires little space but allows for privacy in this bathroom. The bathtub has a cultured marble skirting. (Source: Barbara Huffman)

between areas. Frequently, toilets are not completely compartmentalized but screened by partial walls, shelves, or planters. Lavatories may be located in an alcove visible from the bedroom, with bathing facilities and toilets enclosed in a separate bathroom.

Although bathrooms are smaller than most other rooms, it is desirable to have ample storage in drawers and cabinets for cleaning supplies, personal care items, and bath supplies. An NAHB survey found that 88 percent of individuals wanted a separate linen closet in the bathroom as well. The linen closet should be 2 feet deep and a minimum of 18 inches wide. A clothes hamper can be concealed in the bottom of a linen closet, while shelving above holds bath linens and supplies. Because lavatories consume space inside of vanities, the amount of available storage is reduced

significantly. Additional drawer stacks, case furniture pieces, and cabinets provide space for more storage. A seating unit and a space to lay clean clothing are also desirable.

Luxury bathrooms may have a sauna, a lounging area, an exercise space, a hot tub, or a bathtub designed for multiple users. While most bathroom features are usually hidden from view, luxury features such as these are often partially open—usually to the master bedroom.

For accessibility, the bathroom door should have a minimum width of 32 inches. In homes where there are elderly, infirm, or individuals with limited mobility, it may be desirable for the entry door to open outward rather than into the room. While this obstructs the hallway, it provides a measure of safety if someone falls or needs assistance. In this event, they could obstruct the passage of the door into the room. See Box 15.2 for accessibility suggestions in bathrooms.

Plumbing Fixtures

Plumbing fixtures in bathrooms include lavatories, bathtubs, showers, toilets, and bidets. Urinals may become more important in homes. Fixture choices range from replica models to sleek modern styles.

Lavatories

Lavatories come in a variety of shapes—round, oval, rectangular, triangular, and even more exotic shapes such as seashells. Some lavatories have a soap ledge, which may be perforated for water drainage. Lavatories are made of vitreous china, solid surfacing materials, stone, enameled or stainless steel, copper, or glass.

Bathroom lavatories may be wall-hung, freestanding, or part of a cabinet assembly. Wall-hung lavatories are the least expensive but drain pipes are exposed. Freestanding models may incorporate a pedestal in which the pipes are hidden, presenting an uncluttered appearance, or they may be on legs with the drain pipes exposed. Both wall-hung and freestanding models require little floor space in a room; however, there is no counter space on which to rest hair dryers, toothbrushes, and other items during use.

Pedestal units may be knocked loose if hit and pose a potential danger. Semi-pedestal lavatories have only a partial pedestal covering the pipes that does not extend to the floor. For this reason, they are ideal

---

⊞ In residences, wall-hung and pedestal lavatories are most suitable for half baths where users will not be expected to require space on which to lay objects. In other instances, a small table or shelf can be provided nearby to alleviate the problem presented by the lack of a countertop.

Box 15.2 Designing Bathrooms for Accessibility

- Adapting a conventional bathtub for accessibility can include adding a bench-style seat approximately 10 inches high. A better long-term option is the walk-in bathtub.
- An open area in front of the tub is necessary for accessibility. The minimum size is 30 inches deep and equal to the length of the bathtub.
- A shower stall designed for wheelchair access should be a minimum of 4 feet square with a 3-foot opening.
- A 48 × 48 inch open area is needed in front of the toilet for transferring from a wheelchair.
- An open area 30 × 48 inches in front of the vanity provides minimal space for use from a wheelchair.
- A minimum 5-foot diameter area should be open within the bathroom to allow for turning in a wheelchair.
- D-shaped handles and levers on doors and fixtures facilitate use by individuals with limited mobility.
- Towel bars should not be located at the same level as grab bars because they might be mistaken for grab bars and used for support. Using extra grab bars for towel bars would eliminate this problem.

---

for accessibility from a wheelchair. Freestanding lavatories have two legs supporting the front, although the back is wall-hung. Drain pipes are exposed. All wall-hung lavatories require additional structural support, like any heavy object.

Cabinet assemblies not only conceal the pipes, but also provide a flat counter surface for toiletry articles and storage space beneath. Lavatories in cabinet assemblies can be self-rimming, under-counter, rimmed, and integral models. The vanity may be a piece of traditional furniture with space for the lavatory and the plumbing rather than a typical cabinet. Locating a vanity and lavatory in each bedroom helps to minimize the time spent in the bathroom, making sharing less stressful.

A mirror placed above the lavatory and good lighting are essential for grooming. Storage space for cosmetics, supplies, and appliances should be available nearby in a vanity, closet, wall cabinet, or on shelves. Two lavatories make it easier for two people to use the bathroom for grooming at the same time; however, there should be a minimum distance between the centerlines of the two sinks of 48 inches. This distance may not provide sufficient space for simultaneous use. Separating the lavatories by installing two vanities on different walls or across a divider facilitates simultaneous use. This arrangement is especially desirable in a master bathroom. Sink edges should be located a minimum of 12 inches from a wall or other obstruction to ensure that users are able to swing their arms for tasks such as hair drying without colliding with anything. A minimum of 21 inches of floor area is needed between the front of the counter in which the lavatory is located and any obstruction although more space is desirable. Figure 15.9 illustrates these clearances.

Shampoo sinks may also be installed in bathrooms. A shampoo sink is shallower than a kitchen sink and has a spray attachment to facilitate shampooing.

Bathtubs

Today, homes have one or more bathing facilities. A full bath contains a bathtub. The most popular type of bathtub in the United States is the tub that has walls around three sides and only one finished side on the tub itself. The decorative finished side—called an **apron** or **skirting**—may be an integral part of the bathtub or it may be separate. These bathtubs are

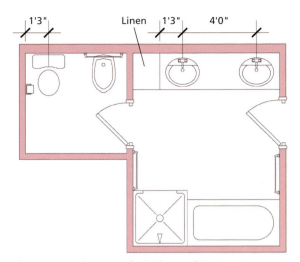

Figure 15.9 Clearances for bathroom fixtures.

often called recessed tubs because they fit into a wall recess. Sunken tubs are difficult to use for bathing young children, and they are difficult to get out of because the user must step up the full height of the tub while standing on a wet surface.

Enameled cast-iron bathtubs are very durable but weigh about 400 pounds, often requiring additional structural support. Because the cast iron is thick, cast-iron bathtubs are fairly quiet. Enameled steel bathtubs can be noisy because they are lightweight. Setting the tub on a sound-deadening block of foam or other material or in sand helps to attenuate the sounds. Insulating the floor beneath the bathtub also helps. Fiberglass and acrylic bathtubs are relatively noisy.

For safety, all tubs should have a slip-resistant surface on the bottom, and many new tubs have this feature built in. Decorative self-stick strips and designs can be applied to others. Grab bars installed around the tub improve the safety of the unit. Grab bars, however, require substantial support in the wall to

For clients who like to wash their hair in the bathtub, a spray arm can be supplied with the bathtub faucet.

ensure the safety of users. There should be sufficient space in front of the bathtub for access; 32 to 36 inches is desirable, although 22 inches will provide for use.

Combination Bathtubs and Showers

Separate shower enclosures may be freestanding or built-in and enclosed in glass, fiberglass, or acrylic. In all types of showers, two or three sides are enclosed with walls, and the other walls have either a waterproof curtain, sliding doors of glass or plastic, or a convoluted entrance that requires no door. When a combination bathtub and shower is used, there are two choices: modular units and one-piece units. Modular units come in two to five pieces. The resulting seams pose potential leakage problems. Modular units are often used in remodeling because the individual pieces are small enough to fit through hallways and doorways.

One-piece units do not have seams, so there is less potential for leakage. They are large and therefore difficult to maneuver around corners and through narrow passageways and doorways. These units are the choice for new construction but their size often precludes their use in remodeling.

Showers

Shower units may be made of fiberglass or acrylic. Shower walls may be made of resins or solid surfacing materials or finished with metal, ceramic, or porcelain

---

❀ American manufacturers are now required to produce 2.5-gallon-per-minute showerheads rather than the older 6-gallon-per-minute models. The International Residential Code stipulates the use of these low-flow showerheads, which conserve not only water but fuel for heating water. According to the U.S. Environmental Protection Agency, replacing a 4.5-gallon-per-minute showerhead with a 2.5-gallon-per-minute model can save a family of four about 20,000 gallons of water per year.

Figure 15.10 Grab bars improve safety around plumbing fixtures and are often installed in accessible bathrooms in homes and public buildings.

tile. Large showers may have one or more seats molded into them. Showers are available with steam units, a foot whirlpool, or even a hydrotherapy spray. Corner showers require less space and are ideal for small areas, although they may not meet IRC minimum size requirements. Grab bars provide additional safety in showers. See Figure 15.10.

The standard height for a single showerhead is 6 feet 6 inches. Some showers have two showerheads —one sufficiently low to prevent the user's hair from getting wet (about 48 inches) and one at standard height. Multiple showerheads are featured in some luxury showers, with water originating from all sides at different levels. Showerheads may be adjustable, permitting the flow to be directed to any location in the shower, or they may be mounted on a bracket from which they can be removed. Spray heads may be adjustable to provide water flow from fine to coarse or a pulsating flow for massage. Rain bars provide a gentle mist, and waterfall spouts deliver a cascade of water. Jet sprays concealed behind shower walls can be programmed for a variety of settings.

Toilets

Toilet bowls may be round or elongated. Elongated or European-style bowls measure 16½ inches from the mounts to the interior of the front edge—about 2 inches longer than round bowls. Although toilets with round bowls are less expensive and use less space, for sanitary reasons the International Building Code requires that public toilets be elongated models with split seats—reducing the possibility of a person's genitalia actually coming in contact with the fixture or the seat. Elongated toilets accommodate standing urination better than round bowls and are therefore more sanitary for men. The disadvantage of elongated toilets is that the vortex action that helps remove wastes is less effective than the action in round bowls.

Some modern toilet models have both a half flush and full-flush option—essentially using the same amount of water for a half flush as does a urinal. Wall-hung models are positioned with the top of the rim 12 to 19 inches from the floor (15 to 16 inches is preferable). Wall-hung models require structural support within the wall.

Some types of toilets are available in both wall-hung and floor models. Wall-hung models are more frequently found in commercial applications than in residences. Wall-hung toilets require no opening in the floor and may be easier to install in existing homes on concrete slabs than floor models. Because they do not touch the floor, wall-hung units are easy to clean around. Floor-mounted toilets are more common; thus, there is a wider variety of choices in color and

Although public men's bathrooms have urinals in them, these fixtures are not commonly found in homes. If water conservation is a goal, families may choose to install at least one urinal. Because most urinals use only 0.75 gallons of water per flush, the water savings could be substantial.

style. Floor models are also less expensive than wall-hung units. Replicas include those with a wall-hung tank installed high on a wall above the bowl, with a long tube connecting the two. A chain pull is used to flush the toilet.

Features that may be found on some toilet models include seats raised to 18 inches rather than the standard 15½ inches, sensor-operated flushing devices, washing wands, lids that automatically lower when the toilet is flushed, and heated seats. There should be a minimum of 15 inches between a side wall and the toilet flange, 1 inch between the back of the toilet tank and a wall, and a minimum 30 × 30 inches of clear area in front of the toilet. The toilet paper holder should be located a minimum of 15 inches from the center of the back of the toilet at a height of 30 inches.

Bidets

Stand-alone bidets resemble toilets. Like toilets, they are generally made of vitreous china. Because the bidet is used immediately after the toilet, it is essential

A few manufacturers produce more decorative toilets for the high-end market. The demand for these toilets is low, often because clients are concerned about the resale value of their homes. Most toilets are designed to match existing plumbing in any home. Installing a toilet is neither expensive nor difficult. It may be possible to specify a decorative toilet if clients realize it can be moved to their next home, keeping their investment. Of course, it will be necessary to replace the toilet in the existing home but a less expensive model can be used for that purpose.

that the two fixtures be adjacent to each other. For aesthetic harmony, they should also be the same height, color, and design. A shelf or fittings for soap, towels, and washcloths should be within reach for an individual using the bidet. Codes concerning the installation of bidets are the same as those for toilets. During use, there is water in the bowl.

Bidets come in a variety of types. The conventional bidet is the modern straddle type. It has faucets on the back, on the wall side. Users adjust the temperature just as with regular faucets, then increase the water pressure by turning the taps on further directing a stream or spray of water.

The Japanese have designed a combination toilet/bidet. It looks and functions like a toilet except that there is a panel extending to one or both sides of the user on which electronic controls are located. At the push of a button, the user can activate a retractable spray arm from beneath the seat, adjust the water temperature and rate of flow, or turn on the electric dryer that blows warm air. Some models prevent the activation of certain operations if there is no one on the seat. One unit even has an air purifier that circulates odiferous air through a charcoal filter. A 120-volt grounded receptacle within four feet is required for operation. Other models are seats designed to install on a regular toilet, making the toilet serve both functions, requiring no additional space. See Figure 15.11. Like the combination toilet/bidet, these bidet seats have a control console and require electricity.

The International Plumbing Code stipulates that both toilets and bidets must not be less than 15 inches from the centerline of the unit to any obstruction: a wall, partition, another fixture, or a cabinet.

⊞ Because bidets require water pressures ranging from 30 to 80 psi, it is necessary to determine actual water pressure at the point of use before deciding which unit to purchase.

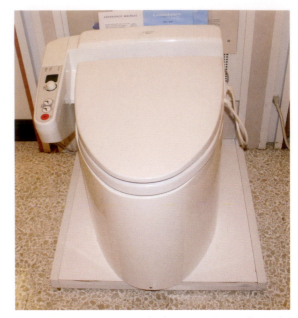

Figure 15.11 The seat on this low, one-piece toilet is designed to fit on a toilet and serve as a bidet. Buttons on the console control water temperature and intensity and the dryer. Combining the toilet and bidet requires no additional space for a second fixture.

The same code requires that there be a minimum of 21 inches of clearance in front of plumbing fixtures. Good design dictates even more space for using fixtures—32 to 36 inches should provide sufficient space for use without crowding.

Bathroom Cabinets

Vanities are often similar to base cabinets, with a drawer blank on the face that covers the area taken up by the lavatory. A major function of the vanity is to conceal the pipes necessary for the lavatory. Stylish vanities may look like furniture and have drawers and enclosed shelving for storage. The depth of vanities is usually 21 inches, although 18-inch units are available. Like base cabinets, widths begin at 18 inches and increase in 3-inch increments to 48 inches.

Toilet cabinets are designed to hang above the toilet tank and are 8 inches deep; linen closets for bathrooms may be 8 inches deep and 84 inches high; and

4-inch-deep wall cabinets with heights from 24 to 30 inches and widths in 3-inch increments from 18 to 48 inches are designed to be installed above a vanity to hold toiletries.

Other Considerations

Although for many years electrical receptacles were not always included in bathrooms, today's large number of electrical personal care appliances has made them a necessity. Receptacles should be within easy reach of the mirror, but the National Electrical Code requires that they be located no closer than 5 feet from a shower or tub. A receptacle that is a part of a lighting fixture does not satisfy this code requirement. The NEC also requires that a bathroom have at least one 20-ampere circuit in addition to the lighting circuit. Hair dryers, electric curlers, and curling irons all require up to 1500 watts of electricity necessitating a 20-ampere circuit. If two or more of the appliances are to be used simultaneously, a second 20-ampere circuit would be desirable. The NEC requires that all bathroom receptacles be protected by ground-fault circuit interrupters. In the United Kingdom, only a single low-voltage receptacle for an electric razor is permitted in the bathroom. Other appliances must be hard-wired into a supply box located outside the bathroom.

A medicine cabinet located out of reach of children, and preferably lockable, may be installed in bathrooms. However, the bathroom is not the best place to store many medicines, because they may be affected by both heat and humidity. A more appropriate location for the medicine cabinet is in a hallway. Some medicine cabinets can be installed between two studs without the necessity of preparing a large opening; others are flush-mounted. Mirrors should be installed at a height suitable for individual users, which is usually between 36 and 42 inches from the floor to the bottom of the mirror. A full-length mirror located in the bathroom aids in grooming as well.

Accessories needed in the bathroom include soap,

Four-inch-deep wall-hung cabinets with storage for toiletries can be installed above a vanity. These cabinets usually have mirrors, some of which can be angled to allow users a three-dimensional view for grooming.

Because recessed medicine cabinets are installed within the wall, it is necessary to ensure that no wires, pipes, or ducts run through the designated space.

glass, and toothbrush holders; towel bars; a toilet paper holder; robe and towel hooks. Towel bars are located between 31 and 43 inches above the floor; towel and robe hooks should be 60 to 66 inches above the floor. Soap dishes, toothbrush holders, and cup holders installed above a lavatory are located 42 inches from the floor. A soap dish associated with a bathtub is located between 24 and 36 inches from the floor. Facilities for towel storage and containers for dirty laundry are also needed in the bathroom or nearby. Grab bars may be installed adjacent to toilets, bathtubs, and showers but require additional wall support for safety.

Outdoor Private Living Areas

Private outdoor living areas include decks and patios. NAHB survey results indicate that 24 percent of individuals desire a rear deck, although there are no data on patios. Private outdoor areas should be located near indoor private areas with doors leading to them. Outdoor living areas are especially desirable in warm-climate areas where they can be used most of the year. These spaces increase living space both for families and for entertaining. Outdoor living areas provide sunshine and fresh air and promote good health. To increase the use of outdoor living areas, comfortable furniture should be included. A cooking area— a barbeque pit or grill, a fireplace, and even a small refrigerator and a water source—can further the desirability of using the space. Windows facing outdoor spaces expand indoor space and, when the outside is well landscaped, also provide a pleasant view.

Fenced-in yards were desired by 29 percent of NAHB survey respondents. Fenced-in yards provide a safe place for children to play, an enclosure for pets, and sometimes visual privacy from neighbors.

Security

People have been concerned with the security of their homes since they began to establish them. However, through the years, cultures have differed in what they consider most threatening and the measures taken to ensure home security. In Morocco, for example, Arabs paint one wall bright blue to protect them from evil spirits. In contemporary Western cultures, locks provide the best security. A lock is a device used for fastening a door, window, or container and is designed to prevent entry by unauthorized individuals.

Types of Locks

The modern pin tumbler cylinder lock was invented by Linus Yale Jr. in the 1860s and is still the most common lock in America. The Yale lock consists of an outer cylindrical shell with a movable inner plug. Holes in the shell correspond with those in the plug when the door is locked. In each of these aligned chambers is a pin tumbler with a spring-activated metal driver. When locked, the drivers or the pins rest partly in the plug and partly in the shell, blocking rotation of the plug. A key with three to seven serrations raises each pin to the proper height. When the tops of all the pins are at the point where the plug meets the cylinder, the plug is free to rotate. A metal arm connects the plug to the bolt.

A variation of the pin tumbler lock that provides even greater security is the magnetic lock. The pins in these locks are magnetized. One or more iron bars in the outer cylinder attract the pins, causing them to rest partly in the chamber and partly in the plug. The key is magnetized at points corresponding to the locations of pins in the lock, which are also magnetized. When the key is inserted, the pins are drawn to it and the lock can be opened. Some magnetic locks are combined with pin tumbler locks, requiring a key with serrated edges as well as magnetized points. A disadvantage of either type of magnetic lock is that whenever the key is not inserted, the door is locked. In emergencies, locating and using the key may cost precious time.

Keyless locks are becoming increasingly used in homes. A series of numbered push buttons controls the lock, which can be set to any desired operating code. The code can be changed in seconds. The operating code may require that a series of buttons be pushed one at a time, several buttons be pushed at the same time, or any combination of these. Most keyless locks are used with **deadbolts**, so they are very secure. They may be connected to an alarm system that goes off after a certain number of unsuccessful attempts to open a lock.

Another type of keyless lock is the **key card lock**, which is opened by a code on a microprocessor chip embedded in a credit-card-sized plastic card. These locks are especially economical in dormitories, apartments, and hotels, where frequent tenant changes make changing locks necessary and expensive. The code is easily changed and entries are logged. Logging entries ensures that owners know who has entered a building or room and the date and time of entry.

Latches and Bolts

A **key-in-knob** lock has a locking button or **thumb turn** in the interior knob and a slot for a key in the exterior knob. When the door is opened or closed, a spring-loaded beveled latch moves in and out of a metal strike plate attached to the jamb. When the locking button or thumb turn is activated, an additional plunger prevents the outside knob from being turned unless the proper key is inserted.

A variation of the key-in-knob lock is the privacy lock, with a thumb turn on the interior and a simple small hole in the exterior. Although the lock comes with a "key" that has a tiny flat edge designed to fit through the hole, almost anything small enough to fit through the hole will unlock the door. These locking knobs are typically used for bathrooms and bedrooms, where security is not important but privacy is.

Although key-in-knob locks are popular, better security is provided by any of several types of locks that include a deadbolt. A deadbolt is a thick metal bar that, when thrown (locked), projects across the gap between the door and the frame. A key is used to throw or retract a deadbolt from the outside. On the inside, deadbolts may be thrown or retracted by means of a thumb turn. Deadbolts require a secondary latch to keep the door closed when it is unlocked.

A **double-cylinder deadbolt** must be operated by a key on both sides, which may be dangerous in emergencies. However, a double-cylinder deadbolt should be used if there is a window or other glass opening within 40 inches of the lock. See Figure 15.12. Otherwise, it would be simple for an intruder to break through the glass and release the lock.

A separate deadbolt can be installed above a regular key-in-knob lock, providing additional security. One type of separate deadbolt lock is mounted in a hole drilled through the door. When thrown, the bolt fits into a strike box that is recessed in the jamb. Another type, called a **rim lock**, is surface-mounted on the inside of the door. The bolt fits into a strike mounted on the frame. Rim locks are not as attractive as more "built-in" locks, but can easily be added to existing doors. One of the most secure locks in existence is a rim lock with a vertical bolt. The lock attached to the door has two or more slots that correspond to projections on the strike. Holes in the projections line up with a bolt that is thrown vertically.

A **mortise lock** combines a deadbolt and beveled latch in one assembly that is installed in a recess cut in

Figure 15.12 A double cylinder deadbolt provides extra security where there is a window in the door. Care must be taken, however, that the door can be quickly unlocked in an emergency.

the edge of the door. Although mortise locks generally look better than separate latches and deadbolts, they are difficult to install. They are usually found in older or custom-built homes.

Sliding glass doors can be inexpensively locked simply by placing a broomstick or dowel along the

Insulated shutters minimize heat loss through windows at night or when a room is unoccupied. They may also serve a security function.

inside floor track to prevent the door from sliding. More sophisticated **charley bars** fit horizontally between the frame and the sliding door, holding it shut, and swing up out of the way when not in use. Special keyed sliding door locks can be installed inside or outside at the bottom or top of the door. These provide better security because a deadbolt fits into an opening in the sash of the stationary unit next to the door.

Window Locks

Windows are another potential means of gaining access to a residence and should be as well protected as doors. For protection from weather as well as intruders, wooden shutters were commonly used for centuries. These could close tightly to cover the window and formed a decorative window treatment when open. Another design element combining decorative and security purposes is a framework of steel or iron that locks in place over each ground-floor window. This system has the disadvantage of interfering with an emergency exit. More commonly, window locks are used to prevent unauthorized entry. Metal grilles can also provide security on windows located some distance from the ground. In this case, a grille prevents accidental falls.

Most windows come with lever locks. However, if the glass is broken, these can easily be unlocked and the window opened. A nail placed in a window slide channel can serve as an inexpensive window lock, but the window cannot then be used for ventilation or an emergency exit. The best solution is a keyed lock that allows the window to be opened easily from the inside, yet effectively secured from intruders when desired.

Appendix

House Plans

This appendix exemplifies drawings that would be part of the contract documents for a residential client. They present a visual summary of the aspects of planning and design covered in detail in the text. The following drawings are included:

- Front rendered view of the exterior
- Front exterior elevation
- Rear exterior elevation
- Left exterior elevation
- Roof plan
- Plot plan
- First floor plan
- Foundation plan
- Electrical plan
- Plumbing plan
- Sanitary plan
- Mechanical plan

Source: These drawings were prepared by Jason Dillbeck, Nuclear Imagery.

ARCHITECTURAL SYMBOLS

- cased opening
- interior swinging door
- exterior swinging door
- pocket door
- bifold door
- sliding door
- overhead garage door
- casement window
- double hung window
- sliding window
- picture window
- pass through

PLUMBING SYMBOLS

- faucet
- towel bar
- bathtub
- bathtub sliding door
- shower
- shower head
- shower with seat
- laundry
- accessible lavatory
- wall lavatory
- bidet
- toilet
- urinal
- double kitchen sink
- single kitchen sink
- triple kitchen sink
- utility or laundry sink
- hosebib

ELECTRICAL SYMBOLS

- ceiling light
- wall mounted light
- track light
- duplex receptacle
- 220-240 receptacle
- waterproof receptacle
- single pole switch
- three-way switch
- four-way switch
- dimmer switch
- exhaust fan
- telephone jack
- doorbell
- television connection
- speaker

HVAC SYMBOLS

- ceiling fan
- thermostat
- HVAC supply vent
- return air vent

SITE SYMBOLS

- deciduous tree
- evergreen tree
- water feature

FRONT ELEVATION
SCALE: 1/8" = 1'-0"

REAR ELEVATION
SCALE: 1/8" = 1'-0"

LEFT ELEVATION
SCALE: 1/8" = 1'-0"

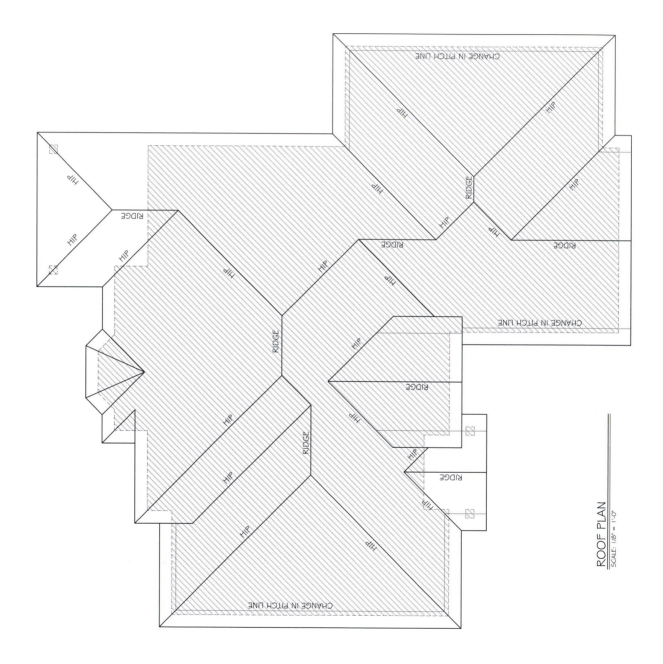

ROOF PLAN
SCALE: 1/8" = 1'-0"

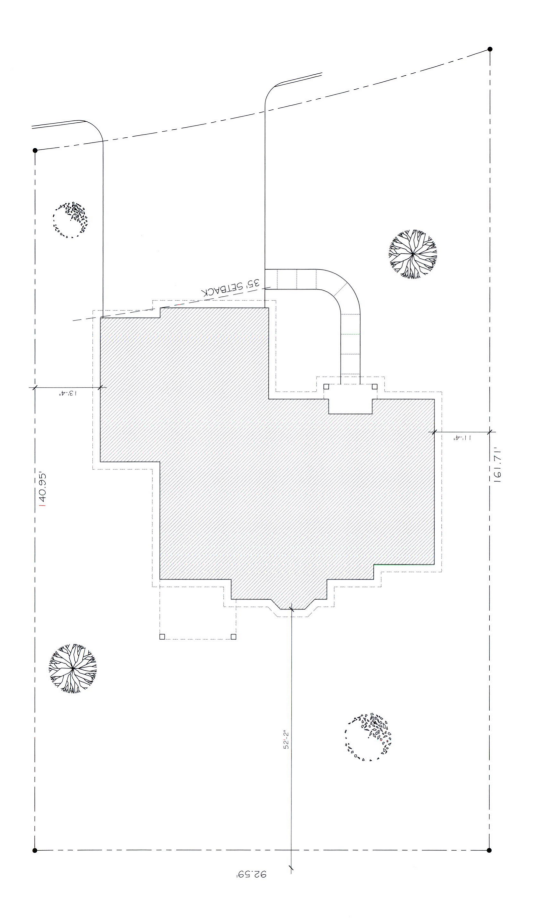

13'-4"

140.95'

35' SETBACK

11'-4"

161.71'

52'-2"

92.59'

PLOT PLAN

SCALE: 1/16" = 1'-0"

N

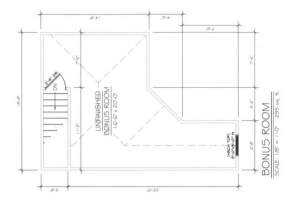

BONUS ROOM 295 sq. ft.
SCALE: 1/8" = 1'-0"

UNFINISHED
BONUS ROOM
16'-6" x 20'-0"

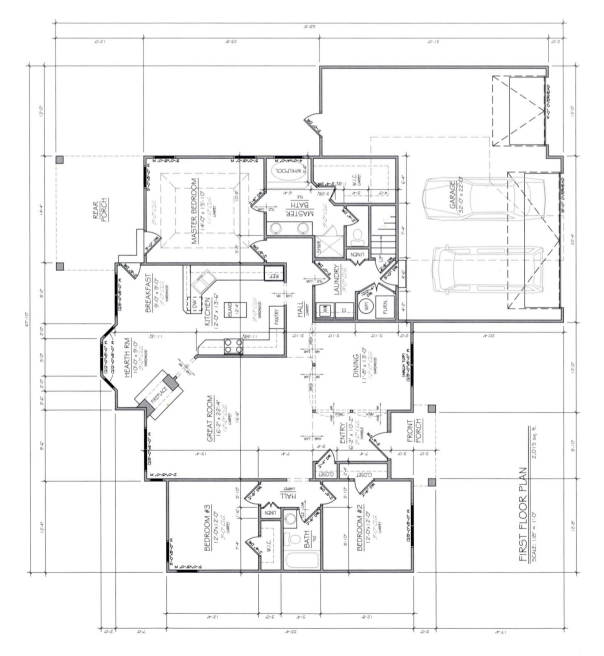

FIRST FLOOR PLAN 2,015 sq. ft.
SCALE: 1/8" = 1'-0"

GARAGE
32'-0" x 22'-0"

MASTER BEDROOM
14'-0" x 15'-10"

MASTER BATH

WHIRLPOOL

W.I.C.

REAR PORCH

BREAKFAST
9'-0" x 9'-0"

KITCHEN
12'-0" x 13'-6"

PANTRY

HEARTH RM
10'-0" x 9'-0"

GREAT ROOM
16'-2" x 22'-4"

FIREPLACE

HALL

LAUNDRY

LINEN

FURN.

DINING
11'-8" x 13'-0"

ENTRY
6'-2" x 10'-2"

FRONT PORCH

CLOSET

CLOSET

BEDROOM #3
12'-0" x 12'-0"

HALL

LINEN

W.I.C.

BATH

BEDROOM #2
12'-0" x 12'-0"

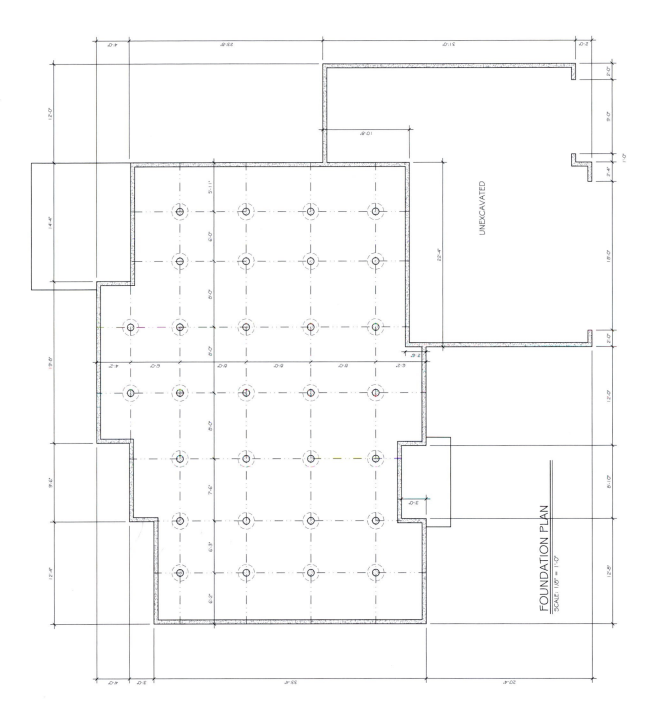

UNEXCAVATED

FOUNDATION PLAN
SCALE: 1/8" = 1'-0"

ELECTRICAL PLAN

SCALE: 1/8" = 1'-0"

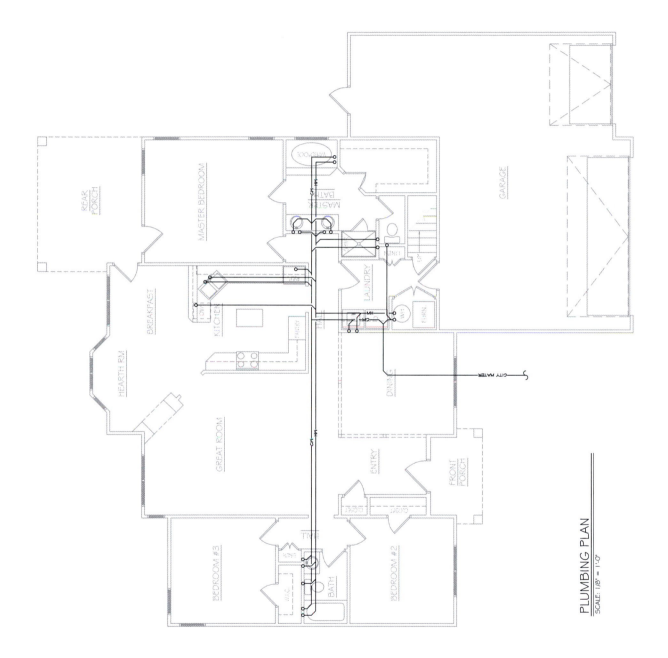

REAR PORCH

MASTER BEDROOM

WHIRL-POOL

MASTER BATH

BREAKFAST

KITCHEN

HEARTH RM

GREAT ROOM

LAUNDRY

DINING

ENTRY

FRONT PORCH

GARAGE

CITY WATER

BEDROOM #3

HALL

BATH

BEDROOM #2

PLUMBING PLAN
SCALE: 1/8" = 1'-0"

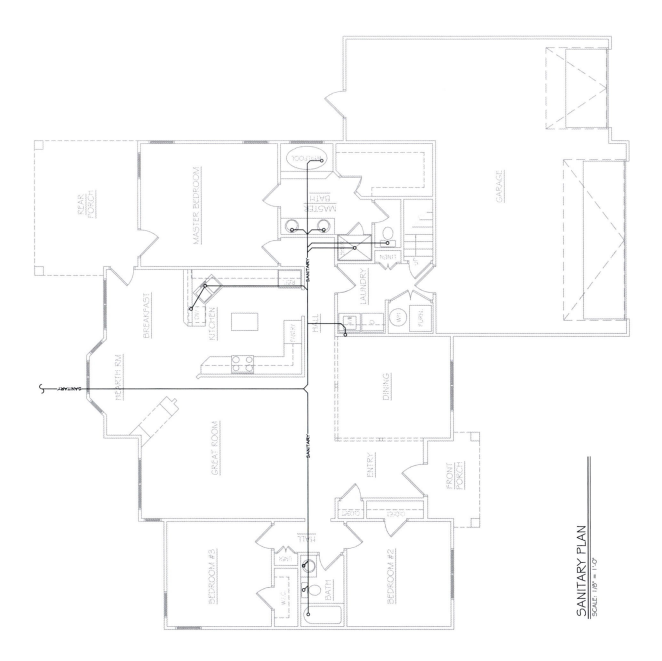

SANITARY PLAN

SCALE: 1/8" = 1'-0"

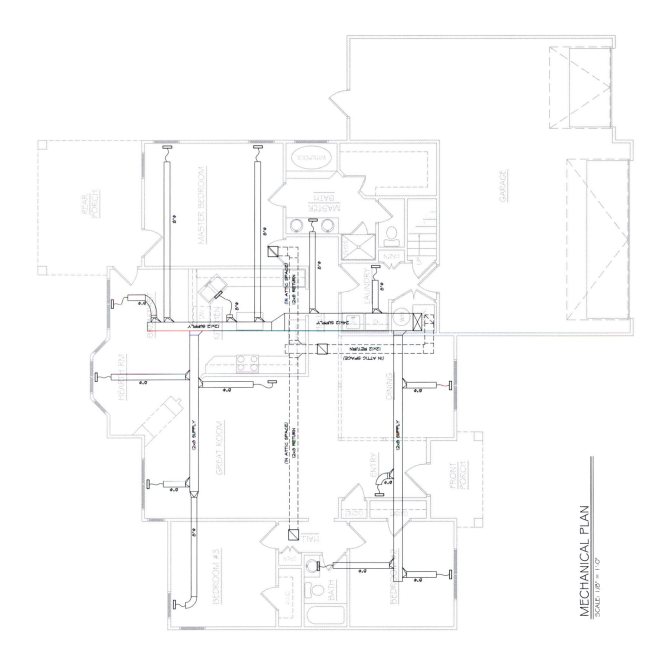

MECHANICAL PLAN
SCALE: 1/8" = 1'-0"

Endnotes

Chapter 1

1. Dutch, German, English, Danish, Swedish, and Icelandic
2. Quoted in "Live Your Best Life," *O* (December 2002): 39.
3. James Ponlewozik, "Home TV: It Hits Us Where We Live," *Time* (October 14, 2002): 75.
4. Kahlil Gibran, *The Prophet* (New York: Alfred A. Knopf, 1961): 34.
5. Mihaly Csikszentmihalyi, and Eugene Rochberg-Halton, *The Meaning of Things: Domestic Symbols and the Self* (Cambridge: Cambridge University Press, 1981), 123.
6. *Domus* means "house"; *celare*, "to conceal, hide, or cover"
7. Only male relatives of the elder to whom the house belongs are considered suitable visitors.
8. Mongols prefer the term *ger* because they associate the term *yurt* with Western invaders who used it.
9. The autonomous regions of Ningxia Hui and Xinjiang Uygur and the provinces of Shaanxi, Gansu, and Qinghai
10. www.aasianst.org/EAA/mccoll.htm
11. The Fan Jibao Residence in Gantangqiao, Wuxing County, Zhejiang Province is an example.

Chapter 2

1. www.epa.gov/cleanenergy/muni.htm
2. http://en.wikipedia.org/wiki/Air_pollution
3. U.S. Census Bureau, "Municipal Solid Waste Generation, Recovery, and Disposal: 1980 to 2001," *Statistical Abstract of the United States: 2004–2005*, Table 363 (Washington, D.C.: Department of Commerce), 222.
4. http://peakstoprairies.org/p2bande/Construction/C&DWaste/whatsC&D.cfm
5. The word *noise* is derived from the Latin word *nausea*, which means "seasickness."
6. www.lhh.org/hrq/25-1/noise.htm, p. 1.
7. U.S. Environmental Protection Agency, Office of Noise Abatement and Control, *Noise: A Health Problem*, (Washington, D.C.: 1978), as quoted by www.nonoise.org/library/epahlth/epahlth.htm, p. 23.
8. Maurice H. Stans, Secretary, U.S. Department of Commerce, *The Noise Around Us: Findings and Recommendations*, Report of the Panel on Noise Abatement to the Commerce Technical Advisory Board (Washington, D.C.: 1970), 9 and 13.
9. Marshall Chasin, *Musicians and the Prevention of Hearing Loss* (San Diego: Singular Publishing Group, 1997). Chasin found that 52 percent of classical musicians and 37 percent of rock musicians have hearing losses. Other studies have shown hearing losses in high school seniors who play in a band.

Chapter 3

1. Defeated by Alexander in 326 B.C.
2. U.S. Census Bureau, "Households with Computers and Internet Access: 1998 and 2003," *Statistical Abstract of the United States: 2004–2005*, Table 1153 (Washington, D.C.: Department of Commerce), 732. Access ranged from a high of 72.7 percent in Alaska to a low of 48.3 percent in Mississippi.

3. http://www.corrosionsource.com/technicallibrary/corrdoctors/Modules/Landmarks/Pillar.htm and Will Durant, *The Story of Civilization: Part 1: Our Oriental Heritage* (New York: Simon and Schuster, 1954), 478.

4. When walls are used instead of posts or columns, this type of device is known as wall and lintel. Post and lintel construction is also known as trabeated construction.

5. The Infinity Room at the House on the Rock is a 218-foot-long walkway that is cantilevered over the valley below. Falling Water, built by Frank Lloyd Wright, incorporates a number of cantilevered decks.

6. U.S. Census Bureau, "Average Length of Time from Start to Completion of New Privately Owned 1 Unit Residential Buildings: 1971 to 2003," *Statistical Abstract of the United States: 2004–2005*, Table 931 (Washington, D.C.: Department of Commerce), 601.

7. U.S. Census Bureau, "New Manufactured (Mobile) Homes Placed for Residential Use and Average Sales Price by Region: 1980 to 2003," *Statistical Abstract of the United States: 2004–2005*, Table 935 (Washington, D.C.: Department of Commerce, 2005), 602.

Chapter 4

1. Trees that have needles rather than broad leaves and that bear seeds in cones

2. Trees that lose their leaves in winter

3. As in pegboard

4. When used in fireplaces, concrete block must be protected by a layer of firebrick to prevent cracking.

5. Gypsum—hydrated calcium sulfate—is a mineral that is the major component of plaster. According to the U.S. Geological Survey, a typical new American home contains more than 7 tons of gypsum.

Chapter 5

1. Just as snowshoes distribute a human's weight over a larger area, making it possible to walk on the surface, the footing spreads weight over a larger area to help insure structural stability.

2. Fifty years is the minimum waiting period for building on filled earth unless it has been compacted and tested.

3. The rebar may be supported on clips until it is totally encased by the concrete.

4. This pipe is actually perforated on only one side. This side is laid toward the bottom, preventing dirt from entering the pipe from the top and clogging it.

5. In seismic zones, rebar must be spaced more closely than in other areas.

6. A steel beam is often called a girder.

7. Called I-beams because their cross-section looks like a capital letter I

8. Floor beams may overhang foundation walls or support posts on one or both sides, and joists are aligned accordingly.

9. Economics Group of the National Association of Home Builders, *What 21st-Century Home Buyers Want: A Survey of Customer Preferences* (Washington, D.C.: Home Builder Press, 2002).

10. Alternatively, it may be expressed as "x:12."

Chapter 6

1. Asbestos fibers were used into the 1980s for shingles. Subsequent controversy over asbestos led to the use of cellulose in place of asbestos. Shingles with cellulose fibers, however, may not last as long as the original asbestos shingles.
2. The painting done by Michelangelo on the Sistine Chapel ceiling is one of the most famous examples.
3. Sometimes simply called coffered ceilings
4. The angle between the seat and back of a seating unit is typically 105 degrees.
5. Historically, a dado or wainscot was made of wood but the term has come to mean any difference in decorative detail from the upper section of a wall.

Chapter 7

1. Johann Schweigger and William Sturgeon developed versions of the electromagnet but neither was powerful enough to be practical.
2. London's Holborn Viaduct power plant was operable by 1880.
3. http://www.winrock.org/GENERAL/PRESREL/RENUREL.html, p. 2
4. Represented by the Greek letter omega (Ω) in formulas without numbers
5. Named for the Italian physicist Alessandro Volta, who invented the battery
6. Terrell Croft and Wilford I. Summers, *American Electricians' Handbook* (New York: McGraw-Hill, 2002), 3.15.
7. According to the Niagara Mohawk Power Corporation, the initial cost of underground electrical service is approximately six times as high as overhead service. Maintenance costs of underground services are higher as well (http://www.nationalgridus.com/niagaramohawk/non_html/constr_undergrnd.pdf).
8. In 1881, the National Association of Fire Engineers developed guidelines to make electrical use safe. These guidelines establish voluntary standards that are used by the building industry. The NEC is revised every three years.
9. Also called the service panel, panel box, and main panel
10. Or ground-fault interrupter (GFI)
11. Also called convenience outlets and duplex receptacles
12. http://www.consumerenergycenter.org/homeandwork/homes/inside/appliances/small.html, p. 1
13. http://www.eia.doe.gov/emeu/reps/enduse/er01_us.html
14. http://www.eia.doe.gov/emeu/recs/recs2001/enduse2001/enduse2001.html
15. Also called metercandles
16. http://www.consumerenergycenter.org/homeandwork/homes/inside/lighting/bulbs.html

Chapter 8

1. A city located on the Indus River and which may have predated the Mesopotamian civilizations
2. Under Sennacherib 705–681 B.C., the Assyrians had an aqueduct that carried water thirty miles from Nineveh.
3. The Greeks used aqueducts before 527 B.C.

4. Prior to 312 B.C., Rome depended on the Tiber, some springs, and wells. It was Appius Claudius the Blind who, at that time, ordered the construction of the first Roman aqueduct to provide a more stable, clean water supply. The aqueduct named in his honor was 11 miles long.

5. Although most of Rome's ancient aqueducts were dysfunctional by the fall of the Western Empire, some have been restored and new ones have been constructed to supply water to modern Rome. The famous Trevi fountain is still supplied by the Aqua Virgo (Will Durant, *The Story of Civilization, Vol. III Caesar & Christ* (New York: Simon and Schuster, 1980), 327).

6. Called tanks in Bermuda. Each home's cistern may hold several hundred gallons.

7. www.pbs.org/now/science/unwater.html, p. 2. Figures were converted from cubic meters as follows. 1844 cubic meters (6146.6 cubic feet × 7.48 gallons = 45,977 gallons per year) for Americans. 664 (2213.3 cubic feet × 7.48 gallons = 16,555 gallons per year) for the world population.

8. www.pbs.org/now/science/unwater.html (8/28/05). Converted from 6 km.

9. In 1871

10. www.un.org/events/water/brochure.htm. *2003 International Year of Freshwater*, p. 1.

11. www.un.org/events/water/brochure.htm, *2003 International Year of Freshwater*, p. 2.

12. www.awwa.org/Advocacy/pressroom/statswp5.cfm, p. 1.

13. Susan S. Hutson, Nancy L. Barber, Joan F. Kenny, Kristin S. Linsey, Deborah S. Lumia and Molly A. Maupin, "Estimated Use of Water in the United States 2000," U.S. Geological Survey Circular 1268 (Reston, VA: U.S. Department of the Interior), p. 1.

14. U.S. Census Bureau, "Water Withdrawals by Source, Type, and Use—State and Other Areas: 2000," *Statistical Abstract of the United States: 2004–2005*, Table 357 (Washington, D.C.: Department of Commerce, 2005), 219. This figure includes Puerto Rico and the Virgin Islands.

15. This text uses the 2003 version of the International Plumbing Code: International Code Council, *International Plumbing Code 2003* (Country Club Hills, IL, 2003).

16. In Bangladesh and other areas of Southeast Asia, some well water contains sufficient amounts of arsenic to cause symptoms of poisoning, according to http://news.nationalgeographic.com/news/2003/06/0605_030605_arsenicwater.html.

17. In conjunction with treatment for purity, many communities add fluorine for protection against tooth decay. This practice is by no means universal and remains controversial. The question of long-range side effects remains to be answered.

18. www.eere.energy.gov/consumerinfo/factsheets/bc1.html, p. 1.

19. www.eere.energy.gov/consumerinfo/factsheets/bc1.html, p. 1.

20. www.census.gov/hhes/www/housing/census/historic/sewage.html.

21. The EPA (www.epa.gov/ow/you/chap3.html) estimates that Americans use 4.8 billion gallons of water per day for flushing toilets. The National Park Service (www.nps.gov/rivers/waterfactshtml) estimates Americans use 6.8 billion gallons per day for the same purpose.

22. The Energy Policy Act of 1992 dictated that as of January 1, 1997, all new toilets consume no more than 1.6 gallons of water per flush.

23. The term *bidet* is derived from an Old French word meaning "young foal" or "pony"—probably because the user sat astride the bidet as on a horse or pony.

Chapter 9

1. The thermal efficiency of the human body is only about 30 percent.

2. People in dry rooms may lose as much as 5 pounds of water a day.

3. In general, Americans desire comfort levels that require greater heating and cooling than individuals in other parts of the world. In Western Europe, for example, even major department stores often do not have air-conditioning and homes rarely do. In the winter, only one or two rooms in a home are heated—and then to a temperature below that considered comfortable by many Americans. This is not to say that all Americans require the same comfort levels. The elderly often require higher temperatures than others to be comfortable. While 68 to 74 degrees Fahrenheit is thermally acceptable to most young and middle-aged Americans, the elderly may prefer 80 degrees Fahrenheit or even higher in the winter.

4. U.S. Census Bureau, *American Housing Survey for the United States: 2003*, www.census.gov/hhes/www/housing/ahs/ahs03/tab1a6.htm, p. 1.

5. U.S. Census Bureau, "Characteristics of New Privately-Owned One-Family Houses Completed: 1990 to 2003," *Statistical Abstract of the United States: 2004–2005*, Table 930 (Washington, D.C.: Department of Commerce), 600.

6. National Association of Home Builders, *What 21st Century Home Buyers Want: A Survey of Customer Preferences* (Washington, D.C.: Home Builder Press), 55.

7. *Kachel* is the term used in German-speaking countries for stove tiles. Wall tiles are known as *fliesen*.

8. Also known as downdraft or downflow furnaces

9. Grilles consist of large open meshes on frames that fit into a wall, ceiling, or floor opening to the duct; registers add adjustable louvers, enabling users to control air flow; diffusers direct the flow of air in one direction—sometimes directing cooled air upward, sometimes directing air outward from beneath cabinets or furnishings. Any of these may be made of metal or plastic. Return air ducts use grilles; supply outlets may use any of these.

10. Meaning "warm stone"

11. The *k'ang* has been common since the Han dynasty. Three types of k'angs have been used in China: the *kao-k'ang*, or sleeping platform; the *ti-k'ang*, which warms the floor much as the Korean ondol system; and the *tong-k'ang*, which uses tubes to warm walls.

12. At this temperature, all particles within molecules cease to move.

13. Also known as swamp coolers

14. The 1987 United Nations Montreal Protocol established cooperation between nations for replacing the chlorofluorocarbon (CFC) (such as Freon) refrigerants then used. CFCs were thought to be one cause of the depletion of ozone in the atmosphere, although that remains controversial. The production of CFCs was stopped in 1992 and replacement hydrofluorocarbons

have not proven as efficient. In fact, HCFCs contain chlorine, which is also a threat to the ozone layer, and these are being phased out. Unfortunately, some of the proposed replacement refrigerants may use more energy, resulting in further depletion of fossil fuels and increased pollution.

15. Since May 19, 1980
16. While the Clinton administration passed an energy act requiring a SEER of 13 by January 2006, legislation in the Senate at this writing may lower the requirement to 12.

Chapter 10

1. www.earthshare.org/tips/trees.html.
2. www.pueblo.gsa.gov/cic_text/housing/cooling/cooling.txt
3. www.conservation.state.mo.us/conmag/1998/03/50.htm
4. Also called air lock entries
5. The American Society of Heating, Refrigerating, and Air Conditioning Engineers, Inc. (ASHRAE) has established many of these formulas.
6. Named for Felix Trombe, one of its French inventors

Chapter 11

1. The dates given for each style indicate when the style was most used. No style begins or ends overnight. In fact, a particular style may not begin in one area until long after it has begun in another. For example, the Renaissance began in Italy about 1420 but did not reach England for another century.
2. Dutch *stoep*
3. New Amsterdam (New York City) and Fort Orange (Albany)
4. Local laws required brick over timber framed construction for fire protection.
5. Also called corbie-step
6. French *galerie*
7. Also called Roman Revival
8. Also known as Carpenter Gothic
9. Also known as Arts and Crafts and Western Stick styles
10. As of this writing, the two largest geodesic domes in the world are located in Japan. The largest geodesic dome in the United States is the Tacoma Dome in Tacoma, Washington, which is 530 feet in diameter.

Chapter 12

1. The study asked about "soundproofing" rather than acoustic control.

Chapter 13

1. American Housing Survey, www.census.gov/hhes/www/housing/ahs/ahs03/tab27.htm
2. In Spanish Colonial homes, the gallery is known as a corredor.
3. National Physical Laboratory, Teddington, Middlesex, U.K. Great Britain's national standards laboratory.
4. L. W. Sepmeyer, *Computer Frequencies and Angular Distribution of the Normal Modes of Vibration in Recording Rooms*, Journal of the Acoustical Society of America, Vol. 37, No. 3, March 1965, 413–423.

5. www.crutchfield.com
6. www.eia.doe.gov/emeu/recs/fax-copiers-compare.html

Chapter 14

1. Their booklet, "Functional Kitchen Storage," published in June 1948, identi-fied the amount of space required for the equipment and food used by a typical family.
2. Becky Love-Yust and Wanda Olson, *Residential Kitchens: Planning Principles for the 1990's*, University of Minnesota, Design, Housing and Apparel Department.
3. This area was originally known as the mixing or mix center.
4. The dishwasher drain is usually hooked into the plumbing system through the garbage disposer, although a separate drain could be provided. This would, of course, require additional piping.
5. National Association of Home Builders, *What 21st Century Home Buyers Want: A Survey of Customer Preferences* (Washington, D.C.: Home Builder Press, 2001), 25, 26, 37, 38, 47.
6. National Association of Home Builders, *What 21st Century Home Buyers Want: A Survey of Customer Preferences* (Washington, D.C.: Home Builder Press, 2001), 45.
7. These midway cabinets are often called appliance garages.
8. National Association of Home Builders, *What 21st Century Home Buyers Want: A Survey of Customer Preferences* (Washington, D.C.: Home Builder Press, 2001), 44.
9. National Association of Home Builders, *What 21st Century Home Buyers Want: A Survey of Customer Preferences* (Washington, D.C.: Home Builder Press, 2001), 51.

Chapter 15

1. The Yagua are indigenous people that live in the rain forest in the Amazon Basin near Iquitos, Peru. They are hunter-gatherers who both fish and hunt.
2. A hallway with apartments or rooms on both sides
3. National Association of Home Builders, *What 21st Century Home Buyers Want: A Survey of Customer Preferences* (Washington, D.C.: 2001).

Glossary

abacus   The square block at the top of a column capital.

absorber plate   The flat back panel inside a solar collector used in active solar heating systems. Insulated on the sides and bottom. Absorbs radiant energy from the sun and transfers it as thermal energy to a fluid in the collector.

AC   Abbreviation for alternating current.

accent lighting   Lighting installed for decorative purposes.

accordion door   A type of folding door made of relatively flexible material. Installed on either a single overhead track or both a top and a bottom track.

accumulator   A plastic container inside the tank of a pressure-assisted toilet. The container is filled with air, which is compressed when water floods into the tank.

acid-resistant brick   A type of brick designed to resist the actions of chemicals.

acoustic sealant   A flexible material used to seal openings such as around electrical boxes to reduce sound transmission.

active solar heating   The collection and distribution of solar energy for heating, using mechanical heat transfer systems. Compare with *passive solar heating*.

adequate housing   One of three categories into which housing is grouped by the U.S. Census Bureau. Adequate housing has the facilities necessary to meet human shelter needs, plus a few conveniences.

adobe   Sun-dried mud or clay mixed with a binder. May or may not be formed into blocks or bricks. When built into walls, exposed surfaces are often plastered with a smooth coating of mud or clay.

AFCI   Abbreviation for arc-fault circuit interrupter.

aggregate   Inexpensive material used to provide bulk in concrete. Usually sand, gravel, or crushed stone. Aggregates minimize the shrinkage of concrete during drying. For good results, aggregates must be coated on all sides by cement mixture.

air infiltration   Air exchange through cracks and gaps in a structure. Exchanges conditioned interior air for exterior air.

alternating current   A type of electric current in which the number of volts alternates from zero to a maximum positive amount, back to zero, then to a maximum negative amount. Abbreviated AC.

amperage   The amount of flow of an electric current.

ampere   One ampere equals approximately 6.28×1018 electrons flowing past a given point in one second. Commonly called an amp.

anchor bent   A type of framework used by Dutch colonists. Consists of three timbers formed into an H shape. The crossbar supports the ceiling, while the vertical posts rising beyond the crossbar provide support for the roof.

anchor bolt   A metal bolt embedded in the masonry foundation while it is still wet. Bolts extend above the foundation, and the sill is attached to them. Provides a wind-resistant joint between the foundation and the frame.

angel stairs   A type of circular stairway similar to spiral stairs, except that there is no central post for support. In fact, there is no apparent support, although the stairs rest on the floor beneath and are attached to the floor above.

apron   1) An interior trim member placed under a window stool. 2) The decorative panel—separate or as an integral component—on the exposed side of a recessed bathtub. Also called skirting.

apron wall   The portion of a wall beneath a window.

aqueduct   Channel that directs water from a water supply such as a reservoir to a public water supplier.

aquifer   Water trapped between layers of rock, sand, or gravel that travels long distances.

arcade   A linear series of arches positioned side by side.

arc-fault circuit interrupter   A safety device that turns off power to a circuit when an arc is detected. Abbreviated AFCI.

arch   A structural member that is usually curved. An arch is made of individual wedge-shaped pieces, with the joints at right angles to the curve. A keystone is located at the top of the arch. Several types of arches are commonly used in building design, each usually typical of an individual architectural style.

architrave   The bottommost molding on a classical entablature.

artesian well   A well formed by drilling an opening through a layer of rock to reach water that flows to the surface under its own pressure.

ash chamber   A storage area where ashes from fires can cool and from which they can be removed. The ash chamber is located beneath the ash dump.

ash dump   A small door in the hearth of a fireplace through which ashes can be dumped into an ash chamber beneath.

ashlar   A type of stonework in which the stones are precisely cut and placed in a specific pattern but in which the faces of the stone are roughly cut.

aspect ratio   The relationship between the width and the height of a viewing screen.

awning window   A type of window that is hinged at the top and opens outward.

balcony   A raised deck or porch, usually projecting from an upper story.

balloon framing A type of framed construction in which studs extend continuously from the sill to the top plate regardless of the number of stories in the building. More dimensionally stable than platform framing and especially desirable when a masonry facade is used. Also called *eastern framing*.

baluster A vertical post, often decorative, that fits between a stair tread or another surface and a handrail.

balustrade A row of balusters supporting a handrail.

bargeboard A decoratively cut band of wood trim installed at the rake. Used especially in Gothic Revival–style homes. Also called a vergeboard.

barrel vault A linear series of arches located behind one another. Also called tunnel vault.

base 1) See *baseboard*. 2) An enlarged portion at the bottom of a column and on which the column rests.

baseboard A plain board or strip of molding nailed around the perimeter of a room to cover the joint between the wall and the floor. May be used with other molding pieces for a decorative effect.

base cabinets Cabinets designed to be installed on the floor. Kitchen base cabinets are typically 34½ inches high and 24 inches deep.

base cap A narrow decorative strip that may be attached to the top of a baseboard. Also called cap molding.

base shoe A narrow convex strip of molding that may be used to cover the joint between a baseboard and the floor.

batten door A door made of two layers of boards nailed together, most frequently used for basements, cellars, sheds, etc.

battered Sloped, rather than vertical, walls or columns. The structural member is larger at the base than at the top.

battlement A type of roof parapet with regularly spaced openings, originally used for defense. Used decoratively on some Gothic Revival and Tudor–style homes.

bay A type of window that forms an angular projection from a building wall.

beam A wood or metal structural member laid beneath floor and ceiling joists to provide intermediate support.

bearing wall construction A type of construction, usually masonry, in which every part of the wall bears the weight of materials above.

belt course See *string course*.

bent Term used to describe each section of post and beam framing that consists of a floor girt, two posts, two rafters, a ridge beam, and any intersecting beams such as a collar beam or additional ceiling or floor girt.

berm An artificial hill.

bevel Siding material that is thicker at the bottom than at the top.

bidet A low bowl-shaped plumbing fixture located in bathrooms. Designed to cleanse the genital and perineal areas, the bidet may also be used for foot bathing or sponge baths when other facilities are not available.

bifold door A type of door consisting of two panels hinged together and attached to one jamb. The two panels fold against each other when the door is open and present a flat surface when the door is closed.

bioconversion The transformation of an organic energy source from one form to another.

black pipe A type of steel pipe that has a coating of varnish for protection. Used for gas lines in residences.

black water Water drained from toilets.

blackout A loss of electricity in a specific area.

board Lumber less than 2 inches thick and 2 inches wide or greater.

board-and-batten A pattern of siding consisting of narrow vertical strips nailed over a layer of wider vertical boards so that the strips (battens) cover the joints between boards.

board-on-board A pattern of siding consisting of vertical boards nailed so that every other board overlaps the edges of the two adjacent boards.

boiserie A wood wall panel that is highly decorative.

bond Patterns used for stone or brick.

boundary furniture Furniture used to define limits of space.

bow window A type of window that forms a curvilinear projection from a building wall.

box cornice An extension of the roofline beyond the wall that is closed in on the bottom side with a soffit.

box header A header in the wall framing above an opening that is constructed of plywood and small pieces of dimensioned lumber.

branch pipe Pipes in a building's plumbing system that run from the distribution pipes to individual fixtures.

brick ledge An extension of the foundation wall designed to support a masonry facade. The brick ledge ends at a point lower than the foundation wall ends.

bridging Wood or metal pieces placed between floor joists, bracing them and helping to distribute weight over several joists. May consist of solid pieces nailed between joists or pairs of strips nailed diagonally to form an X shape.

brightness The intensity of light in a given area.

British thermal unit A measure of heat. The amount of heat needed to raise the temperature of one pound of water one degree Fahrenheit. Abbreviated Btu.

broken pediment   A pediment whose diagonal sides do not meet at the top.

brownfields   Land that has previously been used for industrial purposes.

brownout   When the voltage at which electricity is delivered to an area falls below minimum levels for proper operation of equipment and appliances.

Btu   Abbreviation for British thermal unit.

buffalo box   The underground location near a property line in which the main shutoff valve for a building is located.

building brick   Fired brick that has no special finishes including texturing. Also called common brick.

building felt   Heavy paper saturated with asphalt. Also called tar paper or building paper.

building paper   See *building felt*.

building permit   A permit required by municipal or county government to build new structures or to add to existing homes. Remodeling may require building permits when electric or plumbing work is to be done. Work is inspected at specified intervals and must be approved before the unit can be occupied. Building permits help to insure safe housing.

burn-in   The tendency of some types of video equipment to retain static images, which can be seen as ghost images when viewing other things.

buss bar or **bus bar**   A metal bar in the distribution panel to which ground wires are attached.

buttress   A thickened part of a wall or a pier designed for support. May be used to counteract the thrust of arches.

bypass sliding door   Two sliding doors that move past each other when opened or shut.

cab   The enclosed portion of an elevator or dumbwaiter.

cafe doors   Double-action swinging doors that are not full length.

canister light   Luminaires enclosed in a metal housing, except for one side through which the light is directed.

cantilever   An overhanging portion of a building, without visible support.

capital   The topmost enlarged portion of a column, usually decorative.

cap molding   See *base cap*.

captain's bed   A bed with storage drawers beneath it.

carousel shelves   Three-quarters of a circle shelving with a pie-shaped cutout that rotates around a center point. Installed in a cabinet.

carriage   See *stringer*.

case molding   See *casing*.

cased opening   An opening without a window or door that is trimmed with molding.

casement window   A side-hinged window that opens outward.

casing   1) Trim used around windows and doors to cover the space between the rough opening and the window or door frame. Also called case molding. 2) A solid tube inside the top part of a well that prevents groundwater from seeping into the well.

cast iron   Iron that has carbon in the mixture. Cast iron can be poured into molds while molten but it is too brittle to be hammered into shapes.

cathedral ceiling   A ceiling that slopes upward from the top of a wall.

catslide   A type of roof that extends from a ridge board above a second story to the top of a first-floor wall on one side.

caulking   Flexible material designed to fill cracks where materials meet. Used around window and door frames to reduce air infiltration.

cement   A mixture of lime, silica, iron oxide, alumina, and other ingredients designed to make cement harden slowly, more quickly, underwater, or with other special features. When water is added and the mixture allowed to dry, cement hardens to a permanent rocklike consistency.

cement backer board   A thin panel made of cement with some type of reinforcing, such as a fiberglass mesh to prevent cracking.

centering   The temporary wood structure required during construction of an arch. Masonry units are laid around the centering. When the mortar is dry, the centering is removed.

cesspool   Underground tank made of porous materials and designed to collect sewage and allow it to slowly drain into the surrounding soil. Because liquids can seep out in any direction, little purification occurs.

CFL   Abbreviation for compact fluorescent lamp.

chair rail   Horizontally applied molding at a height approximately equal to the height of the back of a chair.

charley bar   A bar designed to keep a sliding door closed.

check   A defect in wood that runs with the grain but does not go entirely through the board.

chimney effect   A phenomenon in which air warmed by the home heating system rises and leaks from the top of the structure, pulling cold outside air in through lower cracks and gaps.

chlorinated polyvinyl chloride   A type of plastic pipe used in plumbing systems. Known as CPVC, it is rated for hot water use.

chord   The outside members of a truss or wood I-joist to which intermediate supports are attached.

circuit   The path an electrical current follows from the power source and eventually back to the source.

circuit breaker   A device that opens an electrical circuit when the amount of current flowing through exceeds the designed capacity. Unlike a fuse, it does not self-destruct to open the circuit.

circulating hot water   Heated water that constantly circulates from the hot water heater to fixtures and back.

cistern   A waterproof underground tank used to store water prior to use. Roof runoff is often channeled to a cistern through a series of filters and used in the home, though not for drinking.

city   As defined by the U.S. Census Bureau, a city is an area with 50,000 or more inhabitants.

clapboard   A type of siding consisting of plain square-edged boards nailed horizontally in overlapping rows.

cleanout   A door giving access to an ash chamber in a fireplace.

cleat   A narrow board attached to a support and which in turn supports treads in a stairway.

cleat stairs   A stairway that employs cleats for the support of treads.

clerestory window   A window located high on a wall, often projecting upward from the roofline.

clipped gable   See *jerkinhead*.

close cornice   The type of finish given to a roof edge that does not extend past the wall.

closed circuit   A complete circuit with electrical flow from a source and back to the source.

closed plan   A type of floor plan or part of a floor plan in which full-height walls are used between rooms.

cluster housing   Homes built in groups or clusters, with planned green space surrounding them.

coffered and caissoned ceiling   A ceiling with three-dimensional decorative panels formed by moldings.

collar beam   A horizontal brace attached to two rafters on opposite sides of the roof. Collar beams often serve as ceiling joists for finished attic spaces. Also called *collar tie*.

collar tie   See *collar beam*.

colonnade   A row of columns such as may be found across the front of a building.

common brick   See *building brick*.

compact fluorescent lamp   A type of fluorescent lamp in which the tubes are formed into a more compact, convoluted shape so the lamp will fit standard luminaires. Some have screw bases, others pin bases. Abbreviated CFL.

composite A rare type of Roman column that combines both the volutes of the Ionic order and the rows of acanthus leaves of the Corinthian order.

compression strength The ability of a material to support a load that bears directly on it.

conduction The transfer of heat that occurs when objects touch.

conductor A material in which electrons transfer easily from one atom to another, allowing the flow of electrical current.

conduit Metal tubing through which wires can be snaked after it is installed.

convection The transfer of heat from a solid to a fluid.

conventional construction Term used to describe both platform framing and balloon framing. Conventional framing uses small members spaced relatively close together. All labor is done at the site, although prefabricated door and window units are commonly used. Also called on-site or stick-built construction. Compare with *post and beam framing*.

corbel A type of cantilever in which successive layers of materials project beyond the preceding row.

corbie-stepped See *crow-stepped*.

core (1) A prefabricated unit that includes components of some or all of a home's plumbing, electrical, heating, cooling, and ventilation systems. Cores are ready to hook into supply sources without extensive on-site labor. (2) The center layer of material in plywood and other laminated units.

Corinthian A classical order of architecture identified by a slender, fluted shaft, a base, and a capital decorated with two rows of eight acanthus leaves.

corner boards Flat boards used on the corners of Greek Revival structures to simulate pilasters.

corner post An extra stud located at a corner to insure a stable backing for the attachment of sheathing and finishing materials.

cornice 1) The finish of the roof at the eaves. 2) In ancient Greek and Roman architecture, the topmost part of the entablature, located below the pediment.

cornice lighting A concealed luminaire, or row of luminaires, placed on a wall near the ceiling so that the light shines downward.

corredor Term for a covered walkway on the exterior of a Spanish Colonial structure.

counterflow furnace A furnace that forces air downward through the distribution system regardless of the tendency of warmed air to rise.

course A horizontal row of stone or brick.

coursed rubble   A type of stonework using stones that, although not precisely cut or placed, are trimmed to approximately regular shapes and placed to give the impression of rows.

courtyard   A grade-level enclosed area. By definition, a courtyard must be adjacent to a building on at least one side. Other sides may be enclosed with buildings or walls.

cove lighting   A luminaire, or row of luminaires, placed on a wall near the ceiling and concealed in a trough so that the light shines upward.

coverage   The number of layers of roofing material provided at any point by overlapping shingles. Two layers of shingles at every point provides double coverage.

CPVC   Abbreviation for chlorinated polyvinyl chloride.

crawl space   An area beneath the floor of some residences from 1 to 4 feet deep. A crawl space permits access to pipes, electrical wires, and ducts.

cross bridging   A type of bridging between adjacent joists where two diagonal members cross to form an X shape.

crowning   A curve in a board without a change in the plane.

crown molding   The molding that covers the joint between the top of the wall and the ceiling.

crow-stepped   A building facade that reduces in width through a series of step-backs beginning at the eave.

current   A flow of electrons.

curtain wall   A non-load-bearing wall that supports no weight but its own.

cyclopean wall   A wall constructed with uncut stone.

dado   Treatment of the lower portion of a wall with a different material than the material at the top.

damper   A hinged metal flap or circular plate that regulates the upward flow of air in a flue. Operated manually or automatically.

dB   Abbreviation for decibel.

DC   Abbreviation for direct current.

deadbolt   A type of lock in which a steel bolt extends to fit into an opening in a door jamb.

dead load   The weight of all permanent parts of a structure, including the building materials. Compare with *live load*.

decibel   A unit of sound measurement. One decibel is equal to the smallest change in sound intensity that can be discerned by a person with average hearing. Abbreviated dB.

deck   A porch without a roof.

degree day   A unit of measurement used to indicate the need for heating or cooling in the appropriate season. The cumulative total of heating or cooling degree days in a particular area is kept each season. The higher the number of degree days, the more energy is required for heating or cooling. The totals are used to make regional or annual comparisons.

dentils   A series of decorative toothlike projections found at the eaves of Georgian, Federal, and some Colonial Revival–style homes.

dependent stack system   A type of system for stacking modular units in which lower units support those above.

dimension lumber   Lumber that has a minimum thickness and width of 2 inches. The maximum thickness is 5 inches but there is no maximum width.

direct current   Electrical current that flows in one direction. Abbreviated DC.

direct gain   A type of passive solar heating in which sunlight enters the living space before striking a thermal mass.

direct lighting   Light that shines directly on a surface.

direct-view television   A television set designed to be seen from directly in front. May have a curved or flat screen. Both use the same technology.

disappearing stairs   Stairways that fold away out of view when not in use.

distribution panel   The electrical box near the service entrance that separates the incoming current into individual circuits. Each circuit is protected by a fuse or circuit breaker contained within the box.

distribution pipe   The pipe in a building's plumbing system that runs from the main supply line and from which branch supply lines run.

divided-light French door   A door with two stiles and two rails. The center section is glazed with multiple lights separated by muntins.

dome   A series of arches radiating around a center point.

Doric   A classical architectural order that features a fluted column without a base and that has a simple cushion capital. Some examples do not have fluting.

dormer   A vertical projection of the wall through the roof that forms additional space in the upper story. Each dormer has its own roof.

double-action swinging door   A swinging door that swings in both directions.

double-cylinder deadbolt   A deadbolt lock that requires a key to open from either side.

double header   The term used to describe the combination of the header and top plate at the top of wall framing.

double-hung window   A type of window with two separate sashes that slide vertically past each other.

downlight   A luminaire that directs light downward. Can be surface-mounted or recessed.

down point temperature   The lowest temperature at which it is possible to extract heat from a thermal storage medium in an active solar heating system.

downspout   A vertical tubular channel to which gutters are attached and that carries water collected in the gutters to the ground or to a drain.

drain-down system   An active solar heating system in which the water used as a heat transfer medium is automatically drained from the system when temperatures approach freezing.

drawer base   A type of base cabinet that houses a stack of drawers.

dress   The process of planing the surface of lumber to make it smooth.

dressed   Lumber that is smooth on all surfaces.

dressed size   The size of lumber after its surface has been planed until smooth. The planing process removes some of the wood from each side, causing the dressed size to be smaller than the original board. Compare with *nominal size*.

drip cap   An exterior protective strip applied at the top of a window, extending beyond the casing to channel runoff water away from the window.

drop   A carved decoration sometimes found on Colonial-style homes that have an overhanging upper story. When present, drops are suspended from the overhang at the corners. They may also be used beneath the corners of the roof overhang.

drop luminaire   A pendant luminaire that can be adjusted vertically.

dropped ceiling   A portion of a ceiling that is lower than the ceiling in the rest of the room.

dry stone   Dry stone construction uses stone—either cut or uncut—without mortar.

drywall   See *gypsum wallboard*.

duct   A hollow tube, round or rectangular in cross-section, designed to carry air in a heating or cooling system.

ductile iron   Iron that has had magnesium added. Ductile iron has great tensile strength, making it ideal for use in pipes.

dumbwaiter   A small elevator designed to lift objects rather than people.

duplex   A structure that has two housing units under the same roof.

Dutch door   A door separated vertically into two units.

Dutch hip roof   A combination of a hip and a gable roof. The two ends have a gable above a hipped portion called a pent.

Dutch kick   A slight outward curve at the bottom edge of a gambrel roof. Also called a Flemish kick.

dynamic load   A sudden, short-term live load, usually as a result of wind gusts or earthquakes.

earth-contact home   A home that is surrounded by earth on one or more sides and that may have an earth-covered roof.

eastern framing   See *balloon framing*.

eave   The lower edges of a roof where the walls and roof meet.

echo   The reflection of sound from a secondary source that reaches the human ear more than $1/10$ of a second after the original sound.

EER   Abbreviation for Energy-Efficiency Rating.

efficacy   The efficiency of a light source, calculated by dividing the number of lumens by the number of watts of electricity consumed.

efficiency apartment   A type of apartment that has space for normal living activities in one room. A bathroom is separate.

electrohydraulic toilet   A toilet that uses a small motor and/or a pump to accomplish powerful flushes in toilets or to liquefy wastes.

Energy-Efficiency Rating   A measurement of the efficiency of an air conditioner that compares the amount of electricity used with the amount of heat removed:

$$\text{Btus per hour / watts used} = \text{EER.}$$

engaged column   A partial column that is attached directly to a wall or support structure and projects in a curve.

engineered lumber   Lumber manufactured from separated wood fibers, wood chips, or particles with glue under heat and pressure. Engineered lumber is free from defects and has no grain.

entablature   In ancient Greek and Roman structures, the horizontal component that runs across the top of a supporting row of columns. Includes a frieze, architrave, and cornice, the details of which vary with the particular order of architecture.

environmental control glass   Window glass that is designed to reflect or absorb heat from the sun to keep the interior of the home cooler.

escutcheon plate   A decorative covering that fits over a pipe and covers the opening in a wall or floor through which the pipe enters.

evaporative cooler   A cooling system that uses a water-soaked pad to absorb heat from the air. Effective only in dry climates.

exclusionary zoning   A type of zoning that excludes certain groups of individuals from an area, due to limitations on the number of individuals per acre or to minimum criteria for units within the area. These criteria often include a minimum lot size.

expansion tank   Part of a hot water heating system provided to accommodate an excess volume of water as a result of expansion from being heated. Two types are used: open and closed.

exposure The distance from the bottom of one roof shingle to the bottom of the next.

extended hearth A portion of the firebox floor that extends beyond the firebox opening in a fireplace. Made of fireproof materials but designed to be decorative as well.

eyebrow A horizontal projection above a window in an Art Moderne building.

face brick Fired brick that has been treated to improve its appearance.

face frame The frame on the front of a cabinet.

fall The vertical distance a drain pipe travels due to slope.

fanlight A stationary window placed over a door, a window, or a group of openings. Often separated into several lights, resembling the folds of a fan.

fiberboard A panel made of individual wood fibers that are pressed together by rollers.

fiber optic A type of light that uses glass or plastic fibers to transfer light to a remote location.

finish lumber Lumber that has no defects.

finish stringer The decorative covering for a plain stringer.

fireback The back of the firebox. It is designed to absorb heat and radiate it back into the room.

firebox The open boxlike portion of a fireplace or stove in which the fire is contained.

firebrick A brick made of heat-refracting clay that will withstand the high temperatures of combustion in heating devices without cracking or crumbling. Used in chimneys, fireplaces, and woodstoves.

fire-stop A framing member designed to slow the spread of flames. Fire-stops often consist of lumber placed horizontally between studs.

fission The tearing apart of molecules.

flashing A layer of water-impervious material, usually sheet metal strips, installed beneath finish roofing materials where leakage is a potential problem. It is used at valleys, at roof edges, and around chimneys and vents. It is also used at the bottom of a wall behind a masonry facade to direct moisture away from wood members.

flat-panel television A television that uses a different technology to project an image than does a direct-view television. The depth of the set is usually less than 5 inches.

flat-plate collector A type of collector used in active solar heating systems, consisting of a flat absorber plate with a glass or plastic cover and an insulative backing. Air or liquid circulated over the absorber plate carries heat away for storage or use.

flat roof A roof with no incline or only a slight incline.

Flemish kick See *Dutch kick*.

float glass An expensive glass made by floating melted glass on molten tin. Distortion free.

floating slab See *thickened-edge slab*.

floating wall A wall that does not rise completely to the ceiling.

floor furnace A type of warm air heating unit installed directly under the floor. Heat rises into the living area without passing through ducts and without mechanical assistance.

flue An enclosed passage or vent leading from a heating unit to carry away smoke and fumes from the combustion process. Required for any unit that burns fuel (gas, oil, coal, wood) and produces toxic fumes, including hot water heaters, clothes dryers, furnaces, and space heaters.

fluorescent A type of artificial lighting produced by phosphor-coated tubes that convert electrical flow through a vapor to light. Compare with *incandescent*.

flush Type of drawer front construction that allows the drawer when closed to be flush with the face frame.

flush door A door constructed so as to have flat surfaces on both sides. Compare with *panel door*.

flush overlay A type of drawer front that extends the entire width of a cabinet, making it unnecessary to have a face frame.

flush-valve-operated toilet A type of commercial toilet with a flush valve that connects directly to a water supply and requires no tank.

fluted The vertical concave curves in a column shaft.

flying buttress A type of buttress used during the Gothic period that extends beyond a structure, counteracting the thrust of the roof by transferring the force to vertical posts via openwork arches.

folding door Doors that operate on a track and fold into a small area when opened. Accordion and bifold doors are examples.

footcandle The unit used to measure illuminance in the imperial or English system. One footcandle is equivalent to one lumen per square foot.

footing The bottommost portion of most structures, usually consisting of a masonry base beneath a foundation wall, post ,or other component. Footings are designed to distribute the weight of the structure over a large area.

foundation Usually, a masonry perimeter wall, largely below grade level, supporting a structure built on top of it. Together with footings, the foundation provides a stable supporting base for the structure.

four-way switch A type of switch used in conjunction with two three-way switches to enable a receptacle or luminaire to be controlled from three separate locations.

frame construction A type of construction using vertical and horizontal members for support. The covering of the framework supports no weight but its own.

framed door A cabinet door that is framed by stiles and rails.

French door A glazed swinging door. Often used in pairs leading to a patio or porch.

frieze In classical architecture, an often decoratively carved band across a facade just below the cornice.

frost line The depth to which soil freezes in the winter.

furniture lighting Luminaires that illuminate the interior of furnishings, such as a china cabinet, or that illuminate parts of the furniture itself.

furred wall A framed wall constructed adjacent to a masonry wall to provide space for insulation, wiring, pipes, or ductwork. Supports no structural load other than its own weight.

furring strips Wood strips added to a masonry wall to provide a way to fasten finish materials to the wall. Also used on ceilings.

fuse A safety device in an electrical circuit with a metal strip that vaporizes or melts to open the circuit when the amount of current flowing through the circuit exceeds the designed capacity.

fusion The joining of molecular particles.

gable The triangular portion of an exterior wall, extending upward from the top plate to the ridge and formed by a roof with two sloping sides.

gable roof A type of roof having two sloping sides that meet at a ridge.

gain The amount of light reflectance from a viewing screen.

gallery From the French *galerie*. A covered porch or balcony that extends along at least one side of the structure. In different areas, a gallery may be known as a veranda or a loggia.

galvanize The application of coating of molten zinc on steel pipe to help prevent rusting of the material.

gambrel roof A style of roof having two sloping sides similar to a gable roof, but with a change in the steepness of the slope occurring partway up the roof. The lower slope is steeper than the upper slope.

garden apartment An apartment building surrounded by a relatively large landscaped area. Usually located in urban fringes and suburban areas where land is lower in cost than it is in urban areas.

general lighting Low-level background lighting designed for safety.

GFCI Abbreviation for ground-fault circuit interrupter.

giant order Columns that rise more than one story.

gingerbread Decorative wood detailing used on some Victorian-style homes.

girt Horizontal framing member used in post and beam framing.

glazing Glass fitted into an opening, such as a window or a glazed door. Single, double, or triple glazing indicates the number of layers of glass.

grade level The level of the earth surrounding a building.

grayfields Land that has previously been part of a blighted urban area.

gray water Water that drains from bathing fixtures, sinks, and lavatories and which contains no toxic or solid wastes.

great room A living area that is open to a kitchen.

green board A type of gypsum wallboard that has a thin coating of asphalt on the back of the paper faces to resist moisture.

green design Building construction in which the design makes efficient use of land and energy throughout its life cycle and minimizes the impact of the structure on the environment. Also called sustainable construction and high-performance building.

greenhouse effect The phenomenon in which sunlight passes through glass, strikes a heat-absorbing surface, and is changed to long wave heat energy, which is then trapped by the glass.

green lumber Wood that has a moisture content higher than 19 percent.

grounded Term used to describe an electrical system, system component, or appliance that is wired so as to provide an eventual connection with the earth. This connection minimizes the possibility of shock or fire should there be a defect in the appliance or the house wiring.

ground-fault circuit interrupter A sensitive safety device that monitors the current flow in an electrical circuit and breaks the circuit if it detects that current is leaking. Abbreviated GFCI.

ground source heat pump A type of heat pump that extracts heat from air in underground pipes.

guardrail The level railing designed for safety placed around an opening, a stairway, or at the edge of porches and balconies.

gusset A flat wood or metal plate used to attach two pieces of material on the same plane.

gutter A channel that is open at the top and that is attached to the horizontal edge of the roof at the base of the inclined edges for carrying away water.

gypsum wallboard A panel made of plaster covered with paper on both sides. Called drywall, plasterboard, gyp board, and Sheetrock.

half-timbering (1) A type of construction in which timber framing members are left exposed and the spaces between filled with a material such as brick, wattle and daub, or stucco. Characteristic of the English

Tudor and Tudor Revival periods. (2) Decorative wood strips applied to the surface of a structure to give the appearance of half-timbered construction.

hammock   A suspended sleeping unit.

handrail   A railing to aid in climbing stairs or using ramps.

hardboard   A panel made of wood fibers that have been separated using pressurized steam. The fibers are bonded into sheets by applying pressure.

hard water   Water that has a high content of minerals, such as calcium, that react with soap to form a precipitate. Water with 140 parts of minerals per million parts of water is considered hard.

hard-wired appliance   An electrical device that is wired into an electrical system rather than using a plug.

hardwood   Wood from deciduous trees.

head   The topmost horizontal portion of a window or door frame. Also called a lintel.

header   1) A horizontal wall framing member used over windows and doors to support the structure above. Also called a lintel. 2) A floor or ceiling framing member, perpendicular to joists, to which the ends of joists are fastened. Used to frame an opening. 3) A horizontal wall framing member that keeps vertical members in place.

head height   The height above the nosing of a stairway required for human use.

hearth   The floor of the firebox in a fireplace where the fire is built. Made of fireproof materials.

hearth room   A living area in which there is a fireplace.

heat exchanger   The part of a heating system that transfers heat to a fluid (water or air).

heating unit   One hundred cubic feet of natural gas. Also called a therm. Equivalent to approximately 100,000 Btus.

heat producer   The part of a heating system that burns the fuel.

heat pump   A device that uses a refrigerant to move heat from outdoors to indoors in cold weather and from indoors to outdoors in hot weather.

heat sink   A material that absorbs and stores heat when surrounding temperatures are higher. When ambient temperatures fall below the temperature of the heat sink, it reradiates heat to the surroundings.

Hertz   1) The number of pairs of poles passed per second in an alternating current. Abbreviated Hz. 2) The number of sound wave peaks passing a given point in a second.

HID   Abbreviation for high-intensity discharge.

high-intensity discharge   A type of artificial lighting that includes mercury vapor, metal halide, and high-pressure sodium lamps, whereby light is produced by directing an arc through a gas-filled tube that has high pressure.

high-performance building   See *green design*.

hip   One of the raised areas of a hip roof, extending from the ends of the ridge board to an outside corner of the structure.

hip roof   A style of roof having four sloping sides.

hoistway   The open shaft for an elevator.

hopper window   A bottom-hinged window that opens inward.

horseshoe stairs   A pair of curved stairs in mirror images of each other that end at the same landing or platform.

hose bibb   An exterior faucet that has a threaded end to accept a garden hose.

housed stringer   A type of stringer sometimes used against a wall in which grooves are cut to house the edges of the risers and treads.

hub   A centralized location for audio/video equipment and its wiring.

HVAC   Acronym used by the industry to describe the mechanical heating, ventilating, and air-conditioning systems.

hydronic   Term describing a heating system that uses forced hot water as the heat distribution medium.

hyphen   In Georgian architecture, the single-story additions to a house on either side of the main structure. May lead to additional structures.

hypocaust   Ancient Roman central heating system that used a system of tiles to carry heat from a charcoal brazier into the living area.

Hz   Abbreviation for Hertz.

illuminance   The amount of light that reaches a surface.

incandescent   A type of artificial lighting produced when a filament—usually of tungsten—is heated by the flow of electric current. Compare with *fluorescent*.

inclusionary zoning   A type of zoning that ensures that members of different economic groups have access to the same amenities in a given area by specifying a percentage of units for one or more groups.

independent stack system   A type of stacking system for modular units in which each unit is self-supporting and does not support others.

indirect gain   A type of passive solar heating in which the sun strikes a thermal mass without passing through the living space of the home. The sun heats the thermal mass, which in turn warms the interior air.

indirect lighting   Lighting that is directed toward a reflective surface from which it then provides light to a room.

inglenook   A niche in front of or beside a fireplace where the temperature remains warmer than the rest of the room. Frequently used by ill or elderly people before central heating systems were common.

insulator   1) A material with stable electrons that allows little electrical flow. 2) A material with an R-value of two or more per inch that is used to reduce heat loss or gain in a structure.

International Building Code   The model building code established by the International Code Council. This code is replacing other model codes used in different regions.

International Residential Code   The residential portion of the International Building Code. Abbreviated IRC.

intersecting roof   A roof that has slopes running in different directions meeting at any point.

Ionic   Classical order of architecture that consists of a fluted column with a base. The capital has volutes at least on the front and back sides. Some Ionic capitals have angled volutes on all four sides.

IRC   Abbreviation for International Residential Code.

isolated gain   A type of passive solar heating in which heat from the sun is collected away from the house itself. Often uses some of the components of an active solar heating system, but without any mechanical assistance.

jack stud   A shortened stud above or beneath an opening in wall framing.

jali   An openwork screen. Typically used in Muslim structures to provide privacy for women.

jalousie window   A type of window having many panes in the form of narrow horizontal strips, each of which pivots from the top. When closed, the panes overlap.

jamb   A vertical side portion of a window or door frame.

jerkinhead   A type of gable roof in which the end is hipped. Also called clipped gable.

jetty   The overhanging portion of an upper story.

joist   A large horizontal framing member used to support a floor or ceiling.

joist header   A framing member the same size as the joists that is installed perpendicular to joists.

kachelöfen   Type of masonry stove that is covered with glazed earthenware tiles. Heat is produced in a small firebox and must travel through a convoluted system of passages before being exhausted to the outdoors.

key card lock   A lock operated by a card with a magnetic strip.

key-in-knob   A type of lock that uses a thumb turn to engage the lock.

keyless lock A type of lock that uses a number pad from which a code is entered to engage or disengage it.

keystone The masonry unit at the top center of an arch. Because of the wedge shape of units in the arch, the keystone is the final member placed and completes the arch. Once the keystone is in place, each of the wedge-shaped units provides counterthrust for other units, making the arch strong.

keyway A depression in a footing into which the foundation fits. The key prevents movement of the foundation and provides a water-resistant joint between the footing and foundation.

kilowatt A unit of electrical power equal to 1000 watts.

kilowatt-hour A unit of electrical energy consumption equaling 1000 watts in use for one hour. The standard measurement of electricity for billing purposes. Abbreviated kWh.

king stud The extra full-length stud close to a wall opening to which the trimmer is attached.

knee wall A short wall constructed beneath the angle of a roof.

knockdown cabinetry Cabinets that are delivered in pieces and must be assembled on site.

knot A defect in wood formed by a branch.

kWh Abbreviation for kilowatt-hour.

laminated beam A beam formed by gluing lumber together to form a single solid structural member.

lamp The lighting industry's term for a lightbulb.

landing The flat area at the top and bottom of stairways.

lath A base over which plaster or stucco is applied. Wet plaster or stucco works through the openings in the lath and hardens or is chemically bonded to the lath. Lath may consist of narrow horizontal strips of wood, thin perforated metal sheets, or sheets of gypsum board or fiberboard.

lavatory A bowl-like receptacle designed to hold water. Distinguished from a sink in that the bottom of a lavatory is slightly rounded.

lazy Susan A set of rotating circular shelves attached to a center post that rotates 360 degrees. May be installed in a cabinet.

leach field Area of soil in which pipes leading from the septic tank distribute wastewater.

light A separate pane of glass. A window may include one or more lights.

light clutter Light from many sources resulting in sky glow.

light pollution Any light that illuminates the night sky, decreasing the visibility of heavenly bodies.

light trespass Unwanted light from a neighboring source.

linoleum   A type of flooring material made in sheets and that has an asphalt-saturated heavy paper base.

lintel   1) The horizontal member supported by posts. 2) See *head*.

lipped   A drawer front with a rabbet cut on the back that allows the front to be partially recessed into the cabinet when closed.

live load   Temporary weight or force that must be supported by the structure. Common live loads include people, furniture, snow, and the force of high winds. Compare with *dead loads*.

load-bearing partition   A wall that bears a load.

loft bed   A bed located on a platform near the ceiling.

loggia   See *gallery*.

louvered door   A type of panel door. The panels consist of rows of narrow, angled horizontal strips that allow air circulation.

low-e glass   See *low-emissivity glass*.

low-emissivity glass   Double glazing with a metallic coating between the panes that reflects heat waves. The location of the coating depends on whether the glass is used for heating or cooling.

lumen   The amount of light actually produced by a luminaire.

luminaire   The lighting industry's term for a light fixture.

lux   The unit of measurement of illuminance in the metric system. One footcandle is equivalent to 10.76 lux.

maisonette   An apartment that has two stories in the unit.

mansard roof   A style of roof having four sloping sides, similar to a hip roof, but with a change in the steepness of the slope occurring partway up the roof. The upper slope is relatively flat and the lower slope is very steep.

mantel   A decorative shelf or surround for a fireplace.

marquetry   A type of inlay that uses differing materials—varying species of wood or other materials such as tortoiseshell, ivory, and semi-precious stones. An opening is cut in the background material and a marquetry piece cut to fit the opening. When finished, the surface is flat.

mass site construction   The type of building construction in which a number of units are built in the same area, with workers progressing from one to another as work is completed.

megalopolis   See *Standard Metropolitan Statistical Area*.

Mexican quarry tile   A type of quarry tile made by hand that has inconsistent thickness and may have accidental impressions such as those of an animal's foot. These impressions are a result of drying the tiles in the sun.

millwork   Wood molding.

minimal housing   One of three categories into which housing is grouped by the U.S. Census Bureau. Minimal housing meets minimum health and safety standards but provides little else.

mobile home   A manufactured home that has a chassis and wheels and is capable of being towed to its location.

modular unit   A self-contained unit designed as a room or group of rooms for a structure. Modules are finished at the factory prior to delivery and may even have furniture in place. They may be combined vertically or horizontally to form an individual dwelling unit or multifamily dwelling.

molding   Lengths of wood or other material that are shaped.

mortise and tenon   A type of joint in which a projection in one member fits into an opening in another member.

mortise lock   A type of lock that employs both a deadbolt and a beveled latch and that is installed in a hole cut in the edge of a door.

mudroom   A combination entry and laundry area.

mudsill   See *sill*.

mullion   A vertical post separating window sashes that are placed in the same frame.

muntin   A strip that separates the lights in a window. Muntins may be permanent members of a window or snap-out dividers.

Murphy bed   A bed that folds into a cabinet when not in use.

National Electrical Code   A model code dealing with electrical use, published by the National Fire Protection Association and revised every three years.

NEC   Abbreviation for National Electrical Code.

new town   New towns are planned completely before construction is begun. They are built in undeveloped areas near cities.

newel post   A post located at the beginning and end of a staircase and often at platforms to provide support for the balustrade. Newel posts are often highly decorative.

niche   A recessed area in a wall that has curved walls.

NKBA   Abbreviation for the National Kitchen and Bath Association, which establishes guidelines for kitchen and bathroom design.

nogging   Brick used to fill the spaces between timbers in half-timbered structures.

noise   Unwanted sound.

nominal size   The original size of a structural unit. The size of lumber as originally cut and before being smoothed and dried. Also called trade size.

nook   A recessed area in a wall that has angled walls.

nosing   The projection of the tread beyond the riser in a stairway.

obscure glass Glass that has a textured surface. While light passes through, images cannot be distinguished. Also called *patterned glass*.

o.c. Abbreviation for on center.

ohm A measurement of the resistance of a material to the flow of electricity.

on center A way of designating the spacing between two framing members or other objects. The measurement is taken from the center of the thickness of one member to the center of the thickness of the next. Abbreviated o.c.

on-site construction See *conventional construction*.

open circuit A circuit that has a break due to a short or to a switch that is turned off.

open cornice An extension of the roofline beyond the wall that leaves the bottom of the rafters exposed.

open plan A plan or portion of a plan in which rooms or areas are open to one another vertically or horizontally.

oriel A term used for a bow or bay window when located on an upper story and supported by brackets.

oriented-strand board A type of laminated wood panel made of wood chips whose strands are oriented in each layer. Alternate layers have strands oriented perpendicular to adjacent layers. Called OSB.

OSB Abbreviation for oriented-strand board.

outlet A point of end use in an electrical system, such as a luminaire, receptacle, or built-in fan.

overcurrent device A fuse or circuit breaker that limits the amount of current that can flow through an electrical circuit. Designed for safety.

overhang The portion of the roof that extends beyond the wall on any side.

overhead door A garage door that opens by swinging overhead on a track.

overload The condition that results when electrical units attached to a circuit require more power than the circuit can provide.

packaged terminal air conditioner Self-contained air conditioner designed to cool a small area. Contains the compressor, condenser, and refrigeration unit. No ducts are required.

Palladian window A type of window made popular by Andrea Palladio that is in three sections. The center window is usually arched; the side windows are shorter and have square heads.

panel door A type of door having a framework of stiles and rails into which are set panels of wood, glass, or other material. Compare with *flush door*.

panelized   A type of manufactured unit made in flat panels. May be used for floors, walls, ceilings, or roofs.

parapet   An extension of the exterior wall of a structure above the point where the wall and roof meet.

parging   Applying mortar or plaster over structural members such as a foundation wall.

parquet   A type of inlay that uses strips of boards formed into geometric patterns. The patterns are usually small enough to be repeated many times over a large area.

particleboard   Wood fibers coated with glue and pressed into sheets.

party wall   The wall between dwelling units in multi-unit structures.

passive solar heating   The collection and distribution of solar energy for home heating, using building components and natural principles rather than mechanical systems. Compare with *active solar heating*.

patio   Originally a courtyard in Spanish structures. Contemporary use extends the definition to any grade-level space of a different material than the surrounding area that is designed for living activities.

patterned glass   Glass with a textured surface designed to create distortion. Also called obscure glass.

pattern lumber   Long strips with some type of molded edge or finish applied to the surface. Used for tongue-and-groove flooring, siding, and molding. Usually the lumber used has few, if any, defects.

paver   Thin materials such as glass or masonry formed into small units. Masonry units may have the appearance of brick or stone.

pediment   1) In ancient Greek and Roman architecture, the triangular structure, located above the entablature, that is formed by the end of the roof gable. 2) A triangular, semicircular, or other structure used over a door or window, as a porch roof, etc., to suggest a classical pediment.

pendant luminaire   A luminaire that is suspended from the ceiling.

pendentive   A method devised during the Byzantine era to connect a dome with a square structure. The pendentive is curved both horizontally and vertically, fitting the bottom of the dome and reducing in size as it goes downward to a small area that is supported by a square corner.

pent   1) A small roof projecting from a wall at a place other than the roofline. 2) Part of a Dutch hip roof beneath the gable that intersects a hip roof on both sides.

penthouse   An apartment located on the top story of a high-rise building.

performance code   Building codes that specify only that the materials used must be suitable for the structural component and must function appropriately.

phantom load   The electrical usage of an appliance that is turned off.

phase-changing material   A chemical substance that changes from a solid to a liquid and back as its temperature increases or decreases.

photovoltaic cells   Units with materials that react with light to produce electricity under high temperatures.

picture molding   A horizontal molding, installed near the ceiling, that supports hooks for hanging pictures and other objects.

picture window   Large uninterrupted span of glass designed to "frame" a view. Always stationary.

pier   A vertical masonry structure used for structural support. Rows of piers resting on individual footings may take the place of a perimeter foundation wall.

pilaster   A decorative square column that projects a few inches from a wall.

pilotis   Posts that raise a structure off the ground.

pilot light switch   An electrical switch that has a small light on it that glows when the switch is turned on.

pitch   A term used to describe the angle of a roof. Pitch is the ratio of rise to span and is expressed as a fraction reduced to its lowest form. Compare with *slope*.

pivot window   A type of window that operates by means of pivots placed at or near the center of the top and bottom rails. When opened, one side of the window pivots inward and the other outward.

placita   A small courtyard enclosed by a Spanish structure. Short walls or fences may be necessary to enclose the courtyard on sides the structure itself does not enclose.

plain stringer   A lumber support cut in a zigzag pattern to support risers and treads in a stairway. A plain stringer is later covered with a finish material.

plaiting   Braiding of vegetative fibers to form mats or decorative treatments.

plank and beam framing   Term often used to refer to post and beam framing when it is used only for the floor or roof of a structure.

plank flooring   Wood flooring made of strips of lumber 3 to 8 inches wide.

planned unit development   A community that is built in planned clusters near urban areas.

plasterboard   See *gypsum wallboard*.

plate glass   Manufactured by pouring molten glass on a casting table, smoothing the glass with rollers, and polishing it. Has fewer distortions than window glass but more than float glass.

platform   A flat area between the first and last riser of a stairway.

platform framing   A method of framed construction in which a floor platform is constructed for each story before the walls are erected. Studs are a single story in height. Allows sections of walls to be prefabricated and lifted into place. Also called western framing.

plenum   A large duct immediately beyond the heat exchanger in a warm air heating system. From this duct, smaller ducts run to living spaces.

plies (ply)   Thin layers of material—usually wood—that are glued together to form a laminated product.

plinth   A block of molding or trim located at the bottom of other moldings and that is wider than the moldings above it.

plywood   A laminated wood panel formed by using thin plies that alternate directions.

pocket door   A sliding door that disappears into the wall when opened.

polarized plug   An electrical plug having two prongs, one of which is wider than the other. Can be fitted into a receptacle only when properly oriented.

polyvinyl chloride   A type of plastic pipe used in plumbing systems for cold water supply and drains. Also known as PVC.

portico   An entry porch or other roofed projection at the front of a house. Often consists of a pediment supported by columns.

post and beam framing   The use of large timbers that are joined with mortise and tenon joints. The timbers are widely spaced and are visible on the interior. Also called *timber framing*.

post and lintel   An architectural device characterized by vertical posts, columns, or walls that support a lintel.

power   The rate at which work is done. Measured in watts.

power-assisted toilet   A toilet that has an accumulator in the toilet tank from which compressed air quickly forces water during flushing. Also called a pressure-assisted toilet.

precast   A concrete product that is fabricated somewhere other than the position in which it is to be used.

precut   A type of manufactured housing in which each structural member is cut and labeled. The members are put together on the building site.

prefabricated Manufactured components of a structure that are made on a site other than the final building location.

pressure-assisted toilet   See *power-assisted toilet*.

prestressed concrete   A concrete product manufactured by pouring concrete over steel bars under tension. Once the concrete is cured, the tension is released and the bars return to their original configuration.

primary treatment   The first step of treatment where solid matter is removed from sewage by screens and settlement.

proximity ventilation   A type of ventilation system that pulls air downward through a vent in the horizontal plane of a range.

punka   A type of large fan traditionally made from palm leaves and operated by a rope. Modern versions are smaller and powered by electricity.

purlin   A horizontal brace attached to rafters on the same side of the roof. Used to maintain the spacing of rafters and to provide strength and stability at the change in slope of mansard and gambrel roofs.

PVC   Abbreviation for polyvinyl chloride.

quadriplex   A structure that houses four dwelling units.

quarry tile   A type of ceramic tile made of colored clay so the color runs through the entire thickness of the material. Usually, quarry tile is not glazed.

quoins   Decorative treatment of the corners of a building by the use of contrasting or projecting materials.

rabbet   A type of wood joint shaped like an L. Often used on drawer fronts to allow a part of the drawer front to be recessed into the cabinet while the remainder of the front overlaps the face frame.

raceway   A metal or plastic channel mounted on a surface through which wires can be run.

radiation   The transfer of heat without appreciably heating the medium through which the thermal energy travels. Compare with *conduction* and *convection*.

rafter   A sloped roof framing member. Rafters extend from the ridge to the eaves or connect intermediate points on the roof.

rafter tail   The portion of the rafter that extends beyond the exterior wall line.

rail   A horizontal component of a window sash, panel door, or paneled wall.

rake   The inclined edge of a roof at a gable.

random rubble   A type of stonework using irregularly shaped stones in a random pattern.

rebar   Steel rods or bars used to reinforce concrete.

receptacle   An electrical device designed to accept plugs, thereby providing electrical power to lamps, appliances, and tools.

recovery rate   The number of gallons a hot water heater can raise the temperature of in an hour by 100 degrees Fahrenheit.

reeding   A series of convex curves that run vertically on walls or columns.

reflectance   A measurement of the light reflected from a surface.

reservoir A storage tank or area for water used in a public water supply system.

reveal overlay A drawer front that butts against the face frame when the drawer is closed.

reverberation The reflection of a sound wave from a secondary source before the effects of the original sound have dissipated. Generally, this applies to any sound within $\frac{1}{10}$ of a second from the original sound.

reverse-trap toilet A type of toilet with rim holes and a siphonic trap-way.

ridge The line at the highest point of a roof.

ridge board The roof framing member that runs along the highest point of a roof, thus defining the ridge. Rafters are attached to the ridge board.

rim French door A stile and rail door almost completely filled with glass.

rim joist Joists aligned with the outside of the foundation wall, forming a box to which floor or ceiling joists are attached.

rim lock A type of lock that is installed on the inside surface of a door.

rise The distance measured vertically from the top of the walls to the highest point on the roof.

riser The vertical space between one horizontal tread and the next in a stairway.

roofing felt Heavy paper saturated with asphalt. Used on the roof as an underlayment. Lighter-weight material may be used between the wall sheathing and exterior finish materials. Helps to prevent air infiltration, separates layers that may be chemically incompatible, and provides extra protection from leakage.

roof underlayment Material used between roof sheathing and roof finish materials. Isolates the sheathing from finish materials, preventing adverse chemical reactions possible when dissimilar materials are in contact.

rough opening An opening in a framed component that is slightly larger than the window, door, stairway, or other unit that is to be installed within it.

row house A minimum of three dwelling units located beside one another and that share side walls.

rubble Uncut stone.

run 1) The distance measured horizontally from the edge of a roof to a point directly below the ridge. Run is usually one-half the span. 2) A pipe installed horizontally, but with a slight slope, in the drainage portion of a plumbing system. 3) The total horizontal distance required by a stairway.

rural   As defined by the U.S. Census Bureau, a rural area has a population less than 2500.

rustication   The treatment of stone joints that emphasizes the joints themselves.

R-value   A measure of the resistance of a material to the flow of heat. The higher the R-value, the greater the insulative property.

safety glass   A double layer of glass with a layer of plastic sandwiched between.

sash   The wood or metal framework that holds glass in a window.

sash door   A door with at least one glass panel.

Seasonal Energy-Efficiency Ratio   A way to measure air conditioner efficiency. Same as Energy-Efficiency Rating but for an entire cooling season. Abbreviated SEER.

seasoned lumber   Lumber that has been dried in outdoor air or in a kiln to a maximum moisture content of 19 percent.

secondary treatment   The second stage of sewage treatment that uses filtration or aeration.

sectionalized   A type of structure made in two units that are hauled to a site and erected.

sectional overhead door   A type of garage door consisting of several horizontal panels hinged together. Operates on tracks.

SEER   Abbreviation for Seasonal Energy-Efficiency Ratio.

semicustom cabinet   Cabinets in standard sizes for which the ultimate consumer may choose from a variety of options, including wood species, finish, and door style.

semidirect lighting   A combination of direct and indirect lighting.

septic tank   An underground tank in which wastes are decomposed by bacterial action. An alternative to municipal sewage treatment used in rural areas.

series loop   A type of piping layout for forced hot water heating systems. All room distribution units (radiators or convectors) are connected in series so that the water must go through each unit before it recirculates. If one unit is closed, no heat gets to the rooms beyond.

service drop   The cable carrying electric current from a utility pole to the house when overhead wires are used.

service entrance   The point at which wires supplying electrical power enter the home. Often includes the connections leading from the service drop (unless underground cable is used) to the electric meter and from the meter to the distribution panel.

shaft   The vertical portion of a column.

shakes   Wood shingles in uneven lengths and widths.

shampoo sink A shallow sink that may or may not have a faucet but does have a spray attachment.

sheathing The covering applied to a wall or roof framework to provide a flat nailing surface for finish materials.

shed roof A style of roof having a slope in only one direction.

Sheetrock A brand name for gypsum wallboard. Regardless of the manufacturer, many individuals refer to gypsum wallboard as Sheetrock rather than using the generic term.

shingle molding A vertical molding used at the lower edge of the roof to close the spaces between rafters.

shingles Individual roof or wall covering units installed in overlapping rows.

shoe 1) A horizontal piece of metal installed on a wood threshold. 2) A horizontal rail located a few inches above the treads of a stairway. The bottom rail of a balustrade whose balusters do not reach the treads.

shoji screen A type of screen that employs rice paper in its panels.

short circuit A faulty electrical circuit resulting from a loose connection, broken wire, worn insulation, or other defect in wiring. Very hazardous because of the potential to cause shock or start a fire.

shouldered architrave Trim around an opening in which the horizontal top trim extends beyond the vertical trim.

sidelight A tall, narrow window beside a door. May be operable but is typically stationary.

siding Long, narrow strips of finishing material for exterior walls.

sill 1) The framing member located on top of the foundation and to which floor joists are attached in platform framing. 2) The bottom horizontal component of a window frame or an exterior door frame.

sill gasket See *sill sealer*.

sill sealer A material used to minimize air infiltration in the joint between the sill and the foundation. Also called sill gasket.

single-section overhead door A type of garage door made of a single panel. The entire door swings upward on a track.

sink A receptacle designed to hold water. Distinguished from a lavatory in that the bottom of a sink is flat.

siphon-action toilet See *siphon-vortex toilet*.

siphon-jet toilet A toilet that depends on the siphon in the trapway and the jet in the base of the bowl for flushing.

siphon-vortex toilet One-piece toilets that operate very quietly. They depend on rim holes to flush quickly, forming a whirlpool in the bowl. Also called siphon-action.

skeleton construction See *frame construction*.

skip sheathing Roof sheathing installed in strips with spaces between them to allow the installation of certain roofing materials.

skirting See *apron*.

slab door A flush door used on a cabinet. Also called an unframed door.

slab-on-grade A type of foundation structure consisting of a concrete floor slab poured at grade level. There may be separate footings and a foundation wall, or the slab may be thickened at the edge to form a combined floor slab and footing. See *thickened-edge slab*.

sliding door A door that slides horizontally on a track.

sliding window A window in which at least one sash slides horizontally.

slip head window A window that disappears into a wall pocket when open.

slope A term used to describe the angle of a roof. Slope is the ratio of rise to run, expressed as the number of inches of rise for every 12 inches of run. Compare with *pitch*.

sludge Formed by solids in sewage that settle out during treatment.

smart house A house that has wiring designed for high-speed data service and that permits remote or automatic control of electrical devices.

smoke chamber A small area above the smoke shelf in a fireplace that holds smoke before it goes through the flue.

smoke shelf A flat shelf at the top of the fireplace that helps prevent downdrafts that would send smoke into rooms instead of up the flue. It also catches soot and other particles.

SMSA Abbreviation for Standard Metropolitan Statistical Area.

soffit 1) The material that hides the bottom of the rafters from view at the overhang, forming a box cornice. 2) The underside of an interior structural feature, such as an overhead wall cabinet, a projection in the ceiling, etc. See *soffit lighting*.

soffit lighting Concealed luminaires built into a soffit so as to cast light downward.

softwood Wood from coniferous trees.

soil Solid waste and the water that carries it from toilets and, sometimes, garbage disposals.

soil pipe A large pipe that carries wastes from a toilet to the sewage system. Compare with *waste pipe*.

sole The framing member that is laid on its side on top of the subfloor in platform framing to begin the framing of the walls. Studs are attached to the sole plate.

solid bridging A type of bridging between adjacent joists that employs a solid piece of material the same width as the joists and that fills in the space between the joists.

sound masking   The use of one sound to cover another sound.

Sound Transmission Class   The measurement of the resistance of a material to the transmission of sound. Abbreviated STC.

space heater   A device to heat a single area as opposed to central heating.

span   The distance measured horizontally between the exterior walls across the width of the house at the top of the walls.

spandrel wall   A portion of a wall above an opening.

specification code   A building code that specifies acceptable individual materials.

spectrally selective glass   A type of glazing that has a low-emissivity coating that filters a large percentage of infrared rays but allows light through. Used where air-conditioning is of primary concern.

spiral stairway   A curved stairway in which all winders are attached to a central post.

split   A defect in wood that runs with the grain and goes through the thickness of the lumber.

split-entry homes   A type of home that has no living area at the entry level.

split-level house   A type of home with one living level on one side of the structure and two living levels on the other side.

split-wiring   The way in which a receptacle is wired so it has one "hot" outlet and one controlled by a switch.

spring   A natural water supply that exits the ground at low places where the water table is close to the surface.

square   A unit by which roofing materials are purchased. One square provides sufficient materials to cover 100 square feet of area when materials are applied with normal overlap.

stack   A vertical pipe in the drainage portion of a plumbing system.

stainless steel   Steel that is at least 10 percent chromium. The addition of this material makes steel rust-resistant.

Standard Metropolitan Statistical Area   An area that spans many miles, is well developed, and is fairly densely populated. Abbreviated SMSA. Also called megalopolis.

standby loss   1) See *phantom load*. 2) The heat lost by water heaters.

standpipe   A cylindrical container that holds thousands of gallons of water and that serves as a reservoir for water storage.

stationary window   A window with a sash that does not move.

STC   Abbreviation for Sound Transmission Class.

stick-built construction   See *conventional construction*.

stile   A vertical component of a window sash, panel door, or paneled wall.

stool   The finish sill at the bottom of a window.

stoop   A raised platform with steps at the entrance to a home.

stop   The part of a door frame that projects beyond the head and jambs to prevent the door from moving beyond that point.

stop-and-waste valve   A main shutoff valve of a plumbing system that also allows the system to be drained.

straight run stairway   A stairway that goes in one direction only.

strap bridging   A type of bridging between adjacent joists that uses a long board located beneath the joists to tie the joists together.

string course   A horizontal row of brick, stone, or other material that projects slightly from an exterior wall to identify the break between interior levels. Also called a belt course.

stringer   The structural support for risers and treads in a stairway. Also called a carriage.

stringer joists   Joists that fall at the outside edges of a structure and that run parallel to the joists of the floor or ceiling.

strip flooring   Wood flooring made of long, narrow strips 2¼ inches or less in width.

structural lumber   Thick, heavy lumber that is used for large supporting members, such as joists and beams, in construction.

stucco   A smooth-surfaced finish made of plaster or portland cement and sand.

stud   A vertical wall framing member.

studio apartment   See *efficiency apartment*.

subcontractors   Workers in the building industry who specialize in one area. Individuals are responsible for completing work on a job site but may not be responsible for ordering materials or scheduling.

subfloor   The continuous flat surface placed over floor joists and on top of which finish flooring materials are installed. Helps provide dimensional stability.

substandard housing   One of three categories into which housing is grouped by the U.S. Census Bureau. Substandard housing lacks basic amenities, such as running water, cooking facilities, or mechanical equipment, and may have a number of defects. Substandard housing is often also overcrowded.

suburbs   As defined by the U.S. Census Bureau, a suburb is a settled area near a city.

sump   An underground tank used when parts of a home's drainage system are below the level of the sewer system. Wastewater is collected in the sump and pumped up to the sewer outlet. A sump may also be used to collect rainwater, thus preventing flooding in a basement.

supply tube   A small, usually flexible tube that supplies water to faucets and toilets.

surface-mounted ceiling luminaire   A luminaire mounted on the ceiling.

surface-mounted wall luminaire   A luminaire mounted on the wall.

surround   1) The decorative treatment around a door or window. 2) The fireproof front facing of a fireplace.

suspended construction   A type of construction in which the structure is supported from the top by vertical posts or other components via cables or rods.

sustainable construction   See *green design*.

swinging door   Any door that swings on hinges.

tail joist   The shortened joists resulting from cutting an opening in a floor or ceiling.

tambour   A type of door formed with a number of narrow strips mounted on a flexible backing and that rolls up or sideways.

tankless water heater   A water heater that has a coil through which water passes as it is heated. The tankless heater does not store any water.

task lighting   Lighting designed to illuminate a small area more brightly than the surrounding area.

technology   The application of knowledge for a practical purpose.

tempered glass   Glass that has been reheated after initial manufacture, then cooled quickly to improve its integrity under stress.

tempered hardboard   A type of hardboard to which heat and certain chemicals have been added during manufacturing to produce a more moisture-resistant panel than regular hardboard.

tensile strength   The strength of a material when a load is imposed in the middle of a span; the ability of the material to bend.

termite shield   Metal plate with downturned edges. Located between the foundation and the first wood framing member. Prevents termites from reaching the wood frame by crawling up from the earth.

terne   A material used for roofing that is made of metal—usually steel—with a tin alloy coating.

tertiary treatment   The third stage in the treatment of sewage during which chemicals, radiation, or fine treatment are used to purify water.

thatching   The use of grass or reeds tied into bundles and attached to roofs or walls to enclose them.

therm   See *heating unit*.

thermal break construction   An insulative layer, such as vinyl, sandwiched between the interior and exterior metal components in a window or door to interrupt the flow of heat.

thermal mass   A massive structure, such as a thick masonry wall or a row of water-filled drums, that is used in passive solar heating to absorb heat from sunlight. The heat is given off when surrounding air temperatures are cooler.

thermosiphoning   The use of the principles of convection to generate an air flow without mechanical assistance. Air heated in a confined space rises and exits through an upper vent to a room beyond. Cool air from the room is then pulled in through lower vents to continue the cycle. Used especially with passive solar heating.

thermostat   A device used to automatically control temperature. Used in conjunction with heating and air-conditioning units and water heaters.

thickened-edge slab   A type of slab-on-grade construction used in warm climates where frost lines are near the surface. The edges of the slab are thickened, forming the support for the structure. Also called a floating slab.

thin-shell concrete   Concrete sprayed over an inflated form. May have lightweight aggregates.

three-way switch   1) A type of wall switch used in pairs to enable a luminaire to be controlled from two separate locations. See also four-way switch. 2) A lamp switch for use with a three-way bulb to provide three levels of light.

threshold   Durable material that covers the joint between the sill of an exterior door frame and the floor.

threshold size   The minimum-size community that will support an activity or function.

throat   An opening in the top of a fireplace that directs smoke into the smoke chamber.

thumb turn   A raised area in the center of a doorknob that turns to engage the lock.

tie beam   A horizontal structural member designed to counteract the diagonal thrust of the roof.

timbers   Wood with a minimum dimension of 5 inches or more in width and thickness. Used as structural lumber.

time-delay fuse   A fuse that provides a momentary delay before breaking a circuit. Eliminates blown fuses caused by the momentary surge of current when motor-driven equipment starts up.

tongue and groove   A type of interlocking joint in which there is a linear projection from one member that fits into a groove on another piece. Used for siding, flooring, and rigid board insulation.

top plate   A wall framing member laid horizontally across the top of the studs. The top plate maintains the position of the studs and supports the roof. It is usually doubled.

total rise   The total height of a stairway from finished floor level to finished floor level.

town   As defined by the U.S. Census Bureau, a town is an area with a population of 2500 to 50,000.

town house   A row house that has multiple stories.

trabeated   See *post and lintel.* In common usage, refers to stacked posts and lintels.

tracery   Openwork designs in a solid material. Used extensively during the Gothic period.

track lighting   Luminaires, usually downlights, placed in a track attached to the ceiling. The luminaires can be positioned anywhere on the track to direct light where desired.

transformer   A device used to increase or decrease voltage. Found in electrical distribution systems as well as on certain appliances that use lower voltage than that provided by electric lines.

transom   A window above a door. Sometimes operable.

trap   A device associated with a plumbing fixture that "traps" sufficient water to provide a seal between room air and the gases in the sewage system. A trap may consist of a bend in a drainage pipe, as that under a sink, or it may be a part of the design of the fixture itself, as in a toilet.

trapway   Part of the toilet that serves as the trap and carries water from the toilet bowl to the drain during flushing.

travertine   A type of porous limestone formed by mineral springs.

tray ceiling   A recessed portion of a ceiling.

tread   The horizontal portion of a step.

trimmer   (1) A shortened stud used to support the header in a door or window opening. (2) A shortened joist at the side of an opening in the floor frame.

triplex   A structure that houses three dwelling units.

Trombe wall   An interior wall structure used to collect and store heat in some passive solar heating systems. The wall consists of a thermal mass located a few inches behind a large glass area. The wall is oriented to receive sunlight which heats the mass. The room beyond the wall is heated by conduction from the mass, and by thermosiphoning if vents are placed in the mass.

trundle bed   A bed designed to fit beneath another bed when it is not in use.

truss   1) An architectural device that is triangular in form. Its dimensional stability allows the truss to span long distances. 2) Any prefabricated assemblage forming a rigid framework and that is formed with a series of triangles.

tunnel vault   See *barrel vault.*

turbine ventilator   A device for providing attic ventilation consisting of a ball-shaped metal fixture that projects from the roof. Breezes cause the curved blades of the turbine to spin, creating a suction that pulls hot air out of the attic.

Tuscan   A classical order of architecture that features a base, an unfluted shaft, and a simple cushion capital.

type S fuse   A fuse that, as a safety feature, screws into an adapter rather than directly into the socket. Improperly sized replacement fuses will not fit the adapter.

type X gypsum board   A type of gypsum wallboard to which noncombustible fibers have been added to improve the fire-resistance of the material.

underlayment   1) The layer on top of a subfloor designed to be a base for finish flooring. May be of different materials depending on the type of finish flooring to be used. 2) A layer of roofing felt placed between the roof sheathing and finish material.

unframed door   See *slab door*.

universal design   Design for accessibility.

utility cabinet   An 84-inch-tall cabinet designed for storage. May have shelving or other dividers.

U-value   Short for British thermal unit. A measure of the flow of heat through a material. One U is equal to one Btu of heat per square foot per hour for each degree of difference between the inside and outside temperatures.

vacuum-assisted toilet   A relatively new type of toilet that depends on an interconnection between the tank and the trapway to create a vacuum.

valance lighting   A luminaire, or row of luminaires, placed across the top of a window and concealed by a bracket, fabric-covered rod, etc., that directs the light upward and downward.

valley   A low point in a roof formed by the meeting of two sloping surfaces.

vapor barrier   A moisture-proof barrier applied on the warm side of a structural component such as a wall.

veneer   A thin layer of material applied to another—usually less expensive —material. May be wood, mother-of-pearl, metal, or another material.

Venturi principle   The physical principle that describes the relationship between the velocity of a fluid and the space through which it travels. As the size of the space decreases, the velocity of the fluid must increase.

veranda   See *gallery*.

vergeboard See *bargeboard*.

vessel lavatory A lavatory that sits on top of a counter, requiring only a small opening for a drain in the countertop.

video-shielded Speakers that are video-shielded do not interfere with certain types of video signals and can be used near television sets.

viga In Spanish Southwest architecture, the large timbers used for the roof that supported smaller branches and adobe.

vitrified Brick that has been fired to high temperatures and that does not absorb moisture.

volt A unit of measurement of the pressure behind an electric current.

voltage The pressure of an electric current flow as measured in volts.

volume resonator A hollow bottle- or vase-shaped cavity within a structural component into which sounds channel through a small opening. Inside the resonator, the sound is absorbed or converted to heat through friction.

volute A circular design that spirals inward.

voussoir An individual masonry unit that comprises an arch.

waferboard A type of panel made of wood flakes in a random arrangement.

wainscot Wood paneling used on an entire wall. While *dado* is not the same, the terms are often used interchangeably.

wall bracket lighting A luminaire or row of luminaires concealed by a continuous bracket that directs the light upward and downward. Similar to valance lighting but can be placed anywhere on the wall.

wall gable A wall that extends upward to form an isolated gable that has its own roof.

wall washer A type of downlight that allows light to be diffused evenly over the surface of a wall.

warping A defect in wood in which the lumber bends or twists within a plane.

wash-down toilet A relatively inefficient type of toilet that is no longer installed in the United States.

waste pipe A drainage pipe leading from plumbing fixtures other than toilets. Waste pipes carry away wastewater only. Compare with *soil pipe*.

water hammer The noise that results from water under pressure striking a quickly closed valve and creating back pressure on water in the pipe.

water main One of the large pipes that carry purified water from a municipal water supply system to homes. Water mains run underground alongside streets. Individual homes tap into the main.

water spot The area in a toilet bowl that is covered by water.

water table The level at which underground water stands.

watt   A unit of measure of electrical power. Equal to the rate of work represented by a current of one ampere under a pressure of one volt.

wattle and daub   A type of filling used between supporting posts. Made of woven branches (wattle) covered with mud (daub).

weather-stripping   Material used to seal movable joints (such as around the inside edges of door frames and operable windows) against air infiltration.

web   The area between the chords in wood I-joists and trusses.

weep hole   Openings near the bottom of a masonry facade to allow moisture to drain away from wood members.

well   1) The boxed opening leading from a skylight in the roof through the ceiling below. 2) An opening in the ground that extends into the water table.

western framing   See *platform framing*.

wet stone   Stone construction in which mortar is used.

whole-house fan   A type of fan installed horizontally in a ceiling where air can be vented outdoors. Designed to ventilate an entire house.

windbreak   A simple shelter from the wind. Not usually enclosed on all sides.

windchill   A comparison of actual temperature and air velocity to determine perceived temperature.

winder   A wedge-shaped tread in a stairway.

window glass   Sheet glass made by flattening molten glass with rollers.

winged gable roof   A type of gable roof in which the roof at the ridge line extends beyond the roof at the eave.

work triangle   The imaginary triangle formed by the path between the center fronts of the sink, range, and refrigerator in a kitchen.

wrought iron   A mixture of iron and carbon. Purer and more malleable than cast iron. Can be beaten and bent into a variety of intricate shapes. Rust-resistant characteristic makes it suitable for outdoor use.

zapatas   In Spanish Colonial architecture, shaped paired brackets attached to the top of posts to support a structural element above.

zero clearance   A fireplace that requires no minimum distance between it and combustible materials.

Index